Switching to the Mac

Yosemite Edition

the missing manual®

The book that should have been in the box®

Switching to the Mac
Yosemite Edition

the missing manual®
The book that should have been in the box®

David Pogue

O'REILLY®

Beijing | Cambridge | Farnham | Köln | Sebastopol | Tokyo

Switching to the Mac: The Missing Manual, Yosemite Edition
by David Pogue

Published by O'Reilly Media, Inc.,
1005 Gravenstein Highway North, Sebastopol, CA 95472.

O'Reilly Media books may be purchased for educational, business, or sales promotional use. Online editions are also available for most titles: *safari@oreilly. com.* For more information, contact our corporate/institutional sales department: 800-998-9938 or *corporate@oreilly.com.*

January 2015: First Edition.

ISBN: 978-1-491-947180
[M] [01/15]

Table of Contents

Part Three: Yosemite Online

Part Four: Putting Down Roots

The Missing Credits

About the Author

 David Pogue (author, illustrator, indexer) is the founder of Yahoo Tech (*yahootech.com*), a job for which he was groomed by 13 years of writing the weekly tech column for *The New York Times*.

He's also a monthly columnist for *Scientific American*, a two-time Emmy-winning correspondent for *CBS News Sunday Morning*, the host of several *NOVA* miniseries on PBS, and the creator of the Missing Manual series. He's written or co-written more than 75 books, including 30 in this series, six in the For Dummies line (including *Macs, Magic, Opera,* and *Classical Music*), two novels (one for middle-schoolers), *The World According to Twitter,* and *Pogue's Basics: Essential Tips and Shortcuts (That No One Bothers to Tell You) for Simplifying the Technology in Your Life,* a *New York Times* bestseller. In his other life, David is a former Broadway show conductor, a magician, and a funny public speaker. He lives in Connecticut with his wife, Nicki, and three awesome children.

Links to his columns and videos await at *www.davidpogue.com.* He welcomes feedback about his books by email at *david@pogueman.com.*

About the Creative Team

Julie Van Keuren (managing editor) quit her newspaper editing job in 2006 to move to Montana and live the freelancing dream. She and her husband, M.H. (who's living the novel-writing dream), have two teenage sons, Dexter and Michael. Email: little_media@yahoo.com.

Phil Simpson (design and layout) runs his graphic design business from Southbury, Connecticut. His work includes corporate branding, publication design, communications support, and advertising. In his free time, he is a homebrewer, ice cream maker, wannabe woodworker, and is on a few tasting panels. He lives with his wife and several great felines. Email: *phil.simpson@pmsgraphics.com.*

Brian Jepson (**technical consultant**) is an O'Reilly editor and hacker, and co-organizer of Providence Geeks and the Rhode Island Mini Maker Faire. He's also been involved over the years with AS220, a nonprofit arts center. Email: *bjepson@oreilly.com.*

Kirill Voronin (technical editor) is the head of an IT consulting company, aptly called Shortcut, based in Moscow, Russia. He has worked with Macs since the '90s, and he's an Apple Certified System Administrator and Apple Certified Trainer for IT courses. He lives with his wife, Maria, and son, Nil. Email: *kirill.voronin@shortcut.ru.*

Acknowledgments

Over the years, many friends and colleagues have contributed enthusiasm, expertise, and even prose to this book's editions. They include Zachary Brass, Dan Pourhadi, Rich Koster, J.D. Biersdorfer, Teresa Noelle Roberts, Ben Waldie, and Lesa Snider.

In addition to the dream team members identified above, I owe debts of thanks to O'Reilly's Missing Manuals editor-in-chief, Brian Sawyer; Apple's Ryan James and Bill Evans for going beyond the call of duty to chase down tweaky tech answers; Philip Michaels, who wrote about Game Center for this book; fact-checker Judy Le; proofreader Kellee Katagi; John Uppendahl and Kurt Schmucker, who did me some favors capturing the uncapturable; and my assistant Jan Carpenter, whose help redoing this book's 400 illustrations made my very survival possible.

I've never met, or even spoken to, Kirill Voronin; he lives in Moscow. But he submitted so many corrections to the previous edition's Errata page online that I wound up hiring him to be the tech editor for this book—and he knocked it out of the park.

Julie Van Keuren is solely responsible for this book coming out on time. She began her Missing Manual life as a copy editor but, on this edition, also became the adapter, updater, text integrator, and design re-layouter.

Thanks, as always, to David Rogelberg for believing in the idea. Above all, this book owes its existence to the patience and affection of Nicki, Kelly, Tia, and Jeffrey. They make these books—and everything else—possible.

—David Pogue

The Missing Manual Series

Missing Manuals are witty, superbly written guides to computer products that don't come with printed manuals (which is just about all of them). Each book features a handcrafted index; cross-references to specific page numbers (not just "see Chapter 14"); and an ironclad promise never to put an apostrophe in the possessive pronoun *its*.

Here's a list of current and upcoming titles:

For the Mac

- *OS X Yosemite: The Missing Manual* by David Pogue
- *OS X Mavericks: The Missing Manual* by David Pogue
- *AppleScript: The Missing Manual* by Adam Goldstein
- *FileMaker Pro 13: The Missing Manual* by Susan Prosser and Stuart Gripman
- *iMovie: The Missing Manual* by David Pogue and Aaron Miller
- *iPhoto: The Missing Manual* by David Pogue and Lesa Snider

- *iWork: The Missing Manual* by Jessica Thornsby and Josh Clark
- *Office 2011: The Missing Manual* by Chris Grover
- *Switching to the Mac: The Missing Manual, Yosemite Edition* by David Pogue
- *Photoshop CC: The Missing Manual, Second Edition* by Lesa Snider
- *Photoshop CS6: The Missing Manual* by Lesa Snider
- *Photoshop Elements 13: The Missing Manual* by Barbara Brundage

For Windows

- *Windows 8.1: The Missing Manual* by David Pogue
- *Windows 7: The Missing Manual* by David Pogue
- *Access 2013: The Missing Manual* by Matthew MacDonald
- *Excel 2013: The Missing Manual* by Matthew MacDonald
- *Microsoft Project 2013: The Missing Manual* by Bonnie Biafore
- *Office 2013: The Missing Manual* by Nancy Conner and Matthew MacDonald
- *QuickBooks 2105: The Missing Manual* by Bonnie Biafore
- *Photoshop CC: The Missing Manual, Second Edition* by Lesa Snider
- *Photoshop CS6: The Missing Manual* by Lesa Snider
- *Photoshop Elements 13: The Missing Manual* by Barbara Brundage

Electronics

- *iPhone: The Missing Manual, Eighth Edition* by David Pogue
- *David Pogue's Digital Photography: The Missing Manual*
- *Galaxy S5: The Missing Manual* by Preston Gralla
- *Galaxy Tab: The Missing Manual* by Preston Gralla
- *iPad App Development: The Missing Manual* by Craig Hockenberry
- *iPod: The Missing Manual, Eleventh Edition* by J.D. Biersdorfer & David Pogue
- *Kindle Fire HD: The Missing Manual* by Peter Meyers
- *Fire Phone: The Missing Manual* by Preston Gralla
- *Netbooks: The Missing Manual* by J.D. Biersdorfer
- *NOOK HD: The Missing Manual* by Preston Gralla
- *Motorola Xoom: The Missing Manual* by Preston Gralla

Web Technologies

- *Adobe Edge Animate: The Missing Manual* by Chris Grover
- *Creating a Web Site: The Missing Manual, Third Edition* by Matthew MacDonald
- *CSS3: The Missing Manual, Third Edition* by David Sawyer McFarland
- *Dreamweaver CS6: The Missing Manual. Second Edition* by David Sawyer McFarland and Chris Grover
- *Dreamweaver CC: The Missing Manual* by David Sawyer McFarland
- *Flash CS6: The Missing Manual* by Chris Grover
- *Google+: The Missing Manual* by Kevin Purdy
- *HTML5: The Missing Manual, Second Edition* by Matthew MacDonald
- *JavaScript & jQuery: The Missing Manual, Third Edition* by David Sawyer McFarland
- *PHP & MySQL: The Missing Manual, Second Edition* by Brett McLaughlin
- *WordPress: The Missing Manual* by Matthew MacDonald

Life

- *Buying a Home: The Missing Manual* by Nancy Conner
- *Personal Investing: The Missing Manual* by Bonnie Biafore
- *Your Brain: The Missing Manual* by Matthew MacDonald
- *Your Body: The Missing Manual* by Matthew MacDonald
- *Your Money: The Missing Manual* by J.D. Roth

Introduction

What's going on with the Mac these days?

Apple was the only computer company whose sales actually increased during the recession. The Mac's market share has quadrupled since 2005—it's now around 20 percent of computer sales in the U.S. And then there's the most significant statistic of all: you, sitting there reading this book—because, obviously, you intend to switch to (or add on) a Mac.

What's going on?

Maybe it's the "halo effect": the coolness of all those iPads and iPhones is rubbing off onto the rest of Apple's product line. Maybe people have grown weary of boring beige and black boxes. Maybe it's the convenience of the Apple Stores. Maybe potential switchers feel more confident to take the plunge, since more and more of life is moving online, where it makes no difference what kind of computer you have.

Or maybe people have just spent one Saturday too many dealing with viruses, worms, spyware, crapware, excessive startup processes, questionable firewalls, inefficient permissions, and all the other land mines strewn across the Windows world.

In any case, there's never been a better time to make the switch. Mac OS X version 10.10 (nicknamed Yosemite) is gorgeous, easy to understand, and virus-free. Apple's computers are in top form, too, complete with features like built-in hi-def video cameras, built-in Ethernet, illuminated keyboards, and two different kinds of wireless connections. If you're talking laptops, the story is even better: Apple's laptops generally cost less than similarly outfitted Windows laptops, and they weigh less, too. Plus, they look a lot cooler.

And then there's that Intel processor that sizzles away inside today's Macs. Yes, it lets you *run Windows*—and Windows programs—at blazing speed, right there on your Macintosh. (Hell really has frozen over.) Chapter 8 has the details.

That's not to say, however, that switching to the Mac is all sunshine and bunnies. The Macintosh is a different machine, running a different operating system, and built by a company with a different philosophy—a fanatical control freak/perfectionist zeal. When it comes to their missions and ideals, Apple and Microsoft have about as much in common as a melon and a shoehorn.

In any case, you have three challenges before you. First, you'll probably want to copy your Windows stuff over to the new Mac. Some of that is easy to transfer (photos, music, Microsoft Office documents), and some is trickier (email messages, address books, buddy lists).

Second, you have to assemble a suite of Macintosh programs that do what you're used to doing in Windows. Most programs from Microsoft, Adobe, and other major players are available in nearly identical Mac and Windows formats. But, occasionally, it's more difficult: Many programs are available only for Windows, and it takes some research (or Chapter 7 of this book) to help you find Macintosh replacements.

Finally, you have to learn OS X itself; after all, it came preinstalled on your new Mac. In some respects, it resembles the latest versions of Windows: There's a taskbar-like thing, a Control Panel–like thing, and, of course, a Trash can. At the same time, hundreds of features you thought you knew have been removed, replaced, or relocated. (If you ever find yourself groping for an old favorite feature, see Appendix C, The "Where'd It Go?" Dictionary.)

Note: In OS X, the X is meant to be a Roman numeral, pronounced "ten." Unfortunately, many people see "OS X" and say "Oh Ess Ex." That's a sure way to get funny looks in public.

FREQUENTLY ASKED QUESTION

All About "Yosemite"

Why is the operating system called "Yosemite"?

Most software companies develop their wares in secret, using code names for new products. Apple's code names for OS X were first named after big cats: OS X was Cheetah, 10.1 was Puma, 10.2 was Jaguar, 10.3 was Panther, 10.4 was Tiger, 10.5 was Leopard, 10.6 was Snow Leopard, 10.7 was Lion, and 10.8 was Mountain Lion.

(A mountain lion is actually the same thing as a cougar, which is the same thing as a puma. But let's not quibble.)

Usually, the code name is dropped as soon as the product is complete, whereupon the marketing department gives it

a new name. In OS X's case, though, Apple thought its cat names were cool enough to retain for the finished product.

But then it pretty much ran out of species. What was left? Bobcat? Cougar? Ocelot?

So beginning with OS X 10.9, Apple's naming system moved on—to famous places in California. Mavericks is a big-wave surfing spot in Northern California. Yosemite, of course, is a breathtaking national park in the Sierra Nevada mountain range.

Now you know.

What OS X Gives You

These days, a key attraction of the Mac—at least as far as switchers are concerned—is security. Viruses and spyware are almost nonexistent on the Mac. (Even Microsoft Word macro viruses don't run in OS X.) For many people, that's a good enough reason to move to OS X right there.

Along the same lines, Mail, Mac OS X's built-in email program, deals surprisingly well with spam, the unsolicited junk email that's become the scourge of the Internet.

If you ask average people why the Mac isn't overrun by viruses and spyware, as Windows is, they'll probably tell you, "Because the Mac's market share is too small for the bad guys to write for."

That may be true (although 80 million machines isn't too shabby, as targets go). But there's another reason, too: OS X is a relatively young operating system. It was created only in 2001, and with security in mind. (Contrast that with Windows, whose original versions were written before the Internet even existed.) OS X's built-in firewall makes it virtually impossible for hackers to break into your Mac, and the system insists on getting your permission before *anything* gets installed. Nothing can slip in behind your back.

But freedom from gunkware and viruses is only one big-ticket item. Here are a few other joys of becoming a Mac fan:

- **Stability.** Underneath the Mac's shimmering, translucent desktop is Unix, the industrial strength, rock-solid OS that drives many a Web site and a university. It's not new by any means; in fact, it's decades old, and has been polished by generations of programmers. That's precisely why former Apple CEO Steve Jobs and his team chose it as the basis for the NeXT operating system, which Jobs worked on during his 12 years away from Apple and which Apple bought in 1997 to turn into Mac OS X.

- **No nagging.** OS X isn't copy-protected. It's free, too. You can install it on as many Macs as your family owns. When you buy a new Mac, you're never, ever asked to type in a code off a sticker. Nor must you "register," "activate," sign up for ".NET Passport," or endure any other friendly suggestions unrelated to your work. And you won't find any cheesy software demos from other companies clogging up your desktop when you buy a new Mac, either. In short, OS X leaves you alone.

- **Great software.** OS X comes with several dozen useful programs, from Mail (for email) to a 3-D, voice-activated Chess program. The most famous programs, though, are the famous Apple "iApps": iTunes for working with audio files, iMovie for editing video, iPhoto for managing your digital photos, GarageBand for creating and editing digital music, and so on. You also get Messages (a Yahoo-, AOL-, Facebook-, Jabber-, and Google Talk–compatible instant messaging program that also offers videoconferencing) and Calendar, a calendar program, plus iPaddish apps like Maps and iBooks.

• **Simpler everything.** Most applications on the Mac show up as a single icon. All the support files are hidden away inside, where you don't have to look at them. There's no Add/Remove Programs program on the Macintosh; in general, you can remove a program from your Mac simply by dragging that one application icon to the Trash, without having to worry that you're leaving scraps behind.

• **Continuity features.** If you also own an iPhone, you're in for a real treat. In Yosemite, Apple turns the phone into something of a cellular accessory for your Mac.

For example, the Mac can now be a speakerphone, taking and making calls over a wireless connection to your iPhone. You can send and receive standard text messages, too, right from the comfort of your full-sized Mac keyboard. Your phone relays them.

Then there's Handoff, which passes documents between the iPad or iPhone and the Mac. If you've been writing a message on your iPhone, for example, you find a new icon at the left end of the Mac's Dock that you can click to open the same email on the Mac, ready to complete and send.

The same feature works for other Apple programs like Safari (opens the same Web page), Maps, Messages, Reminders, Calendar, Contacts, Notes, Keynote, Numbers, and Pages. It works the other direction, too; if you start something on the Mac, an icon appears on the lower-left corner of your iPhone's Lock screen that opens the same item.

• **Desktop features.** OS X offers a long list of useful desktop features that will be new to you, the Windows refugee.

For example, *spring-loaded* folders let you drag an icon into a folder within a folder within a folder with a single drag, without leaving a wake of open windows. An optional second line under an icon's name tells you how many items are in a folder, what the dimensions of a graphic are, and so on. And there's a useful column view, which lets you view the contents of many nested folders at a glance. (You can think of it as a horizontal version of Windows Explorer's folder tree.)

When your screen gets cluttered with windows, you can temporarily hide all of them with a single keystroke. If you want to see *all* the windows on your screen without any of them overlapping, OS X's Mission Control feature is your best friend (page 161).

A speedy, system-wide Find command called Spotlight is accessible from any program. It searches not only the names of your files and folders, but also the words *inside* your documents, and can even search your email, calendar, address book, Web bookmarks, and about 100 other kinds of data, all at once.

Finally, OS X offers the Dashboard (something like the widgets in Windows Vista and Windows 7). It lets you summon dozens of miniprograms—a calculator, weather forecaster, dictionary, and so on—with a single keystroke, and dismiss them just as easily. You can download thousands more of these so-called widgets from

the Internet, making it even easier to find TV listings, Google search results, local movie showtimes, and more, no matter what program you're using at the moment.

- **Advanced graphics.** Mac programmers get excited about the set of advanced graphics technologies called *Quartz* (for two-dimensional graphics) and *OpenGL* (for three-dimensional graphics). For the rest of us, these technologies translate into a beautiful, translucent look for the desktop, smooth-looking (*antialiased*) onscreen lettering, and the ability to turn any document on the screen into an Adobe Acrobat (PDF) file. And then there are the slick animations that permeate every aspect of OS X: the rotating-cube effect when you switch from one logged-in person to another, the "genie" effect when you minimize a window to the Dock, and so on.

- **Advanced networking.** When it comes to hooking up your computer to others, including those on the Internet, few operating systems can touch OS X. It offers advanced features like *multihoming,* which lets your laptop switch automatically from its cable modem settings to its wireless or dial-up modem settings when you take it on the road.

 If you're not so much a switcher as an *adder* (you're getting a Mac but keeping the PC around), you'll be happy to hear that Macs and Windows PCs can "see" each other on a network automatically, too. As a result, you can open, copy, and work on files on both types of machines as though the religious war between Macs and PCs had never even existed.

- **Voice control, keyboard control.** You can operate almost every aspect of every program entirely from the keyboard—or even by voice. These are terrific timesavers for efficiency freaks. In fact, the Mac can also read aloud *any text in any program,* including Web pages, email, your novel, you name it.

- **Full buzzword compliance.** You can't read an article about OS X without hearing certain technical buzzwords that were once exclusively the domain of computer engineers: *preemptive multitasking, multithreading, symmetrical multiprocessing, dynamic memory allocation,* and *memory protection,* for example.

 What it all adds up to is that OS X is very stable, that a crashing program can't crash the whole machine, that the Macintosh can exploit multiple processors, and that the Mac can easily do more than one thing at once—downloading files, playing music, and opening a program, for example—all simultaneously.

- **A command-line interface.** In general, Apple has completely hidden from you every trace of the Unix operating system that lurks beneath OS X's beautiful skin. For the benefit of programmers and other technically oriented fans, however, Apple left uncovered a tiny passageway into that far more complex realm: Terminal, a program in your Applications→Utilities folder.

 If the idea of an all-text operating system gets you going, you can capitalize on the *command-line interface* of OS X by typing out commands in the Terminal window, which the Mac executes instantly and efficiently. Think DOS prompt, just faster and more useful. (Curious? There's a free online PDF appendix to this book—called

"Terminal Crash Course"—waiting for you. It's on this book's "Missing CD" at *www.missingmanuals.com*.)

What OS X Takes Away

Besides quirks like viruses, spyware, and the Start menu, there are some substantial things on a PC that you lose when you switch to the Mac:

- **Programs.** Certain programs are still Windows-only. You can always search for replacements—using Chapter 7 of this book as a guide, for example—but you may end up having to pay for them. And, of course, there are a *few* programs—like some proprietary accounting and laboratory software, and lots of games—where the Windows versions are simply irreplaceable. For those, you have to keep a PC around or run Windows on your Mac (Chapter 8).

- **Peripherals.** Most add-on devices nowadays work equally well on both Windows PCs and Macs. That includes printers, scanners, digital cameras (still- and video-varieties), and "multifunction" devices that incorporate several of those attributes into one machine.

 Unfortunately, sometimes the Mac software for a gadget isn't as full-featured as the Windows version. Sometimes some of the features on a multifunction printer/scanner aren't available on the Mac. If you have a device made by an obscure manufacturer—especially if the device is more than a few years old—it may not work with your Mac at all.

 Still, all hope is not lost. Chapter 9 can get you out of most hardware ruts you may find yourself in while making the Big Switch.

About This Book

Switching to the Mac: The Missing Manual is divided into five parts, each containing several chapters:

- Part One, **Welcome to Macintosh,** covers the essentials of the Macintosh. It's a crash course in everything you see onscreen when you turn on the machine: the Dock, Sidebar, icons, windows, menus, scroll bars, Trash, aliases, menu, and so on.

- Part Two, **Making the Move,** is dedicated to the actual process of hauling your software, settings, and even peripherals (like printers and monitors) across the chasm from the PC to the Mac. It covers both the easy parts (copying over your documents, pictures, and music files) and the harder ones (transferring your email, address books, buddy lists, and so on). It also covers the steps for running Windows on your Mac, which is an extremely attractive option.

- Part Three, **Yosemite Online,** walks you through the process of setting up an Internet connection on your Mac. It also covers Apple's Internet software suite: Mail, Contacts, Safari, and Messages.

Note: Much of this book is adapted from *OS X Yosemite: The Missing Manual*. That book is a fatter, more in-depth guide to OS X.

- Part Four, **Putting Down Roots**, deals with more advanced topics—and aims to turn you into a Macintosh power user. It teaches you how to use Yosemite's new Continuity features, set up private accounts for people who share a Mac, create a network for file sharing and screen sharing, navigate the System Preferences program (the Mac equivalent of the Windows Control Panel), use the Notification Center, operate the 50 or so freebie bonus programs that come with OS X.

- Part Five, **Appendixes**. At the end of the book, you'll find four appendixes. The first two cover installation and troubleshooting. The third is the "Where'd It Go?" Dictionary—an essential reference for anyone who occasionally (or frequently) flounders to find some familiar control in the new, alien Macintosh environment. The last is a master keyboard-shortcut list for the entire Mac universe.

About→These→Arrows

Throughout this book—and throughout the Missing Manual series—you'll find sentences like this one: "Open the System→Libraries→Fonts folder." That's shorthand for a much longer instruction that directs you to open three nested folders in sequence, like this: "On your hard drive, you'll find a folder called System. Open that. Inside the System folder window is a folder called Libraries; double-click it to open it. Inside *that* folder is yet another one called Fonts. Double-click to open it, too."

Similarly, this kind of arrow shorthand helps to simplify the business of choosing commands in menus, as shown in Figure I-1.

Figure I-1:
If this book says "Choose View→Arrange By→Name," it's describing a logical sequence of steps.

In this example, that would mean clicking the View menu, choosing the Arrange By command from it, and then choosing Name from the submenu.

About MissingManuals.com

If you visit *www.missingmanuals.com,* click the "Missing CD" link, and then click the title of this book, you'll find a neat, organized, chapter-by-chapter list of the shareware and freeware mentioned in this book. (As noted on the inside back cover, having the software online instead of on a CD saved you $5 on the cost of the book.)

The Web site also offers corrections and updates to the book (to see them, click the book's title, and then click Errata). In fact, you're encouraged to submit such corrections and updates yourself. In an effort to keep the book as up to date and accurate as possible, each time we print more copies, we'll make any confirmed corrections you've suggested. We'll also note such changes on the Web site, so that you can mark important corrections into your own copy of the book, if you like.

The Very Basics

To use this book, and indeed to use a Mac, you need to know a few basics. This book assumes you're familiar with a few terms and concepts:

- **Clicking.** This book gives you three kinds of instructions that require you to use the Mac's mouse. To *click* means to point the arrow cursor at something on the screen and then—without moving the cursor—press and release the clicker button on the mouse (or your laptop trackpad). To *double-click,* of course, means to click twice in rapid succession, again without moving the cursor at all. And to *drag* means to move the cursor while holding down the button.

 When you're told to ⌘-*click* something, you click while pressing the ⌘ key (which is next to the space bar). *Shift-clicking, Option-clicking,* and *Control-clicking* work the same way—just click while pressing the corresponding keys.

- **Menus.** The *menus* are the words at the top of your screen: , File, Edit, and so on. Click one to make a list of commands appear.

 Some people click and release to open a menu and then, after reading the choices, click again on the one they want. Other people like to press the mouse button continuously after the initial click on the menu title, drag down the list to the desired command, and only then release the mouse button. Either method works fine.

- **Dialog boxes.** See Figure I-2 for a tour of the onscreen elements you'll frequently be asked to use, like checkboxes, radio buttons, tabs, and so on.

- **Keyboard shortcuts.** If you're typing along in a burst of creative energy, it's disruptive to have to grab the mouse to use a menu. That's why many computer fans prefer to trigger menu commands by pressing certain combinations on the keyboard. For example, in word processors, you can press ⌘-B to produce a **boldface** word. When you read an instruction like "press ⌘-B," start by pressing the ⌘ key, and then, while it's down, type the letter B, and finally release both keys.

Tip: You know what's really nice? The keystroke to open the Preferences dialog box in every Apple program—Mail, Safari, iMovie, iPhoto, TextEdit, Preview, and on and on—is always the same: ⌘-comma. Better yet, that standard is catching on with other software companies, too; Word, Excel, Outlook, and PowerPoint use the same keystroke, for example.

- **Icons.** The colorful inch-tall pictures that appear in your various desktop folders are the graphic symbols that represent each program, disk, and document on your computer. If you click an icon one time, it darkens, indicating that you've just *highlighted* or *selected* it. Now you're ready to manipulate it by using, for example, a menu command.

A few more tips on mastering the Mac keyboard appear in Chapter 1. Otherwise, if you've digested this much information, you have all the technical background you need to enjoy *Switching to the Mac: The Missing Manual*.

Figure I-2:
Knowing what you're doing on the Mac often requires knowing what things are called. Here are some of the most common onscreen elements. They include checkboxes (turn on as many as you like) and radio buttons (only one can be turned on in each grouping).

Pressing Return is usually the same as clicking the default button—the lower-right button that almost always means "OK, I'm done here."

Toolbar Pop-up menu Tabs Text box

Checkboxes Radio buttons Default button

Part One:
Welcome to Macintosh

1

How the Mac Is Different

When you get right down to it, the job description of every operating system is pretty much the same. Whether it's Mac OS X, Windows, or Billy Bob's System-Software Special, any OS must serve as the ambassador between the computer and you, its human operator. It must somehow represent your files and programs on the screen so you can open them; offer some method of organizing your files; present onscreen controls that affect your speaker volume, mouse speed, and so on; and communicate with your external gadgets, like disks, printers, and digital cameras.

In other words, OS X offers roughly the same features as Windows. That's the good news.

The bad news is that these features are called different things and parked in different spots. As you could have predicted, this rearrangement of features can mean a good deal of confusion for you, the Macintosh foreigner. For the first few days or weeks, you may instinctively reach for certain familiar features that simply aren't where you expect to find them, the way your tongue keeps sticking itself into the socket of a newly extracted tooth.

To minimize your frustration, therefore, read this chapter first. It makes plain the most important and dramatic differences between the Windows method and the Macintosh way.

Power On, Dude

As a critic might say, Apple is always consistent with its placement of the power button: It's different on every model.

On iMacs and Mac minis, the power button is on the back panel. On the Mac Pro, it's on the front panel. And on laptop Macs, the button is either a key in the upper-right corner of the keyboard or a round button *near* the upper right of the keyboard. (Then again, if you have a laptop, you should get into the habit of just closing the lid when you're done working and opening it to resume; the power button rarely plays a role in your life.)

In every case, though, the power button looks the same (Figure 1-1): It bears the ⏻ logo.

Figure 1-1:
Every Mac's power button looks like this, although it might be hard to find. The good news: Once you find it, it'll pretty much stay in the same place.

Right-Clicking and Shortcut Menus

You can get terrific mileage out of *shortcut menus* on the Mac, just as in Windows (Figure 1-2).

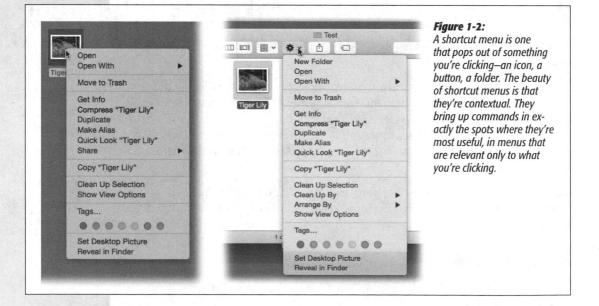

Figure 1-2:
A shortcut menu is one that pops out of something you're clicking—an icon, a button, a folder. The beauty of shortcut menus is that they're contextual. They bring up commands in exactly the spots where they're most useful, in menus that are relevant only to what you're clicking.

They're so important, in fact, that it's worth these paragraphs to explain the different ways you can trigger a "right-click." (Apple calls it a *secondary click,* because not all of these methods actually involve a second mouse button. Also, left-handed people may want to make the *left* mouse button trigger a right-click.)

- **Use the trackpad.** If you have a trackpad (a laptop, for example), you can trigger a right-click in all kinds of ways:

 Out of the box, you do it by clicking the trackpad with *two* fingers. The shortcut menu pops right up.

 Or you can point to whatever you want to click. Rest two fingers on the trackpad—and then click with your thumb.

 But even those aren't the end of your options. In System Preferences→Trackpad, you can turn on even more right-click methods (and even watch little videos on how to do them; see Figure 1-3). For example, you can "right-click" by clicking either the lower-right or lower-left corner of the trackpad—one finger only.

Figure 1-3:
The Trackpad pane of System Preferences looks different depending on your laptop model. But this one shows the three ways to get a "right-click."

- **Control-click.** You can open the shortcut menu of something on the Mac screen by Control-clicking it. That is, while pressing the Control key (bottom row), click the mouse on your target.

• **Right-click.** Experienced computer fans have always preferred the one-handed method: right-clicking. That is, clicking something by pressing the *right* mouse button on a two-button mouse.

"Ah, but that's what's always driven me nuts about Apple," goes the common refrain, "its refusal to get rid of its stupid one-button mouse!"

Well, not so fast.

First of all, you can attach any old $6 USB two-button mouse to the Mac, and it'll work flawlessly. Recycle the one from your old PC, if you like.

Furthermore, if you have a desktop Mac, then you already *have* a two-button mouse—but you might not realize it. Take a look: Is it a white, shiny plastic capsule with a tiny, gray scrolling track-pea on the far end? Then you have a Mighty Mouse. Is it a cordless, flattened capsule instead? Then it's the newer Magic Mouse. Each has a *secret* right mouse button. It doesn't work until you ask for it.

To do that, choose →System Preferences. Click Mouse. There, in all its splendor, is a diagram of the Mighty or Magic Mouse.

Your job is to choose Secondary Button from the pop-up menu that identifies the right side of the mouse.

From now on, even though there aren't two visible mouse buttons, your mouse does, in fact, register a left-click or a right-click depending on which side of the mouse you push down. It works a lot more easily than it sounds like it would.

Logging Out, Shutting Down

If you're the only person who uses your Mac, then finishing up a work session is simple. You can either turn off the machine or simply let it go to sleep, in any of several ways.

Sleep Mode

If you're still shutting down your Mac after each use, you may be doing a lot more waiting than necessary. Sleep mode consumes very little power, keeps everything you were doing open and available, and wakes up almost immediately when you press a key or click the mouse.

To make your machine sleep, do one of the following:

• **Close the lid.** (Hint: This tip works primarily on laptops.)

• **Press the power button** (⏻). In Yosemite, tapping that button makes both laptops and desktops drop off to sleep instantly.

• **Hold down the power button** (⏻) **for 2 seconds.** You get the box shown in Figure 1-4; hit Sleep (or type *S*).

• **Choose →Sleep.** Or press Option-⌘-⏏. (The ⏏ key doesn't appear on laptops—only on the keyboards of some desktop Macs.)

- **Press Control-⏏**. In the dialog box shown in Figure 1-4, click Sleep (or type *S*).

- **Just walk away,** confident that the Energy Saver setting in System Preferences will send the machine off to dreamland automatically at the specified time.

Tip: Ordinarily, closing your MacBook's lid means putting it to sleep. And, ordinarily, putting it to sleep means cutting it off from the world. But OS X's Power Nap feature lets your Mac stay connected to your network and to the Internet, even while it's otherwise sleeping. It can download email, back up your stuff, download software updates, and so on.

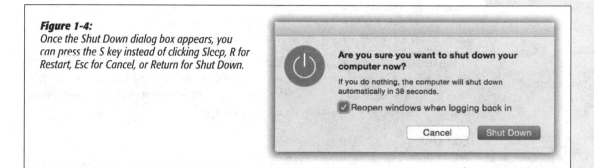

Figure 1-4:
Once the Shut Down dialog box appears, you can press the S key instead of clicking Sleep, R for Restart, Esc for Cancel, or Return for Shut Down.

Are you sure you want to shut down your computer now?

If you do nothing, the computer will shut down automatically in 38 seconds.

☑ Reopen windows when logging back in

Cancel Shut Down

Restart

You shouldn't have to restart the Mac very often—only in times of severe trouble-shooting mystification, in fact. Here are a few ways to do it:

- **Choose ⌘→Restart.** A confirmation dialog box appears; click Restart (or press Return).

Tip: If you press Option as you release the mouse on the ⌘→Restart command, you won't be bothered by an "Are you sure?" confirmation box.

- **Press Control-⌘-⏏.**

- **Press Control-⏏** (or hold down the ⏻ button) to summon the dialog box shown in Figure 1-4; click Restart (or type *R*).

Shut Down

To shut down your machine completely (when you don't plan to use it for more than a couple of days, when you plan to transport it, and so on), do one of the following:

- **Choose ⌘→Shut Down.** A simple confirmation dialog box appears; click Shut Down (or press Return).

Tip: Once again, if you press Option as you release the mouse, no confirmation box appears.

- **Press Control-Option-⌘-⏏.** (It's not as complex as it looks—the first three keys are all in a tidy row to the left of the space bar.)

• **Press Control-⏏** (or hold down the ⏻ button) to summon the dialog box shown in Figure 1-4. Click Shut Down (or press Return).

• **Wait.** If you've set up the Energy Saver preferences to shut down the Mac automatically at a specified time, then you don't have to do anything.

The "Reopen windows" Option

In the Shut Down dialog box illustrated in Figure 1-4, you'll notice a checkbox called "Reopen windows when logging back in." That option does something very useful: The next time you start up your Mac, every running program, and every open window, will reopen exactly as it was at the moment you used the Restart or Shut Down command. The option gives the Mac something like the old Hibernate feature in Windows—and saves you a lot of reopening the next time you sit down to work.

If you turn off that checkbox, then your next startup will take you to the desktop, with no programs running. And if you want the Mac to stop asking—if you never want your programs and windows to reopen—then open ⌘→System Preferences→General and turn on "Close windows when quitting an app."

Log Out

If you share your Mac, then you should log out when you're done. Doing so ensures that your stuff is safe from the evil and the clueless even when you're out of the room. To do it, choose ⌘→Log Out Casey (or whatever your name is). Or, if you're in a hurry, press Shift-⌘-Q.

When the confirmation dialog box appears, click Log Out (or press Return) or just wait for 1 minute (a message performs the countdown for you). The Mac hides your world from view and displays the Log In dialog box, ready for its next victim.

Tip: Last time: If you press Option as you release the mouse on the ⌘→Log Out command, you squelch the "Are you sure?" box.

The Menu Bar

On the Mac, there's only one menu bar. It's always at the top of the screen. The names of these menus, and the commands inside them, change to suit the window you're currently using. That's different from Windows, where a separate menu bar appears at the top of *every* window.

Mac and Windows devotees can argue the relative merits of these two approaches until they're blue in the face. All that matters, though, is that you know where to look when you want to reach for a menu command. On the Mac, you always look upward.

Finder = Windows Explorer

In OS X, the "home base" program—the one that shows you the icons of all your folders and files, the equivalent of Windows Explorer (File Explorer) on the PC—is

called the Finder. This is where you manage your folders and files, throw things away, manipulate disks, and so on. (You will also hear it called the *desktop*, since the items you find there mirror the files and folders you might find on a real-life desktop.)

Finder = Windows Explorer

Getting used to the term "Finder" is worthwhile, though, because it comes up so often. For example, the first icon on your Dock is labeled "Finder," and clicking it always takes you back to your desktop.

Dock = Taskbar

At the bottom of almost every OS X screen sits a tiny row of photorealistic icons. This is the Dock, a close parallel to the Windows taskbar. (As in Windows, it may be hidden or placed on the left or the right edge of the screen instead—options that appeal primarily to power users and eccentrics.)

The Dock displays the icons of all your open windows and programs, which are denoted by small, glowing markers beneath their icons. Clicking these icons opens the corresponding files, folders, disks, documents, and programs. If you click and hold (or right-click) an open program's icon, you'll see a pop-up list of the open windows in that program, along with Quit and a few other commands.

When you close a program, its icon disappears from the Dock (unless you've secured it there for easy access, as described on page 76).

Tip: You can cycle through the various open programs on your Mac by holding down the ⌘ key and pressing Tab repeatedly. (Sound familiar? It's just like Alt-Tabbing in Windows.) And if you just *tap* ⌘-Tab, you bounce back and forth between the two programs you've used most recently.

What you may find confusing at first, though, is that the Dock also performs one function of the old Windows Start menu: It provides a "short list" of programs and files that you use often, for easy access. To add a new icon to the Dock, just drag it there (put programs to the left of the divider line; everything else goes on the right). To remove an icon from the Dock, just drag it away. As long as that item isn't actually open at the moment, it disappears from the Dock with a little animated puff of smoke when you release the mouse button.

The bottom line: On the Mac, a single interface element—the Dock—exhibits characteristics of *both* the Start menu (it lists frequently used programs) and the taskbar (it lists currently open programs and files). (The Windows 8 taskbar does the same thing.)

If you're still confused, Chapter 2 should help clear things up.

Menulets = Tray

Most Windows fans refer to the row of tiny status icons at the lower-right corner of the screen as the *tray,* even though Microsoft's official term is the *notification area.* (Why use one syllable when eight will do?)

Macintosh folks wage a similar battle of terminology when it comes to the little menu-bar icons shown in Figure 1-5. Apple calls them Menu Extras, but Mac fans prefer to call them *menulets*.

In any case, these menu-bar icons are cousins of the Windows tray—each is both an indicator and a menu that provides direct access to certain settings. One menulet lets you adjust your Mac's speaker volume, another shows you the remaining power in your laptop battery, and so on.

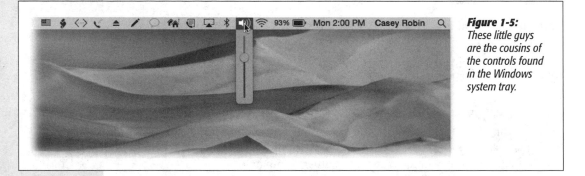

Figure 1-5:
These little guys are the cousins of the controls found in the Windows system tray.

Making a menulet appear usually involves turning on a certain checkbox. These checkboxes lurk on the various panes of *System Preferences* (Chapter 17), which is the Mac equivalent of the Control Panel. (To open System Preferences, choose its name from the menu or click the gear icon on the Dock.)

Here's a rundown of the most useful Apple menulets, complete with instructions on where to find the magic on/off checkbox for each.

- **AirPlay** () lets you send the Mac's screen image to a TV, provided that you have an Apple TV (details on page 35). This menulet turns blue when you're projecting, and its menu lets you turn AirPlay on or off. *To find the Show checkbox:* Open System Preferences→Displays→Display tab.

- **WiFi** () lets you turn your WiFi (wireless networking) circuitry on or off, join existing wireless networks, and create your own private ones. *To find the Show checkbox:* Open System Preferences→Network. Click Wi-Fi.

Tip: You can *Option-click* this menulet to produce a secret menu full of details about the wireless network you're on right now. You see its channel number, password-security method (WEP, WPA, None, whatever), speed, and such geeky details as the MCS Index and RSSI.

- **Battery** () shows how much power remains in your laptop's battery, how much time is left to charge it, whether it's plugged in, and more. When you click the icon to open the menu, you see how many actual hours and minutes are left on the charge. You can also choose Show Percentage to add a percentage-remaining readout (43%) to the menu bar.

This Battery menu also shows something that can be even more useful: a list of the most power-hungry open programs ("Apps Using Significant Energy"). That's handy when you're trying to eke out every last drop of battery life for your laptop. *To find the Show checkbox:* Open System Preferences→Energy Saver.

Tip: If you Option-click the Battery menulet, you get to see the status of your battery's health. A Condition command appears. It might say, for example, "Condition: Normal," "Service Battery," "Replace Soon," or "Replace Now." Of course, we all know laptop batteries don't last forever; they begin to hold less of a charge as they approach 500 or 1,000 recharges, depending on the model.

Is Apple looking out for you, or just trying to goose the sale of replacement batteries? You decide.

- **Bluetooth** (✻) connects to Bluetooth devices, "pairs" your Mac with a cellphone, lets you send or receive files wirelessly (without the hassle of setting up a wireless network), and so on. *To find the Show checkbox:* Open System Preferences→Bluetooth.

UP TO SPEED

Where Your Free Hour of Battery Life Came From

Some of the features Apple works hardest on are things you'll never even see.

One big category: technologies designed to save battery power. Since 75 percent of new Macs are laptops, battery life is a big, big deal.

Here are some of these behind-the-scenes juice-preservation techniques in recent OS X versions, bearing the names Apple has given them:

App Nap. When a program's window is completely covered up by other windows, the Mac slows down that background app. (Ditto for Safari background tabs.)

Slower means less power-hungry—as much as 23 percent, Apple says. (If the app is *doing* something in the background, like downloading or playing music, then App Nap doesn't kick in.) The instant you bring the program to the foreground, it snaps back to full speed.

Timer Coalescing. OS X attempts to consolidate processing tasks and feed them to your Intel chip in bursts. That way,

the processor earns tiny micro-vacations—idle time. More idle time means less power use. Your savings this time: as much as 72 percent.

iTunes HD Playback Efficiency. By reducing the frequency of hard-drive access during iTunes video and audio playback, Apple says the Mac uses up to 35 percent less energy.

Safari Power Saver. Flash videos and animations are famous battery hogs. So when Safari spots a Flash video off at the edges of a Web page—on the side or the top, for example—it concludes that what you've got here is an ad. And it stops the ad from playing until you click on it. (You see a banner on the video that says "Safari Power Saver. Click to start Flash Plug-In.")

Apple says all of its power-saving features together can extend a MacBook Pro's battery charge by as much as an hour. Not bad for a free system-software upgrade, eh?

- **Clock** is the menu-bar clock that's been sitting at the upper-right corner of your screen from Day One. Click it to open a menu where you can check today's date, convert the menu-bar display to a tiny analog clock, and so on. *To find the Show checkbox:* Open System Preferences→Date & Time. On the Clock tab, turn on "Show date and time in menu bar."

- **Time Machine** (⟳) lets you start and stop Time Machine backups (see Chapter 5). *To find the Show checkbox:* Open System Preferences→Time Machine.

- **User** identifies the account holder (Chapter 15) who's logged in at the moment. To make this menulet appear (in bold, at the far-right end of the menu bar), turn on *fast user switching,* which is described on page 514.

- **Volume** (◀⟩), of course, adjusts your Mac's speaker or headphone volume. *To find the Show checkbox:* Open System Preferences→Sound.

To remove a menulet, ⌘-drag it off your menu bar, or turn off the corresponding checkbox in System Preferences. You can also rearrange menulets by ⌘-dragging them horizontally.

These little guys are useful, good-looking, and respectful of your screen space. The world could use more inventions like menulets.

Keyboard Differences

Mac and PC keyboards are subtly different. Making the switch involves two big adjustments: figuring out where the special Windows keys went (like Alt and Ctrl)—and figuring out what to do with the special Macintosh keys (like ⌘ and Option).

Where the Windows Keys Went

Here's how to find the Macintosh equivalents of familiar PC keyboard keys:

- **Ctrl key.** The Macintosh offers a key labeled Control (or, on laptops, "ctrl"), but it *isn't* the equivalent of the PC's Ctrl key. The Mac's Control key is primarily for helping you "right-click" things, as described earlier.

 Instead, the Macintosh equivalent of the Windows Ctrl key is the ⌘ key. It's right next to the space bar. It's pronounced "command," although novices can often be heard calling it the "pretzel key," "Apple key," or "clover key."

 Most Windows Ctrl-key combos correspond perfectly to ⌘-key sequences on the Mac. The Save command is now ⌘-S instead of Ctrl+S, Open is ⌘-O instead of Ctrl+O, and so on.

Note: Mac keyboard shortcuts are listed at the right side of each open menu, just as in Windows. Unfortunately, they're represented in the menu with goofy symbols instead of their true key names. Here's your cheat sheet to the menu keyboard symbols: ⇧ represents the Shift key, ⌥ means the Option key, and ^ refers to the Control key.

- **Alt key.** On North American Mac keyboards, a key on the bottom row is labeled both Alt and Option. This is the closest thing the Mac offers to the Windows Alt key.

 In many situations, keyboard shortcuts that involve the Alt key in Windows use the Option key on the Mac. For example, in Microsoft Word, the keyboard shortcut for the Split Document Window command is Alt+Ctrl+S in Windows, but *Option-*⌘*-T* on the Macintosh.

 Still, these two keys aren't exactly the same. Whereas the Alt key's most popular function is to control the menus in Windows programs, the Option key on the Mac is a "miscellaneous" key that triggers secret functions and special characters.

 For example, when you hold down the Option key as you click the Close or Minimize button on a Macintosh window, you close or minimize *all* open windows in that program. And if you press the Option key while you type *R, G,* or *2,* you get the ®, ©, and ™ symbols in your document, respectively. (See page 228 to find out how you can see which letters turn into which symbols when pressed with Option.)

- ⊞ **key.** As you probably could have guessed, there is no Windows-logo key on the Macintosh. Then again, there's no Start menu to open by pressing it, either.

Tip: Just about any USB keyboard works on the Mac, even if the keyboard was originally designed to work with a PC. Depending on the manufacturer of the keyboard, the Windows-logo key may work just like the Mac's ⌘ key.

- **Backspace and Delete.** On the Mac, the backspace key is labeled "Delete," although it's in exactly the same place as the Windows Backspace key.

 The Delete key in Windows (technically, the *forward delete* key, because it deletes the character to the right of the insertion point) is a different story. On a desktop Macintosh with a full-size keyboard, it's labeled with "Delete" and the ⌦ symbol.

 On small Mac keyboards (like laptop and wireless keyboards), this key is missing. You can still perform a forward delete, however, by pressing the regular Delete key while pressing the fn key in the corner of the keyboard.

- **Enter.** Most full-size Windows keyboards have *two* Enter keys: one at the right side of the alphabet keyboard and one in the lower-right corner of the number pad. They're identical in function; pressing either one serves to "click" the OK button in a dialog box, for example.

 On the Mac, the big key on the number pad still says "Enter," but the key on the alphabet keyboard is labeled "Return." Most of the time, their function is

identical—either can "click" the OK button of a dialog box. Every now and then, though, you'll run across a Mac program where Return and Enter do different things. In Microsoft Word for OS X, for example, Shift-*Return* inserts a line break, but Shift-*Enter* creates a page break.

What the Special Mac Keys Do

So much for finding the Windows keys you're used to. There's another category of keys worth discussing: those on the Mac keyboard you've never seen before.

To make any attempt at an explanation even more complicated, Apple's keyboards keep changing. The one you're using right now is probably one of these models:

- **The current keyboards,** where the keys are flat little jobbers that poke up through square holes in the aluminum (Figure 1-6). That's what you get on current laptops, wired keyboards, and Bluetooth wireless keyboards.

Figure 1-6:
On the top row of aluminum Mac keyboards, the F-keys have dual functions. Ordinarily, the F1 through F4 keys correspond to Screen Dimmer, Screen Brighter, Exposé, and Dashboard. Pressing the fn key in the corner changes their personalities, though.

- **The older, plastic desktop keyboards,** or the white or black plastic laptop ones.

Here, then, is a guided tour of the non-typewriter keys on the modern Mac keyboard:

- **fn.** How are you supposed to pronounce "fn"? Not "function," certainly; after all, the F-keys on the top row are already known as function keys. And not "fun"; goodness knows, the fn key isn't particularly hilarious to press.

 What it *does,* though, is quite clear: It changes the purpose of certain keys. That's a big deal on laptops, which don't have nearly as many keys as desktop keyboards. So for some of the less commonly used functions, you're supposed to press fn and a regular key. (For example, fn turns the ▲ key into a Page Up key, which scrolls upward by one screenful.)

Note: On most Mac keyboards, the fn key is in the lower-left corner. The exception is the full-size Apple desktop keyboard (the one with a numeric keypad); there, the fn key is in the little block of keys between the letter keys and the number pad.

You'll find many more fn examples in the following paragraphs.

- **Numeric keypad.** The number-pad keys do exactly the same thing as the numbers at the top of the keyboard. But with practice, typing things like phone numbers and prices is much faster with the number pad, since you don't have to look down at what you're doing.

Apple has been quietly eliminating the numeric keypad from most of its keyboards, but you can still find it on some models.

- ☼, ☀ (**F1, F2**). These keys control the brightness of your screen. Usually, you can tone it down a bit when you're in a dark room or when you want to save laptop battery power; you'll want to crank it up in the sun.

- ▦ (**F3**). This one fires up Mission Control, the handy window-management feature described in Chapter 4.

- ⊙ or ⊞ (**F4**). Tap the ⊙ key to open Dashboard, the archipelago of tiny, single-purpose widgets like Weather, Stocks, and Movies. Chapter 4 describes Dashboard in detail.

On recent Macs, the F4 key bears a ⊞ logo instead. Tapping it opens Launchpad, which is described on page 152.

- ☀, ☀ (**F5, F6**). Most recent Mac laptops have light-up *keys,* which is very handy indeed when you're typing in the dark. The key lights are supposed to come on automatically when it's dark, but you can also control the illumination yourself by tapping these keys. (On most other Macs, the F5 and F6 keys aren't assigned to anything. They're free for you to use as you see fit.)

- ◄◄, ►▮▮, and ►► (**F7, F8, F9**). These keys work in the programs you'd expect: iTunes, QuickTime Player, DVD Player, and other programs where it's handy to have Rewind, Play/Pause, and Fast Forward buttons.

UP TO SPEED

The Wacky Keystrokes of OS X

OS X offers a glorious assortment of predefined keystrokes for jumping to the most important locations on your Mac: your Home folder, the Applications folder, the Utilities folder, the Computer window, your iDisk, the Network window, and so on.

Better yet, the keystrokes are incredibly simple to memorize: Just press Shift-⌘ and the first letter of the location you want. Shift-⌘-H opens your Home folder, Shift-⌘-A opens the Applications folder, and so on. You learn one,

you've learned 'em all. The point here is that Shift-⌘ means *places.*

The other system-wide key combo, Option-⌘, means *functions.* For example, Option-⌘-D hides or shows the Dock, Option-⌘-H is the Hide Others command, Option-⌘-+ magnifies the screen (if you've turned on this feature in System Preferences→Accessibility→Zoom), Option-⌘-Esc brings up the Force Quit dialog box, and so on. Consistency is always nice.

Tip: Tap either ⏪ or ⏩ to skip to the previous or next track or chapter. Hold one down to rewind or fast-forward.

- ◀, ◀), ◀))) **(F10, F11, F12).** These three keys control your speaker volume. The ◀ key means Mute; tap it once to cut off the sound completely and again to restore its previous level. Tap the ◀) repeatedly to make the sound level lower, the ◀)) key to make it louder.

With each tap, you see a big white version of each key's symbol on your screen, your Mac's little nod to let you know it understands your efforts.

Tip: If you hold down the Shift and Option keys, then tapping the volume keys adjusts the volume by smaller increments, just as with the brightness keys.

- **Home, End.** The Home key jumps to the top of a window, the End key to the bottom. If you're looking at a list of files, then the Home and End keys jump to the top or bottom of the list. In iPhoto (page 658), they jump to the first or last photo in your collection. In iMovie, the Home key rewinds your movie to the very beginning. In Safari, they send you to the top or bottom of the Web page.

(In Word, they jump to the beginning or end of the line. But then again, Microsoft has always had its own ways of doing things.)

On keyboards without a dedicated block of number keys, you get these functions by holding down fn as you tap the ◀ and ▶ keys.

- **Pg Up, Pg Down.** These keys scroll up or down by one screenful. The idea is to let you scroll through word-processing documents, Web pages, and lists without having to use the mouse.

GEM IN THE ROUGH

The Least-Known Typing Feature

This may come as a shock if even to those who know the Mac pretty well, but here goes: OS X actually offers system-wide autocomplete of big words, just like the iPhone.

We're not talking about the spelling checker, and we're not talking about text substitution. We're talking, you start typing a word and the Mac finishes it for you. It's ideal when you're in a hurry, when you're not sure how to finish a word (is it "in-dependance" or "independence"?), or when you're trying to solve a crossword puzzle. It works in

Dear Harold,

It has come to our attention

> attention
> attentive
> attentions
> attentively
> attentiveness
> attention's
> attentional

all the standard Mac programs (TextEdit, Mail, Safari, Pages, and so on).

Once you've begun typing a word, press either F5 or Option-Esc to produce the list of possible word completions shown here. If the Mac correctly anticipates the rest of the word, great; press Tab, Return, or the space bar to accept the suggestion, and then keep right on typing. If it guesses wrong, you can either select a different word in the list (using the mouse or the arrow keys), or tap Esc to ignore the suggestions and continue typing.

On keyboards without a numeric keypad, you get these functions by pressing fn plus the ▲ and ▼ keys.

- **Esc.** Esc stands for Escape, and it means "cancel." It's fantastically useful. It closes dialog boxes, closes menus, and exits special modes like Quick Look, slideshows, screensavers, and so on. Get to know it.

- **Delete.** The Backspace key.

- **⌘.** This key triggers keyboard shortcuts for menu items.

- **Control.** The Control key triggers shortcut menus.

- **Option.** The Option key (labeled "Alt" on keyboards in some countries) is sort of a "miscellaneous" key. It's the equivalent of the Alt key in Windows.

 It lets you access secret features—you'll find them described all through this book—and type special symbols. For example, you press Option-4 to get the ¢ symbol, and Option-Y to get the ¥ (yen) symbol.

- **Help.** In the Finder, Microsoft programs, and a few other places, this key opens up the electronic help screens. But you guessed that.

The Complicated Story of the Function Keys

As the previous section makes clear, the F-keys at the top of modern Mac keyboards come with predefined functions. They control screen brightness, keyboard brightness, speaker volume, music playback, and so on.

But they didn't always. Before Apple gave F9, F10, and F11 to the fast-forward and speaker-volume functions, those keys controlled the Exposé window-management function described in Chapter 4.

So the question is this: What if you don't *want* to trigger the hardware features of these keys? What if you want pressing F1 to mean "F1" (which opens the Help window in some programs)? What if you want F9, F10, and F11 to control Exposé's three modes?

For that purpose, you're supposed to press the fn key. The fn key (lower left on small keyboards, center block of keys on the big ones) switches the function of the function keys. In other words, pressing fn-F10 triggers an Exposé feature, even though the key has a mute symbol (◄) painted on it.

But here's the thing: What if you use those F-keys for software features (like Cut, Copy, Paste, and Exposé) *more often* than the hardware features (like brightness and volume)?

In that case, you can reverse the logic, so that pressing the F-keys *alone* triggers software functions, and they govern brightness and audio only when you're pressing fn. To do that, choose →System Preferences→Keyboard. Turn on the cryptically worded checkbox "Use F1, F2, etc. keys as standard function keys."

And that's it. From now on, you press the fn key to get the functions painted on the keys (◄◄, ►ıı, ►►, ◄, ◄), ◄)), ☀, ☀, and so on).

Disk Differences

Working with disks is very different on the Mac. Whereas Windows is designed to show the names (letters) and icons for your disk *drives*, the Mac shows you the names and icons of your *disks*. You'll never, ever see an icon for an empty drive, as you do in Windows.

As soon as you insert, say, a flash drive, you see its name and icon appear on the screen. In fact, *every* disk inside, or attached to, a Mac is represented on the desktop by an icon (see Figure 1-7). (Your main hard drive's icon may or may not appear in the upper-right corner, depending on your settings in Finder→Preferences.)

Figure 1-7:
You may see all kinds of disks on the OS X desktop (shown here: hard drive, CD, iPod, flash drive)—or none at all, if you've chosen to hide them using the Finder→Preferences command. But chances are pretty good you won't be seeing many floppy disk icons.

If you do decide to hide your disk icons, you can always get to them as you do in Windows: by opening the Computer window (Go→Computer).

If you prefer the Windows look, in which no disk icons appear on the desktop, it's easy enough to recreate it on the Mac; choose Finder→Preferences and turn off the four checkboxes you see there ("Hard disks," "External disks," "CDs, DVDs, and iPods," and "Connected servers.")

Ejecting a disk from the Mac is a little bit different, too, depending on whether it's a CD, DVD, USB flash drive, shared network disk, iDisk, iPod, or external hard drive. You can go about it in any of these ways:

- Hold down the ⏏ key on your keyboard, if you have one (CDs and DVDs only).

- Right-click the disk's desktop icon. From the shortcut menu that appears, choose "Eject [whatever the disk's name is]."

- Click the disk's icon and then choose File→"Eject [disk's name]" (or press ⌘-E).

- Drag the icon of the disk onto the Trash icon at the end of the Dock. (You'll see its icon turn into a giant ⏏ symbol, the Mac's little acknowledgment that it knows what you're trying to do.)

Where Your Stuff Is

If you open the icon for your main hard drive (Macintosh HD) from the Go→Computer window, for example, all you'll find in the Macintosh HD window is a set of folders called Applications, Library, and Users.

Most of these folders aren't very useful to you, the Mac's human companion. They're there for OS X's own use (which is why Apple no longer puts the Macintosh HD icon on the desktop of new Macs, as it did for 25 years). Think of your main hard drive window as storage for the operating system itself, which you'll access only for occasional administrative purposes.

In fact, the folders you really do care about boil down to these:

Applications Folder

Applications is Apple's word for programs.

When it comes to managing your programs, the Applications folder (which you can open by choosing Go→Applications) is something like the Program Files folder in Windows—but without the worry. You should feel free to open this folder and double-click things. In fact, that's exactly what you're supposed to do. This is your complete list of programs. (What's on your Dock is more like a Greatest Hits subset.)

Better yet, on the Mac, programs bear their real, plain-English names, like *Microsoft Word,* rather than abbreviations, like *WINWORD.EXE.* Most are self-contained in a single icon, too (rather than being composed of hundreds of little support files), which makes copying or deleting them extremely easy.

Home Folder

Your documents, files, and preferences, meanwhile, sit in an important folder called your *Home folder.* Inside are folders that closely resemble the My Documents, My Pictures, and My Music folders on Windows.

OS X is rife with shortcuts for opening this all-important folder:

- Choose Go→Home.

- Press Shift-⌘-H.

- Click the ⌂ icon in the Sidebar (page 35). (If you don't see it there, then choose Finder→Preferences→Sidebar and turn on the ⌂ checkbox in the list of Places.)

Within your Home folder, you'll find another set of standard Mac folders. (You can tell the Mac considers them holy because they have special logos on their folder icons.) Except as noted, you're free to rename or delete them; OS X creates the following folders solely as a convenience:

- **Desktop.** When you drag an icon out of a folder or disk window and onto your OS X desktop, it may appear to show up on the desktop. But that's just a visual convenience. In truth, nothing in OS X is really on the desktop. It's actually in this Desktop folder, and mirrored in the desktop area.

You can entertain yourself for hours by proving this point to yourself. If you drag something out of your Desktop folder, it also disappears from the actual desktop. And vice versa. (You're not allowed to delete or rename this folder.)

• **Documents.** Apple suggests that you keep your actual work files in this folder. Sure enough, whenever you save a new document (when you're working in Keynote or Word, for example), the Save As box proposes storing the new file in this folder.

Your programs may also create folders of their own here. For example, you may find a Microsoft User Data folder for your Outlook email, a Windows folder for use with Parallels or VMware Fusion (Chapter 8), and so on.

• **Library.** The main Library folder (the one in your main hard drive window) contains folders for your Mac's system-wide fonts, preferences, help files, and so on.

You have your *own* Library folder, too. It stores the same kinds of things—but they're *your* fonts, your preferences, and so on. It's generally hidden, although you can get to it by pressing Option as you choose Go→Library.

• **Movies, Music, Pictures.** These folders, of course, are designed to store multimedia files. The various OS X programs that deal with movies, music, and pictures will propose these specialized folders as storage locations. For example, when you plug a digital camera into a Mac, the iPhoto program automatically begins to download the photos on it—and stores them in the Pictures folder. Similarly, iMovie is programmed to look for the Movies folder when saving its files, and iTunes stores its MP3 files in the Music folder.

• **Public.** If you're on a network, or if others use the same Mac when you're not around, this folder can be handy: It's the "Any of you guys can look at these files" folder. Other people on your network, as well as other people who sit down at this machine, are allowed to see whatever you've put in here, even if they don't have your password. (If your Mac isn't on an office network and isn't shared, then you can throw this folder away.) More details on sharing and networking on the Mac are in Chapter 16.

Forcing you to keep all your stuff in a single folder has some major advantages. Most notably, by keeping such tight control over which files go where, OS X keeps itself pure—and very, very stable.

System Folder

This folder is the same idea as the Windows or WINNT folder on a PC, in that it contains hundreds of files that are critical to the functioning of the operating system. These files are so important that moving or renaming them could render the computer useless, as it would in Windows. And although there are thousands of files within, many are hidden for your protection.

For maximum safety and stability, you should ignore OS X's System folder just as thoroughly as you ignored the old Windows folder.

Window Controls

As in Windows, a window on the Mac is framed by an assortment of doodads and gizmos (Figure 1-8). You'll need these to move a window, to close it, to resize it, to scroll it, and so on. But once you get to know the ones on a Macintosh, you're likely to be pleased by the amount of thought those fussy perfectionists at Apple have put into their design.

Here's an overview of the various OS X window-edge gizmos and what they do.

Figure 1-8:
When Steve Jobs unveiled Mac OS X at Macworld Expo in 2000, he said his goal was to oversee the creation of an interface so attractive "you just want to lick it." Desktop windows, with their juicy, fruit-flavored controls, are a good starting point.

Title Bar

When several windows are open, the darkened window name and colorful upper-left controls tell you which window is *active* (in front). Windows in the background have gray, dimmed lettering and gray upper-left control buttons. As in Windows, the title bar also acts as a *handle* that lets you move the entire window around on the screen.

Tip: Here's a nifty keyboard shortcut with no Windows equivalent: You can cycle through the different open windows in one program without using the mouse. Just press ⌘-` (that's the tilde key, to the left of the number 1 key). With each press, you bring a different window forward within the current program. It works both in the Finder and in your programs.

After you've opened one folder inside another, the title bar's secret *folder hierarchy menu* is an efficient way to backtrack—to return to the enclosing window. See Figure 1-9.

One more title bar trick: By double-clicking the title bar, you *minimize* the window (see page 34).

Figure 1-9:
Right-click or two-finger click a Finder window's title bar to summon the hidden folder hierarchy menu. This trick also works in most other OS X programs. For example, you can right-click a document window's title to find out where the document is actually saved on your hard drive.

The Folder Proxy Icon

Virtually every Macintosh title bar features a small icon next to the window's name (Figure 1-10), representing the open window's actual folder or disk icon. In the Finder, dragging this tiny icon (technically called the *folder proxy icon*) lets you move or copy the folder to a different folder or disk, to the Trash, or into the Dock, without having to

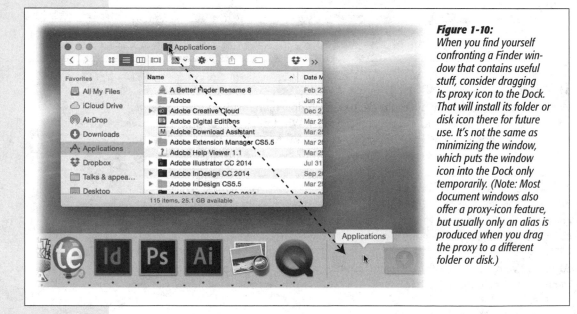

Figure 1-10:
When you find yourself confronting a Finder window that contains useful stuff, consider dragging its proxy icon to the Dock. That will install its folder or disk icon there for future use. It's not the same as minimizing the window, which puts the window icon into the Dock only temporarily. (Note: Most document windows also offer a proxy-icon feature, but usually only an alias is produced when you drag the proxy to a different folder or disk.)

close the window first. (When clicking this proxy icon, hold down the mouse button for half a second, or until the icon darkens. Only then are you allowed to drag it.) It's a handy little function with no Windows equivalent.

Tip: In some programs, including Microsoft Word, dragging this proxy icon lets you move the *actual file* to a different disk or folder—without even leaving the program. It's a great way to make a backup of the document you're working on without interrupting your work.

Close Button

As the tip of your cursor crosses the three buttons at the upper-left corner of a window, tiny symbols appear inside them: ⊗, ⊖, and ⊙. The most important one is the Close button, the red button in the upper-left corner (see Figure 1-8). It closes the window, exactly like the ✕ button at the upper-*right* corner in Windows. Learning to reach for

UP TO SPEED

All My Files

There it is, staring you in the face at the top of the Sidebar in every window: an icon called All My Files. What is this, some kind of geeked-out soap opera?

Nope. It's a massive, searchable, sortable list, all in a single window, of every human-useful file on the computer. That is, pictures, movies, music, documents—no system files, preference files, or other detritus. No matter what folders they're actually in, they appear here in a single window. You can summon it whenever you want, just by clicking the All My Files icon in the Sidebar.

When you first open All My Files, it has your files grouped by type: Contacts, Events & To Dos, Images, PDF Documents, Music, Movies, Presentations, Spreadsheets, Developer (which lists HTML Web site files and Xcode programming files), and Documents (meaning "everything else"). In icon view—the factory setting—each class of icons appears in a single scrolling row. Use a two-finger scroll (trackpad) or one-

finger slide (Magic Mouse) to move through the horizontal list. (If you'd rather not have to scroll, click the tiny Show All button that appears at the right end of each row. Now you're seeing all the icons of this type; click Show Less to return to the single-row effect.)

You can see how this sorting method—which is the new Arrange By command at work (page 52)—might be useful. Suppose you're looking for a certain PowerPoint or Keynote presentation, but you can't remember what you called it or where you filed it. Open All My Files, make sure it's arranged by Kind, and presto: You're looking at a list of every presentation file on your Mac. Using Quick Look (page 68), you can breeze through them, inspecting them one at a time, until you find the one you want.

Apple thinks you'll like All My Files as a starting point for standard file-fussing operations so much that All My Files is the window that appears automatically when you choose File→New Finder Window (or press ⌘-N). (Of course, you can change that in Finder→Preferences.)

the upper-left corner instead of the upper-right will probably confound your muscle memory for the first week of using the Mac.

If you can't break the habit, then learn the keyboard shortcut: ⌘-W (for *window*)—an easier keystroke to type than the Windows version (Alt+F4), which for most people is a two-handed operation. If you get into the habit of dismissing windows with that deft flex of your left hand, you'll find it far easier to close several windows in a row, because you won't have to aim for successive Close buttons.

Tip: If, while working on a document, you see a tiny dot in the center of the Close button, then OS X is trying to tell you that you haven't yet saved your work. The dot goes away when you save the document.

Minimize Button

Click this yellow drop of gel to minimize any Mac window, sending it shrinking, with a genie-like animated effect, into the right end of the Dock, where it now appears as an icon. It's exactly like minimizing a window in Windows, except that the window is now represented by a Dock icon rather than a taskbar button (Figure 1-11). To bring the window back to full size, click the newly created Dock icon. See Chapter 2 for more on the Dock.

Tip: You actually have a bigger target than the tiny Minimize button. The entire title bar is a giant Minimize button when you double-click anywhere on it. Or just press ⌘-M for Minimize.

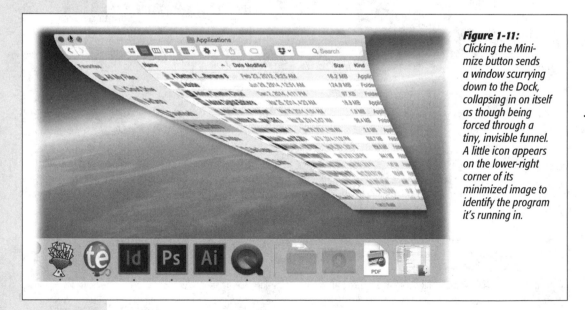

Figure 1-11:
Clicking the Minimize button sends a window scurrying down to the Dock, collapsing in on itself as though being forced through a tiny, invisible funnel. A little icon appears on the lower-right corner of its minimized image to identify the program it's running in.

Full Screen Button

In Yosemite, Apple changed the purpose of this third dot, the green one, on every window's title bar (in most programs, anyway). A click here throws the window into

Full Screen mode, in which the menu bars and window edges disappear, in the name of making your window fill your screen edge to edge. See page 160 for details.

As your cursor approaches this green dot, a little indicator appears inside it: ⊘. That's the hint that you're about to enter Full Screen mode.

And once you're in Full Screen mode, that shape changes to this: ⊕. That's right: It's the universal symbol for "Click me to *leave* Full Screen mode."

In OS X versions before Yosemite, this button was called the Zoom button. It made a desktop window just large enough to reveal all the icons inside it (or, in programs, large enough to reveal all the text, graphics, or music). (The Window→Zoom command does the same thing, and so does double-clicking the title bar of a Finder window.)

If you would prefer that older behavior, just press the Option key as you click. The button sprouts a + button. Now you'll get a zoomed window instead of a full-screen one. (A second Option-click restores the window to its previous size.)

Note: Not all programs permit you to full-screenize their windows. In those apps, this green button displays the + button and, when clicked, merely zooms the window.

The Finder Sidebar

The Sidebar (Figure 1-12) is the pane at the left side of every Finder window, unless you've hidden it. (It's also at the left side of every Open dialog box and every full-size Save dialog box.) It has as many as three sections, each preceded by a collapsible heading.

Tip: If you point to a heading without clicking, a tiny Hide or Show button appears. Click it to collapse or expand that heading's contents.

Here are the headings you'll soon know and love:

- **Favorites.** This primary section of the Sidebar is the place to stash things for easy access. You can stock this list with the icons of disks, files, programs, folders, and the virtual, self-updating folders called *saved searches.*

 Each icon is a shortcut. For example, click the Applications icon to view the contents of your Applications folder in the main part of the window. And if you click the icon of a file or a program, it opens.

 Here, too, you'll find the icons for two recent Mac features: All My Files (see the box on page 33) and AirDrop, the instant-file-sharing feature described on page 484.

- **Shared.** Here's a complete list of the other computers on your network whose owners have turned on File Sharing, ready for access (see Chapter 16 for details).

- **Devices.** This section lists every storage device connected to, or installed inside, your Mac: hard drives, iPhones, iPads, iPods, CDs, DVDs, memory cards, USB flash drives, and so on. (Your main hard drive doesn't usually appear here, but

you can drag it here.) The removable ones (like CDs, DVDs, and i-gadgets) bear a little gray ⏏ logo, which you can click to eject that disk.

- **Tags.** This section lists all your Finder *tags* (color-coded keywords). See page 106 for more on tags.

Note: If you remove everything listed under one of these headings, the heading itself disappears to save space. The heading reappears the next time you put something in its category back into the Sidebar.

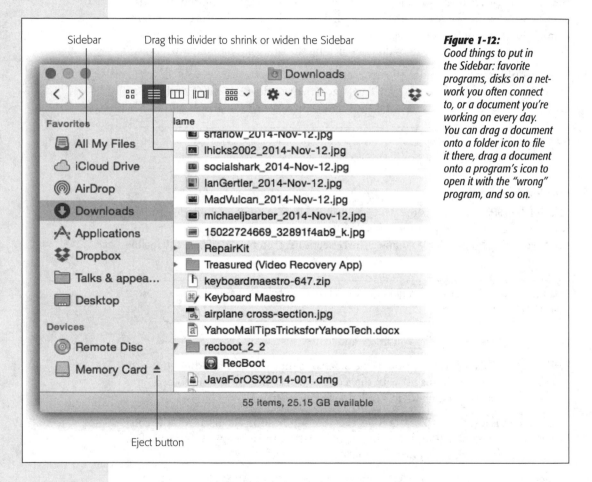

Sidebar Drag this divider to shrink or widen the Sidebar

Figure 1-12:
Good things to put in the Sidebar: favorite programs, disks on a network you often connect to, or a document you're working on every day. You can drag a document onto a folder icon to file it there, drag a document onto a program's icon to open it with the "wrong" program, and so on.

Eject button

Fine-tuning the Sidebar

The beauty of this parking lot for containers is that it's so easy to set up with your favorite places. For example:

- **Remove an icon** by dragging it out of the Sidebar entirely. It vanishes with a puff of smoke (and even a little *whoof* sound effect). You haven't actually removed anything from your Mac; you've just unhitched its alias from the Sidebar.

Tip: You can't drag items out of the Shared list. Also, if you drag a Devices item out of the list, you'll have to choose Finder→Preferences→Sidebar and then turn on the appropriate checkbox to put it back in.

- **Rearrange the icons** by dragging them up or down in the list. For example, hard drives don't appear at the top of the Sidebar, but you're free to drag them into those coveted spots. (You're not allowed to rearrange the computers listed in the Shared section, though.)

- **Rearrange the sections** by dragging *them* up or down. For example, you can drag Favorites to the bottom but promote the Shared category.

- **Install a new icon** by dragging it off your desktop (or out of a window) into any spot in the Favorites list of the Sidebar. Press the ⌘ key after beginning the drag. You can't drag icons into any section of the Sidebar—just Favorites.

Tip: You can also highlight an icon wherever it happens to be and then choose File→Add to Sidebar, or just press Control-⌘-T.

- **Adjust the width** of the Sidebar by dragging its right edge—either the skinny divider line or the extreme right edge of the vertical scroll bar, if there is one. You "feel" a snap at the point when the line covers up about half of each icon's name. Any covered-up names sprout ellipses (…) to let you know there's more (as in "Secret Salaries Spreadsh…").

- **Hide the Sidebar** by pressing ⌘-Option-S, which is the shortcut for the View→Hide Sidebar command. Bring the Sidebar back into view by pressing the same key combination (or by using the Show Sidebar command).

Tip: You can hide and show the Sidebar manually, too: To hide it, drag its right edge all the way to the left edge of the window. Unhide it by dragging the left edge of the window to the right again.

Then again, why would you ever want to hide the Sidebar? It's one of the handiest navigation aids since the invention of the steering wheel. For example:

- **It takes a lot of pressure off the Dock.** Instead of filling up your Dock with folder icons (all of which are frustratingly alike and unlabeled anyway), use the Sidebar to store them. You leave the Dock that much more room for programs and documents.

- **It's better than the Dock.** In some ways, the Sidebar is a lot like the Dock, in that you can stash favorite icons of any sort there. But the Sidebar reveals the names of these icons, and the Dock doesn't until you use the mouse to point there.

- **You can drag onto its folders and disks.** That is, you can drag icons onto Sidebar icons, exactly as though they were the real disks, folders, and programs they represent.

- **It simplifies connecting to networked disks.** Park your other computers' shared folder and disk icons here, as described in Chapter 16, to shave several steps off the usual connecting-via-network ritual.

Window Management

OS X prefers to keep only one Finder window open at a time. That is, if a window called "United States" is filled with folders for the individual states, double-clicking the New York folder doesn't open a second window. Instead, the New York window replaces the United States window, just as in Windows.

So what if you've now opened the New York folder, and you want to backtrack to the United States folder? In that case, just click the tiny ‹ (Back) button or use one of these alternatives:

• Choose Go→Back.

• Press ⌘-[(left bracket).

• Press ⌘-▲.

None of that helps you, however, if you want to copy a file from one folder into another, or to compare the contents of the two windows. In such cases, you'll probably want to see both windows open at the same time.

You can open a second window using any of these techniques:

• Choose File→New Finder Window (⌘-N).

Tip: The window that appears when you do this is the All My Files window (page 33), but you can change that setting in Finder→Preferences→General.

• Double-click a disk or folder icon.

• Choose Finder→Preferences→General, and turn off "Open folders in tabs instead of new windows." Now when you double-click a folder, it opens into a new window.

Scroll Bars

A scroll bar, of course, is the traditional window-edge slider that lets you move through a document that's too big for the window. Without scroll bars in word processors, for example, you'd never be able to write a letter that's taller than your screen.

Apple expects that you'll do most of your scrolling on your trackpad, Magic Mouse top surface, or scroll ball/scroll wheel. You almost never use the antiquated method of dragging the scroll bar's handle manually, with the mouse.

Tip: More reasons nobody uses the mouse to scroll: You can scroll using the keyboard. Your Page Up and Page Down keys let you scroll up and down, one screen at a time, without having to take your hands off the keyboard. The Home and End keys are generally useful for jumping directly to the top or bottom of your document (or Finder window). And if you've bought a mouse that has a scroll wheel on top, you can use it to scroll windows, without pressing any keys at all.

That's a long-winded way of explaining why, in most programs, the scroll bars are hidden. See Figure 1-13 for details.

Note: If the missing scroll bars leave you jittery and disoriented, you can bring them back. Open System Preferences→General and then turn on "Show scroll bars: Always."

Figure 1-13:
Scroll bars don't appear at all while you're working (bottom); you have more screen area dedicated to your work. If you begin to scroll by sliding your fingers across the trackpad or Magic Mouse, the scroll-bar handle appears, so you know where you are (middle).

But if you point to the scroll bar, it fattens up so you can grab it (top).

Resizable Edges

You can change the shape of a window by dragging its *edges*, just as in Windows. Move the mouse carefully to the exact top, bottom, left, or right edge; once its shape changes to a double-headed arrow, you can drag to move that window's edge in or out.

Tip: If you press the Option key while dragging, you resize the *opposite edge* simultaneously. For example, if you Option-drag the bottom edge upward, the top edge simultaneously collapses downward.

If you press Shift as you drag, you resize the *entire* window, retaining its proportions.

And if you Shift-Option-drag, you resize the window around its center, rather than from its edges.

GEM IN THE ROUGH

Using the Scroll Bar with Your Mouse

If you are that rare, special individual who still prefers to operate the scroll bar by clicking it with the mouse, you can do that on a Mac, too.

For example: Ordinarily, when you click in the scroll bar track above or below the dark-gray handle bar, the window scrolls by one screenful. But another option awaits when you choose →System Preferences→General and turn on "Jump to the spot that's clicked." Now when you click the scroll-bar track, the Mac considers the entire scroll bar a proportional map of the document and jumps precisely to the spot you clicked. That is, if you click the very bottom of the scroll-bar track, you see the very last page.

No matter which scrolling option you choose in the Appearance pane, you can always override your decision on a case-by-case basis by *Option*-clicking the scroll-bar track. In other words, if you've selected the "Jump to the spot that's clicked" option, you can produce a "Jump to the next page" scroll by Option-clicking in the scroll-bar track.

Path Bar

This little item appears when you choose View→Show Path Bar. It's a tiny map at the bottom of the window that shows where you are in the folder hierarchy. If it says Casey→Pictures→Picnic, well, then, you're looking at the contents of the Picnic folder, which is inside Pictures, which is inside your Home folder (assuming your name is Casey).

Tip: Each tiny folder icon in this display is fully operational. You can double-click it to open it, right-click it to open a shortcut menu, or even drag things into it.

Status Bar

Out of the box, the Mac hides yet another information strip at the bottom of a window—the status bar, which tells you how many icons are in the window ("14 items," for example) and the amount of free space remaining on the disk. To make it appear, choose View→Show Status Bar.

Terminology Differences

There are enough other differences between Mac and Windows to fill 14 pages. Indeed, that's what you'll find in Appendix C at the end of this book: an alphabetical listing of every familiar Windows feature and where to find its equivalent on the Mac.

As you read both that section of the book and the chapters that precede it, however, you'll discover that some functions are almost identical in OS X and Windows but have different names. Here's a quick-reference summary:

Windows term	Macintosh term
Control Panel	System Preferences
Gadget	Widget
Drop-down menu	Pop-up menu
Program	Application
Properties	Get Info
Recycle Bin	Trash
Search command	Spotlight
Shortcuts	Aliases
Sidebar	Dashboard
Taskbar	Dock
Tray (notification area)	Menulets
Windows Explorer	Finder
Windows folder	System folder

With that much under your belt, you're well on your way to learning the ways of OS X.

Folders, Dock & Windows

These days, the graphic user interface (icons, windows, Trash cans) is standard. Mac, Windows, Chrome OS, Android, iOS—every operating system is fundamentally the same, which is to say a very long way from the lines of typed commands that defined the earliest computers.

That's not to say that the graphic interface hasn't evolved, though; it has. Herewith: a grand tour of the state of the art in computer desktops—the one in Yosemite.

Getting into OS X

When you first turn on a Mac running OS X 10.10, an Apple logo greets you, soon joined by a skinny, helpful progress bar that lets you know how much longer you have to wait.

Logging In

What happens next depends on whether you're the Mac's sole proprietor or have to share it with other people in an office, school, or household.

- **If it's your own Mac,** and you've already been through the setup process described in Appendix A, no big deal. You arrive at the OS X desktop.

- **If it's a shared Mac,** you may encounter the login screen, shown in Figure 2-1. It's like a portrait gallery, set against a blurry version of your usual desktop picture. Click your icon.

 If the Mac asks for your password, type it and then click Log In (or press Return). You arrive at the desktop.

 Chapter 15 offers much more on this business of user accounts and logging in.

Note: In certain especially paranoid workplaces, you may not see the rogue's gallery shown in Figure 2-1. You may just get two text boxes, where you're supposed to type in your name and password. Without even the icons of known account holders, an evil hacker's job is that much more difficult.

Figure 2-1:
On Macs used by multiple people, this is one of the first things you see upon turning on the computer. Click your name. (If the list is long, you may have to swipe the trackpad to find your name—or just type its first few letters.)

Inset: At this point, you're asked to type in your password. Type it, and then click Log In (or press Return). If you type the wrong password, the box vibrates, in effect shaking its little dialog-box head, suggesting that you guess again.

The Elements of the OS X Desktop

The desktop is the shimmering, three-dimensional OS X landscape shown in Figure 2-2. On a new Mac, it's covered by a photo of a spectacular, rugged mountain—its name is Half Dome—in Yosemite National Park (get it?).

If you've ever used a computer before, most of the objects on your screen are nothing more than updated versions of familiar elements. Here's a quick tour.

Note: If your desktop looks even emptier than this—no menus, no icons, almost nothing on the Dock—then somebody in charge of your Mac has turned on *Simple Finder mode* for you. Details on page 499.

Disk icons

In Windows, disk icons remain safely caged in the My Computer window; they don't appear on the desktop automatically. The Mac starts out the same way; to find the icons of disks you've inserted, you have to look in the Sidebar (page 35) or the Computer window (Go→Computer).

If you'd like to save yourself that burrowing, though, you can choose Finder→Preferences, click General, and turn on the checkboxes of the disks whose icons you want on the desktop: hard disks, external disks, iPods, and so on.

The Dock

This row of translucent, almost photographic icons is a launcher for the programs, files, folders, and disks you use often—and an indicator to let you know which programs are already open. They appear to rest on a sheet of transparent smoked glass.

Because the Dock is such a critical component of OS X, Apple has decked it out with enough customization controls to keep you busy experimenting for months. You can change its size, move it to the sides of your screen, hide it entirely, and so on. Page 75 begins a complete discussion of using and understanding the Dock.

Figure 2-2: *The OS X landscape looks like a more futuristic version of the operating systems you know and love. This is just a starting point, however. You can dress it up with a different background picture, adjust your windows in a million ways, and, of course, fill the Dock with only the programs, disks, folders, and files you need.*

Apple menu Menu bar Desktop Menulets

Dock Trash

The menu

The menu houses important Mac-wide commands like Sleep, Restart, and Shut Down. They're always available, no matter which program you're using.

The menu bar

Every popular operating system saves space by concealing its most important commands in menus that drop down. OS X's menus are especially refined:

- **They stay down.** OS X menus stay open until you click the mouse, trigger a command from the keyboard, or buy a new computer, whichever comes first.

Tip: Actually, menus are even smarter than that. If you give the menu name a quick click, the menu opens and stays open. If you click the menu name and hold the mouse button down for a moment, the menu opens but closes again when you release the button. Apple figures that, in that case, you're just exploring, reading, or hunting for a certain command.

- **They're consistently arranged.** The first menu in every program, which appears in bold lettering, tells you at a glance what program you're in (Safari, Microsoft Word, whatever). The commands in this Application menu include About (which indicates what version of the program you're using), Preferences, Quit, and commands like Hide Others and Show All (which help control window clutter, as described on page 191).

 In short, all the Application menu's commands actually pertain to the application you're using.

 The File and Edit menus come next. The File menu contains commands for opening, saving, and closing files. (See the logic?) The Edit menu contains the Cut, Copy, and Paste commands.

 The last menu is almost always Help. It opens a miniature Web browser that lets you search the online Mac help files for explanatory text.

- **You can operate them from the keyboard.** Once you've clicked open a menu, you can highlight any command in it just by typing the first letter (*g* for Get Info, for example). (It's especially great for "Your country" pop-up menus on Web sites, where "United States" is about 200 countries down in the list. You can type *united s* to jump right to it.)

 You can also press Tab to open the next menu, Shift-Tab to open the previous one, and Return to "click" the highlighted command.

Note: The menu bar is partly see-through, for no apparent reason; it's more evident with some desktop pictures than others. Either way, you can turn off the see-throughness if you want. Open System Preferences→ Desktop & Screen Saver→Desktop, and then turn off "Translucent menu bar."

You can also make the menu bar dark gray with white text—a stark, clear, handsome look; see page 597.

The Four Window Views

You can view the files and folders in a desktop window in any of four ways: as icons; as a single, tidy list; in a series of neat columns; or in Cover Flow view, where you can flip through giant document icons like they're CDs in a music-store bin. Figure 2-3 shows the four views.

Every window remembers its view settings independently. You might prefer to look over your Applications folder in list view (because it's crammed with files and folders) but view the Pictures folder in icon or Cover Flow view, where the larger icons serve as previews of the photos.

To switch a window from one view to another, just click one of the four corresponding icons in the window's toolbar (Figure 2-3).

You can also switch views by choosing View→as Icons (or View→as Columns, or View→as List, or View→as Cover Flow), which can be handy if you've hidden the toolbar. Or, for less mousing and more hard-bodied efficiency, press ⌘-1 for icon view, ⌘-2 for list view, ⌘-3 for column view, or ⌘-4 for Cover Flow view.

Figure 2-3:
From the top: the same window in icon view, list view, column view, and Cover Flow view. Very full folders are best navigated in list or column views, but you may prefer to view emptier folders in icon or Cover Flow views, because larger icons are easier to preview and click. Remember that in any view (icon, list, column, or Cover Flow), you can highlight an icon by typing the first few letters of its name. In icon, list, or Cover Flow views, you can also press Tab to highlight the next icon (in alphabetical order), or Shift-Tab to highlight the previous one.

The following pages cover each of these views in greater detail.

Note: One common thread in the following discussions is the availability of the View Options palette, which lets you set up the sorting, text size, icon size, and other features of each view, either one window at a time or for all windows.

Apple gives you a million different ways to open View Options. You can choose View→Show View Options, or press ⌘-J, or choose Show View Options from the ✿ menu at the top of every window.

Icon View

In icon view, every file, folder, and disk is represented by a small picture—an icon. This humble image, a visual representation of electronic bits and bytes, is the cornerstone of the entire Macintosh religion. (Maybe that's why it's called an icon.)

Icon Size

OS X draws those little icons using sophisticated graphics software. As a result, you can scale them to almost any size without losing quality or clarity. If you choose View→Status Bar so that the bottom-edge strip shown in Figure 2-4 appears, you get a size slider that you can drag to the right or left to make that window's icons larger or smaller. (For added fun, make little cartoon sounds with your mouth.)

Figure 2-4:
Once you make the status bar appear, you can choose an icon size to suit your personality. For picture folders, it can often be very handy to pick a jumbo size, in effect creating a slide-sorter "light table" effect. Icons can be an almost ridiculously large 512 pixels square.

Icon Previews

The Mac expands the notion of "an icon is a representation of its contents" to an impressive extreme. As you can see in Figure 2-5, each icon actually looks like a miniature of the first page of the real document.

Because you can make icons so enormous, you can actually watch movies, or read PDF and text documents, right on their icons.

To check out this feature, point to an icon without clicking. A Play button (▶) appears on any movie or sound file; as shown in Figure 2-5, ⊙ and ⊙ page buttons appear on a multipage document (like PDF, Pages, or even presentation documents like PowerPoint and Keynote). You can actually page through one of these documents right there on its icon without having to open the program!

Tip: If you Option-click the little ⊙ and ⊙ buttons on a PDF, PowerPoint, or Keynote icon preview, you jump to the first or last page or slide in the document.

Figure 2-5:
You can page through PDF and presentation icons, or play movies and sounds, right on their icons. (Movie icons even display a circular progress bar so you know how far you are into the video.)

Icon View Options

OS X offers a number of useful icon-view options, all of which are worth exploring. Start by opening any icon-view window, and then choose View→Show View Options (⌘-J). The pane shown in Figure 2-6 appears.

Always open in icon view

It's easy—almost scarily easy—to set up your preferred look for all folder windows on your entire system. With one click on the Use as Defaults button (described below), you can change the window view of 20,000 folders at once—to icon view, list view, or whatever you like.

The "Always open in icon view" option lets you override that master setting, just for this window.

For example, you might generally prefer a neat list view with large text. But for your Pictures folder, it probably makes more sense to set up icon view, so you can see a thumbnail of each photo without having to open it.

That's the idea here. Open Pictures, change it to icon view, and then turn on "Always open in icon view." Now every folder on your Mac is in list view except Pictures.

Note: The wording of this item in the View Options dialog box changes according to the view you're in at the moment. In a list-view window, for example, it says "Always open in list view." In a Cover Flow–view window, it says "Always open in Cover Flow." And so on. But the function is the same: to override the default (master) setting.

Figure 2-6:
Drag the "Grid spacing" slider to specify how tightly packed you want your icons to be. At the minimum setting, they're so crammed it's almost ridiculous; you may not even be able to see their full names. But sometimes you don't really need to. At a more spacious setting (bottom), you get a lot more white space.

Browse in icon view

This option makes sure that any folders inside the current window open up into icon view, too, even if you'd previously set them to open into some other view. So if you're looking at your Pictures folder in icon view and you open the Grand Canyon Jaw-Droppers folder inside it, that folder also will be in icon view.

Arrange By, Sort By

For a discussion of these pop-up menus, see page 52.

Icon size

It's super easy to make all your icons bigger or smaller; just drag the Icon Size slider in the lower-right corner of the window. There's an identical slider in the View Options window as well.

Grid spacing

Listen up, you young whippersnappers! When I was your age, back when computers used Mac OS 9, you could control how closely spaced icons were in a window. Why, if I wanted to see a lot of them without making the window bigger, I could pack 'em in like sardines!

That feature disappeared—for seven years. But back in Mac OS X 10.5, it finally returned. Figure 2-6 shows all.

Text size

Your choices range only from 10 to 16 points, and you still can't choose a different font for your icons' names. But using this pop-up menu, you can adjust the type size. And for people with especially big or especially small screens—or for people with aging retinas—this feature is much better than nothing.

In fact, you can actually specify a different type size for every window on your machine. (Why would you want to adjust the point size independently in different windows? Well, because you might want smaller type to fit more into a crammed list view without scrolling, while you can afford larger type in less densely populated windows.)

Label position

Click either Bottom or Right to indicate where you want an icon's name to appear, relative to its icon. As shown in Figure 2-7 at bottom, this option lets you create, in effect, a multiple-column list view in a single window.

Show item info

While you've got the View Options palette open, try turning on "Show item info." Suddenly you get a new line of information (in tiny blue type) for certain icons, saving you the effort of opening up the folder or file to find out what's in it. For example:

- **Folders.** The info line lets you know how many icons are inside each without having to open it up. Now you can spot empties at a glance.

- **Graphics files.** Certain other kinds of files may show a helpful info line, too. For example, graphics files display their dimensions in pixels.

- **Sounds and QuickTime movies.** The light-blue bonus line tells you how long the sound or movie takes to play. An MP3 file might say "03' 08" " (3 minutes, 8 seconds).

- **.zip files.** On compressed archives like .zip files, you get to see the archive's total size on disk (like "48.9 MB").

Show icon preview

This option is what makes icons display their contents, as shown in Figures 2-4, 2-5, and 2-6. If you turn it off, then icons no longer look like miniature versions of their contents (tiny photos, tiny PDF files, and so on). Everything takes on generic icons.

You might prefer this arrangement when, for example, you want to be able to pick out all the PDF files in a window full of mixed document types. Thanks to the matching icons, it's easy now.

Background

Here's a luxury that other operating systems can only dream about: You can fill the background of any icon-view window on your Mac with a certain color—or even a photo.

Color coordinating or "wallpapering" certain windows is more than just a gimmick. In fact, it can serve as a timesaving visual cue. Once you've gotten used to the fact that your main Documents folder has a sky-blue background, you can look at a screen filled with open windows and pick it out like a sharpshooter. Color-coded Finder windows are also especially easy to distinguish at a glance when you've minimized them to the Dock.

Note: Background colors and pictures show up only in icon view.

Once a window is open, choose View→View Options (⌘-J). The bottom of the resulting dialog box offers three choices, whose results are shown in Figure 2-7.

- **White.** This is the standard option (not shown).

- **Color.** When you click this button, you see a small rectangular button beside the word "Color." Click it to open the Color Picker, which you can use to choose a new background color for the window. (Unless it's April Fools' Day, pick a light color. If you choose a dark one—like black—you won't be able to make out the lettering of the icons' names.)

- **Picture.** If you choose this option, a "Drag image here" square appears. Now find a graphics file—one of Apple's in the Desktop Pictures folder, or one of your own, whatever—and drag it into that "well."

 When you click Select, you see that OS X has superimposed the window's icons on the photo. As you can see in Figure 2-7, low-contrast or light-background photos work best for legibility.

 Incidentally, the Mac has no idea what sizes and shapes your window may assume in its lifetime. Therefore, OS X makes no attempt to scale down a selected photo to fit neatly into the window. If you have a high-res digital camera, therefore, you may see only the upper-left corner of your photo in the window. For better results, use a graphics program to scale the picture down to something smaller than your screen resolution.

Use as Defaults

This harmless-looking button can actually wreak havoc on your kingdom—or restore order to it—with a single click. It applies the changes you've just made in the View Options dialog box to all icon-view windows on your Mac (instead of only the frontmost window).

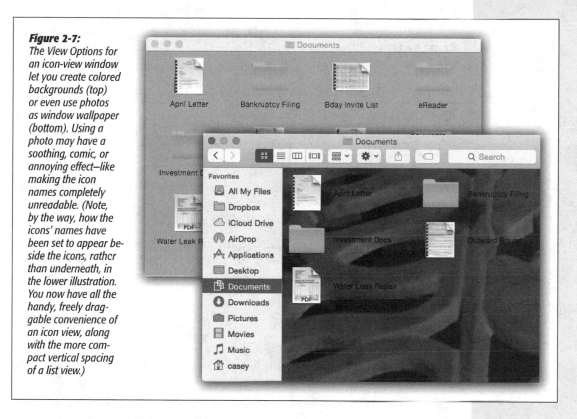

Figure 2-7:
The View Options for an icon-view window let you create colored backgrounds (top) or even use photos as window wallpaper (bottom). Using a photo may have a soothing, comic, or annoying effect—like making the icon names completely unreadable. (Note, by the way, how the icons' names have been set to appear beside the icons, rather than underneath, in the lower illustration. You now have all the handy, freely draggable convenience of an icon view, along with the more compact vertical spacing of a list view.)

If you set up the frontmost window with a colored background, big icons, small text, and a tight grid, and then you click Use as Defaults, you'll see that look in every disk or folder window you open.

You've been warned.

Fortunately, there are two auxiliary controls that can give you a break from all the sameness.

First, you can set up individual windows to be weirdo exceptions to the rule; see page 47.

Second, you can remove any departures from the default window view—after a round of disappointing experimentation on a particular window, for example—using a secret button. Choose View→Show View Options to open the View Options dialog box. Now hold down the Option key. The Use as Defaults button magically changes

to say Restore to Defaults, which means "Abandon all the changes I've foolishly made to the look of this window."

Tip: In the View Options for your Home folder, a checkbox appears: Show Library Folder. The Library folder is usually hidden, to prevent clueless newbies from wreaking havoc with important files. But now OS X is willing to give it back to you—if you know about this sneaky little trick.

Arrange By and Sort By

You can wield two different kinds of control over the layout of files in a Finder window: arranging and sorting.

Tip: You can perform all these obsessive reorganizations in *any view:* icon view, list view, column view, or Cover Flow view. That's a big change from the olden days.

Arranging

Arranging files means "Put my files into related clumps, separated by headings that identify them." You can arrange files in any of the views—icon, list, column, Cover Flow—and there are some incredibly useful options here.

For example, you can arrange your documents into application groups (meaning which program opens each one); now you can see at a glance which files will open in, say, iTunes when you double-click them. Or you can organize your Pictures folder into Date Added groups, with headings like "Today," "Last 7 Days," and "Earlier."

Figure 2-8 shows a few examples.

Tip: In icon view, the icons under each heading appear in a *single row*, scrolling off endlessly to the right. Use the usual sideways-scrolling gesture to flip through a row. (That is, swipe to the left on a trackpad with two fingers, or with one finger on a Magic Mouse.)

If you're not into gestures, or if you don't have a swipeable input device, click the tiny Show All button at the right end of a row. Now you've turned off that one-row-per-heading thing, and all the icons under that heading appear in the usual rows and columns; scroll down to see them all.

Apple wants to make extra, extra sure you're aware of the Arrange commands. It gives you four different ways to find them:

- **Choose View→Arrange By.** Choose one of the criteria from the submenu. Your options are Name (alphabetically); Kind (type of file, like Images, Movies, and Documents); Application (which program opens which documents); Date (Last Opened, Added [to the window], Modified, or Created); Size; or Label (Finder label colors, described on page 106). Marvel as the Finder puts your files into tidy categorized groups.

Note: When you're looking at the Applications folder, you get a special choice: Application Category. It clumps your programs by what they do: Productivity, Social Networking, Music, Video, Board Games, Entertainment, Utilities, Reference, Photography, and so on. Pretty cool, actually.

- **Choose from the ▦▾ icon.** This icon appears in the toolbar of every Finder window. It contains the same options listed in the previous bullet.

- **Right-click (or two-finger-click) an empty spot in an icon-view window; choose from the Arrange By shortcut menu.** Yep, it's those same commands yet again.

- **In the View Options palette (seen in Figure 2-6), use the Arrange By pop-up menu.** Yes, it's a fourth place to find the same six options.

Note: In each case, you can choose None to turn off the grouping altogether.

Figure 2-8:
You can view your Finder-window files in neat little groups, separated by headings.

Top left: The Applications window, in icon view, arranged by application category.

Middle: The Documents folder, in list view, arranged by application (meaning "which program opens this document").

Bottom: The Desktop folder, in column view, arranged by date added.

Remember, arranging (clumping) is not sorting. You can, in fact, sort the icons differently within each arranged group; read on.

Sorting

Sorting means just what it says: You can sort your files alphabetically (by Name), chronologically (by Date), in order of hugeness (by Size), and so on. See Figure 2-9.

Figure 2-9:
Use either the View menu or the View Options window (right) to turn on permanent cleanliness mode. You've told the Mac to keep these icons on the invisible grid, sorted the way you requested. Just don't get frustrated when you try to drag an icon and then discover that it won't budge.

You can sort a window whether or not you've also arranged (grouped) it. You can even sort by different criteria. For example, you might have the programs in your Applications folder arranged by Application Category but sorted alphabetically within each category.

Once again, Apple gives you four ways to sort:

- **While pressing the Option key, choose View→Sort By.** (Pressing Option turns the Arrange By submenu into the Sort By submenu.) Choose one of the criteria: Name, Size, and so on.

- **While pressing the Option key, click the ✿ icon.** Once again, the Option key turns the Arrange By options into Sort By options.

- **Right-click (or two-finger click) an empty spot in an icon-view window. Press the Option key.** And again, Option turns the Arrange By options into Sort By options.

- **In the View Options palette, use the Sort By pop-up menu.** Hey, guess what? You didn't have to press the Option key this time.

Tip: In icon view, you get an additional option: Snap to Grid. It means "Let me drag these icons into any sequence I want, using the trackpad or mouse." When you release each drag, the icon jumps into the nearest position on the underlying spacing grid (unless you press the ⌘ key, which gives you full manual control of the icon's position).

This option appears only if Arrange By is set to None. After all, if you've asked the Mac to arrange your icons into groups, then you've relinquished control of their grid spacing.

Free dragging—and grid spacing

Whenever you've applied an Arrange or a Sort to an icon view, the icons remain rooted to an invisible underlying rows-and-columns grid. You can't budge them.

Tip: You can, however, control how tight or loose that grid is, using the "Grid spacing" slider described on page 48.

But there are two situations when you're allowed to drag icons freely into any order you want:

- **Icons never snap to the grid.** If both Arrange By and Sort By are set to None, then you can go nuts, freely dragging icons into sloppy, off-the-grid positions.

 If, later, you become overwhelmed by shame at your untidiness, you can choose View→Clean Up (if nothing is selected) or View→Clean Up Selection (if some icons are highlighted). Now all icons in the window, or those you've selected, jump to the closest positions on the invisible underlying grid.

 These same commands appear in the shortcut menu when you right-click or two-finger click anywhere inside an icon-view window, which is handier if you have a huge monitor.

 There's even a Clean Up By submenu in the View menu and the shortcut menu. These commands don't just put icons back onto the closest grid positions; they put the icons into their proper sorted positions among the other icons—by name, size, date, and so on.

Tip: If you press Option, then the Mac swaps the wording of the command. Clean Up changes to Clean Up Selection, and vice versa.

- **Icons always snap to the grid.** If Arrange By is set to None but Sort By is set to Snap to Grid, then you can drag icons into any order you like (that is, not in any particular sorted order)—but they'll snap to the grid when you let go of the mouse button.

Tip: If you press the ⌘ key as you release the drag, you can reverse the snapping logic. That is, the icons *will* snap to the grid if Sort By is set to None, but you can drag them freely if it's set to Snap to Grid. (Don't press the key until after you've begun to drag.)

Although it doesn't occur to most Mac fans, you can also apply any of the commands described in this section—Clean Up, Arrange, Sort—to icons lying loose on your desktop. Even though they don't seem to be in any window at all, you can specify small or large icons, automatic alphabetical arrangement, and so on. Just click the desktop before using the View menu or the View Options dialog box.

Note: There's only one View Options dialog box. Once it's open, you can adjust the icon sizes or arrangement options of other windows just by clicking them. Each time you click inside a window, the View Options dialog box remains in front, changing to reflect the settings of the window you just clicked.

Incidentally, you can get rid of the View Options box the same way you summoned it: by pressing ⌘-J.

List View

In windows that contain a lot of icons, list view is a powerful weapon in the battle against chaos. It shows you a tidy table of your files' names, dates, sizes, and so on (Figure 2-10).

You get to decide how wide your columns should be, which of them should appear, and in what order (except that Name is always the first column). Here's how to master these columns.

Figure 2-10:
You control the sorting order of a list view by clicking the column headings (top). Click a second time to reverse the sorting order (bottom). You'll find the ∧ or ∨ triangles–indicating the identical information–in email programs, iTunes, and anywhere else where reversing the sorting order of a list can be useful.

Sorting the List

Most of the world's list-view fans like their files listed alphabetically. It's occasionally useful, however, to view the newest files first, largest ones first, or whatever.

When a desktop window displays its icons in list view, a convenient new strip of column headings appears. These headings aren't just signposts; they're buttons, too. Click Name for alphabetical order, Date Modified to view the newest first, Size to view the largest files at the top, and so on.

Don't miss the tiny ∧ or ∨ that appears in the column you've most recently clicked. It shows you which way the list is being sorted. When it's ∧, then the oldest files, smallest files, or files beginning with numbers (or the letter A) appear at the top of the list, depending on which sorting criterion you have selected.

Tip: It may help you to remember that when the smallest portion of the triangle is at the top (∧), the smallest files are listed first when viewed in size order.

To reverse the sorting order, click the column heading a second time. Now the ∨ shows you that the newest files, largest files, or files beginning with the letter Z appear at the top of the list, as shown in Figure 2-10.

Note: You can also change the sorting order using the Sort By command described earlier (in the View menu, the ⊞▾ pop-up menu, or the View Options dialog box). But, honestly, clicking the column headings is much faster.

Arranging the List

You can arrange your list view into groups by name, date, kind, and so on, with tidy headings that help you make sense of it all. This unsung feature is described under "Arrange By and Sort By" on page 52.

Flippy Triangles

One of the Mac's most attractive features is the tiny triangle that appears to the left of a folder's name in a list view. In its official documents, Apple calls these buttons *disclosure triangles;* internally, the programmers call them *flippy triangles.* (They don't appear if you've sorted the window using the View→Arrange By menu.)

When you click one, the list view turns into an outline, showing the contents of the folder in an indented list, as shown in Figure 2-11. Click the triangle again to collapse the folder listing. You're saved the trouble and clutter of opening a new window just to view the folder's contents.

By selectively clicking flippy triangles, you can in effect peer inside two or more folders simultaneously, all within a single list-view window. You can move files around by dragging them onto the tiny folder icons.

Tip: Once you've expanded a folder by clicking its flippy triangle, you can even drag a file icon out of the folder so that it's loose in the list-view window. To do so, drag it directly upward onto the column headings area (where it says Name, for example). When you release the mouse, you see that the file is no longer inside the expanded folder.

Figure 2-11:
Click a "flippy triangle" (left) to see the list of the folders and files inside that folder (right). Or press the equivalent keystrokes: ▶ (to open) and ◄ (to close).

Your Choice of Columns

Choose View→Show View Options. In the dialog box that appears, you're offered on/off checkboxes for the different columns of information OS X can show you, as illustrated in Figure 2-12.

- **Date Modified.** This date-and-time stamp indicates when a document was last saved. Its accuracy, of course, depends on the accuracy of your Mac's built-in clock.

Note: Many an up-to-date file has been lost because someone spotted a very old date on a folder and assumed that the files inside were equally old. That's because the modification date shown for a folder doesn't reflect the age of its contents. Instead, the date on a folder indicates only when items were last moved into or out of that folder. The actual files inside may be much older, or much more recent.

- **Date Created.** This date-and-time stamp shows when a document was *first* saved.

- **Date Added.** This option shows when a file was added to this folder or window.

- **Size.** With a glance, you can tell from this column how much disk space each of your files and folders is taking up in kilobytes, megabytes, gigabytes, or terabytes—whichever the Mac thinks you'll find most helpful.

Tip: For disks and folders, you see only a dash—at first. You can, however, instruct the Mac to reveal their sizes, as described on page 61.

Figure 2-12:
The checkboxes you turn on in the View Options dialog box determine which columns of information appear in a list-view window. Many people live full and satisfying lives with only the three default columns—Date Modified, Kind, and Size—turned on. But the other columns can be helpful in special circumstances; the trick is knowing what information appears there.

- **Kind.** In this column, you can read what kind of file each icon represents. You may see, for example, Folder, JPEG Image, Application, and so on.

- **Version.** This column displays the version numbers of your programs. For folders and documents, you just see a dash.

- **Comments.** This rarely seen column (Figure 2-13) can actually be among the most useful. Suppose you're a person who uses the Comments feature (highlight an icon, choose File→Get Info, type notes about that item into the Spotlight Comments box). This column displays the first line of those comments about each icon, which comes in handy when tracking multiple versions of your documents.

- **Tag.** Tags are colors and identifying phrases that you can slap onto icons, wherever they appear, to help you categorize and group them. For details, see page 106.

Even with this column turned off, you can still see an icon's color, of course. But only by turning on this column do you get to see the text phrase you've associated with each label.

Figure 2-13:
If your monitor is big enough, you can expand the Comments column to show several paragraphs, all in a single line—enough to reveal the full life history of each icon. (To enter some comments about an icon, type into the Spotlight Comments box in its Get Info pane, as shown here at bottom.)

Other View Options

The View Options for a list view include several other useful settings; choose View→Show View Options or press ⌘-J.

- **Always open in list view.** Turn on this option to override your system-wide preference setting for all windows.

- **Browse in list view.** Ensures that any folder inside this one will also open up in list view, even if its regularly scheduled view is something else.

- **Icon size.** These two buttons offer you a choice of icon sizes for the current window: either standard or tiny. Unlike icon view, list view doesn't give you a size slider.

 Fortunately, even the tiny icons aren't so small that they show up blank. You still get a general idea of what they're supposed to look like.

- **Text size.** You can change the type size for your icon labels, either globally or one window at a time.

- **Show columns.** Turn on the columns you'd like to appear in the current window's list view, as described in the previous section.

- **Use relative dates.** In a list view, the Date Modified, Date Added, and Date Created columns generally display information in a format like this: "Tuesday, March 5, 2015." (The Mac uses shorter date formats as the column gets narrower.) But

when the "Use relative dates" option is turned on, the Mac substitutes the words "Yesterday" or "Today" where appropriate, making recent files easier to spot.

- **Calculate all sizes.** See the box below.

- **Show icon preview.** Exactly as in icon view, this option turns the icons of graphics files into miniatures of the photos or images within.

- **Use as Defaults.** Click to make your changes in the View Options box apply to all windows on your Mac. (Option-click this button to restore a wayward window back to your defaults.)

Rearranging Columns

You're stuck with the Name column at the far left of a window. However, you can rearrange the other columns just by dragging their gray column headers horizontally. If the Mac thinks you intend to drop a column to, say, the left of the column it overlaps, you'll actually see an animated movement—indicating a column reshuffling—even before you release the mouse button.

FREQUENTLY ASKED QUESTION

Calculate All Sizes

When I sort my list view by size, I see only dashes for folder sizes. What am I doing wrong?

Nothing at all; that's normal. When viewing a Finder window, you see a Size statistic for each file. For folders and disks, however, you're shown only an uninformative dash.

Most Mac fans study this anomaly momentarily, scratch their chins, and then get back to their work. Former Windows people don't even scratch their chins; Windows PCs *never* show folder-size or disk-size information in list views.

Here's what's going on: It can take a computer a long time to add up the sizes of all files inside a folder. Your System→Library folder alone, for example, contains over 100,000 files. Instead of making you wait while the Mac does all the addition, OS X simply shows you a dash in the folder's Size column.

On occasion, however, you really do want to see how big your folders are. In such cases, choose View→Show View Options and turn on "Calculate all sizes." You see the folder sizes slowly begin to pop onto the screen, from the top of the window down, as the Mac crunches the numbers on the

files within. (You'll know that the crunching is still in progress, because you'll see the size statistics for some icons appear in light gray. That's the Mac's way of saying, "I'm not totally sure about this folder's size yet.")

In fact, you can even turn on the "Calculate all sizes" option *globally*—that is, for all windows. OS X is multithreaded; it has the opposite of a one-track mind. It's perfectly capable of devoting all its attention to calculating your folder sizes *and* to whatever work you're doing in the foreground.

Now consider this anomaly: Suppose you've opted to sort a particular window by folder size—in other words, you've clicked Size at the top of the column. Turning on "Calculate all sizes" bewilders the unprepared, as folders arbitrarily begin leaping out of order, forcing the list to rearrange itself a couple of times per second.

What's happening, of course, is that all folders begin at the bottom of the list, showing only dashes in the Size column. Then, as the Mac computes the size of your folders' contents, they jump into their correct sorted order at what may seem to be random intervals.

Adjusting Column Widths

If you place your cursor carefully on the dividing line between two column headings, you'll find that you can drag the divider line horizontally. Doing so makes the column to the left of your cursor wider or narrower.

What's delightful about this activity is watching OS X scramble to rewrite its information to fit the space you give it. For example, as you make the Date Modified (or Created) column narrower, "Saturday, March 9, 2015, 2:22 PM" shrinks first to "Sat, Mar 9, 2015, 2:22 PM," then to "3/9/15, 2:22 PM," and finally to a terse "3/9/15."

If you make a column too narrow, OS X shortens the file names by removing text from the middle. An ellipsis (…) appears to show you where the missing text would have appeared. (Apple reasoned that truncating the ends of file names, as in some other operating systems, would hide useful information, like the numbers at the end of "Letter to Marge 1," "Letter to Marge 2," and so on. It would also hide the three-letter extensions, such as Thesis.doc, that may appear on file names in OS X.)

For example, suppose you've named a Word document "Justin Bieber—A Major Force for Humanization and Cure for Depression, Acne, and Migraine Headache." (Yes, file names can really be that long.) If the Name column is too narrow, you might see only "Justin Bieber—A Major…Migraine Headache."

Tip: You don't have to make the column mega-wide just to read the full text of a file whose name has been shortened. Just point to the icon's name without clicking. After a moment, a yellow, floating balloon appears—something like a tooltip in Microsoft programs—to identify the full name.

In fact, now you can move your mouse up or down a list over truncated file names, and their tooltip balloons appear instantaneously. (This trick works in list, column, or Cover Flow views—and in Save and Open dialog boxes, for that matter.)

Column View

The goal of column view is simple: to let you burrow down through nested folders without leaving a trail of messy, overlapping windows in your wake.

The solution is shown in Figure 2-14. It's a list view that's divided into several vertical panes. The first pane (not counting the Sidebar) shows whatever disk or folder you first opened.

When you click a disk or folder in this list (once), the second pane shows a list of everything in it. Each time you click a folder in one pane, the pane to its right shows what's inside. The other panes slide to the left, sometimes out of view. (Use the horizontal scroll bar to bring them back.) You can keep clicking until you're looking at the file icons inside the most deeply nested folder.

If you discover that your hunt for a particular file has taken you down a blind alley, it's not a big deal to backtrack, since the trail of folders you've followed to get here is still sitting before you on the screen. As soon as you click a different folder in one

of the earlier panes, the panes to its right suddenly change, so that you can burrow down a different rabbit hole.

The beauty of column view is that, first of all, it keeps your screen tidy. It effectively shows you several simultaneous folder levels but contains them within a single window. With a quick ⌘-W, you can close the entire window, panes and all. Second, column view provides an excellent sense of where you are. Because your trail is visible at all times, it's much harder to get lost—wondering what folder you're in and how you got there—than in any other window view.

Figure 2-14:
If the rightmost folder contains pictures, sounds, Office documents, or movies, you can look at them or play them right there in the Finder. You can drag this jumbo preview icon anywhere— into another folder or to the Trash, for example.

Column View by Keyboard

Efficiency fans can operate this entire process by keyboard alone. For example:

- **You can jump from one column to the next** by pressing the ◄ or ► keys. Each press highlights the first icon in the next or previous column.

- **You can use any of the commands in the Go menu,** or their keyboard equivalents, or the icons in the Sidebar, to fill your columns with the contents of the corresponding folder—Home, Favorites, Applications, and so on.

- **The Back command** (clicking the ‹ button on the toolbar, pressing ⌘-[, or choosing Go→Back) works as it does in a Web browser: It retraces your steps backward. You can repeat this command until you return to the column setup that first appeared when you switched to column view. Once you've gone back, in fact, you can then go forward again; choose Go→Forward, or press ⌘-].

- **Within a highlighted column,** press the ▲ or ▼ keys to highlight successive icons in the list. Or type the first couple of letters of an icon's name to jump directly to it.

- **When you finally highlight the icon you've been looking for,** press ⌘-O or ⌘-▼ to open it (or double-click it, of course). You can open anything in any column; you don't have to wait until you've reached the rightmost column.

Manipulating the Columns

The number of columns you can see without scrolling depends on the width of the window. That's not to say, however, that you're limited to four columns (or whatever fits on your monitor). You can make the columns wider or narrower—either individually or all at once—to suit the situation, according to this scheme:

- **To make a single column wider or narrower,** drag the fine vertical line that separates it from the column to its right (see Figure 2-15).

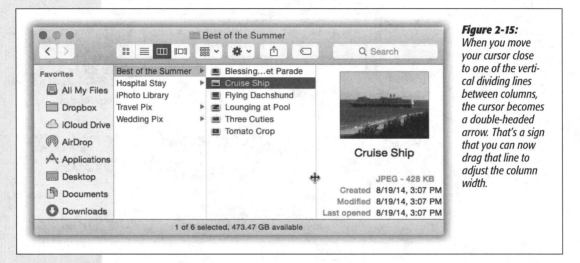

Figure 2-15:
When you move your cursor close to one of the vertical dividing lines between columns, the cursor becomes a double-headed arrow. That's a sign that you can now drag that line to adjust the column width.

- **To make *all* the columns wider or narrower simultaneously,** hold down the Option key as you drag one of the divider lines.

- **To make a column precisely as wide as necessary** to reveal all the names of its contents, double-click the divider line on its right side.

- **To make *all* columns as wide as required**—when you absolutely, positively don't want any names truncated—Option-double-click a column's right-side divider line.

Tip: *If you're having trouble remembering all those key and click combinations, you're not alone. Fortunately, you can use a right-click trick instead.*

If you right-click or two-finger click the divider line at the right side of a column, you get a shortcut menu that offers these commands: Right Size This Column (make it exactly as wide as necessary), Right Size All Columns Individually (make every *column exactly as wide as necessary), and Right Size All Columns Equally (make all columns* the same width, *based on whatever width is necessary to see all the names in the* narrowest *one).*

Grouping the Column Contents

Yes, the Arrange commands are available to column view, too; you can add those gray category headings to the clumps of files in each window. And, once again, you can also use the Sort By commands to change the sequence of files within each grouping. It all works exactly as described starting on page 52.

View Options

Just as in icon and list view, you can choose View→Show View Options to open a dialog box—a Spartan one, in this case—offering additional control over your column views.

- **Always open in column view.** Once again, this option lets you override your system-wide preference setting for all windows.

- **Browse in column view.** Ensures that any folder inside this one will open up in column view when double-clicked.

- **Arrange By, Sort By.** You can put column-view icons into arranged groups—and sort them within those groups—just as described starting on page 52.

- **Text size.** Whatever point size you choose here affects the type used for icons in all column views.

- **Show icons.** For maximum speed, turn off this option. Now you see only file names—not the tiny icons next to them—in all column views. Weird!

- **Show icon preview.** Turn off this option if you don't want the tiny icons in column view to display their actual contents—photos showing their images, Word and PDF documents showing their first pages, and so on. You get generic, identical icons for each file type (text, photo, or whatever).

- **Show preview column.** The far-right Preview column can be handy when you're browsing graphics, sounds, or movie files. Feel free to enlarge this final column when you want a better view of the picture or movie; you can make it really big.

 The rest of the time, though, the Preview column can get in the way, slightly slowing down the works and pushing other, more useful columns off to the left side of the window. If you turn off this checkbox, the Preview column doesn't appear.

Tip: No matter what view you're in, remember this: If you ever start dragging an icon and then change your mind, just press the Esc key or ⌘-period, even while the mouse button is still down. The icon flies back to its precise starting place. Or, if you've already dragged something to a new window and now you regret it, press ⌘-Z (for Undo). Too bad real life doesn't have a similar feature.

Cover Flow View

Cover Flow is a visual display that Apple stole from its own iTunes software, where Cover Flow simulates the flipping "pages" of a jukebox, or the albums in a record-store bin (Figure 2-16). There you can flip through your music collection, marveling as the CD covers flip over in 3-D space while you browse.

The idea is the same in OS X, except that now it's not album covers you're flipping; it's gigantic file and folder icons.

To fire up Cover Flow, open a window. Then click the Cover Flow ▥ button in the toolbar. Or choose View→as Cover Flow, or press ⌘-4.

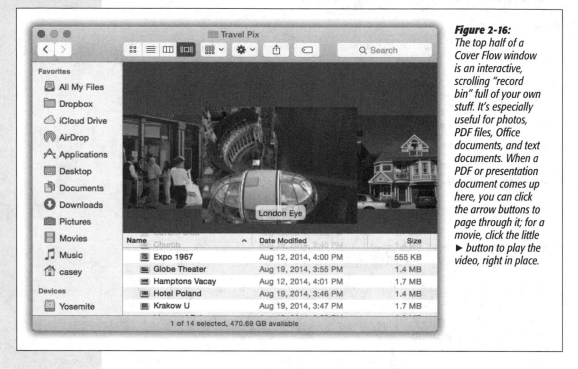

Figure 2-16:
The top half of a Cover Flow window is an interactive, scrolling "record bin" full of your own stuff. It's especially useful for photos, PDF files, Office documents, and text documents. When a PDF or presentation document comes up here, you can click the arrow buttons to page through it; for a movie, click the little ▶ button to play the video, right in place.

Now the window splits. On the bottom: a traditional list view, complete with sortable, arrangeable columns, exactly as described previously.

On the top: the gleaming, reflective-black Cover Flow display. Your primary interest here is the scroll bar. As you drag it left or right, you see your files and folders float by and flip in 3-D space. Fun for the whole family!

The effect is spectacular, sure. It's probably not something you'd want to set up for every folder, though, because browsing is a pretty inefficient way to find something. But in folders containing photos or movies (that aren't filled with hundreds of files), Cover Flow can be a handy and satisfying way to browse.

And now, notes on Cover Flow:

- **You can adjust the size of the Cover Flow display** (relative to the list-view half) by dragging up or down on the grip-strip area just beneath the Cover Flow scroll bar.

- **Multipage documents, presentation files, movies, and sounds are special.** When you point to one, you get either the ▶ button (to play a movie or sound) or ← and → arrow buttons (to flip through a PDF, Pages, PowerPoint, or Keynote document), exactly as you can with icons in icon view.

- **You can navigate with the keyboard, too.** Any icon that's highlighted in the list view (bottom half of the window) is also front and center in the Cover Flow view. Therefore, you can use all the usual list-view shortcuts to navigate both at once. Use the ▲ and ▼ keys, type the first few letters of an icon's name, press Tab or Shift-Tab to highlight the next or previous icon alphabetically, and so on.

- **Cover Flow shows whatever the list view shows.** If you expand a flippy triangle to reveal an indented list of what's in a folder, then the contents of that folder become part of the Cover Flow.

- **The previews are actual icons.** When you're looking at a Cover Flow minidocument, you can drag it with your mouse—you've got the world's biggest target—anywhere you'd like to drag it: another folder, the Trash, wherever.

- **You can use the Arrange and Sort commands.** Yes, you can put the list-view portion of the window into tidy groupings—and sort within those groupings—just as described starting on page 52.

The Preview Pane

The real magic of Cover Flow and Column views has always been the instant previews of what's in each file you highlight. The words in a Word file, the image in a JPEG photo, the numbers in an Excel spreadsheet—you can see them without actually having to double-click an icon. In Cover Flow view, the preview image appears above the list of files (Figure 2-16); in Column view, it appears in the rightmost column.

Figure 2-17:
You can make this preview pane appear in any Finder window, no matter what view it's in. It shows both the contents of the selected file and some handy details about it, like its dimensions, size, and creation date.

But what about Icon and List views? They have charms of their own; don't they deserve some kind of preview column, too?

Why, yes, they do. You can choose View→Show Preview (or press Shift-⌘-P) in any of the Finder's four window views—and you get a full-height preview pane at the right side of the window (Figure 2-17). (To turn off the new pane, choose View→Hide Preview.)

Quick Look

As the preceding several thousand pages make clear, there are lots of ways to view and manage the seething mass of files and folders on a typical hard drive. Some of them actually let you see what's in a document without having to open it—the Preview column in column view, the giant icons in Cover Flow, the new preview pane, and so on.

Quick Look takes this idea to another level. It lets you open and browse a document at nearly full size—without switching window views or opening any new programs (see Figure 2-18). You highlight an icon (or several) and then do one of these things:

- **Press the space bar.** This is by far the best technique to learn. After all, unless you're editing a file's name, what's the space bar ever done for you in the Finder? Nothing. But in OS X, you can highlight any icon and then tap the space bar for an instant preview.

- **Tap with three fingers.** Here's a bonus for laptops. Tap an icon with three fingers on the trackpad (don't fully click down) to open its preview.

- **Press ⌘-Y.** Another keystroke for the same function. The space bar is still better, though.

- **Click the ◉ icon at the top of the window.** But who uses the mouse anymore?

- **Choose File→Quick Look.**

- **Choose Quick Look from the Action menu (✿) at the top of every Finder window.**

- **Right-click (or two-finger click) an icon; from the shortcut menu, choose Quick Look.**

You exit Quick Look in any one of these same ways.

Note: Whenever Quick Look appears in a menu or a shortcut menu, its wording changes to reflect the name of the icon. For example, it might say "Quick Look 'Secret Diary.doc.' "

In any case, the Quick Look window now opens, showing a gigantic preview of the document (Figure 2-18). Rather nice, eh?

The idea here is that you can check out a document without having to wait for it to open in the traditional way—at full size. For example, you can read the fine text in a

Word or PowerPoint document without actually having to open Word or PowerPoint, which saves you about 45 minutes.

Tip: You can use the usual "next page" gesture (two-finger swipe on a trackpad, one-finger swipe on the Magic Mouse) to page through PDF or iWork documents, or to move among photos if you've highlighted a whole bunch. Add the Option key to your finger-swipe to zoom in or out of PDF documents.

Figure 2-18:
Once the Quick Look window is open, you can play a file (movies and sounds), study it in more detail (most kinds of graphics files), or even read it (PDF, Word, and Excel documents). You can also click another icon, and another, and another, without ever closing the preview; the contents of the window simply change to reflect whatever you've just clicked. Supertip: Quick Look works even on icons in the Trash, so you can figure out what something is before you nuke it forever.

It's astonishing how few people are aware of this incredibly useful feature. Learn it!

What Quick Look Knows

You might wonder: How, exactly, is Quick Look able to display the contents of a document without opening it? Wouldn't it have to somehow understand the internal file format of that document type?

Exactly. And that's why Quick Look doesn't recognize all documents. If you try to preview, for example, a Final Cut Pro video project, a sheet-music file, a .zip archive, or a database file, all you'll see is a six-inch-tall version of its generic icon. You won't see what's inside.

Over time, people will write plug-ins for those nonrecognized programs. Already, plug-ins that let you see what's inside folders and .zip files await at *www.quicklookplugins.com*. In the meantime, here's what Quick Look recognizes right out of the box:

- **Graphics files and photos.** This is where Quick Look can really shine, because it's often useful to get a quick look at a photo without having to haul iPhoto or Photoshop out of bed. Quick Look recognizes all common graphics formats, including TIFF, JPEG, GIF, PNG, RAW, and Photoshop documents.

- **PDF and text files.** Using the scroll bar, you can page through multipage documents, right there in the Quick Look window.

- **Audio and movie files.** These begin to play instantly when you open them into the Quick Look window. Most popular formats are recognized (MP3, AIFF, AAC, MPEG-4, H.264, and so on). A scroll bar appears so that you can jump around in the movie or song.

- **Pages, Numbers, Keynote, and TextEdit documents.** Naturally, since these are Apple programs, Quick Look understands the document formats.

- **Microsoft Word, Excel, and PowerPoint documents.** Because these formats are so common, OS X comes with a Quick Look plug-in to recognize them. Move through the pages using the vertical scroll bar; switch to a different Excel spreadsheet page using the Sheet tabs at the bottom.

- **Fonts.** Totally cool. When you open a font file in Quick Look, you get a crystal-clear, huge sampler that shows every letter of the alphabet in that typeface.

- **vCards.** A vCard is an address-book entry that people can send one another by email to save time in updating their Rolodexes. When you drag a name out of Apple's or Microsoft's address books and onto the desktop, for example, it turns into a vCard document. In Quick Look, the vCard opens up as a handsomely formatted index card that displays all the person's contact information.

- **HTML (Web pages) and Safari archived pages.** If you've saved some Web pages to your hard drive, here's a great way to inspect them without firing up your Web browser.

In fact, Quick Look has started seeping even faster into other programs—not just the Finder. For example, you can preview any of the following:

- **A link in a Mail message.** In Mail, there's a tiny ▾ next to each Web link. Click it to view the actual Web page it leads to, right there in a pop-up bubble!

- **An address in Mail or Safari.** If you ever see a street address in an email message or on a Web page, click the tiny ▾ next to it. You're offered the options to add this

person to your address book, or to see a map of that address in Safari, courtesy of Google Maps.

- **An address in Contacts.** In the Contacts program, click the label for an address (like "Work" or "Home"); from the shortcut menu, choose Map This Address. You get to see, once again, an aerial photo of that spot in Safari, thanks to Google.

- **Anything in the Spotlight menu.** When you use the Spotlight search feature described in Chapter 3, point to anything in the results menu without clicking. In a moment, a big Quick Look bubble pops out to the left, showing what's actually in that document or file.

- **Anything in Mission Control, or a Dock menu.** You can also tap the space bar to get a Quick Look preview of anything in the Mission Control view (page 161) or the stack, list, or grid of a Dock folder (page 77).

And you were alive to see the day!

Fun with Quick Look

Here are some stunts that make Quick Look even more interesting:

- **Full screen.** When you click the Full Screen button (the gray ⊗), the Quick Look window expands to fill your screen. Keep this trick in mind when you're trying to read Word, Excel, or PDF documents, since the text is usually too small to read otherwise. (When you're finished with the closeup, click the Full Screen button again to restore the original Quick Look window, or the ⊗ button to exit Quick Look altogether.)

Tip: How's this for an undocumented shortcut? If you press Option-space bar, or Option-click the eyeball icon in any Finder window, you go straight into Full Screen mode without having to open the smaller Quick Look window first. Kewl.

(OK, this is actually part of the slideshow feature described below, but it's also good for super-enlarging a single icon.)

- **Share it.** Click the ⬆ in the title bar to open the Share pop-up menu—a quick way to send this document on to somebody or post it online.

- **Open with [program name].** This button shows up at the top-right corner of your Quick Look window. It might say, for example, "Open with Preview."

 Handy, really. It says: "Oh, so you've been Quick-Looking to find a particular document, and this is the one you wanted? Click me to jump directly into the program that opens it, so you can get to work reading or editing. I've just saved you having to close the window and double-click the icon."

Tip: Actually, you have a much bigger target than the "Open with" button in the corner. You can double-click *anywhere in the Quick Look window* to open the document (in whatever program is named on the "Open with" button).

Better yet: If you click and hold your cursor on that "Open with" button, you get a secret pop-up menu of other programs that could open the file you're looking at.

- **Keep it going.** Once you've opened Quick Look for one icon, you don't have to close it before inspecting another icon. Just keep clicking different icons (or pressing the arrow keys to walk through them); the Quick Look window changes instantly with each click to reflect the new document.

- **Fix the size.** Quick Look tries to display an entire picture or document in a single small window. To view it briefly at actual size, hold down the Option key

The Quick Look Slideshow

OS X is supposed to be all about graphics and other visual delights. No wonder, then, that it offers a built-in, full-screen slideshow feature.

It works like this: Highlight a bunch of icons, and then open Quick Look. Click the ⊙ (Full Screen) button in the top-left corner. The screen goes black, and the documents begin their slideshow. Each image appears on the screen for about 3 seconds before the next one appears. (Press the Esc key or ⌘-period to end the show.) It plays all documents it recognizes, not just graphics.

It's a useful feature when you've just downloaded or imported a bunch of photos or Office documents and want a quick look through them. Use the control bar shown in Figure 2-19 to manage the playback.

Figure 2-19:
Once the slideshow is under way, you can use this control bar. It lets you pause the slideshow, move forward or backward manually, enlarge the current "slide" to fill the screen, or end the show. The Index view is especially handy. (You can press ⌘-Return to "click" the Index View button.) It displays an array of labeled miniatures, all at once—a sort of Exposé for Quick Look. Click a thumbnail to jump directly to the Quick Look document you want to inspect.

Previous, Pause, Next Index View Share Exit Full Screen Exit Quick Look

Note: This same slideshow mechanism is available for graphics in Preview and Mail; Preview even offers crossfades between pictures.

Finder Tabs

The world discovered the miracle of tabs in *Web browsers* years ago. Here's a simple software design idea, modeled after the tabs of file folders, that lets you keep many Web pages open at once in a single window. What convenience! What cleanliness!

But it took until 2013 for someone to realize that tabs might be useful at the desktop, too. That's when Apple added tabs to Finder windows.

They do exactly the same job they do in Safari: They let you keep open the windows of several different containers—folders or disks—in a single window frame. That makes it easy to move icons back and forth between them (Figure 2-20), or even to view the same window twice in different views.

As a convenience, Apple designed the commands, keystrokes, and clicks to work exactly as they do in Safari.

Creating Tabs

There are almost as many ways to open new tabs as there are people:

- **Press the ⌘ key as you open a folder or disk.** (That shouldn't come as a shock; you ⌘-click a link to open a new tab in Safari, too.)

Tip: You can ⌘-click the names of places in the Sidebar of a Finder window, too, like Documents or Pictures.

- **Right-click (or two-finger click) a folder or disk.** From the shortcut menu, choose Open in New Tab.
- **If you already have some tabs, click the + button at the far right.** (Even if you haven't created any tabs yet, that button appears if you've made the Tabs bar visible; choose View→Show Tab Bar.)
- **Drag a disk or folder icon onto the + button at the far right of the tab bar.**
- **Select a folder or disk (or several).** From the ✿ menu, choose Open in New Tab(s).
- **Select a folder or disk (or several),** and then press Control-⌘-O.
- **Choose File→New Tab,** or press ⌘-T, to open a new tab.

Tip: And what will it show? Whatever you've chosen in the Finder→Preferences→General→"New Finder windows show" pop-up menu. It's usually your All My Files window, or maybe the desktop's contents.

Using Tabs

So why bother opening tabs? Because you can perform a few power-usery stunts now that you couldn't before. Like this:

- **Move files around.** You can drag a file or folder icon into another tab as shown in Figure 2-20.

Move an icon to a new window Tabs New Tab

Figure 2-20:
Finder tabs are exactly like tabs in a Web browser. They let you view multiple folders or disks in a single window, which conserves space beautifully.

Tip: If you drag a file onto a new tab (like Recipes, shown here) and let go, you move that icon. If you move it to the Recipes tab and pause, finger still down, the Recipes tab opens so that you can continue your drag into a folder you find there.

- **View the same window twice.** Put one copy of the window in list view, another in icon view. Or view different sections of a very long list of files in two side-by-side tabs.

- **Live in a desktop-free world.** Click the green ⊗ button (upper-left corner) to put your Finder window into Full Screen mode. (See page 160 for more on Full Screen mode.)

Now you can work in tabs, manipulating your files, without ever seeing the desktop.

Tab Management

Once you've got some tabs adorning your window, you can operate them thusly:

- **To switch tabs,** click one, or press Control-Tab. (Add the Shift key to cycle through the tabs in reverse.) If you forget these important keystrokes, they're listed for you as commands in the Window menu.

- **Rearrange tabs** by dragging them horizontally.

- **Turn a tab into a standalone window** by dragging it away from the other tabs. (Or choose Window→Move Tab to New Window.)

Tip: There's no built-in keyboard shortcut for the Window-menu commands like Move Tab to New Window and Merge All Windows. But it's easy enough to add a shortcut of your own, as described on page 199.

- **Move a tab into a different window** by dragging it. That is, you can drag a tab from one window to another.

- **Round up a bunch of open windows** into a single tabbed window: Choose Window→Merge All Windows. That's a good one.

- **To close a tab,** press the usual "close window" keystroke, ⌘-W. (Or, if it's a really slow day, choose File→Close Tab. Or move your cursor onto the tab itself and click the tiny ❌ that appears.)

- **To close all tabs,** add the Option key. For example, press Option-⌘-W or Option-click the window's red Close button.

The Dock

For years, most operating systems maintained two lists of programs. One listed unopened programs until you needed them, like the Start menu (Windows) or the Launcher (Mac OS 9). The other kept track of which programs were open at the moment for easy switching, like the taskbar (Windows) or the Application menu (Mac OS 9).

In OS X, Apple combined both functions into a single strip of icons called the Dock.

Apple's thinking goes like this: Why must you know whether or not a program is already running? That's the computer's problem, not yours. In an ideal world, this distinction should be irrelevant. A program should appear when you click its icon, whether it's open or not—just as on an iPhone or iPad.

"Which programs are open" already approaches unimportance in OS X, where sophisticated memory-management features make it hard to run out of memory. You can have dozens of programs open at once.

And that's why the Dock combines the launcher and status functions of a modern operating system. Only a tiny white dash beneath a program's icon tells you that it's open—and you can even hide that, if you want. (Choose ⌘→Dock→Dock Preferences, and turn off "Show indicator lights for open applications.")

Apple has made it as easy as possible to learn to like the Dock. You can customize the thing to within an inch of its life, use it to control and manipulate windows in elaborate ways, or even get rid of it completely. This section explains everything you need to know.

Setting Up the Dock

Apple starts the Dock off with a few icons it doesn't want you to miss: Finder, Launchpad, Mission Control, App Store, Mail, the Safari Web browser, and so on. But using

your Mac without putting your own favorite icons in the Dock is like buying an expensive suit and turning down the free alteration service. At the first opportunity, you should make the Dock your own.

The concept of the Dock is simple: Any icon you drag onto it (Figure 2-21) is installed there as a button. You can even drag an open window onto the Dock—a Microsoft Word document you're editing, say—using its proxy icon (page 32) as a handle.

Tip: If you right-click a folder, or any other icon, in the *Sidebar* (page 35), you get an Add to Dock command for that icon. Bet you can't guess what it does.

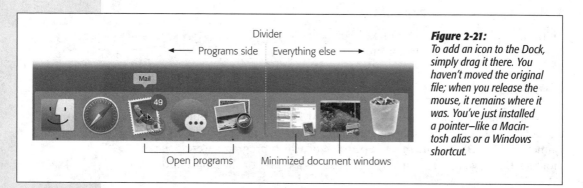

Divider

← Programs side Everything else →

Mail

Open programs Minimized document windows

Figure 2-21:
To add an icon to the Dock, simply drag it there. You haven't moved the original file; when you release the mouse, it remains where it was. You've just installed a pointer—like a Macintosh alias or a Windows shortcut.

A single click, not a double-click, opens the corresponding icon. In other words, the Dock is an ideal parking lot for the icons of disks, folders, documents, programs, and Internet bookmarks that you access frequently.

You can even install batches of icons onto the Dock all at once—just drag them as a group. That's something you can't do with the other parking places for favorite icons, like the Sidebar and the Finder toolbar.

Here are a few aspects of the Dock that may throw you at first:

- **It has two sides.** See the divider line (Figure 2-21)? Everything on the left side is an application—a program. Everything else goes on the right side: files, documents, folders, disks, and minimized windows.

 Remember this division. If you try to drag an application to the right of the line, for example, the Mac teasingly refuses to accept it. (Even aliases observe that distinction. Aliases of applications can go only on the left side, and vice versa.)

- **Its icon names are hidden.** To see the name of a Dock icon, point to it without clicking. You'll see the name appear above the icon.

- **Folders and disks sprout** *stacks*. If you click a folder or a disk icon on the right side of the Dock, a list of its contents sprouts from the icon. It's like X-ray vision without the awkward moral consequences. Read on for details on stacks.

Tip: If you press Shift as you click, the stack opens in slow motion. Amaze your friends.

- **Programs appear there unsolicited.** Nobody but you (and Apple) can put icons on the right side of the Dock. But program icons appear on the left side of the Dock automatically whenever you open one, even one that's not listed in the Dock. Its icon remains there for as long as it's running.

Organizing and Removing Dock Icons

You can move the tiles of the Dock around by dragging them horizontally. As you drag, the other icons scoot aside to make room. When you're satisfied with its new position, drop the icon you've just dragged.

To remove a Dock icon, just drag it away. (You can't remove the icons of the Finder, the Trash, or any minimized document window.) Once your cursor has cleared the Dock, release the mouse button. The icon disappears in a charming little puff of animated smoke. The other Dock icons slide together to close the gap.

Something weird happens if you drag away a Dock program's icon while that program is running. You don't see any change immediately, because the program is still open. But when you quit the program, its previously installed icon disappears from the Dock.

Pop-Up Dock Folders ("Stacks")

When you click a disk or folder icon on the Dock, you witness the effect shown in Figure 2-22. In essence, OS X is fanning out the folder's contents so you can see all of them. If it could talk, it would be saying, "Pick a card, any card."

Tip: You can change how the icons in a particular stack are sorted: alphabetically, chronologically, or whatever. Use the "Sort by" section of the shortcut menu.

In principle, of course, pop-up folders are a great idea, because they save you time and clicking. Click a folder to see what's in it; click the icon you want inside; and you're off and running, without having had to open, manage, and close a window.

Anyway, here's how to operate pop-up Dock folders.

Fan vs. grid vs. list

When you click a disk or folder icon on the Dock, what happens? You see its contents, arrayed in your choice of three displays:

- **Fan.** The fan is a single, gently curved column of icons that pops out of the disk or folder icon. It's ideal for folders that contain very few icons, because there's room for only a handful of items in a fan (the exact number depends on your screen size). After the first few, you see only a "31 more in Finder" button, which you can click to see everything in that folder—but now you've wasted time, not saved it.

Note: When your Dock is positioned on a side of the screen instead of the bottom, the fan option isn't available.

- **Grid.** If you've set a folder to open as a grid, you get to see many more icons in a big rectangular window. File names often get abbreviated because there's not enough horizontal room, but you get to see many more icons this way. Actually, thanks to the scroll bar, you get to see all the icons this way. (You can also type the beginning of an icon's name to select it.)

List view

Fan view

Grid view

Figure 2-22:
What happens when you click a folder in the Dock? You see its contents in one of three views. Here's how you choose the file you're looking for in each:

Top left: In List view, the folder contents appear as a menu; you can "drill down" into subfolders, and you open something by choosing its name.

Top right: In Fan view, click an icon to open it.

Bottom: In Grid view, many more icons appear than can fit in Fan view.

In any of the views, you can get a quick look at a document's contents by using Quick Look. That is, highlight the icon (point without clicking, or use the keyboard to select), and then press the space bar. A window sprouts, showing the actual document contents.

Tip: A cool white-ghostly-highlighting effect is available, which makes it easier to see which icon you're pointing to as you move your mouse around in a grid or a fan. To make it appear, click-and-hold a folder on the Dock—and then, without releasing the mouse, slide onto the grid or fan. The highlighting follows your cursor.

Alternatively, as soon as the grid or fan appears, press the arrow keys on your keyboard to move from icon to icon—complete with ghostly selection square.

- **List.** You can also opt for a simple list of the folder's contents, like a pop-up menu; in Yosemite, you actually see little, tiny icons for the files and folders within. The list appears much faster than a fan or a grid does.

 There's no scroll bar, but you can scroll the list nonetheless just by pointing to the top or bottom of it with your mouse. And, of course, you can type-select.

Tip: The List view also displays a little ▸ to the right of each folder within the Dock folder. That is, it's a hierarchical list, meaning that you can burrow into folders within folders, all from the original Dock icon, and all without opening a single new window. You can stick your entire Home folder, or even your whole hard drive icon, onto the Dock; now you have complete menu access to everything inside, right from the Dock.

- **Automatic.** There's a fourth option in the shortcut menu for a Dock folder, too: Automatic. If you turn this on, then OS X chooses either Fan or Grid view, depending on how many icons are in the folder.

So how do you choose which display you want? Right-click (or two-finger click) the Dock folder's icon, and make a selection from the shortcut menu. Each disk or folder icon remembers its own fan/grid/list setting.

The Finer Points of Pop-Up Dock Folders

Those were the basics of pop-up Dock folders. Here's the advanced course:

- **Ever-Changing Folder-Icon Syndrome (ECFIS).** When you add a folder or disk icon to the Dock, you might notice something wildly disorienting: Its icon keeps changing to resemble whatever you most recently put into it. Your Downloads folder might look like an Excel spreadsheet icon today, a PDF icon tonight, and a photo tomorrow—but never a folder. The annoying part is that you can't get to know a folder by its icon.

 Fortunately, this problem is easy to fix. Right-click (or two-finger click) the Dock folder. From the shortcut menu, in the "Display as" section, choose either Folder (which looks like a folder forever) or Stack (which changes to reflect its contents.)

- **Ready-made pop-up folders.** When you install OS X, you get a couple of starter Dock folders, just to get you psyched. One is Downloads; the other is Documents. (Both of these folders are physically inside your Home folder. But you may well do most of your interacting with them on the Dock.)

 The Downloads folder collects all kinds of online arrivals: files you download from the Web using Safari, files you receive in a Messages file-transfer session, file

attachments you get via Mail, files sent to you using AirDrop (Chapter 16), and so on. Unless you intervene, they're sorted by the date you downloaded them.

It's handy to know where to find your downloads, and nice not to have them all cluttering your desktop.

Tip: Once you've opened a stack's fan or grid, you can drag any of the icons right out of the fan or grid. Just drag your chosen icon onto the desktop or into any visible disk or folder. In other words, what lands in the Downloads folder doesn't have to stay there. (You can't drag out of a list, however.)

- **Hierarchical folders.** The fans and grids are hierarchical—that is, you can drill down from their folders into their folders. Figure 2-23 makes this concept clearer.

Tip: Figure 2-23 shows you how to open a folder in a grid or a list using the mouse—but you can do it all from the keyboard, too. Once a folder is selected, press Return, ⌘-O, or ⌘-▼ to see what's inside it; press ⌘-▲ to backtrack to the original display. When a folder is highlighted, you can press ⌘-Return to open it in a Finder window; add the Option key to open that Finder window without closing the grid or fan.

Figure 2-23:
If you spot a folder inside a list or a grid (left), click it once. You're now looking at a fan or grid of its contents (right). You can go on burrowing like this as deeply as your folders go. You can also "back out" again by clicking the Back button in the upper-left corner.

- **Type selecting.** Once a list, fan, or grid is on the screen, you can highlight any icon in it by typing the first few letters of its name. For example, once you've popped open your Applications folder, you can highlight Safari by typing *sa*. (Press Return to open the highlighted icon.)

Tip: Alternatively, you can "walk" through the fan, grid, or list by pressing the arrow keys. A highlighting effect makes it crystal clear which icon you're selecting. Once an icon is selected, press Return to open it.

- **Two ways to bypass the pop-up.** If you just want to see what's in a folder, without all the graphic overkill of the fan or the grid, then right-click (or two-finger click) the Dock folder's icon and choose the first command—Open "Applications" (or

whatever the folder's name is—from the shortcut menu. You go straight to the corresponding window.

Actually, if you *really* value your time, you'll learn the shortcut: Option-⌘-click the Dock folder's icon. That accomplishes the same thing.

Tip: Alternatively, you can ⌘-click a folder on the Dock–or, indeed, any icon on the Dock–to jump to the window that contains that folder's icon. (Bonus: This same ⌘-clicking trick also works in the list of Spotlight search results.)

Three Ways to Get the Dock Out of Your Hair

The bottom of the screen isn't necessarily the ideal location for the Dock. All Mac screens are wider than they are tall, so the Dock eats into your limited vertical screen space. You have three ways out: Hide the Dock, shrink it, or rotate it 90 degrees.

Auto-hiding the Dock

To turn on the Dock's auto-hiding feature, choose ⌘→Dock→Turn Hiding On (or press Option-⌘-D).

Tip: You also find this on/off switch when you choose ⌘→Dock→Dock Preferences (Figure 2-24), or when you click the System Preferences icon in the Dock, and then the Dock icon. (Chapter 17 contains much more about the System Preferences program.)

When the Dock is hidden, it doesn't slide into view until you move the cursor to the Dock's edge of the screen. When you move the cursor back to the middle of the screen, the Dock slithers out of view once again. (Individual Dock icons may occasionally shoot upward into desktop territory when a program needs your attention—cute, very cute—but otherwise, the Dock lies low until you call for it.)

On paper, an auto-hiding Dock is ideal; it's there only when you summon it. In practice, however, you may find that the extra half-second the Dock takes to appear and disappear makes this feature slightly less appealing.

Many Mac fans prefer to hide and show the Dock at will by pressing the hide/show keystroke, Option-⌘-D. This method makes the Dock pop on and off the screen without requiring you to move the cursor.

Shrinking and enlarging the Dock

Depending on your screen's size, you may prefer smaller or larger Dock buttons. The official way to resize them is shown in Figure 2-24.

There's a much faster way to resize the Dock, though: Just position your cursor carefully on the Dock's divider line so that it turns into a double-headed arrow (shown in Figure 2-25). Now drag up or down to shrink or enlarge the Dock.

Tip: If you press Option as you drag, the Dock snaps to certain canned icon sizes–those that the programmer actually drew. (You won't see the in-between sizes that OS X generally calculates on the fly.)

As noted in Figure 2-25, you may not be able to enlarge the Dock, especially if it contains a lot of icons. But you can make it almost infinitely smaller. This may make you wonder: How can you distinguish among icons if they're the size of molecules?

The answer lies in the →Dock→Turn Magnification On command. What you've just done is trigger the swelling effect shown in Figure 2-24. Now your Dock icons balloon to a much larger size as your cursor passes over them. It's a weird, magnetic, rippling, animated effect that takes some getting used to. But it can actually come in handy when you find your icons shrinking away to nothing.

Tip: You can get Dock magnification à la carte, too. If you press Shift-Control as your cursor approaches the Dock, the icons swell into magnification mode even if magnification is turned off in the →Dock menu. (The icons swell to whatever maximum size you specified in System Preferences (Figure 2-24).

Figure 2-24:
To make your Dock icons bigger or smaller, choose →Dock→Dock Preferences. Leave the Dock Preferences window open on the screen, as shown here. After each adjustment of the Dock size slider, try out the Dock (which still works when the Dock Preferences window is open) to test your new settings.

Moving the Dock to the sides of the screen

Yet another approach to getting the Dock out of your way is to rotate it, so that it sits vertically against a side of your screen. You can rotate it in either of two ways:

- **The menu way.** From the →Dock submenu, choose Position on Left, Position on Right, or Position on Bottom, as you see fit.

- **The mouse way.** While pressing Shift, drag the Dock's divider line, like a handle, to the side of the screen you want.

You'll probably find that the right side of your screen works better than the left. Most OS X programs put their document windows against the left edge of the screen, where the Dock and its labels might get in the way.

Note: When you position your Dock vertically, the "right" side of the Dock becomes the bottom of the vertical Dock. In other words, the Trash now appears at the bottom of the vertical Dock. So as you read references to the Dock in this book, mentally substitute the phrase "bottom part of the Dock" when you read references to the "right side of the Dock."

Figure 2-25:
Look closely—you can see the secret cursor that resizes the Dock. If you don't see any change in the Dock size as you drag upward, then you've reached the size limit. The Dock's edges are already approaching your screen's edges.

Using the Dock

Most of the time, you'll use the Dock as either a launcher (you click an icon once to open the corresponding program, file, folder, or disk) or as a status indicator (the tiny, shiny reflective spots identified in Figure 2-21 indicate which programs are running).

But the Dock has more tricks than that up its sleeve. You can use it, for example, to pull off any of the following stunts.

Switch Applications

The Dock isn't just a launcher; it's also a switcher. Here are some of the tricks it lets you do:

- **Jump among your open programs** by clicking their icons.

- **Drag a document (such as a text file) onto a Dock application** (such as the Microsoft Word icon) to open the former with the latter. (If the program balks at opening the document, yet you're sure the program should be able to open the document, then add the ⌘ and Option keys as you drag.)

- **Hide all windows of the program you're in** by Option-clicking another Dock icon.

- **Hide all other programs' windows** by Option-⌘-clicking the Dock icon of the program you do want (even if it's already in front).

- **Switch windows in one program** by pointing to that program's Dock icon without clicking, and then doing a three-finger downward swipe on your trackpad. (This

feature, called App Exposé, doesn't work until you turn it on in System Preferences→Trackpad→More Gestures.)

This is just a quick summary of the Dock's application-management functions; you'll find the full details in Chapter 4.

Secret Menus

If you right-click (or two-finger click), or click-and-hold on a Dock icon, you see its very useful shortcut menu (Figure 2-26).

Figure 2-26:
Left: Right-click or two-finger click a Dock icon to open the secret menu. In certain recent programs, the top half of the menu lists recently opened documents, followed by currently open ones.

Right: Right-click or two-finger click the divider bar to open a different hidden menu. This one lists a bunch of useful Dock commands, including the ones listed in the ◆→Dock *submenu.*

If you've clicked a minimized window icon, this shortcut menu says only Open (unless it's a minimized Finder window, in which case it also says Close).

But if you've clicked any other kind of icon, you get some very useful hidden commands. For example:

- **[Window names].** The secret Dock menu of a running program usually lists one or more tiny, neatly labeled window icons, like those shown in Figure 2-26. This useful feature means you can jump directly not only to a certain program, but also to a certain open window in that program.

For example, suppose you've been using Word to edit three different chapters. You can use Word's Dock icon as a Window menu to pull forward one particular chapter, or (if it's been minimized) to pull it up—even if a different program is in front of Word. (The checkmark indicates the *frontmost* window, even if the entire program is in the background. A diamond symbol means that the window is minimized and therefore not visible on the screen at the moment.)

In certain Apple showcase programs like TextEdit and the iWork programs, there are actually two lists of documents, separated by a horizontal line. (You can see the effect in Figure 2-26.) The top group lists files you've recently opened in that program; the next batch lists currently open documents.

Tip: The Finder tile that's always at the beginning of the Dock is, in effect, its own Window menu. Its shortcut menu lists all open desktop windows. The Window menu at the top of the Finder screen does the same thing, but the Dock is available no matter what program you're using.

- **Show All Windows/Show Recents.** When a program on the Dock is open, this command says Show All Windows; when it's not running, it says Show Recents. Either way, it takes you to the screen shown in Figure 2-26, where the icons of recently opened documents appear for easy clicking and reopening. (OK, they *may* appear. Apple programs like TextEdit and Pages show these recent icons, but non-Apple programs have to be updated before they'll show you the recent-document icons.)

 To exit the Recents screen, press Esc or ⌘-period.

- **Options.** This submenu contains a bunch of miscellaneous commands:

 Options→Keep In Dock. Whenever you open a program, OS X puts its icon in the Dock—marked with a shiny, white spot—even if you don't normally keep its icon there. As soon as you quit the program, its icon disappears again from the Dock.

Tip: You can get rid of that white "running program" indicator underline, if you like. Open System Preferences→Dock and turn off "Show indicator lights for open applications."

If you understand that much, then the Keep In Dock command makes a lot of sense. It means, "Hello, I'm this program's icon. I know you don't normally keep me in your Dock, but I *could* stay here even after you quit my program. Just say the word." If you find you've been using, for example, Terminal a lot more often than you thought you would, this command may be the ticket.

Tip: Actually, there's a faster way to tell a running application to remain in the Dock from now on. Just drag its icon off the Dock and then right back onto it—yes, while the program is running. You have to try it to believe it.

If you don't want a program's icon to appear on the Dock when it's not running, choose this command again so that the checkmark disappears.

Note: If the program is already running, turning off Keep In Dock doesn't *immediately* remove its icon from the Dock. That's because a program always appears in the Dock when it's open. What you're doing here is saying, "Disappear from the Dock when you're *not* running"—and you'll see the proof as soon as you quit that program.

Options→Open at Login. This command lets you specify that you want this icon to open itself automatically each time you log into your account. It's a great way to make sure your email inbox, your calendar, or the Microsoft Word thesis you've been working on is fired up and waiting on the screen when you sit down to work.

To make this item *stop* auto-opening, choose this command again so that the checkmark no longer appears.

Options→Show In Finder. This command highlights the actual icon (in whatever folder window it happens to sit) of the application, alias, folder, or document you've clicked. You might want to do this when, for example, you're using a program that you can't quite figure out, and you want to jump to its desktop folder in hopes of finding a Read Me file there.

Tip: Once again, there's a much faster way to reveal a Dock icon in its enclosing window: ⌘-click its Dock icon.

- **Hide/Show.** You can hide all traces of the program you're using by choosing Hide from its Dock icon. (You could accomplish the same thing in many other ways, of course; see page 189.)

What's cool here is that (a) you can even hide the Finder and all *its* windows, and (b) if you press Option, the command changes to say Hide Others. This, in its way, is a much more powerful command. It tells all the programs you're *not* using—the ones in the background—to get out of your face. They hide themselves instantly.

Note: Once you've hidden a program's windows, this command changes to say Show, which is how you make them reappear.

- **Quit.** You can quit any program directly from its Dock shortcut menu. (Finder, Launchpad, and Mission Control are exceptions.) The beauty of this feature is that you don't have to switch into a program to get to its Quit command.

(If you get nothing but a beep when you use this Quit command, it's because you've hidden the windows of that program, and one of them has unsaved changes. Click the program's icon, save your document, and then try to quit again.)

Tip: If you hold down the Option key—even after you've opened the pop-up menu—the Quit command changes to say Force Quit. That's your emergency hatch for jettisoning a locked-up program.

- **Miscellaneous.** You might find other commands in Dock shortcut menus; software companies are free to add specialty options to their own programs.

For example, the Finder icon's shortcut menu offers direct access to commands like Find, Connect to Server, and New Finder Window. Microsoft Office programs (Word, Excel, and so on) come with an Open Recent command, with a list of documents you've opened recently. The Mail icon offers Get New Mail and Compose

New Message commands. The Safari icon has a New Window command. The System Preferences icon sprouts a complete list of the preference panes (Sound, Keyboard, Trackpad, and so on). You get the idea.

Tip: If you Control-⌘-click a program's Dock icon, you get an abbreviated shortcut menu. It lists *only* the Options, Hide, and Quit commands and maybe some recent documents—not the full list of commands. If all you want to do is quit a program or something, this abbreviated menu is faster and easier to comprehend.

Drag and Drop

Dock icons are spring-loaded. That is, if you drag any icon onto a Dock folder or disk icon and pause—or, if you're in a hurry, tap the space bar—the Dock icon opens to receive the dragged file.

Note: It opens, that is, *if* the spring-loaded folder feature is turned on in Finder→Preferences→General.

This technique is most useful in these situations:

• **Drag a document icon onto a Dock folder icon.** The folder's Finder window pops open so you can continue the drag into a subfolder.

• **Drag a document into an application.** The classic example is dragging a photo onto the iPhoto icon. When you tap the space bar, iPhoto opens automatically. Since your mouse button is still down, and you're technically still in mid-drag, you can now drop the photo directly into the appropriate iPhoto album or Event.

You can drag an MP3 file into iTunes or an attachment into Mail or Outlook in the same way.

Tip: When you try to drag something into a folder on the Dock, the Dock icons scoot out of the way; the Dock assumes you're trying to put that something *onto* the Dock. But if you press the ⌘ key as you drag an icon to the Dock, the existing icons freeze in place. Without the ⌘ key, you wind up playing a frustrating game of chase-the-folder.

Great Things to Put in Your Dock

Now that you know what the Dock is about, it's time to set up shop, installing the programs, folders, and disks you'll be using most often.

They can be whatever you want, of course, but don't miss these opportunities:

• **Your Home folder.** Many people immediately drag their hard drive icons—or, perhaps more practically, their Home folders—onto the right side of the Dock. Now they have quick access to every file in every folder they ever use.

• **The Applications folder.** Here's a no-brainer: Stash the Applications folder here so you'll have quick pop-up menu access to any program on your machine.

• **Your Applications folder.** As an even more efficient corollary, create a new folder of your own. Fill it with the aliases of just the programs you use most often and

park it in the Dock. Now you've got an even more useful Applications folder that opens as a stack.

- **The Shared folder.** If you're using the Mac's accounts feature (Chapter 15), this is your wormhole to all the accounts—the one place you can put files where everybody can access them (page 513).

- **A tag.** You know those color-coded Finder tags (page 106)? You can drag one directly out of a Finder window's Sidebar and onto the left side of the Dock. When you click its Dock icon, you get a window that displays the icons of everything on your Mac you've tagged that way.

The Finder Toolbar

At the top of every Finder window is a small set of function icons, all in a gradient-gray row (Figure 2-27). The first time you run OS X, you'll find only these icons on the toolbar:

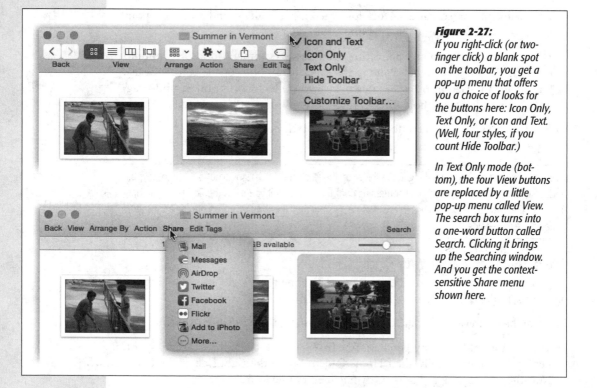

Figure 2-27:
If you right-click (or two-finger click) a blank spot on the toolbar, you get a pop-up menu that offers you a choice of looks for the buttons here: Icon Only, Text Only, or Icon and Text. (Well, four styles, if you count Hide Toolbar.)

In Text Only mode (bottom), the four View buttons are replaced by a little pop-up menu called View. The search box turns into a one-word button called Search. Clicking it brings up the Searching window. And you get the context-sensitive Share menu shown here.

- **Back** (<), **Forward** (>). The Finder works something like a Web browser. Only a single window remains open as you navigate the various folders on your hard drive.

The Back button (<) returns you to whichever folder you were just looking at. (Instead of clicking <, you can also press ⌘-[, or choose Go→Back—particularly handy if the toolbar is *hidden*, as described below.)

The Forward button (>) springs to life only after you've used the Back button. Clicking it (or pressing ⌘-]) returns you to the window you just backed out of.

- **View controls.** The four tiny buttons next to the < button switch the current window into icon, list, column, or Cover Flow view, respectively. And remember, if the toolbar is hidden, you can get by with the equivalent commands in the View menu at the top of the screen—or by pressing ⌘-1 for icon view, ⌘-2 for list view, ⌘-3 for column view, or ⌘-4 for Cover Flow view.

- **Arrange.** This pop-up menu lets you group the files in a window by date, name, or other criteria; see page 52.

- **Action (✿).** You can read about this context-sensitive pop-up menu on page 117.

- **Share (⬆).** You can read about this context-sensitive pop-up menu on page 239.

- **Tags (◁).** Here's the Tags menu described on page 106.

- **Search box.** This little round-ended text box is yet another entry point for the Spotlight feature described in Chapter 3. It's a handy way to search your Mac for some file, folder, disk, or program.

Hiding or Shrinking the Toolbar

With the toolbar, the Dock, the Sidebar, and the large icons of OS X, it almost seems like there's an Apple conspiracy to sell big screens.

Fortunately, the toolbar doesn't have to contribute to that impression. You can hide it by choosing View→Hide Toolbar or by pressing Option-⌘-T. (The same keystroke, or choosing View→Show Toolbar, brings it back.)

You can also just make it smaller by hiding the labels (or the icons), as shown in Figure 2-27.

Rearranging, Customizing, or Removing Toolbar Icons

You can drag toolbar icons around, rearranging them horizontally, by pressing ⌘ as you drag. Taking an icon off the toolbar is equally easy. While pressing the ⌘ key, just drag the icon clear away from the toolbar. You can also get rid of a toolbar icon by right-clicking (two-finger clicking) it and choosing Remove Item from the shortcut menu.

You can also drag a different set of icons onto the toolbar. That's the purpose of the View→Customize Toolbar command.

Getting Help in OS X

It's a good thing you've got a book about OS X in your hands, because the only user manual you get with it is the Help menu, a browser-like program that reads a set of help files that reside in your System→Library folder.

Tip: In fact, you may not even be that lucky. The general-information help page about each topic is on your Mac, but thousands of the more technical pages reside online and require an Internet connection to read.

You're expected to find the topic you want in one of these three ways:

- **Use the search box.** When you click the Help menu, a tiny search box appears just beneath your cursor (Figure 2-28). You can type a few words here to specify what you want help with: "setting up printer," "disk space," whatever.

Tip: You can also hit Shift-⌘-/ (that is, ⌘-?) to open the help search box. And you can change that keystroke, if you like, in System Preferences→Keyboard.

Figure 2-28:
You don't have to open the Help program to begin a search. No matter what program you're in, typing a search phrase into the box shown here produces an instantaneous list of help topics, ready to read.

After a moment (sometimes several moments), the menu becomes a list of Apple help topics pertaining to your search. Click one to open the Help browser described next; you've just saved some time and a couple of steps.

Tip: The results menu does not, however, show all of Help's results—only the ones Apple thinks are most relevant. If you choose Show All Help Topics at the bottom of the menu, the Help browser opens (described below). It shows a more complete list of Help search results.

- **Drill down.** Alternatively, you can begin your quest for assistance by opening the Help browser first. To do that, choose Help→Help Center. (That's the wording in the Finder. In other programs, it might say, for example, "Mail Help." Either way,

this command appears only when nothing is typed in the search box. To empty the search box, click the ✖ button at the right end.)

After a moment, you arrive at the Help browser program shown at top in Figure 2-29. The starting screen offers several "quick click" topics that may interest you—presumably the ones that trigger the most help-hotline calls to Apple. Keep clicking text headings until you find a topic you want to read.

You can backtrack by clicking the ‹ button at the top of the window.

Tip: Annoyingly, the help window still insists on floating in front of all other windows; you can't send it to the back like any normal program. Therefore, consider making the window tall and skinny, so you can put it beside the program you're working in. Drag any edge of the box to change the window's shape.

GEM IN THE ROUGH

Menu Help in the Help Menu

OS X contains a weird, wonderful little enhancement to its online help system. It helps you find menu commands you can't find.

You're floundering in some program. You're *sure* there's a page numbering command in those menus somewhere. But there are 11 menus, and 143 submenus hiding in those menus, and you haven't got time for the pain.

That's when you should think of using the Help menu. When you type *page number* (or whatever) into its search box, the results menu lists, at the top, the names of any menu commands in that program that contain the words you typed. Better still, it actually *opens that menu* for you, and displays a big, blue, animated, floating arrow pointing to the command you wanted. You'd have to have your eyes closed to miss it.

Simply slide your cursor over, click the menu command you wanted, and get on with your life.

Supertip: This feature is especially helpful in Web browsers like Safari and Firefox, because it even finds entries in your Bookmarks and History menus!

In Safari, for example, you can pluck a recently visited site out of the hundreds in the daily History submenus, like the "Wednesday, January 4" submenu. You've just saved yourself a *lot* of poking around menus, trying to find the name of a site you know you've seen recently.

Ultratip: If you think about it, this feature also means you have complete keyboard power over every menu in every program in the world. Hit Shift-⌘-/ (that is, ⌘-?) to open the Help search box, type a bit of the command's name, and then use the arrow keys to walk down the results. Hit Return to trigger the command you want.

- **Use the "Search Help" blank.** Type the phrase you want, like *printing* or *switching applications,* into the search box at the top of the window, and then press Return. As you type, a list of proposed matches drops down from the search box. When you click the closest match, you're shown a list of help-screen topics that may pertain to what you need; see Figure 2-29 for details.

Note: Actually, there's one more place where Help crops up: in System Preferences dialog boxes. Click the circled question-mark button (⑦) in the lower-right corner of most System Preferences panes to open a help page that identifies each control.

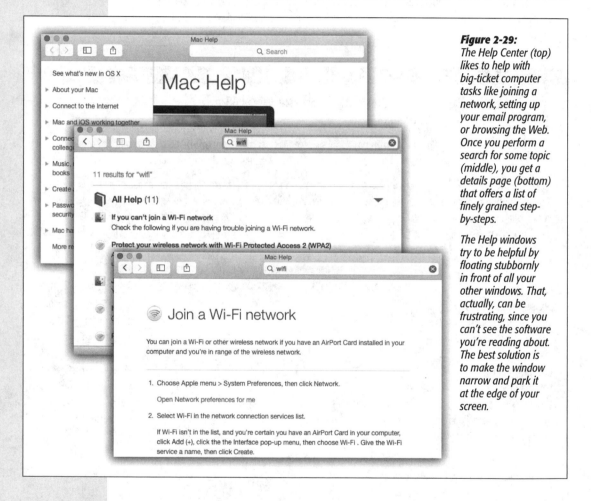

Figure 2-29:
The Help Center (top) likes to help with big-ticket computer tasks like joining a network, setting up your email program, or browsing the Web. Once you perform a search for some topic (middle), you get a details page (bottom) that offers a list of finely grained step-by-steps.

The Help windows try to be helpful by floating stubbornly in front of all your other windows. That, actually, can be frustrating, since you can't see the software you're reading about. The best solution is to make the window narrow and park it at the edge of your screen.

Files, Icons & Spotlight

Every document, program, folder, and disk on your Mac is represented by an *icon:* a colorful little picture that you can move, copy, or double-click to open. In OS X, icons look more like photos than cartoons, and you can scale them to practically any size.

This chapter is all about manipulating those icons—that is, your files, folders, and disks. It's all about naming them, copying them, deleting them, labeling them—and then, maybe most important of all, finding them, using the Mac's famous Spotlight instant-search feature.

Renaming Icons

An OS X icon's name can have up to 255 letters and spaces. Compared with the 31-character or even eight-character limits of older Windows versions, that's quite a luxurious ceiling.

As a Windows veteran, furthermore, you may be delighted to discover that in OS X, you can name your files using letters, numbers, punctuation—in fact, any symbol except the colon (:), which the Mac uses behind the scenes for its own folder-hierarchy designation purposes. And you can't use a period to *begin* a file's name.

To rename a file, click its name or icon (to highlight it) and then press Return. (Or, if you have time to kill, click once on the name, wait a moment, and then click a second time.)

In any case, a rectangle appears around the name (Figure 3-1). At this point, the existing name is highlighted; just begin typing to replace it. If you type a very long name, the rectangle grows vertically to accommodate new lines of text.

Tip: If you simply want to add letters to the beginning or end of the file's existing name, press the ◀ or ▶ key after pressing Return. The insertion point jumps to the beginning or end of the file name.

Figure 3-1:
Click an icon's name (top left) to produce the renaming rectangle (top right), in which you can edit the file's name. OS X is kind enough to highlight only the existing name, and not the suffix (like .jpg or .doc).

Now begin typing to replace the existing name (bottom left). When you're finished typing, press Return or Tab to seal the deal, or just click somewhere else.

You can give more than one file or folder the same name, as long as they're not in the same folder. For example, you can have as many files named "Chocolate Cake Recipe" as you like, provided each is in a different folder. And, of course, files called Recipe.doc and Recipe.xls can coexist in a folder, too.

As you edit a file's name, remember that you can use the Cut, Copy, and Paste commands in the Edit menu to move selected bits of text around, just as though you were word processing. The Paste command can be useful when, for instance, you're renaming many icons in sequence (Quarterly Estimate 1, Quarterly Estimate 2…).

And now, a few tips about renaming icons:

- When the Finder sorts files, a space is considered alphabetically *before* the letter A. To force a particular file or folder to appear at the top of a list view window, insert a space (or an underscore) before its name.

- Older operating systems sort files so that the numbers 10 and 100 come before 2, the numbers 30 and 300 come before 4, and so on. You wind up with alphabetically sorted files like this: "1. Big Day," "10. Long Song," "2. Floppy Hat," "20. Dog Bone," "3. Weird Sort," and so on. Generations of computer users have learned to put zeros in front of their single-digit numbers just to make the sorting look right.

 In OS X, though, you get exactly the numerical list you'd hope for: "1. Big Day," "2. Floppy Hat," "3. Weird Sort," "10. Long Song," and "20. Dog Bone."

- In addition to letters and numbers, OS X also assigns punctuation marks an "alphabetical order," which is this: ` (the accent mark above the Tab key), ^, _, -, space, –, —, comma, semicolon, !, ?, ', ", (,), [,], {, }, @, *, /, &, #, %, +, <, =, ≠, >, |, ~, and $.

Numbers come after punctuation; letters come next; and bringing up the rear are these characters: μ (Option-M); π (Option-P); Ω (Option-Z), and (Shift-Option-K).

Renaming Batches of Files

In Windows, you can highlight a bunch of files and then press F2 to give all of them the same name. You can do that in Yosemite, too—in fact, with more flexibility. You can number them, correct spelling in dozens of files at once, delete a certain phrase from their names, and so on.

To perform this kind of surgery, begin by selecting all the files whose names you want to edit, as shown in Figure 3-2. Then right-click (or two-finger click) any one of them; from the shortcut menu, choose "Rename 12 Items" (or whatever the number is).

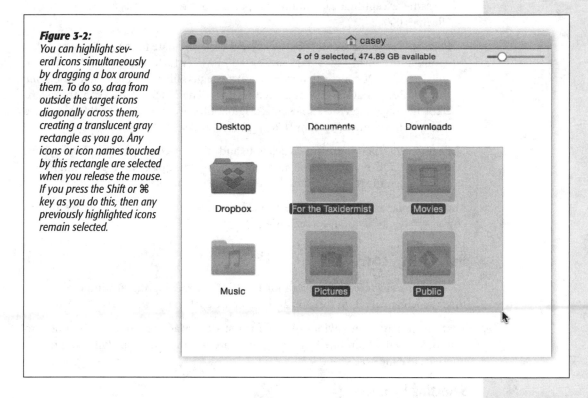

Figure 3-2:
You can highlight several icons simultaneously by dragging a box around them. To do so, drag from outside the target icons diagonally across them, creating a translucent gray rectangle as you go. Any icons or icon names touched by this rectangle are selected when you release the mouse. If you press the Shift or ⌘ key as you do this, then any previously highlighted icons remain selected.

Now you get a box whose pop-up menu offers three ways to rename the icons en masse:

- **Replace Text.** This, ladies and gents, is search-and-replace for text in your files' names. Fill in the "Find" and "Replace with" boxes; click Rename. *Example:* Change "Mom's Recipes—Fish," "Mom's Recipes—Desserts"…into "My Own Recipes—Fish," "My Own Recipes—Desserts"…

- **Add Text** tacks some text onto the files' original names; use the second pop-up menu to specify *where* (beginning or end). *Example:* Change "Mom's Recipes—

Fish," "Mom's Recipes—Desserts"... into "My Mom's Recipes—Fish," "My Mom's Recipes—Desserts"...

- **Format** is complicated but powerful. It completely obliterates whatever the files are called now; instead, it gives them all the same base name (like "Recipes"), differentiating them with a number or the date, either before or after their base names.

 Suppose, for example, that you type "Recipes" into the Custom Format box. That's the base name.

 Now, if you choose "Name and Index" from the second pop-up menu and click Rename, you'll get files named "Recipes 1," "Recipes 2," and so on. You can specify that you want the number (what OS X calls the *index*) either before or after the base name, and what number should begin the sequence. "Name and Counter" is the same, except that each number is padded out to five digits ("Recipes 00001," "Recipes 00002"...).

 Finally, "Name and Date" adds the current time and date to the end of every file's name, in the form "2015-3-19 at 20.20.05 PM" (which means March 19, 2015, at 8:20 p.m.). Of course, that means every selected file will have exactly the *same* name ("Recipes 2015-3-19 at 20.20.05 PM"). The Mac will give you an instant error message, therefore, *unless* the original files are in different folders or have different file name extensions (like .jpg, .doc, and so on).

The new batch-renaming feature is delicious and awesome, but there is some fine print. Don't search-and-replace the file name extensions (like .jpg or .doc); you might not be able to open the files afterward. Don't rename system files or your Home folder.

And use a shareware program like A Better Finder Rename if you want even more power and flexibility in mass-renaming files.

Selecting Icons

To highlight a single icon in preparation for printing, opening, duplicating, or deleting, click the icon once. Both the icon and the name darken in a uniquely OS Xish way.

That much may seem obvious. But most first-time Mac users have no idea how to manipulate *more* than one icon at a time—an essential survival skill in a graphic interface like the Mac's.

Selecting by Clicking

To highlight multiple files in preparation for moving or copying, use one of these techniques:

- **Highlight all the icons.** To select all the icons in a window, press ⌘-A (the equivalent of the Edit→Select All command).

- **Highlight several icons by dragging.** You can drag diagonally to highlight a group of nearby icons, as shown in Figure 3-2. In a list view, in fact, you don't even have

to drag over the icons themselves—your cursor can touch any part of a file's row, like its modification date or file size.

Tip: If you include a particular icon in your diagonally dragged group by mistake, ⌘-click it to remove it from the selected cluster.

- **To highlight consecutive icons in a list.** If you're looking at the contents of a window in list view or column view, you can drag vertically over the file and folder names to highlight a group of consecutive icons, as described above. (Begin the drag in a blank spot.)

There's a faster way to do the same thing; see Figure 3-3.

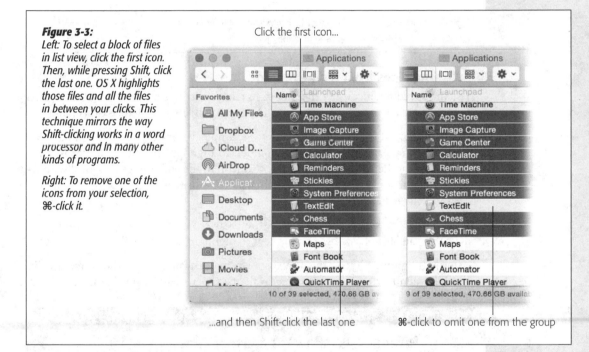

Figure 3-3:
Left: To select a block of files in list view, click the first icon. Then, while pressing Shift, click the last one. OS X highlights those files and all the files in between your clicks. This technique mirrors the way Shift-clicking works in a word processor and In many other kinds of programs.

Right: To remove one of the icons from your selection, ⌘-click it.

Click the first icon...

...and then Shift-click the last one

⌘-click to omit one from the group

- **To highlight arbitrary icons.** If you want to highlight only the first, third, and seventh icons in a window, for example, start by clicking icon No. 1. Then ⌘-click each of the others (or ⌘-drag new rectangles around them). Each icon darkens to show that you've selected it.

If you're highlighting a long string of icons and click one by mistake, you don't have to start over. Instead, just ⌘-click it again so the dark highlighting disappears. (If you do want to start over, you can deselect all selected icons by clicking any empty part of the window—or by pressing the Esc key.) The ⌘ key trick is especially handy if you want to select almost all the icons in a window. Press ⌘-A to select everything in the folder, then ⌘-click any unwanted icons to deselect them.

Tip: In icon view, you can either Shift-click *or* ⌘-click to select multiple individual icons. But you may as well just learn to use the ⌘ key when selecting individual icons. That way you won't have to use a different key in each view.

Once you've highlighted multiple icons, you can manipulate them all at once. For example, you can drag them en masse to another folder or disk by dragging any *one* of the highlighted icons. All other highlighted icons go along for the ride. This technique is especially useful when you want to back up a bunch of files by dragging them onto a different disk, delete them all by dragging them to the Trash, and so on.

When multiple icons are selected, the commands in the File and Edit menus—like Duplicate, Open, and Make Alias—apply to all of them simultaneously.

Tip: Don't forget that you can instantly highlight all the files in a window (or on the desktop) by choosing Edit→Select All (⌘-A)—no icon-clicking required.

Selecting Icons from the Keyboard

For the speed fanatic, using the mouse to click an icon is a hopeless waste of time. Fortunately, you can also select an icon by typing the first few letters of its name.

When looking at your Home window, for example, you can type *M* to highlight the Movies folder. And if you actually intended to highlight the Music folder instead, then press the Tab key to highlight the next icon in the window alphabetically. Shift-Tab highlights the previous icon alphabetically. Or use the arrow keys to highlight a neighboring icon.

(The Tab-key trick works only in icon, list, and Cover Flow views—not in column view, alas. You can always use the ◄ and ► keys to highlight adjacent columns, however.)

After highlighting an icon this way, you can manipulate it using the commands in the File menu or their keyboard equivalents: Open (⌘-O), put it into the Trash

FREQUENTLY ASKED QUESTION

Printing a Window—or a List of Files

How do I print a list of files in a Finder window? The File→Print command prints a selected document, not the list of files.

It's easy enough. Once the window is open on your screen, choose Edit→Select All. Choose Edit→Copy. Now switch to a word processor and paste. (If you're using TextEdit, use Edit→Paste and Match Style instead.) You get a tidy list of all the files in that window, ready to format and print.

This simple file name list isn't the same as printing a window; you don't get the status bar showing how many items are

on the disk and how full the disk is. For that purpose, you can always make a screenshot of the window (page 281) and print that. Of course, that technique is no good if the list of files is taller than the window itself.

Really, what you want is Print Window, a handy shareware program dedicated to printing out your Finder windows, without these workarounds and limitations. You can download it from this book's "Missing CD" page at *www.missingmanuals.com*.

(⌘-Delete), Get Info (⌘-I), Duplicate (⌘-D), or make an alias (⌘-L), as described later in this chapter. By turning on the special disability features described starting on page 572, you can even *move* the highlighted icon using only the keyboard.

If you're a first-time Mac user, you may find it excessively nerdy to memorize key-strokes for jobs the mouse can do. If you make your living using the Mac, however, memorizing these keystrokes will reward you immeasurably with speed and efficiency.

Moving and Copying Icons

In OS X, there are two ways to move or copy icons from one place to another: by dragging them and by using the Copy and Paste commands.

Copying by Dragging

You can drag icons from one folder to another, from one drive to another, from a drive to a folder on another drive, and so on. (When you've selected several icons, drag any *one* of them; the others tag along.) As you drag, you see the ghostly images of all the selected icons moving with your cursor. And the cursor itself sprouts a circled number that reminds you how many files you're moving.

Tip: You can tell that the copying is under way even if the progress bar is hidden. A tiny progress bar appears right on the icon of the copied material in its new home. You can cancel the process either by pressing ⌘-period or by clicking the ⊗ in the progress window.

Understanding when the Mac *copies* a dragged icon and when it *moves* it bewilders many a beginner. However, the scheme is fairly simple when you consider the following:

- On a single disk, dragging from one folder to another *moves* the icon.

- Dragging from one disk (or disk partition) to another *copies* the folder or file. (You can drag icons either into an open window or directly onto a disk or folder icon.)

- If you press the Option key as you release an icon you've dragged, you *copy* the icon instead of moving it. Doing so within a single folder produces a duplicate of the file called "[Whatever its name was] copy."

- If you press the ⌘ key as you release an icon you've dragged from one disk to another, you *move* the file or folder, in the process deleting it from the original disk.

Note: This business of pressing Option or ⌘ *after* you begin dragging is a tad awkward, but it has its charms. For example, it means you can change your mind about the purpose of your drag in mid-movement, without having to drag back and start over.

And if it turns out you just dragged something into the wrong window or folder, a quick ⌘-Z (the shortcut for Edit→Undo) puts it right back where it came from.

Copying or Moving with Copy and Paste

Dragging icons to copy or move them feels good because it's so direct: You actually see your arrow cursor pushing the icons into the new location.

But you pay a price for this satisfying illusion. You may have to spend a moment or two fiddling with your windows to create a clear "line of drag" between the icon to be moved and the destination folder. (A background window will courteously pop to the foreground to accept your drag. But if it wasn't even open to begin with, you're out of luck.)

There's a better way. You can use Copy and Paste to move icons from one window into another, just as in Windows. The routine goes like this:

1. **Highlight the icon or icons you want to move.**

 Use any of the techniques described starting on page 96.

2. **Choose Edit→Copy.**

 Or press the keyboard shortcut: ⌘-C.

Tip: You can combine steps 1 and 2 by right-clicking (or two finger-clicking) an icon and choosing the Copy command from the shortcut menu that appears—or by using the ✿ menu. If you've selected several icons, say five, then the command says "Copy 5 items."

3. **Open the window where you want to put the icons. Choose Edit→Paste.**

 Once again, you may prefer to use the keyboard equivalent: ⌘-V. And once again, you can also right-click (or two-finger click) inside the window and then choose Paste from the shortcut menu that appears, or you can use the ✿ menu.

 If you add the Option key—press Option-⌘-V—you *move* the icons to the new window instead of copying them. That is, the originals disappear after they appear in the new location. (This might make more sense if you use the menu way: If you open the Edit menu and press Option, you'll see the Paste Items command change to say Move Items Here.) It took 27 years, but you can finally *cut* and paste icons, just as in Windows.

GEM IN THE ROUGH

Icon's Progress

Here's an unsung little feature: When you're copying a file or a folder, a tiny progress bar appears right on the icons as they sit in their new location. Animated and everything!

Doesn't matter if it's list view, icon view, or what—you'll see the progress bar.

Blurbs, Brochures,
Notes 2

You'll also see the little ⊗ button at the top-left corner. That, of course, means "Click me to cancel this copying job, since you obviously don't know about the ⌘-period keystroke."

Think of it as a little bit of mistake-recovery insurance.

You can press ⌘-period to interrupt the process. When the progress bar goes away, it means you've successfully transferred the icons, which now appear fully fleshed in the new window.

Dragging from the Title Bar

You may remember from Chapter 1 that the title bar of every Finder window harbors a secret pop-up menu. When you ⌘-click it, you're shown a little folder ladder that delineates your current position in the folder hierarchy. You may also remember that the tiny icon just to the left of the window's name is actually a handle that you can drag to move a folder into a different window.

In many programs, you get the same features in *document* windows, as shown in Figure 3-4. For example, by dragging the tiny document icon next to the document's name, you can perform these three interesting stunts:

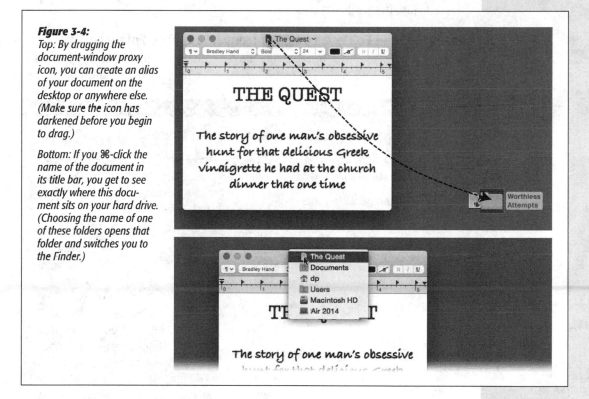

Figure 3-4:
Top: By dragging the document-window proxy icon, you can create an alias of your document on the desktop or anywhere else. (Make sure the icon has darkened before you begin to drag.)

Bottom: If you ⌘-click the name of the document in its title bar, you get to see exactly where this document sits on your hard drive. (Choosing the name of one of these folders opens that folder and switches you to the Finder.)

- **Create an alias on the desktop or the Dock.** By dragging this icon to the desktop or onto a folder or disk icon, you create an instant alias of the document you're working on. (If you drag into the right end of the Dock, you can park the document's icon there, too.) Before the Resume Windows feature came along, this was a useful feature when, for example, you were about to knock off for the night and wanted easy access to the file you'd been working on when you returned the next day.

- **Attach a file to an email message.** You can drag a document (using its proxy icon as a handle) onto the icon of an email program like Mail or Outlook. That process creates a new, outgoing message with the file you dragged already attached. (If an outgoing message is already open in that program, you can drag the file directly into its window, too.) In either case, use the ⌘-Tab switcher (page 159) in mid-drag to switch programs.

- **Launch from a Dock icon.** By dragging this title-bar icon onto another program's *Dock icon,* you open your document in that other program. For example, if you're in TextEdit working on a memo and you decide that you'll need the full strength of Microsoft Word to dress it up, you can drag its title-bar icon directly onto the Word icon in the Dock. Word then launches and opens up the TextEdit document, ready for editing.

Note to struggling writers: Unfortunately, you can't drag an open document directly into the Trash.

Spring-Loaded Folders: Dragging Icons into Closed Folders

You want to drag an icon not just into a folder, but into a folder *inside* that folder. This challenge would ordinarily require you to open the folder, open the inner folder,

GEM IN THE ROUGH

Smart Handling of Identically Named Icons

What if you're dragging a file or folder into some window—and there's already a file or folder there with the same name?

Well, you can Stop (the whole operation) or Replace (the existing items with the ones you were moving).

But there's also a third option: Keep Both. If you click it, OS X adds the number 2 (or 3, or 4…) to the end of each incoming file's name.

Tip 1: If you press Option, the Keep Both button changes to say Skip (meaning "Don't copy *this* file, but keep going with the others I dragged").

> ● ● ●
> An item named "Secret Prototype Info" with extension ".pdf" already exists in this location. Do you want to replace it with the one you're moving?
>
> [Keep Both] [Stop] [Replace]

Tip 2: If you're dragging *several* files whose names match existing files, OS X asks you about each one (Stop, Replace, Keep Both?). If you intend to answer the same way for every single file, save yourself the insanity by turning on the "Apply to all" checkbox before answering the question.

There's another, related feature that comes into play when you paste a *folder* into a spot where there's another folder with the same name. In this case, the Mac offers to *merge the contents* of the two folders.

It might say, for example: "An item named 'Notes' already exists in this location. Do you want to replace it with the one you're moving? Each folder has unique items such as 'Salary Projections' and 'Stealth Projects.doc.' " And your choices are Stop, Keep Both, or Replace All. (These options appear only when you're *pasting* a folder into a new window—not dragging it. They also appear when you Option-drag a folder into a new window to copy it there or when you drag it to a different disk.)

If you click Keep Both, the Finder *combines the contents* of the two folders. The folder you're pasting disappears, but its contents join the contents of the other folder (the one in the destination window) in blissful harmony.

drag the icon in, and then close both windows. As you can imagine, the process is even messier if you want to drag an icon into a sub-subfolder or a *sub*-sub-subfolder.

Instead of fiddling around with all those windows, you can instead use the *spring-loaded folders* feature. Figure 3-5 shows you how it's done.

Tip: You can even drag icons onto disks or folders whose icons appear in the Sidebar (Chapter 1). When you do so, the main part of the window flashes to reveal the contents of the disk or folder you've dragged onto. When you let go of the mouse, the main window changes back to reveal the contents of the disk or folder where you *started* dragging.

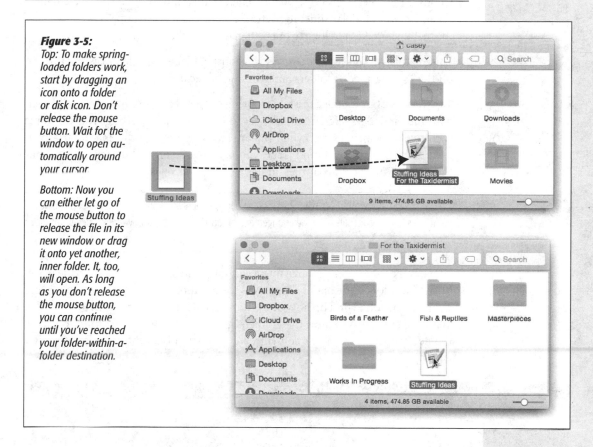

Figure 3-5:
Top: To make spring-loaded folders work, start by dragging an icon onto a folder or disk icon. Don't release the mouse button. Wait for the window to open automatically around your cursor

Bottom: Now you can either let go of the mouse button to release the file in its new window or drag it onto yet another, inner folder. It, too, will open. As long as you don't release the mouse button, you can continue until you've reached your folder-within-a-folder destination.

In short, Sidebar and spring-loaded folders make a terrific drag-and-drop way to file an icon from anywhere to anywhere—without having to open or close any windows at all.

When you finally release the mouse, you're left facing the final window. All the previous windows closed along the way. You've placed the icon into the depths of the nested folders.

Making Spring-Loaded Folders Work

That spring-loaded folder technique sounds good in theory, but it can be disconcerting in practice. For most people, the long wait before the first folder opens is almost enough wasted time to negate the value of the feature altogether. Furthermore, when the first window finally does open, you're often caught by surprise. Suddenly your cursor—mouse button still down—is inside a window, sometimes directly on top of another folder you never intended to open.

Fortunately, you can regain control of spring-loaded folders using these tricks:

- **Choose Finder→Preferences.** On the General pane, adjust the "Spring-loaded folders and windows" delay slider to a setting that drives you less crazy. For example, if the first folder takes too long to open, then drag the slider toward the Short setting.

- **You can turn off this feature entirely** by choosing Finder→Preferences and turning off the "Spring-loaded folders and windows" checkbox.

- **Tap the space bar to make the folder spring open at your command.** That is, even with the Finder→Preferences slider set to the Long delay setting, you can force each folder to spring open when *you* are ready by tapping the space bar as you hold down the mouse button. True, you need two hands to master this one, but the control you regain is immeasurable.

Tip: The space bar trick works even when the "Spring-loaded folders and windows" checkbox (in Finder→ Preferences) is turned off. That's a handy arrangement, because it means folder windows never pop open accidentally.

- **Whenever a folder springs open into a window,** twitch your mouse up to the newly opened window's title bar or down to its information strip. Doing so ensures that your cursor won't wind up hovering on, and accidentally opening, an inner folder. With the cursor parked on the gradient gray, you can take your time to survey the newly opened window's contents, and plunge into an inner folder only after gaining your bearings.

FREQUENTLY ASKED QUESTION

Dragging to Copy a Disk

Help! I'm trying to copy a CD onto my hard drive. When I drag it onto the hard drive icon, I get only an alias—not a copy of the CD.

Sure enough, dragging a disk onto a disk creates an alias.

But producing a copy of the dragged icon is easy enough:

Just press Option or ⌘ as you drag.

Honestly, though: Why are you trying to copy a CD this way? Using Disk Utility (page 701) saves space, lets you assign a password, and usually fools whatever software was on the CD into thinking that it's still *on* the original CD.

Tip: Email programs like Outlook and Mail have spring-loaded folders, too. You can drag a message out of the list and into one of your filing folders, wait for the folder to spring open and reveal its subfolders, and then drag it directly into one of them.

Aliases: Icons in Two Places at Once

Highlighting an icon and then choosing File→Make Alias (or pressing ⌘-L) generates an *alias,* a specially branded duplicate of the original icon (Figure 3-6). It's not a duplicate of the *file*—just of the *icon;* therefore it requires negligible storage space. When you double-click the alias, the original file opens. (A Macintosh alias is essentially the same as a Windows *shortcut.*)

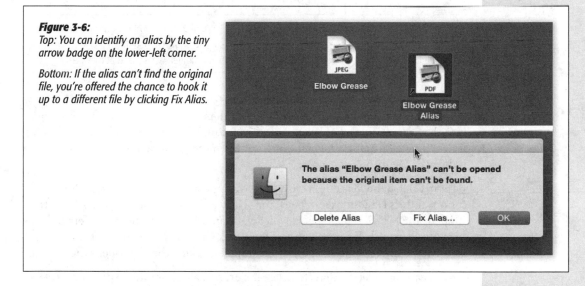

Figure 3-6:
Top: You can identify an alias by the tiny arrow badge on the lower-left corner.

Bottom: If the alias can't find the original file, you're offered the chance to hook it up to a different file by clicking Fix Alias.

You can create as many aliases as you want of a single file; therefore, in effect, aliases let you stash that file in many different folder locations simultaneously. Double-click any one of them, and you open the original file, wherever it may be on your system.

Tip: You can also create an alias of an icon by Option-⌘-dragging it out of its window. (Aliases you create this way lack the word *alias* on the file name—a delight to those who find the suffix redundant and annoying.) You can also create an alias by right-clicking (or two-finger clicking) a normal icon and choosing Make Alias from the shortcut menu that appears, or by highlighting an icon and then choosing Make Alias from the ✿ menu.

What's Good about Aliases

An alias takes up very little disk space, even if the original file is enormous. Aliases are smart, too: Even if you rename the alias, rename the original file, move the alias, and move the original around on the disk, double-clicking the alias still opens the original file.

And that's just the beginning of alias intelligence. Suppose you make an alias of a file that's on a removable disc, like a DVD. When you double-click the alias on your hard drive, the Mac requests that particular disc by name. And if you double-click the alias of a file on a different machine on the network, your Mac attempts to connect to the appropriate machine, prompting you for a password—even if the other machine is thousands of miles away and your Mac must go online to connect.

Here are a couple of ways you can put aliases to work:

- You can file a document you're working on in several different folders, or place a particular folder in several different locations, for convenience.

- You can use the alias feature to save you some of the steps required to access another hard drive on the network. (Details on this trick are in Chapter 16.)

Tip: OS X makes it easy to find the file an alias "points to" without actually having to open it. Just highlight the alias and then choose File→Show Original (⌘-R), or choose Show Original from the ✿ menu. OS X immediately displays the actual, original file, sitting patiently in its folder, wherever that may be.

Broken Aliases

Don't email an alias to the Tokyo office and then depart for the airport, hoping to give the presentation upon your arrival in Japan. When you double-click the alias, now separated from its original, you'll get the message shown the dialog box at the bottom of Figure 3-6.

Be grateful that the Mac doesn't just show you an error message that says " 'NSA Institutional Ethics Handbook' can't be found." Instead, you can click the Fix Alias button. It opens the Fix Alias dialog box, which you can use to navigate the folders on your Mac. When you click a new icon and then click Choose, you associate the orphaned alias with a different file. From now on, double-clicking the alias opens the new file.

Or you can click Delete Alias (to delete the orphan alias) or OK (to do nothing, leaving it where it is).

Tip: You don't have to wait until the original file no longer exists before choosing a new original for an alias. You can perform alias reassignment surgery anytime you like. Just highlight the alias icon and then choose File→Get Info. In the Get Info dialog box, click Select New Original. In the resulting window, find and double-click the file you'd now like to open whenever you double-click the alias.

Finder Tags

Finder tags offer a way to color-code, or apply a keyword to, your icons. After you've applied tags to icons, you can perform some unique file-management tasks—in some cases on all of them simultaneously, even if they're scattered across multiple hard drives. For example:

- **Round up files with Find.** Using the Spotlight search command described start-ing on page 119, you can round up all the icons with a particular tag, no matter which folders they're in.

Note: You can apply more than one tag to an icon, in effect letting it be in more than one place, or sort-able in more than one way. A photo of Aunt Edna in her early days on the farm could be tagged Relatives, Photos, *and* Ancient History.

- **Sort a list view by tag.** No other Mac sorting method lets you create an arbitrary order for the icons in a window. When you sort by tag, the Mac creates alphabetical clusters *within* each tag grouping.

 This technique might be useful when, for example, your job is to process several different folders of documents; for each folder, you're supposed to convert graph-ics files, throw out old files, or whatever. As soon as you finish working your way through one folder, flag it with a tag called Done. The folder jumps to the top (or bottom) of the window, safely marked, leaving the next unprocessed folder at your fingertips, ready to go.

Tip: In a list view, the quickest way to sort by tag is to first make the tag column visible. Do so by choosing View→Show View Options and then turning on the Tags checkbox.

- **Track progress.** Use different-colored tags to track the status of files in a certain project. For example, the first drafts have no tags at all. Once they've been edited and approved, make them blue. Once they've been sent to the home office, make them purple.

 (Heck, you could have all kinds of fun with this: Money-losing projects get red tints; profitable ones get green; things that make you sad are blue. Or not.)

- **Sync across machines.** If you have more than one Mac, and they're signed into the same iCloud account, the same tags are available on all your machines.

Creating Tags

Apple starts you out with a few handy tags, ready to apply to any files you like. They come with ingenious names like "Red," "Yellow," and "Gray."

To create a new tag, use one of the techniques shown in Figure 3-7. You're simultane-ously creating a new tag and applying it to the file(s) in question. The new tag will be available later in the regular Tags menus.

Editing Tag Names and Colors

To change a tag's name, reassign it to a different color, or delete the tag entirely, open the Tags tab of the Preferences dialog box, as shown in Figure 3-8.

Tip: Actually, an identical set of controls appears when you right-click (or two-finger click) one of the tags that appears in the Sidebar of any Finder window.

Two Sets of Favorite Tags

Apple is prepared for Tagageddon; it's created a system that could lead some people to create *hundreds* of tags. That number, of course, is a bit unwieldy. Fortunately, Apple has also equipped you with not one but two sets of "favorites."

Figure 3-7:
Use the File menu, ▱ menu, or shortcut menu to apply label tags to highlighted icons. You can even apply a label within an icon's Get Info dialog box.

Middle: The same menu is your opportunity to create (and simultaneously apply) a new tag. Just type it.

Bottom: You can also apply a tag—or even create a new one—at the moment you're saving a new document. Just type the new tag names into the Tags box that appears just below the Save As box. You can create dozens of different tags (although you can choose from only seven different colors).

- **Sidebar favorites.** The Sidebar at the left side of each Finder window has a section reserved exclusively for displaying the tags you use the most (Figure 3-8, left). To choose which tags you want installed here, open the Preferences dialog box shown

in Figure 3-8 (middle) and turn on the corresponding checkboxes. (Turn off a checkbox to remove its tag from the Sidebar, of course.)

- **Menu favorites.** As shown in Figure 3-8 at right, there's room for only a few favorite tags—their colored dots, anyway—right in the File→Tags menu, or the shortcut menu that appears when you right-click or two-finger click an icon.

Figure 3-8:
Middle: In Finder→ Preferences→ Tags, you can right-click a tag for the shortcut menu shown here. It lets you rename a tag, delete it, or choose a different color.

Left: You can install some favored tags in the Sidebar.

Right: An even smaller set of favorites appears in Finder menus and shortcut menus.

So how do you choose which tags get these exalted positions? In the dialog box shown in Figure 3-8 (middle), drag each favored tag's name into the Favorite Tags box at bottom. (You can remove one by dragging its dot *out* of that box.)

Applying Tags

To apply a tag to a file, highlight the file(s), and then do one of the following:

- **Choose from a menu.** Right-click (or two-finger click) an icon in the Finder or click the ▭ button at the top of the Finder window (Figure 3-7, middle). Or choose File→Tags.

 In each case, you get to see colored dots representing the "menu favorite" tags in your arsenal, as described above. Or you can click Show All to see the complete scrolling list of dozens. (You can apply multiple tags to a single icon.)

- **Use the Sidebar.** You can drag Finder icons *onto* the names of tags in the Sidebar.

- **Apply while saving.** You can tag a file as you're saving it (Figure 3-7, bottom).

- **Apply in the Get Info box.** See page 114.

- **Apply within the app.** Certain Apple programs, like TextEdit, Pages, Numbers, and Keynote, bear a tiny triangle next to the document's name on the title bar (page 31). You can click it to open a Tags box, which lets you edit a document's tags while you're still working on it.

- **Hit a keystroke.** Page 199 describes how you can assign keystrokes to common Mac menu commands. As it turns out, the File→Tags command is available for assignment, too. Give it, say, Control-T, and from now on you can call up the Tags dialog box without even taking your fingers off the keyboard.

 For the application name, use Finder; for the menu title, type *Tags…* (press Option-semicolon to produce that three-dot ellipsis, not three periods).

Once you've applied a tag, you can see it in the Finder. It's represented as a colored dot next to the file's name; see Figure 3-9.

Figure 3-9:
A tag doesn't change the background color of an icon's name. That's because you can apply more than one tag to a single icon.

Instead, tags show up as colored dots—and if you've applied more than one, they show up as stacked, side-by-side colored dots.

Using Tags

OK. So you sat up all weekend, painstakingly tagging each of your thousands of files. Now comes the payoff: *using* tags.

- **Find them all with a click.** Click one of the tag names in the sidebar (Figure 3-8, left). You've instantly performed a Mac-wide search for all files with that tag. They

appear in a single search-results window, regardless of where they're actually sitting on your computer.

Tip: You can drag the name of a tag directly from the Sidebar of any Finder window onto the left (or bottom) side of the Dock. From now on, clicking that Dock icon opens a window that displays every icon on your entire Mac that you've tagged with that color.

- **Find them all using the Find box.** Type a few letters of the tag's name in the Find box at the top-right corner of any Finder window. Use the "Tags" search token (page 110).

- **Find them all with Spotlight.** Into the Spotlight search box (shown on page 120), type *tag:orange* (or whatever the tag name is). The results list shows you all the icons you've tagged that way.

The beauty of these last two methods is that you can combine search criteria. In the Spotlight box, you could search for *tag:orange* and *kind:movie*, for example.

Detagging Files

To remove a tag from an icon, use any of the same menu commands you used to apply the tag in the first place (right-click, File→Tags, click the ⬠ menu). In the Tags drop-down box, just delete the tag name.

The Trash

The Recycle Bin on your old PC is the same idea as the Mac's Trash can, which appears at the end of the Dock. (It's actually a white plastic wastebasket, not a trash can. But who's counting?)

You can discard almost any icon by dragging it into the Trash can. When the tip of your arrow cursor touches the Trash icon, the little wastebasket turns black. When you release the mouse, you're well on your way to discarding whatever it was you dragged. As a convenience, OS X even replaces the empty-wastebasket icon with a wastebasket-filled-with-crumpled-up-papers icon, to let you know there's something in there.

It's worth learning the keyboard alternative to dragging something into the Trash: Highlight the icon, and then press ⌘-Delete (which corresponds to the File→Move to Trash command). This technique is not only far faster than dragging, but it also requires far less precision, especially if you have a large screen. OS X does all the Trash-targeting for you.

Note: If a file is locked, a message appears to let you know; it offers you the chance to fling it into the Trash anyway.

Rescuing Files and Folders from the Trash

File and folder icons sit in the Trash forever—or until you choose Finder→Empty Trash, whichever comes first.

If you haven't yet emptied the Trash, you can open its window by clicking the wastebasket icon once. Now you can review its contents: icons that you've placed on the waiting list for extinction. If you change your mind, you can:

- **Use the Put Back command.** This feature flings the trashed item back into whatever folder it came from, even if that was weeks ago.

 You'll find the Put Back command wherever fine shortcut menus are sold. For example, it appears when you two-finger-click the icon, right-click it, or click the icon and then open the ✿ menu.

Tip: The same keystroke you use to hurl something *into* the trash (⌘-Delete) also works to hurl it *out* again. That is, you can highlight something in the Trash and press ⌘-Delete to put it back where it once belonged.

- **Hit Undo.** If dragging something to the Trash was something you just did, you can press ⌘-Z—the keyboard shortcut for the Edit→Undo command. (The Finder offers a five-level Undo, meaning that you can retrace your last five actions.)

 Undo not only removes a file from the Trash, but also returns it to the folder from which it came. This trick works even if the Trash window isn't open.

- **Drag it manually.** Of course, you can also drag any icon out of the Trash with the mouse, which gives you the option of putting it somewhere new (as opposed to back in the folder it started from).

Emptying the Trash I: Quick and Easy

If you're confident that the items in the Trash window are worth deleting, use any of these three options:

- **Choose Finder→Empty Trash.**

- **Press Shift-⌘-Delete.** Or, if you'd just as soon not bother with the "Are you sure?" message, then throw the Option key in there, too.

- **Right-click the wastebasket icon** (or two-finger click it, or just click it and hold the mouse button down for a moment); choose Empty Trash from the shortcut menu.

GEM IN THE ROUGH

Opening Things in the Trash

Now and then, it's very useful to see what some document in the Trash *is* before committing it to oblivion—and the only way to do that is to open it. Trouble is, you can't open it by double-clicking; you'll get nothing but an error message.

Or at least that's what Apple *wants* you to think.

First of all, you can use Quick Look (page 68) to inspect something in the Trash. But if Quick Look can't open the file—or if you actually want to *edit* it instead of just reading it—then drag the document onto the icon of a program that can open it. That is, if a file called Don't Read Me.txt is in the Trash, you can drag it onto, say, the Word or TextEdit icon in your Dock.

The document dutifully pops open on the screen. Inspect, close, and *then* empty the Trash (or rescue the document).

The Mac asks you to confirm your decision. (Figure 3-10 shows this message.) If you click Empty Trash (or press Return), OS X deletes those files from your hard drive.

Tip: If you'd rather not be interrupted for confirmation every time you empty the Trash, you can suppress this message permanently. To do that, choose Finder→Preferences, click Advanced, and then turn off "Show warning before emptying the Trash."

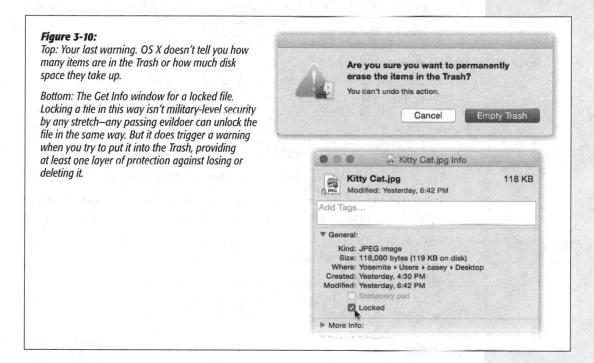

Figure 3-10:
Top: Your last warning. OS X doesn't tell you how many items are in the Trash or how much disk space they take up.

Bottom: The Get Info window for a locked file. Locking a file in this way isn't military-level security by any stretch—any passing evildoer can unlock the file in the same way. But it does trigger a warning when you try to put it into the Trash, providing at least one layer of protection against losing or deleting it.

Emptying the Trash II: Secure and Forever

When you empty the Trash as described above, each trashed icon sure looks like it disappears. The truth is, though, the data *in* each file is still on the hard drive. Yes, the space occupied by the dearly departed is now marked with an internal "This space available" message and, in time, new files may overwrite that spot. But in the meantime, some future eBay buyer of your Mac—or, more imminently, a savvy family member or office mate—could use a program like Data Rescue or FileSalvage to resurrect those deleted files. (In more dire cases, companies like DriveSavers.com can use sophisticated clean-room techniques to recover crucial information—for several hundred dollars, of course.)

That notion doesn't sit well with certain groups, like government agencies, international spies, and the paranoid. As far as they're concerned, deleting a file should *really, really* delete it, irrevocably, irretrievably, and forever.

OS X's *Secure* Empty Trash command to the rescue! When you choose this command from the Finder menu, the Mac doesn't just obliterate the parking spaces around the

dead file. It actually records *new* information over the old—random 0's and 1's. Pure static gibberish.

The process takes longer than the normal Empty Trash command, of course. But when it absolutely, positively has to be gone from this earth for good (and you're absolutely, positively sure you'll never need that file again), Secure Empty Trash is secure indeed.

Tip: You can also direct the Mac to use this secure method *all the time.* To do that, choose Finder→Preferences, click Advanced, and turn on "Empty Trash securely."

Locked Files

By highlighting a file or folder, choosing File→Get Info, and turning on the Locked checkbox, you protect that file or folder from accidental deletion (see Figure 3-10 at bottom). A little 🔒 icon appears on the corner of the full-size icon, also shown in Figure 3-10.

Some notes on how locked files behave:

- **Dragging a locked file into another folder makes a copy;** the original stays put.

- **Putting the locked file into the Trash** produces a warning message: "Item 'Shopping List' is locked. Do you want to move it to the Trash anyway?" If so, click Continue.

- **Once a locked file is in the Trash,** you don't get any more warnings. When you empty the Trash, that item gets erased right along with everything else.

You can unlock files easily enough. Press Option-⌘-I (or press Option as you choose File→Show Inspector). Turn off the Locked checkbox in the resulting Info window. (Yes, you can lock or unlock a mass of files at once.)

Get Info

By clicking an icon and then choosing File→Get Info, you open an important window like the one shown in Figure 3-11. It's a collapsible, multipane screen that provides a wealth of information about a highlighted icon (much like the Properties box in Windows). For example:

- **For a document icon,** you see when it was created and modified, and what programs it "belongs" to.

- **For an alias,** you learn the location of the actual icon it refers to.

- **For a program,** you can turn on Prevent App Nap (page 21).

- **For a disk icon,** you get statistics about its capacity and how much of it is full.

- If *nothing* is selected, you get information about the desktop itself (or the open window), including the amount of disk space consumed by everything on or in it.

- **If you highlight so many icons simultaneously** that their Get Info windows would overwhelm your screen, OS X thoughtfully tallies up their information into a single

summary window. It shows you how many icons you highlighted, breaks them down by type ("23 documents, 3 folders," for example), and adds up their file sizes. That's a great opportunity to change certain file characteristics on numerous files simultaneously, such as locking or unlocking them, hiding or showing their file name suffixes, changing their ownership or permissions (page 541), and so on.

How many icons do you have to highlight to trigger this Multiple Item Info box? That depends on the size of your screen; bigger monitors can hold more Get Info boxes. If you highlight fewer than that magic number of icons, then OS X opens up individual Get Info windows for each one.

Tip: You can force the Multiple Item Info dialog box to appear, though, even if you've highlighted only a couple of icons. Just press Control-⌘-I. (The Option-⌘-I trick described next works for this purpose, too.)

Figure 3-11:
Top: The Get Info window can be as small as this, with all its information panes collapsed.

Bottom: Or, if you click each flippy triangle to open its corresponding pane of information (or Option-click to expand or collapse them all at once), it can be as huge as this—shown here split in two because the book isn't tall enough to show the whole thing. The resulting dialog box can easily grow taller than your screen, which is a good argument for either (a) closing the panes you don't need at any given moment or (b) running out to buy a really gigantic monitor.

And as long as you're taking the trouble to read this caption, here's a tasty bonus: There's a secret command called Get Summary Info. Highlight a group of icons, press Control-⌘-I, and marvel at the special Get Info box that tallies up their sizes and other characteristics.

The Get Info Panes

Apple built the Get Info window out of a series of collapsed "flippy triangles," as shown in Figure 3-11. Click a triangle to expand a corresponding information pane.

Tip: The title-bar hierarchical menu shown on page 32 works in the Get Info dialog box, too. That is, ⌘-click the Get Info window's title bar to reveal where this icon is in your folder hierarchy.

Depending on whether you clicked a document, program, disk, alias, or whatever, the various panes may include the following:

- **Tags.** Yes, here's yet another place where you can add or delete tags for a file.

- **Spotlight Comments.** Here you can type in comments for your own reference. Later, you can view these remarks in any list view if you display the Comments column—and you can find them when you conduct Spotlight searches (page 119).

- **General.** Here's where you can view the name of the icon and also see its size, creation date, most recent change date, locked status, and so on.

 If you click a disk, this info window shows you its capacity and how full it is. If you click the Trash, you see how much stuff is in it. If you click an alias, this pane shows you a Select New Original button and reveals where the original file is. The General pane always opens the first time you summon the Get Info window.

- **More Info.** Just as the name implies, here you'll find more info, most often the dimensions and color format (graphics only) and when the icon was last opened. These morsels are also easily Spotlight-searchable.

- **Name & Extension.** On this pane, you can read and edit the name of the icon in question. The "Hide extension" checkbox refers to the suffix on OS X file names (the last three letters of Letter to Congress.doc, for example).

 Many OS X documents, behind the scenes, have file name extensions of this kind—but OS X comes factory-set to hide them. By turning off this checkbox, you can make the suffix reappear for an individual file. (Conversely, if you've elected to

UP TO SPEED

Compressing, Zipping, and Archiving

OS X comes with a built-in command that compresses a file or folder down to a single, smaller icon—an archive—suitable for storing or emailing. It creates .zip files, the same compression format used in Windows. That means you can now send .zip files back and forth to PC owners without worrying that they won't be able to open them.

To compress something, right-click (or two-finger click) a file or folder and choose "Compress [the icon's name]" from the shortcut menu. (Of course, you can use the File menu or ✿ menu instead.)

OS X thoughtfully creates a .zip archive, but it leaves the original behind so you can continue working with it.

Opening a .zip file somebody sends you is equally easy: Just double-click it. Zip!—it opens.

have OS X *show* all file name suffixes, then this checkbox lets you hide the extensions on individual icons.)

- **Open with.** This section is available for documents only. Use the controls on this screen to specify which program will open when you double-click this document, or any document of its type.

- **Preview.** When you're examining pictures, text files, PDF files, Microsoft Office files, sounds, clippings, and movies, you see a magnified thumbnail version of what's actually *in* that document. This preview is like a tiny version of Quick Look (Chapter 2). A controller lets you play sounds and movies where appropriate.

- **Sharing & Permissions.** This pane is available for all kinds of icons. If other people have access to your Mac (either from across the network or when logging in, in person), this pane lets you specify who is allowed to open or change this particular icon. See Chapter 16 for a complete discussion of this hairy topic.

Shortcut Menus, Action Menus

It's part of the Mac's user-friendly heritage: You can do practically everything using only the mouse. Everything is out front, unhidden, and clickable, whether it's an icon, a button, or a menu.

But as in rival operating systems, you can shave seconds and steps off your workload if you master *shortcut menus:* short menus that sprout out of things you click, offering commands that the software thinks you might want to invoke at the moment, as shown in Figure 3-12.

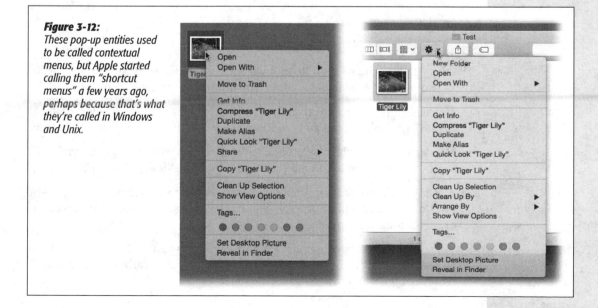

Figure 3-12:
These pop-up entities used to be called contextual menus, but Apple started calling them "shortcut menus" a few years ago, perhaps because that's what they're called in Windows and Unix.

To summon one, just right-click or two-finger click something—an icon, the desktop, a window, a link in Safari, text in a word processor, whatever. You can also trigger these shortcut menus with special clicks on your trackpad or Magic Mouse; see page 14 for additional options.

In any case, a menu drops down listing relevant commands: Get Info, Move to Trash, Copy, and so on. You can click the command you want, or type the first couple of letters of it and then tap the space bar.

These menus become more useful the more you get to know them. The trouble is, millions of Mac fans never even knew they existed. That's why there's a second way to access them. At the top of every Finder window, you'll find a ✿ pop-up menu, technically called the *Action menu* (Figure 3-12, right).

It lists the same sorts of commands you'd find in the shortcut menus, but it's *visible*, so novices stand a better chance of stumbling onto it.

The Finder shortcut menus offer some of the most useful Mac features ever. Don't miss these two in particular:

New Folder with Selection

Imagine this: You've got a bunch of icons scattered on your desktop, or a mass of related files in a window. You can now highlight all of them; right-click any one of them; and from the shortcut menu, choose "New Folder with Selection (12 items)" (or whatever the number of icons is).

With a cool animation, the Finder visibly throws the selected icons into a brand-new folder. It's initially named New Folder With Items (duh), but the hard part is over. All you have to do is rename it—and be grateful that you were spared the 736 steps it would have taken you to do the same job manually.

Share ⬆

Here's a handy menu of ways to send whatever's highlighted to somebody else. In the case of selected Finder icons, you can use these three methods (see Figure 3-13):

- **Mail** whips open Mail and creates a new, outgoing message with the selected file(s) already attached. Address and send, and make a sacrifice to the right-clicky gods.

- **Messages** sends the file to somebody's iPhone. Type a little message and then click Send. Off it goes, just as though you'd sent it from the Messages app (Chapter 13).

- **AirDrop.** AirDrop is a slick, simple way to shoot a file from one Mac to another—or even to or from an iPhone or iPad—without involving any setup, network settings, or user accounts; see page 536.

 But now, you don't have to budge from your current window. Click the file(s) you want to send, click Share→AirDrop, click the name of the nearby destination Mac, iPhone, or iPad, and click Send. Off it goes!

- **Twitter, Facebook, Flickr, Vimeo.** If you have accounts with these Web sites, these options appear, too, making it easy to post your file to those services. For details on these and other Share-menu options, see page 239.

- **Add to iPhoto, Add to Aperture.** If you've selected a photo (or several), these commands send your photographic masterpieces directly into your favorite photo-organizing program.

- **More.** This command opens up a dialog box where you can rearrange the commands in your Share menu, turn off the ones you don't use, and so on.

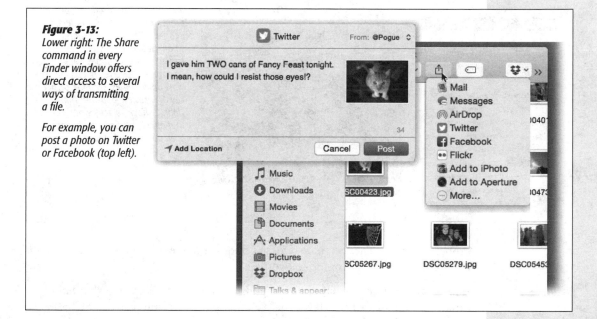

Figure 3-13:
Lower right: The Share command in every Finder window offers direct access to several ways of transmitting a file.

For example, you can post a photo on Twitter or Facebook (top left).

Spotlight

Every computer offers a way to find files. And every system offers several different ways to open them. But Spotlight, a star feature of OS X, combines these two functions in a way that's so fast, so efficient, so spectacular, that it reduces much of what you've read so far to irrelevance.

That may sound like breathless hype, but wait till you try it. You'll see.

See the little magnifying-glass icon (🔍) in your menu bar? That's the mouse-driven way to open the Spotlight search box.

The other way is to press ⌘-space bar. If you can memorize only one keystroke on your Mac, that's the one to learn. It works both at the desktop and in other programs.

In any case, the Spotlight search box appears just below your menu bar (Figure 3-14).

Begin typing to identify what you want to find and open. For example, if you're trying to find a file called *Pokémon Fantasy League.doc,* typing just *pok* or *leag* would

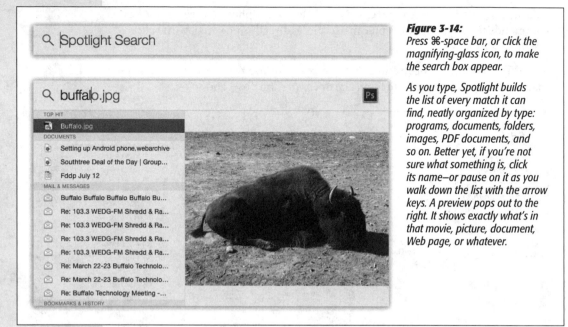

Figure 3-14:
Press ⌘-space bar, or click the magnifying-glass icon, to make the search box appear.

As you type, Spotlight builds the list of every match it can find, neatly organized by type: programs, documents, folders, images, PDF documents, and so on. Better yet, if you're not sure what something is, click its name—or pause on it as you walk down the list with the arrow keys. A preview pops out to the right. It shows exactly what's in that movie, picture, document, Web page, or whatever.

probably suffice. (The search box doesn't find text in the *middles* of words, though; it searches from the beginnings of words.)

A list of results immediately appears below the search box, showing what Spotlight can find containing what you've typed so far. This is a live, interactive search; that is, Spotlight modifies the menu of search results *as you type.*

The results include matches in three categories:

- **Files on your Mac.** As you'd expect, Spotlight rounds up everything with an icon. Every file, folder, program, picture, movie, PDF document, music file, Microsoft Office document, and even font, regardless of its name or folder location. Finally, Spotlight finds things according to their file types (type *.doc* to find Word files), download source (type *cnet.com* to find programs you downloaded from that site), sender (a name or email address), and Finder tag.

- **Data on your Mac.** Spotlight also finds matching information within your Mac programs: every email message, Contacts entry, calendar appointment, Web bookmark, System Preferences pane, To Do item, chat transcript, dictionary definition, and Web site in your History list. Spotlight can also find photos according to *who is in them* (using the Faces feature in iPhoto/Photos) or where they were taken (using its Places feature). If you use Messages (Chapter 13), Spotlight also finds the lucky members of your buddy lists.

- **Online.** In Yosemite, Spotlight also shows you matches it finds on the Internet. You'll often find, for example, a Wikipedia entry in the results, along with matches from the App Store, the iTunes music/movie/TV store, the Maps app's database of restaurants and businesses, Apple's database of movies currently playing, and so on.

As a last resort, you may find general Web-search results from Microsoft's Bing search service—but the beauty of the new Spotlight is that, often, you get the answers you need right in the Spotlight box, without having to venture any farther afield on the Web.

The Preview Pane

Spotlight's window is divided in half. The left side is the traditional list of results.

On the right, though, is a preview pane that shows what's *in each* result. When you click an item in the results list—or use the arrow keys to walk down that list—the preview pane bursts to life, presenting a visual display of that result (Figure 3-14).

Plenty of times, your quest for information *ends* with a glance at the preview pane. If you were hoping to find a dictionary definition, a phone number, an email address, a unit conversion, the address of a business from Maps, or the rating or plot summary of a current movie, for example, that information is now attractively arrayed before you. No need to open anything from here.

In the same way, you can grab yourself a Quick Look preview of what's inside a document. That is, you can see the actual photo when you highlight a JPEG file's name, or you can read the actual text when you highlight a Word document's name.

Tip: You can even copy material out of the preview pane. Just drag through it and then press ⌘-C.

Opening a Result

If you're using Spotlight to find and open an app or a document, double-click it to open it. Or use the arrow keys to walk down the menu, and then press Return to open the one you want.

If you click an application, it opens. If you select a System Preferences pane, System Preferences opens and presents that pane. If you choose an appointment, the Calendar program opens, already set to the appropriate day and time. Selecting an email message opens that message in Mail or Outlook. And so on.

Spotlight is so fast, it eliminates a lot of the folders-in-folders business that's a side effect of modern computing. Why burrow around in folders when you can open any file or program with a couple of keystrokes?

Tip: You can drag icons right out of the results list. For example, you can drag one onto the desktop to park it there, into a window or a folder to move it, into the Trash to delete it, onto the AirDrop icon (in the Sidebar) to hand it over to a colleague, to another disk icon to back it up, and so on.

Spotlight Results Tips

It should be no surprise that a feature as important as Spotlight comes loaded with options, tips, and tricks. Here it is—the official, unexpurgated Spotlight Tip-O-Rama:

- If the very first item—labeled Top Hit—is the icon you were looking for, press Return to open it. This is a huge deal, because it means that in most cases, you can perform the entire operation without ever taking your hands off the keyboard.

 To open Safari in a hurry, for example, press ⌘-space bar (to open the Spotlight search box), type *safa,* and hit Return, all in rapid-fire sequence, without even looking. Presto: Safari is before you.

 And what, exactly, is the Top Hit? OS X chooses it based on its *relevance* (the importance of your search term inside that item) and timeliness (when you last opened it).

Tip: Spotlight makes a spectacular application launcher. That's because Job One for Spotlight is to display the names of matching programs in the results menu. Their names appear in the list nearly instantly—long before Spotlight has built the rest of the menu of search results.

If some program on your hard drive doesn't have a Dock icon, for example—or even if it does—there's no faster way to open it than to use Spotlight.

- You may wonder why Spotlight bothers to display, in big gray lettering, the name of each item you highlight in the results list. It's because sometimes the item's name doesn't match your search term. You might search for *kumquats,* for example, and find it in a document called Frank's Favorite Fruits. The gray lettering tells you the document name.

 The same sort of thing happens when you see a Web site's name in the results. The results list might show the ".com" name for the site (like Amazon.com), and the gray lettering might say "Top Sellers in Electronics."

- To find out where something is on your hard drive—that is, to see its folder path—⌘-click its name. The folder path appears at the bottom of the preview pane (Figure 3-15).

- To jump to (highlight) a search result's Finder icon instead of opening it, ⌘-*double-click* its name. Or arrow-key your way to the result's name and then press ⌘-Return.

- Spotlight's menu shows you, at most, a couple dozen of the most likely suspects, evenly divided among the categories (Documents, Applications, and so on). To see the complete list, you have to open the Spotlight *Searching window* (page 129). Scroll to the bottom of the list and double-click "Show all in Finder."

- It's easy to open something in the results list from the keyboard. Just press ⌘-▲ (or ⌘-▼) to jump from category to category. Once you've highlighted the first result in a category, you can walk through the remaining four by pressing the arrow key by itself. Then, once you've highlighted what you want, press Return to open it.

In other words, you can get to anything in the Spotlight menu with only a few keystrokes.

- The Esc key (top-left corner of your keyboard) offers a two-stage "back out of this" method. Tap it once to close the Spotlight menu and erase what you've typed, so that you're all ready to type in something different. Tap Esc a *second* time to close the Spotlight text box entirely, having given up on the whole idea of searching.

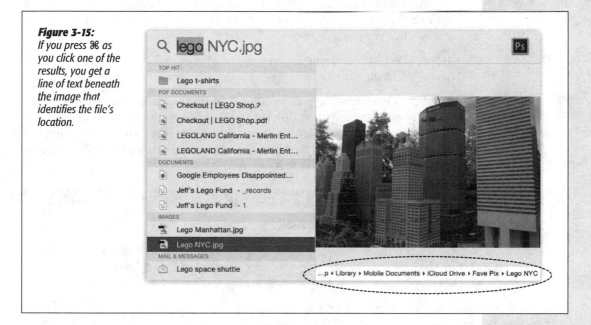

Figure 3-15:
If you press ⌘ as you click one of the results, you get a line of text beneath the image that identifies the file's location.

- Think of Spotlight as your little black book. When you need to look up a number in Contacts, don't bother opening Contacts; it's faster to use Spotlight. You can type somebody's name or even part of someone's phone number.

- Among a million other things, Spotlight tracks the keywords, descriptions, faces, and places you've applied to your pictures in iPhoto. As a result, you can find, open, or insert any photo at any time, no matter what program you're using, just by using the Spotlight box at the top of every Open File dialog box! This is a great way to insert a photo into an outgoing email message, a presentation, or a Web page you're designing. The photo program doesn't even have to be running.

- Spotlight is also a quick way to adjust one of your Mac's preference settings. Instead of opening the System Preferences program, type the first few letters of, say, *volume* or *network* or *clock* into Spotlight. The Spotlight menu lists the appropriate System Preferences pane, so you can jump directly to it.

- While you're pointing to something in the results list, you can press ⌘-I to open the Get Info window for it.

- Spotlight's menu lists only a couple of dozen found items. In the following pages, you'll learn about how to see the rest of the stuff. But, for now, note that you can eliminate some of the categories that show up here (like PDF files or bookmarks), and even rearrange them, to permit more of the *other* kinds of things to enjoy those limited seats of honor. Details on page 140.

- Spotlight shows you only the matches from *your account* and the public areas of the Mac (like the System, Application, and Developer folders)—but not what's in anyone else's Home folder. If you were hoping to search your spouse's email for phrases like "meet you at midnight," forget it.

- If Spotlight finds a different version of something on each of two hard drives, it lets you know by displaying a faint gray hard drive name after each item in the menu.

- Spotlight works by storing an *index*—a private, multimegabyte Dewey Decimal System—on each hard drive, disk partition, or USB flash (memory) drive. If you have some oddball type of disk, like a hard drive that's been formatted for Windows, Spotlight doesn't ordinarily index it—but you can turn on indexing by using the File→Get Info command on that drive's icon.

UP TO SPEED

What Spotlight Knows

The beauty of Spotlight is that it doesn't just find files whose names match what you've typed. That would be *so 2004*!

No, Spotlight actually looks *inside* the files. It can search the contents of text files, RTF and PDF documents, documents from iWork, Keynote, Pages, Photoshop, Microsoft Office (Word, Excel, Entourage, and PowerPoint), and so on.

Over time, software companies can release bits of add-on software–plug-ins–that will make their documents searchable by Spotlight, too. Check periodically by Googling, for example, *spotlight plug-in* and the kind of software you use. For example, free Spotlight plug-ins are available for OmniGraffle, OmniOutliner, TypeIt4Me, MacDraft, REALbasic, Painter, and many others.

But that's only the beginning. Spotlight searches files not only for the text inside them, but also for over 125 other bits of information, including the names of the layers in a Photoshop document, the tempo of an MP3 file, the shutter speed of a digital-camera photo, a document's page size, and on and on.

Technically, this sort of secondary information is called *metadata*. It's usually invisible, although a lot of it shows up in the Get Info dialog box described on page 114.

You might think that typing something into the Spotlight search box triggers a search. But to be technically correct, Spotlight has already done its searching. In the first 15 to 30 minutes after you install OS X–or in the minutes after you attach a new hard drive–Spotlight invisibly collects information about everything on your hard drive. Like a kid cramming for an exam, it reads, takes notes on, and memorizes the contents of all your files. (During this time, if you click the Q icon on the menu bar, you'll be told that Spotlight is indexing the drives.) Once it has indexed your hard drive in this way, Spotlight can produce search results in seconds.

After that initial indexing process, Spotlight continues to monitor what's on your hard drive, indexing new and changed files in the background, in the microseconds between your keystrokes and clicks in other programs.

Tip: Spotlight can even find words inside files on other computers on your network—as long as they're also Macs running Mac OS X Leopard (10.5) or later. If not, Spotlight can search only for the names of files on other networked computers.

Times You Might Not Think of Spotlight

Apple has added so many new functions to Spotlight that, if you're used to thinking of it as a *file* finder, you'll be missing half the fun. It's important, therefore, to get into the habit of hitting ⌘-space when you have a quick question about any of the following:

• **Calculations.** Spotlight is a tiny pocket calculator, always at the ready. Press ⌘-space, type or paste 38*48.2-7+55, and marvel at the first result in the Spotlight menu: 1879.6. There's your answer—and you didn't even have to fire up the Calculator.

(Use the asterisk, *, to mean "times" and the slash, /, as "divided by.")

And Spotlight is not just a four-function calculator, either. It works with square roots: Type *sqrt(25)*, and you'll get the answer 5. It also works with functions like log(x), exp(x), sin(x), sinh(x), and e. You can even type pi to represent, you know, pi.

You can copy the result to the Clipboard by pressing ⌘-C, so that you can paste it into another program.

• **Conversions.** This handy Yosemite feature converts units of measurement for you. It converts time, temperature, mass (weight), length, and even currency.

Usually, you don't have to type anything more than the amount you want to convert; Spotlight instantly converts it to the five most likely other units. For example, if you type *338 feet,* the preview pane shows you the same distance in meters, yards, inches, centimeters, and millimeters (see Figure 3-16).

Figure 3-16:
Spotlight is a units-conversion mastermind. If you simply type a quantity (without saying what you want it converted to), Spotlight displays five different conversions.

But what if what you really wanted was to know how many *miles* that is? Just keep typing. If you type *338 feet in miles,* you get the answer: 0.064 miles.

In the same way, you can convert **volume** (teaspoons, tablespoons, cups, pints, quarts, gallons, cubic feet, fluid ounces, centiliters, milliliters, liters, cubic feet, cubic inches, cubic meters); **weight and mass** (pounds, ounces, kilograms, grams, milligrams, short tons, metric tonnes, long tons); **area** (acres, hectares, square feet, square yards, square meters, square kilometers); **temperature** (Fahrenheit, Celsius, Kelvin—you can abbreviate F, C, or K); **force** (joules, calories, foot pounds, newton meters, British thermal units); and **power** (watts, kilowatts, BTUs per minute). And those are just a few examples.

If you have an Internet connection, you can even convert currencies. Type *134 euros,* for example, and you'll find out that that's $163.13 in U.S. dollars—a lot for a hamburger. (The preview pane also offers the same figure in British pounds, Japanese yen, Canadian dollars, and Swiss francs. If you want a different unit, say so. Type *134 euros in yuan*, for example, to find out how much that's worth in China.

Note: Spotlight doesn't offer to convert the lesser-known units like furlongs, leagues, cubits, and spans. It leaves those conversions to the lucrative market serving biblical scholars and sea captains.

- **Definitions.** The Spotlight menu is a full-blown English dictionary. Or, more specifically, it's wired directly into OS X's own dictionary, which sits in your Applications folder.

 So if you type a word—say, *myrmecophile*—into the search box, you see the Dictionary definition in the results. Click it to see the full-blown entry in the preview pane. (In this example, that would be: "n: an invertebrate or plant that has a symbiotic relationship with ants.")

- **Movies.** Spotlight has a cozy relationship with Fandango.com, the movies database. When you type the name of a movie, past or present, the preview pane shows you a handy dossier about that flick: Its year of release, genre, rating (like PG-13 or R), its rating by viewers (like four stars), run time (hours and minutes long), plot summary, cast and crew lists, and even a button or two that open up your Web browser to play the movie's trailer (Figure 3-17, top).

Tip: For recent movies, you see the critical rating from RottenTomatoes.com, a popular movie-rating site. This rating is expressed as a percentage (like 66 percent, meaning that's how many people liked the movie), as well as with icons. The red tomato indicates a good movie (over 60 percent liked it); the green splatter means a bad one.

- **Music.** Spotlight can find a song in your own iTunes music collection. Type the name of a performer, album, or song to find it.

- **A geographical point of interest.** Spotlight can now speak Maps. You can quickly look up landmarks like "Empire State Building" or "Washington Monument," business names like "Home Depot," and business categories like "sushi" or "pizza."

In each case, the preview pane shows you a snippet of the map of that location, plus handy buttons like Directions to Here, Directions from Here, Add to Favorites, and Add to Contacts. Most of these buttons hand you off to the Maps app to complete the task. (Spotlight finds only the biggest-named businesses. It can't find addresses, coordinates, or smaller companies.)

Figure 3-17:
You can use Spotlight to call up details about any movie, past or present (if your Mac is online). If it's a current movie in theaters, you get the option to look up today's showtimes.

- **The iTunes store.** Want to know if Apple sells or rents a certain movie or TV show? Want a quick way to find that Angry Birds phone game you've heard about? Use Spotlight. It searches Apple's online stores without your having to open the App Store app or your iTunes program. (Only the biggest names show up in these searches; Spotlight doesn't search the entire app, music, or movie store.)

Advanced Menu Searches

Most people just type the words they're looking for into the Spotlight box. But if that's all you type, you're missing a lot of the power of this feature.

Use quotes

If you type more than one word, Spotlight works just the way Google does. That is, it finds things that contain both words *somewhere* inside.

But if you're searching for a phrase where the words really belong together, put quotes around them. You'll save yourself from having to wade through hundreds of results where the words appear *separately*.

For example, searching for *military intelligence* rounds up documents that contain those two words, but not necessarily side by side. Searching for *"military intelligence"* finds documents that contain that exact phrase. (Insert your own political joke here.)

Limit by kind

You can confine your search to certain categories using a simple code. For example, to find all photos, type *kind:image*. If you're looking for a presentation document but you're not sure whether you used Keynote, iWork, or PowerPoint to create it, type *kind:presentation* into the box. And so on.

Here's the complete list of kinds. Remember to precede each keyword type with *kind* and a colon.

To find this:	Use one of these keywords:
A program	app, application, applications
Someone in your address book	contact, contacts
A folder or disk	folder, folders
A message in Mail	email, emails, mail message, mail messages
A Calendar appointment	event, events
A Calendar task	to do, to dos, todo, todos
A graphic	image, images
A movie	movie, movies
A music file	music
An audio file	audio
A PDF file	pdf, pdfs
A System Preferences control	preferences, system preferences
A Safari bookmark	bookmark, bookmarks
A font	font, fonts
A presentation (PowerPoint, iWork)	presentation, presentations

You can combine these codes with the text you're seeking, too. For example, if you're pretty sure you had a photo called "Naked Mole Rat," you could cut directly to it by typing *mole kind:images* or *kind:images mole* (the order doesn't matter).

Limit by recent date

You can use a similar code to restrict the search by chronology. If you type *date:yesterday*, then Spotlight limits its hunt to items you last opened yesterday.

Here's the complete list of date keywords you can use: *this year, this month, this week, yesterday, today, tomorrow, next week, next month, next year*. (The last four items are useful only for finding upcoming Calendar appointments. Even Spotlight can't show you files you haven't created yet.)

Limit by tag

Round up everything with a certain Finder tag using "tag:" as the search prefix. For example, to find everything on your computer that you've tagged as Important, you'd search for *tag:important*.

Limit by metadata

If your brain is already on the verge of exploding, now might be a good time to take a break.

These days, you can limit Spotlight searches by *any* of the 125 different info-morsels that may be stored as part of the files on your Mac: author, audio bit rate, city, composer, camera model, pixel width, and so on. Page 134 has a complete discussion of these so-called *metadata* types. (Metadata means "data about the data"—that is, descriptive info-bites about the files themselves.) Here are a few examples:

- *author:casey.* Finds all documents with "casey" in the Author field. (This presumes that you've actually *entered* the name Casey into the document's Author box. Microsoft Word, for example, has a place to store this information.)

- *width:800.* Finds all graphics that are 800 pixels wide.

- *flash:1.* Finds all photos that were taken with the camera's flash on. (To find photos with the flash *off*, you'd type *flash:0*. A number of the yes/no criteria work this way: Use 1 for yes, 0 for no.)

- *modified:3/7/15-3/10/15.* Finds all documents modified between March 7 and March 10, 2015. You can also type *created:6/1/15* to find all the files you created on June 1, 2015. Type *modified:<=3/9/15* to find all documents you edited *on or before* March 9, 2015.

 As you can see, three range-finding symbols are available for your queries: <, >, and - (hyphen). The < means "before" or "less than"; the > means "after" or "greater than"; and the hyphen indicates a range (of dates, sizes, or whatever you're looking for).

Tip: Here again, you can string words together. To find all PDFs you opened today, use *date:today kind:PDF*. And if you're looking for a PDF document you created on July 4, 2014, containing the word wombat, you can type *created:7/4/14 kind:pdf wombat*—although at this point, you're not saving all that much time.

The Searching Window

As you may have noticed, the Searching window doesn't list *every* match on your hard drive. Unless you own one of those extremely rare 60-inch Apple Skyscraper Displays, there just isn't room.

Instead, Spotlight uses some fancy behind-the-scenes analysis to calculate and display the *most likely* matches for what you typed. But at the bottom of the results list, you usually see that there are many other possible matches; it says, "Show all in Finder," meaning that there are other candidates.

There is, however, a second, more powerful way into the Spotlight labyrinth. And that's to use the *Searching* window, shown in Figure 3-18.

You can open the Searching window in either of two ways.

From Spotlight

If the Spotlight results list—its Most Likely to Succeed list—doesn't include what you're looking for, then click "Show all in Finder" at the bottom. You've just opened the Searching window.

Now you have access to the *complete* list of matches, neatly listed in what appears to be a standard Finder window.

Figure 3-18:
When you type your search term, OS X presents a pop-up menu of suggestions. For example, when you type apple, *it's asking: "Would you like me to limit the search to files with the word 'apple' in their names?" If you ignore the suggestions, the window shows you all matches—including files with the word "apple" inside them.*

From the Finder

When you're in the Finder, you can also open the Searching window *directly,* without using the Spotlight window as a trigger. Actually, there are three ways to get there:

- **⌘-F** (for *Find,* get it?). When you choose File→Find (⌘-F), you get an *empty* Searching window, ready to fill in for your search.

Tip: When the Find window opens, what folder does it intend to search?

That's up to you. Choose Finder→Preferences→Advanced. From the "When performing a search" pop-up menu, you can choose Search This Mac, Search the Current Folder (usually what you want), or Use the Previous Search Scope (that is, either "the whole Mac" or "the current folder," whichever you set up last time).

- **Option-⌘-space bar.** This keystroke opens the same window. But it always comes set to search the currently open window, rather than everything on your Mac, regardless of the setting you made in Preferences (as described in the Tip above).

- **Open any desktop window, and type something into the search box at upper right.** Presto—the mild-mannered folder window turns into the Searching window, complete with search results.

Tip: You can change the Find keystrokes to just about anything you like. See page 140.

The Basic Search

When the Searching window opens, you can start typing whatever you're looking for into the search box at the top.

As you type, the window fills with a list of the files and folders whose names contain what you typed. It's just like the Spotlight results, but without the item-count limit (Figure 3-18).

Where to look

The three phrases at the top of the window—This Mac, [Folder Name], and Shared—are buttons. Click one to tell the Mac where to search:

- **This Mac** means your *entire* computer, including secondary disks attached to it (or installed inside)—minus other people's files, of course.

- **"Letters to Congress"** (or whatever the current window is) limits the search to whatever window was open. So if you want to search your Pictures folder, open it first and *then* hit ⌘-F. You'll see the "Pictures" button at the top of the window, and you can click it to restrict the search to that folder.

- **Shared.** Click this button to expand the search to your *entire network* and all the computers on it. (This assumes, of course, that you've brought their icons to your screen as described in Chapter 16.)

 If the other computers are Macs running Leopard (Mac OS X 10.5) or later, then the Searching window can search their files just the way it does on your own Mac—finding words inside the files, for example. If they're any other kind of computer, Spotlight can search for files only by name.

Tip: If the object of your quest doesn't show up, you can adjust the scope of the search with one quick click on another button at the top of the window, like This Mac or Shared. The Mac updates the results list.

Then again, if you always prefer one of those options, don't forget that you can save yourself a click by choosing it to be the new factory setting. Specify your favorite "where to look" option by visiting Finder→Preferences→Advanced and using the "When performing a search" pop up menu. Your choices are Search This Mac, Search the Current Folder, or Use the Previous Search Scope (that is, "whatever I chose last time").

The suggestions list

When you search, OS X tries to figure out whether you're looking for *file names* or *words inside files.* The Searching window may show you both in the same results list.

But more important, it offers a suggestions pop-up menu. Its purpose is to help you narrow down the results list with one quick click. Whatever you click here is instantly immortalized as a search token, described below.

You may see any of these headings in the suggestions list:

- **Filenames.** The top option is always Filenames; click it to search by the files' names only. If you type *chris* into the box, you want files whose *names* contain that word.

- **Sent by.** If you type *chris,* the Mac wants to know if, by chance, you're looking for email messages and other documents from somebody *named* Chris (or Christina, or Christopher…).

- **Kinds.** If you type *image,* the Kinds option here offers you choices like "image" (any kind), "JPEG image," "Disk image," or "Portable Network Graphics Image." If you type *document,* you get options like "Word document" and "PDF document." If you search for *photo,* the menu lets you pinpoint files whose *file type* contains "photo"—like iPhoto Libraries or Adobe Photoshop files. And so on.

- **Downloaded From.** You see this option when what you type is a Web address. If you type *Macworld* into the search box, then "Downloaded From Macworld.com" appears in the results list—a handy way to round up all the files you've downloaded from a specific site.

- **Dates.** If you type a month (*august* or *august 2015)* or a year into the search box, the suggestions pop-up menu says "Dates: August 2015" (or whatever). Clicking it lets you do a quick roundup of all files you created, modified, last opened, or added during that period.

- **Tags.** Here's yet another way to use the finder tags described on page 106. When you type a search term that matches one of your tags (for example, *green*), the suggestions menu includes "Tags: green."

In each case, the suggestions in this menu reflect only files that actually *exist* on your Mac. If you search for "green," but green isn't one of your Finder tags, then the Tags suggestion doesn't appear. If you haven't downloaded anything from Macworld.com, then that option doesn't appear. And so on.

Once you learn to actually start *using* these suggestions—once you get a hang of the kinds of things they offer—you can get a lot of mileage out of them.

If, on the other hand, you just find them confusing, no big deal. Tap the Esc key to close the suggestions list and reveal the existing Searching window.

Power Searches with Tokens

The real beauty of the Searching window is that it can hunt down icons via more specific searches than you could do using the main Spotlight feature. For example, a feature called *tokens* let you combine criteria, so you find only *music* files sent to you by *Casey.* (A token, in Apple's usage, means "a visual representation of a search criterion.")

Here, for example, is how you might search for pictures of Chris that were last opened in December.

1. **In the Finder, press ⌘-F.**

 The Searching window opens.

2. **In the search box, type *image.***

 Sure enough: The window now shows everything on your Mac that *is* an image or *contains* the word "image" in its name, or even contains the word "image" within the

file. But the list of suggestions that now drops down wants to know: Which do you really want? Files that are images? Or files with the word "image" in their names?

3. **In the suggestions menu, under Kinds, click *Image*.**

You've just pared down the list of results. Now it shows only the files that *are* photos.

Note, too, that the first *token* has appeared. Each time you click a refinement criterion, as you did in this step, OS X enshrines it in the search box as a shaded bubble. In this case, it created a token that says "Kind: Image."

Note: See the tiny ▾ next to the search token's name? You can click it to see a very short pop-up menu of options: the criterion you selected (like "Kind:" or "Date:") and another command that says "Everything." Choosing it undoes the filtering effect of the suggestion, so that this token searches for *any* attribute of your file (like the words inside it).

Why do you need an "Everything" option here? If you'd wanted to search all attributes on your Mac, you could have just typed directly into the search box without even using the suggestions menu.

Three reasons. First, you might want to expand the scope (from "Kind" to "Everything," for example) without having to retype the search term. Second, because you might want to make this token part of a smart folder—a saved search—described at the end of this chapter. Finally, you might want to go on to add another search criterion—another search token—that builds on this search for "Everything."

Now you need to narrow the quest to files containing the word "Chris."

4. **Continue typing in the search box. This time, type *chris*.**

The suggestions appear again, offering options for file names and, probably, a Sent By list that lists everyone named Chris who's ever sent you messages or files. What you want is images whose names contain the *word* "Chris."

5. **Click *Filename*.**

The list of files is much smaller now. It shows only image files with "Chris" in their names.

For your final stunt, you'll screen out all but the December images.

6. **Continue typing in the search box. This time, type *december*.**

This time, the suggestions list offers dates like *December 2014*. You can see the result so far in Figure 3-19.

7. **Click the month you want.**

And voilà: The results list shows you only the December photos of Chris.

To delete a token, click it and then press the Delete key, or backspace over it. You can also edit one: Double-click the right side of the token bubble; now you can retype the search term.

Note: This same feature is also in Mail, where it's even more useful; you have search options like Subject, From, To, and so on.

Figure 3-19:
Each time you add a criterion by clicking the drop-down list of suggestions, the Mac adds a new token (criterion bubble) to the search box.

Power Searching the Old Way

Search tokens are supposed to make multi-criteria searches easier than they used to be. But they're not as powerful as the Old Way, which is still around.

Using the Old Way of power searching, you can set up a search that finds a document whose name begins with the letters *Cro,* is over a megabyte in size, was created after 10/1/14 but before the end of the year, was changed within the past week, has the file name suffix *.doc,* and contains the phrase "attitude adjustment." (Of course, if you knew *that* much about a file, you'd probably know where it is, too. But you get the picture.)

In all, the Old Way lets you specify over 125 different search criteria: date modified, file size, the "last opened" date, color label, copyright holder's name, shutter speed (of a digital photo), tempo (of a music file), and so on. Figure 3-20 illustrates how detailed this kind of search can be.

To set up a complex search like this, use the second row of controls at the top of the window.

And third, and fourth, and fifth. Each time you click one of the + buttons at the right end of the window, a new criterion row appears; use its pop-up menus to specify *what* date, *what* file size, and so on.

Tip: If you press Option, the + button changes into a "…" button. When you click it, you get sub-rows of parameters for a single criterion. A pop-up menu lets you choose Any, All, or None, so that you can build what are called exclusionary searches.

The idea here is that you can set up a search for documents created between November 1 and 7 or documents created between November 10 and 14. Or files named Complaint that are also either Word or InDesign files.

The mind boggles.

Here's a rundown of the ways you can restrict your search, according to the options in the first pop-up menu of a row. Note that after you choose from that first pop-up menu

(Last Opened, for example), you're supposed to use the additional pop-up menus to narrow the choice ("within last," "2," and "weeks," for example), as you'll read below.

Note: It may surprise you that choosing something from the Kind pop-up menu triggers the search instantly. As soon as you choose Applications, for example, the window fills with a list of every program on your hard drive. Want a quick list of every folder on your entire machine? Choose Folders. (Want to see which folders you've opened in the past couple of days? Add another row.)

If you also type something into the search box at the very top of the window—before or after you've used one of these pop-up menus—the list pares itself down to items that match what you've typed.

Figure 3-20:
By repeatedly clicking the + button, you can turn on as many criteria as you'd like; each additional row further narrows the search. To delete a row, click the — button at its right end.

Kind

When the first pop-up menu says Kind, you can use the second pop-up menu to indicate what kind of file you're looking for: Applications, Documents, Executables (programs and Dashboard widgets), Folders, Images, Movies, Music, PDF files, Presentations, Text files, or Other.

For example, when you're trying to free up some space on your drive, you could round up all your movie files, which tend to be huge.

And what if the item you're looking for isn't among those 10 canned choices? What if it's an alias, or a Photoshop plug-in, or some other type?

That's what the Other option is all about. Here you can type in almost anything that specifies a kind of file: *Word, Excel, TIFF, JPEG,* AAC, *final cut, alias,* or whatever.

Last opened date/Last modified date/Created date

When you choose one of these options, the second pop-up menu lets you isolate files, programs, and folders according to the last time you opened them, the last time you changed them, or when they were created.

- **Today, yesterday, this week, this month, this year.** This second pop-up menu offers quick, canned time-limiting options.

- **Within last, exactly, before, after.** If you choose "before," "after," or "exactly," then your criterion row sprouts a month/day/year control that lets you round up items that you last opened or changed before, after, or on a specific day, like 5/27/15. If you choose "within last," then you can limit the search to things you've opened or changed within a specified number of days, weeks, months, or years.

 These are awesomely useful controls, because they let you specify a chronological window for whatever you're looking for.

Tip: You're allowed to add two Date rows—a great trick that lets you round up files you created or edited between two dates. Set up the first Date row to say "is after" and the second one to say "is before."

Science!

Name

Spotlight likes to find text *anywhere* inside your files, no matter what their *names* are. But when you want to search for an icon by the text that's in only its *name,* this is your ticket. (Capitalization doesn't matter.)

Wouldn't it be faster just to click Filename in the suggestions pop-up menu (Figure 3-18)? Yes—but using the Searching window offers you far more control, thanks to the second pop-up menu that offers you these options:

- **Matches.** You'll see files whose names contain entire words you're looking for. If you search for *peas,* you'll find files called "Peas & Crackers" and "Snow Peas"—but not "Appeasement."

- **Contains.** The position of the letters you type doesn't matter. If you type *then,* you find files with names like "Then and Now," "Authentic Cajun Recipes," and "Lovable Heathen."

- **Starts with.** The Find program finds only files beginning with the letters you type. If you type *then,* you find "Then and Now," but not "Authentic Cajun Recipes" or "Lovable Heathen."

- **Ends with.** If you type *then,* you find "Lovable Heathen," but not files called "Then and Now" or "Authentic Cajun Recipes."

- **Is.** This option finds only files named *precisely* what you type (except that capitalization still doesn't matter). Typing *then* won't find any of the file names in the previous examples. It would unearth only a file called simply "Then." In fact, a file with a file name suffix, like "Then.doc," doesn't even qualify.

Contents

You can think of this option as the opposite of Name. It finds *only* the text that's inside your files and completely ignores their icon names.

That's a handy function when, for example, a document's name doesn't match its contents. Maybe a marauding toddler playing Kid Pix renamed your doctoral thesis "xggrjpO#$%////." Or maybe you just can't remember what you called something.

Other

If this were a math equation, it might look like this: *options × options = overwhelming*.

Choosing Other from the first pop-up menu opens a special dialog box containing at least 125 *other* criteria. Not just the big kahunas like Name, Size, and Kind, but far more targeted (and obscure) criteria like "Bits per sample" (so you can round up MP3 music files of a certain quality), "Device make" (so you can round up all digital photos taken with, say, a Canon Rebel camera), "Key signature" (so you can find all the GarageBand songs you wrote in the key of F sharp), "Pages" (so you can find all Word documents that are really long), and so on. As you can see in Figure 3-21, each one comes with a short description.

Figure 3-21:
Here's the master list of search criteria. Turn on the In Menu checkboxes of the ones you'll want to reuse often. Once you've added some of these to the menu, you'll get an appropriate set of "find what?" controls ("Greater than" and "Less than" pop-up menus, for example).

You may think Spotlight is offering you a staggering array of file-type criteria. In fact, though, big bunches of information categories (technically called *metadata*) are all hooks for a relatively small number of document types. For example:

- **Digital photos and other graphics files** account for the metadata types alpha channel, aperture, color space, device make, device model, EXIF version, exposure mode, exposure program, exposure time, flash, f-number, focal length, ISO speed, max aperture, metering mode, orientation, pixel height, pixel width, red eye, resolution height, resolution width, and white balance.

- **Digital music files** have searchable metadata categories like album, audio bit rate, bits per sample, channel count, composer, duration, General MIDI sequence, key signature, lyricist, musical genre, recording date, sample rate, tempo, time signature, track number, and year recorded. There's even a special set of parameters for GarageBand and Soundtrack documents, including instrument category, instrument name, loop descriptors, loop file type, loop original key, and loop scale type.

• **Microsoft Office documents** can contain info bits like authors, contributors, fonts, languages, pages, publishers, and contact information (name, phone number, and so on).

This massive list also harbors a few criteria you may use more often, like Size, File Label, and Visibility (which lets you see all the invisible files on your hard drive).

Now, you could argue that in the time it takes you to set up a search for such a specific kind of data, you could have just rooted through your files and found what you wanted manually. But hey—you never know. Someday, you may remember *nothing* about a photo you're looking for except that you used the flash and an f-stop of 1.8.

Tip: Don't miss the search box in this dialog box. It makes it super-easy to pluck one useful criterion needle—Size, say—out of the haystack. Also don't forget about the In Menu checkbox in the right column. It lets you add one of these criteria to the main pop-up menu, so you don't have to go burrowing into Other again the next time.

What to Do with Search Results

The results window is a regular old Finder window, with all the familiar views and controls (Figure 3-22).

Figure 3-22:
Click a result once to see where it sits on your hard drive (bottom). If the window is too narrow to reveal the full folder path, run your cursor over the folders without clicking. As your mouse moves, the Mac reveals each folder's name, compressing other folders as necessary to make room. (You can drag icons into these folders, too.)

You can work with anything in the results window exactly as though it were in a regular Finder window: Drag something to the Trash, rename something, press the space bar for a Quick Look at it, drag something to the desktop to move it there, drag

something onto a Dock icon to open it with a certain program, Option-⌘-drag it to the desktop to create an alias, and so on.

You can move up or down the list by pressing the arrow keys, scroll a "page" at a time with the Page Up and Page Down keys, and so on. You can also highlight multiple icons simultaneously, the same way you would in a Finder list view: Highlight all of them by choosing Edit→Select All, highlight individual items by ⌘-clicking them, drag diagonally to enclose a cluster of found items, and so on.

Or you can proceed in any of these ways:

- **Change the view (list, column, and so on)** by clicking one of the View icons or choosing from the View menu (see Chapter 2). Actually, Cover Flow is a *great* view for search results; since this list is culled from folders all over the computer, you otherwise have very little sense of context as you examine the file names.

- **Sort the results** by clicking the column headings (in list and Cover Flow views).

- **Arrange the results** by using the Arrange pop-up menu button (▦▾). That way, you group the results as described on page 140. It can be especially useful to clump them by Kind, so that similar file types are clustered together (Documents, Images, Messages, and so on), or to sort by Last Opened, so that the list is chronological.

- **Change the view options.** Press ⌘-J (or choose View→Show View Options) to open the View Options pane for the results window. Here you can add a couple of additional columns (Date Modified, Date Created); change the icon size or text size; or turn on the "always" checkbox at the top, so that future results windows will have the look you've set up here.

- **Get more information** about a result by selecting it and then choosing File→Get Info (⌘-I). The normal Get Info window appears, complete with date, size, and location information.

- **Find out where it is.** It's nice to see all the search results in one list, but you're not actually seeing them in their native habitats: the Finder folder windows where they physically reside.

 If you click once on an icon in the results, the bottom edge of the window becomes a folder map that shows you where that item is.

 For example, in Figure 3-22, the notation in the Path strip means: "The Krakow U icon you found is in the Travel Pix folder, which is in the Pictures folder, which is in Casey's Home folder."

 To get your hands on the actual icon, choose File→Open Enclosing Folder (⌘-R). OS X highlights the icon in question, sitting there in its window wherever it happens to be on your hard drive.

- **Open the file (or open one of the folders it's in).** If one of the found files is the one you were looking for, then double-click it to open it (or highlight it and press either ⌘-O or ⌘-▼). In many cases, you don't know or care where the file was— you just want to get into it.

Tip: You can also double-click to open any of the folders in the folder map at the bottom of the window. For example, in Figure 3-22, you could double-click the selected JPEG icon to open it, or the Travel Pix folder to open it, and so on.

- **Move or delete the file.** You can drag an item directly out of the found-files list and into a different folder, window, or disk—or straight to the Dock or the Trash. If you click something else and then re-click the dragged item in the results list, the folder map at the bottom of the window updates itself to reflect the file's new location.

- **Start over.** If you'd like to repeat the search using a different search phrase, just edit the text in the search box. (Press ⌘-F to empty the search box and the Searching window.)

- **Give up.** If none of these avenues suits your fancy, you can close the window as you would any other (⌘-W).

Customizing Spotlight

You've just read about how Spotlight works fresh out of the box. But you can tailor its behavior, both for security reasons and to fit it to the kinds of work you do.

Here are two ways to open the Spotlight preferences center:

- **Use Spotlight itself.** Hit ⌘-space bar, type *spotl*, and press Return.

- **Choose ⌘→System Preferences. Click Spotlight.**

In any case, you wind up face to face with the dialog box shown in Figure 3-23.

You can tweak Spotlight in three ways here, all very useful:

- **Turn off categories.** The list of checkboxes identifies what Spotlight tracks. If you find that Spotlight uses up valuable menu space listing, say, Web bookmarks or fonts—stuff you don't need to find very often—then turn off their checkboxes. Now the Spotlight menu's limited precious slots are allotted to icon types you care more about. "I'm perfectly capable of looking up movies online," you might say. "I don't need to clutter my Spotlight results list with movie names." Fine—turn off Movies.

- **Prioritize the categories.** This dialog box also lets you change the *order* of the category results; just drag a list item up or down to change where it appears in the Spotlight menu.

 The factory setting is for Applications to appear first in the results. That makes a lot of sense if you use Spotlight as a quick program launcher (which is a great idea). But if you're a party planner who spends all day on the phone, and the most important Spotlight function for you is its ability to look up someone in your address book, then drag Contacts to the top of the list. You'll need fewer arrow-key presses once the results menu appears.

- **Change the keystroke.** Ordinarily, pressing ⌘-space bar highlights Spotlight in your menu bar, and Option-⌘-space bar opens the Searching window. If these

keystrokes clash with some other key assignment in your software, though, you can reassign them to almost any other keystroke you like.

Most people notice only the pop-up menu that lets you select one of your F-keys (the function keys at the top of your keyboard). But you can also click inside the white box that lists the keystroke and then press *any* key combination—Control-S, for example—to choose something different.

Apple assumes no responsibility for your choosing a keystroke that messes up some other function on your Mac. ⌘-S, for example, would not be a good choice.

On the other hand, if you choose a Spotlight keystroke that OS X uses for some other function, a little yellow alert icon appears in the Spotlight pane. This icon is actually a button; clicking it brings you to the Keyboard pane, where you can see exactly which keystroke is in dispute and change it.

Figure 3-23:
Here's where you can specify what categories of icons you want Spotlight to search, which order you want them listed in the Spotlight menu, and what keystroke you want to use for highlighting the Spotlight search box.

Privacy Settings

You can hide certain folders from Spotlight searches. Maybe you have privacy concerns—for example, you don't want your spouse Spotlighting your stuff while you're away from your desk. Maybe you just want to create more focused Spotlight searches, removing a lot of old, extraneous junk from its database.

Either way, the steps are simple. Open the Spotlight pane of System Preferences, as described previously. Click the Privacy tab. Figure 3-24 explains the remaining steps.

Tip: When you mark a disk or folder as non-searchable, Spotlight actually deletes its entire *index* (its invisible card-catalog filing system) from that disk. If Spotlight ever seems to be acting wackily, you can use this function to make it rebuild its own index file on the problem disk. Just drag the disk into the Privacy list and then remove it again. Spotlight deletes, and then rebuilds, the index for that disk.

(Don't forget the part about "remove it again," though. If you add a disk to the Privacy list, Spotlight is no longer able to find *anything* on it, even if you can see it right in front of you.)

Figure 3-24:
You can add disks, partitions, or folders to the list of non-searchable items by dragging them into this window. Or, if the private items aren't visible at the moment, click +, navigate to your hard drive, select the item, and then click Choose. To remove something from this list, click it and then press the Delete key or click the — button.

Once you've built up the list of private disks and folders, close System Preferences. Spotlight now pretends the private items don't even exist.

Smart Folders

A *smart folder* is a self-updating folder. It always contains exactly the items that match criteria you've specified in advance. (Smart folders are a lot like smart albums in iTunes, smart mailboxes in Mail, and so on.)

The key to creating one, as it turns out, is the little Save button in the upper-right corner of the Searching window when you've built a search request.

Here's a common example. You choose File→Find. You set up the pop-up menus to say "last opened date" and "this week." You click Save. You name the smart folder something like Current Crises, and you turn on Add to Sidebar (Figure 3-25).

Tip: Behind the scenes, smart folders are special files in your Home→Library→Saved Searches folder.

Figure 3-25:
OS X can preserve your search as a smart folder listed in the Sidebar—at least, it does as long as Add to Sidebar is turned on. You can stash a smart folder in your Dock, too, although it doesn't display a stack of its contents, as normal folders do.

From now on, whenever you click that smart folder, it reveals all the files you've worked on in the past week or so. These items' *real* locations may be all over the map, scattered around your Mac and your network. But through the magic of the smart folder, they appear as though they're all in one neat folder.

Tip: If you decide your original search criteria need a little fine-tuning, click the smart folder. From the ✿ menu, choose Show Search Criteria. You're back on the original setting-up-the-search window. Use the pop-up menus and other controls to tweak your search setup, and then click the Save button once again.

To delete a smart folder, just drag its icon out of the Sidebar. (Or if it's anywhere else, like on your desktop, drag it to the Trash like any other folder.)

Documents, Programs & Mission Control

T he beauty of life in the Era of Switchers is that most of the big-boy programs are available in nearly identical versions for both Mac and Windows. Microsoft Word, Excel, Outlook, and PowerPoint; Adobe Photoshop, Illustrator, and InDesign; iTunes; Quicken; Web browsers; and many other programs are available for both systems. Sometimes you have to buy the Mac version separately; sometimes it comes in the same package.

The best part: The documents you create with the Mac versions are generally *identical in format* to the ones created in Windows. A Microsoft Word document, for example, requires no conversion when transferred from a Mac to a PC or vice versa. It is what it is—a .doc or .docx file.

Same thing with Excel spreadsheets (.xls), PowerPoint slideshows (.ppt), Photoshop documents (.psd), and on and on. You may occasionally encounter a tiny formatting difference—a line thickness change, a movie file that requires a plug-in—but most documents open flawlessly when moved between Macs and PCs. (Chapter 7 offers more detail on finding Mac versions of your favorite PC programs.)

But even if switching to the Mac versions of your programs is relatively easy, learning how Mac programs *in general* operate may require some study. As this chapter will make clear, the relationship between programs and their documents differs in several substantial ways from the way things work in Windows.

The Mac App Store

For years, people installed software onto their computers by buying disks: floppies, CDs, and, later, DVDs.

But starting with the iPhone, people installed software onto their phones by downloading it directly from the Internet. Once everybody saw how convenient (and profitable) that system was, it didn't take Apple long to realize it could bring the same convenience to the Mac.

So now there's the Mac App Store—or, as the program is called in your Applications folder, just App Store (Figure 4-1). It's an online catalog of software from huge software companies, tiny one-person software companies, and everything in between. You can read about the programs, check out customer reviews, and download them directly to your Mac. (As you probably know, Yosemite itself is an App Store download.)

Figure 4-1:
Top: Mastering the App Store won't take you much time; just about everything you need is in the toolbar at the top, including a search box and buttons like Featured, Top Charts, and Categories, which are meant to help you dive into the enormous catalog of Mac software. The Purchases tab shows everything you've ever bought using your Apple account, for easy re-downloading.

Bottom: As with the iPhone/iPad App Store, you can read reviews of each piece of software, written by other people who've tried it.

There are some huge advantages to this system. Since there's no box, disc, registration card, shipping, or stocking, the software can cost a lot less; Apple's own programs certainly reflect this price advantage. Plenty of programs in the App Store are actually free.

Furthermore, Apple controls the transaction on both ends—it knows who you are—so there are no serial numbers to type in. The installation no longer interrupts you with warnings like "Please enter your password to install this software" or "This software appears to have been downloaded from the Internet"; once you click Buy, the software downloads and installs itself *automatically,* without any interaction from you.

And there are no discs to store and hunt down later. If you ever get a new Mac, or if you ever need to reinstall a program from the App Store, you just re-download it from the Purchases tab; the App Store remembers that you're a legitimate owner. Better yet,

you'll be downloading the latest version of that program; you won't have to install all the ".01" patches that have come along since.

Tip: To hide an app you've bought so it no longer appears in Purchases, right-click its name and choose Hide Purchase. (To unhide it later, click the Account link on the main page of the App Store; under the "iTunes in the Cloud" heading, choose View Hidden Purchases.)

And speaking of updates: Since Apple knows what programs you have, it can let you know when new versions are available. And it does: In Yosemite, a numbered badge appears next to the $\bullet$→App Store command (there's no more Software Update control panel to notify you). The updates are small files, so they download fast; the App Store delivers only the pieces that have actually changed.

Some details:

- You can opt to have new versions of your programs quietly and automatically downloaded and installed in the background, so that you're never bugged about their arrival. (Open System Preferences→App Store. "Download newly available updates in the background" downloads the new versions but asks your permission before installing them. "Install app updates" goes the next step and installs them without consulting you.)

- "Automatically download apps purchased on other Macs" (also in System Preferences→App Store) ensures that when you download an app on one Mac, it auto-downloads on all your other ones, too (assuming they're logged in with the same iCloud account). Handy, really.

- If the App Store app indicates that new versions of your programs are available, then right-click (or two-finger click) the Update All button. There, for your time-shifting pleasure, is a shortcut menu containing options like Install Now, Try in an Hour, Try Tonight, and Remind Me Tomorrow. The point is to set up a downloading session for a time when (a) you're in a WiFi hotspot or (b) you're asleep and these big downloads won't slow down anybody's Internet work.

One final advantage of the App Store concept: If you decide to use Launchpad, described in the following pages, anything you've bought from the App Store is easy to delete with a single click.

The only people bemoaning the App Store Era are people with slow Internet connections (or whose Internet services are limited to a certain amount of data each month). Apple cheerfully invites them to take their Macs to an Apple Store, where there's a free, high-speed, in-store WiFi network.

To use the Mac App Store, open the App Store program in your Applications folder (or on your Launchpad).

In general, the App Store here works exactly like the iPhone/iPad App Store. Click a program's icon to open its details page. Here you'll find reviews and ratings from other people, a description, pictures (screenshots) of the program, and much more information to help you make a good buying decision. See Figure 4-1 for more details.

When you buy an app, Launchpad opens automatically, so you can see where it went.

Other Ways to Get Mac Software

In general, new programs arrive on your Mac via one of two avenues: as an Internet download (whether from the App Store or not), or on a CD or DVD.

Downloading Compressed Files

Programs you download from the Web (not the App Store) generally arrive in a specially encoded, compressed form (Figure 4-2). And unless you've changed the settings, they arrive in the Downloads folder on your Dock.

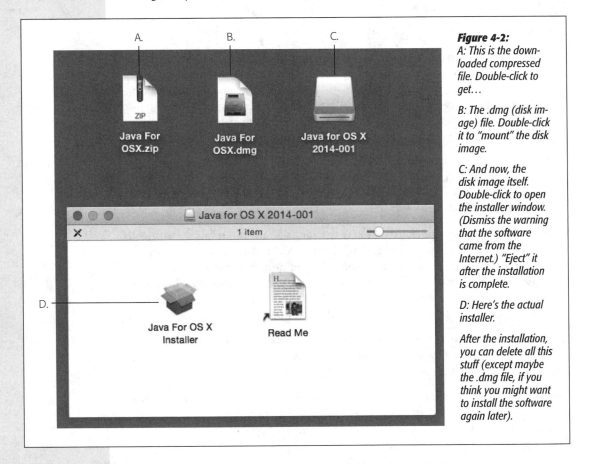

A. B. C.

ZIP

Java For OSX.zip **Java For OSX.dmg** **Java for OS X 2014-001**

Java for OS X 2014-001

1 item

D.

Java For OS X Installer **Read Me**

Figure 4-2:
A: This is the downloaded compressed file. Double-click to get...

B: The .dmg (disk image) file. Double-click it to "mount" the disk image.

C: And now, the disk image itself. Double-click to open the installer window. (Dismiss the warning that the software came from the Internet.) "Eject" it after the installation is complete.

D: Here's the actual installer.

After the installation, you can delete all this stuff (except maybe the .dmg file, if you think you might want to install the software again later).

The downloaded file's name usually has a file name extension like .zip (the standard compression file format for Windows and Mac files) or .dmg (a disk image file, described below).

You may occasionally run into .tar files (*tape archive,* an ancient Unix utility), .gz (*gzip,* a standard Unix compression format), or combo formats like .tar.gz or .tgz.

Fortunately, you generally don't have to worry about any of this; most Web browsers, including Safari, automatically unzip and unstuff downloads of all types.

Disk images (.dmg files)

Once you've downloaded a program, it often takes the form of a disk image file, whose name ends with the letters .dmg (middle top in Figure 4-2).

Disk images are common in OS X. All you have to do is double-click the .dmg icon. After a moment, it magically turns into a disk icon on your desktop, which you can work with just as though it were a real disk (top right in Figure 4-2). For example:

- Double-click it to open it. The software you downloaded is inside.

- Remove it from your desktop by dragging it to the Trash (whose icon turns into a big silver ⏏ key as you drag), highlighting it and pressing ⌘-E (the shortcut for File→Eject), clicking its ⏏ button in the Sidebar, or right-clicking (two-finger clicking) it and then choosing Eject from the shortcut menu.

 You've still got the original .dmg file you downloaded, so you're not really saying goodbye to the disk image forever.

When you've finished unzipping or unstuffing a downloaded file, you may have several icons on your desktop or in the Downloads folder. It's generally safe to throw them away—the .sit, .tar, .gz, or .tgz file you originally downloaded, for example, or the .dmg icon.

The disk image icon, the one that contains the actual software or its installer (top right in Figure 4-2), is a phantom drive, held in memory, that will go away by itself when you log out. So after installing its software, feel free to drag it to the Trash (or highlight it and press ⌘-E to "eject" it).

Performing the installation

Once you've got a disk icon on your desktop—either a pseudo-disk from a disk image or a CD or DVD you've inserted—you're ready to install the software. You can install many OS X programs just by dragging their icons or folders to your hard drive (usually the Applications folder). Others offer a traditional installer program that requires you to double-click, read and accept a license agreement, and so on.

Uninstalling Software

If you got a program from the App Store, it's easy to delete from the Launchpad (page 152).

If you got it from some other source, well, there's generally no Uninstall program. To uninstall a program, you just drag it (or its folder) to the Trash.

Some programs leave harmless scraps of themselves behind; to check for them, look for preference files or folders bearing the dearly departed program's name in your Library folders (especially in Application Support) and in your Home→Library→Preferences folder.

Cocoa and Carbon

OS X can run two different kinds of programs, each with different characteristics: *Cocoa and Carbon.*

The explanation involves a little bit of history. When Mac OS X came along in 2001, Apple gave software companies a choice: They could either *adapt* their existing software to the new operating system—or rewrite it from the ground up.

If programmers were willing to put *some* effort into getting with the OS X program, they could update their existing software. These are what Apple calls *Carbonized* programs, named for the technology (Carbon) that permits them to run on OS X.

But as OS X became popular, more and more software companies opted to create programs exclusively for it. The geeks call such programs *Cocoa* applications. Although they look exactly like Carbonized programs, they feel a bit more solid. And they offer a number of special features that Carbonized programs don't offer:

Note: The following features appear in almost all Cocoa programs. That's not to say that you'll never see these features in Carbonized programs; the occasional Carbon program may offer one of these features or another.

- **The Fonts pane:** When you use a Carbon program, you usually access these fonts the same way as always: using a Font menu. But when you use a Cocoa program, you get the Fonts *pane,* which makes it far easier to organize, search, and use your font collection. Chapter 9 describes fonts, and the Fonts pane, in more detail.

- **Retina friendliness:** In general, Cocoa programs automatically sharpen up their text when you view it on a Retina display—Apple's name for super-high-resolution screens like the one on its latest MacBook laptops. Text in Carbonized programs, on the other hand, looks blotchy and awful until their software companies make the effort to make them Retina-friendly.

- **Title bar tricks:** By dragging the tiny icon next to the document's name in an open window, you can perform stunts—like dragging that little icon to the desktop or to the Dock icon of a different program for opening—right from your document's title bar.

- **Secret keyboard shortcuts:** If you're a card-carrying member of KIAFTMA (the Keyboard Is Always Faster Than the Mouse Association), you'll love these additional keyboard navigation strokes:

 Control-A. Moves your insertion point to the beginning of the paragraph. (*Mnemonic:* A = beginning of the Alphabet.)

 Control-E. Deposits your insertion point at the end of the paragraph. (*Mnemonic:* E = End.)

 Control-D. Forward delete (deletes the letter to the *right* of the insertion point).

 Control-K. Instantly deletes all text from the insertion point to the right end of the line. (*Mnemonic:* K = Kills the rest of the line.)

Control-O. Inserts a paragraph break, much like Return, but leaves the insertion point where it was, above the break. This is the ideal trick for breaking a paragraph in half when you've just thought of a better ending for the first part.

Control-T. Moves the insertion point one letter to the right—and, along with it, drags whichever letter was to its left. (*Mnemonic:* T = Transpose letters.)

Option-Delete. Deletes the entire word to the left of the insertion point. When you're typing along in a hurry and discover that you've just made a typo, this is the keystroke you want. It's much faster to nuke the previous word and retype it than to fiddle around with the mouse and the insertion point just to fix one letter.

- **Cool text-selection tricks:** By holding down certain keys while dragging through text in a Cocoa program, you gain some wild and wacky text-selection powers (especially useful in, for example, TextEdit and Pages):

Highlight only one column by Option-dragging. Instead of highlighting all the text, margin to margin, you get only the text within your selection rectangle.

Highlight several passages simultaneously by ⌘-dragging. Each time you ⌘-drag, you highlight another block of text, even though the earlier blocks are still selected (see Figure 4-3).

These days, almost every name-brand program is a true Cocoa application, including Photoshop, Microsoft Office, FileMaker, iMovie, iPhoto, Safari, Messages, TextEdit, Stickies, Mail, Contacts, and so on.

Figure 4-3:
The beauty of being able to select multiple blobs of text is that you can format all of them simultaneously (making them bold, for example) with one click. You can also copy the selected portions; when you paste them into a different document, you get a tidy excerpt containing only the parts you wanted, all run together.

Opening OS X Programs

You can launch (open) an application in any of several ways:

- **Single-click an icon on the Launchpad,** described on the following pages.

- **Single-click a program's icon on the Dock, the Sidebar, or the Finder toolbar.**

- **Use Spotlight.** Hit ⌘-space bar, type the first letters of the program's name, and then press Return.

- **Double-click an app's icon in the Finder.**

- **If you've added the Applications folder to your Dock,** click the Dock icon to open the pop-up fan, grid, or list of icons. Then click the program you want (or even type the first few letters of its name and then press Return).

- **Highlight an application icon and then press ⌘-O** (short for File→Open) or ⌘-▼.

- **Use the submenus** of the menu's Recent Items→Applications command.

Note: OS X stores a list of your recently used programs in a text file called com.apple.recentitems.plist, located in your Home folder→Library→Preferences folder. And with about a dollar, that information will buy you a cup of coffee in most restaurants.

- **Open a *document* icon in any of these ways,** or drag a document onto the icon of a program that can open it (whether in the Dock, the Finder toolbar, the Sidebar, or a folder window).

Tip: If you press Option as you open an application (or anything else) in the Finder, you automatically close the window that contains its icon. Later, when you return to the Finder, you find a neat, clean desktop—no loitering windows.

Launchpad

The Launchpad app presents a dark background with evenly spaced icons that represent all your programs (Figure 4-4). You can open one with a single click.

Why did Apple feel the need to create yet *another* way to open programs?

First, because Launchpad fits right into the general theme of making the Mac look and work more like the iPad. Launchpad is a dead ringer for the Home screens of an iPad, iPhone, or iPod Touch.

Second, it's a much less intimidating place for technophobes to learn to love than, say, the Applications folder.

And third, it's a lot quicker to get to than the Applications folder. You can summon it instantly, using any of these methods:

- **Put four fingers on your trackpad and pinch them together.** The Launchpad appears instantly, no matter what program you were in; you don't have to duck back into the Finder, navigate to the Applications folder, and so on.

- **Press the Launchpad key.** Recent Macs have a special Launchpad icon painted right on the F4 key (⌘).

- **Click its icon on the Dock.** It's the second one, resembling a rocket (⌖).

- **Press a keyboard shortcut of your choice.** To set that up, choose ⌘→System Preferences→Keyboard. Click the Shortcuts tab, and then click Launchpad & Dock in the left-side list. On the right, make sure Show Launchpad is turned on—and then double-click in the blank space to the right of it and press the key combination you want.

- **Move the cursor into one of the screen's four corners.** To set up these options, open ⌘→System Preferences→Mission Control. Click Hot Corners to choose a corner of the screen for Launchpad.

- **Open it as you would any other program.** It's in your Applications folder.

One thing's for sure: Sooner or later, you'll wind up in Launchpad.

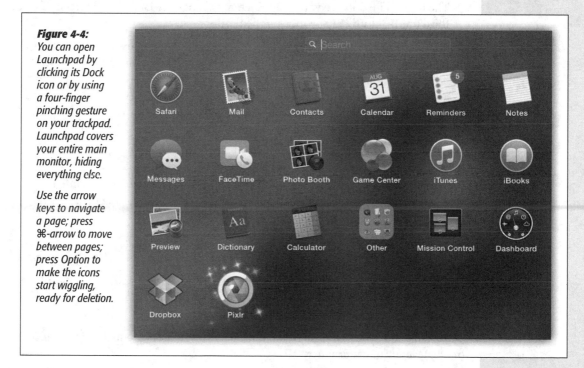

Figure 4-4:
You can open Launchpad by clicking its Dock icon or by using a four-finger pinching gesture on your trackpad. Launchpad covers your entire main monitor, hiding everything else.

Use the arrow keys to navigate a page; press ⌘-arrow to move between pages; press Option to make the icons start wiggling, ready for deletion.

Only three visual elements appear there:

- **Icons.** Each icon represents one of your programs. Apple's programs are listed first, in alphabetical order: App Store, Automator, Calculator, and so on. Then come all your other programs, again in A-to-Z order. Click one to open that program.

 Sparkly animated twinkles surround any new app you've installed. (You can see them at lower left in Figure 4-4.)

Note: The only program icon that *doesn't* appear in Launchpad…is Launchpad's. That's a good thing. You wouldn't want to wind up in an infinite loop, would you?

- **Search box.** This box at the top of the screen lets you pluck one needle from your haystack of apps, no matter what page it's on. You don't have to click there first—just start typing when Launchpad is before you. With each letter you type, Launchpad hides everything but the matching app icons.

- **Home page dots.** As you install more and more programs, Launchpad makes room for them by creating additional screens. You can spread your new programs' icons across an unlimited number of launch screens.

 The little white dots are your map. Each represents one Launchpad screen. If the third one is "lit up," then you're on the third screen.

 To move among the screens, press ⌘-arrow keys, or swipe horizontally with two fingers on the trackpad. (Magic Mouse: one finger.) Or tap directly on one of the little dots to jump to the corresponding screen.

Tip: To exit Launchpad without opening anything, click a blank spot, tap the Esc key, or—most fun of all— *spread* the same four fingers on the trackpad.

Redesigning the Launchpad Screens

If you use Launchpad a lot, it's worth taking a moment to arrange its icons into logical categories or a sensible sequence. As it turns out, you can freely drag them into new spots; the other icons scoot aside to make room.

Tip: You can even drag an icon directly to the Dock to install it there for quicker access.

You can create additional screens, too. To do that, drag an icon to the right edge of the screen; keep your mouse button down. The first screen slides off to the left, leaving you on a new, blank one where you can deposit the icon.

You can organize your icons on these Home pages by category, frequency of use, color, or whatever tickles your fancy.

Folders

The Launchpad just wouldn't be like the iPad if it didn't also let you organize your apps into *folders*. Folders let you organize your apps, de-emphasize the ones you don't use often, and restore order to that horribly flat, multipage display of icons.

To create a folder, drag one app's icon *on top of another*. OS X puts both of them into a single new folder (Figure 4-5). If they're the same kind of app, it even tries to figure out what category they both belong to—and names the new folder accordingly ("Music," "Photos," "Games," or whatever). This new name is only a proposal; an editing window also appears so that you can type a custom name you prefer.

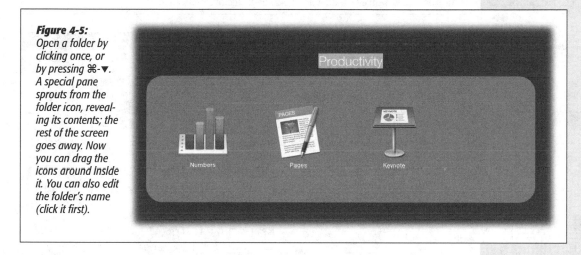

Figure 4-5:
Open a folder by clicking once, or by pressing ⌘-▼. A special pane sprouts from the folder icon, revealing its contents; the rest of the screen goes away. Now you can drag the icons around inside it. You can also edit the folder's name (click it first).

A folder can hold several rows' worth of icons; if you add more apps than that, Launchpad adds additional "pages" that you scroll horizontally. (Little white dots indicate which page you're on.)

Take an app out of a folder by dragging its icon anywhere else on the screen. The other icons scoot aside to make room. If you remove all but one app from a folder, the folder disappears.

Move a folder around by dragging, as you would any other icon.

Deleting App Store Programs

If you've downloaded some apps from the App Store, you'll find a bonus feature here in Launchpad: They're especially fun to delete.

Start by holding the mouse down on any icon until, after about a second, all the icons begin to—what's the correct term?—*wiggle*. (If you have an iPhone, iPad, or iPod Touch, this should look familiar.)

Tip: You can also just press the Option key to trigger the wiggling. Sometimes, every second counts.

At this point, you may notice that some of them have sprouted little red X's. Those are the ones you downloaded from the App Store.

To delete an App Store program you don't need anymore, click that X to make it say bye-bye—instantly and for good. It doesn't even have a layover in the Trash.

Note: You can't delete non–App Store apps this way, so no X appears on those icons. Why not? Because this deletion method is so fast and permanent. It's not much of a risk for App Store apps, because you can always download them again—but that would not be true of other apps.

UP TO SPEED

When Programs Are Actually Folders

OS X programs don't seem to have 50,000 support files strewn across your hard drive. Most programs just sit there, naked and shivering, in your Applications folder—seemingly unaccompanied by libraries, dictionaries, foreign language components, and other support files and folders.

The question is: Where did all those support files go?

OS X features *packages* or *bundles*, which are folders that behave like single files. Every properly written OS X program looks like a single, double-clickable application icon. Yet to the Mac, it's actually a folder that contains both the actual application icon and all its hidden support files. (Even documents can be packages, including iDVD project files, Keynote files, and some TextEdit documents.)

If you'd like to prove this to yourself, try this experiment. Choose Go→Applications. See the Calculator program? Right-click (or two-finger click) it. From the shortcut menu, choose Show Package Contents. You're asking OS X to show you what's inside the Calculator's "application icon" folder.

The Calculator package window opens, revealing a Contents folder you've never seen before. If you open this folder, you'll find a handful of strange-looking, Unix-named folders and files that are, behind the scenes, pieces of the Calculator program itself.

The application-as-folder trick is convenient for you, of course, because it means you're generally free to move the application to a different window—or to uninstall the program by dragging this single icon to the Trash—without worrying that you're leaving behind its entourage of support files. It's also convenient for programmers, because they can update certain aspects of their applications just by replacing one of these component files, without having to rewrite the entire program.

You can even try out this programmery benefit for yourself. In the case of the Calculator and many other OS X programs, the Resources folder contains individual graphics files—PDF or TIFF files—that serve as the graphic elements you see when using the program. For example, the file lcd.tiff in the Calculator's Resources folder contains the image of the calculator's screen (where the numbers appear as you punch the calculator buttons).

Using a graphics program, you can change the background of this light-yellow calculator screen to, say, light blue. The next time you double-click Calculator—which you now realize is actually a folder behind the scenes—you'll see your modified calculator design.

(P.S. There are still hundreds or thousands of support files that aren't embedded within their programs' icons. They're sitting in your Library→Application Support folder, organized by software company.)

Windows That Auto-Reopen

When you open a program, the Mac reads its computer code, which lies on your hard drive's surface, and feeds it quickly into RAM (memory). During this brief interval, the icon of the opening program jumps up and down eagerly in your Dock.

Tip: You don't have to wait for the application to finish bouncing—you're wasting perfectly good computing time. Just switch to another program and get back to work; the newly opened program keeps right on launching in the background. This means you, Photoshop and Final Cut nerds.

For decades, opening a program on the Mac presented exactly the same thing every time: a blank screen, or maybe a welcome screen. It was up to you to specify what *document* you then wanted to work on.

Now, though, whatever documents were open when you last quit that program magically *re*open, ready for you to get back to work. Everything is *exactly* as it was, including your window and palette positions. Incredibly, any text that was highlighted when you last quit the program is still highlighted, and the insertion point is just where you left it.

This is all extremely handy if you tend to work on the same documents day after day; the auto-reopened document serves as a nice refresher on what you were in the middle of doing. You can skip fussing with the Open command, remembering what you were doing, rearranging the windows the way you like them, and so on.

Then again, maybe you can't stand this feature.

Fortunately, it's easy to turn it off, either globally, on a per-program basis, or on a per-Quit basis.

- **Turn off auto-reopen for good.** Open System Preferences→General, and turn off "Restore windows when quitting and re-opening apps."

- **Prevent your current setup from being memorized.** You can also prevent just *one particular* program from reopening its documents the next time—at the time you're quitting it. To do that, press Option while you quit the program (for example, when you choose Safari→Quit or press ⌘-Q). The Quit command magically changes to say "Quit and Discard Windows." The next time you open the program, it will have forgotten all about your window setup.

 (On the other hand, if you've turned *off* the "Restore windows" feature in System Preferences, pressing the Option key makes the Quit command say "Quit and *Keep* Windows.")

- **Make a program forget its window setup as you reopen it.** If it's too late for the tip in the previous paragraph, you can force a program to start up in its empty, virginal state by pressing the Shift key as it opens. That forces the program to forget the previous window setup.

The Application Menu

In every app, the very first menu (to the right of the menu) appears with bold lettering and identifies the program you're using. It might say iTunes, or Microsoft Word, or Stickies.

This Application menu (Figure 4-6) offers a number of commands pertaining to the entire program and its windows, including About, Quit, and Hide.

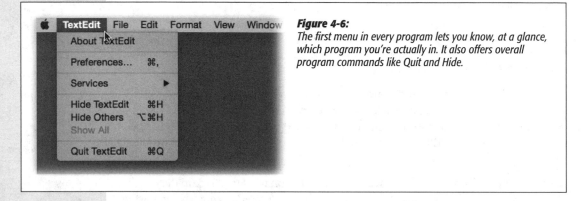

Figure 4-6:
The first menu in every program lets you know, at a glance, which program you're actually in. It also offers overall program commands like Quit and Hide.

Quitting Programs

You quit a program by pressing ⌘-Q, the keyboard equivalent of the Quit command. (The Quit command is always at the bottom of the Application menu.)

But OS X offers two much more fun ways to quit a program:

- Right-click (or two-finger click) a program's Dock icon to make its shortcut menu appear. Then choose Quit. (Or, if you do the *click-and-hold* thing on a program's Dock icon, a Quit button appears just above your cursor.)

- When you've pressed ⌘-Tab to summon the "heads-up display" of open programs, type the letter Q without releasing the ⌘ key. The highlighted program quits without further ado.

Force Quitting Programs

OS X is a rock-solid operating system, but that doesn't mean that *programs* never screw up. Individual programs are as likely as ever to freeze—or, rather, to *hang* (lock up and display the "spinning beach ball of death" cursor). In such cases, you have no choice but to *force quit* the program—the computer equivalent of terminating it with a blunt instrument.

Doing so doesn't destabilize your Mac; you don't have to restart it. In fact, you can usually reopen the very same program and get on with your life.

You can force quit a stuck program in any of several ways:

- **Click-and-hold on the program's Dock icon,** or two finger click it, or right-click it. A Quit button appears just above your cursor. Press the Option key to make the button say Force Quit. Click it. Bingo—that program is outta here.

- **Press Option-⌘-Esc,** the traditional Mac force-quit keystroke, or choose ⌘→ Force Quit. Either way, proceed as shown in Figure 4-7.

Figure 4-7:
When you press Option-⌘-Esc or choose Force Quit from the ⌘ menu, a tidy box listing all open programs appears—something like the Task Manager in Windows. Just click the one you want to abort, click Force Quit, and click Force Quit again in the confirmation box. (Using more technical tools like the Unix kill command, there are other ways to jettison programs. But this is often the most convenient.)

The only downside to force quitting a program is that you lose any unsaved changes to your open documents, along with any preference settings you may have changed while the program was open.

The "Heads-Up" Program Switcher

Just as in Windows , there's a handy keystroke for switching from one open program to another: the ⌘-Tab keystroke (Figure 4-8).

You can use this feature in three different ways, which are well worth learning:

- **If you keep the ⌘ key pressed,** each press of the Tab key highlights the Dock icon of another program, in left-to-right Dock order. Release both keys when you reach the one you want. OS X brings the corresponding program to the front. (To move *backward* through the open programs, press *Shift-⌘-Tab.*)

- **If you leave the ⌘ key pressed,** you can choose a program by clicking its icon with your mouse or by pressing the ◀ or ▶ keys.

- **A single press of ⌘-Tab** takes you to the program you used most recently, and another, separate ⌘-Tab bounces back to the program you started in.

Imagine, for example, that you're doing a lot of switching between two programs, like your Web browser and your email program. If you have five other programs open, you don't want to waste your time ⌘-tabbing your way through all the open programs just to get back to your Web browser.

Tip: Here's a related keystroke, equally awesome. If you press ⌘-tilde (the ~ key next to the number 1), you switch to the next window in the *same* program.

Figure 4-8:
Apple calls this row of open program icons a "heads-up display," named after the projected data screen on a Navy jet windshield that lets pilots avoid having to look down at their instruments.

Full Screen Mode

Features are great and all. But the more of them your software accumulates, the more toolbars and icon panes fill the screen, and the bigger the clutter-problem becomes. After a while, all that "chrome" (as software designers call it) winds up crowding out the document you're actually trying to work on.

That's why Apple invented Full Screen mode. It's not available in all programs, but it's showing up in more and more of them—including almost all Apple programs: App Store, Calendar, Chess, Final Cut Pro, Font Book, Game Center, GarageBand, iBooks, iMovie, iPhoto, iTunes, Keynote, Mail, Maps, Messages, Notes, Photo Booth, Preview, Safari, and so on.

To take a program into Full Screen mode, click the Full Screen button. It's the round, green dot in the upper-left corner of the document window. (And how do you know if your program even offers Full Screen mode? As your cursor approaches the green dot button, a tiny double-arrow logo appears inside the dot, like this: ⊗.)

When you click the green dot, the Mac hides the menu bar, scroll bars, status bars, and any other bars or palettes surrounding your work area. The window's edges expand all the way to the edges of the screen (Figure 4-9).

Tip: You may as well learn the keyboard shortcut to enter Full Screen mode: Control-⌘-F. The same keystroke *leaves* Full Screen mode, but you can also tap the Esc key for that purpose.

The menu bar is still available; move the pointer to the top of the screen to make it reappear. Click the green dot again to *exit* Full Screen mode.

Figure 4-9:
Top: So much for the glorious Web. You're seeing a Web page segment, swimming in an ocean of toolbars, scroll bars, status bars, menu bars, and distracting desktop.

Bottom: In Full Screen mode, Safari stretches to the very edges of your screen, and everything else disappears. (Your address bar and tab bars are still available in this case.)

Each Full Screen app becomes its own desktop in Mission Control. And you can put a Full Screen app on each of your monitors, too.

To leave Full Screen mode, move your cursor to the top of the screen so that the menu bar reappears. Click the green dot once again (top left of your document window).

Mission Control: Death to Window Clutter

In its day, the concept of overlapping windows on the screen was brilliant, innovative, and extremely effective. (Apple borrowed this idea—well, bought it in a stock swap—from a research lab called Xerox PARC.) In that era before digital cameras, MP3 files, and the Web, managing windows was easy this way; after all, you had only about three of them.

These days, however, managing all the open windows in all the open programs can be like herding cats. Off you go, burrowing through the microscopic pop-up menus of your Dock, trying to find the window you want. And heaven help you if you need to

duck back to the desktop—to find a newly downloaded file, for example, or to eject a disk. You'll have to fight your way through 50,000 other windows on your way to the bottom of the "deck."

Mission Control tackles this problem in a fresh way. The concept is delicious: With one mouse click, keystroke, or finger gesture, you shrink all windows in all programs to a size that fits on the screen (Figure 4-10), like index cards on a bulletin board, clumped by open program. Now you feel like an air-traffic controller, with all your screens arrayed before you. You click the window or program you want, and you're there. It's fast, efficient, animated, and a lot of fun.

Figure 4-10:
Top: Quick! Where's the Finder in all this mess?

Bottom: With a four-finger upward swipe on the trackpad, you can open Mission Control and spot that window, shrunken but not overlapped. Each program's thumbnail cluster offers an icon and a label to help you identify it. These aren't static snapshots of the windows at the moment you Mission Controlled them. They're live, still-updating windows, as you'll discover if one of them contains a QuickTime movie or a Web page that's still loading.

Starting and Stopping Mission Control

Mission Control is a program, just like any other. So you can open it with a click on its Dock icon, from Launchpad, from the Applications folder, and so on.

But it's really meant to be opened quickly, fluidly, naturally, whenever the mood seizes you—with a *gesture*. On the trackpad, that's a swipe upward with three fingers. (On the Magic Mouse, it's a double-tap with *two* fingers—taps, not clicks.)

Note: You can change this gesture so that it requires *four* fingers, if you like, in System Preferences→Trackpad (or Mouse)→More Gestures→Mission Control. Use the pop-up menu.

Or you can press the dedicated ▦ key, if you have one, on the top row of your keyboard. Substitute the F9 key if you don't.

And even that's just the beginning of the ways you can open Mission Control; read on.

Note: To *exit* Mission Control without clicking any of your windows or virtual screens, swipe *down* with three fingers. Or tap the Esc key.

Mission Control keystrokes

You can reassign the Mission Control functions to a huge range of other keys, with or without modifiers like Shift, Control, and Option. To view your options, choose →System Preferences and then click the Mission Control icon.

Here you'll find four pop-up menus. The first, Mission Control, lets you specify how you want to open Mission Control. The other three—"Application windows," "Show Desktop," and "Show Dashboard"—correspond to functions of other Mac features, Exposé and Dashboard, described later in this chapter.

Within each pop-up menu, for example, you'll discover that all your F-keys—F1, F2, F3, and so on—are available as triggers. If, while the pop-up menu is open, you press one or more of your modifier keys (Shift, Option, Control, or ⌘), all these F-key choices *change* to reflect the key you're pressing; now the pop-up menu says Shift-F1, Shift-F2, Shift-F3, and so on. That's how you can make *Shift*-F1 trigger Mission Control, for example.

These pop-up menus also contain choices like Left Shift, which refers to the Shift key on the left side of your keyboard. That is, instead of pressing F9 to open Mission Control, you could simply tap the Shift key.

Note: This is only an example. Repeat: This is only an example. *Actually* using the Shift key to open Mission Control is a terrible, terrible idea, as you'll quickly discover the next time you try to type a capital letter. This feature is intended exclusively for hunt-and-peck typists who never use the Shift key on one side.

If you have a laptop, you'll also find out that you can tap the fn key alone for Mission Control—and this time, it's a great choice, because fn otherwise has very little direction in life.

If your mouse has more than one button, you'll see a second column of pop-up menus in System Preferences (Figure 4-11). Each pop-up menu offers choices like Right Mouse Button and Middle Mouse Button. Use these pop-up menus to assign Mission Control (or Exposé or Dashboard) to the various clickers on your mouse: right-click to hide all windows, middle-click to reveal the desktop, and so on.

Figure 4-11:
You can trigger Mission Control in any of five ways: by clicking its icon, with a finger gesture, by twitching your cursor into a certain corner of the screen (Hot Corners), by pressing a key (bottom half of this box), or by clicking the extra buttons on a multibutton mouse, including Apple's Mighty Mouse.
Of course, there's nothing to stop you from setting up all of these ways, so you can press or swipe in some situations and twitch or click in others.

Note, by the way, that on a laptop, the wording isn't "right mouse button"—it's "secondary mouse button." Which means "right-click." Which means that on a laptop, you can set it up so that a "right-click" *trackpad gesture* triggers one of these functions. See page 14 for all the different ways you can trigger a right-click.

Screen corners

If you click Hot Corners, you see something like Figure 17-11 (page 591). The four corners here represent the corners of your screen. Using these menus, you can assign a window-management feature to each corner; for example, if you choose Mission Control from the first pop-up menu, then when your pointer hits the upper-left corner of the screen, you'll open Mission Control. (Launchpad and Notification Center are options here, too.)

Depending on the size of your screen, this option can feel awkward at first. But if you've run out of keystrokes that aren't assigned to other functions, be glad that Apple offers you this alternative.

Note: In previous versions of OS X, whipping the pointer into a corner was one good way to turn on your *screensaver.* Apple hasn't forgotten about that, which is why you'll also find commands called Start Screen Saver and Disable Screen Saver in the pop-up menus. Apple wants to make sure you don't get confused and assign two different functions to the same corner.

Managing Windows in Mission Control

Once you open Mission Control, you see two major elements: your *Spaces* (virtual screens) at the top, and the actual window thumbnails below that.

You can click anything here to jump to it: Jump to a different Space (desktop) by clicking its thumbnail, switch to a different program by clicking its icon, or click one of the window miniatures.

Tip: Try holding down the Shift key as you do it. You'll enjoy watching all your windows shift around with OS X's patented slow-motion animation, which can be quite a sight.

Or, if you decide to abandon ship and return to whatever you were doing, swipe *down* with three fingers on the trackpad (two on the Magic Mouse), or press the Esc key.

The trouble with miniaturized windows is that, well, they're miniaturized. The more windows you have open, the smaller they are, and the harder it is to see what's in them.

If you need a little help identifying a window miniature, you have three options:

- **Point to the cluster of windows in one app** and do a two-finger swipe up on the trackpad. OS X helpfully spreads the window thumbnails out and enlarges them a little bit, so it's easier to tell them apart and click the one you want.

- **Point to a window thumbnail without clicking.** OS X puts a colored border on it to show that it's highlighted; now press the space bar. That, of course, is the Quick Look keystroke, and it works here, too. It magnifies the window you're pointing to, making it full size—big enough for you to read its contents and identify it.

- **Press ⌘-~.** That keystroke takes you into Exposé, described later in this chapter.

Spaces in Mission Control

Mission Control's other star feature, Spaces, gives you up to 16 *full-size monitors.* Ordinarily, of course, attaching so many screens to a single computer would be a massively expensive proposition, not to mention detrimental to your living space and personal relationships.

Fortunately, Spaces monitors are *virtual.* They exist only in the Mac's little head. You see only one at a time; you switch using Mission Control or a gesture.

But just because the Spaces screens are simulated doesn't mean they're not useful. You can dedicate each one to a different program or *kind* of program. Screen 1 might contain your email and chat windows, arranged just the way you like them. Screen 2 can hold Photoshop, with an open document and the palettes carefully arrayed. On Screen 3: your Web browser in Full Screen mode.

You can also have the *same* program running on multiple screens—but with different documents or projects open on each one.

These desktops are also essential to OS X's *Full Screen apps* feature, because each full-screen app gets its own Spaces desktop.

Now, virtual screens aren't a new idea—this sort of software has been available for years. But until the Mac came along, it had never been a standard feature of a consumer operating system, and rarely has it been executed with such finesse.

Creating a Desktop

Mission Control starts you off with two Spaces (or "desktops," as they're labeled). One of them shows the Dashboard, described later in this chapter; the other shows your regular Mac world. If you've clicked the ⊗ button in an app to make it full screen, it fills an additional desktop unto itself.

To create another desktop, enter Mission Control. You can now proceed in either of two ways:

- **The long way.** Point to the upper-right corner of the screen, or just press the Option key; a big + button slides into view (Figure 4-12). Click it to create a new mini desktop in the top row.

Figure 4-12:
Create a new blank Space by clicking the big + button. Or save time and energy by dragging a window, or a whole program's icon, into the empty space at the right end of the Spaces thumbnails. You've just created a Space and loaded it up with windows in one fell swoop.

Now it's time to park some windows onto the new desktop. Either drag a window thumbnail onto the blank desktop—or, to move *all* of one program's windows there, drag the application icon. All the windows go along for the ride.

Note: If you've positioned your Dock against the right side of the screen, the + button appears when you point to the upper-*left* corner. And to create a new screen by dragging a window's or program's icon (see "The short way," next), drag to the upper-left corner of the screen.

- **The short way.** Drag one window thumbnail into a blank spot at the upper-right corner of the screen—or, to move *all* of one program's windows there, drag the application icon. Again, all the windows go along for the ride.

Tip: There are two ways to move a window to a different Space without opening Mission Control first. First, you can drag a window (using its title bar as a handle) all the way to the edge of the screen. Stay there with the mouse button still down. After about a second, you'll see the adjacent screen slide into view; you've just moved the window.

Second, switch to the new Space. Hold your mouse down on the app's icon; from the shortcut menu, choose Options→Assign To→This Desktop. The Mac whisks that app's windows from whatever *other* screen they're on to *this* screen.

Switching Spaces

Once you've got Spaces set up and turned on, the fun begins. Start by moving to the virtual screen you want; it's like changing the channel. Here are some ways to do that:

- **Swipe horizontally on your trackpad with three fingers.** (On the Magic Mouse, it's two fingers.) If you have a trackpad or a Magic Mouse, this is definitely the method to learn; it's fast, fluid, and happy.

 You can change this gesture so that it requires an additional finger, if you like, in System Preferences→Trackpad (or Mouse)→More Gestures.

Tip: If you perform this swipe *slowly,* you can drag the next Space only *partway* onto the screen. That's sometimes handy when you want to get your bearings or to just *peek* into the next screen.

- **Enter Mission Control.** Click the desktop you want.

- **Press Control-◀ or Control-▶** to rotate to the previous or next desktop.

- **While pressing the Control key,** type the number of the desktop you want. For example, hit Control-3 to jump to your third screen. (You have to turn on this feature first, though. See Figure 4-13.)

When you make a switch, you see a flash of animation as one screen flies away and another appears. Now that you're "on" the screen you want, open programs and arrange windows onto it as usual.

Tip: What if you're using Spaces, and you want to drag something from one screen (like a photo in iPhoto) into a window that's on a different screen (like an outgoing email message)?

There are two ways; take your pick. First, you can start dragging whatever it is—and then, in mid-drag, press the keystroke for Mission Control (usually fn-F9); complete the drag directly onto the other Space, and even into the relevant window *in* that Space.

Another approach: Start dragging. With the mouse button still down, press ⌘-Tab to open the application switcher. Continue the drag onto the *icon* of the receiving program, and still keep the mouse button down. OS X switches to the appropriate virtual screen automatically.

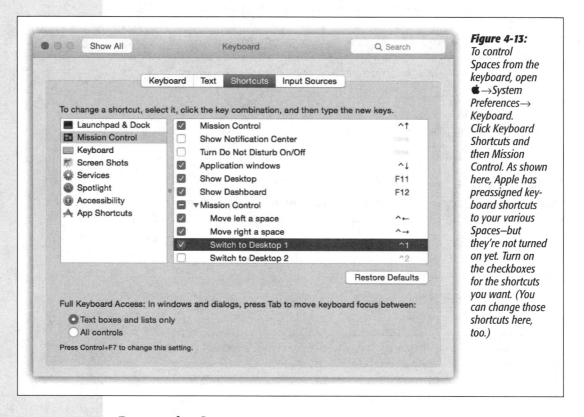

Figure 4-13:
To control Spaces from the keyboard, open →*System Preferences*→ *Keyboard. Click Keyboard Shortcuts and then Mission Control. As shown here, Apple has preassigned keyboard shortcuts to your various Spaces—but they're not turned on yet. Turn on the checkboxes for the shortcuts you want. (You can change those shortcuts here, too.)*

Rearranging Spaces

Here's something handy: You can *rearrange* the Spaces. Open Mission Control, and then drag the Space thumbnails around horizontally.

You can even drag the Dashboard out of its traditional left-side position. Put it off to the right of the other Spaces, for all Apple cares.

Spaces and Multiple Monitors

Here's another favor Apple's done for you: If you have a second monitor connected to your Mac (or even several), each one can have its own set of Spaces.

Make sure "Displays have separate Spaces" is turned on in the Mission Control pane of System Preferences. (You can see this checkbox in Figure 4-11.)

From now on, each monitor has its own set of Spaces. When you use one of the gestures or keystrokes for switching Spaces, you affect the Spaces on only one monitor: the one that contains your cursor at the moment.

Two Eccentric Spaces Settings

Deep in System Preferences→Mission Control, two settings govern the way Spaces works:

- **Automatically rearrange Spaces based on most recent use.** If this option is turned on, then OS X will constantly rearrange your virtual desktops so that the most recently used ones are first. (The most recent one becomes Desktop #2, since Desktop #1 is always your main desktop.)

 The point, of course, is to make it quick and easy to return to whatever you were doing most recently. But if you find it disorienting to have your desktops constantly changing their sequence, you can turn this option off.

- **When switching to an application, switch to a Space with open windows for the application.** There must be some clearer way to write this checkbox.

 In any case, it means that when you click the Dock icon for a running program, you jump to the Space that contains that program's open windows already, instead of leaving you on the current Space.

 For example, suppose you're working in your browser on Desktop #3. Then you click the Mail icon on the Dock. If this option is turned on, you jump to Desktop #2 (or wherever you've been already working in Mail). If it's not turned on,

GEM IN THE ROUGH

Pinning One App to One Space—or to All Spaces

Usually, you slap each app (or each window) onto only one Spaces desktop. Your Web browser on Space 1. Email on Space 2. iTunes on Space 3. And so on.

Sometimes, though, you might find it useful to keep an app's windows on *all* your desktops—perhaps because you use it so often, you want it always with you. The Finder and System Preferences are great examples. Or maybe your calendar app, your browser, or your email program.

To do that, make sure the program's icon is in your Dock (either because you've put it there or because the program is running). Hold the mouse button down on the program's

icon until the shortcut menu appears. From this menu, choose Options.

You'll see two useful options. One, Assign To→All Desktops, puts this program's windows on all your desktops. Wherever you go, there you are.

The other one, Assign To→This Desktop, gives you yet another quick way to *move* an app's windows—from whatever desktop they're on now to the one you're using at the moment. You've just "pinned" that app to that Space, and that's where it will stay. That's a convenience for neat freaks who like to know exactly where each app will live.

Mail jumps to the foreground, but you won't see any windows—they're stranded back on Desktop #2.

Pictures for Every Desktop

Unless you intervene, OS X uses your main desktop's background picture for all additional Spaces.

Coolly enough, though, you can set a different wallpaper photo (desktop background) to each Space. You might find it easier to get your bearings that way. When you restart the computer, the Mac will remember not just which Spaces you had open and what was on them, but also what pictures lay behind them.

You can go about assigning desktop pictures in two ways. First, switch to the Space whose picture you want to change. Then:

• Open System Preferences→Desktop & Screen Saver→Desktop.

• Right-click (or two-finger click) a blank spot on the existing desktop background. From the shortcut menu, choose Change Desktop Background.

Note: In both cases, you may have to move the System Preferences window onto your current Space. You can do that by popping into Mission Control.

Either way, you wind up in the Preferences pane for choosing desktop wallpaper. Click the backdrop you want for this screen. Then switch to the next Space and repeat.

Deleting a Desktop

To delete a desktop, enter Mission Control. Point to one of the screen thumbnails without clicking until a ⊗ appears in its corner; click it. The desktop disappears, and whatever windows were on it get shoved onto Desktop #1, your main desktop.

Tip: If you don't have the 1½ seconds to wait for the — to appear, then press Option as you point. The Close button appears instantly.

By the way, this trick doesn't work for apps running in Full Screen mode. You can't get rid of their desktops unless you first switch to them and get out of Full Screen mode.

Dashboard

As you know, the essence of using a computer is running *programs*, which often produce *documents*. In OS X, however, there's a third category: a set of weird, hybrid entities that Apple calls *widgets*. They appear, all at once, on a virtual desktop (Figure 4-14)—the leftmost of the ones in Mission Control, unless you've moved your desktops around.

(Yes, the information modules of your Today pane [page 616] are *also* called widgets. But those are much newer—and they may even be a sign that the Dashboard's days are numbered. For now, however, these duplicate features coexist.)

Note: Apple thought that parking the Dashboard widgets on their own little virtual screen was a convenient place to keep them. They do, after all, feel like they constitute a separate little software world.

But if you can also make widgets appear *in front* of whatever window you have open. To do that, open →
System Preferences. Click Mission Control, and then turn off Show Dashboard as a Space. From now on, Dashboard widgets appear as a constellation of little app windows on top of whatever else you were doing.

Figure 4-14:
The Dashboard is a fleet of mini-programs that convey or convert all kinds of useful information, on a Spaces screen all their own. You get rid of the Dashboard either by pressing the same key again (F4 or whatever), by swiping three fingers to the right on your trackpad, or by clicking anywhere except on a widget.

Here, for example, is how you can find them:

- **If your F4 key bears the Dashboard logo (☉),** then press it.

Note: On recent Macs, F4 bears a Launchpad icon (⬚⬚⬚) instead. On the very oldest Yosemite-capable Macs, the Dashboard keystroke is usually F12. Or, on laptops where F12 is the ☉ key, you have to hold down the fn key (lower-left corner).

In all of these cases, you can change the Dashboard keystroke to whatever you like, as described below.

- **Swipe to the left with three fingers on your trackpad**—repeatedly, if necessary—until you reach the far-left "desktop." (On the Magic Mouse, swipe with *two* fingers.)

- **Open Mission Control;** click the Dashboard thumbnail at the top left of the screen.

- **Dashboard is an actual program,** with an icon of its own in your Applications folder. You can open it with a double-click or by using any of the usual program-opening tricks.

In any case, you now see the display shown in Figure 4-14. Welcome to the Dashboard.

These weird, hybrid entities aren't really programs or documents. What they most resemble, actually, are little Web pages. They're meant to display information, much of it from the Internet, and they're written using Web programming languages like HTML and JavaScript.

Mastering the basics of Dashboard won't take you long at all:

- **To move a widget,** drag it around the screen. (Click anywhere except on a button or a control.)

- **To close a widget,** press the Option key as you move the mouse across the widget's face. You'll see the ⊗ button appear at the widget's top-left corner; click it.

- **To open a closed widget,** click the big ⊕ button at the bottom of the screen. Now the Widget browser appears (Figure 4-15), as described in the following section. Open the widget you want by clicking its icon.

- **To hide one of Apple's widgets,** or to delete one you've installed yourself, use the Widget browser described next.

Note: As mentioned, the Dashboard may be on its way to the great software graveyard in the sky; Yosemite's new Notification Center widgets do almost exactly the same thing. But for now the Dashboard is still yours to enjoy.

The Widget Browser

The Widget browser screen appears when you click the big ⊕ button at the bottom of the Dashboard. As shown in Figure 4-15, it's simply a master collection of every

Figure 4-15:
The Widget browser works exactly like the Launchpad. Move widget icons around by dragging. Drag one widget on top of another to create a folder. Search using the box at the top of the screen. Start them wiggling, for ease of mass deletion, by holding your cursor down on any icon, or by clicking the big — button. Read pages 152–156 again, taking care to mentally substitute the word "widget" for "app."

widget on your Mac, even the ones that you haven't dragged onto the main Dashboard screen. Its goal in life: managing all your *other* widgets.

For example, you can enter icon-deleting mode by holding your cursor down on any one of them; they all start wiggling—and displaying the ⊗ button at the top-left corner.

Note: Even in wiggling-icon mode, you're not allowed to delete Apple's widgets—only ones you've downloaded and installed yourself.

But what you'll do here most often is simply *click* a widget's icon to install it onto the main Dashboard screen.

(To close the browser without pulling a new icon out of it, click anywhere on the background.)

The Widget browser also harbors the godlike power of the More Widgets button, described later in these pages.

Dashboard Tips

Dashboard is crawling with cool tips and tricks. Here are a few of the biggies:

- **To refresh a certain widget**—for example, to update its information from the Internet click it and press ⌘-R. The widget instantly *twist-scrambles* itself into a sort of ice-cream swirl (you've got to see it to believe it) and then untwists to reveal the new data.

- **You can open more than one copy of the same widget.** Just click its icon more than once in the Widget browser. You wind up with multiple copies of it on your screen: three World Clocks, two Stock Trackers, or whatever. That's a useful trick when, for example, you want to track the time in more than one city, or when you maintain two different stock portfolios.

- **If you keep the Shift key pressed** when you click the big ⊕ button, the Widget browser fades in in gorgeous *slow motion*. Aren't you just glad to be alive?

Dashboard Preferences

To change the Dashboard keystroke to something other than F4 or F12, choose →System Preferences and then click Mission Control.

Here you'll discover that you can choose almost any other keyboard combination to summon and dismiss the Dashboard, or even choose a screen corner that, when your mouse lands there, acts as the Dashboard trigger. This works exactly as described on page 164.

Note: Yes, yes, you can also change the Dashboard keystroke on the Keyboard→Shortcuts pane of System Preferences. But if you use the Mission Control pane instead, then you can set up a screen corner or a mouse button to trigger Dashboard—not just a keyboard combo.

Widget Catalog

Here's a rundown of the 15 standard widgets that come preinstalled. True, they look awfully simple, but some of them harbor a few secrets.

Calculator

Here's your basic four-function pocket calculator, with one-number memory storage. Begin by clicking to make it active; once it is, any typing you do on the number keys gets intercepted by this little calculator. (Using the keyboard is much faster than clicking the onscreen numbers.)

There's not a lot to this calculator. If you need scientific and hexadecimal features, or even square root functions, use the regular Calculator described on page 622.

Calendar

Sure, you can always find out today's date by clicking the clock on your menu bar. But this one is so much nicer looking. And besides, you can use this calendar to look ahead or back, or to check your schedule for the day. As you click this widget, it cycles through three degrees of expansion; see Figure 4-16.

Tip: Press Shift as you click to see the panes expanding or collapsing in slow motion.

Figure 4-16:
Click the "today's date" pane to expand the second pane, which shows the month. (Click ◄ and ► to move a month at a time.) Click a third time to reveal whatever's on the calendar for the remainder of the day today, as recorded in Calendar.

Contacts

The concept is to give you faster access to your own address book. (Trudging off to the actual Contacts program takes way too long when you just want to look up a number.) It's filled with clickable shortcuts. For example:

• **Search box.** Type a few letters of somebody's name here. As you type, the widget fills with matching names from the Contacts program.

Tip: Actually, it shows you entries with text that match any part of each person's "card," not just names. For example, you could type *212* to find everyone with that area code, or *cherr* to find someone whose name you've forgotten—but you know she lives on Cherrystone Avenue.

When you spot the name of the person you're looking for, click it to open that person's full Rolodex card.

- **Phone number.** Click it to fill your screen with the phone number, big enough to see from outer space. Or at least from across the room as you dial the number on your desk phone.

- **Email address.** Click to fire up your email program, complete with a fresh outgoing message already addressed to this person. All you have to do is type your message and click Send.

- **Mailing address**. Clicking the mailing address fires up your Web browser and takes you to Apple's Maps program, already opened up to a map that reveals the pinpoint location of the specified address. Very, very slick.

Dictionary

Apple has provided about 65,000 different ways to access its built-in dictionary/ thesaurus (like the Dictionary app or Spotlight), and here's another one. Just type the word you want and press Return. Instantly, a handy definitions pane drops down. Use the ⟨ and ⟩ buttons in the upper-left corner to walk through your most recent lookups and the pop-up menu to specify whether you want to search the dictionary, the thesaurus, or the Apple terminology glossary.

Tip: See how the first letter of your word appears in a special rounded tab at the left edge of the pane? If you click that letter, you get to see the word you looked up in its alphabetical context among all the other words in the dictionary. It's a neat way to check for additional word forms, to see if perhaps you've misspelled the word, or to scrabble your way out of a tight situation when you're playing the word game Ghost with someone.

ESPN

This widget shows the current or final scores of college and professional sports games. (If the game hasn't started yet, you see the start time.) Click the ❶ button to choose the sport you want to track. Click the News button to see headlines—and click a headline to visit ESPN's full article online.

Flight Tracker

This handy widget (Figure 4-17) lets you find out which flights fly between which cities—and if the flight is already en route, it shows you where it is on the map, how high it's flying, how fast, and whether it's going to be on time.

This may look like a small window, but there's a lot going on here:

- **Flight Finder.** If you're planning a trip, the widget can show you a list of flights that match your itinerary. Use the pop-up menus to specify the arrival and departure cities, and which airline you want to study, if any. (Actually, it's usually faster to *type* the name of the city into the box, if you know how to spell it, or, better yet, its three-letter airport code.) Then click Find Flights or press Return.

 After a moment, the right side of the screen becomes a scrolling list of flights that match your query. You can see the flight number, the departure and arrival times, and the name of the airline.

This is a great tool when a friend or relative is flying in and you're unsure of the flight number, airline, or arrival time.

- **Flight Tracker.** Most of the time, the status column of the results says "Scheduled," meaning that you're looking at some future flight. Every now and then, however, you get lucky and it says "Enroute." This is where things get really fun: Double-click that row of results to see the plane's actual position on a national or international map (Figure 4-17, bottom).

Tip: If you click the little ❶ button before performing a flight search, the pane flips around to reveal the logo of the company that supplies the flight data. Click the logo to open its Web page.

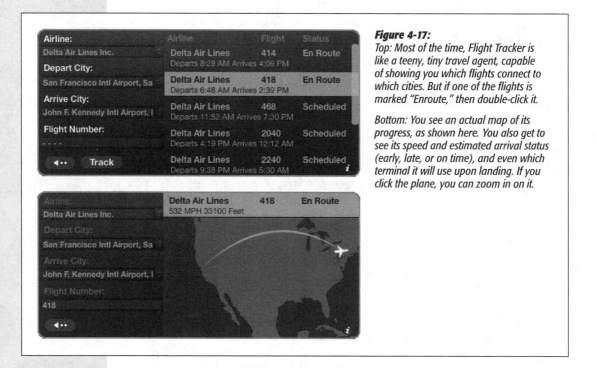

Figure 4-17:
Top: Most of the time, Flight Tracker is like a teeny, tiny travel agent, capable of showing you which flights connect to which cities. But if one of the flights is marked "Enroute," then double-click it.

Bottom: You see an actual map of its progress, as shown here. You also get to see its speed and estimated arrival status (early, late, or on time), and even which terminal it will use upon landing. If you click the plane, you can zoom in on it.

Movies

Yosemite's steroid-enhanced Spotlight feature is the quickest way to look up local movie-theater listings without having to endure the hassle of the newspaper, the hellish touch-tone labyrinth of a phone system, or the flashing ads of a Web site. But Dashboard's original movie-lookup widget is still around, too.

When you open this widget, a miniature poster changes to a different current movie every 3 seconds. At any point, you can click the poster itself to see something like Figure 4-18.

In the left column, you get a scrolling list of movies in your area. Click one of them to see, at bottom, all the details: release date, rating, length, cast, genre, a plot synopsis,

and a link to the preview (trailer). (After you've watched the trailer, go back to the list by clicking the left-pointing arrow button at the lower-left corner of the widget.)

The center column lists the theaters near you where the selected movie is playing. Click a theater to see the movie showtimes in the right column.

Tip: So how does the widget know what's "near you"? Because you've told it. You've clicked the ❶ button to flip the widget around to the back, where you can input your Zip code or your city and state.

Figure 4-18:
The Movies widget starts out with a slideshow of movie posters.

But on the back, shown here, you can read about current movies in theaters, find out which theaters they're in, and see today's showtimes. The pop-up menu at upper right lets you see the schedule for today, tomorrow, and the following four days.

Incidentally, you're not stuck with this "Choose a movie, and we'll show you the theaters" view. See at the top left, where the titles "Movies" and "Theaters" appear? Click Theaters to reverse the logic. Now you're in "Choose a theater, and we'll show you what movies are playing there" mode. This view is much better when, for example, there's only one theater nearby and you want to know what your options are there.

Tip: To return to the original cycling movie-poster display, click an empty part of the title bar.

Stickies

Stickies is a virtual Post-it note widget that lets you type out random scraps of text—a phone number, a Web address, a grocery list, or whatever.

Of course, OS X already comes with a Stickies program. So why did Apple duplicate it in Dashboard? Simple—because you can call this one up with a press of your Dashboard keystroke, making it faster to open.

On the other hand, the Stickies widget isn't quite as flexible as the Stickies application. For example, you can't resize the Stickie. And to add a second or a third note, you have to open the Widget browser and then click the Stickies icon for each new page.

On the *other* other hand, this Stickies isn't quite as bare bones as you might think. If you click the little ❶ button at the bottom-right corner, the note spins around to reveal, on the back, a choice of paper colors, fonts, and font sizes.

Stocks

Hey, day traders, this one's for you. This widget lets you build a stock portfolio and watch it rise and fall throughout the day (Figure 4-19, top right).

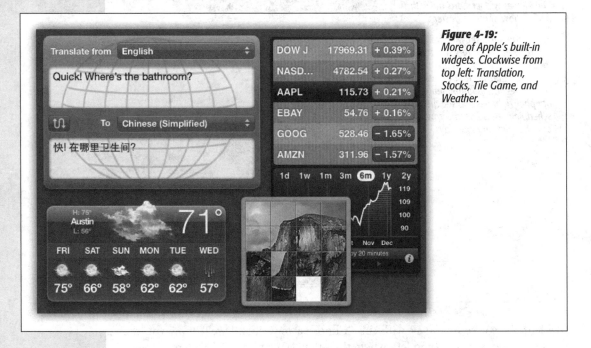

Figure 4-19:
More of Apple's built-in widgets. Clockwise from top left: Translation, Stocks, Tile Game, and Weather.

To set up your portfolio, click the little ❶ button at the bottom of the window. The widget flips around, revealing the configuration page on the back:

- **Add a stock to your list** by typing its name or stock abbreviation into the box at the top; then click the + button or press Return. If there's only one possible match—Microsoft, for example—the widget adds it to the list instantly. If there's some question about what you typed, or several possible matches, you'll see a pop-up menu listing the alternatives so you can click the one you want.

- **Remove a stock from the list** by clicking its name and then clicking Remove.

Tip: Ordinarily, the widget displays the ups and downs of each stock as a dollar amount ("+.92" means up 92 cents, for example). But if you turn on "Show change as a percentage," then you see these changes represented as percentages of their previous values.

But why bother? Once you're looking at the actual stock statistics, you can switch between dollar and percentage values just by clicking any one of the red or green up/down status buttons.

Click Done to return to the original stock display. Here's your list of stocks, their current prices (well, current as of 20 minutes ago), and the amount they've changed—green if they're up, red if they're down. Click a stock's name to see its chart displayed at the bottom. (You control the time scale by clicking one of the little buttons above the graph: "1d" means one day, "3m" means three months, "1y" means one year, and so on.)

Finally, if you double-click the name of the stock, you fly into your Web browser to view a much more detailed stock-analysis page for that stock.

Tile Game

For generations, Microsoft Windows had its Solitaire game—and for generations, the Mac has had the Tile Game. The idea, of course, is to click the squares of the puzzle, using logic to rearrange them back into the original sequence, so that the put-together photograph reappears.

Tip: The widget starts you out with a handsome photo of Yosemite National Park (the standard desktop picture, in fact). But you can substitute any photo you like.

To pull this off, begin by exiting the Dashboard. Go find the photo you prefer (on the desktop or in iPhoto, for example). Now begin dragging it in any direction. While the mouse is still down, press F4 (or whatever your Dashboard keystroke is) and drop the dragged graphic directly on the Tile Game puzzle. You've just replaced the existing graphic with your new one. (Figure 4-19 shows an example.)

The first time you use the Tile Game, click inside it to trigger the animated tile-scrambling process. Click a second time to stop the scrambling; in other words, Apple leaves it up to you to decide just how difficult (how scrambled) the puzzle is.

And what should you do if you get frustrated and give up, or if you miss the old photo? Just open the Widget bar and open a fresh copy of the Tile Game.

Translation

The next time you travel, go somewhere that has wireless Internet access wherever you go (yeah, right). You'll be able to use this module to translate your utterances—or those of the natives—to and from 13 languages.

Just choose the language direction you want from the "from" and "to" pop-up menus, and then type a word, sentence, or paragraph into the Translate From box. In a flash, the bottom of the window shows the translation, as shown at top left in Figure 4-19. (Don't click the curvy double-headed arrow button to perform the translation; that button means "Swap the 'to' and 'from' languages.")

Of course, these translations are performed by automated software robots on the Web. As a result, they're not nearly as accurate as what you'd get from a paid professional. On the other hand, when you're standing in the middle of a strange city and you don't know the language—and you desperately need to express yourself—what Dashboard provides may just be good enough.

Tip: Your first instinct may be to assume that this module is designed for translating things you want to say into the local language. However, you may find it even more useful for translating foreign-language paragraphs—from email or Web pages, for example—into your own language so that you can read them.

Unit Converter

Yosemite's Spotlight feature (page 119) is, in general, the best and fastest way to convert units—meters, grams, inches, miles per hour, and so on. But Dashboard did it first.

From the upper pop-up menu, choose the kind of conversion you want: Temperature, Area, Weight, or whatever. (Take a moment to enjoy the clever graphic at the top of the window that helps identify the measurement you've selected.)

Use the lower pair of pop-up menus to specify which units you want to convert to and from, like Celsius to Fahrenheit. Then type in either the starting or ending measurement. To convert 48 degrees Celsius to Fahrenheit, for example, type *48* into the Celsius box. You don't have to click anything or press any key; the conversion is performed for you instantly and automatically as you type.

Weather

This famous Dashboard module shows a handy current-conditions display for your city (or any other city) and, if you choose, even offers a six-day forecast (Figure 4-19, lower left).

Before you get started, the most important step is to click the ❶ button at the lower-right corner. The widget flips around, and on the back, you'll see where you can specify your city and state or Zip code. You can also specify whether you prefer degrees Celsius or degrees Fahrenheit and whether you want the six-day forecast to show both highs and lows. (It ordinarily shows only the highs.) Click Done.

Now the front of the widget displays the name of your town, today's predicted high and low, the current temperature, and a graphic representation of the sky conditions (sunny, cloudy, rainy, and so on). Click anywhere to reveal the six-day forecast.

Tip: Evidently, the Weather widget team members at Apple were really proud of their artwork. Lest you miss out on seeing all the beautiful weather graphics, they've given you a secret keystroke that reveals all 19 of the gorgeous and witty sky-weather graphics.

All you have to do is hold down ⌘ and Option as you click repeatedly on the widget. You'll see that, for the town of Nowhere, the weather changes every time you click.

Web Clip

Web Clip lets you make your *own* widgets with one click. This particular widget, however, is nothing more than a little ad for the Web Clip feature—and a reminder that you must start your Web Clip adventure in Safari, not Dashboard. See "Web Clips" starting below.

World Clock

Sure, this clock shows the current time, but your menu bar does that. The neat part is that you can open up several of these clocks—click World Clock in the Widget bar repeatedly—and set each one to show the time in a different city. The result looks like the row of clocks in a hotel lobby, making you look Swiss and precise.

To specify which city's time appears on the clock, click the ❶ button at the lower-right corner. The widget flips around, revealing the pop-up menus that let you choose a continent and city.

More Widgets

Thousands of new widgets, written by other people, are available on the Web: games, chat and email notifiers, gas-price reporters, calculators and translators, news and sports updaters, finance and health trackers, and on and on.

To see Apple's current list of goodies, use one of these tactics:

- **The short way.** Right-click (or two-finger click) the Dashboard icon in the Dock. From the shortcut menu, choose More Widgets.

- **The long way.** In Dashboard, open the Widgets browser; click More Widgets.

Either way, you go to the Apple Dashboard downloads page. Some of the most intriguing widget offerings include the Yahoo Local Traffic widget (gives you the traffic conditions in your area), Air Traffic Control (identifies wireless AirPort base stations within range of your laptop), and TV Tracker (shows what you could be watching on TV right now instead of working). There are also FedEx package trackers, joke-of-the-day widgets, comic-strip-of-the-day widgets, and many other varieties.

Installing a widget

When you download a widget, OS X asks if you're sure you want to install it. If you confirm, OS X downloads it and then displays it proudly in the Widget browser. Click it to open. (Behind the scenes, it's been copied into your Home→Library→Widgets folder. Only you will see that Dashboard widget, because it's been copied into the Widgets folder of *your account.* Anyone else who has an account on this Mac won't see it.)

Web Clips

You can also make a Dashboard widget of your own.

Web Clips exploit an inescapable characteristic of widgets: An awful lot of them exist to deliver real-time information from the Web—weather, stocks, flights, and so on.

But what if your interest isn't snowstorms, stocks, or sports? What if it's *The New York Times* front page? Or the bestselling children's books on Amazon? Or the most-viewed video on YouTube? Or some cool Flash game?

That's the beauty of Web Clips, a joint venture of Dashboard and the Safari Web browser. They let you turn *any section of any Web page* into a Dashboard widget that updates itself every time you open it. It's like having a real-time keyhole peek at all your favorite Web sites at once.

Creating a Web Clip widget

Here's how you go about creating a do-it-yourself widget:

1. **In Safari, go to the Web page that contains the information you want to snip. Choose File→Open in Dashboard.**

 The screen goes dark, with only a small window of white. As you move your cursor around the page, the white rectangle conveniently snaps to fit the various rectangular sections of the page (Figure 4-20).

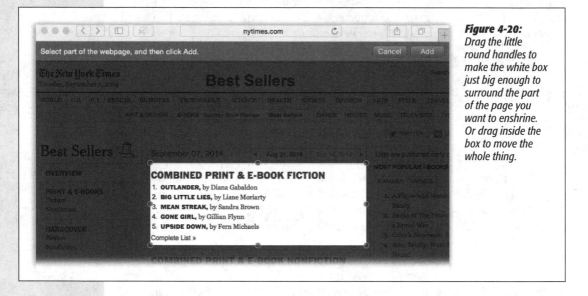

Figure 4-20:
Drag the little round handles to make the white box just big enough to surround the part of the page you want to enshrine. Or drag inside the box to move the whole thing.

Your job is to make a frame around the part of the page that usually shows the information you want. If the Web site ever redesigns its pages, it'll wreck your widget—but what the heck; it takes only 5 seconds to make it again.

2. **Adjust the corner or side handles to enclose the piece of page you want. When you're finished, click Add or press Return.**

 Now Dashboard's Widget browser opens automatically. But wait—what's this? There's a new widget here that wasn't here before.

At this point, you can dress up your widget, adding a little polish to this raw clipping you've ripped out of a Web page. Click the ❶ button that appears when you move your mouse to the lower-right corner. The widget flips around to reveal the controls shown in Figure 4-21.

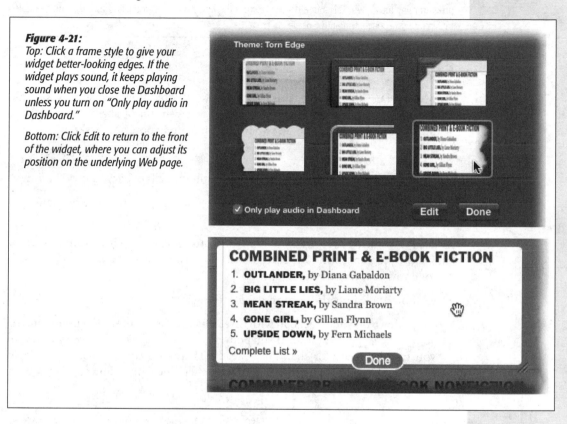

Figure 4-21:
Top: Click a frame style to give your widget better-looking edges. If the widget plays sound, it keeps playing sound when you close the Dashboard unless you turn on "Only play audio in Dashboard."

Bottom: Click Edit to return to the front of the widget, where you can adjust its position on the underlying Web page.

Here you can click one of the frame styles to give your widget a better-looking border.

If you click Edit, the widget flips around to face you again, and here's where it gets weird: You can reposition your widget's contents as though they were a window on a Web page that's visible behind it. Drag the widget contents in any direction within the frame, or resize the frame using the lower-right resize handle. Click Done.

You can make as many Web Clip widgets as you want.

But here's a big screaming caution: If you close one of these homemade widgets, it's gone forever (or at least until you recreate it). Web Clips are never represented as icons on the Widget bar, as ordinary widgets are. Ah, well—easy come, easy go, right?

Note: If you're of the programmer persuasion—if you're handy in JavaScript and HTML, for example—it's easy to write widgets. (Not just Web Clips widgets, but *real* widgets.)

All you need is Dashcode, an easy-to-use widget-assembly environment. It's part of Apple's Xcode software programming toolkit, which is a free download from the Mac App Store. You'll find tutorials and examples by typing *dashcode tutorial* into Google.

Exposé

Before Mission Control, there was Exposé. It was flexible, it was novel, it was a little confusing. It was meant to help you manage a screen full of chaotic, overlapping windows. And it's still around, in two forms: one-app Exposé and desktop Exposé.

One-App Exposé

When you trigger Mission Control, you see the thumbnails of *all* windows in *all* apps.

But sometimes it's useful to see only the windows of *one* app arrayed before you—the app you're *using*.

That's great when you're Web browsing or word processing. This Exposé function makes the program's windows spread out, and shrink if necessary, so you can click the one you want (Figure 4-22, top).

Here's how Apple intends for most people to trigger this option:

- **Swipe down on your trackpad with three fingers.** You're shown the miniatures of your current app's windows. If you point to an icon *on the Dock* before you swipe, you trigger Exposé for that app instead. (There's no equivalent on the Magic Mouse—although if you install the free BetterTouchTool, you can dream up a gesture of your own.)

Note: You have to turn this feature on in System Preferences→Trackpad→More Gestures. Once you've done that, you can change this gesture to four fingers on the trackpad using the pop-up menu—handy if you find yourself triggering the function by accident.

- **Press Control-F3 (▦).** That's the keystroke on aluminum keyboards. (If you have a plastic keyboard, press F10 or fn-F10, whichever works.)

Tip: As noted in the box on page 187, you can also press fn-F10 or, with some tweaking, F10 alone. Or you can change the keystroke altogether as described on page 199.

- **Enter Exposé from the heads-up display.** The heads-up display is the OS X application switcher—the row of "These are your open programs" icons—which appears when you press ⌘-Tab.

The cool thing is that once you've got that heads-up display open, you can press
▲ or ▼ to enter Exposé for whatever program's icon is highlighted! From there,
release the keys and hit Tab to cycle through your open apps.

Figure 4-22:
*Top: When you
trigger one-app
Exposé, you get a
clear shot at any
window in the current
program (TextEdit,
in this example). In
the meantime, the
rest of your screen
attractively dims. In
model Apple apps,
like TextEdit and
Preview, you even get
a little row of icons
at the bottom. They
represent recently
opened files, ready
for clicking.*

*Bottom: Trigger desk-
top Exposé when you
need to duck back
to the desktop for a
quick administrative
chore. Here's your
chance to find a file,
throw something
away, eject a disk,
or whatever, without
having to disturb
your application
windows.*

*Tap the same key
again to turn off
Exposé. Or click a
window edge peeking
out from all four
edges of the screen.*

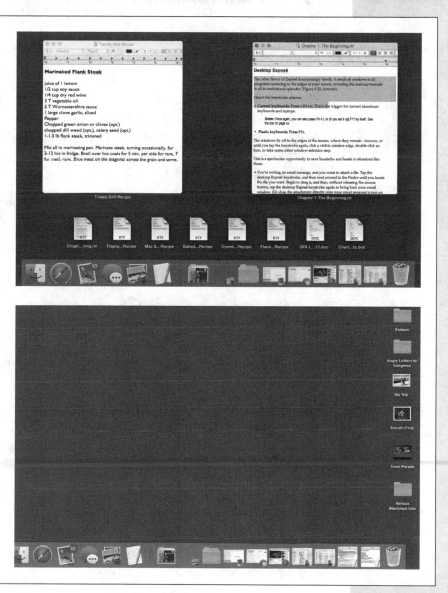

- **Use Dock Exposé.** Click the program's Dock icon and hold the button down for
half a second. (Or, for faster service, right-click or two-finger click the program's
Dock icon.)

This feature has one chief advantage over the keystroke method: You can Exposé-ize *any* program's windows, not just the one you're using at the moment.

- **Shove your mouse into whatever corner of the screen you've chosen.** See page 164 for instructions.

Once you've triggered Exposé, you're not quite finished yet. As shown in Figure 4-22, beneath the window thumbnails, you get to see the icons of documents you've worked on recently in this app (at least in enlightened Apple programs like TextEdit).

Desktop Exposé

The other flavor of Exposé is surprisingly handy. It sends *all* windows in *all* programs cowering to the edges of your screen, revealing the desktop beneath in all its unclut-tered splendor (Figure 4-22, bottom).

Here's the keystroke scheme:

- **Current keyboards: Press ⌘-F3 (▦).** That's the trigger for current aluminum keyboards and laptops.

Note: Once again, you can also press fn-F11, or (if you set it up) F11 by itself. See the box on the facing page.

- **Plastic keyboards: Press F11.**

The windows fly off to the edges of the screen, where they remain—forever or until you tap the keystroke again, click a visible window edge, double-click an icon, or take some other window-selection step.

This is a spectacular opportunity to save headache and hassle in situations like these:

- **You're writing an email message, and you want to attach a file.** Tap the desktop Exposé keystroke, and then root around in the Finder until you locate the file you want. Begin to drag it, and then, without releasing the mouse button, tap the desktop Exposé keystroke again to bring back your email window. (Or drag the attachment directly onto your email program's icon on the Dock and pause until its window thumbnails appear.)

 Move your cursor, with the file in mid-drag, directly over the outgoing message window; release the cursor to create the attachment. You've just added an attach-ment from the desktop in one smooth motion.

Tip: You can apply the same life-changing shortcut to dragging a graphic into a page-layout program, a folder of photos into iPhoto, a sound or graphic into iMovie, and so on.

- **You want to open a different document.** For many people, having access to the entire Finder beats the pants off having to use the Open dialog box. Double-clicking the icon you want automatically opens it and turns off Exposé.

- **You're on the Web, and you want to see if some file has finished downloading.** Trigger desktop Exposé to survey the situation on your desktop.

If the layer of open programs is the atmosphere, the Finder is the earth below—and the ability to teleport back and forth is a huge timesaver.

Tip: You can switch between the two Exposé modes (one-app or desktop), even after you've triggered one. For example, if you three-finger downswipe to shrink only that program's windows, you can then press ⌘-F3 to see the desktop. In fact, you can also get to one-app Exposé from within Mission Control—just press ⌘-~.

Exposé Tip-O-Rama

Just having your world o' windows spread out like index cards is magic enough. But these windows are *live.* You can work with them. Let us count the ways:

- **Tab through Exposé'd apps.** Once you've started one-app Exposé and a program's windows are arrayed before you, *press the Tab key.* With each tap, you cycle through the open apps, each getting the Exposé treatment in turn. It's an informative way to inspect what's happening in each open program without losing your way. (Pressing ⌘-~ does the same thing.) Shift-Tab, as usual, cycles through the programs in the opposite direction.

Tip: You can also switch to another app's micro-windows by clicking its Dock icon.

- **Change Exposé'd apps using the heads up display.** Here's another way to change programs once you're in one-app Exposé: Press ⌘-Tab to bring up the heads-up display (yes, even while your windows are shrunken). Tab your way through the

TROUBLESHOOTING MOMENT

A Tedious Side Note about the Aluminum Apple Keyboards

You used to be able to trigger the three Exposé modes described on these pages with three simple keystrokes: F9, F10, and F11.

Then Apple's aluminum keyboards and laptops came along. On these, Apple devoted the F3 key to Exposé functions—and reassigned the F9, F10, and F11 keys to speaker-volume control!

You *can* make them operate as in the days of yore—by adding the fn key. That is: fn-F9 for Mission Control, fn-F10 for one-app Exposé, and fn-F11 for desktop Exposé. (Details on the fn key appear on page 24.)

So here's the point: On modern Macs, you have a choice of two Exposé keystroke suites: the F3 key (by itself, with

Control, and with ⌘)—or fn-F9 (Mission Control), fn-F10 (one-app Exposé), and fn-F11 (desktop Exposé).

Actually, it's even more complicated than that. If you find yourself using Exposé more than you use the volume keys, you can get rid of the requirement to press fn. Open System Preferences→Keyboard→ Keyboard. Here you'll find a checkbox that reverses this logic. It's called "Use all F1, F2, etc. keys as standard function keys."

If that checkbox is *on,* then you can use F9, F10, and F11 to trigger Mission Control and Exposé. Now you need the fn key only when you want those keys to go back to adjusting the *volume.*

program icons (Figure 4-22) until the one you want is selected, and then release the keys. That program's windows spring to the front, still miniaturized and arrayed for your selection pleasure.

- **Hold down instead of two presses.** Most of the time, you'll probably use Exposé in two steps. You'll tap the keystroke once to get the windows out of the way and tap it again to bring them back (if, indeed, you haven't *clicked* a window to bring them back).

 In some cases, though, you may find it easier to *hold down* the relevant key. For example, hold down ⌘-F3 (Show Desktop) to see if a file is finished copying to the desktop, and then release the keys to bring back all the windows. (Actually, you can let go of the ⌘ key as soon as you've entered Exposé.) For quick window-clearing situations, that method saves you the step of having to press the keystroke a second time to turn off Exposé.

- **Use the spring-loaded Dock.** This trick is great when you want to drop a file from one program into a particular window belonging to another.

 The most common example: You want to add an attachment to an outgoing email message. In the Finder, locate the file's icon. Drag it directly onto your email program's Dock icon—and *pause* with your finger still on the button. After a half-second, Exposé happens, showing all your email program's open windows. Now continue your drag onto the miniaturized window of the outgoing message so it's highlighted, tap the space bar to open it, and then release. Presto! The file is attached.

 This trick also works great when you want to drop a photo into a newsletter, for example, or a text clipping into a word-processing document.

- **Dip into Quick Look.** Once you've got shrunken windows on the screen, tap your arrow keys to highlight a window (or point with your mouse at them without clicking). A bright-blue border moves from window to window.

 At any point, you can press the space bar to make that one window return to life size. You haven't really activated it—you can't edit it—but at least you can see it at full size.

 And here's the very cool part: Once you've triggered Quick Look like this, you can press the arrow keys to zap *other* miniwindows back to full size, without having to exit Quick Look. Or, again, point to other windows without clicking. Each zooms in to 100 percent size. (All of this is much easier to do than to imagine.)

 You can keep examining your windows at full size until you spot the one you're after; now tap Return (or click the mouse in the window) to exit Quick Look *and* Exposé. You've just opened that window, and you're ready to roll.

Tip: Keep in mind that you can change all of these Exposé triggers—keyboard shortcuts, hot corners, and so on. See page 184.

Hiding Programs the Old-Fashioned Way

When it comes to getting windows out of your way, nothing can touch Mission Control and Exposé for speed and entertainment value. Once you've mastered those features, the traditional rituals of hiding windows will seem charmingly quaint. "When I was your age," you'll tell your grandchildren, "we used to have to *hold down the Option key* to hide windows!"

But you know the drill at software companies: They giveth, but they never taketh away. All the old techniques are still around for the benefit of Mac fans who use them by force of habit.

Hiding the Program You're Using

For the purposes of this discussion, when a program is *hidden,* all its windows, tool palettes, and button bars disappear. You can bring them back only by bringing the program to the front again (by clicking its Dock icon again, for example).

If your aim is to hide only the frontmost program, OS X offers a whole raft of approaches. Many of them involve the Option key, as listed here:

- **Option-click any visible portion of the desktop.** The program you were in vanishes, along with all its windows.

- **Option-click any other program's icon on the Dock.** You open that program (or bring all its windows to the front) *and* hide all the windows of the one you were using.

- **Option-click any visible portion of another program's windows.** Once again, you switch programs, hiding the one you were using at the time.

- **From the Application menu, choose Hide iPhoto (or whatever the program is).** The Application menu is the boldfaced menu that bears the program's name.

- **From the program's Dock icon shortcut menu, choose Hide.** You open the shortcut menu, of course, by right-clicking (or two-finger clicking). You also get a Hide button if you click-and-hold on the Dock icon for half a second.

- **When you've highlighted a program's icon by pressing ⌘-Tab to rotate through the running programs, press the letter H key.** The program hides itself instantly. Leave the ⌘ key down the whole time and, after pressing the H, press Tab again to move on to the next program. If you release the keys while "stopped" on the program instead, you'll bring it forward rather than hiding it.

- **Press ⌘-H.** This may be the easiest and most useful trick of all (although it doesn't work in a few oddball programs). Doing so hides the program you're in; you then "fall down" into the next running program.

Tip: Consider this radical timesaving proposal: Never quit the programs you use frequently. Instead, simply hit ⌘-H whenever you're finished working in a program. That way, the next time you need it, the program launches with zero wait time.

There's a limit to this principle; if you have only 2 gigabytes of memory and you keep 20 programs open, and one of them is Photoshop, you'll incur a speed penalty. In more moderate situations, though, OS X's virtual-memory scheme is so good that there's almost no downside to leaving your programs open all the time.

To unhide a program and its windows, click its Dock icon again, choose the Show All command in the Application menu, or press ⌘-Tab to summon the heads-up application display.

Tip: The Dock continues to display the icons of all running programs without any indication that you've hidden them. Fortunately, that's easy enough to fix. All you need is the free program TinkerTool, which is available on this book's "Missing CD" page at *www.missingmanuals.com.* It offers a simple checkbox that makes hidden programs appear with transparent Dock icons.

GEM IN THE ROUGH

Window Layering

OS X takes a layered approach to your programs' windows. They're not all in front or all in back; it's entirely possible to wind up with the windows of different programs sandwiched and layered, front to back.

Suppose, for example, you have Microsoft Excel in the foreground but Word in the background. If you click within a visible portion of a background window, you bring only that window of Word to the front.

The remedy for this situation, if it bothers you, is the Window→Bring All to Front command, which appears in the Finder and many other programs. It brings all a program's windows to the front. (You can do the same thing by simply clicking

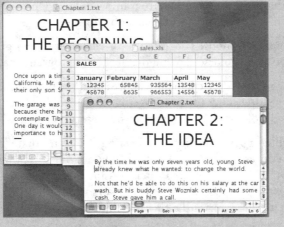

the program's Dock icon, or using the ⌘-Tab "heads-up" display.)

Layered windows shine when you're comparing two documents in two different programs, because they free you of the window clutter of other open documents. But the time will come when you're ready to bring all a background program's windows to the front. Get into the habit of clicking its Dock icon, or pressing ⌘-Tab to select its icon, rather than clicking inside one window. When you do that, all open windows in that application come forward, from wherever they may be.

Hiding All Other Programs

Choosing Hide Others from your program's Application menu means, of course, "Hide the windows of every program but this one." It even hides your Finder (desktop) windows, although desktop icons remain visible.

Better yet, there's a keystroke for this command: Option-⌘-H. That's one small step for keystrokes, one giant leap for productivity geeks.

Tip: If you right-click (or two-finger click) a program's Dock icon, you get its shortcut menu, including a Hide command. If you press Option, it changes to say Hide Others. It's a lot more work than the methods described above, but, you know. One strives for thoroughness.

If this trick interests you, you might also enjoy its corollary, described next.

The Bring-Forward, Hide-All-Others Trick

Here's a terrific technique that lets you bring one program to the front (along with all its open windows) and hide all other windows of all *other* open programs—all with one click.

You might think of it as Hero mode, or Front-and-Center mode, or Clear My Calendar mode.

In any case, the trick is to Option-⌘-click the lucky program's icon on the Dock. As it jumps to the fore, all other windows on your Mac are instantly hidden. (You can bring them back, of course, by clicking the appropriate Dock icons.)

Hiding (Minimizing) Individual Windows

You can also hide or show *individual windows* of a single program. In fact, Apple must believe that hiding a window will become one of your favorite activities, because it offers at least three ways to do it:

- **Choose Window ›Minimize Window,** if your program offers such a command, or press ⌘-M.

- **Click the Minimize button** on the window's title bar.

- **Double-click the window's title bar.** (If this doesn't work, choose →System Preferences→Dock. Make sure "Double-click a window's title bar to minimize" is turned on.)

In any case, the affected window shrinks down until it becomes a new icon on the right side of the Dock. Click that icon to bring the window back.

How Documents Know Their Parents

Every operating system needs a mechanism to associate documents with the applications that created them. When you double-click a Microsoft Word document icon, for example, it's clear that you want Microsoft Word to launch and open the document.

So how does OS X know how to find a document's mommy? It actually has two different mechanisms:

- **File name extensions.** A *file name extension* is a suffix following a period in the file's name, as in *Letter to Mom.doc*. (It's usually three letters long, but it doesn't have to be.) These play a role in determining which documents open into which programs.

 That's how Windows identifies its documents, too. If you double-click something called *memo.doc*, it opens in Microsoft Word. If you double-click *memo.wri*, it opens in Microsoft Write, and so on.

Note: OS X comes set to hide most file name extensions, on the premise that they make the operating system look more technical and threatening. If you'd like to see them, however, then choose Finder→Preferences, click the Advanced button, and then turn on "Show all filename extensions." Now examine a few of your documents; you'll see that their names display the previously hidden suffixes.

 You can hide or show these suffixes on an icon-at-a-time basis, too (or a clump-at-a-time basis). Just highlight the icon or icons you want to affect, and then choose File→Get Info. In the resulting Info window, proceed as shown in Figure 4-23.

- **Your preferences.** If you've used the Always Open With command to *specify* which program opens your document, that's the one that opens; this preference overrides the file name extension system. OS X memorizes that new pairing.

It's possible to live a long and happy life without knowing anything about these suffixes and relationships. Indeed, the vast majority of Mac fans may never even encounter

Figure 4-23:
Top: In the Info window, open the Name & Extension pane. Now you can see what OS X really thinks your file is called. Turn "Hide extension" on if you'd rather not see the file name suffix in the Finder.

Bottom: If you try to add a suffix of your own, OS X objects, in effect saying, "Hey–I've already got a file name extension for this, even if you can't see it. Are you sure you know what you're doing?" (And you can turn off this warning, if you like. Choose Finder→Preferences→Advanced pane. Turn off "Show warning before changing an extension.")

them. But if you're prepared for a little bit of technical bushwhacking, you may discover that understanding document-program relationships can be useful in troubleshooting, keeping your files private, and appreciating how OS X works.

Reassigning Documents to Programs

Unfortunately, file name extensions aren't always especially specific. Suppose you've downloaded a graphic called Sunset.jpg. Well, almost any program these days can open a JPEG graphic—Photoshop, Pages, Word, Preview, Safari, and so on. How does OS X know which of these programs to open when you double-click the file?

Fortunately, *you* can decide. You can *reassign* a document (or all documents of its kind) to a specific program. Here's the rundown.

Reassigning a certain document—just once

Double-clicking a graphics file generally opens it in Preview, the graphics viewer included with OS X. Most of the time, that's a perfectly good arrangement. But Preview has only limited editing powers. What if you decide to edit a graphics file more substantially? You'd want it to open, just this once, into a different program—Photoshop Elements, for example.

To do so, you must access the Open With command. You can find it in three places:

• Highlight the icon and then choose File→Open With.

• Highlight the icon and then open the ✿ menu. In the menu, choose Open With.

• Right-click (or two-finger click) the file's icon. From the shortcut menu, choose Open With.

Study the submenu for a moment (Figure 4-24, top). The program whose name says "(default)" indicates which program *usually* opens this kind of document. From this pop-up menu, choose the name of the program you'd *rather* open this particular file, right now, just this once.

Reassigning a certain document—permanently

After opening a TIFF file in, say, Photoshop Elements for editing, you haven't really made any changes in the fabric of your Mac universe. The next time you double-click that file, it opens once again in Preview.

If you wish this particular file would *always* open in Photoshop Elements, the steps are slightly different. In fact, there are three different ways:

• In the Choose an Application dialog box (the one that appears when you double-click a document whose "parent" program isn't clear), turn on Always Open With (shown at bottom in Figure 4-24).

• Start out with one of the previously described techniques (for example, File→Open With, or right-click the file's icon and choose Open With)—but after you see the menu, press the Option key, too. Before your very eyes, the Open With command changes to say *Always* Open With.

- Highlight the icon, and then choose File→Get Info. Open the "Open with" pane. Choose a new "parent" program's name from the pop-up menu. You'll see that the word "(default)" changes position, now tacking itself onto the name of the program you've chosen.

Tip: You can use a similar trick to reassign the parenthood of a whole *flock* of selected icons at once. Once you've selected them, keep the Option key pressed as you choose File→Show Inspector. In the Open With section of this specialized Get Info window, choose a new program from the pop-up menu. The message at the top of the window—"22 items," for example—reminds you that you're changing the whole batch at once.

Figure 4-24:
Top: The shortcut menu offers a list of programs capable of opening an icon. If you were to press the Option key right now, the words "Open With" would suddenly change to say "Always Open With."

Bottom: If you choose Other, you're prompted to choose a different program. Turn on Always Open With if you'll always want this document to open in the new parent program. Otherwise, this is a one-time reassignment.

Reassigning all documents of one type

So much for reassigning one document (or a group of documents) at a time. What if you're writing, say, a book about OS X, and you've been taking a lot of screenshots? OS X saves each captured screen illustration as a graphics file in something called PNG format. That's all fine, except that every time you double-click one of these, it opens into Preview, where you can't paint out unwanted details.

You could reassign all these files, one at a time, to a different program, but your grand-children would have grandchildren by the time you finished. In this case, you want to tell OS X, "For heaven's sake, make *all* PNG files open in Photoshop from now on!"

To make it happen, start by highlighting *any* PNG file. Choose File→Get Info. (The shortcut menus won't help you in this case.) Open the "Open with" pane.

From its pop-up menu, choose the program you want to open this kind of document from now on.

Tip: If the one you prefer isn't listed, use the Other option, which opens the Choose an Application dialog box so you can navigate to the one you want, as shown in Figure 4-24 at bottom. Find and double-click the program.

Or, instead of choosing Other, you can also choose App Store. It's Apple's way of saying, "Hey—if you don't have a program that can open this document, maybe you should just *go buy one right now!"*

This time, follow up by clicking Change All beneath the pop-up menu. (This button is dimmed until you've actually selected a different program from the pop-up menu.) Confirm by clicking Continue or pressing Return.

From now on, double-clicking any similar kind of document opens it in the newly selected program.

Keyboard Control

OS X offers a fantastic feature for anyone who believes life is short: keyboard-controllable menus, dialog boxes, pop-up menus, and even Dock pop-up menus. You can operate every menu in every program without the mouse.

In fact, you can operate every control in every dialog box from the keyboard, including pop-up menus and checkboxes. And you can even redefine many of the built-in OS X keystrokes, like Shift-⌘-3 to capture the screen as a graphic.

In fact, you can even add or change *any menu command in any program*. If you're a keyboard-shortcut lover, your cup runneth over.

Here are some of the ways you can control your Mac mouselessly. In the following descriptions, you'll encounter the factory settings for the keystrokes that do the magic—but as you'll see in a moment, you can change these key combos to anything you like. (The System Preferences→Keyboard→Shortcuts tab contains the on/off switches for these features.)

Note: On modern-day aluminum keyboards, the keystrokes described below may not work unless you also press the fn key simultaneously.

If that seems clumsy, you can eliminate the fn-key requirement either by using the "Use all F1, F2, etc. keys as standard function keys" option described in the box on page 187—or by choosing a different keystroke altogether (page 199).

Control the Menus

When you press Control-F2, the menu is highlighted. At this point, you can "walk" to another menu by pressing the ◄ or ► keys (or Tab and Shift-Tab). When you reach the menu you want, open it by pressing ▼, space, or Return.

Walk down the commands in the menu by pressing ▲ or ▼, or jump directly to a command in the menu by typing the first couple of letters of its name. Finally, "click" a menu command by pressing Return or the space bar.

You can also close the menu without making a selection by pressing Esc or ⌘-period.

Control the Dock

Once you've pressed Control-F3, you can highlight *any* icon on the Dock by pressing the appropriate arrow keys (or, once again, Tab and Shift-Tab).

Then, once you've highlighted a Dock icon, you "click" it by pressing Return or the space bar. Again, if you change your mind, press Esc or ⌘-period.

Tip: Once you've highlighted a disk or folder icon, you can press the ▲ or ▼ keys to make its shortcut menu appear. (If you've positioned the Dock vertically, then use ◄ or ► instead.)

Cycle Through Your Windows

Every time you press Control-F4, you bring the next window forward, eventually cycling through *every window in every open program*. Add the Shift key to cycle through them in the opposite order.

You may remember that OS X offers a different keystroke for cycling through the different windows in your *current* program (it's ⌘-~, the tilde symbol at the upper left on your keyboard). Control-F4, on the other hand, tours all windows in *all* programs. Both keystrokes are useful in different situations.

Control the Toolbar

This one is on the unpredictable side, but it more or less works in most programs that display an OS X–style toolbar: the Finder, System Preferences, and so on.

When you press Control-F5, you highlight the first button on that toolbar. Move the "focus" by pressing the arrow keys or Tab and Shift-Tab. Then tap Return or the space bar to "click" the highlighted button.

Control Tool Palettes

In a few programs that feature floating tool palettes, you can highlight the frontmost palette by pressing Control-F6. At this point, use the arrow keys to highlight the various buttons on the palette. You can see the effect when, for example, you're editing text in TextEdit and you've also opened the Font palette. Pressing Control-F6 highlights the Font palette, taking the "focus" off your document.

Control Menulets

Here's a gem you may not have heard about: You can operate *menulets*—those menu-bar status indicators for your speaker volume, wireless networks, and so on—from the keyboard, too.

This time, the trick is to hit Control-F8. That highlights the leftmost Apple menulet. Now you can use your ◀ and ▶ arrow keys to move around the menu bar; when you've highlighted the one you want, press Return or the space bar to "click" that menu and open it.

Control Dialog Boxes

You can also navigate and manipulate any *dialog box* from the keyboard.

See the dialog box shown in Figure 4-25? If you turn on "All controls" at the bottom, then pressing the Tab key highlights the next control of any type, whatever it may be—radio button, pop-up menu, and so on. Press the space bar to "click" a button or to open a pop-up menu. Once a menu is open, use the arrow keys (or type letter keys) to highlight commands on it, and use the space bar to "click" your choice.

Changing a Menu Keyboard Shortcut

Suppose you love iPhoto (and who doesn't?). But one thing drives you crazy: The Revert to Original command, which discards all the changes you've ever made since taking the photo, has no keyboard shortcut. You must trek up to the menu bar every time you need that command.

This is why OS X lets you add keyboard shortcuts to menu commands that lack them—or change the commands in programs whose key assignments break with tradition. (It works in any program that uses the standard OS X menu software, which rules out older versions of Microsoft Office.) Here's the routine:

1. **Choose** ⌘→**System Preferences→Keyboard. Click the Shortcuts tab, and then click App Shortcuts in the left-side list.**

 You're shown a list of any keyboard assignments you've created so far.

2. **Click the + button just beneath the list.**

 The dialog box shown in Figure 4-25 appears.

3. Indicate which program needs behavior modification.

In this example, you'd choose iPhoto from the Application pop-up menu. (If the program's name doesn't appear in the pop-up menu, then choose Other; navigate to, and double-click, the program you want.)

Figure 4-25:
If you choose All Applications from the top pop-up menu, you can change the keyboard combo for a certain command wherever it appears. You could, for example, change the keystroke for Page Setup in every program at once. (Beware the tiny yellow triangles; they let you know if a chosen keystroke conflicts with another OS X keystroke.)

4. Carefully type in the name of the menu command whose keyboard shortcut you want to change or add.

Type it *exactly* as it appears in the menu, complete with capitalization and the little ellipsis (…) that may follow it. (You make the ellipsis character by pressing Option-semicolon.)

5. Click in the Keyboard Shortcut box. Press the new or revised key combo you want.

For example, press Control-R for iPhoto's Revert to Original command. You'll see the Mac's notation of your keystroke appear in the Keyboard Shortcut box—unless, of course, the combo you selected is already in use within that program. In that case, you hear only an error sound that means "Try again."

6. Click Add.

The dialog box closes. By scrolling down in your Keyboard Shortcuts list, you see that the keystroke you selected has now been written down for posterity under

the appropriate program's flippy triangle. (To get rid of it, click its name and then click the — button beneath the list.)

The next time you open the program you edited, you'll see that the new keystroke is in place.

Tip: To delete or change one of your custom menu shortcuts, open System Preferences→Keyboard→Shortcuts. Click App Shortcuts in the list at left. Click the command you'd like to edit. Press Delete to get rid of it; or, to try a different key combo, click where the existing keyboard shortcut appears and then press a new one.

Redefining a Keystroke

As you've no doubt become painfully aware, there are *hundreds* of keyboard combinations for the various OS X functions and settings. That's good, because keyboard shortcuts are efficient and quicker than using the mouse. But that's also bad, because there's no *way* you'll be able to remember all of them—and some of the most useful shortcuts are ridiculous, multikey affairs that you'll never remember at all.

In the keyboard-shortcut center, shown in Figure 4-26, you can look over all the common OS X hidden keyboard functions—for Mission Control, Exposé, Spotlight, Dashboard, the Dock, and many others—and *change them.*

Here's how it goes:

1. **Choose →System Preferences. Click Keyboard. Click the Shortcuts tab.**

 You arrive at the dialog box shown in Figure 4-26.

2. **In the left-side list, click the category or function you want.**

 Your choices include Launchpad & Dock, Mission Control, Keyboard, and so on. When you click a category name, you see the available shortcuts.

Tip: You don't have to be content with *changing* one of these keyboard shortcuts. You can also *turn it off* by clicking the corresponding checkbox. That's great if one of Apple's predefined keystrokes–for a function you don't even use–is interfering with one in a program you like.

3. **Click the command you want to change. Then click the current keyboard combination (or the "add shortcut" button, if there is no existing shortcut).**

 Suppose, for example, that you wish the Show Desktop Exposé keystroke were something easier to remember, like Control-D. So in step 2, you'd click Mission Control. In this step, you'd click Show Desktop. Then you'd click where it currently says "F11."

4. **Press a new key combination.**

 In this example, you'd press Control-D.

 Be careful, though. OS X keystrokes take precedence over *all others.* So if you choose a keystroke like ⌘-P for something, well, by golly, you'll no longer be able to use

⌘-P to print anything in any of your programs. Think before you assign. Run a couple of tests afterward.

Figure 4-26:
The keyboard-shortcut center lets you redefine the keystrokes that trigger many basic OS X features, menu commands in your programs, and software you've built yourself using Automator.

The Save and Open Dialog Boxes

When you choose File→Save, you're asked where you want the new document stored on your hard drive, what you want to call it, and what Finder tags (page 106) you want applied to it. The resulting dialog box is a miniature Finder. All the skills you've picked up working at the desktop come into play here.

To give it a try, launch any program that has a Save or Export command—TextEdit, for example. Type a couple of words, and then choose File→Save. The Save sheet appears (Figure 4-27).

Tip: In most programs, a quick glance at the Close button in the upper-left corner of a document window tells you whether it's been saved. When a small dot appears in the red button, it means you've made changes to the document that you haven't saved yet. (Time to press ⌘-S!) The dot disappears as soon as you save your work.

In programs that offer the Auto Save and Versions features described later in this chapter, like TextEdit, the red-dot convention has been retired. Instead, when you've made changes to a document since saving it, you see the light-gray word *Edited* in the title bar.

Sheets

In the days of operating systems gone by, the Save dialog box appeared dead center on the screen, where it commandeered your entire operation. Moreover, because it seemed stuck to your *screen* rather than to a particular *document,* you couldn't actually tell which document you were saving—a real problem when you quit out of a program that had three unsaved documents open.

In most Mac programs, there's no mystery regarding which document you're saving, because a little Save dialog box called a *sheet* slides directly out of the document's title bar.

Figure 4-27:
Top: The Save dialog box, or sheet, often appears in its compact form.

Right: If you open the Where pop-up menu, you'll find that OS X lists all the places it thinks you might want to save your new document: online (iCloud), on the hard drive, in a folder you've put into your Sidebar ("Favorites"), or into a folder you've recently opened.

Bottom: If you want to choose a different folder or to create a new folder, click the ▼ button (next to the Save As box) to expand the dialog box. Here you see the equivalent of the Finder—with a choice of icon, list, or column view. Even the Sidebar is here, complete with access to other disks on the network.

Tip: In most programs, you can enlarge the Save or Open dialog box by dragging one of its edges. You can also adjust the width of the Sidebar by dragging its right edge.

Compact Save sheet

Expanded Save sheet

Better still, this little Save box is a sticky note attached *to the document*. It stays there, neatly attached and waiting, even if you switch to another program, another document, the desktop, or wherever. When you finally return to the document, the Save sheet is still there, waiting for you to type a file name and save the document.

The Mini Finder

Of course *you,* o savvy reader, have probably never saved a document into some deeply nested folder by accident, never to see it again. But millions of novices (and even a few experts) have fallen into this trap.

When the Save sheet appears, a pop-up menu shows you precisely where the Mac proposes to put your newly created document: usually in the Documents folder of your own Home folder. For many people, this is an excellent suggestion. If you keep everything in your Documents folder, it will be extremely easy to find, and you'll be able to back up your work just by dragging that single folder to a backup disk.

As shown at top in Figure 4-27, the Where pop-up menu gives you direct access to some other places where you might want to save a newly created file. (The keystrokes for the most important folders work here, too—Shift-⌘-H for your Home folder, for example.)

In any case, when you save a file, the options in the Where pop-up menu have you covered 90 percent of the time. Most people work with a limited set of folders for active documents.

But when you want to save a new document into a new folder, or when you want to navigate to a folder that isn't listed in the Where pop-up menu, all is not lost. Click the ▾ button identified in Figure 4-27. The Save sheet expands into a very familiar sight: a miniature version of the Finder.

Tip: You can switch back and forth between the compact and expanded versions of this dialog box by pressing the undocumented shortcut ⌘-=.

There's your Sidebar, complete with access to the other computers on your network, and your iCloud Drive. There are the ◄/► buttons. There are your little buttons for icon, list, column, and (in most programs) even Cover Flow views.

Incredibly, you can even add new folders to the Favorites listing (drag them into the Sidebar here, either from the desktop, if it's visible, or right out of the dialog box in front of you) or remove them (drag them out of the Sidebar here). You can even drag files into folders here. The whole Save box is getting to be more Findery every year.

Tip: In column view, your first instinct should be to widen this window, making more columns available. Do so by carefully dragging either edge of the dialog box. The Mac remembers the size for this Save sheet independently in each program.

And in list view, how's this for a tip? If you right-click (or two-finger click) one of the column headings, like Name or Date Modified, you get a secret pop-up menu of column names: Last Opened, Size, Kind, Label, and so on. That's right: You can customize the list view within an Open or Save dialog box. You can sort, too, by clicking one of the column headings, just as at the desktop.

Most of the familiar Finder navigation shortcuts work here, too. For example, press the ◄ and ► keys to navigate the columns, or the ▲ and ▼ keys to highlight the disk and folder names *within* a column. Once you've highlighted a column, you can also type to select the first letters of disk or folder names.

In fact, you can use Quick Look (page 68) in the Open or Save dialog box, too. Highlight a file or folder in the list and tap the space bar to view it in a full-size window.

Tip: Even in the Save or Open dialog box, you can highlight an icon (or several) and then press ⌘-I. You switch back to the Finder, where the Get Info box is waiting with the date, size, and other details about the selected icons.

When you're finished playing around, open the folder where you want to save your newly created document and then click Save to store it there.

Tip: Here's one of the weirdest tricks yet. When the Open or Save dialog box is open before you, you can press Shift-⌘-period to make all your Mac's *hidden* files appear. (As a Unix-based outfit, OS X is crawling with these invisible files, which are of primary interest to technical types.) Press that keystroke again to re-hide the hidden files. Fun for geeks!

If you use a non-American number-formatting system (where one thousand is 1.000, for example), use Shift-⌘-comma instead.

Alternatively, click New Folder (or press the usual New Folder keystroke, Shift-⌘-N) to create a new folder *inside* the folder you're looking at.

You'll be asked to type the new name for the folder. After you've done so, click Create (or press Return). The new folder appears and opens before you, empty. You can now proceed with saving your new document into it, if you like.

The next time you save a new document, the Save sheet reappears in whatever condition you left it. That is, if you used column view the last time, it's still in column view. At any time, you can collapse it into simplified view, shown at top in Figure 4-27, by clicking the ▲ button to the right of the Save As pop-up menu.

Tip: For years, there's been a keyboard shortcut for the Don't Save button that appears when you close a new document without saving it: ⌘-D. But in many modern Apple programs, including TextEdit, Preview, Grab, Pages, and Keynote, the button says Delete instead of Don't Save. In those cases, press ⌘-Delete to "click" it instead of using the mouse.

Spotlight

The search box at the top of the Open or Save dialog box is a clone of the Finder's search box (Chapter 3). Press ⌘-F to make your insertion point jump there. Type a few letters of the name of the file or folder you're looking for, and up it pops, regardless of its actual hard-disk location.

Your savings: 5 minutes of burrowing through folders to find it, and several pages of reading about how to navigate the Save and Open boxes.

Insta-Jumping to a Folder Location

Whether you're using the mini-sheet or the expanded view, you can save yourself some folder-burrowing time by following this very weird tip: You can specify a folder location by dragging the icon of any folder or disk *from your desktop* directly into the Save or Open sheet. OS X instantly displays the contents of that folder or disk. This feature is totally undocumented—but well worth learning.

Tip: If, when the Save box is in its expanded condition, you click the name of an existing file, OS X thoughtfully copies the name of the clicked file into the Save As text box (which otherwise said "Untitled" or was blank).

This trick can save you time when you're saving a second document with a slightly modified name ("Oprah and Me: The Inside Story, Chapter 1" and then "Oprah and Me: The Inside Story, Chapter 2"). It's also useful if you want to replace the original file with the new one you're saving. Instead of having to type out the entire name of the file, you can just click it.

The File Format Pop-Up Menu

The Save dialog box in many programs offers a pop-up menu of file formats below the Save As box. Use this menu when preparing a document for use by somebody else—somebody whose computer doesn't have the same software. For example, if you've used a graphics program to prepare a photograph for use on the Web, this menu is where you specify JPEG format (the standard Web format for photos).

The Open File Dialog Box

The dialog box that appears when you choose File→Open is almost identical to the expanded Save File sheet. Because you encounter it only when you're opening an existing file, this dialog box lacks a Save button, a Tags box, a file name field, and so on.

Note: Furthermore, the Open dialog box gives you access only to disks, folders, and documents that you can actually open at this moment. For example, when you're using GarageBand, picture files show up dimmed.

But the Open box adds a special Sidebar category called Media (see Figure 4-28), which gives you direct access to all your photos, music, and movies. Apple figures you might want to import these items *into* a document you're working on.

Figure 4-28:
The Media Browser is built right into the Open box. You get miniature listings of your iTunes, iPhoto, and movie files right in the Sidebar, for convenience in importing them into (for example) Keynote, PowerPoint, or a Web design program.

Most of the other Save File dialog box controls are equally useful here. That handy Spotlight search bar is still there, only a ⌘-F away. Once again, you can begin your navigation by seeing what's on the desktop (press ⌘-D) or in your Home folder (Shift-⌘-H). Once again, you can find a folder or a disk by beginning your quest with the Sidebar and then navigate using icon, list, or column view. And once again, you can drag a folder, disk, or file icon off your desktop directly into the dialog box to specify where you want to look. (If you drag a *file* icon, you're shown the folder that contains it.)

When you've finally located the file you want to open, double-click it or highlight it (which you can do from the keyboard), and then press Return or ⌘-O.

In general, most people don't encounter the Open File dialog box nearly as often as the Save File dialog box. That's because the Mac offers many more convenient ways to *open* a file—double-clicking its icon in the Finder, choosing its name from →Recent Items, and so on—but only a single way to *save* a new file.

There are, however, some nifty techniques hiding in the Open dialog box; see Figure 4-29.

Figure 4-29:
There are some useful tricks in the Open and Save boxes that might not occur to you.

First, you can open or save a document directly to or from your iCloud Drive, of course (page 211). But certain anointed apps, like TextEdit and Pages, have special folders of their own on your iCloud Drive, named after themselves. When you save or open, you can choose either this special folder or your iCloud Drive in general (top).

Second, you can rename a document right in the Open box's list of files (bottom). Just right-click (or two-finger click) its name; from the shortcut menu, choose Rename.

Who knew?

Auto Save and Versions

In the beginning, Jobs created the Save command—because computers were slow.

Every time you saved, your work was interrupted for a few seconds (or a lot of seconds) as the very slow program on your very slow computer saved your work onto a very slow floppy disk.

And *that*, ladies and gentlemen, is why most programs still don't autosave: because the interruptions were just too annoying.

Apple figured it's high time the world revisit that scenario. Computers now have plenty of horsepower. They could be saving your work *continuously*, and you'd never even know it. Why shouldn't *all* programs save your work as you go, automatically and invisibly? As long as you also have the option to rewind and take your document in a different direction, what could possibly be the harm?

And so it is that, in OS X today, Auto Save is here. Unfortunately, it's available in only a few programs. You'll find it in Apple's showcase programs: Pages, Keynote, Numbers, Preview, and TextEdit.

In these programs, your document is saved every time there's even the tiniest pause in your typing or working—in the background. No progress bar, no interruption. If you quit or close the document without remembering to save, no problem: Your work will be there when you open the document again later.

Note: "But wait a minute," cry the masses—"I *like* being able to close a document without saving changes! Sometimes all I wanted to do was fool around, play 'what-if' games—and then close it without saving changes!"

Just for you, Apple offers a pair of sneaky little checkboxes in System Preferences→General. First, "Ask to keep changes when closing documents." If that's turned on, then when you close a document with unsaved changes, the Mac asks if you want to keep the edits, just as it does in all other programs.

But if you *quit* the program without saving, your changes *are* auto-preserved; Auto Save apps autosave your documents when you quit their programs, so you can pick up where you left off the next time. You can override that, too, if you like; turn on "Close windows when quitting an application," also in System Preferences→General. Now you'll get the "Save changes?" box when you quit the app with unsaved changes.

Versions

In those enlightened programs that work with Auto Save, there's a more complicated but more powerful feature at work: Versions. It's an invisible paper trail of every in-progress condition of your document—and you can return to any earlier version at any time. You can even return to an earlier version and copy just a *chunk* of it into the current version, which is great when one paragraph of your previous draft was gold but the rest was junk.

Here's what you need to know about the Versions world of document management:

- **All the version information is stored in the same original document file.** (It's not like there's a rat's nest of icons for each thing you're working on.) But when you send the document to somebody else (by email or network, for example), the Mac sends only the current version, stripping out all the history. Nobody will ever know how much you labored over your work (or how little).

Note: Behind the scenes, the various versions of each document are saved in an invisible folder on your hard drive called *.DocumentRevisions-V100*. But you probably guessed that.

- **OS X creates a new snapshot of your document once an hour.** You can also create new snapshots manually at even shorter intervals—by using the File→Save command (⌘-S), as you always have.

These snapshots, or *versions*, represent rewind points that you can return to later, even months or years after you first created the document. Thoughtfully enough, the Mac records, invisibly, only what's *changed* between versions, so your files don't get all big and bloated.

Note: All right, you don't have *total* time-rewinding control. OS X stores hourly versions for a day, daily versions for a month, and weekly versions for all previous months.

- **There's a secret menu in the title bar.** Point to the name of your document. In Auto Save–compatible files, a little ∨ appears in the title bar (Figure 4-30).

Figure 4-30:
Point to the title of your document to see this secret menu. It lets you rename the document, change its tags, or file it into a new folder, without ever leaving the window.

- **The Save As command is hidden in these programs.** It appears in the File menu only when you hold down the Option key.

Apple is hoping that you'll learn to use the new way. When you want to spin off a different version of a document—to experiment with taking it into a radical new direction, for example—choose File→Duplicate. Before your very eyes, a copy of the open window springs into existence. If the original was called "Kumquat Tarts," then the new one is called "Kumquat Tarts copy"—but that name is highlighted, selected, right in the title bar.

To leave your duplicated document in the same folder as the original, just type a new name and press Return. To file it in a different folder, choose File→Save. You get the standard Save dialog box, where you can choose a name and a folder for it.

Tip: You can also choose to move a document to a different folder later right there in the program. Just choose File→Move To and choose a new storage bin for it. (You can even store it in iCloud at this point; see page 211.) Or use the secret menu-bar menu shown in Figure 4-30.

Rewinding to an earlier version

The point of all of this, of course, is to make it easy to go back in time—to undo the mediocre work you've done, or to resurrect some genius work that you later deleted.

The quick way is to choose File→Revert to→Last Saved (or Last Opened). That command restores the document to the last snapshot version (or to the way it was when you most recently opened it, if no new versions have been created). That, of course, is nothing new; lots of programs have Revert to Saved commands that work similarly.

What's cool is that you can revert your document to *any* snapshot, even an ancient one from weeks or months ago.

To do that, choose File→Revert to→Browse All Versions.

After a moment, you see the stunning display shown in Figure 4-31. On the left, you see your document in its current condition. On the right, you see a stack of windows that represent all the different snapshots of your document, going back in time. (And behind it all, you see another sort of version: Apple's animated, starry version of the galaxy.)

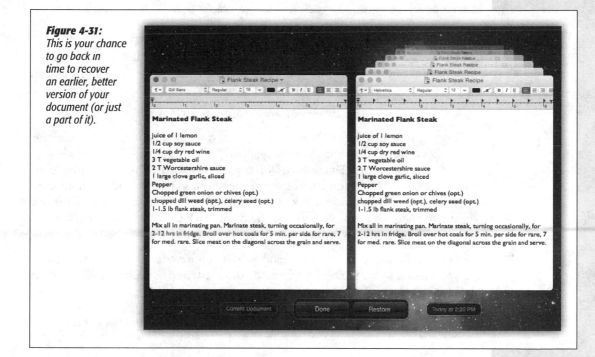

Figure 4-31:
This is your chance to go back in time to recover an earlier, better version of your document (or just a part of it).

You can have all kinds of productive fun in this version browser:

- **Compare the current version (on the left) with the next-most-recent one (on the right).** These are live documents, so you can scroll through them as necessary. If you decide to stick with the latest edition on the left, just click Done. You leave the starry version-history world and go back to editing.

- **Zoom back in time to inspect older versions (snapshots) of your document.** On the right side of the screen, you see earlier versions of the document—maybe even dozens of them, stretching back in time.

 You can click individual windows' title bars to see what's in them. You can also click or drag your cursor through the notches at the right side. It's like a time ruler that flies through the windows into the past. (As you go, the time/date stamp below the right-side window identifies where you are in time—that is, which version you're examining.)

- **Restore an earlier version.** If you finally find the incarnation of the document you consider superior to your current one, click Restore. You leave Starry Versionland and return to your document, which has now been rewound to its earlier condition.

 If you later decide you should not have gone back to that earlier version, no problem. Your later version—the one you started out with—is still in the version browser, too. So you can fast-forward to it, if necessary.

Tip: If you press Option, then the Restore button changes to say Restore a Copy. In other words, you'll create a previous-version duplicate of the document, without disturbing the current condition of the one you've just been working on.

- **Restore *part* of an earlier version.** Often, the current version of your work is *generally* good, but you really wish you could recover *one* magical sentence or paragraph or section—something you've since edited or deleted.

 You can do that in Starry Versionland, too, because Copy and Paste work here!

 Use the time ruler to find the earlier edition of your document, the one containing the good stuff. Then drag through the desired text or graphics in the window on the right, as shown in Figure 4-31. Now copy the highlighted material (either press ⌘-C or move your mouse to the top of the screen so that the menu bar appears, and choose Edit→Copy). Click in the *current* version of the document, the one at left, and now paste (⌘-V, or use the menu bar). Click Done to complete this astonishing act of salvation.

- **Delete a version.** Once you've found a draft you never want to see again, move your cursor to the top of the screen; the menu bar appears. Choose File→Revert To→Delete This Version.

Tip: If you press Option, the command says Delete Old Versions; it gets rid of *all* old versions of the file.

Revert

Even though Auto Save is constantly backing up your document, it also remembers how the file looked the moment you opened it. And you want to know what's crazy? It can revert to that condition even if you've been manually saving your work all along! Just choose File→Revert to→Last Saved (or Last Opened).

iCloud Drive

Truth is, "cloud" is an annoying buzzword. Most of the time, when people say "in the cloud," they mean "on the Internet"—a term that has served us perfectly well for years.

In any case, you can save your files online, into an online "hard drive" called iCloud Drive—Apple's version of the OneDrive (SkyDrive) in Windows. It makes your files available for opening or editing from any computer or gadget you use, including iPhones, iPads, and iPod Touches.

iCloud Drive Defined

iCloud Drive is like a magic folder. In the Finder, it's represented by an iCloud Drive icon in the Sidebar of every window.

Whatever you put into it appears, almost instantly, in the iCloud Drive folder on all your other machines: Macs, iPhones, iPads, and even Windows PCs. In fact, your files will even be available at iCloud.com, so you can grab them even when you're stranded on a desert island with nothing but somebody else's computer. (If this concept reminds you of the popular free program Dropbox, then you're very wise.) Figure 4-32 shows the idea.

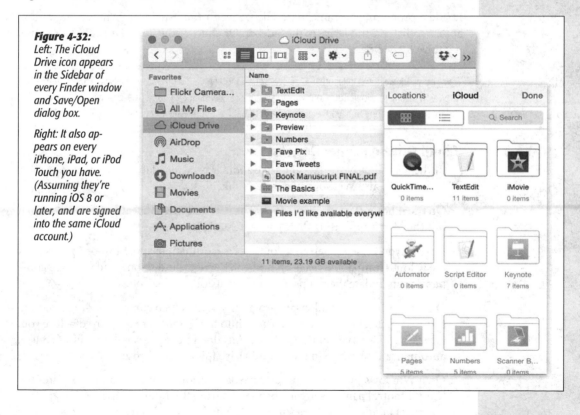

Figure 4-32:
Left: The iCloud Drive icon appears in the Sidebar of every Finder window and Save/Open dialog box.

Right: It also appears on every iPhone, iPad, or iPod Touch you have. (Assuming they're running iOS 8 or later, and are signed into the same iCloud account.)

This is an incredibly useful feature. No more emailing files to yourself. No more carrying things around on a flash drive. After working on some document at the office, you can go home and resume from right where you stopped; the same file is waiting for you, exactly as you left it.

iCloud Drive also makes a gloriously simple, effective backup disk. Anything you drag into this "folder" is instantly copied to all your devices and computers. And, as you know, the more copies that exist of something (and in the more locations), the better your backup. Even if your main Mac is stolen or burned to aluminum dust, your iCloud Drive files are safe.

Your drive holds 5 gigabytes of files for free. You can pay extra for more space: $1 a month for 20 gigs, $4 a month for 200 gigs, $10 for 500 gigs, or $20 a month for one terabyte (1,000 gigabytes).

Putting Files onto the iCloud Drive

On the Mac, you use the iCloud Drive just as you would a folder or a flash drive. Click its name in the Sidebar to see what's in there. Drag files into its window to copy them there. Make folders, add files, delete files, rename them—whatever. Any changes you make are reflected on your other Apple (and Windows) gadgets within seconds.

Inside a program, you can choose File→Save in the usual way. When the Save box appears, click iCloud Drive in the Sidebar. Or choose an iCloud Drive folder's name, if you've made one.

Tip: The window shown in Figure 4-32 shows your iCloud Drive documents and lets you open them, even when you're offline. How? Turns out your Mac stores a secret "local" copy. The changes you make won't update the online copy until you're online again, but at least you're never cut off from your own files.

iCloud Drive on Other Devices

So: If the iCloud Drive behaves just like a folder on your Mac, how does it appear on iPhones, iPads, and Windows computers? Like this:

- **On the iPhone, iPad, or iPod Touch.** The iCloud Drive is a feature of iOS 8 or later, but there's no app sitting there called iCloud Drive.

 Instead, you have to open an iCloud Drive–compatible app. Most of Apple's apps are iCloud-compatible (Pages, Numbers, Keynote, and so on), and software companies can update their apps to recognize iCloud Drive, too.

 Once you're in an iCloud-aware program, use the Open command—the first time an Open dialog box has ever been built into the iPhone. There, arrayed before you, are all the folders of your iCloud Drive. Any document you save here will, of course, automatically show up in the iCloud Drive folders of all your other machines.

- **On a Windows PC.** Your computer needs Windows 7 or later, and it requires the iCloud control panel. (You can download it from this book's "Missing CD" at *www.missingmanuals.com*.) It does just what you'd expect: It creates an iCloud Drive icon in your File Explorer windows, exactly as on the Mac.

Data: Typing, Dictating, Sharing & Backing Up

The original 1984 Mac didn't make jaws drop because of its speed, price, or sleek looks. What amazed people was the simplicity and elegance of the user interface. At some point in every Apple demo, the presenter copied a graphic drawn in a painting program (MacPaint) and pasted it directly into a word processor (MacWrite), where it appeared neatly nestled between typed paragraphs of text.

We take these examples of data input and data exchange for granted today. But, in those days, that little stunt struck people like a thunderbolt. After all, if this little computer let you copy and paste between different programs, it could probably do anything.

Today, the Mac is even more adept at helping you enter, move, and share your hard-won data. OS X offers several ways to move information within a single document, between documents, between programs, and even between the Mac and Windows computers. This chapter leads you through this broad cycle of data: from entering it with the mouse and keyboard, to moving it around, to backing it up.

Power Typing

Something strange has been quietly taking place at Apple: *Typing* has been getting a lot of attention.

It began when Apple created *system-wide* spelling and grammar checkers. For the first time in computer history, the *operating system* took over typos and grammos. You didn't have to maintain a separate spelling checker for each program you used. Now there's just one, and it works in most programs: TextEdit, Stickies, Messages, Mail, Calendar, Safari, Pages, iPhoto, iMovie, and so on. Add a word to the dictionary in one program, and it's available to all the others.

Today, there's much more. There's text substitution, where you type *addr* and the system types out "Irwina P. McGillicuddy, 1293 Eastport Lane, Harborvilletown, MA, 02552." (The same system autocorrects common typos like *teh* instead of *the*.) There's also a case-flipping feature that can change selected text to ALL CAPS, all lowercase, or First Letter Capped. Both of these features are available in most Apple programs and in any other programs that tap into OS X's built-in text-processing circuitry (although not, alas, Microsoft programs).

The OS X Spelling and Grammar Checker

Your Mac can give you live, interactive spelling and grammar checking, just as in Microsoft Word and other word processors. That is, misspelled words or badly written sentences or fragments get flagged with a dashed red underline (for grammar problems, a green underline) the moment you type them. Here's the crash course:

- **Check the spelling of one word:** Highlight the word. Choose Edit→Spelling and Grammar→Show Spelling and Grammar. The spell-check dialog box opens, with the proposed corrections visible.

- **Check spelling as you type.** Choose Edit→Spelling and Grammar→Check Spelling While Typing. (If Check Grammar With Spelling is turned on in the same submenu, you'll get a grammar check, too.)

Now, as you type, you'll see those red and green underlines on words the Mac thinks represent spelling or grammar mistakes. To fix one, right-click (or two-finger click) the underlined word, and proceed as shown in Figure 5-1.

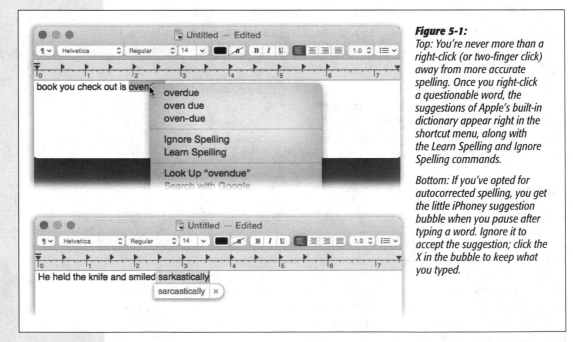

Figure 5-1:
Top: You're never more than a right-click (or two-finger click) away from more accurate spelling. Once you right-click a questionable word, the suggestions of Apple's built-in dictionary appear right in the shortcut menu, along with the Learn Spelling and Ignore Spelling commands.

Bottom: If you've opted for autocorrected spelling, you get the little iPhoney suggestion bubble when you pause after typing a word. Ignore it to accept the suggestion; click the X in the bubble to keep what you typed.

Tip: In TextEdit, the factory setting for error-underlining is On. To turn it off for all new documents, choose TextEdit→Preferences, click New Document, and then turn off "Check spelling as you type."

- **Check spelling after the document is finished.** Choose Edit→Spelling and Grammar→Show Spelling and Grammar (or press ⌘-:). The Spelling dialog box appears. The first error it spots appears in the top box, with the proposed corrections in the bottom one.

 If you like one of Apple's proposals, click it and then click Change. If the word was correct already (for example, the guy's last name really is Teh), then click Find Next ("Leave the word as I typed it"), Ignore ("It's OK everywhere in this document"), or Learn ("Never flag this word again").

 Handily enough, you can also click Define to look up a highlighted word (one of the spelling suggestions, for example) in the Mac's built-in Dictionary app. Also handily enough, the spelling checker is smart enough to maintain different spelling checkers (dictionaries) for different languages—and to recognize, within a single document, which language you're using!

- **Fix spelling as you type.** Note the difference. *Checking* your spelling just means "finding the misspelled words." *Fixing* means autocorrecting the errors as they occur, as you type. You might not even notice that it's happening!

 This most tantalizing option is found in Edit→Spelling and Grammar→Correct Spelling Automatically. And sure enough, when this option is turned on, common typos like *teh* and *frmo* and *dont* get fixed as you type; you don't have to do anything to make it happen.

Note: If you're typing slowly enough, you might see the suggestion bubble illustrated in Figure 5-1. That, of course, is a feature Apple brought to the Mac from the iPhone/iPad. It's saying, "Here's the word I *think* you meant—and if you just keep on typing, I'll go ahead and make the change I'm proposing. If you disagree, click on the X in the word bubble to make me shut up and leave what you typed, just as you typed it."

It's not perfect. It doesn't correct all errors (or even most of them). It occasionally even corrects a word you didn't mean to have corrected. (When it makes a mistake, hit ⌘-Z, the Undo command, to restore what you typed.) And sometimes it doesn't make the change until you're halfway through the sentence.

Still, though. Kind of cool.

Text Substitution (Abbreviation Expansion)

This useful feature autoreplaces *one* thing you type with something else. Why? Because it can do any of these things.

Insert the proper typographical symbols

For example, the Mac can insert attractive "curly quotes" automatically as you type "straight ones," or em dashes—like this—when you type two hyphens (--like that).

You can see the list of built-in substitutions—and create your own—in the System Preferences→Keyboard→Text tab, as shown in Figure 5-2.

Figure 5-2:
This is where you can manage OS X's typographic substitutions.

You can add all kinds of auto-typo corrections and even boilerplate text paragraphs.

Apple doesn't want to drive you nuts, though, so it makes sure *you're* sure you really want these swappings to take place. So you have to turn on each of these features manually, in each program. (These commands are available anywhere you do a *lot* of typing, like TextEdit, Mail, and Stickies. Look for the Edit→Substitutions submenu.)

- **Auto-quotes.** To make the quotes curlify themselves, choose Edit→Substitutions→ Smart Quotes, so that a checkmark appears.

Note: In the System Preferences→Keyboard→Text tab, you can specify which kind of fancy quotation mark you prefer: «this kind,» „this kind," or whatever. You international thing, you!

- **Auto-dashes.** To turn double hyphens into these (—) long dashes, choose Edit→ Substitutions→Smart Dashes, so that a checkmark appears.

- **Smart links.** There's also an option to create smart links, where any Web address you type turns into a blue, underlined, *clickable* link to a Web page. Turn on Edit→ Substitutions→Smart Links.

Tip: You can also choose Edit→Substitutions→Show Substitutions to make a floating pane appear, complete with on/off checkboxes for all these features.

Replace abbreviations with much longer phrases

You can program *addr* to type your entire return address. Create two-letter abbreviations for big legal or technical words you have to type a lot. Set up *goaway* to type out a polite rejection letter for use in email. And so on.

This feature has been in Microsoft Office forever (called AutoCorrect), and it's always been available as a shareware add-on (TypeIt4Me and TextExpander, for example). But now it's built right into most Apple programs, plus any others that use Apple's text-input plumbing.

You build your list of abbreviations in the System Preferences→Keyboard→Text tab, shown in Figure 5-2. See the list at left? Click the + to create a new row in the scrolling table of substitutions.

Click in the left column and type the abbreviation you want (for example, *addr)*. Click in the right column and type, or paste, the text you want OS X to type instead.

GEM IN THE ROUGH

Instant Accented Characters, Courtesy of the iPhone

It's been a problem since the dawn of computing: How do you produce accented characters—líké thêsë—on a keyboard with only 26 letter keys?

For most of computing history, the answer has been: You bring up some special palette on the screen, or you memorize key combinations. And yes, those options are still available in OS X.

But today, there's a new option, which Apple stole from its own iPhone software: Hold down the letter you want accented—*e,* for example. After a moment, you get a pop-up pane of possible accented versions. You can click the one you want, or, if you'd rather not lift your hands off the keyboard, you can type the corresponding number that appears in light gray beneath each letter.

This feature works in almost all programs, although there may be some where it doesn't...pop up.

Now, if you're the kind of person who needs accents from time to time, you're probably delighted with this new, clever way to get them. But if holding down a key produces

an accented character, that means holding down a key no longer *repeats* the key, right? It means you can no longer type, "You go, grrrrrrrrrrl!" or "rated XXXXXXXX" or "I love you SOOOOOOOOOOO much!" Right?

Right. A few characters that people routinely type lines of, like ***** and and ____, still repeat when you hold them down. But none of the 26 letter keys repeat anymore.

There is, fortunately, a quick and easy way to restore the old key-repeating behavior, if you're a "SOOOOO much" kind of person.

Open up Terminal (page 714). Type this one line, exactly as it appears here:

```
defaults write -g ApplePressAnd-
HoldEnabled -bool false
```

...and then press Return. Log out and back in.

Either way, you've just flipped off the switch for the accent picker. Now every key repeats, just as it always used to.

Tip: Don't be shy–you're not limited to short snippets. The replacement text can be pages long, which is handy if you're a lawyer and you build your contracts out of boilerplate chunks of canned text.

You can even create multiple paragraphs–but not by hitting Return when you want a new line; no, hitting Return means "I'm finished entering this text" and closes up the box. Instead, press Option-Return when you want a paragraph break.

That's it! Now, whenever you type one of the abbreviations you've set up, the Mac instantly replaces it with your substituted text.

And not just the Mac, either; your abbreviations auto-sync to iPhones, iPads, iPod Touches, and other Macs. If, that is, you've turned on System Preferences→iCloud→ Documents & Data.

(Remember, you can *turn off* the text-replacement feature in individual programs, if you like—TextEdit, Mail, Stickies, and so on. To do that, choose Edit→Substitutions→ Text Replacement, so that a checkmark disappears.)

Case Swapping

The final chunk in OS X's text-massaging tool chest is case swapping—that is, changing text you've already typed (or pasted) from ALL CAPS to lowercase or Just First Letters Capitalized.

This one's simple: Select the text you want to change, and then choose from the Edit→ Transformations submenu. Your options are Make Upper Case (all caps), Make Lower Case (no caps), and Capitalize (first letters, like a movie title).

Keep that in mind the next time some raving lunatic SENDS YOU AN EMAIL THAT WAS TYPED ENTIRELY WITH THE CAPS LOCK KEY DOWN.

Tip: Here's a sneaky one: You can double-tap a word with three fingers on your trackpad to get a pop-up dictionary and thesaurus definition. (That's a light double-*tap,* not a full double-*click*.) This trick doesn't work in all programs, and it requires you to turn it on in System Preferences→Trackpad→Point & Click. And it's a tad bit finicky.

But once you have it working, check it out: It also works in text documents you're examining in Quick Look!

Dictation

Dictation is built into the Mac, just as it is on iPhones and iPads (and Windows). You can speak to type text anywhere, into any program. (Behind the scenes, it's using the same Nuance recognition technology that powers Dragon Dictate.) You can blather away into an email, fire off a text message, or draft a memo without ever looking at the screen.

Now, before you get all excited, here are the necessary footnotes:

- Voice typing works best if there's not a lot of background noise. It works even better on Macs that have dual microphones, like MacBooks with Retina Displays;

those two mikes create a "beam array"—a directional alignment that helps them differentiate your voice from the background noise.

- Voice typing isn't always practical, since everybody around you can hear what you're doing.

- Voice typing isn't 100 percent accurate. Very often, you'll have to correct an error or two. (Your accuracy is much, much better when you wear a headset.)

On the other hand, how's this for some good news? You don't need an Internet connection to use voice typing; an option called Enhanced Dictation downloads the conversion software right to your Mac. And with Enhanced Dictation, you're not limited in how long your dictations can be. You can keep on blabbing away until you've dictated your entire dissertation or letter to Congress. And the words appear on the screen *as you speak*.

Unfortunately, Enhanced Dictation is not quite as accurate as non-Enhanced. So the following pages describe both the standard and the Enhanced features, in order.

All right—expectations set? Then here's how to type by speaking.

Dictation Step by Step

First, fire up some program where you can type. TextEdit, Mail, Word, whatever. Dictation works in any program.

Now tap the fn key twice. (You can also choose the Start Dictation command, which magically appears in almost every program's Edit menu. Or you can choose a different keystroke, as described in the box below.)

GEM IN THE ROUGH

The Mac Reads to You

Most Apple programs have a Start Speaking command built right in: Safari, Mail, TextEdit, Messages, Stickies, Pages, and so on. Just right-click (or two-finger click) inside a window full of text and, from the pop-up menu, choose Speech→Start Speaking. Your Mac can read your email or a Web article to you while you're getting dressed for the day.

But that's kid stuff. Truth is, the Mac can read almost anything you like: text you pass your cursor over, alert messages, menus, and any text document in any program. To configure the Mac's voice, revisit the Dictation & Speech pane of System Preferences. Click the Text to Speech tab at the top of the

window. Specify which of the Mac's voices you want your computer to use, as well as how fast it should speak. (Some of the voices—like Alex, Jill, Samantha, and Tom—sound scarily like professional human voice-over artists.)

The first time you turn on "Speak selected text," you specify a keystroke. Choose one that doesn't conflict with the program you're using, like Control-T. Now highlight some text in any program and press the keystroke. The Mac reads it aloud immediately. To stop, press the same keystroke again.

And be glad you were alive to see the day.

Note: The first time you trigger dictation, the Mac asks for confirmation that you do, indeed, want to turn on dictation. It offers to turn on Enhanced Dictation, too (page 219).

And it warns you that proceeding means that the Mac will send the names in your Contacts app to Apple, so that you'll be able to say things like "Dear Mr. Szvredyk" and get a correct transcription. If that prospect unnerves you—if you think that it means that some Apple or Nuance employee will wind up reading the list of names in your personal Rolodex—then you shouldn't proceed.

See the tiny microphone button that appears next to the insertion point (Figure 5-3, top)? When it appears, you hear a single xylophone note. Say what you have to say. You don't have to speak slowly, loudly, or weirdly; speak normally.

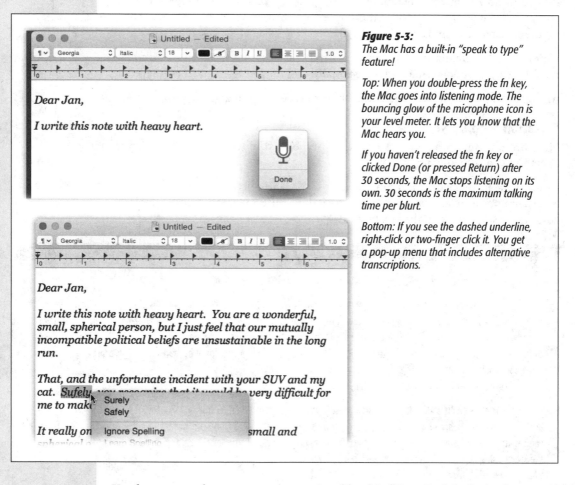

Figure 5-3:
The Mac has a built-in "speak to type" feature!

Top: When you double-press the fn key, the Mac goes into listening mode. The bouncing glow of the microphone icon is your level meter. It lets you know that the Mac hears you.

If you haven't released the fn key or clicked Done (or pressed Return) after 30 seconds, the Mac stops listening on its own. 30 seconds is the maximum talking time per blurt.

Bottom: If you see the dashed underline, right-click or two-finger click it. You get a pop-up menu that includes alternative transcriptions.

You have to speak your own punctuation, like this: "Dear Dad (colon): Please send money (dash)—as much as you can (comma), please (period)." The table at the end of this section describes all the punctuation symbols you can dictate.

After you finish speaking, click Done or press Return.

Tip: Here's a shortcut. You can also *hold down the fn key* on the second tap; do your speaking; and then release the key when you're done. In other words, you can use it like a push-to-talk button on a walkie-talkie. That saves you the final press of the Return key.

The Mac plays another xylophone note—higher, this time—and transmits the audio data to distant computers. They analyze your speech and transmit the resulting typed-out text back to your screen. (During this time, three blinking purple dots occupy the text area where you dictated. You can click Cancel if you're getting impatient.) The transcribed text appears all at once, in a big blob.

If the transcription contains errors, you can click to edit them, exactly as you would fix an error in something you typed. Better yet, if the Mac *knows* it made errors, it underlines them, and you can often fix them with a quick click (Figure 5-3, bottom). Or, if the whole thing is a mess, you can press ⌘-Z, the universal keystroke for Undo.

Usually, you'll find the accuracy pretty darned good, considering you didn't have to train the software to recognize your voice. You'll also find that the accuracy is better when you dictate complete sentences, and long words fare better than short ones.

Punctuation

Here's a handy table that shows you what punctuation you can say, and how to say it.

Say this:	To get this:	For example, saying this:	Types this:
"period" or "full stop"	. [space and capital letter afterward]	"Best (period) date (period) ever (period)"	Best. Date. Ever.
"dot" or "point"	. [no space afterward]	"My email is frank (dot) smith (at sign) gmail (dot) com"	My email is frank. smith@gmail.com
"comma," "semicolon," "colon"	, ; :	"Mom (comma) hear me (colon) I'm dizzy (semicolon) tired"	Mom, hear me: I'm dizzy; tired
"question mark," "exclamation point"	? ! [space and capital letter afterward]	"Ellen (question mark) Hi (exclamation point)"	Ellen? Hi!
"inverted question mark," "inverted exclamation point"	¿ ¡	"(inverted question mark) Que paso (question mark) "	¿Que paso?
"ellipsis" or "dot dot dot"	…	"Just one (ellipsis) more (ellipsis) step (ellipsis)"	Just one… more… step…
"space bar"	[a space, especially when a hyphen would normally appear]	"He rode the merry (space bar) go (space bar) round"	He rode the merry go round

Say this:	To get this:	For example, saying this:	Types this:
"open paren" then "close paren" (or "open bracket/close bracket," or "open brace/close brace")	() or [] or { }	"Then she (open paren) the doctor (close paren) gasped"	Then she (the doctor) gasped
"new line"	[a press of the Return key]	"milk (new line) bread (new line) Cheez Whiz"	milk bread Cheez Whiz
"new paragraph"	[two presses of the Return key]	"autumn leaves (new paragraph) softly falling"	autumn leaves softly falling
"quote," then "unquote"	" "	Her perfume screamed (quote) available (unquote)	Her perfume screamed "available"
"numeral"	[writes the following number as a digit instead spelling it out]	"Next week she turns (numeral) eight"	Next week she turns 8
"asterisk," "plus sign," "minus sign," "equals sign"	*, +, −, =	"numeral eight (asterisk) two (plus sign) one (minus sign) three (equals sign) fourteen"	8*2+1−3=14
"ampersand," "dash"	&, −	"Barry (ampersand) David (dash) the best (exclamation point)"	Barry & David—the best!
"hyphen"	- [without spaces]	"Don't give me that holier (hyphen) than (hyphen) thou attitude"	Don't give me that holier-than-thou attitude
"backquote"	'	"Back in (backquote) (numeral) fifty-two"	back in '52
"smiley," "frowny," "winky" (or "smiley face," "frowny face," "winky face")	:-) :-(;-)	"I think you know where I'm going with this (winky face)"	I think you know where I'm going with this ;-)

You can also say "percent sign" (%), "at sign" (@), "dollar sign" ($), "cent sign" (¢), "euro sign" (€), "yen sign" (¥), "pounds sterling sign" (£), "section sign" (§), "copyright sign" (©), "registered sign" (®), "trademark sign" (™), "greater-than sign" or "less-than sign" (> or <), "degree sign" (°), "caret" (^), "tilde" (~), "vertical bar" (|), and "pound sign" (#).

Capitalization

The software automatically capitalizes the first new word after a period, question mark, or exclamation point. But you can also force it to capitalize words you're dictating by saying "cap" right before the word, like this: "Dear (cap) Mom, I've run away to join (cap) The (cap) Circus (comma), a nonprofit cooperative for runaway jugglers."

Here's another table—this one shows the other commands for capitalization, plus spacing and spelling commands.

Say this:	To get this:	For example, saying this:	Types this:
"cap" or "capital"	Capitalize the next word	"Give me the (cap) works"	Give me the Works
"caps on," then "caps off"	Capitalize the first letter of every word	"Next week, (caps on) the new england chicken cooperative (caps off) will hire me"	Next week, The New England Chicken Cooperative will hire me
"all caps," then "all caps off"	Capitalize everything	"So (all caps on) please please (all caps off) don't tell anyone"	So PLEASE PLEASE don't tell anyone
"all caps"	Type just the next word in all caps	"We (all caps) really don't belong here"	We REALLY don't belong here
"no caps"	Type the next word in lowercase	"see you in (no caps) Texas"	see you in texas
"no caps on," then "no caps off"	Prevents any capital letters	"I'll ask (no caps on) Santa Claus (no caps off)"	I'll ask santa claus
"no space"	Runs the next two words together	"Try new mega (no space) berry flavor"	Try new megaberry flavor
"no space on," then "no space off"	Eliminates all spaces	"(No space on) I can't believe you ate all that (no space off) (comma) she said excitedly"	Ican'tbelieveyou ateallthat, she said excitedly
[alphabet letters]	Types the letters out, though usually not very accurately	"The stock symbol is A P P L"	The stock symbol is APPL

You don't always have to dictate these formatting commands, by the way. The Mac automatically inserts hyphens into phone numbers (you say, "2125561000," and it types "212-556-1000"); formats two-line street addresses without your having to say "New line" before the city; handles prices automatically ("six dollars and thirty-two cents" becomes "$6.32"). It formats dates and Web addresses well, too; you can even use the nerdy shortcut "dub-dub-dub" when you want the "www" part of a Web address.

The Mac recognizes email addresses, too, as long as you remember to say "at sign" at the right spot. You'd say, "harold (underscore) beanfield (at sign) gmail (dot) com" to get harold_beanfield@gmail.com.

Enhanced Dictation

In Enhanced Dictation mode, you can dictate without an Internet connection. You're not limited to 30-second utterances, and the words appear on the screen as you speak them. The only downside: The accuracy isn't as good as non-Enhanced Dictation.

If, after you've searched your soul, you decide to give Enhanced a try, open System Preferences→Dictation & Speech. Turn on Use Enhanced Dictation. (Or accept Yosemite's invitation to turn it on when you first attempt to dictate. If you say yes, you're treated to a 785-megabyte download.)

When the downloading is over, everything about dictation works just as described on the previous pages, except you can dictate offline, you can dictate forever, and the accuracy—well, you know.

Note: You'll also discover that your words fly onto the screen as you speak them. But as you speak more of a sentence, and the Mac uses context clues to figure out what you intended, you'll see words flip around and revise themselves. That, too, is part of Enhanced, and it's all in the name of giving you the best possible transcription.

Speech Settings

In System Preferences→Dictation & Speech, you can fiddle with several settings:

- **On/Off.** If you turn Dictation off, you can no longer dictate to type; the little microphone button won't appear.

- **Use Enhanced Dictation.** As described above.

- **Language.** What language and accent do you have? The options here include English in three accents—American, British, and Australian—plus (if you choose Add Language) German, Italian, Japanese, Korean, Spanish, Chinese, and French. Apple says it will add more languages over time.

- **Shortcut.** Here's where you specify what key you want to double-tap in order to dictate. From this pop-up menu, you can choose the fn key (on laptops) or the right or left ⌘ key—or you can choose Customize to make up any keystroke you want. The Shortcut box goes empty; press a key combination you prefer (Control-S, for example).

- **About Dictation and Privacy.** Here you can read more about that business of your utterances and address-book names being transmitted to Apple.

Note: You can also issue spoken commands to your Mac—"Open Safari," for example, or "Select the last paragraph" and "Bold that." This feature is hiding in System Preferences→Accessibility. For details, see page 579.

The Many Languages of OS X Text

Apple has always taken pride in its language-friendliness. You can shift from language to language on the fly, as you type, even in midsentence—without reinstalling the operating system or even restarting the computer.

OS X's facility with language, though, goes the extra overseas mile. It lets you type vertical Japanese and Chinese text; includes fonts for 20 more non-Roman alphabets (including the ones you need for five Indian languages); offers "filtering by tones, ordering and filtering by radical or stroke count, and improved pinyin-han conversion accuracy" (you have to be a Chinese speaker to appreciate those tweaks); and much more.

Figure 5-4:
Top: You can flip your copy of OS X into any of about 165 languages. Click the + button to see them all—and add them to the list of Preferred Languages. You're asked, when you add a language, if you want it to be the Mac's primary language.

Bottom: Here's what your Mac looks like running in Dutch. Actually understanding Dutch would be useful at a time like this—but even if you don't, it can't help but brighten up your workday to choose commands like Spraakfunctie or Knip.

First, tell your Mac which languages you'd like to have available. Open System Preferences→Language & Region. You see a listing of the languages the Mac can switch into, in the corresponding languages—Français, Español, and so on. Just drag one of the languages to the top of the list to select it as your primary language, as shown in Figure 5-4.

Note: You can mix English with right-to-left languages like Hebrew and Arabic. There's even a split-cursor option that makes the pointer flip directions at the boundary between right-to-left and left-to-right text.

Now launch Safari, TextEdit, Mail, or Stickies. Every menu, button, and dialog box is now in the new language you selected! If you log out and back in (or restart) at this point, the entire Finder will be in the new language, too.

Note: Programs differ widely in their "language awareness." If you use a language beyond the 33 in the top part of the list, adding it (with the Edit List button) ensures that its relevant features will be available in all programs. (You may still have to add additional language software to make your menus and dialog boxes change.)

Formats

Of course, if you're *really* French (for example), you'll also want to make some formatting changes on the System Preferences→Language & Region pane.

First, choose your French-speaking country from the Region pop-up menu, so that time and date formats, number punctuation, and currency symbols also conform to your local customs.

For example, the decimal and thousands separator characters for displaying large numbers differ from country to country. (The number 25,600.99, for example, would be written as "25 600,99" in France, and as "25.600,99" in Spain.) And what appears to an American to be July 4 (the notation "7/4"), to a European indicates April 7.

Similarly, for Calendar purposes, you'll want to specify what you consider to be the first day of the week and which calendar style you observe. (Hint: If you're reading this book, it's probably Gregorian.)

Choose the French *keyboard layout* from the Input Sources tab, as explained next.

Input Sources

While the Mac can display many different languages, *typing* in those languages is another matter. The symbols you use when you're typing in Swedish aren't the same as when you're typing in English. Apple solved this problem by creating different keyboard layouts, one for each language. (Apple calls them *input sources*, because not all of them technically use a keyboard.) Each rearranges the letters that appear when you press the keys. For example, when you use the Swedish layout and press the semicolon key, you don't get a semicolon (;)—you get an ö.

Apple even includes the famous Dvorak layout and the not-very-famous Colemak layout. Both are scientific rearrangements of the standard layout that put the most common letters directly under your fingertips on the home row. Fans of the Dvorak layout, and the more modern Colemak layout, claim greater accuracy, better speed, and less fatigue.

To set up an input source, see Figure 5-5.

Tip: The icon of the Input menulet changes. It becomes a colorful flag to show the currently selected language.

Figure 5-5:
Bottom: Click the + button to view a list of keyboard layouts; choose one to add to this list.

When you do so, "Show input menu in menu bar" turns on. That option puts a tiny flag in your menu bar (top)—a keyboard menulet that lets you switch layouts just by choosing their names.

If you turn on "Automatically switch to a document's input source," then each document stays put with the keyboard you've been using in it, even if you've switched to a different input source in other documents.

The Character Viewer

There you are, two-thirds of the way through your local matchmaker newsletter, when it hits you that you need a heart symbol. Right now.

You can't help wishing there were an easy way to find those special symbols that hide among your fonts—fancy brackets, math symbols, special stars and asterisks, and so on.

The Keyboard Viewer, described next, can generate a few of them. But to see the full range of symbols available, you need the Character Viewer. To make it appear, choose Edit→Special Characters.

Most programs have this command. If yours doesn't, here's the long way: Open System Preferences→Keyboard→Input Sources tab, and then turn on "Show Input menu in menu bar." You've just installed the Keyboard menulet.

Then, next time you're word processing or doing page layout, choose Show Character Viewer from this menu. The resulting window (Figure 5-6, top) rounds up all symbols from all your fonts at once. To find a particular symbol, click the "by Category" tab, and then click the various category headings: Arrows, Bullets/Stars, Math Symbols, and so on.

Figure 5-6:
Top: You can preview variations of the same symbol in the Font Variation pane. You can also use the search box to find a symbol by name: "heart" or "yen" or "asterisk," for example. And if you click the ✿ menu in the top left, you can choose Customize List—and you'll have access to a staggering array of even more symbol categories, including wacky symbols from other alphabets.

Bottom: How do you make a π? Keyboard Viewer reveals the answer. When you press the Option key, the Keyboard Viewer shows that the pi character is mapped to the P key. To insert the symbol into an open document, just click it in the Keyboard Viewer window.

When you find the symbol you want, double-click it. The correct symbol pops into your document. (If not, you may get the correct character in the wrong font. In that case, change the font of the inserted character manually. To find out what font it came from, click the symbol in the Font Variation pane to see the font name.)

Keyboard Viewer

Keyboard Viewer consists of a single window containing a tiny onscreen keyboard (Figure 5-6, bottom). When you hold down any of the modifier keys on your keyboard (like ⌘, Option, Shift, or Control), you can see exactly which keys produce which characters. The point, of course, is to help you learn which keys to press when you need special symbols or non-English characters, such as © or ñ, in each keyboard layout.

Note: Keyboard Viewer shows only the symbols you can produce by typing keystrokes. A font may contain thousands of other characters that can't actually be typed; the Character Viewer is the only way to access these other symbols.

It's a great tool—if you can find it. The secret is to open System Preferences→Keyboard→Keyboard tab. Then turn on "Show Keyboard and Character Viewers in menu Bar." You open the Keyboard Viewer by choosing its name from the new menulet that appears.

GEM IN THE ROUGH

Draw Those Chinese Characters

Apple has made a huge push to appeal to Chinese Mac fans. There's a Chinese dictionary and text input; eight Chinese fonts; compatibility with popular Chinese mail services like QQ, 163, and 126; built-in Safari searching using Baidu (like a Chinese Google); and Share button posting directly to Youku Tudou (like YouTube) and Weibo (a microblogging service).

If you want to write in Chinese, you can draw the characters you want, right on your laptop's trackpad.

To set this up, open the System Preferences→Keyboard→Input Sources pane. Turn on Chinese–Simplified (or Chinese–Traditional), choose the Chinese writing system you prefer, and then turn on Trackpad Handwriting.

Then, when you're actually writing, use the flag (Input) menulet to choose Show Trackpad Handwriting (or press

Shift-Control-space bar) to make the writing pane appear, as shown here.

The trick is to understand that the pane is a full map of your trackpad. Draw your character by dragging across the trackpad; white lines appear as you go.

On both sides of the onscreen pane, you see the Mac's interpretations of your character; to choose one, tap the corresponding spot on the outside edges of your actual trackpad. (Or, to backspace–delete your most recent line–tap the upper-left corner of your trackpad.) The Mac drops the character into your document.

Press Shift-Control-space bar again to hide the pane, or press Esc to exit it momentarily, and shake your head in wonder.

To see the effect of pressing the modifier keys, either click the onscreen keys or press them on your actual keyboard. The corresponding keys on the onscreen keyboard light up as they're pressed.

Tip: You're not stuck viewing the characters in a 12-point font size—a good thing, because some of them are hard to read when displayed that small. You can make the Keyboard Viewer window nearly fill the screen by clicking its Zoom button. That will magnify the Keyboard Viewer window and its font size.

Data Detectors

Here's a cool step-saver, something no other operating system offers—a little something Apple likes to call *data detectors*.

In short, Mac programs like Mail and TextEdit can recognize commonly used bits of information that may appear in your text: a physical address, a phone number, a date and time, and so on. With one quick click, you can send that information into the appropriate program, like Calendar, Contacts, or your Web browser (for looking up an address on a map).

Here's how it works: When you spot a name, address, date, or time, point to it without clicking. A dotted rectangle appears around it. Right-click (or two-finger click) inside the rectangle, or click the ▾ at the right side.

A shortcut menu appears. Its contents vary depending on what you're pointing to:

- **A mailing address.** You can choose Show Address in Google Maps from the shortcut menu; your Web browser opens automatically and shows you that address on a Google map.

 Alternatively, you can choose Create New Contact (to add a Contacts entry for this address) or Add to Existing Contact (if the *person* is in your address book—just not the *address*). Like magic, a little editing box sprouts out of the data-detected rectangle, prefilled with the information from the message, so that you can approve it.

GEM IN THE ROUGH

Styled Text

When you copy text from, for example, Microsoft Word, and then paste it into another program, such as Mail, you may be pleasantly surprised to note that the formatting of that text—bold, italic, font (size, color, and so on)—appears intact in Mail. You're witnessing one of the Mac's most useful but underpublicized features: its handling of styled text on the Clipboard.

Almost all Mac programs transfer the formatting along with the copied text. Every time you paste formatted text copied from one of these programs, the pasted material appears with the same typographical characteristics it had in the original program. Over time, this tiny timesaver spares us years' worth of cumulative reformatting effort—yet another tiny favor the noble Macintosh does mankind.

- **A date and time.** When you click the ▾, you get the amazing pop-up menu shown in Figure 5-7. It shows you the actual Calendar day view where Yosemite is proposing adding the appointment. The logic of this feature is overwhelming; after all, when someone emails you to ask if you're free for drinks next Thursday at 10, what's the first thing you usually want to do? Check your calendar, of course.

Tip: If, while working in Calendar, you ever forget where this event came from, double-click it. In the Info balloon, you'll see a link that takes you right back to the original Mail message that started it all.

Figure 5-7:
When a data detector detects a date and time, it can suggest an appointment on your calendar automatically. It even shows you the proposed new Calendar entry (in dotted lines), in context with all your existing appointments, so you'll know whether to accept or decline the new appointment. If everything looks good, click Add to Calendar. Or, if Mail's parsing of the appointment needs a little tweaking, click Edit; the box expands so that you can edit the details.

- **A phone number.** As with mailing addresses, the shortcut menu here offers you things like Create New Contact and Add to Existing Contact. The third one, Large Type, is great when you want to call this person right now—it displays the phone number in *huge* type, filling your screen, so you can see it from across your mansion.

- **A flight number.** When you highlight flight information (for example, "AA 152"), the data detector offers a Show Flight Information command. It opens the Flights widget of Dashboard so you can see the flight's departure time, arrival time, and other details. It works only if the airline is represented as a two-letter code.

- **A Web address.** When you click the ▾ next to a URL (like *www.nytimes.com*), you get a pop-up balloon that contains the *actual Web page!* You get a quick look, without even having to leave your email message.

- **A package tracking number.** When you send a package using a service like FedEx, UPS, or the U.S. Postal Service, you usually get a confirmation email. A data detector can recognize such numbers and, when you click the ▾, offer you a Track Shipment command. Choosing it displays a pop-up window right there at your cursor, showing the courier company's tracking page for that package, and thereby letting you know exactly where your package is right now.

Tip: In the unlikely event that you don't actually care for data detectors and would rather not see those dotted lines and ▾ buttons, you can shut down the whole feature. To do that, open Terminal (page 714). Carefully type this command, and then press Return:

```
defaults write com.apple.mail DisableDataDetectors YES
```

You can always turn them back on again by repeating that step—and substituting *NO* for the final word.

Moving Data Between Documents

You can't paste a picture into your Web browser, and you can't paste MIDI music information into your word processor. But you can put graphics into your word processor, paste movies into your database, insert text into Photoshop, and combine a surprising variety of seemingly dissimilar kinds of data.

Cut, Copy, and Paste

The original copy-and-paste procedure of 1984—putting a graphic into a word processor—has come a long way. Most people have learned to trigger the Cut, Copy, and Paste commands from the keyboard and without even thinking. Here's how it works:

1. **Highlight some material in a document.**

 Drag through some text in a word processor, for example, or highlight graphic, music, movie, database, or spreadsheet information.

2. **Use the Edit→Cut or Edit→Copy command.**

 Or press the keyboard shortcuts ⌘-X (for Cut—think of the X as a pair of scissors) or ⌘-C (for Copy). The Mac memorizes the highlighted material, socking it away on an invisible storage pad called the Clipboard. If you chose Copy, nothing visible happens. If you chose Cut, the highlighted material disappears.

3. **Click to indicate where you want the material to reappear.**

 This may entail switching to a different program, a different document, or simply a different place in the same document.

4. **Choose the Edit→Paste command (⌘-V).**

 The copy of the material you had originally highlighted now appears at your insertion point—*if* you're pasting into a program that can accept that kind of information. (You won't have much luck pasting, say, a block of spreadsheet numbers into World of Warcraft.)

The most recently cut or copied material remains on your Clipboard even after you paste, making it possible to paste the same blob repeatedly. On the other hand, whenever you next copy or cut something, whatever was already on the Clipboard is lost forever.

Drag-and-Drop

As useful and popular as it is, the Copy/Paste routine doesn't win any awards for speed. After all, it requires four steps. In many cases, you can replace that routine with the far more direct (and enjoyable) drag-and-drop method. Figure 5-8 illustrates how this works.

Note: Most Cocoa programs (page 150) require you to press the mouse button for a split second before beginning to drag.

Virtually every Apple program works with the drag-and-drop technique, including TextEdit, Stickies, Mail, QuickTime Player, Preview, iMovie, iPhoto, and System Information, not to mention other popular programs like Microsoft applications, Web browsers, and so on.

When to use drag-and-drop

As shown in Figure 5-8, drag-and-drop is ideal for transferring material between windows or between programs—from a Web page into Photoshop, for example. It's especially useful when you've already copied something valuable to your Clipboard, since drag-and-drop doesn't involve (and doesn't erase) the Clipboard.

Its most popular use, however, is rearranging text within a single document. In Word or Pages, for example, you can rearrange entire sections, paragraphs, sentences, or even individual letters, just by dragging them—a wonderfully efficient editing technique.

Figure 5-8:
To use drag-and-drop, highlight some material. Click anywhere in the highlighted area and press the mouse button for about half a second. Now, with the button still pressed, drag to another place in the document, into a different window, or into a different application. As your cursor enters the target window, a shaded outline appears inside the window's boundaries–the Mac's way of letting you know it understands your intention. When you release the mouse, the highlighted material appears instantly in its new location.

Tip: When you use drag-and-drop to move text within a document, the Mac moves the highlighted text, deleting the highlighted material from its original location. If you press Option as you drag, however, you make a copy of the highlighted text.

Drag-and-drop to the desktop

You can also use drag-and-drop in the one program you use every single day: the Finder itself. As shown in Figure 5-9, you can drag text, graphics, sounds, and even movie clips out of your document windows and directly onto the desktop. Graphics and movies generally turn into ordinary graphic or movie files; text becomes an icon called a *clipping file*.

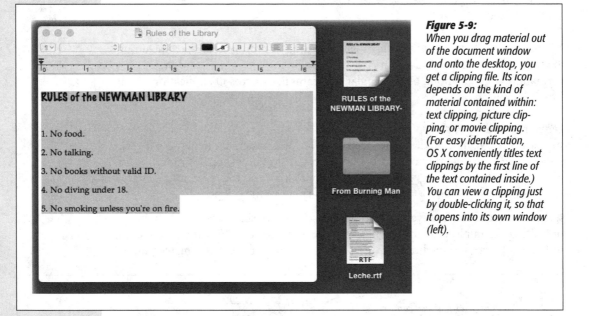

Figure 5-9:
When you drag material out of the document window and onto the desktop, you get a clipping file. Its icon depends on the kind of material contained within: text clipping, picture clipping, or movie clipping. (For easy identification, OS X conveniently titles text clippings by the first line of the text contained inside.) You can view a clipping just by double-clicking it, so that it opens into its own window (left).

Later, you can examine a clipping's contents using Quick Look—just select its icon and then tap the space bar. Or you can double-click a clipping file and then select a portion of the text to copy.

When you drag a clipping from your desktop *back* into an application window, the material in that clipping reappears. Drag-and-drop, in other words, lets you treat your desktop itself as a giant, computer-wide pasteboard—an area where you can temporarily stash pieces of text or graphics as you work.

Tip: When the material you drag to the desktop contains nothing but an Internet address, such as an email address or a Web page URL, it gets a special icon and a special function: an Internet location file. You can stash it in a folder, double-click it for quick access, and so on.

Export/Import

When it comes to transferring large chunks of information—especially address books, spreadsheet cells, and database records—from one program to another, none of the data-transfer methods described so far in this chapter does the trick. For these purposes, use the Export and Import commands found in the File menu of almost every database, spreadsheet, email, and address-book program. (In some programs, the Save As command serves this function.)

These Export/Import commands aren't part of OS X, so the manuals (if any) of the applications in question should be your source for instructions. For now, however, the power and convenience of this feature are worth noting—it means that your four years' worth of collected addresses in, say, some old email program can find their way into a newer program, like Contacts, in a matter of minutes.

Exchanging Data with Other Macs

Considering how many ways there are to move files back and forth between Macs, it seems almost comical that anybody complained when Apple discontinued built-in floppy disk drives. Here's a catalog of the different ways you can move your files from one computer to another, including some that might not have occurred to you.

By Network

You can shoot a file to another Mac with a single drag-and-drop operation, thanks to AirDrop (536) or another file-sharing method. You can open files from the other drives, copy stuff back and forth—anything you would do with your own disk. Step-by-step instructions are in Chapter 16.

Best for files of any size, when the computers are in the same building.

Tip: And for $0, you can create an *ad hoc* network, meaning a tiny wireless network between just two computers (or a handful). Great when you're in the car somewhere, or in the airport waiting lounge, or a hotel lobby, and someone says, "Hey, can I have a copy of that?" Details are on 534.

By Email

High on convenience; computers can be in different countries.

And the built-in Mail program can cheerfully send huge file attachments to anyone, no matter what kind of computer she uses. See page 387 for details.

Using Dropbox

Dropbox is a free service, almost universally adored, that lets you create synchronized folders on multiple computers. Add a file to, say, your New Projects folder on your home Mac, and it appears instantly in the matching folder on your Windows folder at work.

You can use Dropbox to share folders with other people, too. Just drag a new file into a shared folder, and marvel as your associates get an auto-generated email message

letting them know that you've posted a new document. They open the shared folder on their *own* desktops, and there are your files, waiting. (Details are at *www.dropbox. com/help/19.*)

The great thing about services like Dropbox is that you don't have to worry about the small file-size limits imposed by email. (There's a 2-gigabyte storage limit on Dropbox's free accounts, but you can upgrade to larger storage capacities for a fee; you also get more storage granted when you refer a friend to Dropbox.)

Via iCloud Drive

In many ways, Yosemite's new iCloud Drive is identical to Dropbox. It, too, acts as a magic folder that reproduces itself on as many Macs as you own.

It's a fantastic way to transfer big files among your own computers. But because it requires that each machine be logged into the same iCloud account, it's not so great for sending big files to *other* people.

By CD or DVD

You can always burn your files onto a blank CD or DVD and then carry or mail it to the recipient. Awfully slow and clumsy, but it does result in a safety copy of whatever you're transferring.

FireWire Disk Mode/Thunderbolt Disk Mode (Target Disk Mode)

FireWire Disk Mode/Thunderbolt Disk Mode is a brilliant but little-known Macintosh-only feature that lets you turn one Mac into an external hard drive for another. This is by far the fastest method yet for transferring a lot of data—even faster than copying files over a network. It's extremely useful in any of these situations:

- **You're traveling with a laptop.** You want to copy your life onto it from your main Mac, including your entire 5 GB email folder and project files, before taking it on a trip, and then unload it when you return.

- **You have a new Mac.** You want to copy everything off the old one, without having to wait all night.

- **One Mac won't start up.** You want to repair it, using another Mac as a "front end."

Unfortunately, not all Macs have a FireWire or Thunderbolt jack. If you're among the lucky, though, you can use the following trick. (In the following steps, suppose your main Mac is an iMac and you want to use a MacBook as an external hard drive for it.)

1. **Connect the FireWire (Thunderbolt) jacks of both computers with a cable.**

 If you have an older Mac with a FireWire 400 jack, you need a *6-pin* FireWire cable—*not* the one that connects a camcorder to a Mac. The one you need has the same large connector on both ends.

 Modern Macs have Apple's FireWire 800 jacks, which require a 9-pin FireWire cable (and give you much greater speed). If only one Mac has a FireWire 800 jack, then use that computer's traditional FireWire 400 connector instead. Otherwise,

you need either a special FireWire 800–to–FireWire 400 cable, or the 400-to-800 adapter that came with your Mac.

2. **On the MacBook, choose →System Preferences. Click Startup Disk.**

 The Startup Disk pane opens.

3. **Click Target Disk Mode. In the confirmation box, click Restart.**

 The MacBook turns off and then on again. A giant gray FireWire icon (⚲) or Thunderbolt icon (↯) bounces around the laptop screen.

 Now take a look at the iMac's screen: Sure enough, there's the MacBook's hard drive icon on the desktop. You're ready to copy files onto or off of it, at extremely high speeds, and go on with your life.

4. **When you're finished working with the MacBook, eject it from the iMac's screen as you would any disk. Then turn off the laptop by pressing the power button.**

The next time you turn on the MacBook, it'll start up from its own copy of OS X, even if the cable is still attached. (You can disconnect the cable whenever you please.)

Note: The steps above describe the modern method of setting up Target Disk Mode. But an old way still works, too. Leave the iMac turned on, but shut down the MacBook. (Make sure it's plugged in. You wouldn't want the battery to die in the middle of this process.) Now turn the MacBook on again, but hold down the T key immediately after the chime. After a moment, you see the big Y-shaped FireWire icon (⚲) on the laptop screen, and the laptop's hard drive shows up on the iMac's desktop. Continue from step 4 above.

This method is arguably quicker, because you don't have to open up System Preferences. And this method works when the Mac is too sick even to start up.

Via Flash Drive

A flash drive, also called a thumb drive, is one of those keychain-like doodads that plug into your USB jack. Inside is a big chunk of memory that acts like a miniature hard drive. When the flash drive is plugged into your Mac, its icon shows up on the desktop as a disk. Use it as a tiny, 8-gigabyte hard drive (or whatever size you've bought).

The beauty of a flash drive is that it works instantly and automatically with any Mac *or* any Windows machine, without software installation or configuration. It's small and light enough to carry around on your keychain…and it's *so darned cool.* If you regularly transfer documents between Macs or between Macs and PCs, a flash drive will change your life.

Via Bluetooth

Bluetooth is a cable-elimination technology. It's designed to let Bluetooth-equipped gadgets communicate within about 30 feet, using radio signals.

Bluetooth comes built into most computers and cellphones, plus the occasional printer, pocket organizer, even camera or camcorder.

Bluetooth is built into all recent Macs. It's ready, therefore, to connect with Apple's wireless keyboard and mouse, to get on the Internet using a Bluetooth cellphone as a cordless modem, to listen to music through wireless headphones or speakers, and to transfer files through the air to similarly equipped gear.

Bluetooth is pretty slow. (You get transfer speeds of 30 to 150 K per second, depending on the distance.) But when you consider the time you'd have taken for wiring, passwords, and configuration using any other connection method, you may find that Bluetooth wins, at least in casual, spur-of-the-moment, airport-seat situations.

And Bluetooth works no matter what the gadget—Mac, Windows, cellphone—so it's great as a universal file-exchange translator, too.

Note: For more details on configuring your Mac for Bluetooth connections, see page 581.

Sending a file

To shoot a file or two across the airwaves to a fellow Bluetooth-equipped Mac fan, first *pair* your Mac with the other Bluetooth machine, as described on page 582. In System Preferences→Bluetooth, make sure your Mac is Discoverable. *Discoverable* means "Other Bluetooth gadgets can see me." (Check the receiving gadget, too, to make sure *it's* in Discoverable mode.) Then you're ready to send:

1. **From the Bluetooth ✶ menulet, choose the device's name—and, from the submenu, Send File to Device (Figure 5-10).**

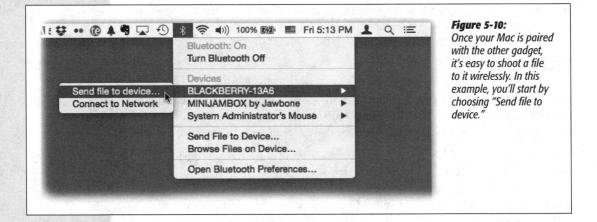

Figure 5-10:
Once your Mac is paired with the other gadget, it's easy to shoot a file to it wirelessly. In this example, you'll start by choosing "Send file to device."

If you don't *have* the Bluetooth menulet on your menu bar, then open System Preferences. Click Bluetooth, and turn on "Show Bluetooth status in the menu bar."

After a moment, the Select File to Send dialog box appears. (You've actually succeeded in opening a program called Bluetooth File Exchange, which sits in your Applications→Utilities folder.)

2. **Navigate to, and select, the files you want to send.**

 A new Send File dialog box appears, showing the list of Bluetooth machines within range. (If you've never Bluetoothed to one of the computers before, you may first have to *pair* with it.)

3. **In the list of found machines, click the name of the one you want to send your files to, and then click Send.**

 What happens now depends on how the receiving machine has been set up. In most cases, a dialog box tells the receiver that files are arriving; if he clicks Accept, then the download proceeds. He's then offered the chance to either (a) open each transferred file or (b) reveal its highlighted icon in the Finder.

Tip: In System Preferences→Sharing→Bluetooth Sharing, you can control what happens when someone sends you files via Bluetooth. Usually, you'll want your Mac to ask whether or not to accept these files. (That's what the option "Ask What to Do" means.) You can also specify where you want received files to wind up—for example, in your Downloads folder.

Fetching a file

You can also perform this entire procedure in reverse. That is, you can go fishing through your buddy's files without her explicitly having to send anything.

To make a Mac invadable, the person to be invaded must open System Preferences→ Sharing and turn on Bluetooth Sharing. Here's also where she can specify what folder is available to you for examination (the Mac proposes her Home→Public folder), and what kind of security she wants to set up.

Then all you have to do is choose Browse Files on Device from your own menulet (you can see it in Figure 5-10)—and let the rummaging begin!

Exchanging Data with Windows PCs

Documents can take one of several roads between your Mac and a Windows machine: via disk (such as a CD), flash drive, iCloud Drive, Dropbox, network, email, Bluetooth, iPod, Web page, FTP download, and so on.

But since transferring your life's work from your existing PC to your new Mac is such an important first hurdle, the PC-to-Mac transition gets a whole chapter unto itself—Chapter 6.

The Share Button (⬆)

In its never-ending efforts to bring the best of the iPad to the Mac, Apple has built the Share button into many spots. It's a quick, one-click way to send something (text, link, photo, video) to somebody else (by email, Twitter, Facebook, text message, AirDrop).

If you've seen an iPhone or iPad, then you've probably seen this Share icon: ⬆. On the Mac, this button, or a command that just says Share, pops up in all kinds of pro-

grams: the Finder's shortcut menus. Quick Look panes. The Open File dialog box in Apple programs. OS X programs like Contacts, Notes, Preview, Safari, Photo Booth, TextEdit, iPhoto, and so on. Other companies can add it to their programs, too, or install new commands into the Share menu for transmitting stuff to new channels.

To use this feature, select or open some text, a photo, a video, a file icon, a Web link, or something else that you want to send to friends. When you click this button or command, you're offered various ways to share the selected item. The choices vary according to the program you're using, but here are some examples:

- **Email.** The Mac copies the selected material into a new, outgoing email message, or attaches the selected file to an outgoing message. Just add a few explanatory notes, address the message, and send.

- **Twitter.** Opens up the Twitter share sheet pictured in Figure 5-11. A counter helps you keep your message under the legal limit of 140 characters. Explain what your linked item is about, and then click Post.

- **Facebook.** Attaches the selected photo, video, or text to the Facebook share sheet shown at bottom in Figure 5-11. This tiny box offers two pop-up menus. The one at top left lets you specify who gets to see this post: Only Me, Friends, Friends and Networks, Everyone, or one of your Facebook lists, if you've set them up. If you're posting a photo or video, a second pop-up menu at top right lets you indicate what album you want this item to land in—your Timeline or an existing photo album.

- **Messages.** Puts the selected material into an outgoing message, ready to send as a text message or an iMessage (Chapter 13). Just address and send.

Tip: In the Finder, the Share command offers a brilliantly simple way to send a file to somebody. Just right-click (or two-finger click) a file icon, choose Share→Message, and then enter the person's phone number (to send to an iPhone) or Apple ID (to send by iMessage). Click Send—off it goes!

- **AirDrop.** As you can read on 536, AirDrop lets you shoot Finder files to nearby Macs, iPhones, and iPads—wirelessly, without having to fuss with passwords, file sharing, mounting disks, and so on.

 In the Finder, right-click (or two-finger click) the file icon (or icons) that you want to send to another Mac. From the shortcut menu, choose AirDrop. In a flash, you get the AirDrop share sheet shown in Figure 5-11, lower right. It lists every nearby Mac, iPhone, or iPad. Click the one you want, and then click Send; if the other guy clicks Accept, then the file is on its way to his Apple gadget.

- **Vimeo.** When you select a video (in the Finder, for example), you have the option of posting it to Vimeo, which is a lot like YouTube but smaller and with a more mature tone. You're asked for a name, description, and tags (keywords) for your video, and you're given the option to keep it private (rather than public). When you click Send, the movie goes on its way. After the upload, a tiny status box appears, showing you the link that takes you to the newly posted video; click the ⊙ to jump to it in your Web browser.

- **Flickr.** You can post a photo from your Mac directly to this popular photo-sharing site, even from the Finder. You're asked to provide a title and description for the photos, and then off it goes to your online Flickr account. After the upload, the tiny status box shows you the link.

All the online services mentioned here—Twitter, Facebook, Flickr, Vimeo—require free accounts. And using the Share button assumes that you've entered your account name and password in System Preferences→Internet Accounts. Once you've recorded your account info there, it's stored; you can use the corresponding Share options in any program without having to log in again.

This list of options in the Share menu isn't complete; you may find other oddball options in the Share menus of certain programs. For example, in Photo Booth, you also get choices like Add to iPhoto, Set Buddy Picture, Set Account Picture, or Change

Figure 5-11:
Top: Here's how you might tweet a link to a page from Safari. Choose Twitter from the □ button; type a comment; click Post.

Bottom: Other share sheets you might encounter. Lower left: posting a photo to Facebook. (Note the tiny pop-up menus. One lets you control who sees this post; the other specifies where it goes—which album, for example.)

Lower right: sending a file using AirDrop.

Keyboard fans: For Twitter or Facebook, press Shift-⌘-D to "click" the Send or Post button.

Twitter Profile Picture—all handy things to do with a picture you've just taken with your Mac's built-in camera.

Editing the Share Menu

You get to choose which options appear in your Share menu, and in which order they appear.

For that, you can thank the pane in System Preferences called Extensions. (One quick way to open it: From the Share menu itself, choose More.) If you click Share Menu in the left-side list, you're treated to a System Preferences box where you can turn off the Share-menu options you never use. You can also drag items' names up or down, so that the most useful ones appear at the top of the Share menu from now on. (You're not allowed to turn off the Big Three: Mail, Messages, and AirDrop.) For more on Extensions, see page 596.

Time Machine

There are two kinds of people in the world: those who have a regular backup system—and those who *will.*

You'll get that grisly joke immediately if you've ever known the pain that comes with deleting the wrong folder by accident, or making changes that you regret, or worst of all, having your hard drive die. All those photos, all that music you've bought online, all your email—gone.

Yet the odds are overwhelming that at this moment, you do not have a complete, current, automated backup of your Mac. Despite about a thousand warnings, articles, and cautionary tales a year, guess how many do? About *four percent.* Everybody else is flying without a net.

If you don't have much to back up—you don't have much in the way of photos, music, or movies—you can get by with using a free online backup system like iCloud Drive, Dropbox, or CrashPlan. But those methods leave most of your Mac unprotected: all your programs and settings.

What you really want, of course, is a backup that's rock-solid, complete, and *automatic.* You don't want to have to remember to do a backup, to insert a disc, and so on. You just want to know you're safe.

That's the idea behind Time Machine, a marquee feature of OS X. It's a silent, set-it-and-forget-it piece of peace of mind. You sleep easy, knowing there's a safety copy of your *entire* system: your system files, programs, settings, music, pictures, videos, document files—*everything.* If your luck runs out, you'll be *so* happy you set up Time Machine.

Setting Up Time Machine

Here's the bad news: Time Machine requires a second hard drive. That's the only way to create a completely safe, automatic backup of your *entire* main hard drive.

That second hard drive can take any of these forms:

- An external USB, FireWire, or Thunderbolt hard drive.

- An Apple Time Capsule. That's an AirPort wireless base station/network backup hard drive in one; it's available in gigantic capacities.

- Another internal hard drive.

- A *partition* of any one of those drives.

- The hard drive of another Mac on the network (Mac OS X 10.5 or later) that you've mounted on your screen.

Tip: It's perfectly OK to back up several Macs onto the same external hard drive, as long as it's got enough room. You can also back up onto a hard drive that has other stuff on it, although of course that means you'll have less room for Time Machine backups.

In all cases, the backup disk must be bigger than the drive you're backing up (preferably *much* bigger).

Here's what you *can't* use as the backup disk: a CD or your startup drive.

Note: The backup drive must be a standard Mac-formatted hard drive—yet many new drives bought by Mac fans come preformatted as Windows disks. Fortunately, Time Machine automatically reformats them to the Mac OS Extended (Journaled) scheme, which it requires. Thoughtful, really.

Sure, it sounds like an Apple plot to sell more hard drives. But you'd be surprised at how cheap hard drives are. At this writing, you can buy an external USB 2-*terabyte* hard drive (2,000 gigabytes) for $80, for goodness' sake—and hard drive prices-per-gigabyte go only down.

The first time the Mac sees your second hard drive, it invites you to use it as Time Machine's backup drive ("Do you want to use 'Seagate 2TB Drive' to back up with Time Machine?"). That could be the moment you connect an external drive, or the first time you turn on the Mac after installing an internal drive.

Note: Time Machine still works if there's other stuff on the drive, but life is simpler if you don't use that drive for anything but Time Machine.

If you click Use as Backup Disk, you're taken immediately to the Time Machine pane of System Preferences (Figure 5-12). Here's where you see that Time Machine is turned on and has a drive it can use for backup.

Soon enough, the Mac starts copying *everything* on your hard drive, including OS X itself, all your programs, and everyone's Home folders. You know that because you see the ↻ symbol in the Sidebar (next to the backup disk's name), and the menu-bar Time Machine icon looks like ↺.

And that, ladies and gentlemen, is the easiest setup for a backup program in history.

Note: Unless you turn on encryption (see the box on the facing page), Time Machine doesn't use any compression or encoding; it's copying your files exactly as they sit on your hard drive, for maximum safety and recoverability. On the other hand, it does save some space on the backup drive, because it doesn't bother copying cache files, temporary files, and other files you'll never need to restore.

Now go away and let the Mac do its thing. The first backup can take hours as the Mac duplicates your entire internal hard drive onto the second drive. The Mac may feel drugged during this time.

Tip: You can create multiple backups on different disks—a great feature if you have a laptop that you carry between work and home. You can have a backup drive at both places; Time Machine will seamlessly switch between them. To set this up, just choose another backup disk in System Preferences→Time Machine. Time Machine will automatically back up to that drive, too.

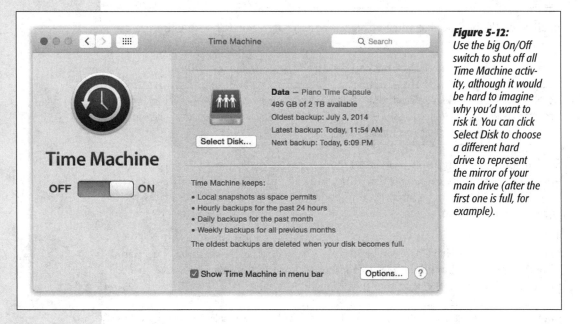

Figure 5-12:
Use the big On/Off switch to shut off all Time Machine activity, although it would be hard to imagine why you'd want to risk it. You can click Select Disk to choose a different hard drive to represent the mirror of your main drive (after the first one is full, for example).

How the Backups Work

From now on, Time Machine quietly and automatically checks your Mac once an hour. If any file, folder, or setting has changed, it gets backed up at the end of the hour. These follow-up backups are quick; Time Machine backs up only what's changed.

So, should disaster strike, the only files you can lose are those you've changed within the past 59 minutes.

Tip: And even then, you can force more frequent backups if you want to. Just choose Back Up Now from the Time Machine menulet. Or choose Back Up Now from the shortcut menu of the Dock's Time Machine icon.

You can pause the backup the same way—if you need to use the backup drive for another quick task, for example. Open System Preferences→Time Machine and turn the big switch Off. Don't forget to turn the backing-up on again when you're finished.

By the end of the day, you'll have 24 hourly backups on that second disk, all taking up space. So at day's end, Time Machine replaces that huge stash with a single *daily* backup. You can no longer rewind your system to 3:00 p.m. last Monday, but you can rewind to the way it was at the *end* of that day.

Similarly, after a month, Time Machine replaces those 30 dailies (for example) with four weekly backups. Now you may not be able to rewind to October 14, but you can rewind to November 1. (Apple assumes it won't take you a whole week to notice that your hard drive has crashed.)

Tip: You can see these backups, if you want. Open your backup drive, open the *Backups.backupdb* folder, and then open the folder named for your computer. Inside, you'll find a huge list of backup folders, bearing names like 2014-07-22-155831. That's the backup from July 22, 2014, at 15:58 (that is, 3:58 p.m.) and 31 seconds.

The point is that Time Machine doesn't just keep *one* copy of your stuff. It keeps *multiple* backups. It remembers how things were in every folder—not just yesterday, but last week, last month, and so on. It keeps on making new snapshots of your hard drive until the backup drive is full.

POWER USERS' CLINIC

Encrypted Time Machine Backups

Time Machine can encrypt your backups.

Without encryption, an evildoer could theoretically bust into your house, steal your backup disk, and have full, unfettered access to all your backed-up files. It's never happened yet, but—you know. It could.

If you're interested in encrypting your backups, there are some prerequisites. The hard drive must use HFS (Journaled) formatting—a Mac hard drive, in other words. The drive has to be physically, directly connected to your Mac using USB, FireWire, or Thunderbolt—or else a wireless Apple Time Capsule.

To turn this feature on, open System Preferences→Time Machine. Click Select Disk. Turn on "Encrypt backup disk." You're asked for a password. Type it in, and whatever you

do, don't forget it! Without that password, you won't be able to recover your files if something goes wrong. Keep that password somewhere safe—on the bottom of the backup drive, for example. (Joke! That's a joke.)

Once you click OK, the encryption begins. It takes a long time. Go away for the weekend.

Once it's done, you won't notice any difference—until the day comes when you need to recover your files. At that point, you'll be asked for your password when you enter Time Machine.

If something serious ever happens to your Mac, you can connect the encrypted Time Machine drive to any other Mac that's running Lion or later. You'll be able to enter your password there and recover your files onto that different Mac.

At that point, the oldest ones get deleted to make room for new ones.

Tip: Ordinarily, Time Machine alerts you when it has to start deleting old backups. If you'd rather have it just do it without bothering you, then open System Preferences, click Time Machine, click Options, and then turn off "Notify after old backups are deleted."

By the way, if a backup is interrupted—if you shut down the Mac, put it to sleep, or take your laptop on the road—no big deal. Time Machine resumes automatically the next time you're home and connected.

Local Snapshots

If you're among the 75 percent of Mac fans with a laptop, Time Machine used to be something of a bust in one regard: Whenever you were away from your backup disk (at home or the office, for example), you lost the benefits of Time Machine.

Today, crazy as this may sound, Time Machine keeps on working even on a laptop that's far from home. Thanks to a feature called local snapshots, Time Machine works as usual by making its backups right on the laptop's own hard drive.

Of course, this system won't help you if your hard drive dies; your backup is on the same drive, so you'll lose the originals and the backups simultaneously. But what local snapshots do provide is a safety net—a way to recover a file that you deleted or changed during this time away. Better yet, once you're home again, when your laptop rejoins the network, the local snapshots are intelligently merged with the master Time Machine backups, as though you'd never been away.

If Time Machine is turned on on your laptop, it makes local snapshots automatically— once an hour, as usual. As time goes on, Time Machine condenses those backups to daily or weekly snapshots to save disk space.

Note: If your laptop gets really low on disk space, Time Machine stops making new snapshots and may even delete old ones so that you can keep using your Mac. When you make more space, snapshots resume automatically.

If you need to recover a file, enter Time Machine as usual. Your local snapshots show up on the same timeline as backups made on your regular, external backup disk, but they're color-coded: pink tick marks for external backups, gray for local ones. If the pink bars are dimmed, it's because you're not hooked up to your external Time Machine backup drive.

Tip: To see how much disk space your local snapshots are eating up, choose →About This Mac. Click More Info. Click the Storage tab. The color-coded graph clearly indicates the space being used for backups.

Changing Time Machine Settings

Time Machine has four faces. There's the application itself, which sits in your Applications folder; open it only when you want to enter Restore mode. There's its Dock

icon, which also enters Restore mode, but which has a shortcut menu containing useful commands like Back Up Now (and Stop Backing Up).

There's the Time Machine menulet, which may be the handiest of all. It identifies the time and date of the most recent backup, offers Back Up Now/Stop Backing Up commands, and has direct access to Time Machine's restore mode and preferences pane.

Tip: If you Option-click the Time Machine menulet, you get two secret new commands: Verify Backups (just in case you're a little nervous about your backups' integrity) and Browse Other Backup Disks. Yes, it's perfectly possible to back up onto multiple hard drives—to keep one offsite so you won't be hosed in case of fire, flood, or burglary, for example—and this is how. (Right-clicking or two-finger clicking the Time Machine icon on the Dock is another way to get this command.)

Finally, then there's its System Preferences pane, where you adjust its settings (Figure 5-12). To see it, choose →System Preferences→Time Machine. Or choose Time Machine Preferences from Time Machine's Dock icon or menulet.

Recovering Lost or Changed Files

All right, you've got Time Machine on the job. You sleep easy at night, confident that your life is in order—and your stuff is backed up.

Then, one day, it happens: Your hard drive crashes. Or you can't find a file or folder you know you had. Or you save a document in some non–Auto Save program and then wish you could go back to an earlier draft. Some kind of disaster—sunspots, clueless spouse, overtired self—has befallen your files. This is Time Machine's big moment.

Start by pinpointing what you're looking for, in one of these two ways:

• Open the disk or folder window where the missing or changed item was.

FREQUENTLY ASKED QUESTION

The End of Time

What happens when my backup drive gets full?

Good question. The whole idea of Time Machine is that it preserves multiple backups, so that you can rewind a window or a drive not just to *a* backup, but to *any* date in the past. The bigger the hard drive, the farther back those monthly backups are preserved.

Eventually, of course, your backup drive runs out of space. At that point, Time Machine notifies you and offers you a choice: "Your backup disk is now full. The oldest remaining backup disk is..." (and then the date).

You can keep using that drive; Time Machine will begin deleting the oldest backups to make room for newer ones.

Or you can install a new Time Machine backup drive. New backups will go on that one; your older backups will still be available on the original drive.

If you ever need to retrieve files or folders from the older disk, right-click (or two-finger click) the Time Machine icon in the Dock; from the shortcut menu, choose Browse Other Time Machine Disks. In the list of disks, choose the older one. Then click the Time Machine icon on the Dock to enter the Restore mode.

- Type what you're looking for into the search box at the top of any Finder window. Click the location button that makes the most sense: "This Mac" or the name of the window you're in.

 In the case of deleted files or folders, the search will probably come up empty; that's totally OK.

Now click the Time Machine icon on the Dock, or choose Enter Time Machine from the menulet (Figure 5-13, top). Don't look away; you'll miss the show.

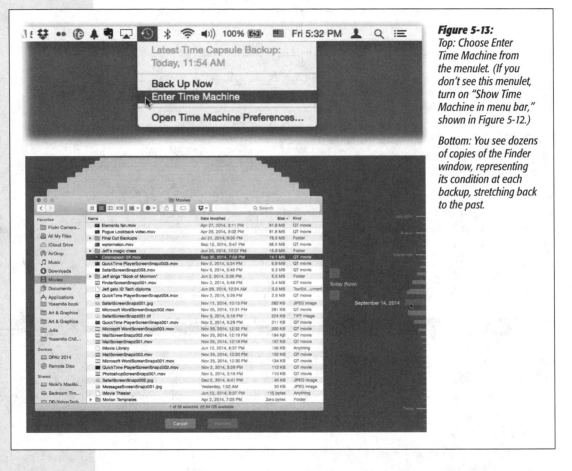

Figure 5-13:
Top: Choose Enter Time Machine from the menulet. (If you don't see this menulet, turn on "Show Time Machine in menu bar," shown in Figure 5-12.)

Bottom: You see dozens of copies of the Finder window, representing its condition at each backup, stretching back to the past.

Your desktop *slides down the screen* like a curtain that's been dropped from above. Front and center is your Finder window—or, rather, dozens of them, stretching back in time (Figure 5-13, bottom). Each is a snapshot of that window at the time of a Time Machine backup.

You have four ways to peruse your backup universe:

- **Click individual windows to see what's in them.**

- **Drag your cursor through the timeline at the right side.** It's like a master dial that flies through the windows into the past.

- **Click one of the two big, flat perspective arrows.** The one pointing into the past means "Jump directly to the most recent window version that's *different* from the way it is right now."

In other words, it's often a waste of time to go flipping through the windows one at a time, because your missing or changed file might have been missing or changed for the last 25 backups (or whatever). What you want to know is the last time the contents of this window *changed*. And that's what the big flat arrows do. They jump from one *changed* version of this window to another. (Or, if you began with a search, the arrow takes you to the most recent backup with a matching result.)

- **Use the search box in the corner of the window.** You can search for whatever you're missing in the current backup.

As you go, the very bottom of the screen identifies where you are in time—that is, which backup you're examining.

Tip: OK, it's all very dazzling and all. But if you're technically inclined, you don't have to sit still for the big show. Just open the backup disk itself, whose icon appears on your desktop. Inside, you'll find nested folders, neatly representing every computer, every backup, every day, and every hour—which you can rummage through by hand.

In many ways, the recovery mode is just like the Finder. You can't actually open, edit, rename, or reorganize anything here. But you can use Quick Look to inspect the documents to make sure you've got the right version. And you can use icon, list, column, or Cover Flow views to sort through the files you're seeing.

If you're trying to recover an older *version* of a file or folder, highlight it and then click the flat arrow button that's pointing away from you; Time Machine skips back to the most recent version that's *different* from the current one.

If you're trying to restore a deleted file or folder that you've now located, highlight it and then click Restore (lower right). The OS X desktop rises again from the bottom of the screen, there's a moment of copying, and then presto: The lost file or folder is back in the window where it belonged.

Note: Time Machine prides itself not just on recovering files and folders, but also on putting them back where they belong.

If you recover a different version of something that's still there, OS X asks if you want to replace it with the recovered version—or to keep both versions.

And if you're recovering a document whose original folder no longer exists, Time Machine automatically recreates the folder so that the recovered item feels at home.

Recovering from Contacts and Mail

The Finder isn't the only program that's hooked into Time Machine's magic. Contacts and Mail work with Time Machine, too. Other software companies can also revise their own applications to work with it.

In other words, if you want to recover certain addresses or email messages that have been deleted, you don't start in the Finder; you start in Contacts or Mail.

Then click the Time Machine icon on the Dock. Once again, you enter the recovery mode—but this time, you're facing a strange, disembodied, stripped-down copy of Contacts or Mail.

You're ready to find your missing data. Click the Jump Back arrow to open the most recent version of your address book file or email stash that's different from what you've got now. (You can also use the timeline on the right if you remember the date when things went wrong.)

POWER USERS' CLINIC

Declaring Stuff Off-Limits to Time Machine

The whole point of Time Machine is to have a backup of your entire hard drive. That's how most people use it.

It's conceivable, though, that you might want to exclude some files or folders from the Time Machine treatment. There are two reasons.

First, you might not want certain, ahem, private materials to be part of your incriminating data trail.

Second, you might want to save space on the backup drive, either because it's not as big as your main drive or because you'd rather dedicate its space to more backups of the essential stuff. For example, you might decide not to back up your collection of downloaded TV shows, since video files are enormous. Or maybe you use an online photo-sharing Web site as a backup for all your photos, so you don't think it's necessary to include those in the Time Machine backup.

To eliminate certain icons from the backup, open the Time Machine pane of System Preferences. Click Options.

In the resulting list, click the + button; navigate to your hard drive, and then select the files or folders you don't want backed up. Or just find their actual icons in the Finder and drag them into the list here. (Use the — button to remove items from the list, thereby excluding them from the excluded list.)

Exclude these items from backups:

/Applications	6.98 GB
~/Desktop/Billing	392.2 MB
~/Desktop/Incriminating photos	1.2 MB
System Files and Applications	3.1 GB

Estimated size of full backup: 184.47 GB

☐ Back up while on battery power
☑ Notify after old backups are deleted

Cancel Save

If you're strapped for disk space, one logical candidate to exclude is the System folder on your main hard drive—that is, OS X itself. After all, if you lose your hard drive, you already have a copy of OS X: the original App Store installer.

When you add the System folder to the exclusion list, Time Machine makes another space-saving offer: "Would you like to also exclude other files installed with Mac OS X, such as system applications and UNIX tools?"

Agreeing (by clicking Exclude All System Files) saves you another several gigabytes of backup space.

Tip: If you're looking for something particular, specify that before you start clicking. For example, type a name into the Contacts search box first.

At this point, you can select individual Contacts entries or email messages to restore; just click the Restore button.

Often, though, you'd rather reinstate the *entire* Contacts file or email collection from the backup. That's what the Restore All button is for.

If you click it, the experience is slightly different. Contacts may discover a lot of duplicate name-and-address entries and invite you to step through them, deciding which ones "win" (the old or the new).

Note: When you finish restoring in Mail, you'll find the restored messages in the On My Mac ›Time Machine→Recovered folder at the left side of the window.

Recovering the entire hard drive

Every hard drive will die at some point. You just hope it won't happen while *you* own the computer. But if it does, you, as a Time Machine aficionado, won't care. You'll just repair or replace the hard drive, and then proceed as follows.

1. **Connect the Time Machine backup disk to the Mac. Start the recovery mode.**

 There are actually three ways to recover a dead Mac or a dead hard drive, none of which require an actual DVD, as in the days of yore. If the hard drive is fine but it just can't start up your Mac, hold down ⌘-R during startup. If the hard drive is empty, you can restart from the Internet itself (if it's a Mac released since Lion came out). And if all else fails, you can always use the Recovery Disk Assistant that you wisely made long in advance of your horror-story dead-disk day.

 Appendix B covers all three of these recovery modes in more detail. The point is, however, that all three of them present "Restore from a Time Machine backup" as one of the options.

2. **Choose "Restore from a Time Machine backup." Click Continue.**

 Now you're shown a list of Time Machine backup disks. You probably have only one.

3. **Click your Time Machine backup disk. In the list, click the most recent backup.**

 The installer goes about copying *everything* from the backup disk onto your new, empty hard drive. When it's all over, you'll have a perfect working system, just the way it was before your series of unfortunate events.

Beware, however: Restoring your earlier version also *erases any files* you've created or changed since you installed the update. Back them up manually before you proceed!

Then follow the steps; when you're asked to choose a backup to restore, choose the most recent one. When it's all over, copy the latest files (the ones that you manually backed up) back onto the hard drive.

Recovering to another Mac

Weirdly enough, you can also use Time Machine to bring over some or part of any Time Machine backup to a totally different Mac.

On the new machine, connect your backup disk. In the Applications→Utilities folder, open the program called Migration Assistant. On the first screen, click "From another Mac, PC, Time Machine backup, or other disk." The subsequent screens invite you to choose which backup, which Home folder, and which elements (applications, settings, files) you want to bring over.

Frequently Asked Questions

Time Machine is a very different kind of backup program, and a real departure for longtime Mac addicts. A few questions, therefore, are bound to come up—like these:

- **Can I back up more than one Mac onto the same disk?** Yes. Each Mac's backup is stored in a separate folder on that disk.

- **Can I use more than one backup disk—like one at the office and one at home?** Yes. Just use the Time Machine pane of System Preferences (or the Time Machine Dock icon's shortcut menu) to select the new backup drive each time you switch.

- **Can I delete something for good, from all the backups at once?** Yes. Click the Time Machine icon on the Dock to enter the Restore mode. Find and select the file or folder you want to obliterate. From the ✿ menu, choose Delete All Backups of [the Thing's Name]. (Sneaky, huh? That command is never in the ✿ menu *except* when you're in Time Machine restoring mode.)

Part Two: Making the Move

2

Transferring Your Files to the Mac

A huge percentage of "switchers" do not, in fact, *switch*. Often, they just *add*. They may get a Macintosh (and get *into* the Macintosh), but they keep the old Windows PC around, at least for a while. If you're in that category, get psyched. It turns out that communicating with a Windows PC is one of the Mac's most polished talents.

That's especially good news in the early days of your Mac experience. You probably have a good deal of stuff on the Windows machine that you'd like to bring over to the Mac. Somewhere along the line, somebody probably told you how easy this is to do. In fact, the Mac's reputation for simplicity may even have played a part in your decision to switch.

In any case, this chapter describes the process of building a bridge from the PC to the Mac, so that you can bring all your files and settings into their new home. It also tells you where to *put* them all.

As it turns out, files can take one of several roads from your old PC to your new Mac. For example, you can transfer them on a disk (such as a CD or iPod), by a network, or as an attachment to an email message.

Tip: The first part of this chapter covers the mechanical aspects of moving files and folders from your Windows PC to the Mac. On page 261, you'll find a more pointed discussion of where to put each kind of data (mail, photos, music, and so on) once it's on the Mac.

Transfers by Apple Genius

By far the easiest way to transfer all the stuff from your PC to your new Mac is to let Apple do it for you. Yes, that's right: Those busy Geniuses who work at the 400 Apple Stores around the world are prepared to bring your music, pictures, documents, address book, email, bookmarks, and other things to their new home on your Mac.

This service is included in the $100 One on One program, which is worth a look. (You're supposed to buy One on One at the time you buy the Mac.)

One on One gives you a year's worth of weekly *one-hour private lessons* at an Apple Store from an Apple rep. They'll teach you the Mac, help you organize your photos, teach you the software, whatever you need. That's gotta be the best private-lessons price ever offered for anything.

Once you're signed up, the Apple Genius will take your old PC and your new Mac and do the transferring for you. For example, all your Windows pictures (even if they're in Picasa or special photo-editing programs from HP or Kodak) get brought over to the Mac and imported into iPhoto. All your music is imported into iTunes on the Mac. Your documents and movies get copied to the Documents and Movies folders on the Mac. Your Web bookmarks from Internet Explorer or Firefox get transferred to Safari on the Mac. Even your email, address book, and calendar get transferred from Outlook or Outlook Express on the PC and brought into Mail, Contacts, and Calendar on the Mac.

The rest of this chapter covers do-it-yourself ways to transfer your stuff. But, man, there's nothing like having a professional do it for you.

The Windows Migration Assistant

If you don't really need the year's worth of private Mac lessons, then here's another low-effort option: Let the Windows Migration Assistant do the transferring for you.

Now, this app has a reputation for bugginess. But if it works on your system, it's a nearly effortless automatic tool that copies all your important data from a Windows PC (running Windows XP SP3 or later) to your Mac. (And if it doesn't work, page 259 offers manual techniques that can do the same job.)

On the Mac, you'll find the Migration Assistant program in your Applications→Utilities folder. Before you open it, make sure your Mac and your PC are connected to the same network (WiFi or wired), as described in Chapter 16.

Now open Migration Assistant. Choose the first option: "From another Mac, PC, Time Machine backup, or other disk." Click Continue. (Enter your password if you're asked for it.)

When all is said and done, here's what it accomplishes:

- **Transfers your email** into Mail from Outlook, Outlook Express, Windows Mail, or Windows Live accounts (POP or IMAP). Your messages even show up correctly

marked as having been read, replied to, and flagged (except if they originated in Windows Live).

- **Transfers your address book** into Contacts from Outlook and Outlook Express contacts, and from Windows contacts in the Contacts folder on your PC.

- **Transfers your calendar** into Calendar from Outlook's calendar.

- **Transfers your iTunes** collection into iTunes for the Mac from iTunes on Windows. Everything comes over, including music, photos, videos (but not rentals), and apps and games for iPhone/iPad/iPod Touch.

- **Transfers everything in your Windows Home folder** into the corresponding Mac Home-folder folders: Music, Pictures, Desktop, Documents, and Downloads.

- **Transfers your browser bookmarks and preferred home page** into Safari from Explorer, Firefox, and Safari for Windows.

- **Transfers your account settings** like language and even your desktop wallpaper.

All of this winds up in a new user account on your Mac. The migration program doesn't make any attempt to merge your Windows world into your *existing* account on the Mac.

Now, the Migration Assistant app (in your Utilities folder) represents only the *Mac* end of this transaction. You also need the Windows end.

For that, download the free Windows Migration Assistant program. It's waiting at *www.apple.com/migrate-to-mac*. Install it on your PC, which is a matter of clicking through three screens. In your Control Panel, turn off Windows Updates.

Now you're ready to begin.

1. **Make sure the PC and the Mac are on the same network.**

 It can be a WiFi network, but you'll get a much faster transfer, with much less risk of interference, if you connect them to a wired network. For example, connect each with an Ethernet cable to your router.

2. **On the PC, open the Windows Migration Assistant program that you downloaded. Click Continue.**

 The PC is now ready for action.

3. **On the Mac, quit all programs. In your Applications→Utilities folder, open the Migration Assistant program.**

 You're offered two choices: "From another Mac, PC, Time Machine backup, or other disk" and "To another Mac" (see Figure 6-1).

4. **On the Mac, click "From a Windows PC." Click Continue. Provide your name and password, and click Continue again. Click "From another Mac or PC," and click Continue.**

At this point, your Mac should "see" the PC on the network. You'll know, because you'll see the PC's name and icon in the dialog box shown in Figure 6-1, middle.

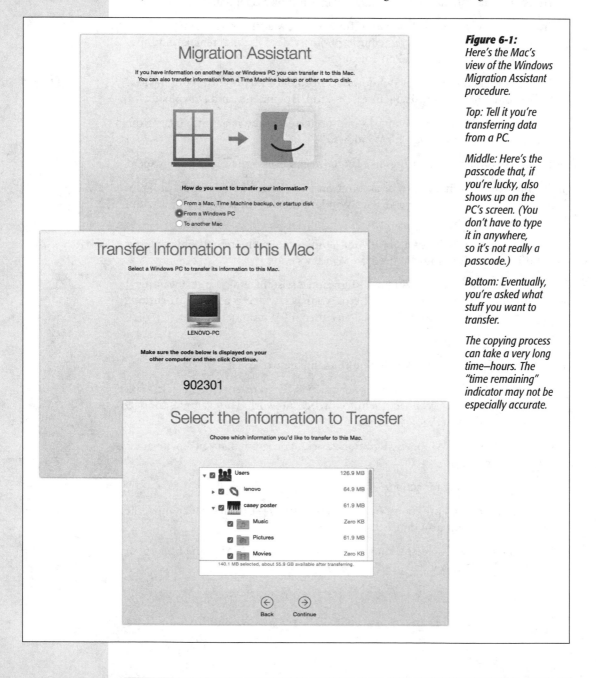

Figure 6-1:
Here's the Mac's view of the Windows Migration Assistant procedure.

Top: Tell it you're transferring data from a PC.

Middle: Here's the passcode that, if you're lucky, also shows up on the PC's screen. (You don't have to type it in anywhere, so it's not really a passcode.)

Bottom: Eventually, you're asked what stuff you want to transfer.

The copying process can take a very long time—hours. The "time remaining" indicator may not be especially accurate.

5. **Click Continue.**

On the Mac, you see something like Figure 6-1, middle: a big passcode. On the PC, you're supposed to see a matching passcode.

If you don't see the passcode on the PC, then something—your firewall, your antivirus program, Migration Assistant flakiness—is getting in the way. You may have to opt for the manual procedures described on page 259.

6. **If you see the passcode on the PC's screen, then click Continue.**

After a few minutes of whirring and thinking, the Mac displays a list of files that it can transfer from the PC (Figure 6-1, bottom).

7. **On the Mac, turn on the checkboxes of the items you want copied. Click Continue to begin the transfer.**

If all goes well, after a few hours, the Mac says, "Your information has been transferred successfully."

8. **On the Mac, click Quit.**

If you choose →Log Out, you'll see that there's a new account on your Mac, named after the account you transferred from the PC. If you try to sign into it, you're asked to provide a password for this new Mac account. (If you didn't *want* your Windows stuff to wind up in a new Mac account, then you can always copy it back into your main account using the Users→Shared folder as a tunnel between accounts.)

Tip: The Migration Assistant puts all your mail into Apple's Mail program, the one described in Chapter 11. If you'd prefer to use Microsoft Outlook for the Mac as your email program, here are the steps for transferring the mail stash from Mail to Outlook: http://j.mp/xtsGwi.

Manual Network Transfers

As you may have guessed from the paragraphs above, Macs and PCs can "see" each other on a network (wired or wireless). Seated at the Mac, you can open or copy files from any folders you've shared on a PC. In fact, you can go in the other direction, too: Your old PC can see shared folders on your Mac.

Chapter 16 offers a crash course in setting up a network. When it's all over, you'll be seated at the Mac, looking at the contents of your Windows PC in a separate window. At that point, you can drag whatever files and folders you want directly to the proper places on the Mac, as described on page 261.

Transfers by Dropbox, iCloud Drive, or OneDrive

Dropbox is a free service (for up to 2 gigabytes) that puts a magic folder on your desktop—of every machine you own, including your tablet, phone, Mac, and PC. iCloud Drive is Apple's version. It gives you 5 gigabytes of storage for free; it, too, is

available on Mac, Windows, iPhone, or iPad. And OneDrive is Microsoft's version of the same thing; it gives you an amazing *15* gigabytes of free storage.

Anything you put in there on one machine magically shows up on all the others. There's no reason you couldn't transfer your stuff from PC to Mac, a few gigabytes at a time, by dragging it into your Dropbox, iCloud Drive, or OneDrive icon on the PC, and then opening the Dropbox, iCloud Drive, or OneDrive icon on the Mac a few minutes later and moving your files from there into their new homes.

Transfers by Disk

Another way to transfer Windows files to the Mac is to put them onto a disk that you then pop into the Mac. (Windows can't read all Mac disks without special software, but the Mac can read Windows disks.)

This disk can take any of these forms:

- **An external hard drive or iPod.** If you have an external hard drive (USB or IEEE 1394, what Apple calls *FireWire*), then you're in great shape. While it's connected to the PC, drag files and folders onto it. Then unhook the drive from the PC, attach it to the Mac, and marvel as its icon pops up on your desktop, its contents ready for dragging to your Mac's built-in hard drive. (The Mac can read Windows disks and flash drives, which use unappetizingly named formatting schemes like FAT32 and NTFS, but Windows can't read Mac hard drives or flash drives.)

 Most iPods work great for this process, too; they can operate as external hard drives—even the iPod Nano.

- **A Time Capsule.** An Apple Time Capsule is a sleek, white box that contains a huge hard drive plus a wireless base station. The idea, of course, is to create a WiFi network for your house or office and include a built-in disk for backing up all your computers, automatically and wirelessly.

 That also means the Time Capsule makes a great transfer station between a PC and a Mac, since its icon shows up on the desktops of both.

- **A USB flash drive.** These small keychainy sticks don't hold nearly as much data as, say, a hard drive. But they're cheap, and they work on both Macs and PCs. Like a mini-external hard drive, a flash drive plugs directly into your USB port, at which point it shows up on your desktop just like a normal disk. You copy files to it from your PC, plug it into your Mac, and copy the files off, just like you would for any other disk. And you're left with a backup copy of the data on the drive itself.

- **Move the hard drive itself.** This is a grisly, technical maneuver best undertaken by serious wireheads—but it can work. You can install your PC's hard drive directly into a Mac Pro, as long as it was prepared using the older FAT or FAT32 formatting scheme. (The Mac can handle FAT hard drives just fine, but it chokes with NTFS hard drives.)

When you insert a Windows-formatted disk, whatever the type, its icon appears in the Mac's Computer window (or on the desktop, if you've turned on the relevant checkbox in the Finder→Preferences→General tab).

Transfers by File-Sending Web Site

Free Web sites like *hightail.com* and *sendthisfile.com* are specifically designed for sending huge files from one computer to another, without worrying about email file attachments or size limits.

On the Windows PC, zip up your files into a great big .zip file. Upload it to one of these free sites, and provide your Mac's email address.

On the Mac, click the link that arrives by email—and, presto, that huge zip file gets downloaded onto your Mac. It's free, and you can download the big file(s) at any time within three days of sending them. The only price you pay is a little bit of waiting while the stuff gets uploaded and then downloaded.

Tip: If you have your own Web site—a *.com* of your own, for example, or a free site through a university—you can also use *that* Web space as a transfer tool. Follow the uploading instructions you were given when you signed up for the space. (Hint: It usually involves a so-called *FTP* program.) Then, once all your files are on the site, download them onto your Mac.

Transfers by Email

Although sending files as email attachments might seem to be a logical plan, it's very slow. Furthermore, remember that many email providers limit your attachment size to 5 or 10 megabytes. Trying to send more than that at once will clog your system. If you've got a lot of stuff to bring over from your PC, then use one of the disk- or network-based transfer systems described earlier in this chapter.

But for smaller transfer jobs or individual files, sending files as plain old email attachments works just fine.

Where to Put Your Copied Files

Getting your PC files onto the Mac is only half the battle. Now you have to figure out where they *go* on the Mac.

Here's the short answer: Everything goes into your Mac's Home folder. (Choose Go→Home, or click the ⌂ icon in your Sidebar.)

Some of the more specific "where to put it" answers are pretty obvious:

- **My Documents.** Put the files and folders from the PC's My Documents folder into your Home→Documents folder. Here's where you should keep all your Microsoft Office files, PDF files, and other day-to-day masterpieces.

- **My Music.** Your Windows My Music folder was designed to hold all your MP3 files, AIFF files, WAV files, and other music. As you could probably guess, you should copy these files into your Mac's Home→Music folder.

 After that, you can import the music directly into iTunes. If you used iTunes on your PC, for example, see the steps on page 265 for specific transfer instructions.

 If you used some *other* music program on your PC (like Windows Media Player or MusicMatch), things are a little different. On your Mac, choose iTunes→Import, and navigate to the folder that contains all your music. (In either case, click Choose in the resulting dialog box.)

- **My Pictures.** Windows also offers a My Pictures folder, which is where your digital camera photos probably wound up. OS X has a similar folder: the Home→Pictures folder.

 Here again, after copying your photos and other graphics faves over to the Mac, you're only halfway home. If you fire up iPhoto (in your Applications folder), choose File→Import, and choose the Pictures folder, you'll *then* be able to find, organize, and present your photos in spectacular ways.

- **My Videos.** The My Videos folder of Windows XP and later versions contains the video clips you've downloaded from your camcorder (presumably so that you can edit them with, for example, Microsoft's Movie Maker software). Once you've moved them to your Home→Movies folder, though, you're in for a real treat: You can now edit your footage (if it's *digital* footage) with iMovie, which, to put it kindly, runs rings around Movie Maker.

Other elements of your Windows world, though, are trickier to bring over. For example:

Desktop Pictures (Wallpaper)

Especially in recent versions of Windows, the desktop pictures, better known in the Windows world as *wallpaper,* are pretty cool. Fortunately, you're welcome to bring them over to your Mac and use them on your new desktop.

To find the graphics files that make up the wallpaper choices in Windows (version Me or later), proceed like this:

1. **Open My Computer, double-click your hard drive's icon, and open the Windows or WINNT folder.**

 If you see a huge "These files are hidden" message at this point, or if the window appears empty, click "Show the contents of this folder" or "View the entire contents of this folder" at the left side of the window.

2. **In the Windows or WINNT window, open the Web folder.**

 You're looking for a folder inside it called Wallpaper.

3. **Open the Wallpaper folder.**

It's filled with .bmp or .jpg files ready for you to recycle for use on the Mac. See page 170 for instructions on choosing wallpaper for your Mac.

Note: In Windows 95 or 98, the wallpaper files are in your Program Files→Plus!→Themes folder instead.

Sound Effects

The Mac doesn't let you associate your own sound effects to individual system events (Low Battery Alarm, Maximize, Minimize, and so on) as Windows does. It lets you choose *one* sound effect for all attention-getting purposes.

Still, there's nothing to stop you from harvesting all the fun little sounds from your Windows machine for use as the Mac's error beep.

To find them on the PC, repeat step 1 of the preceding instructions. But in the Windows or WINNT folder, open the Media folder to find the WAV files (standard Windows sound files).

Once you've copied them to your Mac, you can double-click one to listen to it. (It opens up in something called QuickTime Player, which is the rough equivalent of Windows Media Player. Press the space bar to listen to the sound.)

To use these sounds as error beeps, you'll have to convert them from the PC's WAV format into the Mac's preferred AIFF format. You'll find step-by-step instructions in the free downloadable appendix for this chapter, "Converting WAV Sounds to Mac Error Beeps." It's on this book's "Missing CD" page at *www.missingmanuals.com*.

Bookmarks (Favorites)

Moving your Favorites (browser bookmarks) to a Mac is easy. The hardest part is exporting them as a file, and that depends on which browser you've been using on the PC.

- **Internet Explorer.** Fire up Internet Explorer; choose File→Import and Export. (In Internet Explorer 7, click the double-star icon in the upper-left corner of the window. From the pop-up menu, choose Import and Export.)

 When the Import/Export Wizard appears, click Next; on the second screen, click Export Favorites, and then click Next again. On the third screen, leave the Favorites folder selected, and click Next. Click Browse to choose a location for the exported bookmarks file. For now, save it to your desktop. Click Next, Finish, and then OK.

- **Firefox.** In Firefox, choose Bookmarks→Organize Bookmarks. In the Bookmarks Manager window, choose File→Export. Save the Bookmarks file to your desktop.

Tip: Firefox is available for the Mac, too (*www.getfirefox.com*). You can transfer your exported Windows bookmarks file into the Mac version by choosing Bookmarks→Manage Bookmarks; then, in the Bookmarks Manager window, choose File→Import. Find and select the exported bookmarks file.

Or you can let Firefox synchronize your PC bookmarks with your Mac automatically and wirelessly. Details are at *http://j.mp/1eH7PBl*.

- **Chrome.** In Chrome, use the Chrome menu (≡) on the toolbar. Select Bookmarks→Bookmark manager→Organize menu→Export bookmarks. Save the HTML file to your desktop.

Tip: Chrome is available for the Mac, too (*www.google.com/chrome*). If you sign into your Google account on each computer (PC and Mac), you'll find your bookmarks already magically present in the Mac version of Chrome. Your tabs, history, and other browser preferences are auto-synced, too.

Now you've got an exported Bookmarks file on your desktop. Transfer it to your Mac using any of the techniques described earlier in this chapter (network, email, whatever).

WORKAROUND WORKSHOP

Transferring Your Mail and Contacts

If you're lucky, you can use the Windows Migration Assistant to bring your PC's files over to the Mac—including your email stash and your contacts. Those are very difficult to transfer manually—the files themselves require conversion—so if the Migration Assistant doesn't work, you might wonder where to turn next.

Four solutions await you. None is free, fast, and easy—but each is either free, fast, *or* easy.

The Thunderbird method. Thunderbird is the free, open-source email companion to the Firefox Web browser. Among other virtues, it can easily open Outlook or Outlook Express email collections on the PC—and convert them into formats that Mac email programs can use. You can find step-by-step instructions online— for example, at *http://j.mp/1dZ657s.*

The O2M solution. For several years, the easiest and most flexible method of transferring your email and contacts was a shareware program called O2M (short for Outlook2Mac). Unfortunately, the company that wrote it has disappeared without a trace. You might still be able to find a copy of O2M floating around online, though.

The 8Convert solution. For $14, you can buy 8Convert, a shareware program especially for extracting your data from Outlook (not Outlook Express). It handles your email (complete with attachments and date ranges that you choose), address book, and calendar; the online instructions (*www.eighthoof.com*) show you how to bring these three items into Mail, Contacts, and Calendar on the Mac. (Similar shareware: MessageSave, *www.techhit.com.*)

The Gmail trick. You can use an online (IMAP) email account as an intermediary between Outlook and the Mac.

Sign up for a free Gmail account. Then, in Windows, open Outlook and add your Gmail account. Now copy the mail folders from your Outlook list into the Gmail account. (Don't drag-and-drop; that moves the messages instead of copying.) This process can take a very long time.

Then, in Mail on the Mac, add the same Gmail account, and after a while, presto: All your mail now shows up on the Mac.

Now open the Mac's Web browser, Safari (it's in your Applications folder). Choose File→Import Bookmarks. Navigate to, and double-click, the exported Favorites file to pull in the bookmarks.

iTunes Music

If you've kept your Windows music collection in iTunes, you can transfer it to the Mac with everything intact: play counts, ratings, playlists, and so on.

Before you begin, though, you have to do some Windows housekeeping. On the PC, open iTunes and choose Edit→Preferences→Advanced. Turn on "Keep iTunes media folder organized" and "Copy files to iTunes media folder when adding to library." Then choose File→Library→Organize Library, turn on Consolidate Files, and click OK. If the option called "Upgrade to iTunes Media organization" is available, then turn that on, too. (All these steps put all of your music and video files in the main iTunes Media folder, which you'll copy to the Mac.)

You may have to wait for iTunes to complete these steps. Once they're finished, copy the iTunes folder from your PC to the Mac. Here's where to find it on the PC:

- **Windows XP.** Documents and Settings→[your user name]→My Documents→My Music→iTunes
- **Windows Vista, Windows 7 or 8.** [your user name] ›Music ›iTunes

Copy that entire iTunes folder to your Mac using one of the methods described in this chapter. It goes into your Home→Music folder.

If there is already an iTunes folder, it's OK to replace it. (Unless, of course, you've imported music into the Mac version of iTunes; in that case, you'll have to copy the Music files from it into the incoming PC's iTunes folder.)

Now, when you open iTunes on the Mac, you'll see your iTunes collection, safely transferred. All of it: music, videos, ratings, playlists, everything.

Tip: If you plan to abandon or sell your PC, don't forget to "deauthorize" its iTunes account so that it doesn't count as one of the five machines that are allowed to play your copy-protected iTunes songs. Do that by opening iTunes. From the Store menu, choose Deauthorize This Computer.

Document Conversion Issues

Most big-name programs are sold in both Mac and Windows flavors, and the documents they create are freely interchangeable.

Files in standard exchange formats don't need conversion, either. These formats include JPEG (the photo format used on Web pages), GIF (the cartoon/logo format used on Web pages), PNG (a newer image format used on Web pages), HTML (raw Web-page documents), Rich Text Format (a word-processor exchange format), plain text (no formatting), QIF (Quicken Interchange Format), MIDI files (for music), and so on.

One reason: both Windows and OS X use filename extensions to identify documents. ("Letter to the Editor.doc," for example, is a Microsoft Word document on *either* operating system.) Common suffixes include these:

Kind of document	Suffix	Example
Microsoft Word	.doc, .docx	Letter to Mom.doc
text	.txt	Database Export.txt
Rich Text Format	.rtf	Senior Thesis.rtf
Excel	.xls, .xlsx	Profit Projection.xls
PowerPoint	.ppt, .pptx	Slide Show.ppt
FileMaker Pro	.fp5, .fp6, .fp7…	Recipe file.fp7
JPEG photo	.jpg, .jpeg	Baby Portrait.jpg
GIF graphic	.gif	Logo.gif
PNG graphic	.png	Dried fish.png
Web page	.htm, .html	Index.htm

Note: Recent versions of Microsoft Office for Mac and Windows offer a more compact file format ending with the letter x. For example, Word files are .docx, Excel files are .xlsx, and so on. The older, more widely compatible format doesn't have the x (.doc, .xls, and so on).

The beauty of OS X is that most Mac programs add these file name suffixes automatically and invisibly—and recognize such suffixes from Windows with equal ease. You and your Windows comrades can freely exchange documents without ever worrying about this former snag in the Macintosh/Windows relationship. (You may, however, encounter snags in the form of documents made by Windows programs that don't exist on the Mac, such as Microsoft Access. Chapter 7 tackles these special cases one by one.

Special Software, Special Problems

B e glad you waited so long to get a Mac. By now, all the big-name programs look and work almost exactly the same on the Mac as they do on the PC. Once you've mastered the basic differences between the Mac and Windows (keyboard shortcuts, the menu bar, and so on), you'll find that programs from Microsoft, Adobe, and other major software companies feel distinctly familiar in their Mac incarnations. In fact, the documents that they create are in the same format and generally need no conversion.

Still, there are more software programs available for Windows than for the Mac. Sooner or later, you'll probably run into a familiar Windows program for which there's no equivalent on the Mac.

One solution is simply to run those Windows programs *on* the Mac, as described in Chapter 8. For thousands of people, that's the screamingly obvious, and extremely convenient, approach. Each time you read, "There's no Mac equivalent of this program" in this chapter, add, in your head, "but you can always run the Windows version."

Still, in other cases, you may not want to fool around with Windows anymore. You may prefer to identify Mac replacements for your favorite Windows programs. That's the purpose of this chapter: to guide you in finding Mac equivalents for the most popular Windows programs (listed here alphabetically), and to guide you in bringing your data and settings over from Windows to the Mac whenever possible.

ACDSee

As digital photography becomes more popular, so do programs like ACDSee, a Windows program that serves as a digital shoebox and basic retouching program for

digital photos. Your Mac, of course, stands ready to run a far more elegant equivalent: iPhoto. It's one of the world's most pleasant photo-organizing programs—and it's free.

In its most recent incarnation, iPhoto has a pretty complete set of image-retouching features. Still, if you need more editing power, consider Photoshop Elements, a program that's available for both Mac and Windows and has won rave reviews on both platforms.

In any case, ACDSee doesn't have any documents of its own—it does all its work on your existing digital photos, wherever you keep them on your hard drive. All you have to do, then, is move the photos themselves to the Mac, using any of the techniques described in Chapter 6. From there, drag them into the iPhoto window to import them.

Acrobat Reader

Acrobat Reader, which lets you read Acrobat (PDF) files, works precisely the same on the Mac as it does in Windows. If you like, you can download Acrobat Reader from *www.adobe.com.*

However, you have a much nicer PDF-reading program right there in your Applications folder, called Preview.

Preview can display PDFs with the best of them—but it's got Acrobat Reader beat on several other counts. Preview can annotate PDFs with virtual yellow sticky-notes—a great tool for marking up book layouts before they go to press, for example. Also, Preview's search feature is so fast and convenient, it blows Acrobat Reader out of the water. And finally, Preview opens in a matter of seconds, while Acrobat Reader can take a minute or so to launch. (For more on Preview, see page 67.)

Act

No Mac version of this Contacts/calendar program is available, but don't let that stop you. Export and Import commands are the bread and butter of address and calendar programs. Your Act life can find a happy home in any of several Mac programs:

- **OS X's free, built-in Contacts app.**

Tip: Contacts syncs with Google Calendar on the Web, which opens up a fascinating possibility: All of your computers (Macs, Windows, iPhone) can maintain synchronized calendars, with Google Calendar serving as the mother ship.

- **Outlook for Mac** (part of Microsoft Office for Mac).

- **BusyCal** *(www.busycal.com)*, which is networkable. That is, if you have more than one computer in the house, you can check your Rolodex from any machine on the network.

In any case, here are the instructions for transferring your addresses from Act (version 5 or later) to the Mac:

1. **In Act for Windows, start by choosing File→Data Exchange→Export.**

 The Export Wizard dialog box appears.

2. **From the "File type" drop-down list, choose Text-Delimited. Specify a folder location and name for your exported file (call it Exported Contacts, for example). Click Next, and click Next on the next screen, too.**

 Now you're asked, "Which contact or group records do you want to export?"

3. **Click "All records," and then click Next.**

 Now you see a list of the *fields* (information tidbits like City, State, and Zip) that Act is prepared to export. You can save yourself time later if you take a moment now to remove the ones you don't need (click a name and then click Remove Field).

4. **Click Finish.**

 If you plan to import your addresses into a commercial program like BusyCal, transfer the Exported Contacts file to the Mac (see Chapter 6), and then import them into BusyCal.

 If your aim is to import the addresses into Microsoft Entourage on the Mac, or OS X's own Contacts program, though, read on.

5. **Open Outlook Express or Windows Mail.**

 Yes, Outlook Express for Windows (or, in Windows 7/8, Windows Mail), the free program that comes on every PC. You'll use it as a glorified converter program.

6. **Follow the instructions on page 264 for exporting the contacts into a format suitable for your Mac.**

 That page outlines several ways to get your contacts from Outlook Express into OS X's Contacts—your Act info's final resting place.

Ad Subtract (Pop-Up Stopper)

Nothing quite spoils the fun of the Web like pop-ups—those annoying miniature advertising windows that sprout in front of the Web page you're trying to read.

Safari, OS X's Web browser, has a built-in command for blocking pop-ups: Safari→Preferences→Privacy→Block Pop-Up Windows. Nowadays, so does just about every other Web browser made for the Mac—Firefox, Netscape, Chrome, and so on. In other words, you don't even *need* Ad Subtract.

If you're interested in some of Ad Subtract's other features, like blocking animated ads or zapping all ads on Web pages, consider SafariBlock (for Safari) or Adblock (for Firefox). Or, for Safari, the awesome ClickToFlash, which simply neutralizes all

of those annoying *blinking* ads. All three are free and available for download from this book's "Missing CD" at *www.missingmanuals.com*.

Adobe [your favorite program here]

Most of Adobe's bestsellers are available in Mac versions, including Photoshop, Photoshop Elements, After Effects, Illustrator, InDesign, GoLive, Acrobat, Acrobat Reader, Premiere, and so on.

You don't have to do any document conversion. A Windows Photoshop document is exactly the same thing as a Macintosh Photoshop document, for example.

AOL

Truth is, you don't actually need an AOL *program* on your Mac. You can access all your AOL mail, as well as all of AOL's features, on the Web at *www.aol.com*.

AIM (AOL Instant Messenger)

If you're an online chat junkie, switching to the Mac involves very little disruption to your routine. AIM is available for the Mac, too, and it awaits your download at *www.aim.com*. Better yet, the minute you fire it up, you'll discover that your entire Windows-version Buddies list is intact and ready to use. (That's because it actually lives on the America Online network, not on your Windows PC.)

Tip: Actually, you might have a lot more fun—and save a lot of effort—by just using Messages. It's a built-in OS X chat program that's compatible with the whole AIM network, as described in Chapter 13.

Children's Software

Thanks to the vast number of Macs in schools, a huge percentage of educational software programs are available in both Mac and Windows versions—often on the same CD. That includes most programs from The Learning Company (including the Arthur, Carmen Sandiego, Little Bear, and Reader Rabbit series), Broderbund (Mavis Beacon, The Print Shop, and so on), Humongous Entertainment (series like Putt-Putt and Freddi Fish), and other major educational publishers.

Chrome

See "Google Chrome."

Easy CD Creator

You don't need any add-on software at all to burn CDs in OS X. You can just drag files and folders onto the icon of a blank CD, if you have an external drive.

If you want fancier features—recording less common disc formats, for example—what you need is Toast for the Macintosh. It comes from the same company that makes Easy CD Creator.

Its main rival is Discribe *(www.charismac.com)*. Both programs can create audio CDs, video CDs, data DVDs, and so on. Both come with a program that helps you turn old vinyl records and tapes into digital CDs, too.

The only disappointment: Neither program can treat a CD as a glorified floppy disk, as Easy CD Creator for Windows can, so that you can add and delete files freely (rather than burning the CD all at once).

There's a workaround, though: Copy the contents of a rewriteable CD (a CD-RW disc) to a folder on your desktop; make whatever changes you like to the contents of this folder; and then burn the CD-RW again. (Use the Disk Utility program in your Applications→Utilities folder to erase the disc first.)

Tip: Ordinarily, the CD-burning feature of OS X burns the entire CD each time, even if you've only filled a small portion of it. But if you download the handy $17 shareware program called CD Session Burner, you can perform additional "mini-burns" of new data to the CD until all the space is used up. Each such *session* shows up on your desktop with its own icon, as though it's a separate disc. You can download this program from *www.sentman.com/CD_Session_Burner.html*.

Encarta

Microsoft's bestselling encyclopedia program isn't available for the Macintosh. The World Book Encyclopedia is, however. (Details at *www.worldbook.com*.)

But most people just use Wikipedia, the Web-based encyclopedia.

Eudora

The ancient Mac version of Eudora no longer runs in OS X. Your only option is to import your mail into a more modern Mac mail program, like Mail or Outlook for Mac.

Excel

See "Microsoft Office" in this chapter.

Firefox

On Windows, Firefox is a faster, more secure, better-featured Web-browsing alternative to Internet Explorer. If you'd like, you can download the identical Mac version from *www.getfirefox.com,* and then follow the instructions on page 263 for transferring your bookmarks.

Alternatively, you can switch to OS X's built-in, super-fast Safari browser. Chapter 12 houses the coverage of the Safari adventure.

Games

Nobody switches to the Mac to play games; of the top 250 computer games for Windows, only about 150 are available for the Macintosh.

Still, that number includes the majority of the big-name titles and series, including Guitar Hero, Spore, Civilization, Madden NFL, Tiger Woods PGA, the various Sims games, Civilization, Quake, Harry Potter, Spider-Man, Tomb Raider, Warcraft, Jedi Knight, Soldier of Fortune, Max Payne, Links Championship Edition, Age of Empires, Medal of Honor, Return to Castle Wolfenstein, and hordes of others.

And once you do get these programs going on the Mac, you're likely to be impressed. Recent Macs generally come equipped with pleasantly high-horsepower graphics cards—the kind that serious computer gamers crave.

If you're a game nut, you can stay in touch with what's new and upcoming by reading the articles (and watching the game "trailers") at *www.apple.com/games,* not to mention *www.insidemacgames.com, www.macgamer.com,* and *www.macgamefiles.com.*

Google Desktop Search

OS X's Spotlight feature does everything that Google Desktop does—searching inside files, finding favorite Web sites, and so on. Spotlight just does it better.

Google Earth

Google's wicked-cool searchable, navigable digital version of the planet Earth is available for the Mac, too. Download it at *www.earth.google.com.*

Google Chrome

Google's fast, popular Web browser is available for the Mac, just as it is in Windows. You can download it from *www.google.com/chrome.* (Details on transferring your bookmarks are in the previous chapter.)

ICQ

If you're a fan of this Internet-wide chat program, look no further than ICQ for Mac or one of its many shareware rivals.

Internet Explorer

Microsoft once wrote an Internet Explorer version for the Mac, but abandoned it years ago. Safari (Apple's built-in Web browser) blocks pop-up windows, loads pages faster, and doubles as an RSS reader for news sites. See Chapter 12.

If some Web site (like a banking site) refuses to work with Safari, then download Chrome or Firefox for the Mac instead; they work with almost everything.

iTunes

If you grew used to iTunes on Windows, you'll be glad to know that the Mac version is already sitting in your Applications folder. Read all about it on page 323.

Just move your iTunes Library folder from the Music folder of your old PC into the Music folder on your Mac. That's all there is to it!

McAfee VirusScan

There's a Mac version of VirusScan, all right—but don't buy it. You don't even need a virus program for OS X. (If you run Windows on your Mac, as described in the next chapter, then you can install your antivirus program onto that side of the computer, by all means.)

Microsoft Access

Microsoft has never been interested in creating a Macintosh equivalent of its flagship database program (which comes with the higher-priced versions of Microsoft Office for Windows). FileMaker, a much easier-to-use database program, towers over the Macintosh database market like the Jolly Green Giant (and has a decent following on the Windows side, too). Resistance, Microsoft apparently assumes, is futile.

It's easy enough to get your data out of Microsoft Access; just choose File→Export. In the resulting dialog box, you can choose from a number of common export formats that can serve as intermediaries between the Windows and Mac worlds (see Figure 7-1).

Among them is Microsoft Excel—that is, you can turn your database into a spreadsheet. The beauty here is that FileMaker on the Macintosh can turn Excel documents into FileMaker databases without even batting an eye. You just drag the exported Excel document onto the FileMaker icon, and FileMaker does the rest.

UP TO SPEED

Viruses in OS X (Not!)

One of the greatest perks of moving to Macintosh is that viruses are practically nonexistent. At this writing, in fact, not a *single widespread virus* for OS X has turned up.

The only viruses that manage to sneak into OS X are Microsoft Word macro viruses that hide in ordinary Word files sent to you by your Windows friends.

> **Warning**
>
> The document you are opening contains macros or customizations. Some macros may contain viruses that could harm your computer.
>
> If you are sure this document is from a trusted source, click Enable Macros. If you are not sure and want to prevent any macros from running, click Disable Macros.
>
> [Tell Me More]
>
> [Enable Macros] [Do Not Open] [Disable Macros]

Fortunately, on the Mac version of Word, most of these don't run at all. Also, whenever you try to open a document that contains macros that you didn't create yourself, you see the message shown here. All you have to do is click Disable Macros. The file opens normally, 100 percent virus free.

Unfortunately, there's more to an Access database than just its data. Your database may well have fancy forms (layouts), complete with letterhead and other graphic elements, not to mention relational links between database files. In these cases, the situation isn't quite so hopeful—there's no way to export layouts and relational links to the Macintosh.

Your best bet might be to run Microsoft Access itself on the Macintosh, as described in Chapter 8.

Figure 7-1:
When you export your data from Access, you can choose from any of several formats. The idea is that you'll transfer the resulting exported file onto your Mac and then import it into a proper database program there.

Microsoft Money

Microsoft has abandoned its Money personal-finance program, so you would have had to export your Money data to Quicken whether you switched to the Mac or not.

It's easy enough to export your Money data into Quicken for the Mac, although not every scrap of information comes through alive. You'll lose your Money abbreviations, comments, and Lifetime Planner information. Fortunately, the important stuff—your accounts and the transactions in them, including categories, classes, and stocks that you've set up—come through in one piece.

Unfortunately, you have to export one account at a time. Furthermore, you'll be creating something called a QIF (Quicken Interchange Format) file as an intermediary between Windows and the Mac—and this file format can't handle category names longer than 15 characters. Before you begin, then, you might want to take a moment either to shorten them or to make a note of which ones might get truncated in the transfer.

Ready? Fire up Money on your Windows PC and then proceed like this:

1. **Choose File ›Export.**

 The Export dialog box appears. It wants to know if you are exporting your information to another version of Money ("Loose QIF") or to some other, rival financial program that shall, as far as Microsoft is concerned, remain nameless.

2. **In the resulting dialog box (Figure 7-2), choose Strict QIF, and then click OK.**

 Now you're supposed to name and save the exported file. Make sure you give each account a descriptive name (like Citibank Savings).

Figure 7-2:
Use the Strict QIF option. It lops off category names longer than 15 characters.

3. **Specify a name and a folder on your PC for the exported file, and then click OK.**

 Repeat these three steps for each of your Money accounts.

4. **Specify the kind of account (usually you'll want Regular, not Investment), and which one of your accounts to export.**

 Click OK when the exporting is done.

5. **Transfer the exported files to the Mac.**

 You can do it via network, email, or any of the other techniques described in Chapter 6. Then move to the Macintosh, open Quicken, and create a new file (see the Quicken instructions). Then, once you've got an empty "check register" before you, continue like this:

6. **Choose File→Import QIF. In the "Select a QIF file" dialog box, navigate to, and open, the first exported account file.**

 When the dust settles, you'll see your Money transactions safely ensconced in Quicken. (If you see a message that some transactions couldn't be completed, don't

worry; it's usually just telling you that some of your category names were longer than 15 characters and have been marked with asterisks to help you spot them.)

If you have more than one account, choose File→New Account to set it up, and then repeat from step 4 to bring in your other Money accounts.

Microsoft Office

Microsoft Office is available for the Mac in what some critics have declared to be a more attractive, less frustrating version than the Windows incarnation. At this writing, the current version is called Office for Mac 2011.

The beauty of Microsoft Word, Excel, and PowerPoint documents is that their format is the same on Mac and Windows. You can freely exchange files without having to go through any kind of conversion. (The big exception, as noted earlier, is Access; Microsoft doesn't make a database program for the Mac.)

In heavily formatted documents, you may occasionally see some strange differences: Windows documents containing many numbered paragraphs sometimes become confused on the Mac, for example. And if the Mac and the originating PC don't have the same fonts installed, you'll see different fonts, too. Otherwise, documents look identical despite having been shuttled to a different kind of computer.

Tip: With Office 2007 for Windows, Microsoft introduced a set of new file formats (.docx for Word, .pptx for PowerPoint, and so on) that are more compact than the previous set (.doc, .ppt, and so on). When you save a document, you can choose which format you want to use: the old one, which 400 million other people can open on their Macs and PCs, or the new one, which only recent upgraders can open.

Exactly the same conundrum presents itself on the Mac. Office 2008 and 2011 can open and create those same newfangled files, but the previous versions (like Office 2004 for the Mac) can open only the older formats.

Microsoft Publisher

Microsoft Publisher is a comprehensive page-layout program, complete with canned designs, clip art, and so on.

There's no Mac version of it, but you can perform most of the same tasks using Pages. (Pages is part of Apple's $80 iWork software suite; you can download a 30-day trial from *www.apple.com/iwork*.) Like Publisher, Pages offers dozens of attractive, ready-to-use page-design templates that you can adapt as you see fit.

There are also plenty of standalone page-design programs—this is the Mac, after all—including professional powerhouses like Adobe InDesign and QuarkXPress.

Microsoft Visio

If flowcharts, org charts, network diagrams, family trees, project processes, office layouts, and similar diagrams are part of your own personal workflow, you're in luck—at

least some luck. Microsoft Visio isn't available in a Macintosh version, but you'll probably find that OmniGraffle for OS X is a satisfactory, even delightful, replacement (see Figure 7-3). The Pro version even lets you import and export Visio documents.

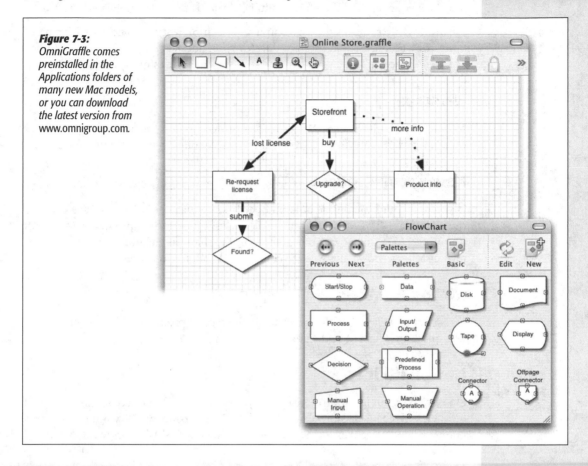

Figure 7-3:
OmniGraffle comes preinstalled in the Applications folders of many new Mac models, or you can download the latest version from www.omnigroup.com.

Minesweeper

Time wasters, rejoice! There are a number of free Minesweeper programs for OS X, including CocoaMines and Aqua Mines. You can download them from the Mac App Store.

NaturallySpeaking

Speech-recognition programs have traditionally been far more advanced on Windows than on the Macintosh. Windows programs like Dragon NaturallySpeaking transcribe your dictated text with almost *Star Trek*–like accuracy, and even let you make corrections and manipulate the computer itself using all voice commands.

Fortunately, the Mac program called Dragon Dictate for Mac (*www.macspeech.com*) uses precisely the same "recognition engine" as NaturallySpeaking. If you just can't use the keyboard, or don't want to, you'll be amazed at its speed and accuracy, although it's much younger (and therefore less fully featured) than NaturallySpeaking.

Finally, of course, there's the Mac's built-in Dictation feature (page 218). It's a bare-bones, down-and-dirty transcription feature that doesn't give you the same accuracy as Dragon Dictate. But it's built-in and free, which is worth quite a bit.

Netscape

Netscape, on both Mac and Windows, has grown up into the beloved Web browser called Firefox. It comes in an OS X version—free, of course—from *http://getfirefox.com.*

Newsgroup Readers

If you're a fan of the online bulletin boards known as *newsgroups,* you've come to the right place. The Mac is crawling with newsgroup-reading programs. Microsoft Entourage, for instance, has one built in. In the shareware world, you can take your pick of MT-NewsWatcher X, NewsHunter, and Halime, to name a few.

Norton AntiVirus

You can buy Norton AntiVirus for the Macintosh, no problem (*www.symantec.com*). The question is, why? See the box on page 273.

Norton Utilities

On Windows, this program defragments your hard drive, helps recover files in case of disaster, and repairs disk problems. There's no Mac version, but very similar Mac programs are available; for example, Mac veterans swear by DiskWarrior (*www.alsoft.com).*

Notepad

If you're an aficionado of this beloved note-taking tool in the standard Windows Start menu, you're in luck. OS X's Stickies program is even more powerful, because it offers formatting and even graphics. Or, for more of a word-processor effect, check out TextEdit.

Outlook/Outlook Express/Windows Mail

OS X's built-in Mail program is similar to Outlook Express for Windows (or Windows Mail in Vista and Windows 7), just more powerful and a lot better-looking. Chapter 6 describes the process of switching, and Chapter 11 covers the rest of the Mail experience.

If you want all the features from *Outlook,* though, you'd probably be better off using Microsoft Outlook for Mac, which is available as part of Microsoft Office for Mac.

PaintShop Pro

If your goal is to retouch and edit digital photos, the closest you can come to Paint-Shop on the Mac is probably Photoshop Elements, a terrific OS X program (about $100) that belongs on the hard drive of any serious digital camera owner. (Any digital camera owner who doesn't own the full-blown Photoshop program, that is.)

If your goal is to organize and *use* your photos, rather than paint on them, remember that iPhoto is already on your hard drive.

Finally, if opening and converting graphics to other formats is your main concern, try Preview (page 67), whose exporting feature is surprisingly powerful. You may also want to investigate the beloved shareware program GraphicConverter, which may be the last graphics editing/converting program you'll ever need.

Picasa

Google's Picasa, one of several Windows photo organizers, is also available for the Mac. Now, therefore, you have a choice; you can edit, organize, and order prints of your images with either Picasa or iPhoto.

PowerPoint

PowerPoint is available on the Mac; see "Microsoft Office" in this chapter. Remember, too, that Apple's own Keynote presentation program (available as part of iWork for $80) is the same idea as PowerPoint, but with more spectacular graphic effects.

QuickBooks

If you've been happily using QuickBooks for Windows to manage your small business—to prepare estimates and invoices, track bills, maintain lists of inventory and customers, and so on—there's good news and bad news. The good news is that QuickBooks is available on the Mac, and the steps for transferring your company files aren't difficult.

The bad news is that the transfer isn't perfect. Along the way, you might lose your memorized transactions, custom report designs, and reconciliations. Note, too, that you may not be able to send an older Windows file (like QuickBooks 2007) to an older version on the Mac (like QuickBooks 2006).

It's not especially hard; heck, there's a File→Utilities→Copy Company File for Quick-Books Mac command right in QuickBooks for Windows. You can find the rest of the step-by-step instructions in two places:

- **Open the electronic Help for QuickBooks for Mac,** and search for this topic: "Converting a QuickBooks file from Windows to Mac."

- **Follow the do-it-yourself procedure** described on Intuit's Support Web page (here's a short link to it: *http://j.mp/xS9PuS*).

Quicken

If you've been keeping track of your personal finances in Quicken on your PC, you'll feel right at home when you move to the Mac. Quicken 2015 is available for OS X.

In general, switching over is quick and painless. You can import into the Mac version of Quicken all of the actual transaction information, including accounts, the categories and classes you've used to group them, and stock holdings. Certain kinds of Windows Quicken information—like schedule transactions, QuickFill transactions, online account information, stock histories, and loan information—don't make it, however.

For the official manual on transferring your Quicken data from Windows to the Mac, download the free "Transferring Quicken" PDF appendix from this book's "Missing CD" at *www.missingmanuals.com*.

If the technology gods are smiling, the Mac version of Quicken should take only a moment to import all of your Windows data, which now appears neatly in your Register windows, ready to use. Make sure the final balances match the final balances in Quicken for Windows. (If they don't, scan your Mac registers for duplicate or missing transactions.)

RealPlayer

Want to listen to Internet music and watch Internet video in Real format, just as you did on your PC? No sweat. Visit *www.real.com* and download RealPlayer Cloud for OS X, either in the free basic edition or the fancy paid version.

If you just want to listen to music on your *hard drive,* though, you'd be better off using iTunes (page 331).

RssReader

RSS is a technology for reading quick Web site summaries, and it's taken the Net by storm. RSS returns the Internet to real utility, free from pop-up ads and the other annoyances of Web life.

To take advantage of RSS, however, you need a program to *subscribe* to Web sites that support RSS—and then to display the resulting summaries. In Windows, you might use a program like RssReader. On the Mac, you can download any number of great, free RSS readers from the Mac App Store—or use a Web-based RSS reader like *www.feedly.com*.

Skype

For making Internet-based phone calls, it's hard to beat Skype. If you call from one computer to another, you pay absolutely nothing—no matter how far away your recipient is.

Luckily, you can download a Mac version from *www.skype.com*. From there, you can audiochat with all your Mac- and PC-using Skype buddies until you lose your voice.

Tip: Messages, Apple's own instant-messaging program, also offers free audiochats. If you and your buddy both have Web cams or video cameras, in fact, you can make free, Internet *video* calls. See Chapter 13 for the details.

Snagit (Screenshots)

If you prepare instructions for using any kind of computer or software—computer books, magazine articles, or how-to materials of any kind—you may already be familiar with this amazing screen-capture program. It captures any window, menu, or area of the Windows screen and saves it as a graphics file that you can print or pop into a layout program.

In OS X, this feature is built right in. Here's how to capture:

- **The whole screen.** Press Shift-⌘-3 to create a picture file on your desktop, in PNG format, that depicts the entire screen image. A satisfying camera-shutter sound tells you that you were successful.

 The file is called *Picture 1*. Each time you press Shift-⌘-3, you get another file, called Picture 2, Picture 3, and so on. You can open these files in Preview, Photoshop, or another graphics program, in readiness for editing or printing.

- **One section of the screen.** You can capture only a rectangular *region* of the screen by pressing Shift-⌘-4. When you drag and release the mouse, you hear the camera-click sound, and the Picture file appears on your desktop as usual.

- **One menu, window, icon (with its name), or dialog box.** Once you've got your menu or window open onscreen, or the icon visible (even if it's on the Dock), press Shift-⌘-4. But instead of dragging diagonally, press the space bar.

 Now your cursor turns into a tiny camera. Move it so that the misty highlighting fills the window or menu you want to capture—and then click. The resulting Picture file snips the window or menu neatly from its background. (Press the space bar a second time to exit "snip one screen element" mode and return to "drag across an area" mode.)

Tip: If you hold down the Control key as you release your fingers from the click or drag (using any of the techniques described above), you copy the screenshot to your *Clipboard,* ready for pasting, rather than saving it as a new graphics file on your desktop.

OS X also offers another way to create screenshots: a program called Grab, which offers a timer option that lets you set up the screen before it takes the shot. It's in your Applications→Utilities folder.

But if you're really serious about capturing screenshots, you should opt instead for Snapz Pro X (*www.ambrosiasw.com*), which can capture virtually anything on the screen—even movies of onscreen procedures, along with your narration—and save it in your choice of format.

Solitaire

Ah yes, Solitaire: possibly the most overused Windows software in the world.

The Mac doesn't come with a preinstalled copy of Solitaire (neither does Windows 8, actually), but the world is crawling with free and shareware solitaire games for the Mac. Open the Mac App Store app on your hard drive; in the search box, type *solitaire*.

When you click Go or press Return, you'll see a substantial list of solitaire games, ready to download: FreeCell, Klondike, and so on.

Street Atlas USA

Mapping software is, alas, a weak spot in the Mac software catalog. Street Atlas USA and Route 66, for example, are no longer available for the Mac.

Then again, who cares? You live in the age of Google Maps (*http://maps.google.com*). It's fast, it's convenient, it works the same on both Mac and Windows, it gives spectacularly good driving directions, and it's free.

TaxCut, TurboTax

Both TaxCut and TurboTax are available for the Mac. You can even buy state versions of TurboTax for the states that require income tax returns. You can buy them wherever fine Mac programs are sold.

Winamp, MusicMatch

When it comes to playing MP3 files, creating MP3 files, burning music CDs, and otherwise organizing your music library, you'd be hard-pressed to beat iTunes, the free OS X program that's already on your Mac (and a free download from *www.apple.com/itunes*).

Windows Media Player

The Macintosh equivalent for Windows Media Player is, of course, QuickTime Player. It handily plays and shows almost any kind of movie, picture, or sound (although you'll want to use iTunes for most music playback).

There are a few entertainment sources that come in the Windows Media format, however, notably Windows Media Video (.wmv) movies that play on Web sites. By itself, QuickTime Player can't play them.

Microsoft actually went to the trouble of creating a Macintosh version of Windows Media Player (never mind the irony of its name). You can download it from *www.microsoft.com/mac,* but it's officially been abandoned.

The more modern, equally free solution is to download and install Flip4Mac. It's technically a plug-in for QuickTime Player, but you don't need to know that. All you need to know is that once you've installed it, you can suddenly play all those Web videos that you couldn't play before. You can download it from this book's "Missing CD" at *www.missingmanuals.com.*

WinZip

In OS X, you create a .zip file by right-clicking any Finder icon and choosing "Compress [the icon's name]" from the shortcut menu. You decompress a .zip file by simply double-clicking its icon in the Finder.

Word

See "Microsoft Office" in this chapter.

WordPerfect

Unfortunately, WordPerfect lost the battle with Microsoft Word on the Mac side pretty much the way it did on the Windows side. If you're a die-hard WordPerfect fan, your best bet might be to invest in Microsoft Word and capitalize on its keystroke-customizing features to turn it into a living simulation of WordPerfect.

Or, if you'd rather not spend a significant portion of your life's savings on a word processor, use the free Word-importing and -exporting features of TextEdit (page 689).

Yahoo Messenger

The equivalent chat program on the Mac is, of course, Yahoo Messenger for OS X. It's a free download from *http://messenger.yahoo.com.* (But Messages, described in Chapter 13, can also handle Yahoo.)

Windows on the Mac

T he very moment Apple announced in 2006 that all new Mac models would come with Intel chips inside, the geeks and the bloggers started going nuts. "Let's see," they thought. "Macs and PCs now use exactly the same memory, hard drives, monitors, mice, keyboards, networking protocols, *and processors.* By our calculations, it ought to be possible to make a Mac run Windows!"

Now, some in the Cult of Macintosh were baffled by the very idea. Who on earth, they asked, wants to pollute the magnificence of the Mac with a headache like Windows?

Lots of people, as it turns out. Think of all the potential switchers who are tempted by the Mac's sleek looks, yet worry about leaving Windows behind entirely. Or the people who love Apple's iLife programs, but have jobs that rely on Microsoft Access, Outlook, or some other piece of Windows corporateware. Even true-blue Mac fans occasionally look longingly at some of the Windows-only games, Web sites, or movie download services they thought they'd never be able to use.

Today, there are two ways to run Windows 7 (or later) on a Mac:

- **Restart it in Boot Camp.** Boot Camp is a little Apple program that lets you *restart* your Mac into Windows.

 At that point, it's a full-blown Windows PC, with no trace of the Mac on the screen. It runs at 100 percent of the speed of a real PC, because it is one. Compatibility with Windows software is excellent. The only downsides: Your laptop battery life isn't as good, and you have to restart the Mac *again* to return to the familiar world of OS X.

Tip: What's cool, though, is that even when you're running Windows, you can still access your Mac files and folders, as described below.

- **Run Windows in a window.** For $80 or so, you can eliminate the Boot Camp Bummer—the business of having to restart the Mac every time you want to switch its operating-system personality. You can buy a program like Parallels or VMware Fusion, which let you run Windows *in a window.*

You're still running OS X, and all your Mac files and programs are still available. But you've got a parallel universe—Microsoft Windows—running in a window simultaneously.

Compared with Boot Camp, this *virtualization software* offers only 90 percent of the speed. But for thousands of people, the convenience of eliminating all those restarts—and gaining the freedom to copy and paste documents between OS X and Windows programs—makes the Windows-in-a-window solution nearly irresistible.

Tip: There's nothing wrong with using *both* on the same Mac, by the way (Boot Camp plus a virtualization program). In fact, both Parallels and Fusion can use the *same copy of Windows* as Boot Camp, so you save disk space and don't have to manage two different Windows worlds.

Both techniques require you to provide your own copy of Windows. And both are described on the following pages.

Boot Camp

To set up Boot Camp, you need the proper ingredients:

- **A copy of Windows 7 or later.** OS X requires the Home Premium, Pro, or Ultimate editions of Windows 7—or any version of Windows 8 or 8.1. In all cases, it has to be the *64-bit version* of Windows, and it has to be a full installation copy—not an upgrade version.

FREQUENTLY ASKED QUESTION

The Virus Question

Doesn't running Windows on my Mac mean that I'll be exposed to the nightmare of viruses and spyware, just like the rest of the Windows world?

Yep!

If you install Windows on your Mac, you should also install Windows antivirus and antispyware software to protect that half of the computer. The world is crawling with commercial programs that do the job. There are also lots of free programs, like Microsoft Security Essentials, which protects you against both viruses and spyware.

The good news is that even if your Windows installation gets infected, the Mac side of your computer is unaffected. Just as OS X can't run Windows-only software like, say, Microsoft Access, it also can't run Windows virus software.

Some people, therefore, run Windows naked—without virus protection (especially when using Windows-in-a-window programs like Parallels and VMware Fusion). If a virus does strike, no big deal; they just drag the infected copy of Windows to the Trash and install a fresh one!

A DVD copy of Windows is fine—if your Mac has a DVD drive. Since it probably doesn't, you need an electronic copy of Windows, which you can download as a simulated disk called an *ISO disk image*. (You can also *make* an ISO out of a DVD copy of Windows—for example, at a friend's house. A friend with a DVD drive.)

- **At least 10 gigs of free hard drive space** on your built-in hard drive, or a second internal drive. (You can't install Windows on an external drive using Boot Camp.)

- **The keyboard and mouse that came with your Mac.** You can also use a generic USB keyboard and mouse; what you *can't* use is a non-Apple cordless keyboard and mouse.

- **A USB flash drive or USB hard drive.** You have to use Disk Utility (page 701) to format it using the MS-DOS (FAT) formatting scheme. This drive will hold the drivers your Mac needs once it's running in Windows. So let's call this the "drivers drive."

- **A DVD drive, or a second USB flash drive.** If you have Windows on a disc, then of course you also need a DVD drive for your Mac. If you plan to use the ISO disk image version of Windows, you need a *second* USB flash drive (8 gigabytes or bigger) to hold the Windows image. Let's call this one the "Windows flash drive."

- **At least 30 gigabytes of free space** on your Mac's internal hard drive. Windows is not svelte.

Before you begin, Apple strongly recommends that you back up your Mac, make sure it's running the latest version of Yosemite, and ensure that you have the latest version of Boot Camp (visit *www.apple.com/support/bootcamp*). If you're using a laptop, plug it in for the surgery.

Installing Boot Camp

To begin, connect the drivers drive to your Mac.

Phase 1: Build the drivers drive

Open your Applications→Utilities folder. Inside, open the program called Boot Camp Assistant.

Click Continue. You arrive at the Select Tasks screen (Figure 8-1), where you have three options:

- **Create a Windows 7 or later install disk.** This checkbox means "Use the ISO image of Windows, because I don't have a DVD drive." When you click Continue, Boot Camp Assistant will copy the ISO image to your Windows flash drive.

 If you plan to install Windows from its DVD, on the other hand, you can leave this off (if, indeed the option appears at all).

- **Download the latest Windows support software from Apple.** One of Boot Camp's primary jobs is to teach Windows to recognize and operate all your Mac's hardware components: keyboard, trackpad, camera, WiFi, and so on. And, as you may know, Windows does that by requiring an installed *driver* (software nugget) for each one

of these components. Well, guess what? Out of the box, Windows does not know about any Apple hardware elements. Surprise, surprise.

So your first job is to create an installation disk that contains these drivers. That's the purpose of the drivers drive.

Figure 8-1:
Boot Camp plans to guide you through preparing the three primary ingredients in the Boot Camp recipe. Set aside a whole afternoon for this.

• **Install Windows 7 or later version.** This option will guide you through partitioning (subdividing) your hard drive, and installing Windows onto one of the partitions.

Once you click Continue, the Mac downloads the Windows drivers it will need; allow 10 or 20 minutes, depending on your Internet speed.

Phase 2: Create the Windows partition on your Mac

When those setup tasks are complete, Boot Camp Assistant now asks you to *partition*, or subdivide, your hard drive. You're setting aside a certain amount of space that will hold your copy of Windows and all the PC software you decide to install. This partitioning process doesn't involve erasing your whole hard drive; all your stuff is perfectly safe. (You can't install Boot Camp if your hard drive is already partitioned—except for OS X's own Recovery partition, of course.)

The dialog box offers a Divide Equally button, but it also lets you drag a space-divider handle to divide up your drive space between the Mac and Windows sides; see Figure 8-2.

Note: Most people choose to dedicate a swath of the main internal hard drive to the Windows partition. But if you have a second internal hard drive, you can also choose one of these options: "Create a Second Partition" (the Boot Camp Assistant carves out a Windows partition from that drive) and "Erase Disk and Create a Single Partition for Windows" (just what it says).

When you click Install, you're in for another 10 or 20 minutes of waiting, as your Mac subdivides your main hard drive.

Phase 3: Install Windows

Now your Mac restarts. At this point, Apple steps back and Microsoft takes charge; the usual Windows installation process gets under way.

Begin by choosing your preferred language, time and currency formats, and text-input method. Click Next.

Figure 8-2:
Top: How much hard drive space do you want to dedicate to your "PC"? It's not an idle question; whatever you give Windows is no longer available for your Mac.

Apple recommends that for Windows 8 or 8.1, the Windows partition should be at least 30 gigabytes.

Drag the handle between the Mac and Windows sides of this diagram.

Bottom: Choose the partition called "Disk 1 Partition 3 BOOTCAMP." (The number may be different, but it will say "BOOTCAMP.")

Then click "Drive options (advanced)," click Format, click OK, and finally click Next. Your Windows partition is now formatted (it uses the NTFS formatting scheme, if anybody asks).

On the next screen, click Install Now. After some more waiting, you're asked to enter your Windows serial number (product key), and then agree to whatever Microsoft's lawyers say.

Now comes the only even remotely tricky part: At this point, Microsoft's installer asks which partition you want to put Windows on. It's *really* important to pick the right one. Play your cards wrong, and you could erase your whole *Mac* partition.

See Figure 8-2, bottom, for guidance.

Now your Mac looks just like a PC that's having Windows installed. Be patient; sit around for half an hour as the Windows installer flits about, restarts, does what it has to do.

When it's all over, a crazy, disorienting sight presents itself: your Mac, running Windows. There's no trace of the desktop, Dock, or menu; it's Windows now, baby.

Walk through the Windows setup screens, creating an account, setting the time, and so on.

At this point, your Mac is actually a true Windows PC. You can install and run Windows programs, utilities, and even games; you'll discover that they run *really* fast and well.

Phase 4: Install the Mac drivers

But as Windows veterans know, every hardware feature of Windows requires a *driver*—a piece of software that tells the machine how to communicate with its own monitor, networking card, speakers, and so on. And it probably goes without saying that Windows doesn't include any drivers for *Apple's* hardware components.

That's why, at this point, you need the drivers drive you created earlier. It contains all the drivers for the Mac's graphics card, Ethernet and WiFi networking, audio input and output, built-in camera, brightness and volume keys, ⏏ key, multitouch trackpad gestures, and Bluetooth transmitter. (It also installs a new Control Panel icon and system tray pop-up menu.)

When you insert this disc or flash drive, the drivers installer opens and begins work automatically. (If it doesn't, double-click the *setup.exe* file in the WindowsSupport or Boot Camp folder.)

Click past the Welcome and License Agreement screens, and then click Install. You'll see a lot of dialog boxes come and go; just leave it alone. Don't click any Cancel buttons. If you get a complaint that the software hasn't passed Windows Logo testing, click Continue Anyway.

Tip: If the installation seems to stall, Windows may be waiting for you to click OK or Next in a window that's hidden behind other windows. Inspect the taskbar and look behind open windows.

When it's all over, a dialog box asks you to restart the computer; click Restart. When the machine comes to, it's a much more functional Windows Mac. (And it has an online Boot Camp Help window waiting for you on the screen.)

Note: Once you're running Windows, you might wonder: How am I supposed to right-click? I don't have a two-button mouse or two-button trackpad!

Yes, you do. See page 16 for a panoply of options.

Forth and Back, Windows/Mac

From now on, your main interaction with Boot Camp will be telling it what kind of computer you want your Mac to be today: a Windows machine or a Mac.

Presumably, though, you'll prefer one operating system *most* of the time. Figure 8-3 (top and middle) shows how you specify your favorite.

Tip: If you're running Windows and you just want to get back to OS X right now, you don't have to bother with all the steps shown in Figure 8-3. Instead, click the Boot Camp system-tray icon and, from the shortcut menu, choose Restart in OS X.

From now on, each time you turn on the Mac, it starts up in the operating system you've selected.

UP TO SPEED

Removing Windows

Maybe you're a switcher who held onto Windows because you were worried that you'd need it. Maybe you're finished with the project, the job, or the phase of life that required you to use Windows on your Mac. One way or another, there may come a time when you want to get rid of your Windows installation and reclaim all the hard drive space it was using.

You can, and the process doesn't touch anything that's already on the Mac side. You don't have to erase your entire hard drive or anything—OS X simply erases what's on the Windows partition of your hard drive, and then adds that disk space back to your main *Mac* partition.

To do this, start by making sure you've rescued anything worth saving from the Windows side of your computer—it's about to be erased.

Start up in OS X, quit all open programs, and make sure nobody's logged in but you. Now open up the Boot Camp Assistant program in your Applications→Utilities folder.

On the Select Tasks screen, click "Install or remove Windows 7 or a later version." On the next screen, you're warned: "The Windows volume and all of its contents will be permanently lost." But you knew that. Click Restore.

That's all there is to it.

Special notes for special setups: If you installed Windows on a separate hard drive, rather than a partition of your main hard drive, don't bother with all this. Just erase the Windows hard drive using Disk Utility, as described on page 701, and format it as a Mac drive.

On the other hand, if your Mac has more than one internal hard drive and you created a Windows partition on one of them (rather than taking it over completely), then open Boot Camp Assistant as described above. Click the partition with Windows on it, and then click "Restore to a single Mac OS partition." Then click Continue.

If you ever need to switch—when you need Windows just for one quick job, for example—press the Option key as the Mac is starting up. You'll see something like the icons shown in Figure 8-3 (bottom).

Figure 8-3:

Top: To choose your preferred operating system—the one that always starts up unless you intervene—choose →System Preferences. Click Startup Disk, and then click the icon for either OS X or Windows. Next, either click Restart (if you want to switch right now) or close the pane. The identical controls are available when you're running Windows, thanks to the new Boot Camp control panel.

Middle: To open the Boot Camp control panel, choose its name from its icon in the Windows system tray.

Bottom: This display, known as the Startup Manager, appears when you press Option during startup. It displays all the disk icons or partitions that contain bootable operating systems. Click the one you want, and then click the up-arrow button.

Keyboard Translation Guide

Now, if you really want to learn about Windows, you need *Windows 7: The Missing Manual* or *Windows 8.1: The Missing Manual.*

But suggesting that you go buy *another* book would be tacky. So here's just enough to get by.

First of all, a Mac keyboard and a Windows keyboard aren't the same. Each has keys that would strike the other as extremely goofy. Still, you can trigger almost any keystroke Windows is expecting by substituting special Apple keystrokes, like this:

Windows keystroke	Apple keystroke
Ctrl+Alt+Delete	Control-Option-Delete
Alt	Option
⊞ key	⌘
Backspace	Delete
Delete (forward delete)	⌦ (laptops: fn-Delete)
Enter	Return
Num lock	Clear (laptops: fn-F6)
Print Screen	F14 (laptops: fn-F11)
Print active window	Option-F14 (laptops: Option-fn-F11)

The keyboard shortcuts in your programs are *mostly* the same as on the Mac, but you have to substitute the Ctrl key for the ⌘ key. So in Windows programs, Copy, Save, and Print are Ctrl+C, Ctrl+S, and Ctrl+P.

Similarly, the Alt key is the Windows equivalent of the Option key.

Tip: You know that awesome two-finger scrolling trick on Mac laptops? It works when you're running Windows, too.

If you really want to understand how your Mac keyboard corresponds to your old PC keyboard, don't miss Apple's thrilling document on the subject at *http://support. apple.com/kb/HT1167.*

Accessing Mac Files from the Dark Side—and Vice Versa

When you've started up in one operating system, it's easy to access documents that "belong" to the other one. For example:

• When you're running OS X, you can get to the documents you created while you were running Windows, which is a huge convenience. Just double-click the Windows disk icon (called NO NAME or Untitled), and then navigate to the Documents and Settings→[your account name]→My Documents (or Desktop).

You can only copy files *to* the Mac side, or open them without the ability to edit them.

Tip: You can rename the Windows disk, if you want, so it doesn't say NO NAME the rest of its life—as long as you do it while you're running Windows.

• When you're running Windows, you can get to your Mac documents, too. Click Start→Computer. In the resulting window, you'll see an icon representing your Mac's hard drive partition. Open it up.

You can see and open these files. But if you want to edit them, you have to copy them to your Windows world first—onto the desktop, for example, or into a folder. (The Mac partition is "read-only" in this way, Apple says, to avoid the possibility that your Mac stuff could get contaminated by Windows viruses.)

Tip: If you did want to edit Mac files from within Windows, one solution is to buy a $50 program called MacDrive (*www.mediafour.com*). Another solution: Use a disk that both OS X and Windows "see," and keep your shared files on *that*. A flash drive works beautifully for this. So does a shared drive on the network.

Windows in a Window

The problem with Boot Camp is that every time you switch to or from Windows, you have to close down everything you were working on and restart the computer—and reverse the process when you're done. You lose 2 or 3 minutes each way. And you can't copy and paste between Mac and Windows programs.

There is another way: an $80 utility called Parallels Desktop for Mac (*www.parallels.com*), or its rival, VMware Fusion (*www.vmware.com*). These programs let you run Windows and OS X *simultaneously;* Windows hangs out in a window of its own, while the Mac is running OS X (Figure 8-4). You're getting about 90 percent of Boot Camp's Windows speed—plenty fast for everything but 3-D games.

Figure 8-4:
The strangest sight you ever did see: OS X and Windows. On the same screen. At the same time. Courtesy of Parallels Desktop. VMware Fusion is very similar.

Once again, you have to supply your own copy of Windows for the installation process. This time, though, it can be any version of Windows, all the way back to Windows 3.1—or even Linux, FreeBSD, Solaris, OS/2, or MS-DOS. And Windows 8.1 works great.

Having virtualization software on your Mac is a beautiful thing. You can be working on a design in iWork, duck into a Microsoft Access database (Windows only), look up an address, copy it, and paste it back into the Mac program.

And what if you can't decide whether to use Boot Camp (fast and feature complete, but requires restarting) or Parallels/Fusion (fast and no restarting, but no 3-D games)? No problem—install both. They coexist beautifully on a single Mac and can even use the same copy of Windows.

Together, they turn the Macintosh into the Uni-Computer: the single machine that can run nearly 100 percent of the world's software catalog.

Virtualization Tip-O-Rama

Mastering Parallels or Fusion means mastering Windows, of course, but it also means mastering these tips:

- You don't *have* to run Windows in a window. With one keystroke, you can make your Windows simulator cover the entire screen. You're still actually running two operating systems at once, but the whole Mac world is hidden for the moment so you can exploit your full screen. Just choose View→Full Screen.

Tip: Or use the keystroke Control-⌘-F (Parallels) or Control-⌘-Return (Fusion) to enter and exit Full Screen mode. (These keystrokes tend to change from version to version. You've been warned.)

- Conversely, both Parallels and Fusion offer something called *Coherence* or *Unity* mode, in which there's no trace of the Windows desktop. Instead, each Windows

POWER USERS' CLINIC

Beyond the Big Names

Parallels and VMware Fusion are bloodthirsty rivals. New versions tumble out with alarming frequency, each designed to one-up the competitor's.

Both also let you specify which program—Mac or Windows—opens when you double-click documents of specific types (like .jpeg or .doc). That's yet another way Windows becomes a full player on the Mac team.

Still, these aren't the only options. Several efforts are afoot to create software that lets you run Windows software without Windows. The most promising one is a $60 program called

CrossOver (*www.codeweavers.com*). It's a commercialized version of Wine, a Unix-based Windows simulator.

Sure enough, CrossOver-compatible Windows programs open up and run in OS X just as though they were real Mac programs—without your having to own, install, or fire up a copy of Windows itself.

Unfortunately, the list of compatible programs is tiny. The CrossOver Web site lists 9,000 Windows apps that work, but only about 1,000 of them work perfectly. Still, you owe it to yourself to check the list to see if what you need is CrossOver-friendly.

program floats in its own disembodied window, just like a Mac program; the OS X desktop lies reassuringly in the background.

> **Tip:** In Fusion's Unity mode and Parallels' Coherence mode, you can access your Computer, Documents, Network, Control Panel, Search, and Run commands right from Fusion's or Parallels' Dock icon or launch palette, so you won't even care that there's no Start menu.

In Parallels, press Control-⌘-Return to enter or exit Coherence mode. In Fusion, hit Control-⌘-U for Unity mode.

> **Tip:** In Fusion, in Unity mode, you can use the usual Mac keystrokes for Cut, Copy, and Paste within Windows applications (⌘-X, ⌘-C, and ⌘-V). In Parallels, on the other hand, you can remap *all* Windows Ctrl-key shortcuts to the ⌘ key in Preferences.

- To send the "three-fingered salute" to shut down, restart, or lock Windows (usually Ctrl+Alt+Delete), press Control-Option-Delete (Fusion) or Control-fn-Alt-Delete (Parallels). Or use the Send Control-Alt-Del command in the menus.

- You can drag files back and forth between the Mac and Windows universes. Just drag icons into, or out of, the Windows window.

- If you have a one-button mouse, you can "right-click" in Parallels by Control-Shift-clicking. In Fusion, Control-click instead. On Mac laptops, you can right-click by putting two fingers on the trackpad as you click.

- When you quit the virtualization program, you're not really shutting down the PC; you're just *suspending* it, or putting it to sleep. When you double-click the Parallels/VMware icon again, everything in your Windows world is exactly as you left it.

- Your entire Windows universe of files, folders, and programs is represented by a single file on your hard drive. In Parallels, it's in your Home→Documents→Parallels folder. In Fusion, it's in your Home→Documents→Virtual Machines folder.

 That's super convenient, because it means you can back up your entire Windows "computer" by dragging a single icon to another drive. And if your Windows world ever gets a virus or spyware infestation, you can drag the entire thing to the Trash—and restore Windows from that clean backup.

Life with Microsoft Exchange

In the corporate world, Microsoft Exchange is the 800-pound gorilla. It's the networking software that runs the email, address books, and calendars for hundreds or thousands of employees. All of this communicates with a central master database whose heart beats away in some closet or back room at your company's headquarters.

For years, Macs have been second-class citizens in Corporate America. As long as they couldn't talk to the Exchange brain, they weren't much use outside the graphic-design department. (You could buy add-on software or muck with workarounds, but you always felt like a weirdo.)

Now, however, Exchange compatibility is built in. In the Mac's Calendar, your company's Exchange calendar shows up. In Mail, you can get all your corporate email. Best of all, this information shows up side by side with your own personal data, so you can have it all in one place. All the conveniences of OS X now apply to your corporate email: Spotlight, Quick Look, data detectors, and so on.

If your company is using Exchange 2007 or later (Service Pack 1, Update Rollup 4 and later), setting this up could not be easier.

Connecting to Exchange

To connect to your company's Exchange system, open System Preferences→Internet Accounts. Click the big Microsoft Exchange button, and then proceed as shown in Figure 8-5.

Figure 8-5:

Top: In System Preferences, fill in your Exchange information—your email address and password—as provided by your cheerful network administrator.

Middle: If you entered your information correctly and your Exchange server recognized you, then this box appears, summarizing the Mac's understanding of your Exchange account. You're all set.

If your Mac doesn't find the server, then either (a) your company doesn't use Exchange 2007 or later, or (b) your network geek hasn't turned on Exchange Autodiscover. In that case, you have no choice but to call that person over to your desk and either (a) harangue him for not turning on Autodiscover, or (b) have him fill in the server address and other boxes by hand.

Bottom: Which elements of your Exchange account do you want your Mac to display? If you choose Mail, for example, then your Mail app will display your Exchange email account. Contacts, Calendars, Notes, and Reminders will all show Exchange's information as specially identified accounts, which you can hide or show with one click.

Exchange in Mail

Once everything is set up, open Mail. If you have a lot of mail, it may take time for Mail to synchronize with the Exchange server and display your messages. But it gets there eventually. Your Exchange account appears with its own heading, beneath your personal accounts.

Now you can send and receive email, create notes and to-do items, respond to emailed invitations, and so on. All the Mail features described in Chapter 11 are ready to go: Spotlight can search all your accounts simultaneously, Smart Folders can round up messages from one account or all of them, Quick Look can show you attachments without your having to open them in a separate program, and so on.

Your corporate appointments now show up in the Mac's calendar (page 624), neatly filed under their own heading in the Calendars list.

And in Contacts, your company's Global Address Lists show up as a group in the Groups list.

GEM IN THE ROUGH

Delegating Your Calendars

Once you're all Exchanged up, you can even delegate your calendar—that is, permit someone else on your corporate network to see (and, if you wish, edit) your calendar from across the network. That's handy when you're a busy executive and you want your personal assistant to help you manage your busy life, or when you're going to be out of town and you've authorized a trusted minion to carry on with your calendar in your absence.

(This is not the same as publishing your calendar as described on page 636. Your Exchange calendar isn't actually going to move. It'll sit right there on the server—you're just giving someone else access to it.)

To set this up, choose Calendar→Preferences→Accounts. (If you have more than one account, choose the one you want to share from the Accounts list.)

Click Delegation. Click Edit. On the Manage Account Access screen, click +, and type the name of the person you want

to share your calendar with. You can also specify how much access you want that person to have; Read Only means she can just see your life, and Read & Write means she can actually edit it. You can grant different levels of access to your calendar and your Tasks list.

Finally, click Done.

Now change hats. Suppose you're the trusted assistant.

On your Mac, choose Calendar→Preferences→Accounts. You'll find the account that's been shared with you on "Delegation – Accounts I can access."

Finally, turn on the Show checkbox. Close the Preferences dialog box to return to the main Calendar display. Here your boss's calendars (appointment categories) show up in the left-side list; turn on the checkboxes of the ones you want to appear on the calendar grid.

Hardware on the Mac

Most of the discussion in this book so far has covered *software*—not only the OS X operating system that may be new to you, but also the programs and documents you'll be using on it. But there's more to life with a computer than software. This chapter covers the finer points of using Macintosh-compatible printers, cameras, disks, monitors, and keyboards.

Mac Meets Printer

Printing has always been one of the Mac's strong suits—and you're about to find out why.

Setting Up a Printer

Setting up a printer is incredibly easy. The first time you want to print something, follow this guide:

1. **Connect the printer to the Mac, and then turn the printer on.**

 Inkjet printers connect to your USB jack. Laser printers hook up either to your USB jack or to your network (Ethernet or wireless).

2. **Open the document you want to print. Choose File→Print. In the Print dialog box, choose your printer's name from the Printer pop-up menu (or one of its submenus, if any, like Nearby Printers). See Figure 9-1.**

 Cool! Wasn't that easy? Very nice how the Mac autodiscovers, autoconfigures, and autolists almost any USB, FireWire, Bluetooth, or Bonjour printer.

 Have a nice afternoon. The End.

Oh—unless your printer *isn't* listed in the Printer pop-up menu. In that case, read on.

Note: "Nearby Printers" refers to printers that aren't connected directly to your Mac but are accessible anyway: a printer connected to an Apple Time Capsule or an AirPort base station, certain network printers that speak Bonjour, or printers connected to other Macs that you've shared, as described later in this chapter.

3. **From the Printer pop-up menu (Figure 9-1, top), choose Add Printer.**

A special setup window opens (Figure 9-1, bottom), which is even better at auto-detecting printers available to your Mac. If you see the printer's name here, click it and then click Add.

You're all set. Have a good time. Unless, of course, your printer *still* isn't showing up. Proceed to step 4.

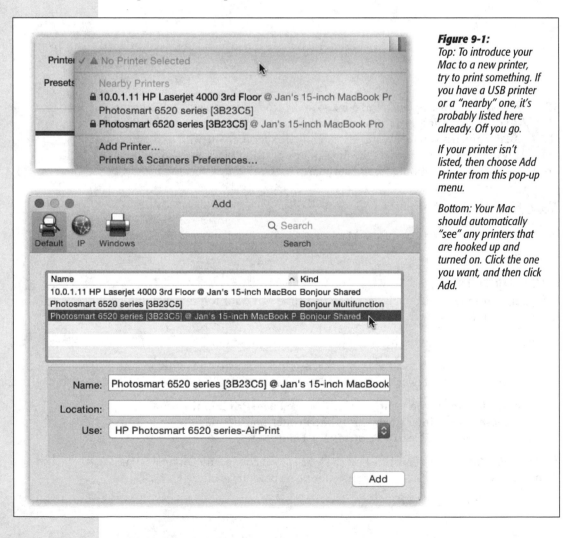

Figure 9-1:
Top: To introduce your Mac to a new printer, try to print something. If you have a USB printer or a "nearby" one, it's probably listed here already. Off you go.

If your printer isn't listed, then choose Add Printer from this pop-up menu.

Bottom: Your Mac should automatically "see" any printers that are hooked up and turned on. Click the one you want, and then click Add.

4. **Click the icon for the *kind* of printer you have: Default, IP, or Windows.**

 Default usually does the trick, especially if you have an inkjet printer. Choose IP if you have a network printer that's not showing up in Default. And choose Windows if there's a Windows-only printer out there on your office network.

 After a moment, the names of any printers that are turned on and connected appear in the printer list. For most people, that means only one printer—but one is enough.

5. **Click the name of the printer you want to use.**

 As an optional step, you can open the Use pop-up menu at the bottom of the dialog box. Choose "Select a driver to use," and then, in the list that appears, choose your particular printer's model name, if you can find it. That's how your Mac knows what printing features to offer you when the time comes: double-sided, legal size, second paper tray, and so on.

6. **Click Add.**

 After a moment, you return to the main Printer Browser window, where your printer now appears. You're ready to print.

Note: If you still don't see your printer's name show up, ask yourself this: Is my Mac on a corporate network? Does the network have an LPR (Line Printer Remote) printer? If you and your company's network nerd determine that the printer you want to use is, in fact, an LPR printer, then click IP Printing at the top of the Printer Browser dialog box. Fill in the appropriate IP address and other settings, as directed by your cheerful network administrator.

Finally: Is your printer one of those ancient AppleTalk models? OS X no longer works with AppleTalk printers, but there's a workaround. Check the free PDF appendix to this chapter, "The Death of AppleTalk." It's on this book's "Missing CD" page at *www.missingmanuals.com*.

Printer Preferences

If you're lucky enough to own several printers, then repeat the steps above for each one. Eventually, you'll have introduced the Mac to all the printers available to it, so all their names show up in the printer list.

To see the printer list so far, open System Preferences→Print & Scan. You can have all kinds of fun here (Figure 9-2):

- **Choose a default printer.** As indicated by the Default Printer pop-up menu, OS X intends, conveniently enough, to use whichever printer you used for the last printout for the next one. Most people, after all, don't switch printers much.

 Still, you can choose one particular printer from this pop-up menu to set it as the default printer—the one the Mac uses unless you intervene by choosing from the Printer pop-up menu in the Print dialog box.

- **Create desktop printer icons.** *This* handy, little-known feature gives you drag-and-drop access to your printers.

From the Print & Scan pane of System Preferences, just drag a printer's icon out of the window and onto the desktop (or wherever you like). Repeat for your other printers. From now on, you can print a document on a certain printer just by dragging the document's icon onto the appropriate printer icon.

- **Check the ink level.** Click a printer, and then click Options & Supplies, to see how your inkjet ink or laser-printer toner level is. That way you won't be caught short when you're on a deadline and your printer is out of ink. You now get a bright yellow "low ink" warning in the dialog box that actually appears when you print.

Figure 9-2:
You know that stuff you read about earlier? Setting up printers from the Print dialog box? You can do the same work here. Click the + button below the left-side list.

Making the Printout

You can't miss the Print dialog box. It appears, like it or not, whenever you choose File→Print in one of your programs.

The options you encounter depend on the printer you're using. They also depend on whether or not you *expand* the dialog box by clicking the Show Details button. That reveals a *lot* of useful options, including a handy preview; see Figure 9-3.

If you expand the box, the options you find vary by printer. But here are the common options:

- **Printer.** If you have more than one printer connected to your Mac, then you can indicate which you want to use for a particular printout by choosing its name from this pop-up menu.

- **Presets.** Here's a way to preserve your favorite print settings: Once you've proceeded through this dialog box, specifying the number of copies, which printer trays you want the paper taken from, and so on, you can choose Save As from the pop-up

menu and then assign your settings set a name (like "Borderless, 2 copies"). Thereafter, you'll be able to recreate that elaborate suite of settings simply by choosing its name from this pop-up menu.

- **Copies.** Type the number of copies you want printed. The Collated checkbox controls the printing order for the pages. For example, if you print two copies of a three-page document, the Mac generally prints the pages in this order: 1, 2, 3, 1, 2, 3. If you turn off Collated, on the other hand, it prints in this order: 1, 1, 2, 2, 3, 3.

- **Pages.** You don't have to print an entire document—you can print, say, only pages 2 through 15.

Tip: You don't have to type numbers into both the From and To boxes. If you leave the first box blank, the Mac assumes you mean "From page 1." If you leave the second box blank, the Mac understands that you mean "To the end." To print only the first three pages, in other words, leave the first box blank and type *3* into the second box. (These page numbers refer to the physical pages you're printing, not to any fancy numbering you've set up in your word processor. As far as the Print dialog box is concerned, the first printed page is page 1, even if you've told your word processor to label it "page 455.")

- **Paper Size, Orientation.** Here you can choose your paper size (such as letter or legal) and whether you want to print horizontally or vertically.

- **PDF.** A *PDF* file, of course, is an Adobe Reader (Acrobat) document—a file that any Mac, Windows, Linux, or Unix user can view, read, and print using either Preview or the free Adobe Reader (included with every PC and Mac operating system).

Figure 9-3:
Left: Most of the time, all you want is one darned copy of what's on your screen. So the standard Print dialog box is basic: a preview, page controls, and a Print button.

Right: But when you click Show Details, you get a new world of options: orientation, magnification, and so on.

You can easily save any document as a PDF file instead of printing it—a truly beautiful feature that saves paper, ink, and time. The document remains on your hard drive, and the text inside is even searchable using Spotlight.

And that's just the beginning. Apple has added a long list of additional PDF options (like password-protected PDFs, emailed ones, and so on). But Apple faced a design quandary: How could it offer a new list of PDF-related options without junking up the Print dialog box?

Its solution was a strange little item called a pop-up *button,* shown in Figure 9-3, bottom. Use it like a pop-up menu. The command you'll use most often is probably Save as PDF, which turns the printout into a PDF file instead of sending it to the printer. For details on the other PDF-related options here, see page 307.

If you examine the unnamed pop-up menu near the middle of the dialog box, you'll find dozens of additional options. They depend on your printer model and the program you're using at the moment, but here are some typical choices:

- **Media & Quality.** Here's where you specify the print quality you want, the kind of paper you're printing on, and so on. (The name of this pane varies by manufacturer.)

- **Layout.** You can save paper and ink or toner cartridges by printing several miniature "pages" on a single sheet of paper.

- **Paper Handling, Paper Feed.** If you chose the correct printer model when setting up your printer, then this screen "knows about" your printer's various paper trays. Here's where you specify which pages you want to come from which paper tray. (By far the most popular use for this feature is printing the first page of a letter on company letterhead and the following pages on blank paper from a second tray.) You can also opt to print your pages in reverse order so they stack correctly, or you can print just odd or just even pages so you can run them through again for double-sided printing.

Tip: Here's one for the technically inclined. Open your Web browser and enter this address: *http://127.0.0.1:631.* You find yourself at a secret "front end" for CUPS (Common Unix Printing System), the underlying printing technology for OS X. This trick lets your Mac communicate with a huge array of older printers that don't yet have OS X drivers. Using this administration screen, you can print a test page, stop your printer in its tracks, manage your networked printers and print jobs, and more—a very slick trick.

Printing

When all your settings look good, click Print (or press Return) to send your document to the printer.

Managing Printouts

After you've used the Print command, you can either sit there until the paper emerges from the printer, or you can *manage* the printouts-in-waiting. That option is attractive primarily to people who do a lot of printing, have connections to a lot of printers, or share printers with many other people.

Start by opening the printer's window. If you're already in the process of printing, just click the printer's Dock icon. If not, open →System Preferences→Print & Scan, click the printer's name, and then click Open Print Queue.

At this point, you see something like Figure 9-4. The printouts that will soon be sliding out of your printer appear in a tidy list.

Figure 9-4:
Waiting printouts appear in this window. You can pause (⏸), restart (↻) or cancel (✕) each printout with a click (the ↻ button shows up only after you've paused a printout.) Choosing Printer→Supply Levels will show you the amount of ink you have left in each cartridge (for some printers). If your printer is also a scanner, then clicking the scanner icon will pull up a basic scanner utility.

Here are some of the ways in which you can control these waiting printouts, which Apple collectively calls the *print queue:*

- **Delete them.** By clicking an icon, or ⌘-clicking several, and then clicking the Delete toolbar button, you remove items from the list of waiting printouts. Now they won't print.

- **Pause them.** By highlighting a printout and then clicking the Hold button, you pause that printout. It doesn't print until you highlight it again and then click the Resume button. (Other documents continue to print.) This pausing business could be useful when, for example, you need time to check or refill the printer, or when you're just about to print your letter of resignation as your boss drops by (maybe to offer you a promotion).

- **Halt them all.** You can stop all printouts from a printer by clicking Pause Printer. (They resume when you click the button again, which now says Resume Printer.)

You can't rearrange printouts by dragging them in the queue list. But remember that you can resequence the printing order by choosing the Scheduler option; you can also drag waiting printouts *between* these lists, shifting them from one printer to another.

Tip: As you now know, the icon for a printer's queue window appears automatically in the Dock when you print. But it also *stays* in the Dock for the rest of the day; it doesn't disappear when the printing is complete. If you wish it would, right-click (or two-finger click) the printer's Dock icon; from the shortcut menu, choose Auto Quit.

Printer Sharing

Printer sharing is for people (or offices) with more than one Mac, connected to a network, who'd rather not buy a separate printer for each machine. Instead, you connect the printer to one Mac, flip a couple of software switches, and then boom: The other Macs on the network can send their printouts to the printer without actually being attached to it—even wirelessly, if they're on an AirPort network.

Figure 9-5:
Top: On the Mac with the printer, open the Sharing pane of System Preferences. Turn on Printer Sharing and then turn on the checkboxes for the printers you want to share. Switch to the Print & Scan pane, and turn on "Share this printer on the network" for the printer(s) you want to share.

Bottom: To use a shared printer elsewhere on the network, open the document you want to print, and then choose File→Print. In the Print dialog box, the shared printer is identified under the Nearby Printers heading.

Note: Of course, this feature is most useful when you're sharing printers that can hook up to only one Mac at a time, like USB inkjet photo printers. Office laser printers are often designed to be networked from Day One.

Setting up printer sharing is easy; see Figure 9-5, top. Then, to make a printout from across the network, see the instructions in Figure 9-5, bottom.

Tip: You can control *which* account holders on your network are allowed to use the printer you've shared. You know that idiot in Accounting who's always using up your cartridges by printing 200-page documents? Cut that sucker off! Just add the lucky guests' names to the Users column in System Preferences→Sharing→Printer Sharing, as shown in Figure 9-5, top.

If your PC-wielding friends install Bonjour for Windows (a free download from this book's "Missing CD" page at *www.missingmanuals.com*), then they can even print to your Mac's shared printer, too.

Tip: Of course, your Mac (the one attached to the printer) must be turned on in order for the other computers to print. In part, that's because the documents-in-waiting from other people pile up on *your* hard drive.

Faxing

Apple has never been afraid to abandon technologies that strike it as obsolete, and faxing has made the list. Heck, Yosemite can't even fax if you have one of Apple's own USB fax modems.

But if you still need to fax, you have a couple of options. First, you can sign up for a service like eFax or Faxaway, which let you send and receive faxes online. Second, you're welcome to buy a non-Apple fax modem, some of which work fine. Whatever you buy comes with its own software and instructions.

PDF Files

Sooner or later, almost everyone with a personal computer encounters PDF (portable document format) files. Many a software manual, Read Me file, and downloadable "white paper" come in this format. Until recently, you needed the free program called Adobe Reader if you hoped to open or print these files. Windows devotees still do.

PDF files, however, are one of OS X's common forms of currency. In fact, you can turn *any document* (in any program with a Print command) into a PDF file—a trick that once required a $250 program called Adobe Acrobat Distiller. (Maybe Apple should advertise: "Buy Acrobat for $250, get OS X free—and $120 cash back!")

Note: All right, that joke about Acrobat is an exaggeration. OS X alone creates *screen-optimized* PDF files: compact, easy-to-email files that look good onscreen but don't have high enough resolution for professional printing. For high-end purposes and more optimization for specific uses (Web, fancy press machines, and so on), you still need a program like Adobe Acrobat, Illustrator, or InDesign.

But why would you want to create PDFs? What's the big deal about them? Consider these advantages:

- **Other people see your layout.** When you distribute PDF files to other people, they see precisely the same fonts, colors, page design, and other elements you put in your original document. And here's the kicker: They get to see all of this even if they don't *have* the fonts or the software you used to create the document. (Contrast with the alternative: Say you're sending somebody a Microsoft Word document. If your correspondent doesn't have precisely the same fonts you have, then he'll see a screwy layout. And if he doesn't have Word or a program that can open Word files, he'll see nothing at all.)

- **It's universal.** PDF files are very common in the Macintosh, Windows, Unix/Linux, and even smartphone worlds. When you create a PDF file, you can distribute it (by email, for example) without worrying about what kinds of computers your correspondents are using.

- **It has very high resolution.** PDF files print at the maximum quality of any printer. A PDF file prints great both on cheapo inkjets and on high-quality image-setting gear at professional print shops. (Right now you're looking at a PDF file that was printed at a publishing plant.)

- **You can search it.** A PDF file may look like a captured graphic, but behind the scenes, its text is still text; Spotlight can find a word in a PDF haystack. That's an especially handy feature when you work with electronic software manuals in PDF format.

Opening PDF Files

There's nothing to opening up a PDF file: Just double-click it. Preview takes over from there and opens the PDF file on your screen. (Or highlight its icon in the Finder and tap the space bar for a Quick Look at it.)

Creating PDF Files

Opening, schmopening—what's really exciting in OS X is the ability to create your *own* PDF files. The easiest way is to click the PDF pop-up button in the standard Print dialog box (Figure 9-6). When you click it, you're offered a world of interesting PDF-creation possibilities:

- **Open PDF in Preview** lets you convert whatever document you're on the verge of printing into a frozen PDF file that opens into Preview for your inspection. The point here is that you can have a look at it *before* you print it.

- **Save as PDF** saves your document to the disk as a PDF document instead of printing it.

- **Save as PostScript** gives you a PostScript file instead of a PDF. (PostScript is a format preferred by some designers and print shops. It consists of highly precise "what to draw" instructions for PostScript laser printers.)

Figure 9-6:
The PDF button is crawling with neat ways to process a document while it's still open—and you can add to this pop-up button's list, too. For example, you can create even more elaborate pathways for documents you want to print or convert to PDF using an Automator workflow you've built yourself, if you're that kind of technical.

- **Add PDF to iBooks** converts the document into a PDF file and stores it in, of all places, iTunes. (Yes, iTunes can manage PDF documents.)

- **Mail PDF** generates a PDF file and then attaches it to an outgoing message in Mail. Great for exchanging layout-intensive documents with collaborators who don't have the same fonts, layout software, or taste as you.

- **Save PDF to Web Receipts Folder** is one of the simplest and sweetest features in all of OS X.

 You use it when you've just ordered something on a Web site, and the "Print this receipt" screen is staring you in the face. Don't waste paper and ink (and, later, time trying to find it)! Instead, use this command. You get a perfectly usable PDF version, stored in your Home→Documents→Web Receipts folder, where you can use Spotlight to find it later, when you need to consult or print it because your gray-market goods never arrived.

- **Send PDF via Messages.** The Mac opens up Messages and starts a new message for you, with your PDF already attached.

Note: You may see other commands here, too, as you install other companies' software programs.

Fonts—and Font Book

OS X type is all smooth, all the time. Fonts in OS X's formats—called TrueType, PostScript Type 1, and OpenType—always look smooth onscreen and in printouts, no matter what the point size.

OS X also comes with a program that's *just* for installing, removing, inspecting, and organizing fonts. It's called Font Book (Figure 9-7), and it's in your Applications folder.

Figure 9-7:
Each account holder can have a separate set of fonts; your set is represented by the User icon. You can drag fonts and font families among the various Fonts folders represented here—from your User account folder to the Computer icon, for example, making them available to all account holders.

Where Fonts Live

Brace yourself. In OS X, there are *three* Fonts folders. The fonts you actually see listed in the Font menus and Fonts panes of your programs are combinations of these Fonts folders' contents.

Here's a rundown:

• **Your private fonts (your Home folder→Library→Fonts).** This Fonts folder sits right inside your own Home folder. You're free to add your own custom fonts to this folder. Go wild—it's your font collection and yours alone. Nobody else who uses the Mac can use these fonts; they'll never even know you have them.

Note: Your Home→Library folder is ordinarily hidden. The quickest way to see it is to press Option as you choose Go→Library in the Finder.

- **Main font collection (Library→Fonts).** Any fonts in this folder are available to everyone to use in every program. (As with most features that affect everybody who shares your Mac, however, only people with Administrator accounts can change the contents of this folder.)

- **Essential system fonts (System→Library→Fonts).** This folder contains the fonts that the Mac itself needs: the typefaces you see in your menus, dialog boxes, icons, and so on. You can open this folder to *see* these font suitcases, but you can't do anything with them. Remember that, for stability reasons, the System folder is sealed under glass forever. Only the Unix entity known as the *superuser* can touch these files—and even that person would be foolish to do so.

With the exception of the essential system fonts, you'll find an icon representing each of these locations in your Font Book program, described next.

Note: And just to make life even more exciting, Adobe's software installers may donate even *more* fonts to your cause, in yet *another* folder: your Home→Application Support folder.

Font Book: Installing and Managing Fonts

One of the biggest perks of OS X is its preinstalled collection of over 50 great-looking fonts—"over $1,000 worth," according to Apple, which licensed many of them from type companies. In short, fewer Mac users than ever will wind up buying and installing new fonts.

But when you do buy or download new fonts, you're in luck. There's no limit to the number of fonts you can install.

Looking over your fonts

Right off the bat, Font Book is great for looking at samples of each typeface. For example, click Computer, click the first font name, and then press the ▼ key. As you walk down the list, the rightmost pane shows you a sample of each font (Figure 9-7).

You can also click any font family's flippy triangle (or highlight its name and then press ▶) to see the font *variations* it includes: Italic, Bold, and so on.

Tip: When you first open Font Book, the actual text of the typeface preview (in the right pane) is pretty generic. Don't miss the Preview menu, though. It lets you substitute a full display of every character (choose Repertoire)—or, if you choose Custom, it lets you type your *own* text.

Printing a reference sheet

You can print a handy, whole-font sampler of any font. Click its name and then choose File→Print. In the Print dialog box, click the Show Details button to expand the dialog box, if necessary.

As shown in Figure 9-8, you can use the Report Type pop-up menu to choose from three reference-sheet styles:

- **Catalog** prints the alphabet twice (uppercase and lowercase) and the numbers in each selected font; use the Sample Size slider to control the size. This style is the most compact, because more than one print sample fits on each sheet of paper.

- **Repertoire** prints a grid that contains every single character in the font. This report may take more than one page per font.

- **Waterfall** prints the alphabet over and over again, with increasing type sizes, until the page is full. You can control which sizes appear using the Sample Sizes list.

When everything looks good, click Print.

*Figure 9-8:
From the Report
Type pop-up
menu, choose the
style you want.
The preview screen
shows you each
one before you
commit it to paper.
Type-size controls
always appear in
the lower right.*

Eliminating duplicates

Since your Mac accesses up to three folders containing fonts, you might wonder what happens in the case of *conflicts*. For example, suppose you have two slightly different fonts, both called Optima, which came from different type companies and are housed in different Fonts folders on your system. Which font do you actually get when you use it in your documents?

The scheme is actually fairly simple: OS X proceeds down the list of Fonts folders in the order shown on page 310, beginning with your own home Fonts folder. It acknowledges the existence of only the *first* duplicated font it finds.

If you'd rather have more control, open Font Book. A bullet (•) next to a font's name is Font Book's charming way of trying to tell you that you've got copies of the same font in more than one of your Fonts folders. You might have one version of Comic Sans in your own Home→Library→Fonts folder, for example, and another in your Mac's main Fonts folder.

Click the one you want to keep, and then choose Edit→Resolve Duplicates. Font Book turns off all *other* copies, and the bullet disappears.

Adding, removing, and hiding fonts

Here's what you can do with Font Book:

- **Install a font.** When you double-click a font file's icon in the Finder, Font Book opens and presents the typeface for your inspection pleasure. If you like it, click Install Font. You've just installed it into *your account's* Fonts folder so that it appears in the Font menus of all your programs. (If you'd rather install it so that it appears in *all* account holders' Font menus, see Figure 9-7.)

- **Remove a font.** Removing a font from your machine is easy: Highlight it in the Font Book list, and then press the Delete key. (You're asked to confirm the decision.) Before taking such a drastic and permanent step, however, keep in mind that you can simply *disable* (hide) the font instead. Read on.

- **Disable a font.** When you disable a font, you're simply hiding it from your programs. You might want to turn off a font so that you can use a different version of it (bearing the same name but from a different type company, for example), or to make your Font menus shorter, or to make programs like Microsoft Word start up faster. You can always turn a disabled font back on if you ever need it again.

Tip: How's this for a sweet feature? OS X can activate fonts *automatically* as you need them. When you open a document that relies on a font it doesn't have, OS X activates that font and keeps it available until that particular program quits.

Actually, it does better than that. If it doesn't see that font installed, it *searches your hard drive* on a quest to find the font—and then it asks you if you want it installed, so the document will look right.

To disable a font, just click it or its family name and then click the checkbox button beneath the list (or press Shift-⌘-D). Confirm your decision by clicking Disable in the confirmation box. (Turn on "Do not ask me again" if you're the confident sort.)

The font's name now appears gray, and the word "Off" appears next to it, making it absolutely clear what you've just done. (To turn the font on again, highlight its name, and then click the now-empty checkbox button, or press Shift-⌘-D again.)

Note: When you install, remove, disable, or enable a font using Font Book, you see the changes in the Font menus and panes of your *Cocoa* programs immediately. You won't see the changes in open Carbon programs, however, until you quit and reopen them.

Font collections

A font *collection,* like any of the ones listed in the first Font Book column, is a subset of your installed fonts. Apple starts you off with collections called things like PDF (a set of standard fonts used in PDF files) and Web (fonts you're safe using on Web pages—that is, fonts that are very likely to be installed on the Macs or Windows PCs of your Web visitors).

But you can create collections called, for example, Headline or Sans Serif, organized by font type. Or you can create collections like Brochure or Movie Poster, organized by project. Later, you can switch these groups of fonts on or off at will, or jump right to them in programs that use the standard Fonts pane, which saves you time wading through hundreds of fonts.

To create a new collection, click the leftmost + button to create a new entry in the Collection column, whose name you can edit. Then click one of the font storage locations—User or Computer—and drag fonts or font families onto your newly created collection icon. (Recognize this process from playlists in iTunes, or albums in iPhoto?) Each font can be in as many different collections as you want.

To remove a font from the collection, click its name and then press Delete. You're not actually removing the font from your Mac, of course—only from the collection.

Tip: Each time you create a new font collection, OS X records its name and contents in a little file in your Home folder→Library→FontCollections folder.

By copying these files into the Users→Shared folder on your hard drive, you can make them available to anyone who uses the Mac. If your sister, for example, copies a file from the Shared folder into her own Home folder→Library→FontCollections folder, then she'll see the name of your collection in her own Fonts pane. This way, she can reap the benefits of the effort and care you put into its creation.

Smart collections

Font Book can create a collection *for* you, too. If you choose File→New Smart Collection, a new dialog box lets you specify criteria for this always-updated collection. For example, you might use the + buttons to specify "Kind name is TrueType" and "Design style is Sans-serif." The effect is exactly like smart folders in the Finder (page 142) or smart playlists in iTunes (page 326): Once you set up the smartness, the set stays up to date as your font collection changes.

Font libraries

Don't get confused; a font *library* is not the same as a font *collection.*

A font library is a set of fonts *outside* Font Book that you can install or uninstall on the fly. They don't have to be in any of your Fonts folders; Font Book can install them from wherever they happen to be sitting on your hard drive (or even on the network). Font Book never copies or moves these font files as you install or remove them from libraries; it simply adds them to your Font menus by referencing them right where they sit.

Tip: That can be a handy arrangement if you periodically work on different projects for different clients. Why burden your day-to-day Font menu with the 37 fonts used by *Beekeepers Quarterly* magazine when you need to work with those fonts only four times a year?

Once you've added some fonts to a library, you can even set up collections *within* that library.

To create a library, choose File→New Library; the library appears in the Collection list at the left side of Font Book. Now you can drag fonts into it right from the Finder or set up collections inside it by highlighting the library's icon and choosing File→New Collection.

Exporting fonts

Next time you submit a design project to a print shop or a graphics bureau, you won't have to worry that it won't have the right fonts. It's easy to collect all the fonts you used in a document and export them to a folder, ready to submit along with your file.

Use the Services→Font Book→Create Collection From Text command. Font Book opens and shows you the new collection it's created, containing all the fonts used in your document. Click the collection and then choose File→Export Collection. The software prompts you to name and choose a location for the exported fonts folder.

Note: The Create Collection From Text command doesn't work in all programs, but you can always build and export a collection manually.

The Fonts Pane

As noted in Chapter 4, some existing Mac programs have simply been touched up—*Carbonized*, in the lingo—to be OS X–compatible. To choose a font in these programs, you simply choose a typeface name from the Font menu or from a formatting palette.

Things get much more interesting when you use the more modern *Cocoa* programs, like TextEdit, iMovie, Pages, Keynote, Numbers, iPhoto, and Mail. They offer a standard OS X feature called the Fonts pane. If you're seated in front of your OS X machine now, fire up TextEdit or Pages and follow along.

Choosing fonts from the Fonts pane

Suppose you've just highlighted a headline in TextEdit and now you want to choose an appropriate typeface for it.

In TextEdit, you open the Fonts pane (Figure 9-9) by choosing Format→Font→Show Fonts (⌘-T). Just as in Font Book, the first column lists your Collections. The second column, Family, shows the names of the actual fonts in your system. The third, Type-face, shows the various style variations—Bold, Italic, Condensed, and so on—available in that type family. (Oblique and Italic are roughly the same thing; Bold, Black, and Ultra are varying degrees of boldface.)

The last column lists a sampling of point sizes. You can use the Size slider, choose from the point-size pop-up menu, or type any number into the box at the top of the Size list.

Designing collections and favorites

At the bottom of the Fonts pane, the ✿ menu offers a few useful customization tools:

- **Add to Favorites.** To designate a font as one of your favorites, specify a font, style, and size by clicking in the appropriate columns of the Fonts pane. Then use this command. From now on, whenever you click Favorites in the Collections column, you'll see a list of the typefaces you've specified.

- **Show Preview.** The Fonts pane is great and all that, but you may have noticed that, until you choose this option, it doesn't actually *show* you the fonts you're working with—something of an oversight in a window designed to help you find your fonts. See Figure 9-9 for details. (Choose Hide Preview to get rid of the preview.)

> **Note:** Once you've opened the preview pane, feel free to click the different sizes, typeface names, and family names to see the various effects.

Figure 9-9:
The Fonts pane, generally available only in Cocoa programs, offers elaborate controls over text color, shadow, and underline styles.

See the handy font sample shown here above the font lists? To get it, choose Show Preview from the ✿ pop-up menu. Or use the mousy way: Place your cursor just below the title bar (where it says Fonts) and drag downward.

- **Hide Effects.** The "toolbar" of the Fonts pane lets you create special text effects—colors, shadows, and so on—as shown in Figure 9-9. This command hides that row of pop-up buttons.

- **Color.** Opens the Color Picker, so you can specify a color for the highlighted text in your document.

- **Characters.** Opens the Character Viewer, so you can choose a symbol without having to remember the crazy keyboard combo that types it.

- **Typography.** Opens the Typography palette (see Figure 9-10).

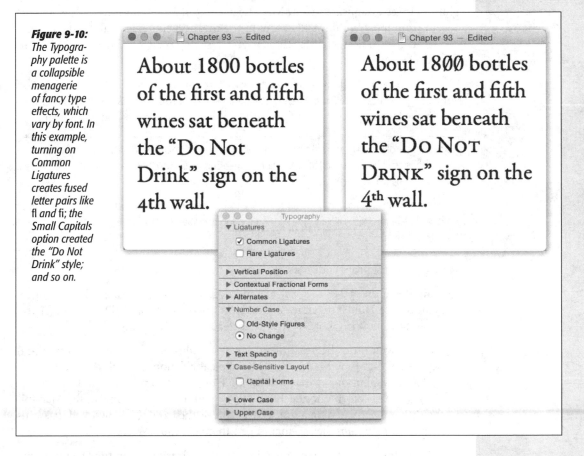

Figure 9-10:
The Typography palette is a collapsible menagerie of fancy type effects, which vary by font. In this example, turning on Common Ligatures creates fused letter pairs like fl and fi; the Small Capitals option created the "Do Not Drink" style; and so on.

- **Edit Sizes.** The point sizes listed in the Fonts pane are just suggestions. You can actually type in any point size you want. By choosing this command, in fact, you can edit this list so that the sizes you use most often are only a click away.

- **Manage Fonts.** Opens Font Book, described earlier in this chapter.

Digital Cameras

Like Windows, OS X is extremely camera-friendly. The simple act of connecting a digital camera to its USB cable stirs OS X into action—namely, it opens iPhoto, Apple's digital-photo shoebox program.

If it's a digital *video* camera you plugged in, OS X opens iMovie instead.

(If iPhoto and iMovie intrigue or baffle you, entire Missing Manuals await you on those topics. Just sayin'.)

Disks

Floppy drives disappeared from Macs beginning in 1997—and these days, they're absent from most Windows PCs, too. In the meantime, there are all kinds of other disks you can connect to a Mac these days: CDs and DVDs, hard drives, iPods, USB flash drives, and so on.

When you insert a disk, its icon may show up in any of three places (depending on your Finder preferences): on the right side of the desktop, in the Computer window, and in the Sidebar. To see what's on a disk you've inserted, double-click its icon.

Tip: You can make the Mac work like Windows, if you choose. For example, to open a single window containing icons of all currently inserted disks, choose Go→Computer (which produces the rough equivalent of the My Computer window).

To save you that step, though, you can tell OS X to put disk icons on the desktop, too. Just choose Finder→Preferences, click General, and turn on the top checkboxes—"Hard disks," "External disks," and "CDs, DVDs, and iPods."

To remove a disk from your Mac, use one of these methods:

- **Hold down the ⏏ key on your keyboard,** if it has one. It's usually in the upper-right corner. Hold it down for a moment to make a CD or DVD pop out. (If you don't have an ⏏ key, hold down F12 instead.)

- **Drag its icon onto the Trash icon.** For years, this technique has confused and frightened first-time Mac users. Their typical reaction: Doesn't the Trash mean "delete"? Yes, but only when you drag *file or folder* icons there—not *disk* icons. Dragging a disk icon into the Trash (at the end of the Dock) makes the Mac spit the disk out. (If you drag a *disk image* icon or the icon of a networked disk, this maneuver *unmounts* them—that is, gets them off your screen.)

 The instant you begin dragging a disk icon, the Trash icon on the Dock changes form, as though to reassure the novice that dragging a disk icon there will only eject the disk. As you drag, the wastebasket icon morphs into a giant-sized ⏏ logo.

- **Highlight the disk icon,** and then choose File→Eject (or press ⌘-E). The disk pops out.

- **Right-click the disk icon.** Choose Eject from the shortcut menu.

- **Click the ⏏ button** next to a disk's name in the Sidebar.

Any of these techniques also work to get network disks and disk images off your screen.

Note: If you try to eject a disc and the Mac tells you, "This disk is in use," the message tells you exactly which program is still holding on to the disk. Switch to that program, close whatever document is causing the problem, and then eject the disk.

Erasing a Disk

OS X doesn't have an Erase Disk command at the desktop. When you want to erase a disk (such as a DVD-RW disc), you're supposed to use Disk Utility, which sits in your Applications→Utilities folder. This is the same program you use to erase, repair, or subdivide *(partition)* a hard drive.

Once you've opened Disk Utility, click the name of the disk (in the left-side list), click the Erase tab, and then click the Erase button.

You won't be able to do so, though, if:

- The disk is a standard CD-ROM, DVD, a previously recorded CD-R disc, or a disk elsewhere on the network.

- You're trying to erase the startup disk. You can't wipe out the disk that contains the currently running System folder any more than you can paint the floor directly beneath your feet. (To erase your built-in hard drive, for example, you must start up from the OS X DVD.)

Burning CDs and DVDs

At one time, burning a CD or DVD was great for backing up stuff, transferring stuff to another computer (even a Windows PC), mailing to somebody, or offloading (archiving) older files to free up hard drive space.

These days, those discs are too small to use for backups or archives, too slow to burn for transferring files ridiculous to send by mail. WiFi and Internet services have deprived CDs and DVDs almost completely of their few reasons for being.

But OS X Yosemite can still burn those discs, if you buy an external disc drive. In that case, the free downloadable appendix to this chapter, "Burning CDs and DVDs.pdf," offers step-by-step instructions. You can find it on this book's "Missing CD" at *www. missingmanuals.com.*

Startup Disks

When you turn the Mac on, it hunts for a *startup disk*—a disk containing a System folder. If you've ever seen the dispiriting blinking folder icon on a Mac's screen, you know what happens when the Mac *can't* find a startup disk. It blinks like that forever, or until you find and insert a disk with a viable System folder on it.

Usually, a startup disk is a DVD or a hard drive (internal or external—any properly formatted USB, FireWire, or Thunderbolt drive). You can even put a stripped-down, emergency copy of Yosemite onto a flash drive and start up your Mac that way; see page 725.

Selecting a Startup Disk

It's perfectly possible to have more than one startup disk simultaneously attached to your Mac. Some veteran Mac fans deliberately create other startup disks—using external hard drives, for example—so that they can easily start the Mac up from a backup disk or from a different version of the OS.

Only one System folder can be operational at a time. So how does the Mac know which to use as its startup disk? You make your selection in the Startup Disk pane of System Preferences (Figure 9-11).

Tip: If you're in a hurry to start the machine up from a different disk, just click the disk icon and then click Restart in the System Preferences window. You don't have to close the System Preferences window first.

Figure 9-11:
In the Startup Disk pane of System Preferences, the currently selected disk—the one that will be "in force" the next time the machine starts up—is always highlighted. You also see the System folder's version, the name of the drive it's on, and its actual name.

DVD Movies

If your Mac has an external DVD drive, watching movies on your screen couldn't be simpler: Just insert a movie DVD. Unless you've fiddled with your preference settings, the DVD Player program opens and begins playing the movie in Full Screen mode. (Even the menu bar disappears. To make it reappear, move your cursor to near the top of the screen.)

Note: If DVD Player *doesn't* open automatically when you insert a DVD movie, you can open it yourself. It's sitting there in your Applications folder. (Then fix the problem, using System Preferences→CDs & DVDs.)

Playing a Movie

Once DVD Player starts playing your movie, you can move your mouse to the bottom of the screen, at any time, to bring up the control bar.

Or just use the keyboard controls, which appear here in this clip 'n' save cheat sheet:

Function	Keystroke
Play, Pause	space bar
Fast-forward, rewind	Shift-⌘-▶, Shift-⌘-◀ (press repeatedly to cycle to 3, 8, 16, and 32 times normal speed)
Skip forward/back 5 seconds	Option-⌘-▶, Option-⌘-◀
Louder, quieter	⌘-▲, ⌘-▼
Mute/Unmute	Option-⌘-▼
Next/previous "chapter"	▶, ◀
Full-screen mode on/off	⌘-F
Half, normal, maximum size	⌘-1, ⌘-2, ⌘-3
Eject	⌘-E
Add a bookmark	⌘-= (equal sign)

Language Fun

Most Hollywood DVDs have been programmed with onscreen subtitles to help those with hearing impairments and people sitting in noisy bars. The Subtitle button offers a pop-up menu of alternative languages and subtitle options.

Tip: For real fun, turn on English subtitles but switch the soundtrack to a foreign language. No matter how trashy the movie you're watching, you'll gain much more respect from your friends and family when you tell them you're watching a foreign film.

FREQUENTLY ASKED QUESTION

Region Changing

The first time I tried to play a DVD, I got this weird message about initializing the region code. What's up with that?

Hollywood generally releases a movie in different parts of the world at different times. A movie may come out on video in the U.S. when it's just hitting theater screens in Europe. We certainly can't have people watching a DVD before the movie studio says it's OK! That's why many discs are region-locked, so that they play back only on players in certain geographic regions.

As a DVD player in disguise, your Mac is just doing its duty. You can change its region (you'll be offered the chance to do so when you insert a region-locked DVD from another region), but only five times—and then it's frozen forever in the fifth version.

The dialog box shows you which region your DVD is designed for: 1 for the U.S. and Canada; 2 for Japan, Europe, South Africa, and the Middle East; 3 for Southeast and East Asia; 4 for Australia, New Zealand, Pacific Islands, Central America, Mexico, South America, and the Caribbean; 5 for Eastern Europe, Africa, and North Korea; 6 for China; and 8 for airplanes, cruise ships, and so on. Any DVD that you burn yourself is assigned region 0, meaning that it will play anywhere.

(There's no region 7. Maybe it's reserved for the empty spot in movie executives' hearts.)

Chapter Thumbnails

A standard Hollywood DVD comes programmed with chapters—invisible markers that let you jump from the beginning of one important scene to the next. To see them in DVD Player, just move your mouse to the top of the screen. A row of chapter thumbnail images appears, which you can click to jump around in.

You can create your own scene thumbnails, too. That might not be an especially tempting feature when you're playing Hollywood DVDs. But on homemade DVDs, made either by you or by somebody else, these custom scene markers can be handy signposts.

First choose Window→Chapters (⌘-B) to open the chapter thumbnail palette. Here you'll find the existing scene breaks, which may or may not already have "poster frame" images.

All the action takes place in the Action menu (✿) at the bottom of the pane. For example, it contains the Generate Missing Thumbnails command, for use on DVDs that have chapter breaks but no little poster frames to represent them.

Whether there's a poster frame for a particular chapter or not, you can substitute an image of your own. Find the exact frame of the movie that you think looks better than what's already in the Chapters palette; click the chapter in the palette, and, from the ✿ pop-up menu, choose Use Current Frame for Thumbnail. Presto: You've replaced the unhelpful (or nonexistent) chapter image with one that works better.

The Big Picture

Now, watching a movie while sitting in front of your Mac is not exactly the great American movie-watching dream. Fortunately, every recent Mac has a video-output jack; with the proper cables, you can connect the Mac to your TV for a much more comfortable movie-watching experience.

Of course, if you have an Apple TV, then you can pull off the same stunt without any wires at all, using AirPlay. Read on.

GEM IN THE ROUGH

Parental Controls

The DVD parental controls in OS X aren't much. You can't say, for example, "Don't play anything rated PG-13 or above"; you have to rate each DVD yourself, one at a time.

But that's better than nothing.

Insert the DVD you're worried about. Choose File→Get Disk Info. Click the Parental Controls tab.

Click the 🔒 button and enter your administrator's password. (Unless your 8-year-old is the administrator instead of you, in which case this DVD is the least of your problems.)

Now you can select either "Always ask for authorization" or "Always allow to be played," depending on your feelings about the movie. Click OK.

All you've done so far, however, is to specify what happens when you turn on parental controls—and you haven't done that yet. Choose Features→Enable Parental Control.

When parental control is turned on, nobody can watch the "Always ask for authorization" DVDs without correctly inputting your administrator's password.

Which nobody knows except you. (Right?)

iTunes: The Digital Jukebox

iTunes, in your Applications folder, is the ultimate software jukebox (Figure 9-12).

The first thing to understand is that iTunes is three apps in one. It's designed to be the viewer for all the music, videos, apps, and ebooks in three places: (1) on your computer, (2) on your i-gadget, and (3) in Apple's online store.

Apple loves to play with the design of this program; every couple of years, it gets another overhaul. The following pages describe version 12.

Figure 9-12:
iTunes can play music CDs; tune in to Internet radio stations; load up your iPod, iPhone, or iPad; and play music files (including those in the Internet's favorite format, MP3). It can also turn selected tracks from your music CDs into MP3 files, so that you can store favorite songs on your hard drive to play back anytime—without having to dig up the originals.

In this version, it's not as clear when you're looking at the stuff that's already on your computer—or the stuff that's on the iTunes Store. The icons at top left (♫, ⊟, and ⌐, and so on) affect what *kind* of file you're viewing; the buttons at top center affect whether you're looking on your computer or online.

Tip: You can install or remove file-type icons from this top-left "shelf." For starters, you might want to add the Apps icon (A), so that you can manage your phone's apps in iTunes. See Figure 9-13.

The playback and volume controls are at the top-left corner of iTunes. At the upper-right corner is a search box that lets you pluck one track out of a haystack.

The following pages take you through the three worlds—computer, store, iPhone—one by one.

Your Stuff

The key to understanding iTunes' new layout is the "shelf" of file-type icons at top left. These represent your music, movies, TV shows, apps, and other files that iTunes can manage: ♫ (Music), ⊟ (Movies), ⌷ (TV Shows), ⋏ (Apps), ⦿ (Podcasts), ⪜ (iTunes U), ⌕ (Audiobooks), and △ (Tones). (Some are probably hiding in the **...** button.)

To view the music, videos, apps, and ebooks that you've downloaded to your Mac, click the corresponding "shelf" icon, and then click one of the "My" buttons at top center (My TV Shows, My Music, and so on).

Click to edit the shelf

The shelf

Figure 9-13:
*To edit the "shelf," click the **...** button; from the shortcut menu, choose Edit. Click to place checkmarks next to the file types you want to appear on the shelf, as shown here at right.*

The button at top right can sort your files or show them as a list. For example, if you clicked ♫, you can see them *displayed* as Songs, Albums, Artists, Composers, or Genres. And that's just how they're displayed; an additional control in this menu governs how they're *sorted*.

You may see wildly different things here, depending on which display you've chosen. For example, if you click Songs, you see a huge alphabetical list; if you click Albums, you see a square grid of album covers.

Three Ways to Fill Your Library

iTunes gives you at least three ways to get music and video onto your computer—ready for transferring to your devices, if you want:

- **Let iTunes find your files.** The first time you open iTunes, it offers to search your Mac for music files and add them to its library.

- **Visit the iTunes Store.** Another way to feed your library is to shop at the iTunes Store, as described on page 327.

- **Import music from a CD.** iTunes can also convert tracks from audio CDs into digital music files. Just start up iTunes and then stick a CD into your Mac's CD drive. The program asks if you want to convert the songs to audio files for iTunes. (If it doesn't ask, click the CD icon at the top of the window.) Click Yes to import all the songs, or No to view a list of songs and turn off the duds. (Then click Import CD near the top of the window.)

The program downloads song titles and artist information from the CD and begins to add the songs to the iTunes library. (For more control over this process, choose iTunes→Preferences→General (Mac). Use the "When you insert a CD" pop-up menu.)

In that same Preferences box, you can also click Import Settings to choose the *format* (file type) and *bit rate* (amount of audio data compressed into that format) for your imported tracks. The factory setting is the AAC format at 128 kilobits per second.

Most people think these settings make for fine-sounding music files, but you can change your settings to, for example, MP3, another format that lets you cram big music into a small space. Upping the bit rate from 128 to 256 kbps makes for richer-sounding music files—which also take up more room.

Once the importing is finished, each imported song bears a green checkmark, and you have some brand-new files in your iTunes library.

Playlists

A *playlist* is a list of songs you've decided should go together. For example, if you're having a party, you can make a playlist from the current Top 40 and dance music in your music library. Some people may question your taste if you, say, alternate tracks from *La Bohème* with Queen's *A Night at the Opera*, but hey—it's your playlist.

To create a playlist in iTunes, press ⌘-N or choose File→New→Playlist. Type a name for it: "Cardio Workout," "Shoe-Shopping Tunes," "Hits of the Highland Lute," or whatever.

Now click Add To. The screen is now divided into three sections: all your music at left, the selected music in the middle, and your playlist-in-the-making at right. Use any of the buttons in the pop-up menu at top right—Songs, Albums, Artists, whatever—to help you find the songs (or videos); then drag their names into your playlist at far right.

Tip: Instead of making an empty playlist and then dragging songs into it, you can work the other way. You can scroll through a big list of songs, selecting tracks as you go by ⌘-clicking—and then, when you're finished, choose File→New→Playlist From Selection. All the songs you selected immediately appear on a brand-new playlist.

When you drag a song title onto a playlist, you're not actually moving or copying the song. In essence, you're creating an *alias* or *shortcut* of the original, which means you can have the same song on several different playlists.

iTunes even starts you out with some playlists of its own devising, like "Top 25 Most Played" and "Purchased" (a convenient place to find all your iTunes Store goodies listed in one place).

Smart playlists

Smart playlists constantly rebuild themselves according to criteria you specify. You might tell one smart playlist to assemble 45 minutes' worth of songs you've rated higher than four stars but rarely listen to, and another to list your most-often-played songs from the '80s.

Tip: To rate a song, make the window wide enough that you can see the Rating column. (If you don't see this column, right-click any column heading and choose Rating from the list of options.) Then just click the Rating column for a selected song. The appropriate number of stars appears—one, two, three, four, or five—depending on the position of your click. You can change a song's rating as many times as you like—a good thing, considering the short shelf life of a pop hit these days.

To make a smart playlist, choose File→New Smart Playlist (Option-⌘-N). The dialog box shown in Figure 9-14 appears. The controls here are designed to set up a search of your music database. Figure 9-14, for example, illustrates how you'd find up to 74 minutes of Beatles tunes released between 1965 and 1968—that you've rated three stars or higher and that you've listened to no more than twice.

Figure 9-14:
A smart playlist is a powerful search command for your iTunes database. You can set up certain criteria, like the hunt for particular Beatles tunes illustrated here. The "Live updating" checkbox makes iTunes keep this playlist updated as your collection changes, as you change your ratings, as your play count changes, and so on.

Editing and deleting playlists

A playlist is easy to change. Here's what you can do with just a little light mousework. Start by making sure you're viewing your library and your music, and click Playlists at the top:

- **Change the order of songs in the playlist.** Drag song titles up or down within the playlist window to reorder them.

- **Add new songs to the playlist.** Click Add To (upper right), and then tiptoe through your iTunes library and drag more songs into a playlist.

- **Delete songs from the playlist.** If your playlist needs pruning, or that banjo tune just doesn't fit in with the brass-band tracks, you can ditch it quickly: Click the song in the playlist window and then hit Delete or Backspace to get rid of it. When iTunes asks you to confirm your decision, click Remove.

 Deleting a song from a playlist doesn't delete it from your music library it just removes the title from your playlist.

- **Delete the whole playlist.** To delete an entire playlist, click its name in the list of playlists (far left) and then press Delete. Again, this zaps only the playlist itself, not all the songs you had in it. (Those are still in your computer's iTunes folder.)

iTunes Store

The iTunes software's second purpose is to be the face of Apple's online iTunes Store. (Click a file type on the "shelf," like ♫ or ⌨, and then click iTunes Store at top center).

Once you land on the store's main page and set up your iTunes account, you can buy and download songs, audiobooks, ebooks, apps, and videos. This material goes straight into your iTunes library, just a sync away from your i-devices.

UP TO SPEED

iTunes Match

Anything you've ever bought from the iTunes music store is now available for playing on any Apple gadget you own. We get it.

A lot of people, however, have music in their collections that *didn't* come from the iTunes store. Maybe they ripped some audio CDs into their computers. Maybe they acquired some music from, ahem, a friend.

What a sad situation! You've got some of your music available with you on any computer or mobile gadget, and some that's stranded at home on your computer.

Enter iTunes Match. It's an Apple service that lets you store your *entire* collection, including songs that didn't come from Apple, online, for $25 a year.

The iTunes software analyzes the songs in your collection. If it finds a song that's also available in iTunes, then—*bing!*—that song becomes available for your playback pleasure, without

your actually having to transfer your copy to Apple. Apple says, in effect: "Well, our copy of the song is just as good as yours, so you're welcome to listen to our copy on any of your machines."

Truth is, in fact, Apple's copy is probably *better* than your copy. You get to play back the song at iTunes' 256-Kbps quality, no matter how grungy your own copy was.

If there's a song or two in your collection that are *not* among Apple's 20 million tracks, you can upload them to Apple.

The advantages of forking over the $25 a year are (a) you can listen to *all* your music from any computer/phone/tablet, (b) using the song-matching system saves you hours or days of uploading time, and (c) that audio-quality upgrade. And, oh yeah: (d) You can listen to iTunes Radio (page 331), without any ads.

The disadvantage: You're paying $25 a year.

Tip: iTunes doesn't have a monopoly on music sales. Amazon, Google, Rhapsody, and other services sell songs in MP3 format, meaning no copy protection (and Apple compatibility). eMusic.com has great MP3 prices, but the music comes from lesser-known bands. And Amazon's MP3 Downloader software can whip your purchases right into iTunes.

To navigate the iTunes Store, click the buttons on the file-type "shelf": ♫ (Music), ⊟ (Movies), ▭ (TV Shows), or whatever.

Music (♫)

Here it is, the store that made Apple a powerhouse in the music industry: the Music store. Here are millions of songs, individually downloadable, all without copy protection, for 79 cents, $1, or $1.29, depending on popularity.

There are all kinds of ways to slice, dice, and search this catalog. On the right side of the screen, there's a Genres pop-up menu that sorts the offerings by music type. Use the search box (top right) to find a song by name, album name, band, composer, and so on.

The various buttons on the front page of the Music store represent music Apple thinks you might like: new releases, big hits, Genius recommendations (songs Apple thinks you'll like based on an analysis of what's already in your library), and so on.

If you scroll down the right side of the window, you can find lists of the top-selling songs and albums. A handy way to see what the rest of your fellow music lovers are buying, if you don't mind being a sheep.

Learning these tools for finding songs is handy, because the same tools are available for finding TV shows, movies, podcasts, audiobooks, and so on.

TV (▭), movies (⊟), and movie rentals

The iTunes store also offers an increasingly vast selection of downloadable TV episodes ($2 apiece, no ads) and movies (some you can buy for $10 to $20, others you buy *or* rent for $3 to $56).

Once you rent a movie, you have 30 days to start watching—and once you start, you have 24 hours to finish before it turns back into a pumpkin (it deletes itself from your computer or phone).

(If you download a rental movie to your iPhone, you can't move it to any other gadget. But if you download it to iTunes, you can move it from Mac to iPad, or whatever, although it can exist on only one machine at a time.)

Note: If you're one of the few, the proud, who own a DVD drive, you can play back DVD movies using OS X's aging but perfectly functional DVD Player app. You can find instructions on its features in the free downloadable appendix to this chapter, "DVD Player.pdf." You can find it on this book's "Missing CD" at *www.missingmanuals.com*.

Podcasts (⊙)

Not everything in the iTunes Store costs money. In addition to free iPhone apps, there are plenty of free audio and video podcasts in the Podcasts area of the store. See page 333 for more on podcasts.

iTunes U (⊜)

Here, for your personal-growth pleasure, are hundreds of thousands of downloadable college courses, all of them free and many of them amazing. Watch the videos of the professors, follow along with the reading materials. You won't actually earn a college degree this way, but you *will* attain a degree of enlightenment.

Audiobooks (⊡)

Some people like to curl up with—or listen to—a good book, and iTunes has plenty to offer, both as ebooks (which you buy and read in the iBooks app) and as audiobooks (which you listen to as you work in the garden or drive).

If iTunes doesn't offer the audiobook you're interested in, you can find a larger collection (over 50,000 of them) at Audible.com. This Web store sells all kinds of audiobooks, plus recorded periodicals like *The New York Times* and radio shows. To purchase Audible's wares, though, you have to go to the Web site and create an Audible account.

The files land in iTunes automatically when you buy them.

Apps (⊼)

Here's where you grab apps for your iPad or iPhone, using your computer as a loading dock.

Internet Radio (⊙)

iTunes offers two ways to use the Internet as the world's biggest AM/ FM radio. First, there's iTunes Radio—the custom radio stations, based on songs or singers you like, and delivered to you with full pause/skip capabilities and the occasional ad. It's exactly the same service that's described on page 331—but in iTunes, you get to it by clicking the iTunes Radio link in the list at the right side.

Before iTunes Radio, the iTunes program offered the option to listen to live Internet radio broadcasts—from radio stations and colleges all over the world. That feature is still around; see the box on page 333.

Authorizing computers

All movies and TV shows, and some old music files, are still copy protected.

When you create an account in iTunes, you automatically *authorize* that computer to play copy-protected songs from the iTunes Store. Authorization is Apple's way of making sure you don't go playing those music tracks on more than five computers, which would greatly displease the music studios.

You can copy those songs and videos onto a maximum of four other computers. To authorize each one to play music from your account, choose Store→Authorize Computer. (Don't worry; you have to do this just once per machine.)

When you've maxed out your limit and can't authorize any more computers, you may need to *deauthorize* one. On the computer you wish to demote, choose Store→ Deauthorize Computer.

Syncing an iPad or iPhone

The third function of iTunes is to load up, and back up, your iPhone, iPad, or iPod Touch. You can connect it to your computer either wirelessly, over WiFi, or wirefully, with the white USB cable that came with it. (To save precious swaths of forest trees, the rest of this chapter refers to "iPhone" when it means "iPhone, iPad, or iPod Touch.")

Once the phone is connected, click the ☐ at the top-left corner of the iTunes screen. Now you can look over the phone's contents or sync it (read on).

Note: If you have more than one i-device, and they're all connected, this button is a pop-up menu. Choose the name of the one you want to manipulate.

Connecting the phone with a cable

Pretty simple: Plug one end of the white cable (supplied with your iPhone) to your computer's USB jack. Connect the other end to the phone. If the phone is turned on and awake, it's officially connected.

Connecting over WiFi

The familiar white USB cable is all well and good—but the iPhone is a wireless device, for Pete's sake. Why not sync it to your computer wirelessly?

WORKAROUND WORKSHOP

iPod Independence

Out of the box, the iPod (or iPad, or iPhone) and iTunes come set for automatic synchronization. That is, as soon as you hook them together, iTunes sends your complete music library (the contents of your Library "folder" in iTunes) to the iPod. The iPod's songs and playlists always match the Mac's.

Apple's idea here was to ensure that you don't use the iPod as a convenient piracy machine. Your iPod gets its music from your Mac, but it can't put its songs onto a Mac.

At least that's the theory. But what if your hard drive self-destructs, vaporizing the 945 MP3 files that you've made from your paid-for CD collection? You legally own those copies. Shouldn't you have the right to retrieve them from your own iPod?

If you believe the answer is yes, then a quick search at *www. download.com* will bring up a list of programs like Senuti (iTunes spelled backward, get it?), which let you copy music from the iPod to the Mac.

These programs know that the name of the super-secret music folder on the iPod, called *iPod_Control*, is invisible, which is why you can't see it on your desktop without the help of these utilities.

The phone can be charging in its bedside alarm clock dock, happily and automatically syncing with your laptop somewhere else in the house. It transfers all the same stuff to and from your computer—apps, music, books, contacts, calendars, movies, photos, ringtones—but through the air instead of via your USB cable.

Your computer has to be turned on and running iTunes. The phone and the computer have to be on the same WiFi network.

To set up wireless sync, connect the phone using the white USB cable, one last time. Ironic, but true.

Now open iTunes and click ☐ at top left. On the Summary tab, scroll down; turn on "Sync with this iPhone over Wi-Fi." Click Apply. You can now detach the phone.

From now on, whenever the phone is on the WiFi network, it's automatically connected to your computer, wirelessly. You don't even have to think about it. (Well, OK—you have to think about leaving the computer turned on with iTunes open, which is something of a buzzkill.)

Just *connecting* it doesn't necessarily mean *syncing* it, though; that's a more data-intensive, battery-drainy process. Syncing happens in either of two ways:

- **Automatically.** If the iPhone is plugged into power (like a speaker dock, an alarm-clock dock, or a wall outlet), and it's on the same WiFi network, it syncs with the Mac all by itself.

- **Manually.** You can also trigger a sync manually—and this time, the iPhone doesn't have to be plugged into power. To do that, open Settings→General→iTunes Wi-Fi Sync and tap Sync Now. (You can also trigger a WiFi sync from within iTunes—just click the Sync button. It says "Sync" only if, in fact, anything has changed since your last sync.)

Once your iPhone is connected to the computer and you've clicked its name at the upper-left corner of iTunes, the left column of the iTunes window reveals word buttons: Summary, Apps, Music, Movies, TV Shows, Podcasts, Books, Photos, Info, and On This iPhone. For the most part, these represent the categories of stuff you can sync to your device. They let you specify exactly what you want copied to it—which songs, which TV shows, which apps, and so on.

Once you've made your selections, click the Summary tab and then click Apply. (The Apply button says Sync instead if you haven't actually changed any settings.)

iTunes Radio

In OS X, Apple has given you an amazing gift: your own radio station. Your own *empire* of radio stations, in fact.

The iTunes Radio service (Figure 9-15) lets you listen to exactly the kind of music you want to hear. It doesn't just distinguish among genres like *jazz* or *rock*; your choices are far more specific, like "upbeat male vocals with driving brass section" versus "slow lovesick ballads with lots of strings."

You don't get to choose the exact songs or singers you want to hear. Instead, you specify a "seed" song, singer, or musical genre, and iTunes Radio does the rest. For example, if you choose Billy Joel as your "seed," then you'll hear a lot of Billy Joel, but also a lot of other music that sounds more or less like his.

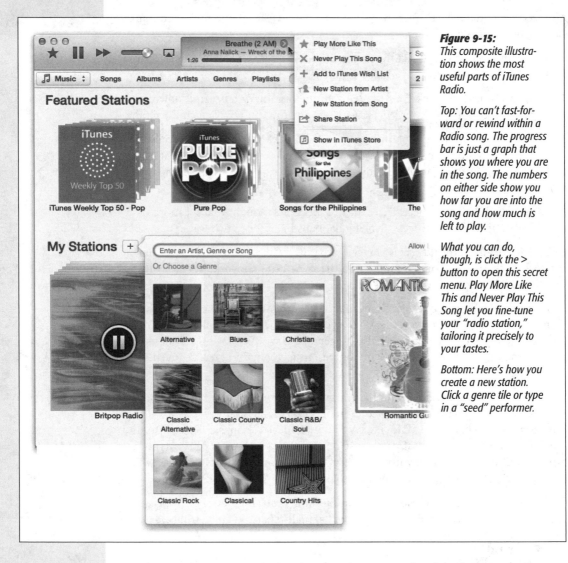

Figure 9-15:
This composite illustration shows the most useful parts of iTunes Radio.

Top: You can't fast-forward or rewind within a Radio song. The progress bar is just a graph that shows you where you are in the song. The numbers on either side show you how far you are into the song and how much is left to play.

What you can do, though, is click the > button to open this secret menu. Play More Like This and Never Play This Song let you fine-tune your "radio station," tailoring it precisely to your tastes.

Bottom: Here's how you create a new station. Click a genre tile or type in a "seed" performer.

Here's something you can't do when you listen to real radio: Skip past a song you don't like. When you tap the ▶▶ button, iTunes Radio instantly skips to the next song it would have played. In fact, you can even tell it Play More Like This or Never Play This Song to shape your radio station's future.

Note: You're allowed to skip up to six songs per hour per station. When you've reached your skip limit, the Skip button is dimmed for an hour.

In exchange for all this magic, you have to listen to the occasional ad between songs—unless you subscribe to iTunes Match (page 327), in which case you never hear any ads.

The idea of a "seed song"–based radio service isn't new, of course. It's the same idea as Pandora, a Web site and app that has offered precisely the same features for years. But iTunes Radio is built in, it syncs with the Apple TV, iPhone, and iPad, and it's so nice to use.

Playing iTunes Radio

When you open iTunes and look at your library, choose Music from the top-left pop-up menu; then click Radio on the top bar.

Internet Radio and Podcasts

iTunes Radio may be all the rage. But the Internet radio feature that's been in iTunes for years is still around, too. It lets you tune in to hundreds of Internet-based radio stations, which may turn out to be the most convenient music source of all. They're free, they play 24 hours a day, and their music collections make yours look like a drop in a bucket.

You can also download and listen to podcasts, which are like Web-distributed personal radio shows—some commercial (like NPR) and some homemade (sometimes *very* homemade).

For radio, choose Music from the top-left corner pop-up menu. Click Internet at the top of the screen. (If you don't see Radio there, then choose iTunes→Preferences→General and turn on Internet Radio.)

In the main list, if you're connected to the Internet, you'll see categories like Blues, Classic Rock, Classical, and so on, as shown here. Click the flippy triangle to see a list of Internet radio stations in that category.

When you see one that looks interesting, double-click it. (The higher the number in the Bit Rate column, the better the sound quality.) Wait a moment for your Mac to connect to the appropriate Internet site, and then let the music begin!

Without add-on shareware (like Audio Hijack Pro), there's no easy way to capture Internet broadcasts or to save them onto your hard drive. You can, however, drag a radio station's name into a playlist to make it easier to access later on. If you discover other Internet radio stations that sound interesting, choose File→Open Stream, type in the station's Web address (URL), and press Return.

To grab a podcast, click iTunes Store at top right. At the top of the screen, click Podcasts. Now you can browse a vast list of available podcasts. When you click one that looks promising, you can either listen to it on the spot, or—and here's the real fun—click Subscribe.

Once you do that, choose Podcasts from the top-left pop-up menu in your Library view to find the latest episodes of the podcasts you've subscribed to. Sync those babies to your iPod or iPhone, and you've got interesting material—or, at least fresh material—to listen to every day of the week.

Across the top, you get a horizontally scrolling set of "album covers" (Figure 9-15). They represent ready-made "radio stations" that Apple has supplied for you. Click the one called "iTunes Top 100: Pop," for example, and your Mac instantly begins playing the biggest current pop hits.

Below these, you see bigger "album covers" for radio stations you've created yourself, as described below. Don't forget to scroll down to see them all.

As a station plays, the control panel at the top center shows the song's name, band, and album name. And, of course, the price; Apple would be thrilled if you came across a song you liked so much that you wanted to buy it. That's why the price button ($1.29, for example) is so prominent. When you tap it, the price changes to say Buy Song; tap again to download the song directly. Now you can listen to it again, on command, without being subject to the randomness of iTunes Radio.

Make your own station

You can set up a new "radio station" of your own in either of two ways: by choosing one of Apple's canned, ready-to-use stations or by typing in a song or performer you like.

- **Prefab stations.** Tap the + button. Boom: There's a huge, scrolling list of music genres—Blues, Christian, Classical, Indie Rock, and so on (Figure 9-15). Tap one to see a list of prefab radio stations, ready to hear.

 If you tap Jazz, for example, the options include Bop, Early Jazz, Jazz Rock, Latin Jazz, and The Big Band Era. Tap the ▶ to listen a little bit. If you like what you hear, tap Add, just to its right. You've just added a new "radio station" to the iTunes Radio main screen.

- **Type in a "seed."** Tap +, and then tap the tiny search box at the top. Type in the name of a singer, band, song, or kind of music ("show tunes" or "a cappella," for example).

 In the results, tap the entry that looks most promising ("A Cappella Radio," for example). You've just created a new station, and it begins instantly. Its details page opens, too, so you can fine-tune it.

Tip: If a song comes on that you especially like, the New Station from Artist and New Station from Song buttons (Figure 9-15) instantly create a new station that will play more music that sounds like this performer or this song. In effect, you get to branch your original station into one that's more finely tuned to a particular taste.

Deleting or editing a station

On the main Radio screen, in the My Stations row, tap the icon of the station you want to mangle or obliterate.

Now you can rename your station (click its existing name) or share it. Using the Play More Like This and Never Play This sections, you can add performers, songs, or genres that you want more of or don't want to be part of this station anymore.

Finally, Delete a station by right-clicking (or two-finger clicking) its icon.

Tip: Click ☰ (top of the screen) to view a list of every song you've heard on each of your stations. It's an amazing way to find out the name of some great song whose name you didn't catch while it was playing. This list also, of course, includes a Buy button for each of those songs.

Playing with Playback

To play a song or video in iTunes, double-click it. Or click iTunes' Play button (▶) or press the space bar. The Mac immediately begins to play the songs whose names have checkmarks in the main list, or from the CD currently in your Mac.

Tip: The central display at the top of the window shows not only the name of the song and album, but also where you are in the song, as represented by the horizontal strip. Drag the handle, or click elsewhere in the strip, to jump around in the song.

As music plays, you can control and manipulate the music and the visuals of your Mac in all kinds of interesting ways. Some people don't move from their Macs for months at a time.

Turning on visuals

Visuals are onscreen light shows that pulse, beat, and dance in sync to the music. (For real party fun, invite some people who grew up in the '60s to your house to watch.)

To summon this psychedelic display, choose View→Show Visuals, or just press ⌘-T. The show begins immediately—although it's much more fun if you choose View→Enter Full Screen (Control-⌘-F) so the show takes over your whole monitor. True, you won't get a lot of work done, but when it comes to stress relief, visuals are a lot cheaper than a hot tub.

Keyboard control

You can control iTunes' music playback using its menus, of course, but the keyboard can be far more efficient. Here are a few of the control keystrokes worth noting:

Function	Keystroke
Play, Pause	space bar
Next song/previous song	▲, ▼ or ◀, ▶
Louder, quieter	⌘-▲, ⌘-▼
Rewind, fast-forward	Option-⌘-◀, Option-⌘-▶
Eject the CD	⌘-E
Turn Visuals on	⌘-T
Turn Visuals off	⌘-T or mouse click
Full Screen mode	Control-⌘-F
Exit full-screen visuals	⌘-T, ⌘-F, Esc, or mouse click

Tip: You can also control CD playback from the Dock. Right-click (or two-finger click) the iTunes icon to produce a pop-up menu offering playback commands like Pause, Next Song, and Previous Song, along with a display that identifies the song currently being played.

Sound Check: Preventing ear-blast syndrome

Here's a clever touch: In iTunes→Preferences→Playback, you see a checkbox called Sound Check. Its function is to keep the playback volume of all songs within the same basic level so you don't have to adjust the volume to compensate for different recorded levels. (This setting, too, gets transferred to your iPod, iPad, or iPhone.)

Come to think of it, you could while away quite a few happy afternoons just poking through the Preferences dialog box. It grows richer with every successive version of iTunes.

Playing with the graphic equalizer

If you choose Window→Equalizer, you get a handsome control console that lets you adjust the strength of each musical frequency independently (Figure 9-16).

Figure 9-16:
Drag the sliders (bass on the left, treble on the right) to accommodate the strengths and weaknesses of your speakers or headphones (and listening tastes). Or save yourself the trouble—use the pop-up menu above the sliders to choose a canned set of slider positions for Classical, Dance, Jazz, Latin, and so on. These settings even transfer to your i-gadgets.

AirPlay

If you'd shown this new feature to the masses in 2005 or so, they'd have fallen down and worshiped it as a god. With one click, you can send whatever is on your Mac's screen to your TV's screen, in hi-def. No wires. In Yosemite, you can make the TV either a mirror of your Mac's screen or an extension of it.

You can present photo slideshows on the TV from your laptop. Or play movies you've found online. Or give presentations from PowerPoint or Keynote. Or present software lessons to a class.

This trick requires both a fairly recent Mac model (mid-2011 or later) and an Apple TV. That's a tiny, $90 black box that connects to a hi-def TV and lets you watch videos from services like YouTube, Netflix, MLB.TV, NBA, NHL, and Vimeo. It can also play videos, music, and photos from Macs or PCs on the network.

But with AirPlay, the Apple TV (and therefore your TV) can now play anything you can see on your Mac, including services like Hulu that aren't available on the Apple TV alone. You can play your iTunes music while watching those cool screensavery visual-

izers on your HDTV. And you can carry your Apple TV around with you to corporate boardrooms to project your pitches, rather than a $1,500 projector.

Tip: If the Apple TV is the third generation or later, the two machines don't even have to be on the same wireless network. This feature, called peer-to-peer AirPlay, is terrific. It makes life so much simpler when you want to give a presentation at some company or school whose WiFi network is complicated and secure; now your Mac doesn't have to be on it at all. (It does, however, have to have Bluetooth turned on.)

Using AirPlay is so simple, it would confuse only an AirHead. The ⊡ menulet (Figure 9-17) offers controls like these:

- **Connect to AirPlay Display: Apple TV.** Here's how you start projecting to your TV. (It changes to say Disconnect once you're connected.)

Figure 9-17:
Make sure the Apple TV is on the same WiFi network as your Mac. At that point, the ⊡ menulet appears automatically.

From it, choose the name of your Apple TV, and presto: Whatever is playing on your Mac simultaneously plays on your big screen, both stereo audio and 720p hi-def video.

Top: Use the ⊡ menulet to control whether the TV displays a mirror image of your Mac or an extension of it. To stop sending your Mac's A/V to your TV, choose Disconnect AirPlay Display from the same menulet.

Bottom: Whenever two monitors are going, the Arrangement tab lets you specify which one gets the menu bar and where the monitors think they are relative to each other.

- **Mirror Built-in Display/Extend Desktop.** Choose Mirror if you want the Mac and the TV to show the same thing. Choose Extend if you want the TV to serve as additional screen real estate, off to the right (or left, or top, or bottom) of your Mac's screen.

- **Match Desktop Size.** Your Mac and your TV probably don't have the same proportions and resolution. So the menu is asking: Which screen "wins"?

 The factory setting is "Apple TV." Your TV screen will be completely filled, although you might see black letterbox bars on your Mac's screen. But if you're watching TV shows or movies, for example, you won't care.

 If you choose This Mac instead, then the picture will look normal on your Mac, but you might see black letterbox bars on the TV. That might be better for a PowerPoint or Keynote presentation, for example, where you want the TV to show *exactly* what the Mac shows.

 Your choice here may affect the magnification of the image on your TV, too, since its resolution and your Mac's probably don't match.

System Preferences

In System Preferences→Displays, you'll find an AirPlay Mirroring pop-up menu that duplicates the AirPlay menulet described above. You'll also find a checkbox called "Show mirroring options in the menu bar when available." That's the on/off switch for the AirPlay menulet. When this option is turned on, and the Mac uses The Force to detect the presence of a nearby Apple TV, the AirPlay menulet appears automatically.

Keyboards

As you know by now, switching to the Mac entails switching your brain, especially when it comes to the old keyboard shortcuts. All of those Ctrl-key sequences become, on the Mac, ⌘-key sequences. (Check your Macintosh keyboard: The ⌘ key is right next to the space bar, usually on both sides.)

GEM IN THE ROUGH

AirPlay Audio

Before there was AirPlay video, there was AirPlay audio. Your Mac can easily send audio to your Apple TV (or your AirPort Express base station), and from there to what's presumably a better sound system than your Mac's puny built-in speakers.

The official way to do that: Open System Preferences→Sound→Output. Click the name of the Apple TV or AirPort Express in the list of speakers.

But there are two faster ways:

Press Option as you open the ◀)) menulet. The items in this menu magically sprout previously invisible choices—like Apple TV and your other AirPlay gear.

If you just want to play music that's in iTunes, you can choose your Apple TV's name (or AirPort Express's name) from the ⊡ pop-up menu at the top left of the window.

But plenty of other Mac keys may seem unfamiliar. For your reassurance, Chapter 1 offers a rundown of what they do.

Text-Navigation Keystrokes

In Windows, you may have grown accustomed to certain common keystrokes for navigating text—key combinations that make the insertion point jump to the beginning or end of a word, line, or document, for example.

OS X programs offer similar navigation keystrokes, as you can see here:

Function	Windows keys	Mac keys
Move to previous/next word	Ctrl+←, Ctrl+→	Option-◄, Option-►
Move to beginning/end of line	Home/End	Home/End*
Move to previous/next paragraph	Ctrl+↑, Ctrl+↓*	Option-▲, Option-▼*
Move to top/bottom of window	Home/End	Home/End (but see below)
Select all text	Ctrl+A	⌘-A
Select text, one letter at a time	Shift+↑, Shift+↓	Shift-▲, Shift-▼
Select text, one word at a time	Ctrl+Shift+arrow keys	Option-Shift-arrow keys
Undo	Ctrl+Z	⌘-Z
Cut, Copy, Paste	Ctrl+X, C, V	⌘ X, C, V
Close window	Alt+F4	⌘-W
Switch open programs	Alt+Tab	⌘-Tab
Hide all windows	⊞+D	F11

* in some programs

Incidentally, the keystroke for jumping to the *top or bottom* of a window varies, depending on the program. You need ⌘-Home/End in Microsoft Word, ⌘-up/down arrow in TextEdit and Stickies, and Home/End in iPhoto and Finder list windows.

Mouse

Most USB mice work as soon as you plug them into your Mac—even two-button, scroll-wheel mice. Using System Preferences, you can program your spare mouse buttons to invoke cool features like Exposé and the Dashboard.

That's not to say, however, that you shouldn't install your mouse's driver software. If your mouse *came* with such software (or if you find it on the manufacturer's Web site), you may well find that your mouse learns a few new tricks—making its "back" and "forward" buttons work properly in Safari, for example. Otherwise, a shareware program like USB Overdrive ($20, from *www.usboverdrive.com*) can unlock those features.

Monitors

Your Mac can use standard monitors of the type found in the Windows world. Every Macintosh can drive *multiple* screens at the same time, too, meaning that you can generally use your old PC screen either as your Mac's main monitor or as a second, external screen.

If one of those arrangements appeals to you, the only complication might be the connector. Most PC screens, of course, have a standard VGA connector (or a more modern DVI connector) at the tip of their tails. Over the years, however, Apple has "standardized" on enough different screen-plug types to fill a catalog. There's been DVI, Mini-DVI, Micro-DVI, Mini DisplayPort, Thunderbolt—you get the idea.

For the proper fee, Apple will be happy to sell you whatever adapter cable you need to accommodate the monitor you've got.

Tip: It's even possible to connect *both* your Mac and your PC to the *same* monitor, and to switch from one to the other at will. If this arrangement appeals to you, you'll need a so-called KVM switch (which also lets you switch your keyboard and mouse between the two computers). You can find KVM switches for sale at electronics stores and online from manufacturers like Belkin (*www.belkin.com*).

In any case, the center of operations for all your monitor settings is the System Preferences→Displays pane. Here you set your monitor's resolution, calibrate color balance and brightness, and turn AirPlay on and off—a cool feature that duplicates whatever is on your Mac screen on a TV set. Wirelessly.

Tip: You can open up this pane with a quick keystroke from any program on the Mac. Just press Option as you tap one of the screen-brightness keys on the top row of your keyboard.

The specific controls depend on the kind of monitor you're using, but here are the ones you'll most likely see.

Display Tab

This tab is the main headquarters for your screen controls. It governs these settings:

- **Resolution.** All Mac screens today can make the screen picture larger or smaller, thus accommodating different kinds of work. You perform this magnification or reduction by switching among different *resolutions* (measurements of the number of dots that compose the screen).

 When you use a low-resolution setting, such as 800×600, the dots of your screen image get larger, thus enlarging (zooming in on) the picture—but showing a smaller slice of the page. Use this setting when playing a small Web movie, for example, so that it fills more of the screen. (Lower resolutions usually look blurry on flat-panel screens, though.) At higher resolutions, such as 1280×800, the screen dots get smaller, making your windows and icons smaller, but showing more overall area. You could use this kind of setting when working on two-page spreads in your page-layout program, for example.

If you select "Best for built-in display," the Mac uses the highest resolution possible for your Mac's screen—the one that makes it look sharpest. The list of other resolution settings your monitor can accommodate—800 × 600, 1024 × 768, and so on—doesn't appear unless you turn on Scaled.

Tip: Option-click the Scaled button to see some additional, less common display resolutions.

- **Brightness.** This slider lets you make the screen look good in the prevailing lighting conditions. Of course, most Apple keyboards have brightness-adjustment *keys,* so this software control is included just for the sake of completeness.

- **Automatically adjust brightness.** Your laptop's light sensor dims the screen automatically in dark rooms—*if* this checkbox is turned on.

Arrangement Tab (Multiple Monitors)

From the dawn of the color-monitor era, Macs have had a terrific feature: the ability to exploit multiple monitors all plugged into the computer at the same time. Sometimes you want the Mac to project the same thing on both screens (*mirror mode*); that's useful in a classroom when the "external monitor" is a projector. Other times, you want to make one monitor act as an *extension* of the next. For example, you might have your Photoshop image window on your big monitor but keep all the Photoshop controls and tool palettes on a smaller screen. Your cursor passes from one screen to the other as it crosses the boundary.

To connect a second monitor or a projector, you have a couple of options:

- **The wired way.** Connect the appropriate cable or adapter to your Mac's video-output jack. This jack may be any of three types these days. Mac laptops and iMacs use a weird, tiny connector called a *Mini DisplayPort*; you need an adapter cord to connect it to the VGA, DVI, or HDMI input that most monitors or projectors expect.

 All Macs these days also have something called Thunderbolt jacks. You can connect them to a few Thunderbolt-equipped external monitors, notably Apple's.

 Finally, there's the black, cylindrical Mac Pro. It also has an HDMI jack, which is the easiest of all to connect to screens and projectors.

 To set this up, hook up the monitor or projector. Your Mac should discover (and start projecting to) the external screen automatically; if it doesn't, close and then reopen the lid (if you're using a laptop), or choose Detect Displays from the Displays *menulet.*

- **The wireless way.** You can also connect your Mac to a TV wirelessly—if you have an Apple TV. This feature is called AirPlay, and it's described on page 336.

Once you've connected a second screen, with a cable or without, a different System Preferences→Displays window appears on each screen. The idea is that you can change the color and resolution settings independently for each. Your Displays menulet shows two sets of resolutions, too—one for each screen.

The Arrangement tab (Figure 9-17, bottom) shows a miniature version of each monitor. By dragging these thumbnails around within the window, you can specify how you want the second monitor's image "attached" to the first. Most people position the second monitor's image to the right of the first, but you're also free to position it on the left, above, below, or even directly on top of the first monitor's icon (the last of which produces a video-mirroring setup). For the least likelihood of going insane, consider placing the real-world monitor in the same position.

For committed multiple-monitor fanatics, the fun doesn't stop there. See the microscopic menu bar on the first-monitor icon? You can drag that tiny strip onto a different monitor icon, if you like, to tell Displays where you'd like your menu bar to appear. (And check out how most screensavers correctly show different stuff on each monitor!)

Tip: If you close your laptop while it's connected to an external monitor, the machine doesn't go to sleep. Instead, it keeps the external monitor on. The laptop remains on, so you can keep right on working, as though the laptop were the brains for a big-screen Mac.

When you're not mirroring, here's what you can expect:

- **The menu bar** appears on every monitor. It's bright and alive on only one screen at a time, though; on the other screens, it's dimmed and unavailable until you click it.

- **The Dock** appears on only one screen at a time. As you start working on a different screen, move your cursor to the bottom edge to make the Dock jump there. (That's if you've positioned the Dock at the bottom. If you've placed it on the left or right, vertically, it stays on the leftmost or rightmost monitor all the time.)

- **Mission Control** appears independently on every screen. That is, when you do the three-finger swipe upward, whatever programs are on each screen shrink down. You can even create separate sets of Spaces on each screen; it's exactly as though you're using multiple *Macs* and not just multiple screens.

Color Tab

This pane offers a list of *color profiles* for your monitor (or, if you turn off "Show profiles for this display only," for *all* monitors). Each profile represents colors slightly differently—a big deal for design and photography types.

When you click Calibrate, the Display Calibrator Assistant opens to walk you through a series of six screens, presenting various brightness and color-balance settings in each screen. You pick the settings that look best to you; at the end of the process, you save your monitor tweaks as a ColorSync profile, which your Mac uses to adjust the screen for improved color accuracy.

Scanners

OS X gives you two programs that can operate any standard scanner: Image Capture and Preview. The controls are identical in both programs.

To scan in Image Capture, turn on your scanner and click its name in the left-side list. Put your photos or documents into the scanner.

Now you have a couple of decisions to make:

- **Separate and straighten?** If you turn on "Detect separate items" in the Scan Size menu, OS X will perform a nifty little stunt indeed: It will check to see if you've put *multiple* items onto the scanner glass, like several small photos. (It looks for rectangular images surrounded by empty space, so if the photos are overlapping, this feature won't work.)

 If it finds multiple items, Image Capture automatically straightens them, compensating for haphazard placement on the glass, and then saves them as individual files.

- **Where to file.** Use the "Scan to" pop-up menu to specify where you want the newly scanned image files to land—in the Pictures folder, for example. You have some other cool options beyond sticking the scans in a folder; for example, you can send the resulting image to iPhoto, Preview, or Mail.

Once you've put a document onto it or into it, click Scan. The scanner heaves to life. After a moment, you see on the screen what's on the glass. It's simultaneously been sent to the folder (or post-processing task) you requested using the "Scan to" pop-up menu.

More Power to You

As you can see, Apple has tried to make *basic* scanning as simple as possible: one click. That idiotproof method gives you very few options, however.

If you click Show Details before you scan, though, you get a special pane on the right side of the window that's filled with useful scanning controls (Figure 9-18).

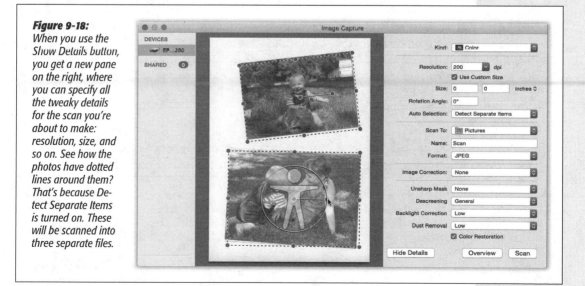

Figure 9-18:
When you use the Show Details button, you get a new pane on the right, where you can specify all the tweaky details for the scan you're about to make: resolution, size, and so on. See how the photos have dotted lines around them? That's because Detect Separate Items is turned on. These will be scanned into three separate files.

Here are some of the most useful options:

- **Resolution.** This is the number of tiny scanned dots per inch. 300 is about right for something you plan to print out; 75 is standard for graphics that will be viewed on the screen, like images on a Web page.

- **Name.** Here, specify how you want each image file named when it lands on your hard drive. If it says *Scan,* then the files will be called *Scan 1, Scan 2,* and so on.

- **Format.** Usually, the file format for scanned graphics is TIFF. That's a very high-res format that's ideal if you're scanning precious photos for posterity. But if these images are bound for the Web, you might want to choose JPEG instead; that's the standard Web format.

- **Image Correction.** If you choose Manual from this pop-up menu, then, incredibly, you'll be treated to a whole expando-pane of color correction tools: brightness, tint, saturation, a histogram, and so on.

Opening the Details pane has another handy benefit, too: It lets you scan only a *portion* of what's on the scanner glass.

Once you've put the document or photo into the scanner, click Overview. Image Capture does a quick pass and displays on the screen whatever is on the glass. You'll see a dotted-line rectangle around the entire scanned image—unless you've turned on "Detect separate images," in which case you see a dotted-line rectangle around *each* item on the glass.

You can adjust these dotted-line rectangles until you've enclosed precisely the portion of the image you want scanned. For example, drag the rectangles' corner handles to resize them; drag inside the rectangles to move them; drag the right end of the line inside the rectangle to rotate it; preview the rotation by pressing Control and Option.

Finally, when you think you've got the selection rectangle(s) correctly positioned, click Scan to trigger the actual scan.

Note: These instructions apply to the most common kind of scanner—the *flatbed* scanner. If you have a scanner with a document feeder—a tray or slot that sucks in one paper document after another from a stack—the instructions are only slightly different.

You may, for example, see a Mode or Scan Mode pop-up menu; if so, choose Document Feeder. You'll want to use the Show Details option described above. You may also be offered a Duplex command (meaning "Scan both sides of the paper"—not all scanners can do this).

Part Three: Yosemite Online

3

Internet Setup & iCloud

A s Apple's programmers slogged away on the massive OS X project, there were
areas where they must have felt like they were happily gliding on ice: network-
ing and the Internet. For the most part, the Internet already runs on Unix,
and hundreds of extremely polished tools and software chunks were already available.

There are all kinds of ways to get your Mac onto the Internet these days:

- **WiFi.** Wireless hotspots, known as WiFi (or, as Apple used to call it, AirPort), are
glorious conveniences, especially if you have a laptop. Without stirring from your
hotel bed, you're online at high speed. Sometimes for free.

- **Cable modems, DSL.** Over half of the U.S. Internet population connects over
higher-speed wires, using *broadband* connections that are always on: cable modems,
DSL, or corporate networks. (These, of course, are often what's at the other end
of an Internet hotspot.)

- **Cellular modems.** A few well-heeled individuals enjoy the go-anywhere bliss of
USB cellular modems, which get them online just about anywhere they can make
a phone call. These modems are offered by Verizon, Sprint, AT&T, and so on, and
usually cost around $50 a month.

Note: A MiFi is sort of a cellular modem, too. It's a pocketable, battery-operated, portable hotspot. It converts
the cellular signal into a WiFi signal, so up to five people can be online at once, while the MiFi itself sits
happily in your pocket or laptop bag.

- **Tethering.** *Tethering* is letting your cellphone act as a glorified Internet antenna
for your Mac, whether connected by a cable or a Bluetooth wireless link. You pay
your phone company extra for this convenience.

• **Dial-up modems.** Their numbers are shrinking, but some people still connect to the Internet using a modem that dials out over ordinary phone lines. The service is cheap, but the connection is slow.

This chapter explains how to set up each one of these. It also describes some of OS X's offbeat Internet featurettes. It tackles Internet Sharing, which lets several computers in the same household share a single broadband connection; the system-wide Internet bookmarks known as *Internet location files*; and iCloud, Apple's suite of free online syncing tools.

Network Central and Multihoming

In this chapter, you'll be spending a lot of time in the Network pane of System Preferences (Figure 10-1). (Choose →System Preferences; click Network.) This list summarizes the ways your Mac can connect to the Internet or an office network—Ethernet, WiFi, Bluetooth, cellular modem card, VPN, and so on.

Figure 10-1:
You set up your network connections here, and you can connect to and disconnect from them here. The listed network connections are tagged with color-coded dots. A green dot means turned on and connected to a network; yellow means the connection is working but some other setting is wrong (for example, your Mac can't get an IP address); and red means there's no connection or you haven't yet set up a connection.

Multihoming

The *order* of the network connections listed in the Network pane is important. That's the sequence the Mac uses as it tries to get online. If one of your programs needs Internet access and the first method isn't hooked up, then the Mac switches to the next available connection automatically.

In fact, OS X can maintain multiple simultaneous network connections—Ethernet, WiFi, dial-up, even FireWire—with a feature known as *multihoming*.

This feature is especially relevant for laptops. When you open your Web browser, your laptop might first check to see if it's plugged into an Ethernet cable, which is the fastest, most secure type of connection. If there's no Ethernet, then it looks for a WiFi network.

Here's how to go about setting up the connection-attempt sequence you want:

1. **Open System Preferences. Click the Network icon.**

 The Network status screen (Figure 10-1) brings home the point of multihoming: You can have more than one network connection operating at once.

2. **From the ✿ pop-up menu, choose Set Service Order.**

 Now you see the display shown in Figure 10-2. It lists all the ways your Mac knows how to get online, or onto an office network.

Figure 10-2:
The key to multihoming is sliding the network connection methods' names up or down. Note that you can choose a different connection sequence for each location. (Locations are described later in this chapter.)

Service Order:

- Bluetooth DUN
- USB Ethernet
- Wi-Fi
- Bluetooth PAN
- Thunderbolt Bridge

Drag services to change order.

[Cancel] [OK]

3. **Drag the items up and down the list into priority order.**

 If you have a wired broadband connection, for example, you might want to drag Built-in Ethernet to the top of the list, since that's almost always the fastest way to get online.

4. **Click OK.**

 You return to the Network pane of System Preferences, where the master list of connections magically re-sorts itself to match your efforts.

Your Mac will now be able to switch connections even in real time, during a single Internet session. If lightning takes out your Ethernet hub in the middle of your Web surfing, your Mac will seamlessly switch to your WiFi network, for example, to keep your session alive.

All right, then: Your paperwork is complete. The following pages guide you through the process of setting up these various connections.

Broadband Connections

If your Mac is connected wirelessly or, um, *wirefully* to a cable modem, DSL, or office network, you're one of the lucky ones. You have a high-speed broadband connection to the Internet that's always available, always on. You never have to wait to dial.

Automatic Configuration

Most broadband connections require *no setup whatsoever.* Take a new Mac out of the box, plug in the Ethernet cable to your cable modem—or choose a wireless network from the 🛜 menulet—and you can begin surfing the Web instantly.

That's because most cable modems, DSL boxes, and wireless base stations use *DHCP.* It stands for *dynamic host configuration protocol,* but what it means is "We'll fill in your Network pane of System Preferences automatically." (Including techie specs like IP address and DNS Server addresses.)

Manual Configuration

If, for some reason, you're not able to surf the Web or check email the first time you try, it's remotely possible that your broadband modem or your office network *doesn't* offer DHCP. In that case, you may have to fiddle with the Network pane of System Preferences, preferably with a customer-support rep from your broadband company on the phone.

On the Network pane, click your Internet connection (Wi-Fi, built-in Ethernet, cellular modem, whatever). Click Advanced; click TCP/IP. Now you see something like Figure 10-3. Don't be alarmed by the morass of numbers and periods—it's all in good fun. (If you find TCP/IP fun, that is.)

Figure 10-3:
Here's the setup for a cable-modem account with a static IP address, which means you have to type in all these numbers yourself.

To get the information to fill in here, you can call your Internet provider (cable or phone company) for help—or you can copy your Windows configuration onto the Mac. Read on.

Settings from Windows 2000, XP, Vista, Windows 7, or Windows 8

Your first task is to get to the Properties dialog box for your connection:

- **Windows 2000.** Choose Start→Settings→Network and Dial-up Connections.

- **Windows XP.** Choose Start→Control Panel. Open Network Connections.

- **Windows Vista.** Choose Start→Control Panel. Open Network and Sharing Center. Click "Manage network connections."

- **Windows 7.** Choose Start→Control Panel. Open Network and Sharing Center. Click "Change adapter settings."

- **Windows 8.** At the desktop, right-click the lower-left corner of the screen; from the pop-up menu, choose Control Panel. Open Network and Sharing Center. Click "Change adapter settings."

You wind up with a window full of icons that represent the various ways you can connect (3G Connection, Wireless Network Connection, Local Area Connection—that is, Ethernet cable—and so on).

Continue by right-clicking the icon for your broadband connection; from the shortcut menu, choose Properties. (In Windows Vista, you get an "Are you sure?" box at this point; click Continue.)

In the resulting dialog box, click the row that says "Internet Protocol (TCP/IP)."

If the resulting screen says "Obtain an IP address automatically," then leave Using DHCP selected in the Mac's Configure pop-up menu; your Mac should teach itself the correct settings automatically.

If the Windows screen says, "Use the following IP address" instead, then select Manually from the Mac's Configure pop-up menu, and copy the relevant numbers into the Mac's Network pane (see Figure 10-3).

Similarly, if the Internet Protocol (TCP/IP Properties) dialog box says "Use the following DNS server addresses," then type the numbers from the "Preferred DNS server" and "Alternate DNS server" boxes into the Mac's DNS Servers text box. (Press Return to make a new line for the second number.)

Note: If your Mac plugs directly into the cable modem (that is, you don't use a router), then you'll have to turn the cable modem or DSL box off and then on again when you've switched from the PC to the Mac.

Settings from Windows 98, Windows Me

Choose Start→Settings→Control Panel. In the Control Panel window, double-click Network. Double-click the TCP/IP row that identifies how your PC is connected to the broadband modem. (It may say "TCP/IP→3Com Ethernet Adapter," for example.)

Click the IP Address tab. If it says "Specify an IP address," then copy the IP Address and Subnet Mask numbers into the same ones on the Mac's Network pane. Then click the Gateway tab and copy the "Installed gateway" number into the Mac's Router box.

Finally, click the DNS Configuration tab. Copy the strings of numbers you see here into the Mac's DNS Servers text box. (Press Return to make a new line for the second number, if necessary.)

Applying the settings

That's all the setup; on the Mac, in the Network pane of System Preferences, click Apply. If your settings are correct, you're online, now and forever. You never have to worry about connecting or disconnecting.

Ethernet Connections

The beauty of Ethernet connections is that they're super fast and super secure. No bad guys sitting across the coffee shop, armed with shareware "sniffing" software, can intercept your email and chat messages, as they theoretically can when you're on wireless.

And 99 percent of the time, connecting to an Ethernet network is as simple as connecting the cable to the Mac. That's it. You're online, quickly and securely, and you never have to worry about connecting or disconnecting.

WiFi Connections

Your Mac can communicate with a wireless base station up to 300 feet away, much like a cordless phone. Doing so lets you surf the Web from your laptop in a hotel room, for example, or share files with someone across the building from you.

Chapter 16 has much more information about *setting up* a WiFi network. The real fun begins, however, when it comes time to *join* one.

Sometimes you just want to join a friend's WiFi network. Sometimes you've got time to kill in an airport, and it's worth a $7 splurge for half an hour. And sometimes, at some street corners in big cities, WiFi signals bleeding out of apartment buildings might give you a choice of several free hotspots to join.

POWER USERS' CLINIC

PPPoE and DSL

If you have DSL service, you may be directed to create a *PPPoE service.* (You do that on the Network pane of System Preferences; click the + button, choose PPPoE, select the connection you're using to PPPoE, and then click Create.)

It stands for PPP over Ethernet, meaning that although your DSL "modem" is connected to your Ethernet port, you still have to make and break your Internet connections manually, as though you had a dial-up modem.

Fill in the PPPoE dialog box as directed by your ISP (usually just your account name and password). From here on in, you start and end your Internet connections exactly as though you had a dial-up modem.

Your Mac joins WiFi hotspots like this:

- First, it sniffs around for a WiFi network you've used before. If it finds one, it connects quietly and automatically. You're not asked for permission, a password, or anything else; you're just online. (It's that way, for example, when you come home with your laptop every day.) For details on this memorization feature, see the box on page 355.

- If the Mac can't find a known hotspot, but it detects a new hotspot or two, a message appears on the screen, displaying their names. Double-click one to connect.

Tip: If you don't *want* your Mac to keep interrupting you with its discoveries of new hotspots—it can get pretty annoying when you're in a taxi driving through a city—you can shut them off. In System Preferences, click Network, click Wi-Fi, and then turn off "Ask to join new networks."

- If you're in the presence of a commercial hotspot—one that requires payment or reading some kind of insipid legal agreement—OS X opens a miniature Web page, shoving it right into your face, even if your Web browser isn't open; see Figure 10-4.

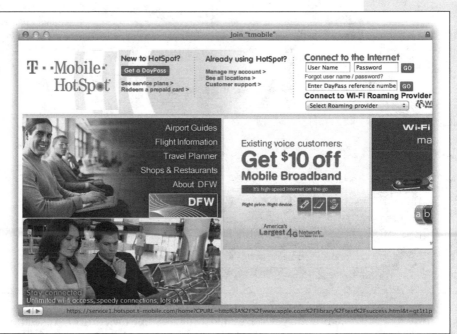

Figure 10-4:
OS X auto-opens a page like this whenever it senses that you're in a commercial WiFi network, one that requires you to sign in. (That's a big improvement from the old way, where you'd join a network and then have no clue that you wouldn't be able to get any further until you opened up your Web browser to find that login screen.)

- If you missed the opportunity to join a hotspot when the message appeared, or if you joined the wrong one or a non-working one, then you have another chance. You can always choose a hotspot's name from the 🛜 menulet, as shown in Figure 10-5. A 🔒 icon indicates a hotspot that requires a password, so you don't waste your time trying to join it (unless, of course, you *have* the password).

Tip: It always takes a computer a few seconds—maybe 5 or 10—to connect to the Internet over WiFi. In OS X, the 🛜 menulet itself *pulses,* or rather ripples, with a black-and-gray animation to let you know you're still in the connection process. It's an anti-frustration aid. (Oh, and also, each hotspot's signal strength appears right in the menulet.)

Figure 10-5:
Top: Congratulations—your Mac has discovered new WiFi hotspots all around you! You even get to see the signal strength right in the menu. Double-click one to join it. But if you see a 🔒 icon next to the hotspot's name, beware: It's been protected by a password. If you don't know it, then you won't be able to connect.

Bottom: Later, you can always switch networks using the WiFi menulet.

Or, if you have an iPhone or cellular iPad with Instant Hotspot turned on (page 481), you can hop right onto your own private network.

Before you get too excited, though, some lowering of expectations is in order. There are a bunch of reasons why your 🛜 menulet might indicate that you're in a hotspot, but you can't actually get online:

- **It's locked.** If there's a 🔒 next to the hotspot's name in your 🛜 menulet, then it's password protected. That's partly to prevent hackers from "sniffing" the transmissions and intercepting messages and partly to keep random passersby like you off the network.

- **The signal isn't strong enough.** Sometimes the WiFi signal is strong enough to make the hotspot's name show up in your 🛜 menu but not strong enough for an actual connection.

- **You're not on the list.** Sometimes, for security, hotspots are rigged to permit only *specific* computers to join (see the box below), and yours isn't one of them.

- **You haven't logged in yet.** Commercial hotspots (the ones you have to pay for) don't connect you to the Internet until you've supplied your payment details on a special Web page that appears automatically when you open your browser, as described below.

- **The router's on, but the Internet's not connected.** Sometimes wireless routers are broadcasting, but their Internet connection is down. It'd be like a cordless phone that has a good connection back to the base station in the kitchen—but the phone cord isn't plugged into the base station.

Commercial Hotspots

Choosing the name of the hotspot you want to join is generally all you have to do—if it's a *home* WiFi network.

Unfortunately, joining a *commercial* WiFi hotspot—one that requires a credit card number (in a hotel room or an airport, for example)—requires more than just connecting to it. You also have to *sign into* it before you can send so much as a single email message.

The Super-Secret Hotspot Management Box

If you open System Preferences→Network, click Wi-Fi in the left-side list, and then click Advanced, you see the dialog box shown here. It lets you manage the list of WiFi hotspots that OS X has memorized on your travels.

For example, you can delete the old ones. Or you can drag the hotspots' names up and down the list to establish a priority for making connections when more than one is available.

Ordinarily, OS X memorizes the names of the hotspots you join on your travels. It's kind of nice, actually, because it means you're interrupted less of-

ten by the "Do you want to join?" box. But if you're alarmed at the massive list of hotspots OS X has memorized—for privacy reasons, say—here's where you turn off "Remember networks this computer has joined."

Finally, for added security on your Mac, you can turn on any of these three checkboxes that prevent the unauthorized from making changes—creating computer-to-computer networks, changing networks, or turning WiFi on or off—without an administrator's password.

To do that, open your Web browser—if, in fact, OS X doesn't auto-open the sign-up screen (page 353). You'll see the "Enter your payment information" screen either immediately or as soon as you try to open a Web page of your choice. (Even at free hotspots, you might have to click OK on a welcome page to initiate the connection.)

Supply your credit card information or (if you have a membership to this WiFi chain, like Boingo or T-Mobile) your name and password. Click Submit or Proceed, try *not* to contemplate how this $8 per hour is pure profit for somebody, and enjoy your surfing.

Cellular Modems

WiFi hotspots are fast and usually cheap—but they're *spots.* Beyond 150 feet away, you're offline.

No wonder laptop luggers across America are getting into *cellular* Internet services. All the big cellphone companies offer USB sticks that let your laptop get online at high speed *anywhere* in major cities. No hunting for a coffee shop; with a cellular Internet service, you can check your email while zooming down the road in a taxi. (Outside the metropolitan areas, you can still get online wirelessly, though slowly.)

Verizon, Sprint, and AT&T all offer cellular Internet networks with speeds approaching a cable modem's. So why isn't the world beating a path to this delicious technology's door? Because it's expensive—maybe $60 a month on top of your phone bill.

To get online, insert the USB stick; it may take about 15 seconds for the thing to latch on to the cellular signal.

Now you're supposed to make the Internet connection using the special "dialing" software provided by the cellphone company. Technically, though, you may not need it. You can start and stop the Internet connection using a menulet—no phone-company software required.

Tethering (Personal Hotspot)

If you have an iPhone, Android phone, or another app phone, you don't even need a cellular modem; you've already got one. Most app phones nowadays offer *tethering,* where the cellphone tunes into the Internet for the benefit of your laptop (or even your desktop computer). The phone connects to your laptop either with a USB cable or wirelessly (Bluetooth or WiFi).

The nice part is that you can get online almost anywhere there's cellphone coverage. The less-nice part is that the connection isn't always blazing fast, and you have to pay your cellphone company for the privilege. (It's usually $20 or $30 on top of your regular monthly phone plan; for that, you're allowed to send and receive 2 gigabytes of data each month. If you go over the limit, you pay overage fees. Good luck figuring that out.)

Here's a typical example: Suppose you have an iPhone. You open Settings→General→ Network→Personal Hotspot. You turn it on. You assign a password to your private little hotspot. The iPhone asks how you'll be connecting to the phone; let's say you tap Wi-Fi.

Now, on your laptop, you choose your iPhone's name from the 🛜 menulet. (If the phone has iOS 8.1 or later, the menulet shows the iPhone's name even if it's asleep and Instant Hotspot is turned off, as described on page 481.)

You enter your hotspot password (just this time—later, your laptop will remember), and presto: Your laptop is online. A bright-blue "Personal Hotspot: 1 Connection" banner appears on your iPhone to remind you, and your 🛜 menulet changes to become the International Symbol for Apple Tethering: ⚭.

Now, tethering eats up your phone's battery like crazy; you'll be lucky to get 3 hours out of it. So you probably shouldn't count on watching Netflix on your laptop via your phone.

But for email, emergency Web checks, and other mobile crises, tethering is a convenient, useful feature. And when you're on the road for a couple of weeks, it's a heck of a lot cheaper than paying your hotel $13 a night for WiFi.

Dial-Up Modem Connections

If you ask Apple, dial-up modems are dead. Macs haven't come with built-in modems for years. You can get a non-Apple USB modem for $50, but clearly Apple is trying to shove the trusty dial-up technology into the recycling bin.

Still, millions of people never got the memo. If you're among them, then you need to sign up for Internet service. Once you've selected a service provider, you plug its settings into the Network pane of System Preferences. You get the necessary information directly from your ISP by consulting either its Web page, the instruction sheets that came with your account, or a help-desk agent on the phone.

Further details on OS X's dial-up modem setup are in the free appendix to this chapter, "Setting Up a Dial-Up Connection." It's available on this book's "Missing CD" page at *www.missingmanuals.com*.

Switching Locations

If you travel with a laptop, you may find yourself frequently opening up System Preferences→Network so you can switch between Internet settings: Ethernet at the office, WiFi at home.

The simple solution is the →Location submenu, which appears once you've set up more than one Location. As Figure 10-6 illustrates, all you have to do is tell it where you are. OS X handles the details of switching Internet connections.

Creating a New Location

To create a *Location,* which is nothing more than a set of memorized settings, open System Preferences, click Network, and then choose Edit Locations from the Location pop-up menu. Continue as shown in Figure 10-6 at bottom.

Tip: You can use the commands in the ✿ menu to rename or duplicate a Location.

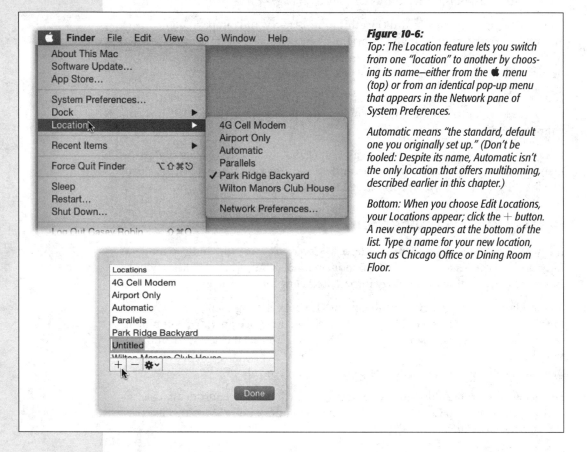

Figure 10-6:
Top: The Location feature lets you switch from one "location" to another by choosing its name—either from the ⌘ menu (top) or from an identical pop-up menu that appears in the Network pane of System Preferences.

Automatic means "the standard, default one you originally set up." (Don't be fooled: Despite its name, Automatic isn't the only location that offers multihoming, described earlier in this chapter.)

Bottom: When you choose Edit Locations, your Locations appear; click the + button. A new entry appears at the bottom of the list. Type a name for your new location, such as Chicago Office or Dining Room Floor.

When you click Done, you return to the Network pane. Take this opportunity to set up the kind of Internet connection you use at the corresponding location, just as described on the first pages of this chapter.

If you travel regularly, you can build a *list* of Locations, each of which "knows" the way you like to get online in each city you visit.

A key part of making a new Location is putting the various Internet connection types (Ethernet, Wi-Fi, Modem, Bluetooth) into the correct order. Your connections will be slightly quicker if you give the modem connection priority in your Hotel setup, the Wi-Fi connection priority in your Starbucks setup, and so on.

You can even turn off some connections entirely. For example, if you use nothing but a cable modem when you're at home, you might want to create a location in which *only* the Ethernet connection is active. Use the Make Service Inactive command in the ✿ menu.

Conversely, if your laptop uses nothing but WiFi when you're on the road, your Location could include *nothing* but the Wi-Fi connection. You'll save a few seconds each time you try to go online, because your Mac won't bother hunting for an Internet connection that doesn't exist.

Making the Switch

Once you've set up your various Locations, you can switch among them using the ✿→Location submenu, as shown in Figure 10-6. As soon as you do so, your Mac is automatically set to get online the way you like.

Tip: If you have a laptop, create a connection called Offline. From the Show pop-up menu, choose Network Port Configurations; make *all* the connection methods in the list inactive. When you're finished, you've got yourself a laptop that will *never* attempt to go online. It's the laptop equivalent of Airplane Mode on a cellphone.

Internet Sharing

If you have cable modem or DSL service, you're a very lucky individual. You get terrific Internet speed and an always-on connection. Too bad only one computer in your household or office can enjoy these luxuries.

It doesn't have to be that way. You can spread the joy of high-speed Internet to every Mac (and PC) on your network in either of two ways:

- **Buy a router.** A *router* is a little box, costing about $50, that connects directly to the cable modem or DSL box. In most cases, it has multiple Internet jacks so you can plug in several Macs, PCs, and/or wireless base stations. As a bonus, a router provides excellent security, serving as a firewall to keep out unsolicited visits from hackers on the Internet.

- **Use Internet Sharing.** OS X's Internet Sharing feature is the software version of a router: It distributes a single Internet signal to every computer on the network. But unlike a router, it's free. You just fire it up on the one Mac that's connected directly to the Internet—the *gateway* computer.

 But there's a downside: If the gateway Mac is turned off or asleep, then the other machines can't get online.

Most people use Internet Sharing to share a broadband connection like a cable modem or DSL. But there are other times when it comes in handy. If you have a cellular modem, for example, you might want to share its signal via WiFi so the kids in the backseat can get online with their iPod Touches.

The only requirement: The Internet-connected Mac must have some *other* kind of connection (Ethernet, WiFi, Bluetooth, FireWire) to the Macs that will share the connection.

Turning On Internet Sharing

To turn on Internet Sharing on the gateway Mac, open the Sharing pane of System Preferences. Click Internet Sharing, as shown in Figure 10-7, but don't turn on the checkbox yet.

Figure 10-7:
Ka-ching! You and your buddy are about to save money. In this example, an Ethernet wire is getting this Mac online. But it's sharing that Internet connection with other Macs via WiFi. They can get online, too.

Before you do that, you have to specify (a) how the gateway Mac is connected to the Internet, and (b) how it's connected to the other Macs on your network:

- **Share your connection from.** Using this pop-up menu, identify how *this Mac* (the gateway machine) connects to the Internet—via built-in Ethernet, WiFi, cellular modem, or Bluetooth DUN (dial-up networking—that is, tethering to your cellphone or iPad).

- **To computers using.** Using these checkboxes, specify how you want your Mac to rebroadcast the Internet signal to the others. (It has to be a *different* network channel. You can't get your signal via WiFi and then pass it on via WiFi.)

Note: Which checkboxes appear here depends on which kinds of Internet connections are turned on in the Network pane of System Preferences. If the gateway Mac doesn't have WiFi circuitry, for example, or if WiFi is turned off in the current configuration, then the Wi-Fi option doesn't appear.

Now visit each of the other Macs on the same network. Open the Network pane of System Preferences. Select the network method you chose in the second step above: Wi-Fi, Built-in Ethernet, or FireWire. Click Apply.

If the gateway Mac is rebroadcasting using WiFi—by far the most common use of this feature—you have one more step. In your 🛜 menulet, you'll see a strange new "hotspot" that wasn't there before, bearing the name of the gateway Mac. (It might say, for example, "Casey's MacBook Air.") Choose its name to begin your borrowed Internet connection.

As long as the gateway Mac remains on and online, both it and your other computers can get onto the Internet simultaneously, all at high speed, even Windows PCs. You've created a *software* base station. The Mac itself is now the transmitter for Internet signals to and from any other WiFi computers within range.

Tip: You can let a wired Mac share a *wireless* connection, too. Suppose, for example, that you and a buddy both have laptops in a hotel lobby. You're online, having paid $13 to use the hotel's WiFi network. If you set up Internet Sharing appropriately, your buddy can connect to your Mac via an Ethernet cable and surf along with you—no extra charge.

POWER USERS' CLINIC

Internet Sharing as a Bridge

Ordinarily, only one Mac has Internet Sharing turned on: the one that's connected directly to the Internet.

But sometimes, you might want another Mac "downstream" to have it on, too. That's when you want to *bridge* two networks.

Consider the setup shown here. There are really two networks: one that uses WiFi, and another connected to an Ethernet hub.

If you play your cards right, all these Macs can get online simultaneously, using a single Internet connection.

Set up the gateway Mac so that it's a WiFi base station, exactly as described on these pages.

Start setting up the *bridge* Mac the way you'd set up the other WiFi Macs—with Wi-Fi selected as the primary connection method, and Using DHCP turned on in the Network pane.

Then visit the bridge Mac's Sharing pane. Turn on Internet Sharing here, too, but this time select "To computers using: Built-in Ethernet."

The bridge Mac is now on both networks. It uses the WiFi connection as a bridge to the gateway Mac and the Internet—and its Ethernet connection to share that happiness with the wired Macs in its own neighborhood.

Meet iCloud

In your time with the Mac, you'll see frequent references to Apple's free iCloud service. So what is iCloud?

It's a huge array of features that are designed to make you glad you belong in the Apple ecosystem. iCloud synchronizes information across all your Macs, iPhones, iPads, iPod Touches, across family members, across the world, wirelessly and automatically. It keeps track of every song, book, movie, app, and TV show you've bought from Apple, so that you can download them onto any other gadget with an Apple logo on the back. It lets you find a lost Apple gadget. It gives you an email account. And a lot more.

The rest of this chapter details each of iCloud's goodies, one at a time. They're described in the order they appear in System Preferences→iCloud (Figure 10-8).

Figure 10-8:
The headquarters of iCloud's features. You'll find a nearly identical pane on your iPhone, iPad, or iPod Touch (in Settings→iCloud).

iCloud Drive

The iCloud Drive is Apple's version of Dropbox. It's a folder, present on every Mac, iPhone, iPad, and iPod Touch, that lists whatever you've put into it—an online "disk" that holds 5 gigabytes (more, if you're willing to pay money).

The iCloud Drive is a perfect place to put stuff you want to be able to access from any Apple gadget, wherever you go. It's a great backup, too.

If you click Options (shown in Figure 10-8), you find two tabs. The first, Documents, lists all the Mac apps that have stored files or preference settings on your Drive. "Look Me Up by Email" is a list of apps that permit other iCloud members to find you by looking up your address.

You can read more about iCloud Drive on page 362.

Photos

For most people, pictures are extremely important data. iCloud takes the worry out of maintaining your collection by making sure they're backed up and available online.

In System Preferences→iCloud, click Options to see two on/off checkboxes. "My Photo Stream" and "iCloud Photo Sharing" are the master switches for Photo Streams and iCloud Photo Sharing.

My Photo Stream

Every time a new photo enters your life—when you take a picture with an i-gadget, for example, or import one onto your Mac—it gets added to your Photo Stream. In other words, it appears automatically on all your *other* iCloud machines. Here's where to find them:

- **iPhone, iPad, iPod Touch.** Open your Photos app. There it is: a listing called My Photo Stream. It shows the most recent 1,000 photos you've taken with any of your *other* i-gadgets, or that you've imported to your computer from a scanner or digital camera (Figure 10-9).

Figure 10-9:
Left: Why, look! It's photos you imported onto your Mac at home. How'd they get here on the iPhone? iCloud!

Middle: To rescue one of these photos from the 1,000-photo rule, open it. Then tap the □ button.

Right: Finally, tap Save to Camera Roll (bottom row, center). Now, even after that photo disappears from the Photo Stream, having been displaced by the 1,001st incoming photo, you'll still have your permanent copy.

Now, Apple realizes that your i-gadget doesn't have nearly as much storage available as your Mac; you can't yet buy an iPad with 750 gigabytes of storage. That's why, on your iPhone/iPad/iPod, your Photo Stream consists of just the last 1,000 photos. (There's another limitation, too: The iCloud servers store your photos for 30 days. As long as your gadgets go online at least once a month, they'll remain current with the Photo Stream.)

Once a photo arrives, you can save it to your Camera Roll, where it's permanently saved. See Figure 10-9.

Note: Photo Stream is the one iCloud feature that doesn't sync over the cellular airwaves. It sends photos around only when you're in a WiFi hotspot or connected to a wired network.

- **On the Mac.** In iPhoto, your Photo Stream photos appear in a new album called, of course, Photo Stream. (On a Windows PC, you'd get a Photo Stream folder in your Pictures folder.)

 You don't have to worry about that 30-day, 1,000-photo business. Once pictures appear here, they're here until you delete them.

 This, in its way, is one of the best features in all of iCloudland, because it means you don't have to sync your iPhone over a USB cable to get your photos onto your computer. It all happens automatically, wirelessly over WiFi.

- **Apple TV.** When you're viewing your photos on an Apple TV, a new album appears there called Photo Stream. There they are, ready for showing on the big plasma.

iCloud Photo Sharing

The term "iCloud Photo Sharing," introduced in 2014, is what used to be called a shared Photo Stream. It lets you send photos or videos to other people's gadgets. After a party or some other get-together, you could send your best shots to everyone who attended; after a trip, you could post your photographic memories for anyone who might care.

The lucky recipients can post comments about your pix, click a "like" button to indicate their enthusiasm, or even submit pictures and videos of their own. It's like having a tiny Instagram network of your very own, consisting solely of people you invite.

Photo Sharing does have certain requirements:

- **iPhone, iPad, or iPod Touch** with iOS 7 or later. The On switch is in Settings→ iCloud→Photos; turn on iCloud Photo Sharing.

- **A Mac** with OS X Mavericks (10.9) or later *and* iPhoto 9.5 or Aperture 3.5 or later. Open System Preferences→iCloud. Make sure Photos is turned on; click Options and confirm that Photo Sharing is on, too.

- **A PC** with Windows 7 or later. The On switch is in the iCloud Control Panel for Windows (a free download from Apple's Web site).

- **An Apple TV** (2nd generation) with Software Update 6.0 or later.

Instructions for working with iCloud Photo Sharing—for every kind of computer and handheld gadget—await at *http://help.apple.com/icloud/#mmc0cd7e99*.

It's a bit pointless to describe the steps for creating shared albums in iPhoto or Aperture on the Mac, since Apple intends to kill off both programs and replace them with a new one, simply called Photos. But to give you a flavor of the process, here are the steps to share some of your photographic masterpieces with your adoring fans in iPhoto:

1. **Select the photos and videos you want to share. Click ⤴, then iCloud, then click "New photo stream."**

 A dialog box appears, called New Photo Stream. You're being asked for the email addresses of your lucky audience members.

2. **Specify the invitees.**

 Enter their addresses in the "To:" box just as you would address an outgoing email. For your convenience, a list of recent sharees appears below the "To:" box.

 Also name the stream ("Chris's Wedding" or whatever). Add a comment, if you like. And see Figure 10-10 for guidance on setting up the checkbox options.

Figure 10-10:
If you turn on Subscribers Can Post, your subscribers will be able contribute photos and videos to your album. That's a fantastic feature for an event where there was a crowd: a wedding, show, concert, picnic, badminton tournament. Now everyone who was there can enhance the gallery with shots taken from their own points of view with their own phones or cameras.

And if you turn on Public Website, then even people who aren't members of the Apple cult will be able to see these photos. The invitees will get an email containing a Web address. It links to a hidden page on the iCloud Web site that contains your published photos.

3. Click Share.

 Your Mac gets busy uploading the photos, and your recipients are invited by email to see them.

 Later, you can adjust these settings. In iPhoto, click iCloud (in the left-side column); click the icon of your shared album; and then click Info at the bottom of the screen.

iCloud Photo Library

If learning the difference between My Photo Stream and iCloud Photo Sharing isn't hard enough, then hold on to your lens cap. Apple has introduced yet another online photo feature: the iCloud Photo Library.

The idea this time is that all your Apple gadgets will keep all your photos and videos backed up online and synced. *All* your photos and videos are always backed up, and always accessible from any of your gadgets.

iCloud Photo Library began life in 2014 as a beta (test) program for iPhones and iPads—but it won't be available for Macs until the Photos app arrives later this year.

Tip: Even if you're using, say, an iPhone to post your iCloud Photo Library, there is a way to see your photos on a Mac: at iCloud.com. You can click Photos to view your photos and videos, no matter what machine you're using. The Moments and Albums tabs here correspond to the tabs in the phone's Photos app. Click a photo to open it full size, whereupon the icons at the top of the screen let you delete, download, or "favorite" it.

Mail

Apple offers an email address as part of each iCloud account. Of course, you already *have* an email account. So why bother? The first advantage is the simple address: *YourName@me.com.* (It may look like what you've got is *YourName@icloud.com,* but mail sent to *YourName@me.com* comes to exactly the same place. These addresses are aliases of each other.)

Second, me.com addresses are integrated into OS X's Mail program, as you'll see in Chapter 11. You can also read your me.com email from any computer anywhere in the world, via the iCloud.com Web site, or on your iPhone/iPod Touch/iPad.

Besides, it's always great to have a backup account, one you never enter on Web sites so that it never gets overrun with spam. Or vice versa: Let this be your junk account, the address you use for online forms. Either way, it's great to have a second account.

To make things even sweeter, your me.com or icloud.com mail is completely synced. Delete a message on one gadget, and you'll find it in the Deleted Mail folder on another. Send a message from your iPhone, and you'll find it in the Sent Mail folder on your Mac. And so on.

Contacts, Calendars, Reminders, Safari, Notes, Keychain

iCloud began life as a *synchronization* service. It can keep your calendar, address book, reminders, notes, bookmarks, and documents updated and identical on all your gadgets: Mac, PC, iPhone, iPad, iPod Touch. Also your Web passwords and credit card numbers. And all your photos, too, rounded up from all your Apple gadgets.

It's a huge convenience—almost magical. It's one of the great payoffs of living within Apple's ecosystem of gadgets. It offers both a huge convenience factor—all your stuff is always on all your gadgets—and a safety/backup factor, since you have duplicates everywhere.

It works by storing the master copies of your stuff—email, notes, contacts, calendars, Web bookmarks, and documents—on the Web. (Or "in the cloud," as the product managers would say.)

Whenever your Macs, PCs, or i-gadgets are online—over WiFi or cellular—they connect to the mother ship and update themselves. Edit an address on your iPhone, and shortly thereafter you'll find the same change in Contacts (on your Mac) and Outlook (on your PC). Send an email reply from your PC at the office, and you'll find it in your Sent Mail folder on the Mac at home. Add a Web bookmark anywhere and find it everywhere else. Edit a spreadsheet in Numbers on your iPad and find the same numbers updated on your Mac.

Actually, there's even another place where you can work with your data: on the Web. Using your computer, you can log into *www.icloud.com* to find Web-based clones of Calendar, Contacts, and Mail.

Figure 10-8 shows the on/off switches for these sync features. They include these:

- **Contacts, Calendars.** There's nothing as exasperating as realizing that the address book you're consulting on your home Mac is missing somebody you're sure you entered—on your phone. This option keeps all your address books and calendars synchronized. Delete a phone number on your computer at home, and you'll find it gone from your phone. Enter an appointment on your iPhone, and you'll find the calendar updated everywhere else.

- **Reminders.** This option refers to the to-do items you create in the phone's Reminders app; very shortly, those reminders will show up on your Mac (in Reminders, Calendar, or BusyCal) or PC (in Outlook). How great to make a reminder for yourself in one place and have it reminding you later in another one!

- **Safari.** If a Web site is important enough to merit bookmarking while you're using your phone, why shouldn't it also show up in the Bookmarks menu on your desktop PC at home, your Mac laptop, or your iPad? This option syncs your Safari Reading List, too.

- **Notes.** This option syncs the notes from your phone's Notes app into the Notes app on the Mac, the email program on your PC, your other i-gadgets, and, of course, the iCloud Web site.

- **Keychain.** The iCloud Keychain keeps all your online name/password combinations synchronized across all your Apple machines, so you don't have to memorize them or even type them as you log into various sites. Credit card numbers, too. See page 526.

To set up syncing, turn on the checkboxes for the items you want synced. That's it. There is no step 2.

Note: You may notice that there are no switches here for syncing stuff you buy from Apple, like books, movies, apps, and music. They're not so much synced as they are stored for you online. You can download them at any time to any of your machines.

Back to My Mac

The option to grab files from one of your other Macs across the Internet is now a part of iCloud. It lets you access the contents of one Mac from another one across the Internet. See page 567.

Find My Mac (or iPhone, or iPad)

Did you leave your iPhone somewhere? Did your laptop get stolen? Has that mischievous 5-year-old hidden your iPad again?

Now you can check into iCloud.com to see exactly where your Mac, iPhone, or iPad is. You can even make it beep loudly for 2 minutes, so you can figure out which couch cushion it's under, or which jacket pocket you left it in. If the missing item is an iPad or an iPhone, you can make it beep even if the ringer switch is off, and even if the device is asleep. You can also make a message pop up on the screen; if you actually left the thing in a taxi or on some restaurant table, you can use this feature to plead for its return. The bottom line: If you ever lose your Apple gear, you have a fighting chance at getting it back.

(That's *if* it's online, and *if* you turned on Find My Mac in the iCloud pane of System Preferences.)

If an ethical person finds your phone, you might get it back. If it's a greedy person who says, "Hey, cool! A free iPhone!" then maybe you can bombard him with so many of these messages that he gives it back in exasperation.

If not, you can either lock the gadget with a password (yes, by remote control) or even avail yourself of one more amazing last-ditch feature: Remote Wipe.

That means *erasing your data by remote control,* from wherever you happen to be. The evil thief can do nothing but stare in amazement as the phone, tablet, or Mac suddenly erases itself, winding up completely empty.

Note: And by the way: That evil thief can't erase your stolen phone or tablet himself, thanks to Apple's ingenious Activation Lock feature. It prevents the phone or tablet from being erased without your Apple ID and password. Good luck with that, bad guy!

To set up your Mac so you can find it remotely, open System Preferences→iCloud. Make sure Find My Mac is turned on. Later, if the worst should come to pass and you can't find your Mac, go to any computer and call up *www.icloud.com*. Log in with your Apple name and password. Click Find My Mac. If you're asked for your password again, type it; Apple wants to make sure it's really, *really* you who's messing around with your account settings.

Immediately, the Web site updates to show you, on a map, the current location of your Macs (and iPhones, iPod Touches, and iPads); see Figure 10-11.

Note: If they're not online, or if they're turned all the way off, you won't see their current locations. If they're just asleep—even if your laptop's lid is closed—you will.

If just knowing where the thing *is* isn't enough to satisfy you, click the little pushpin that represents your Mac (or choose its name from the menu at top center), and try one of these three buttons:

- **Play Sound.** When you click this button, a very loud sonar-like pinging sound instantly chimes on your Mac, wherever it is, no matter what its volume setting. Even if your laptop is closed and asleep, it will ring. The idea is to help you find it in whatever room of the house you left it in.

 When it's all over, Apple sends an email confirmation to your @me.com address.

- **Lock.** What if you worry about the security of your Mac's info, but you don't want to erase it completely and just want to throw a low-level veil of casual protection over the thing? Easy: Lock it by remote control.

 The Lock button lets you make up a four-digit passcode (which overrides the one you already had, if any). Without it, the sleazy crook can't get into your Mac, and can't even erase it.

 You're also offered the opportunity to type a message; it will appear on the Unlock screen, below the four boxes where you're supposed to type in the four-digit code. You might type something like, "Thank you for finding my lost laptop! Please call me at 212-556-1000 for a delicious frosty reward."

- **Erase.** This is the last-ditch security option, for when your immediate concern isn't so much the Mac as all the private stuff that's on it. Click this button, confirm the dire warning box, and click Erase All Data. By remote control, you've just erased everything from your Mac, wherever it may be. (If it's ever returned, you can restore it from your Time Machine backup.)

Figure 10-11:
The location process can take a couple of minutes. You can zoom into or out of the map, click Satellite to see an overhead photo of the area, or click Hybrid to see the photo with street names superimposed.

The big green dot indicates that one of your Apple gadgets isn't as lost as you thought.

Once you've wiped the Mac, you can no longer find it or send messages to it using Find My Mac.

Family Sharing

It might have taken years, but Apple has finally acknowledged a fundamental fact of American life: Many of us have *families.*

If you have kids, it's always been a hassle to manage your Apple life. What if they want to buy a book, movie, or app? They have to use your credit card—and you have to reveal your iCloud password to them. Or what if they want to see a movie that you bought? Do they really have to buy it again?

Not anymore. Once you've turned on Family Sharing and invited your family members, here's how your life will be different:

- **One credit card to rule them all**. Up to six of you can buy books, movies, apps, and music on your master credit card.

- **Ask before buy**. When your kids try to buy stuff, your phone pops up a permission request. You have to approve each purchase.

- **Younger Appleheads**. Within Family Sharing, you can now create Apple accounts for tiny tots; 13 is no longer the age minimum.

- **Shared everything**. All of you get instant access to one another's music, video, iBooks, and app purchases—again, without having to know each other's Apple passwords.

- **Find one another**. You can use your phone to see where your kids are, and vice versa (with permission, of course).

- **Find one another's phones**. The miraculous Find My iPhone feature (page 368) now works for every phone in the family. If your daughter can't find her phone, you can find it for her with your phone.

- **Mutual photo album, mutual calendar, and mutual reminders**. When you turn on Family Sharing, your Photos, Calendar, and Reminders apps each sprout a new category that's preconfigured to permit access by everyone in your family.

Setting Up Family Sharing

You can turn on Family Sharing either on the Mac (in System Preferences→iCloud) or on the phone. Since this book is about the Mac, here are the steps to do it there (Figure 10-12).

In System Preferences→iCloud, tap Set Up Family. Read about the juicy features, and then click Continue. The next screen asks you to confirm that you are the sage adult, the Organizer—the one with the power, the wisdom, and the credit card. Click Continue (unless it's listing the wrong Apple ID account, in which case, you can fix it now).

On successive screens, you read about the idea of shared Apple Store purchases; you're shown the credit card that Apple believes you want to use; you're offered the chance to share your location with the others. Each time, read and click Continue or Confirm.

Finally, you're ready to introduce the software to your family. Click the + button at lower left. Then:

- **If the kid has an iCloud account and is standing right there with you in person:** Type in her name or email address. (Your child's name must already be in your Contacts; if not, go add her first. By the way, you're a terrible parent.)

 You're asked to confirm that you're actually present with her by entering the security code for your credit card. When you click Continue, she can now enter her iCloud password on your Mac to complete her setup (Figure 10-12, bottom).

Figure 10-12:
Top: The iCloud pane of System Preferences is the central hub of Family Sharing planning. The setup process involves a bunch of dialog boxes, but at least you have to walk through them only once.

Middle: Adding a new member to your circle starts with an email address.

Bottom: If the prospective family member is standing with you, she can enter her password on the spot.

(That doesn't mean you'll learn what her password is; your Mac stores it but hides it.)

On the next screen, she has a couple of decisions to make (Figure 10-13, bottom).

- **If the kid has an iCloud account but isn't with you at the moment:** Type in his email address. Click Send an Invitation.

 Your little darling gets an email at that address. He must open it on his Apple gadget—the Mail app on the iPhone, or the Mail program on his Mac, for example. When he hits View Invitation, he can either enter his iCloud name and password (if he has an iCloud account), or get an Apple ID (if he doesn't).

 Once he accepts the invitation, he can choose a picture to represent himself; tap Confirm to agree to be in your family; enter his iCloud password to share the stuff he's bought from Apple; agree to Apple's lawyers' demands; and, finally, opt in to sharing his location with the rest of the family.

- **If the kid is under 13:** Your kid doesn't have an iCloud account, because until Family Sharing came along, you had to be over 13 to get an iCloud account. No longer!

 Choose "Create an Apple ID for a child who doesn't have an account." Click Continue. On the screen that follows, you'll enter the kid's name and birth date (Figure 10-13, top).

Figure 10-13:

Top: You'll notice that the dialog box requires a birth year that confirms your kid's age under 13. If your kid is over 13, you should set up an iCloud account in the usual way—at iCloud.com, for example, or in System Preferences→iCloud.

Bottom: A newly added family member has some decisions to make. First, the Purchases pop-up menu lets her specify her iCloud address—the one whose purchases she'll be pooling with the family. (It's usually the same address you just specified, but not always.)

Second, here she can turn on location sharing. In other words: The rest of the family will be able to see where she is, using Messages, Find My Mac, and the Find My Friends app on the iPhone or iPad.

Make up a name and password for the new iCloud account, too. Decide whether you want the family to be able to see where the kid is at all times. Click Continue.

On the Parent Privacy Disclosure screen, enter the security code for your credit card yet again (to prove that you're you, and not, for example, your naughty kid).

On the next screen, you choose and answer three security questions for this new iCloud account. Click Continue. Then more legalese on two screens (click "I agree," then Agree).

You can, of course, repeat this cycle to add additional family members, up to a maximum of six. Their names and ages appear on the Family screen.

From here, you can click someone's name to perform stunts like these:

- **Delete a family member.** Man, you guys really don't get along, do you? Anyway, click the — button.

- **Turn Ask To Buy on or off.** This option appears when you've selected a child's name. If you decide your kid is responsible enough not to need your permission for each purchase, you can turn this option off.

Note: If you turn off Ask To Buy for someone after she turns 18, you can't turn it on again.

- **Turn Parent/Guardian on or off.** This option appears when you've selected an adult's name. It gives Ask To Buy approval privileges to someone else besides you—your spouse, for example.

- **Turn "Allow [this person] to see your location" on or off.** Do you want this person to be able to see where you are (by using Messages, Find My Mac, or Find My Friends)?

Once kids turn 13, by the way, Apple automatically gives them more control over their own lives. They can, for example, turn off Ask To Buy *themselves,* on their own Macs

UP TO SPEED

The Price of Free

A free iCloud account gives you 5 gigabytes of online storage. That may not sound like much, especially when you consider how big some music, photo, and video files are. Fortunately, anything you buy from Apple—like music, apps, books, and TV shows—doesn't count against that 5-gigabyte limit. Neither do the photos in your Photo Stream.

So what's left? Some things that don't take up much space, like settings, documents, and pictures you take with your iPhone, iPad, or iPod Touch—and some things that take up

a lot of it, like email, commercial movies, and anything you put on your iCloud Drive.

You can, of course, expand your storage if you find 5 gigs constricting. You can expand that to 20, 50, 500, or 1,000 gigabytes—for $12, $48, $120, or $240 a year. You can upgrade your storage online, on your phone, or right on the Mac (in System Preferences→iCloud→Manage→Buy More Storage).

or phones. They can even express their disgust for you by leaving the Family Sharing group. (On her own phone, for example, your daughter can visit Settings→iCloud→ Family, tap her name, and then tap Leave Family. Harsh!)

Life in Family Sharing

Once everything's set up, here's how you and your nutty kids will get along.

- **Purchases.** Whenever one of your kids (for whom you've turned on Ask To Buy) tries to buy music, videos, apps, or books from Apple—even free items—he has to ask you (Figure 10-14).

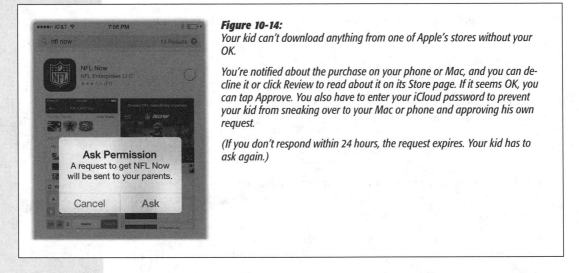

Figure 10-14:
Your kid can't download anything from one of Apple's stores without your OK.

You're notified about the purchase on your phone or Mac, and you can decline it or click Review to read about it on its Store page. If it seems OK, you can tap Approve. You also have to enter your iCloud password to prevent your kid from sneaking over to your Mac or phone and approving his own request.

(If you don't respond within 24 hours, the request expires. Your kid has to ask again.)

Furthermore, each of you can see and download everything that everyone else has bought. To do that, open the appropriate program: App Store, iTunes, or iBooks. Click Purchased, and then tap the family member's name, to see what she's got; tap the ☁ to download any of it yourself.

Tip: Anything you buy, your kids will see. Keep that in mind when you download a book like *Tough Love: Sending the Unruly Child to Military School.*

However, you have two lines of defense. First, you can hide your purchases so nobody sees them. On the Mac, in iTunes, click iTunes Store; then click the relevant category (♫, @, whatever). Click Purchased (right side). Point to the thing you want to hide, click the ⊗, and click Hide. Second, remember that you can set up parental control on each kid's Mac or phone, shielding their impressionable eyes from R-rated movies and stuff. See page 498.

- **Where are you?** Go to iCloud.com and click Find My iPhone (see page 368) to see where their phones are right now, which may or may not be with their owners. Or, on an iPhone or iPad, use the Find My Friends app to see where in town (or in the world) your posse is right now.

Note: If one of you needs secrecy for the afternoon (Apple sweetly gives, as an example, shopping for a gift for your spouse), open System Preferences →iCloud. Click Manage Family. Click the person you want to hide from. Turn off "Allow [this person] to see your location." Now you're untrackable until you turn the switch on again.

- **Photos, appointments, and reminders.** In Calendar, Photos, and Reminders, each of you will find a new category, called Family, that's auto-shared among you all. You're all free to make and edit appointments in this calendar, to set up reminders in Reminders ("Flu shots after school!"), or to add photos or videos (or comments) to this album; everyone else will see the changes instantly.

More iCloud Features

Not all of iCloud's goodies are represented as checkboxes in System Preferences→ iCloud. Don't forget that iCloud's online hub is waiting for you—available from any computer, tablet, or phone—at iCloud.com (Figure 10-15).

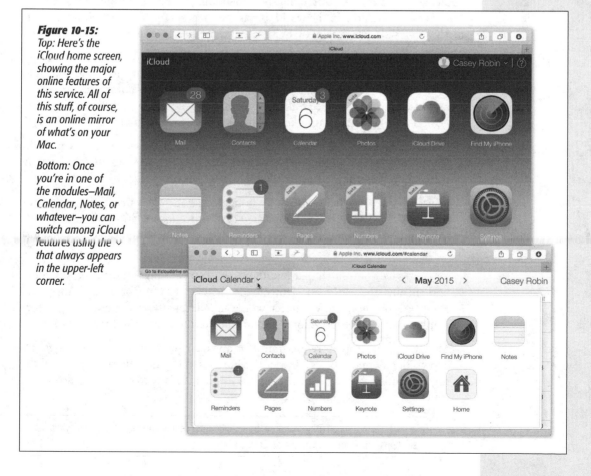

Figure 10-15:
Top: Here's the iCloud home screen, showing the major online features of this service. All of this stuff, of course, is an online mirror of what's on your Mac.

Bottom: Once you're in one of the modules—Mail, Calendar, Notes, or whatever—you can switch among iCloud features using the ⌄ that always appears in the upper-left corner.

And even that's not all there is to iCloud. For example:

Automatic backup

If you have an iPhone, iPad, or iPod Touch, iCloud can back it up, automatically and wirelessly (over WiFi, not over cellular connections). It's a quick backup, since iCloud backs up only the changed data.

Continuity

If you have an iPhone, and it's running iOS 8.1 or later, you're in for a treat. The set of features Apple calls Continuity turn the iPhone into a part of the Mac. They let you make calls from your Mac as though it were a speakerphone. They let you send and receive text messages from your Mac—to any cellphone on earth. They let you AirDrop files between computer and phone, wirelessly. And more.

Continuity gets its own chapter (Chapter 14).

Books, Music, Apps, Movies: The Locker in the Sky

Apple, as if you hadn't noticed, has become a big seller of multimedia files. It has the biggest music store in the world. It has the biggest app store, for both i-gadgets and Macs. It sells an awful lot of TV shows and movies. Its ebook store, iBooks, is no Amazon.com, but it's chugging along.

When you buy a song, movie, app, or book, you've always been allowed to copy it to all your other Apple equipment—no extra charge. But iCloud automates, or at least formalizes, that process. Once you buy something, it's added to a tidy list of items that you can download to all your *other* machines. Here's how to grab them:

- **iPhone, iPad, iPod Touch.** Open the App Store icon (for apps), the iBooks program (for books), or the iTunes Store app (for songs or TV shows; tap the category you want). Tap More. Tap Purchased. Tap Not on This iPhone.

 There they are: all the items you've bought on your *other* machines using your Apple ID. To download anything listed here onto *this* machine, tap the ⟳ button. Or tap an album name to see the list of songs on it so you can download just *some* of those songs.

 You can save yourself all that tapping by opening Settings→iTunes & App Store and turning the Automatic Downloads switches to On (for Music, Apps, and Books). From now on, whenever you're in WiFi, stuff you've bought on other Apple machines gets downloaded to this one *automatically*, in the background.

- **Mac.** Open the App Store program (for apps) or the iTunes app (for songs, TV shows, books, and movies). Under the Purchased heading, there they are: all the digital goodies you've bought using this Apple ID, ready to open or re-download if necessary.

Tip: To make this automatic, open iTunes. Choose iTunes→Preferences→Store. Under Automatic Downloads, turn on Music, Apps, and Books, as you see fit. Click OK.

Mail & Contacts

You know how every copy of Windows comes with a free, basic email program like Outlook Express or Windows Mail? Well, every copy of OS X comes with Mail, a slightly fancier email program that's also free. Mail is a surprisingly complete, refreshingly attractive program, filled with shortcuts and surprises. Together with the high-octane Contacts program included with OS X, you may never pine for your Windows setup again.

Setting Up Your Accounts

The beauty of today's Web-based email accounts (like Gmail, Yahoo Mail, Outlook. com, AOL) and IMAP accounts (like your company's mail system) is that you don't have to transfer the messages from your old PC to your Mac. Just set up the account correctly, and marvel as the mail arrives on your Mac directly from the Internet— complete with folders full of sent mail, deleted mail, and so on.

The first time you open Mail, you're offered the chance to set up those account types; just enter your email address and password, and you're on your way. To add another email account later, choose Mail→Add Account.

If you have a POP account (the older type, where each message is downloaded to your computer and stored only there), see page 264 for details on importing your existing message stash to the Mac.

Checking Your Mail

You get new mail and send mail you've already written using the Get Mail command. You can trigger it in any of several ways:

- Click the ✉ button on the toolbar.

- Choose Mailbox→Get All New Mail (or press Shift-⌘-N).

Note: If you have multiple email accounts, you can also use the Mailbox→Get New Mail submenu to pick just *one* account to check for new mail.

- **Right-click (or two-finger click) Mail's Dock icon, and choose Get New Mail from the shortcut menu.** (You can use this method from within any program, as long as Mail is already open.)

- **Wait.** Mail comes set to check your email automatically every few minutes. To adjust its timing or to turn this feature off, choose Mail→Preferences, click General, and then choose a time interval from the "Check for new messages" pop-up menu.

Tip: If you choose Automatically, then you'll get incoming messages the instant they arrive—at least in any accounts that offer "push" email.

Now Mail contacts the mail servers listed in the Accounts pane of Mail's preferences, retrieving new messages and downloading any files attached to those messages. It also *sends* any outgoing messages that couldn't be sent when you wrote them.

Tip: The far-left column of the Mail window has a tiny Mail Activity monitor tucked away; click the second button (▣) at the lower-left corner of the Mail window to reveal Mail Activity. If you don't want to give up mailboxes-list real estate, or if you prefer to monitor your mail in a separate window, you can do that, too. The Activity window gives you a Stop button, progress bars, and other useful information. Summon it by choosing Window→Activity, or by pressing ⌘-0.

Also, if you're having trouble connecting to some (or all) of your email accounts, choose Window→Connection Doctor. There, you can see detailed information about accounts that aren't responding. If your computer's Internet connection is at fault, you can click Network Diagnostics to try to get back online.

The Mailboxes List

The mailboxes pane, the leftmost list on the screen, lists all your email accounts' folders (and subfolders, and sub-subfolders) for easy access.

Tip: You can also collapse or expand the various sections of the mailboxes list (On My Mac and Reminders, for example) by clicking the Hide or Show button next to each one. That button doesn't appear, however, until you *point* to the capitalized section title (like MAILBOXES or ON MY MAC).

Under the Mailboxes heading, you may find these folders:

- **Inbox** holds mail you've received. If you have more than one email account, you can expand the triangles to see separate folders for each of your accounts. You'll see this pattern repeated with the Sent, Junk, and other mailboxes, too—separate accounts have separate subheadings.

Tip: If Mail has something to tell you about your Inbox (like, for instance, that Mail can't connect to it), a tiny warning triangle (⚠) appears on the right side of the Mailboxes heading. Click it to see what Mail is griping about. If you see a wavy ◔ icon, that's Mail's way of announcing that you're offline. Click the icon to try to connect to the Internet.

- **VIPs** displays messages from the most important people in your life—those you've designated as VIPs (page 409). This folder doesn't appear if you haven't identified any VIPs.

- **Flagged.** If you've flagged any messages, the flag headings appear here, too. (Flags are described on page 401.)

- **Outbox** holds mail you've written but haven't yet sent. If you have no mail waiting to be sent, then the Outbox disappears.

- **Drafts** holds messages you've started but don't want to send just yet.

- **Sent,** unsurprisingly, holds copies of messages you've sent.

- **Trash** works a lot like the Trash on your desktop, in that messages you put there don't actually disappear. They remain in the Trash folder until you permanently delete them—or until Mail's automatic trash-cleaning service deletes them for you.

- **Junk** appears when you use Mail's spam filter, as described later in this chapter.

- **Mail Activity.** You don't need to summon a separate window to see how much more of that message with the giant attachment the program still has to send. To reveal the Mail activity pane, click the tiny ◳ icon below the Mailboxes list.

Tailoring the Look of Mail

Apple put a lot of energy into exploiting the size and shape of your screen. In a program made for managing lists and reading messages, you need all the room you can get.

You've always been able to tweak Mail's look, layout, and proportions—but now you have both the modern layout (three columns) and the classic layout (list above, message below). The following pages offer advice in modifying the design of *both* layouts.

Tweaking the Three-Column Layout

The three-column view is shown in Figure 11-1 at top. Here's some of the plastic surgery you can perform:

- **Try Full Screen mode.** Click the green ◉ dot in the upper-left corner to make the Mail window expand to fill your monitor. (See page 160 for details on Full

Screen mode.) Full Screen mode is a natural for space-hungry email, especially on a small laptop screen.

Note: In Full Screen mode, any *individual* message that you double-click pops front and center; the rest of the screen, including all your lists and panes and other messages, fades and becomes inactive. That means you can't copy and paste from another message, refer to another message, or drag to or from another message. If you want to do something like that, you have to exit Full Screen mode first.

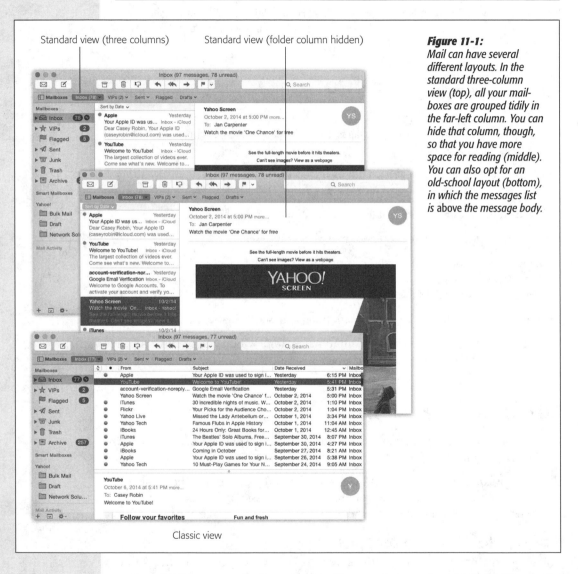

Standard view (three columns) Standard view (folder column hidden)

Classic view

Figure 11-1:
Mail can have several different layouts. In the standard three-column view (top), all your mailboxes are grouped tidily in the far-left column. You can hide that column, though, so that you have more space for reading (middle). You can also opt for an old-school layout (bottom), in which the messages list is above the message body.

- **Install folders onto the Favorites bar.** You can drag any icon in the mailboxes list onto the Favorites toolbar, where it becomes a button or a pop-up menu. The button works exactly like a folder: For example, you can drag a message onto one to

file it there, or you can click one of these folder buttons (or use its pop-up menu) to see what's inside.

The Favorites bar comes with starter buttons already installed, like Inbox, Sent, Notes, and so on. But you can, and should, install your *own* favorites there, and remove the ones you don't want. (To move a button around, ⌘-drag it. To get rid of it, just drag it away from the toolbar.)

Tip: You can also hide this Favorites bar when you feel the urge. Choose View→Hide Favorites Bar, of course.

- **Hide the mailboxes pane completely.** To do that, click the ⊡ button above it. Now you have much more screen space to work with.

Tip: Hey, here's a thought! *Combine* the previous two ideas. Install the most important folders onto the Favorites bar, so you can get at them, and *then* hide the mailboxes list. Now you have easy access to the most important folders, but your mailboxes list isn't eating up a lot of screen space. This glorious, space-efficient result is shown in Figure 11-1, middle.

- **Label the toolbar buttons.** Out of the box, the buttons on the toolbar (⊠, 🗑, and so on) have no labels. But if you right-click (or two-finger click) the toolbar, you get a pop-up menu that offers you other styles for those buttons: Icon & Text, Icon Only, Text Only (which is *very* space-efficient), and None (which is even more space-efficient—provided you know the keyboard shortcuts for all the buttons you've just hidden away).

- **Change the type size/icon size for the folders in the mailboxes pane.** To do that, open System Preferences→General. Use the "Sidebar icon size" pop-up menu to choose Small, Medium, or Large.

Note: Whatever you choose here also affects the font and icon sizes in the *Finder window Sidebar.* Apple figures that if you're that eagle-eyed (or that vision-impaired), you'll want the same size adjustment in both apps.

- **Redesign the New Message window.** What signature do you want stamped on every outgoing message? Do you want the Cc and Bcc lines to show up? How about the Priority pop-up menu? You can make all these settings using the little ≣⌄ menu in the New Message window; see Figure 11-2.

- **Adjust the message window width.** Drag the very right edge of the window inward or outward to adjust the width of the message itself. Double-click the edge of the messages list to hide the *message* completely. Now you have only the mailboxes list and the very wide messages list; to read a message, you have to double-click it to open it into a new window. (Double-click the right edge of the window to restore the message-reading pane.)

- **Adjust the width of the mailboxes or messages list.** Similarly, you can drag the right edges of the first two columns to adjust their width. Or double-click the right edge to make the column exactly as wide as Mail thinks it should be.

- **Change what morsels show up in the messages list.** The messages list (center column) usually shows the sender's name, subject line, and the first few lines of the message itself. But you can add additional info to the list—message size, mailbox, date sent, and so on—by choosing from the View→Message Attributes submenu.

- **Change what details show up in the header.** The *header* is the top part of a message, where you see the details of how the message reached you. Ordinarily, Mail shields you from the geekiest details of the header; if you really want to see it all, choose View→Message→All Headers.

Figure 11-2:
To redesign the New Message window, use the little pop-up menu shown here. Turn on the pieces you want in your everyday email composing.

But if you'd rather, you can tailor the standard header so that Mail always shows you exactly the information you want. In Mail→Preferences→Viewing, use the "Show header detail" pop-up menu to choose Custom. Now you can add just the details you always want to see: Attachments, Bcc, Cc, Flag, From, Reply-To, and so on.

- **Control how many lines of preview text appear.** In Mail→Preferences→Viewing, you can use the List Preview pop-up menu to control how many lines of each message you want to appear, in light gray, as a preview of what's in the message itself. You can choose up to five lines, or choose None to hide the preview completely.

- **Sort the messages.** Use the "Sort by" pop-up menu above the messages list ("by Date," "by Attachment," "by Unread," and so on). Use the bottom two commands—Ascending or Descending—to control *which way* the sorting goes (A to Z, Z to A, or whatever).

Tip: If you click the "Sort by" bar above the message list, you jump directly to the top—just like you do on the iPhone or iPad. Some ideas, you just can't keep down.

The Toolbar

In either layout—classic or standard—you have full control over the toolbar. You can rearrange or remove icon buttons (by ⌘-dragging them); add interesting new buttons to the toolbar (View→Customize Toolbar); change its display to show just text

labels or just icons (choose View→Customize Toolbar, and then use the Show pop-up menu); or hide the toolbar entirely (using the View→Hide Toolbar command).

Tip: Even when the toolbar is hidden, you can still hit Option-⌘-F to use the search box. (Press ⌘-F by itself to search the *current message.*)

Writing Messages

To send an email, click ✎ in the toolbar or press ⌘-N. The New Message form, shown in Figure 11-3, opens.

Figure 11-3:
If you want to use formatting, click the Show Format Bar icon (A) on the toolbar to open the Format bar—a strip of buttons for font, style, color, justification, bulleted lists, indentation, and so on. (The Format menu contains menu versions of the same stuff.)

Here's how you go about writing a message:

1. In the To field, type the recipient's email address.

If somebody is in your Contacts, type the first couple of letters of the name or email address; Mail automatically completes the address. (If the first guess is wrong, then type another letter or two until Mail revises its guess.)

Tip: If Mail constantly tries to autofill in the address of someone you don't really communicate with, you can zap that address from its memory by choosing Window→Previous Recipients. Click the undesired address, and then click Remove From List.

As in most dialog boxes, you can jump from blank to blank (from To to Cc, for example) by pressing Tab. To send this message to more than one person, separate the addresses with commas: *bob@earthlink.net, billg@microsoft.com,* and so on.

Tip: If you send most of your email to addresses within the same organization (like *reddelicious@apple.com, grannysmith@apple.com,* and *winesap@apple.com*), Mail can automatically turn all *other* email addresses red. It's a feature designed to avoid sending confidential messages to outside addresses.

To turn this feature on, choose Mail→Preferences, click Composing, turn on "Mark addresses not ending with," and then type the "safe" domain (like *apple.com*) into the blank.

2. To send a copy to other recipients, enter their addresses in the Cc field.

Cc stands for *carbon copy*. Getting an email message where your name is in the Cc line implies: "I sent you a copy because I thought you'd want to know about this correspondence, but I'm not expecting you to reply."

Tip: If Mail recognizes the address you type into the To or Cc box (because it's someone in your Contacts, for instance), then the name turns into a shaded, round-ended box button. In addition to looking cool, these buttons sprout a ∨ when you point to them; when you click there, you get a list of useful commands (including Show Contact Card).

These buttons are also drag-and-droppable. For example, you can drag one from the To field to the Cc field, or from Contacts to Mail.

3. Type the topic of the message in the Subject field.

It's courteous to put some thought into the subject line. (Use "Change in plans for next week," for instance, instead of "Yo.") On the other hand, don't put the *entire* message into the subject line, either.

4. Specify an email format.

There are two kinds of email: *plain text* and *formatted* (which Apple calls Rich Text). Plain text messages are faster to send and open, are universally compatible with the world's email programs, and are greatly preferred by many veteran computer fans. And even though the message itself is plain, you can still attach pictures and other files. (If you want to get really graphic with your mail, you can also use the *Stationery* option, which gives you preformatted message templates to drop in pictures, graphics, and text. Flip to page 391 for more on using stationery.)

Resourceful geeks have even learned how to fake some formatting in plain messages: They use capitals or asterisks instead of bold formatting (**man* is he a GEEK!*), and pseudo-underlines for emphasis (*I _love_ Swiss cheese!*). By contrast, formatted messages sometimes appear without any formatting at all in some email programs.

To control which kind of mail you send on a message-by-message basis, choose from the Format menu either Make Plain Text or Make Rich Text. To change the factory setting for new outgoing messages, choose Mail→Preferences; click the Composing icon; and choose from the Message Format pop-up menu.

(But note: Even if you choose Rich Text, Mail sends a plain text message if you don't actually *use* a formatting command—choose a new font, size, or whatever.)

Tip: If you plan to send formatted mail, remember that your recipients won't see the fonts you use unless their machines have the same ones installed. Bottom line: For email to Mac and Windows owners alike, stick to universal choices like Arial, Times, and Courier.

5. **Type your message in the message box.**

 You can use all standard editing techniques, including dictation, copy and paste, drag-and-drop, and so on. If you selected the Rich Text style of email, you can use word processor–like formatting (Figure 11-3).

 As you type, Mail checks your spelling, using a dotted underline to mark questionable words. You can read much more about OS X's built-in spelling/grammar checker (and typing expander) in Chapter 5.

 If you're composing a long message, or if it's one you don't want to send until later, press ⌘-S or choose File→Save. You've just saved the message in your Drafts folder. It'll still be there the next time you open Mail. To reopen a saved draft later, click the Drafts icon in the mailboxes column and then double-click the message.

6. **Click Send ✑ (or press Shift ⌘ D).**

 Mail sends the message.

Tip: To resend a message you've already sent, click it and then choose Message→Send Again, or press Shift-⌘-D.

If you'd rather have Mail place each message you write in the Outbox folder instead of connecting to the Net when you click Send, choose Mailbox→Take All Accounts Offline. While you're offline, Mail refrains from trying to connect, which is a great feature when you're working on a laptop at 39,000 feet and didn't feel like paying for WiFi. (Choose Mailbox→Take All Accounts Online to reverse the procedure.)

Attaching Files to Messages

Sending little text messages is fine, but it's not much help when you want to send somebody a photograph, a sound, or a Word document. To attach a file to a message you've written, use one of these methods:

- Drag the icons you want to attach directly off the desktop (or out of a folder) into the New Message window. There your attachments appear with their own hyperlinked icons (visible in Figure 11-3), meaning that your recipient can simply click to open them.

Tip: Exposé was *born* for this moment. Hit ⌘-F3 to make all open windows flee to the edges of the screen, revealing the desktop. Root around until you find the file you want to send. Begin dragging it; without releasing the mouse, press ⌘-F3 again to bring your message window back into view. Complete your drag into the message window.

Mail makes it look as though you can park the attached file's icon (or the full image of a graphics file) *inside* the text of the message, mingled with your typing. Don't be fooled, however; on the receiving end, all the attachments will be clumped together at the end of the message (unless your recipient also uses Mail or you've sent pictures with Stationery).

- Drag the icons you want to attach from the desktop onto Mail's *Dock icon*. Mail dutifully creates a new outgoing message, with the files already attached.

- Click the ⏀ on the New Message toolbar, choose File→Attach Files, or press Shift-⌘-A. The Open File sheet appears so you can find the files you want to include. (You can choose multiple files simultaneously in this dialog box. Just ⌘-click or Shift-click them as though you were selecting them in a Finder window.)

Once you've selected them, click Choose File (or press Return). You return to the New Message window, where the attachments' icons appear, ready to ride along when you send the message.

UP TO SPEED

Bcc, Reply-To, and Priority

A blind carbon copy is a secret copy. This feature lets you send a copy of a message to somebody secretly, without any of the other recipients knowing that you did so. To view this field when composing a message (if it's not already visible), choose View→Bcc Address Field.

You can use the Bcc field to quietly signal a third party that a message has been sent. For example, if you send your co-worker a message that says, "Chris, it bothers me that you've been cheating the customers," you could Bcc your supervisor to clue her in without getting into trouble with Chris.

The Bcc box is useful in other ways, too. Many people send email messages (corny jokes, for example) to a long list of recipients. You, the recipient, have to scroll through the long list of names the sender placed in the To or Cc field.

But if the sender used the Bcc field to hold all the recipients' email addresses, you won't see anybody else's names at the top of the email. In the To box, you might see the sender's name, or "undisclosed recipients," or nothing at all. (Spammers have also learned this trick, which is why it usually looks like you're the only recipient of a junk message when there are actually millions of other people who received the same message.)

Another hidden field you can add to your messages is *Reply-To.* (Choose View→Reply-To Address Field.) That field has one simple purpose: to make the recipient's email program reply to a different email address than the one you sent the message from.

For example, if your business email address isn't working but you absolutely *have* to send a field report to your boss, you can send the message from your personal email account but put your business address in the Reply-To field. That way, when your boss emails you back to congratulate you, the email goes to your business account.

Finally, if you click the ≡∨ on the left side of an email message, you can enable one more hidden header option: Priority. (It's the pop-up menu with an exclamation mark in it.) If you turn on the checkbox next to that pop-up menu and click OK, all your email messages let you set how important they are on a three-tiered scale.

The good part about this system is that it lets your recipient see that an email you've sent is, for example, urgent. The bad part is that not every email program displays the priority of email—and even if your recipient's email program *does* display your message's priority, there's no guarantee that it'll make him respond any faster.

To remove an attachment, drag across its icon to highlight it, and then press the Delete key. (You can also choose Message→Remove Attachments.)

Mail Drop: Sending Huge Attachments

Since the dawn of email, we, the downtrodden masses, have been told over and over again: Don't attach big files! Anything over about 5 megabytes is too big for most email systems. Best case, your entire message will bounce back to you; worst case, you'll clog the recipients' inboxes so that they can't receive any more mail.

So the world has slogged along with crude workarounds—sites like SendThisFile.com, or services like Dropbox that require signup and software installation.

Today, that era is over. If you use Mail in OS X, you'll probably never have to think about the file sizes of your attachments again. Go ahead—attach a whole video. Attach a gigantic Photoshop document, or several, or dozens. Attach a gigantic Keynote or PowerPoint file. Your file-size limit is now 5 *gigabytes*—about 1,000 times what it used to be.

The first time you attach a big file to an outgoing message and then click Send, Mail offers the message shown in Figure 11-4.

Figure 11-4:
There's no reason not to use Mail Drop. In fact, there's no reason not to turn on "Don't ask again for this account," too. From now on, Mail Drop will work just like magic—invisibly.

You can attach a bunch of files to a single message, as long as the grand total is under 5 gigabytes.

Their icons show up right in the body of the message.

Note: Mail Drop is an iCloud feature. It works only if your Mac is currently signed into your iCloud account. (The files you send don't count toward your iCloud storage limit, though.)

Behind the scenes, Mail Drop uploads your file to iCloud's computers, where it sits there for 30 days, waiting for your recipient to get a clue and download it.

If the recipient also has Yosemite Mail, the attachment is quietly auto-downloaded in the background, so that it's on his Mac already when he opens the message. He'll click, it'll open, and he'll probably never even consider the miracle of what just happened.

If you're sending to any other computer or mail program, your message contains an indication of the file's 30-day expiration date, and a "Click to download" link. (Clicking it opens the recipient's Web browser, where the file begins to download immediately.) It's a little waiting—but that's what people get for not drinking the Apple Kool-Aid.

And now, Apple's entirely reasonable fine print and limits:

- Mail Drop allows you to send a maximum of 200 messages a day, or messages to more than 1,000 recipients a day from your iCloud account. A single message sent via iCloud can have a maximum of 100 recipients.

- iCloud's holding tank for Mail Drop attachments doesn't hold more than 1 terabyte. In other words, once you've Mail Dropped that many attachments, you won't be able to send any more until those files have been downloaded or expire.

Mail Drop is fantastic.

GEM IN THE ROUGH

When You Want to Be Nudged about Incoming Mail

The Notification Center (Chapter 18) consolidates all the different programs and features that might want your attention—Mail, Reminders, Twitter, Facebook, software updates, and so on—into a single tidy list.

But if a little Notification Center alert bubble appeared on your screen every time *any* new Mail message came in, you'd go quietly mad. Fortunately, a new Mail setting lets you tell Mail, "Don't disturb me unless it's really important. Like if it's from my accountant."

Here's how to set up this useful filter. Choose Mail→Preferences→General. See the "New message notifications" pop-up menu?

Here you can choose **Inbox only** (all incoming messages trigger alert bubbles); **VIPs** (perhaps the most useful option—only messages from these essential people produce alerts); **Contacts** (messages from anyone in your address book trigger alerts—just not messages from strangers); or **All Mailboxes** (every single incoming message flags you).

You can also choose the name of a smart mailbox, if you've created one. That's a pretty potent feature. It means that you can set up incoming messages to alert you only if they match whatever criteria your smart mailbox uses. For example, you might not want to be disturbed except when a message comes from one of your best friends *and* it has an attachment *and* it mentions "money I owe you."

You may have noticed, by the way, that there's no option here for "Don't show me Mail message bubbles at all." That's because you do that in System Preferences.

Open System Preferences→Notifications, click Mail, and turn off Show in Notification Center. Now you'll be left in peace when new mail arrives, no matter who it's from.

Marking Up, Signing, and Drawing on Attachments

You can mark up PDF and graphics attachments at the moment of sending them. Add your signature to a contract, circle a typo, draw arrows on a diagram, and so on. All this magic awaits in the Markup toolbar.

First, you have to attach a graphic—a photo, PDF file, or other kind of image—using any of the tricks described on page 385.

Once the image appears in your outgoing message, click to select it. At that point, the tiny ∨ icon appears in its upper-right corner; from it, choose Markup (Figure 11-5).

Figure 11-5:
Top: This button doesn't appear until you attach a graphic and then select it.

Bottom: The buttons on this toolbar let you draw and type on your image. Don't miss the ∂ tool, which auto-perfects your attempts to draw lines, circles, and angles.

What you'll quickly discover is that this entire markup feature is shared, pixel for pixel, with the markup feature in your Preview program. And it's described in detail on page 679.

Signatures

Signatures are bits of text that get stamped at the bottom of your outgoing email messages. A signature might contain a name, a postal address, a pithy quote, or even a scan of your *real* signature, as shown in Figure 11-6.

You can customize your signatures by choosing Mail→Preferences→Signatures. Here's what you should know:

- **To build up a library of signatures that you can use in any of your accounts:** Select All Signatures in the leftmost pane, and then click the + button to add each new signature (Figure 11-6). Give each new signature a name in the middle pane, and then customize the signatures' text in the rightmost pane.

Tip: If you ever get tired of a signature, you can delete it forever by selecting All Signatures→[your signature's name], clicking the — button, and then clicking OK.

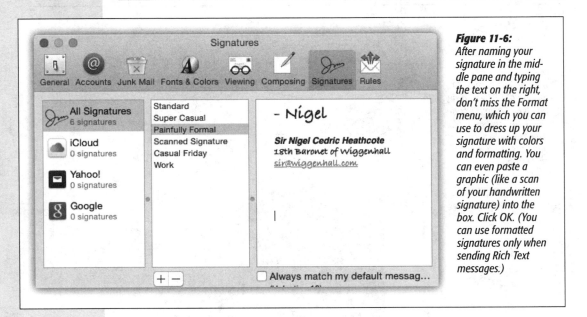

Figure 11-6:
After naming your signature in the middle pane and typing the text on the right, don't miss the Format menu, which you can use to dress up your signature with colors and formatting. You can even paste a graphic (like a scan of your handwritten signature) into the box. Click OK. (You can use formatted signatures only when sending Rich Text messages.)

- **To make a signature available in one of your email accounts:** Drag the signature's name from the middle pane onto the name of the account in the leftmost pane. In other words, you can make certain signatures available to only your work (or personal) account, so you never accidentally end up appending your secret FBI contact signature to the bottom of a birthday invitation you send out.

- **To assign a particular signature to one account:** In the left pane, click an account; pick from the Choose Signature pop-up menu. Each time you compose a message from that account, Mail inserts the signature you selected.

Tip: To make things more interesting for your recipients, pick At Random; Mail selects a different signature each time you send a message. Or, if you're not that much of a risk-taker, choose In Sequential Order; Mail picks the next signature in order for each new message you write.

Remember that you can always change your signature on a message-by-message basis, using the Signature pop-up menu in any new email message.

- **To use the signature feature as a prefix in replies:** Turn on "Place signature above quoted text." If you turn on this setting, your signature gets inserted *above* any text that you're replying to, rather than below. You'd use this setting if your "signature" said something like, "Hi there! You wrote this to me!"

Tip: If you're into consistent typographical styling, also turn on "Always match my default font." That setting makes sure that any messages you send contain the signature in the same font as the rest of the message, lending it an air of professionalism.

Stationery

Rich Text—and even plain text—messages are fine for your everyday personal and business correspondence. After all, you really won't help messages like, "Let's have a meeting on those third-quarter earnings results" much by adding visual bells and whistles.

But suppose you have an occasion where you *want* to jazz up your mail, like an electronic invitation to a bridal shower or a mass-mail update as you get your kicks down Route 66.

These messages just cry out for Mail's *Stationery* feature. Stationery means colorful, predesigned mail templates that you make your own by dragging in photos from your own collection. Those fancy fonts and graphics will certainly get people's attention when they open the message.

Note: They will, that is, *if* their email programs understand HTML formatting. That's the formatting Mail uses for its stationery. (If *HTML* rings a bell, it's because this HyperText Markup Language is the same language used to make Web pages so lively and colorful.)

It might be a good idea to make sure everyone on your recipient list has a mail program that can handle HTML; otherwise, your message may look like a jumble of code and letters in the middle of the screen. Here's how to make a stylized message with Mail Stationery:

1. **Create a new message.**

 Click File→New Message, press ⌘-N, or click ☑ on the Mail window toolbar.

2. **On the right side of the toolbar in the New Message window, click ▦.**

 A pane opens up, showing you all the available templates, in categories like Birthday and Announcements (Figure 11-7).

3. **Click a category; click a stationery thumbnail image to apply it to your message.**

 The body of your message changes to take on the look of the template.

4. **If you like what you see, click ▦ on the toolbar again to fold up the stationery-picker pane.**

Now, Apple's canned stationery looks fantastic. The only problem is, the photos on most of the templates are pictures of *somebody else's* family and friends. Unless you work for Apple's modeling agency, you probably have no clue who they are.

Fortunately, it's easy to replace those placeholder photos with your *own* snaps.

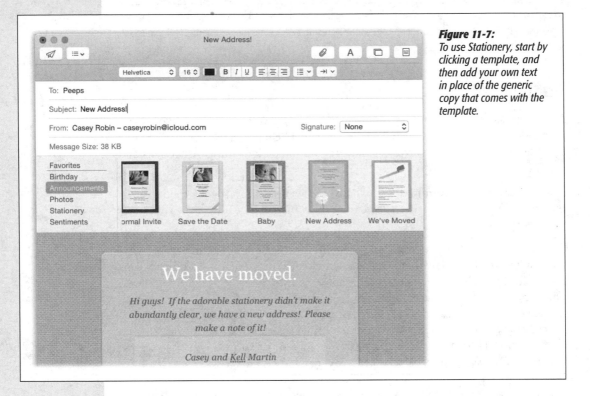

Figure 11-7:
To use Stationery, start by clicking a template, and then add your own text in place of the generic copy that comes with the template.

5. **Add and adjust pictures.**

 Click the Photo Browser icon (□) on the toolbar to open up a palette that lists all the photos you've stored in iPhoto, Aperture, and Photo Booth.

Tip: If you don't keep your pictures in any of those programs, you can drag any folder of pictures onto the Photo Browser window to add them.

 Now you can drag your own pictures directly onto Apple's dummy photos on the stationery template. They replace the sunny models. You don't have to know a lick of HTML to use the templates—it's all drag, drop, and type, baby.

 To resize a photo in the template, double-click it. A size slider appears. Drag the mouse around the photo window to reposition the picture relative to its frame.

6. **Select the fake text and type over it with what you really want to say.**

 As you type, your words are autoformatted to match the template design.

Once you've got your message looking the way you want it, address it just as you would any other piece of mail, and then click ✐ to get it on its way.

Tip: You're not stuck with Apple's designs for your stationery templates; you can make your own. Just make a new message, style the fonts and photos the way you want them, and then choose File→Save as Stationery. You can now select your masterwork in the Custom category, which appears down at the end of the list in the stationery-picker pane.

If you decide that the message would be better off as plain old text, click Show Stationery on the message window. In the list of template categories, click Stationery and then Original to strip the color and formats out of the message.

Tip: If you find you're using one or two templates a lot (if, for example, all your friends are having babies these days), drag your frequently used templates into the Favorites category so you don't have to go wading around for them.

To remove one from Favorites, click it, and then click the ⊗ in the top-left corner of the thumbnail.

Reading Email

Mail puts all incoming email into your Inbox; the statistic after the word *Inbox* lets you know how many messages you haven't yet read. New messages are also marked with light-blue dots in the main list.

Tip: The Mail icon in the Dock also shows you how many new messages you have waiting; it's the number in the red circle. In Mail→Preferences→General, you can specify *which* mailbox it's tallying up—or have it tally up all of them.

Click the Inbox folder to see a list of received messages. If it's a long list, press Control-Page Up and Control-Page Down to scroll. (Page Up and Page Down without the Control key scroll the message pane instead.)

Tip: If you ⌘-click more than one mailbox folder, you can combine them (and their total-message counts) into one unified messages list.

Click the name of a message once to read it in the message window, or double-click a message to open it into a separate window. (If a message is already selected, pressing Return also opens its separate window.)

When you click the name of a message in the messages list (or press the ▲ and ▼ keys to highlight successive messages in that list), you see the message itself, along with any attachments, in the message pane.

Tip: Instead of reading your mail, you might prefer to have OS X read it *to* you, as you sit back in your chair and sip a strawberry daiquiri. Highlight the text you want to hear (or choose Edit→Select All), and then choose Edit→Speech→Start Speaking. To stop the insanity, choose Edit→Speech→Stop Speaking.

At the top of a message, you see its *header*—date, subject, addresses, and some handy buttons that don't appear until you point to them (Figure 11-8).

Once you've viewed a message, you can respond to it, delete it, print it, file it, and so on. The following pages should get you started.

Figure 11-8:
If you point to the header without clicking, you get to see the ghosts of four useful buttons: Trash, Reply, Reply All, and Forward.

Conversation View

Threading is one of the most useful mail-sorting methods to come along in a long time. It groups all messages that are part of the same back-and-forth conversation as a *single item* in the main messages list. (In this discussion, let's call that one item the *main message.* In Mail, it's always the most recent message in the conversation.)

Less sophisticated email programs figure out which messages go together by matching only their subject lines. But Mail is much smarter; it also studies the message headers, senders, recipients, and dates. Even if someone changes the subject line along the way, Mail still knows that a conversation is a conversation.

As shown in Figure 11-9, Conversation view, as Apple calls it, hides all the usual awful indents, repetitions, forwards of forwards, and so on. You see only neatly numbered scrolling blocks, each representing the *newly added* text in each back-and-forth.

To turn on threading, choose View→Organize by Conversation. Each main message in the messages list sprouts a little numbered badge, like "3»," to indicate messages that have been clustered together (Figure 11-9, bottom).

Note: When Organize by Conversation is turned on, you might be wondering: What happens to chronological order? In other words, if the messages in a certain thread took place over several days or weeks, where does Mail wind up listing them when it sorts your messages list by date?

Answer: They're all clumped together in the main message—the *most recent* message. That is, if the messages on a certain topic arrived July 1, 4, 7, and 11, you'll find all four grouped with the July 11 message. They're essentially pulled *out* of the chronological list to join the latest one, for your reviewing pleasure.

Here are some powerful ways to use threading:

- **View all the messages in a conversation** by clicking the main message in the messages list. In the message pane, you see all the back-and-forths, minus all the duplication and the replies to replies.

- **Expand a list of the messages in a conversation** by clicking the small gray number-of-messages badge—or by clicking the main message and then pressing the ▶ key. A tiny message-conversation list sprouts out of the one listed message, as shown in the inset in Figure 11-9. (Or you can make *all* conversations display their sub-messages like this; to do that, choose View→Expand All Conversations.)

Once you've expanded the mini-list, you can walk through it by pressing the up/down arrow keys.

The messages from the current mailbox are numbered—those are the big gray digits in the upper-right corner. Those numbers help you figure out where you are in all the back-and-forths.

- **Examine messages from multiple mailboxes.** Normally, conversations display only messages held in the *same* mailbox, but that's not especially convenient when you

Figure 11-9:
In Mail's version of thread-ing, called Conversation view, the back-and-forths are represented extremely concisely. All the duplica-tion and redundancy is hidden. (You can see it, if you really want to, by clicking the See More link at the bottom of each message.)

Lower right: Click the tiny number, as shown here by the cursor, to view a list of the messages within the clump.

want to see, for example, both messages you've received (from your Inbox) and your replies (from your Sent box). To work around that problem, turn on "Include related messages" in Mail→Preferences→Viewing. These options mean, "Include messages in *other* mailboxes, too, like Sent messages—not just this one mailbox." Now your conversations seamlessly combine related messages from all mailboxes.

Note: When "Include related messages" is turned on, the related messages do *not* display the big gray numbers in the corner; only the ones in the current mailbox sprout numbers.

- **Move all the messages in a conversation to a new mailbox** by dragging the main message. You might find this useful, for example, when you've just finished a project and want to file away all the email related to it quickly. You can even delete all the messages in a thread at once by deleting its main entry.

Note: If you just drag *one* message of a conversation to a different folder, though, it becomes a "related" message, no longer numbered, as described in the previous Note.

- **Send someone all the messages in a thread** by selecting the main message and then clicking Forward as usual. Mail automatically copies all the messages of the thread into a new message, putting the oldest at the top. You might find this useful, for instance, when you want to send your boss all the correspondence you've had with someone about a certain project.
- **Manipulate an individual message in a conversation** by first clicking it in the message-reading pane. For example, if you have five messages in a conversation, and you want to forward only the juicy one, which happens to be message #2, click #2 and then use the Forward command—or Reply, Delete, or whatever. (You can also click one of the four light-gray buttons that appear when you point to the message header—Delete, Reply, Reply All, Forward.)

Tip: In Mail→Preferences→Viewing, you'll find a bunch of fine-tuning tweaks that apply to conversations. For example, you can ask that messages that are part of the same conversation show up highlighted in a color you choose—even when conversation grouping is turned *off*. And you can request that, when a conversation message is clicked in the messages list, the resulting messages are shown in reverse chronological order—oldest at the top.

Adding the Sender to Contacts

When you choose the Message→Add Sender to Contacts command, Mail memorizes the email address of the person whose message is on the screen. In fact, you can highlight a huge number of messages and add *all* the senders simultaneously using this technique.

Thereafter, you'll be able to address a new message to somebody just by typing the first few letters of her name or email address.

Data Detectors

Data detectors are described on page 230. They're what you see when OS X recognizes commonly used bits of written information: a physical address, a phone number, a date and time, a flight number, and so on. With one quick click, you can send that information into the appropriate OS X program, like Calendar, Contacts, the Flight Tracker widget in Dashboard, or your Web browser (for looking an address up on a map).

This is just a public-service reminder that data detectors are especially useful—*primarily* useful, in fact—in Mail. Watch for the dotted rectangle that appears when you point to a name, address, date, time, or flight number.

Opening File Attachments

Just as you can attach files to a message, so can people send files to you. Sometimes they don't even bother to type a note; you wind up receiving an empty email message with a file or two attached. Only the presence of the file's icon in the message body tells you there's something attached.

Mail stores downloaded files in a hidden folder on your hard drive. To bring them out into the open, you must proceed in one of these ways:

- **Click the Quick Look button** in the message header. Instantly, you're treated to a nearly full-size preview of the file's contents. Yes, Quick Look has come to email. It works exactly as described in Chapter 2.

Tip: If the attachments are pictures, then clicking Quick Look gives you a full-screen slideshow of every attached image. If you jiggle the mouse a little during the slideshow, you get a useful row of slideshow-control buttons along the bottom of the screen, too.

- **Click the Save button** in the message header to save it to your Downloads folder, nestled within easy reach in the Dock. (It's a pop-up menu, which is handy if there's more than one attachment. You can either save *all* attachments at once, or choose from the pop-up menu to save them individually.)

Tip: If you don't want to use the Downloads folder, you can choose a new autosave location for attachments by choosing Mail→Preferences→General→Downloads folder.

- **Drag the attachment icon** (it appears at the bottom of the message) out of the message window and onto any visible portion of your desktop or any visible folder window.

- **Double-click the attachment's icon,** or single-click the blue link underneath the icon. If you were sent a document (a photo, Word file, or Excel file, for example), it now opens in the corresponding program.

Note: After the attachment is open, use the File→Save As command to save the file into a folder of your choice. Otherwise, any changes you make to the document will be lost.

• **Right-click (or two-finger click)** the attachment's icon at the bottom of the message. From the shortcut menu, you can open it, save it, Quick Look it, and so on.

Replying to a Message

To answer a message, click the Reply ◄ button on the message toolbar (or choose Message→Reply, or press ⌘-R). If the message was originally addressed to multiple recipients, you can send your reply to everyone simultaneously by clicking Reply All ◄◄ instead (Shift-⌘-R).

A new message window opens, already addressed. As a courtesy to your correspondent, Mail places the original message at the bottom of the window, set off by a vertical bar, as shown in Figure 11-10.

Figure 11-10:
If you highlight some text before clicking Reply, Mail pastes only that portion of the original message into your reply. That's a great convenience to your correspondent, who now knows exactly which part of the message you're responding to.

In Mail messages formatted with Rich Text (not to be confused with Rich Text Format word processing format, which is very different), a reply includes the original message, marked in a special color (which you can change in Mail→Preferences) and with a vertical bar to differentiate it from the text of your reply. (In plain-text messages, each line of the reply is >denoted >with >brackets, although only your recipient will see them.)

The original sender's name is automatically placed in the To field. The subject is the same as the original subject with the addition of "Re:" (shorthand for Regarding). You're now ready to type your response.

At this point, you can add or delete recipients, edit the subject line or the original message, attach a file, and so on.

Tip: Use the Return key to create blank lines in the original message. Using this method, you can splice your own comments into the paragraphs of the original message, replying point by point. The brackets preceding each line of the original message help your correspondent keep straight what's yours and what's hers.

When you're finished, click Send (✒).

Forwarding Messages

Instead of replying to the person who sent you a message, you may sometimes want to pass the note on to a third person.

To do so, click the Forward ➡ toolbar button (or choose Message→Forward, or press Shift-⌘-F). A new message opens, looking a lot like the one that appears when you reply. You may wish to precede the original message with a comment of your own, along the lines of: "Frank: I thought you'd be interested in this joke about your mom."

Finally, address it as you would any outgoing piece of mail.

Redirecting Messages

A *redirected* message is similar to a forwarded message, with one useful difference: When you forward a message, your recipient sees that it came from you. When you redirect it, your recipient sees the *original* writer's name as the sender. In other words, a redirected message uses you as a low-profile relay station between two other people.

Treasure this feature. Plenty of email programs don't offer a Redirect command at all. You can use it to transfer messages from one of your own accounts to another, or to pass along a message that came to you by mistake.

GEM IN THE ROUGH

The Email Answering Machine

If you're going on vacation, you can turn Mail into an email answering machine that sends a canned "I'm away until the 15th" message to everyone who writes you.

To do so, set the first set of pop-up menus in the Rules dialog box so that they say Account and the name of your account. In the bottom half of the dialog box, select Reply to Message from the pop-up menu. Click "Reply message text," and then type your outgoing message in the resulting box.

Keep in mind, though, that mail rules work only when Mail is open and connected to the Internet. If your computer is set to turn off after a certain period of time, therefore, make sure to disable that feature before you go on vacation.

Also: If you subscribe to mailing lists, set up another mail rule that intercepts and files them *before* your answering-machine rule kicks in. Otherwise, you'll incur the wrath of other Internet citizens by littering their email discussion groups with copies of your auto-reply message.

To redirect a message, choose Message→Redirect, or press Shift-⌘-E. You get an outgoing copy of the message—this time without any quoting marks.

Printing Messages

Sometimes there's no substitute for a printout. Choose File→Print, or press ⌘-P to summon the Print dialog box.

Filing Messages

Mail lets you create new mailboxes (mail folders) in the mailboxes list. You might create one for important messages, another for order confirmations from Web shopping, still another for friends and family, and so on. You can even create mailboxes *inside* these mailboxes, a feature beloved by the hopelessly organized.

Tip: You can drag mailbox folders up and down in the list to rearrange them. Sweet.

Mail even offers *smart mailboxes*—self-updating folders that show you all your mail from your boss, for example, or every message with "mortgage" in its subject. It's the same idea as smart folders in the Finder or smart playlists in iTunes (Figure 11-11).

Figure 11-11:
Mail lets you create self-populating folders. In this example, a smart mailbox will automatically display all messages from Momma Smith that you've received in the past week.

The commands you need are all in the Mailbox menu. For example, to create a new mailbox folder, choose Mailbox→New Mailbox, or click the + button at the bottom of the column. To create a smart mailbox, choose Mailbox→New Smart Mailbox.

Mail asks you to name the new mailbox. If you have more than one email account, you can specify which one will contain the new folder. (Smart mailboxes, however, always sit outside your other mailboxes.)

Tip: If you want to create a folder inside a folder, use slashes in the name of your new mailbox. (If you use the name *Cephalopods/Squid,* for example, then Mail creates a folder called Cephalopods, with a subfolder called Squid.) You can also drag the mailbox icons up and down in the drawer to place one inside another.

None of those tricks work for smart mailboxes, however. The only way to organize smart mailboxes is to put them inside a smart mailbox *folder,* which you create using Mailbox→New Smart Mailbox Folder. You might do that if you have several smart mailboxes for mail from your coworkers ("From Jim," "From Anne," and so on) and want to put them together in one collapsible group to save screen space.

When you click OK, a new icon appears in the mailboxes column, ready for use.

You can move a message (or group of messages) into a mailbox folder in any of three ways:

- **Drag it out of the messages list onto a mailbox icon.**

- **Highlight one or more messages,** and then choose from the Message→Move To submenu, which lists all your mailboxes.

- **Right-click (or two-finger click) a message,** or one of several that you've highlighted. From the resulting shortcut menu, choose Move To, and then, from the submenu, choose the mailbox you want.

Of course, the only way to change the contents of a *smart* mailbox is to change the criteria it uses to populate itself. To do so, double-click the smart mailbox icon and use the dialog box that appears.

Flagging Messages

Sometimes you'll receive email that prompts you to some sort of action, but you may not have the time (or the fortitude) to face the task at the moment. ("Hi there... it's me, your accountant. Would you mind rounding up your expenses for 1999 through 2011 and sending me a list by email?")

That's why Mail lets you *flag* a message, summoning a little flag icon in a new column next to the message's name. In fact, you can use seven differently *colored* flags.

These indicators can mean anything you like—they simply call attention to certain messages.

UP TO SPEED

All the Little Symbols

The left edge of the messages list shows little symbols that let you know at a glance how you've processed certain messages. The most common one is, of course, the light-blue dot (●), which means "new message." (After reading a message, you can mark it once again as an *unread* message by choosing Message→Mark→As Unread [Shift-⌘-U]—or by right-clicking (or two-finger clicking) the message's name and then choosing Mark→As Unread from the shortcut menu.)

You might also see these symbols, which represent messages you've replied to (↩), forwarded (➡), redirected (⇗), or flagged (⚑).

A well-guarded secret, however, is that the "replied to" and "forwarded" symbols aren't just indicators—they're also

buttons. When you see one of these symbols next to your original message, click it to jump straight to your reply (or forwarded message). You're spared the trouble of having to search through all your mailboxes.

Incidentally, you may have noticed that Mail marks a message as having been read the moment you click it. You can change it back to unread by using its shortcut menu, as just described—but there's also a more permanent workaround.

If you hide the message pane by double-clicking the divider bar to its right (or, in Classic view, above it), Mail no longer marks messages "read" just because you clicked them in the list.

Once you've applied some flags, you can use their power in all kinds of ways. For example, you can view all of them in one place—in the Flagged folder that appears near the top of the mailboxes list.

You can also sort your mail list by flag color (choose Sort by→Flags at the top of the messages list). You can search for flagged messages using the search box. Better yet, you can view all messages with a certain flag color—magically rounded up from all your different accounts and mailboxes—by clicking the corresponding icon in the Flagged folder of the mailboxes list.

Tip: Just in case you don't find "Red," "Orange," "Yellow," and so on to be the most descriptive possible flag names, you can change them.

First, though, make sure you've applied a couple of flags to different messages already. That's necessary to make the Flagged mailbox appear in the mailboxes list. If you open the flippy triangle, you'll see the names of the flags you've applied so far. You can change a flag's name just the way you'd name a file–start by double-clicking it.

To flag a message in this way, select the message (or several messages) and then choose one of the colored flags in the Message→Flag submenu. Or right-click (or two-finger click) the message's name in the list and, from the shortcut menu, choose one of the seven flag colors. (To clear the flags, repeat the procedure, but use the Message→ Flag→Clear Flag command instead.)

If you're using only one flag to simply mean "flag this," and you don't need all the colors, you can also press Shift-⌘-L.

Finding Messages

The box in the upper-right corner of the main mail window is Mail's own private Spotlight—a fast, powerful search command. That's essential when you have to deal with masses of email (see Figure 11-12).

This search box incorporates the same pop-up suggestions lists and "search tokens" as regular file searching in the Finder. Here's how it works:

1. **Press Option-⌘-F (or click in the search box).**

 The cursor jumps up there.

2. **Start typing what you're looking for.**

 As you type, the messages list changes to show only the matching messages from all your mail folders.

 If you see the message you're looking for, great. Click it, and off you go.

 But this initial search is a pretty broad one. Mail is rounding up messages that match your search term *in any way*. If you type *veg*, you see messages from Murray Vegelstein, messages from vegan@militanteaters.org, and messages with the subject line "HOT DEALS IN VEGAS." All of them in one big stew.

To help you sort through it, Mail produces a Suggestions list, which sprouts from the search box. As in the Finder, it's Mail's way of asking what sort of *thing* your search term is. Is it a person? A subject? The status of a message? A date? Figure 11-12 shows the idea.

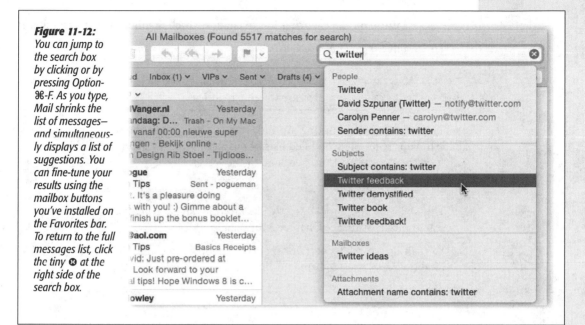

Figure 11-12:
You can jump to the search box by clicking or by pressing Option-⌘-F. As you type, Mail shrinks the list of messages—and simultaneously displays a list of suggestions. You can fine-tune your results using the mailbox buttons you've installed on the Favorites bar. To return to the full messages list, click the tiny ⊗ at the right side of the search box.

3. **Click the suggestion you want.**

 Mail filters the list. For example, if you click Murray Vegelstein, you'll see *only* the messages to or from Murray.

4. **Edit the search token.**

 The *search token* is the little bubble that appears in the search box after you've clicked one of the suggestions. You can click the little ▾ in the search token to change it. For example, if you've clicked somebody's name, that pop-up menu says To, From, or Entire Message (including the header and the body).

 You can also type more into the search box to add *another* search token. For example, the first token might limit the search to messages from one person; you could then create another one that limits the search to a certain date.

Tip: Once you've built up a complicated search like this, save yourself the effort next time by *saving* that search. Click the Save button just below the search box. You get the Smart Mailbox dialog box, already filled out with the search setup you've specified. All you have to do is give it a name and click OK to transform your search into a smart mailbox that you can open anytime.

You've done a lot of refining of this search. But you still haven't limited your results by *account or folder*. Mail is showing you results from either *all* mailboxes, or from only the most recent mailbox you've searched. Fortunately, your Favorites bar has now sprouted two new buttons: one called All, and one that names the folder you most recently clicked.

5. **Click a button on the Favorites bar to change which mailbox is being searched.**

 The results list updates itself.

Tip: *If you ⌘-click several mail folders before you search, you can limit the search to that particular set of mailboxes. (In that case, you see a button on the Favorites bar called Selected Mailboxes.)*

When you're finished hunting around, you can empty out the search box, and get back to your regularly scheduled lists of email, by clicking any other mailbox, or by clicking the ⊗ button at the right end of the search box.

A few last notes on searching:

- The Mail search is almost exactly like Finder searching, right down to the saved-search mechanism. See Chapter 3 for details.

- You can also search for certain text *within* an open message. Choose Edit→Find→ Find (or press ⌘-F) to bring up the Find dialog box (Figure 11-13).

Figure 11-13:
The Find box works just as it does in a word processor, except that the Replace function works only on messages you've written yourself—Mail doesn't let you change the words of mail you've received. (Lawyers would have a field day with that one.)

- As with regular Spotlight, Mail matches your search term by looking only at the *beginnings* of words. Searching for *flag* will find messages that contain the words *flagstone* and *flagellum*, but not *Redflag Incorporated*.

- In Mail→Preferences→General, you can specify whether or not you want Mail to include the Trash folder, Junk folder, and encrypted messages when you search all mailboxes.

Deleting Messages

Sometimes it's junk mail. Sometimes you're just done with it. Either way, it's a snap to delete a selected message, several selected messages, or a message that's currently before you on the screen. You can press the Delete key, click the Delete 🗑 button on the toolbar, choose Edit→Delete, or drag messages out of the list window and into your Trash mailbox—or even onto the Dock's Trash icon.

Tip: If you delete a message by accident, the Undo command (Edit→Undo or ⌘-Z) restores it.

All these commands move the messages to the Trash folder. If you like, you can then click its icon to view a list of the messages you've deleted. You can even rescue messages by dragging them back into a mailbox (back to the Inbox, for example).

Emptying the Trash folder

Mail doesn't vaporize messages in the Trash folder until you "empty the trash," just like in the Finder. You can empty the Trash folder in any of several ways:

- **Click a message (or several) within the Trash folder list,** and then click the Delete 🗑 icon on the toolbar (or press the Delete key). Now those messages are *really* gone.

- **Choose Mailbox→Erase Deleted Items (Shift-⌘-Delete).** (If you have multiple accounts, choose Erase Deleted Items→In All Accounts.)

- **Right-click (or two-finger click) the Trash mailbox icon,** and then choose Erase Deleted Items from the shortcut menu. Or choose the same command from the ⚙ pop-up menu at the bottom of the window.

- **Wait.** Mail will permanently delete these messages automatically after a week.

 If a week is too long (or not long enough), you can change this interval. Choose Mail→Preferences, click Accounts, and select the account name from the list at left. Then click Mailbox Behaviors, and change the "Permanently erase deleted messages when" pop-up menu. If you choose Quitting Mail from the pop-up menu, Mail will take out the trash every time you quit the program.

Turning deleted mail invisible

Mail offers another—and very unusual—method of deleting messages that doesn't involve the Trash folder at all. Using this method, pressing the Delete key (or clicking

TROUBLESHOOTING MOMENT

Rebuilding Your Mail Databases

Mail keeps your messages in your Home→Library→Mail folder. (Your Library folder is usually invisible, but you can jump to it by pressing Option as you choose Go→Library in the Finder.)

Over time, as you add and delete hundreds of messages from these database files, some digital sawdust gets left behind, resulting in general Mail sluggishness. You also wind up with *massive* message files hidden on your hard drive, which can consume hundreds of megabytes of disk space. That's a particular bummer if you like to copy your message databases to your laptop when you go on a trip.

Fortunately, it's easy enough to *rebuild the message databases.* Doing so cleanses, repairs, and purges your message files. As a result, you wind up with a much more compact and healthy database.

To rebuild a mailbox, highlight it in the mailboxes column in Mail. (Highlight several by ⌘-clicking, if you like.) Then choose Mailbox→Rebuild. OS X takes several minutes (or hours, depending on the size of your mailboxes) to repair and compact your database—but if you're experiencing Mail weirdness or slowness, it's well worth the sacrifice.

the Delete 🗑 toolbar button) simply hides the selected message in the list. Hidden messages remain hidden, but they don't go away for good until you use the rebuild mailbox command described in the box on page 405.

If this arrangement sounds useful, choose Mail→Preferences; click Accounts and select the account from the list on the left; click Mailbox Behaviors; and then turn off the checkbox called "Move deleted messages to a separate folder" or "Move deleted messages to the Trash mailbox." (The checkbox's wording depends on what kind of account you have.) From now on, messages you delete vanish from the list.

They're not really gone, however. You can bring them back, at least in ghostly form, by choosing View→Show Deleted Messages (or pressing ⌘-L). Using this system, in other words, you never truly delete messages; you just hide them.

At first, you might be concerned about the disk space and database size involved in keeping your old messages around forever like this. Truth is, OS X is perfectly capable of maintaining many thousands of messages in its mailbox databases—and with the sizes of hard drives nowadays, a few thousand messages aren't likely to make much of a dent.

Meanwhile, there's a huge benefit to this arrangement. At some point, almost everyone wishes he could resurrect a deleted message—maybe months later, maybe years later. Using the hidden-deleted-message system, your old messages are always around for reference. (The downside to this system, of course, is that SEC investigators can use it to find incriminating mail that you thought you'd deleted.)

When you do want to purge these messages for good, you can always return to the Mailbox Behaviors dialog box and turn the "Move deleted mail to a separate folder" checkbox back on.

Archiving messages

There's one final option for getting unwanted messages out of your hair: *archiving*. It just means "Get it out of my sight for now." Archiving sweeps the selected message into a folder called Archived, where it will stay until you deal with it further (by moving or deleting it). There's one of these folders per account.

To archive a selected message, a group of selected messages, or a conversation, choose Message→Archive, or click the Archive icon on the toolbar.

POWER USERS' CLINIC

Secrets of the Mailbox Files

Mail keeps your messages in a series of mailbox folders in your Home→Library→Mail folder, inside folders (Outbox, Deleted Messages, and so on) named for each account.

Knowing this permits you to perform a number of interesting tricks. First of all, now you know what files to back up for safekeeping. (To see the invisible Library folder, press Option as you choose Go→Library in the Finder.)

Second, if you have messages on an old Mac that you'd like to copy to your new one, now you know where they're stored.

Exporting Mailboxes

Time Machine (Chapter 5) backs up its data regularly—including your email. If you ever delete a message by accident or otherwise make a mess of your email stash, you can duck into Time Machine right from within Mail.

But not everybody wants to use Time Machine, for personal reasons—lack of a second hard drive, aversion to software named after H.G. Wells novels, whatever.

Yet having a backup of your email is critically important. Fortunately, there's a second good way to back up your email—*export it*, like this:

1. **In the mailboxes column, choose which mailbox or mailboxes you want to archive.**

 If you have multiple mailboxes in mind, ⌘-click each one until you've selected all the ones you want.

2. **At the bottom of the Mail window, open the ✿ pop-up menu and choose Export Mailbox(es).**

 You can also get to this command by choosing Mailbox→Export Mailbox.

3. **In the box that appears, navigate to the place you want to stash this cache of valuable mail, like a server, a flash drive, or a folder. Click Choose.**

 Your exported mailboxes are saved to the location you've chosen. You can now go back to work writing new messages.

 Later, if you need to pull one of those stashes back into duty, choose File→Import Mailboxes. Choose the Apple Mail option and then navigate back to the place where you stored your mailboxes.

Message Rules

Once you know how to create folders, the next step in managing your email is to set up a series of *message rules* (filters) that file, answer, or delete incoming messages automatically based on their contents (such as their subject, address, and/or size). Message rules require you to think like the distant relative of a programmer, but the mental effort can reward you many times over. Message rules turn Mail into a surprisingly smart and efficient secretary.

Setting up message rules

Here's how to set up a message rule:

1. **Choose Mail→Preferences. Click the Rules icon.**

 The Rules pane appears, as shown at top in Figure 11-14.

2. **Click Add Rule.**

 Now the dialog box shown at bottom in Figure 11-14 appears.

3. **Use the criteria options (at the top) to specify how Mail should select messages to process.**

For example, if you'd like the program to watch out for messages from a particular person, you would set up the first two pop-up menus to say "From" and "Contains," respectively.

To flag messages containing *loan, $$$$, XXXX, !!!!*, and so on, set the pop-up menus to say "Subject" and "Contains."

You can set up *multiple* criteria here to flag messages whose subjects contain any one of those common spam triggers. (If you change the "any" pop-up menu to say "all," then *all* the criteria must be true for the rule to kick in.)

Figure 11-14:
Top: Mail rules can screen out junk mail, serve as an email answering machine, or call important messages to your attention. All mail message rules you've created appear in this list. (The color shading for each rule is a reflection of the colorizing options you've set up, if any.)

Bottom: Double-click a rule to open the Edit Rule dialog box, where you can specify what should set off the rule and what it should do in response.

4. **Specify which words or people you want the message rule to watch for.**

 In the text box to the right of the two pop-up menus, type the word, address, name, or phrase you want Mail to watch for—a person's name, or *$$$$*, in the previous examples.

5. **In the lower half of the box, specify what you want to happen to messages that match the criteria.**

 If, in steps 1 through 4, you've told your rule to watch for junk mail containing *$$$$* in the subject line, here's where you can tell Mail to delete it or move it into, say, a Junk folder.

With a little imagination, you'll see how the options in this pop-up menu can do absolutely amazing things with your incoming email. Mail can colorize, delete, move, redirect, or forward messages—or even play a sound when you get a certain message.

By setting up the controls as shown in Figure 11-14, for example, you'll have specified that whenever your mother sends something to you that mentions a visit, you'll hear a specific alert noise as the email is highlighted in a bright red, so it will jump out at you in the Inbox.

6. **In the very top box, name your mail rule. Click OK.**

At this point, Mail offers to apply your freshly minted rule to all the messages that are in the mailboxes that are currently selected. It's your one chance to go back in time—because from now on, the rule will apply only to *new* messages. Click either Apply or Don't Apply.

Now you're back to the Rules pane (Figure 11-14, top). Here you can choose a sequence for the rules you've created by dragging them up and down. Here, too, you can turn off the ones you won't be needing at the moment, but may use again one day.

Tip: Mail applies rules as they appear, from top to bottom, in the list. If a rule doesn't seem to be working properly, it may be that an earlier rule is intercepting and processing some messages before the "broken" rule even sees them. To fix this, try dragging the rule (or the interfering rule) up or down in the list.

VIPs

In the real world, VIPs are people who get backstage passes to concerts, or special treatment at business functions (it stands for "very important person"). In Yosemite, it means "somebody whose mail is important enough that I want it brought to my attention immediately when it arrives."

So who should your VIPs be? That's up to you. Your spouse, your boss, and your doctor come to mind.

To designate someone as a VIP, follow the steps shown in Figure 11-15. From now on, lots of interesting things happen:

- A new mailbox, called VIPs, appears in your mailboxes list. Click it to see all the mail from all your VIPs (even messages you've deleted). Or click the flippy triangle to see your VIPs' names, each representing messages from that person.

- A new menu button appears on your Favorites toolbar called VIPs. Click to see all VIP messages, or click the ▾ to see a pop-up menu of all the VIPs' names. Here again, the point is that you can jump to the messages from just that person.

- If you use iCloud, the same person is now a VIP on all your other Macs (running Mountain Lion or later), plus iPhones and iPads (running iOS 6 or later).

• Best of all, you can set up your Mac so that when a new message from a VIP comes in, an alert bubble appears in the top-right corner of your screen (Figure 11-15, bottom). That feature, of course, is part of the Notification Center, and it's described in Chapter 18. See the box on page 388 for instructions on setting this up.

Figure 11-15:
Top: To designate a VIP, open a message she's sent you. Point to her name. A hollow star appears; click there. The star darkens. (Or choose Add to VIPs from the pop-up menu that appears when you point to her name.) Note: If that person one day insults you, fires you, or dumps you, then you can remove her VIP status by clicking that same star again.

Bottom: OS X can alert you when VIP messages arrive. And in Yosemite, you can reply right on the spot.

The Anti-Spam Toolkit

Spam, the junk that now makes up more than 80 percent of email, is a problem that's only getting worse. Luckily, you, along with Mail's advanced spam filters, can make it better—at least for *your* email accounts.

Using the Junk Mail Filter

You'll see the effects of Mail's spam filter the first time you check your mail: Certain message titles appear in brown. These are the messages that Mail considers junk.

Note: Out of the box, Mail doesn't apply its spam-targeting features to people whose addresses are in your Contacts, to people you've emailed recently, or to messages sent to you *by name* rather than just by email address. You can adjust these settings in the Mail→Preferences→Junk Mail tab.

During your first couple of weeks with Mail, your job is to supervise Mail's work. That is, if you get spam that Mail misses, click the message, and then click the Junk button on the toolbar. On the other hand, if Mail flags legitimate mail as spam, slap it gently on the wrist by clicking the Not Junk button. Over time, Mail gets better and better at filtering your mail.

The trouble with this so-called Training mode is that you're still left with the task of trashing the spam yourself, saving you no time whatsoever.

Once Mail has perfected its filtering skills to your satisfaction, though, open Mail's preferences, click Junk Mail, and then click "Move it to the Junk mailbox." From now on, Mail automatically files what it deems junk into a Junk mailbox, where it's much easier to scan and delete the messages en masse.

Tip: Don't miss the "Trust Junk Mail headers" option in the Junk Mail pane of the Preferences window. If you turn on that checkbox, then Mail takes your Internet provider's word that certain messages are spam, giving you a *double* layer of spam protection.

More Anti-Spam Tips

The Junk filter goes a long way toward cleaning out the spam from your mail collection—but it doesn't catch everything. If you're overrun by spam, here are some other steps you can take:

- **Rules.** Set up some message rules, as described on the preceding pages, that autoflag as spam messages that have subject lines containing trigger words like "Viagra," "Herbal," "Mortgage," "Refinance," "Enlarge," "Your"—you get the idea.

- **Create a private account.** If you're overrun by spam, consider sacrificing your current address, using it for the public areas of the Internet, like chat rooms, online shopping, Web site and software registration, and newsgroup posting. Reserve a separate email account for person-to-person email.

 Spammers use automated software robots that scour every public Internet message and Web page, recording email addresses they find. (In fact, that's probably how they got your address in the first place.)

 Using this technique, at least you're now restricting the junk mail to a secondary mail account.

- **For goodness' sake, don't *order* anything sold by the spammers.** If only one person in 500,000 does so, the spammer makes money.

Contacts

Contacts is OS X's little-black-book program—an electronic Rolodex where you can stash the names, job titles, addresses, phone numbers, email addresses, and Internet chat screen names of all the people in your life. It can also hold related information, like birthdays, anniversaries, and any other tidbits of personal data you'd like to keep at your fingertips (Figure 11-16).

The best part: It's *centralized*. This one address list appears everywhere: in Mail, Messages, and so on. And it synchronizes with your iPhone, iPad, and (via iCloud) your other computers.

Once you make Contacts the central repository of all your personal contact information, you can call up this information in a number of convenient ways:

- **You can open Contacts and then search for a contact** by typing just a few letters in the search box.

- **Regardless of what program you're in,** you can use a single keystroke (the ⊙ key on aluminum keyboards, or ⌸ on more recent ones) to summon the Contacts Dashboard widget. There you can search for any contact you want. When you're done, hide the widget with the same quick keystroke.

- **When you're composing messages in Mail,** Contacts automatically fills in email addresses for you when you type the first few letters.

Tip: If you choose Window→Address Panel (Option-⌘-A) from within Mail, you can browse all your addresses without even launching the Contacts program. Once you've selected the people you want to contact, just click the To button to address an email to them—or, if you already have a new email message open, to add them to the recipients.

Figure 11-16:
Contacts is meant to look like a physical address book. On the left, the full list of names; on the right, the card for the one person whose name you've clicked. (You can hide the names list by choosing View→Card Only, or bring it back with View→List and Card.)

- **When you use Messages to chat** with people in Contacts, the pictures you've stored of them automatically appear in chat windows.

- **The free iCloud service can synchronize your contacts** to the Web so you can see them while you're away from your Mac.

- **Contacts can sync with an iPod, iPhone, or iPad,** giving you a "little black book" that fits in your shirt pocket, can be operated one-handed, and comes with built-

in musical accompaniment. You can have that happen wirelessly, using iCloud, or wirefully, when you connect your iPod/iPhone/iPad to your Mac. (To set this up, open iTunes while your i-gadget is connected. Click the i-gadget's icon; on the Contacts or Info tab, turn on Synchronize Contacts.)

You can find Contacts in your Applications folder or in the Dock.

Importing Addresses

The easiest way to add people to Contacts is to import them from another service, like Yahoo or Exchange, or another program, like Microsoft Outlook (for Mac) or Entourage.

Importing from Yahoo, Google, Exchange, or another Internet service

Contacts can synchronize its contacts with online Rolodexes that may be very important to you: your Gmail (Google) contacts, Yahoo contacts, iCloud address book, or your company's Microsoft Exchange master address book (Figure 11-17).

Figure 11-17:
Contacts can sync your digital Rolodex with online contact managers like Yahoo and Google. Turn on the appropriate checkbox to enter your account name and password. For other account types, like Exchange, click the + button below the list to begin.

In Contacts, choose Contacts→Preferences→Accounts. There, staring you in the face, are checkboxes that let you sync your contacts with iCloud, Yahoo, Google. Turn on the checkbox you want, click Configure, agree to the legalese, enter your account information, and boom—you're done. Contacts is now synced with your online accounts. Change information in one place, and it's also changed in the other. Even your contacts' photos, if your online address book has them, show up in Contacts!

Tip: You can also enter this information in the Internet Accounts pane of System Preferences.

If some other online service maintains your address book, Contacts can sync with it, too, as long as it uses one of the standard sharing formats (Exchange, CardDAV, or Lightweight Directory Access Protocol, known by the pros as LDAP). To teach Contacts about those, choose Contacts→Preferences→Accounts. Click the + button in the lower left, enter your account information on the resulting screen, click Create, and away you go.

> **Note:** Contacts may display an advanced Account Settings screen, where you have to enter more detailed information. If you're a hands-on sort of nerd, you can also force this screen to open on your command. To do that, press Option and point to the Create button, which now says Continue. Click it.

Once you've set up a Contacts account, you can also change its settings, right there in the same Preferences dialog box. Specify how often you want your Mac to sync changes with the online account, for example.

Importing from another address-book program

Contacts can also slurp in contact info from other address-book or list programs, like Microsoft Outlook (Entourage), Palm Desktop, Excel, and others. Not directly, of course; that would be too easy. But most of those programs can *export* their information as an intermediary file in one of four popular formats: vCard, LDAP Interchange Format (LDIF), tab-delimited, or comma-separated value (CSV).

TROUBLESHOOTING MOMENT

Resolving Conflicts and Duplicates

Suppose you tell Contacts to sync its information with one of your online accounts. And suppose that someone is listed in both places—with a different phone number in each place. Which address-book information "wins"? What's the Mac supposed to do?

Ask you, of course.

And that's exactly what it does.

The first warning you may see lets you know that the other address book is very different from the one on your Mac—more than, say, 25 percent different. If you know what you're doing, go ahead and click Sync Contacts. If you'd like to inspect the differences name by name, click Show Details instead. You'll see a summary box that indicates how many people need to be added to one list or the other, and how many people's information is different.

That "these two address books are radically different" warning isn't quite the same thing as the warning you may get about sync conflicts. That's when you've entered the same

person into each address book source, but with different information. Maybe one has a different phone number, for example. If you click Review Now, you're shown one conflict after another—the complete address cards—so that you can make a ruling on which version "wins."

One other problem may crop up when you're combining accounts: You may wind up with duplicates.

Fortunately, Contacts is ready for you here. On the Groups page (press ⌘-3), click the account with the problem (or All Contacts). Choose Card→Look for Duplicates.

The program lets you know about any duplicates it finds, even if only the name is the same and everything else is different. It even flags cards that have duplicate bits of information, like the same phone number twice. All you have to do is click Merge; Contacts merges the multiple cards into a single one, preserving all the details that are unique to each. (If there were duplicate photos, whichever one was on the first card becomes the new photo.)

For example, Microsoft's programs can export addresses as vCards; Thunderbird can export in LDIF format; Excel can export tab-delimited or CSV files.

It's a fine art, this importing business; all kinds of things can go wrong. The fields (like Name, Street, Phone) may not be in the right order. Tab-separated export files may not have the right number of empty fields. And so on.

For best results, choose Contacts→Help, and search for "Importing contacts from other applications." The resulting page gives special tips for each kind of export/ import file format. (Fortunately, if the fields are out of order, Contacts will offer you the chance to straighten them out.)

About vCards

Contacts exchanges contact information with other programs primarily through *vCards*. vCard is short for *virtual business card*. More and more email programs send and receive these electronic business cards, which you can identify by their .vcf file name extensions (if, that is, you've set your Mac to display these extensions in Finder→Preferences→Advanced).

If you ever receive an email with a vCard file attached, drag the .vcf file into your Contacts window to create an instant entry with a complete set of information. You can create vCards of your own, too. Just drag a name out of your Contacts and onto the desktop (or into a piece of outgoing mail).

Tip: In addition to letting you create vCards of individual entries, Contacts makes it easy to create vCards that contain several entries. To do so, ⌘-click the entries in the Name column that you want included, and drag them to the desktop. There they'll appear all together as a single vCard. You can even drag an item from the Group page to the desktop to make a vCard that contains all the group's entries.

This trick is especially helpful when you want to copy all your contacts from your old PC to your new Mac. By creating a single vCard containing all your contacts, you've made it trivial to import them into the copy of Contacts running on your new Mac.

Creating Address Cards

Each entry in Contacts is called a *card*—like a paper Rolodex card, with predefined spaces to hold all the standard contact information.

To add a new person, choose File→New Card, press ⌘-N, or click the + button beneath the Name column. Then type in the contact information, pressing the Tab key to move from field to field, as shown in Figure 11-18.

Tip: If you find yourself constantly adding the same fields to new cards, check out the Template pane of Contacts' Preferences (Contacts→Preferences). There you can customize exactly which fields appear for new cards.

Figure 11-18 shows some unusual fields that you can plug into your address cards. There's a Birthday field and even a place to store the contact's Game Center, Twitter, Facebook, and Flickr handles. To add fields like these, choose from the Card→Add Field menu.

Each card also contains a free-form Note field at the bottom, where you can type any other random crumbs of information you'd like to store about the person (pet's name, embarrassing nicknames, favorite Chinese restaurant, and so on).

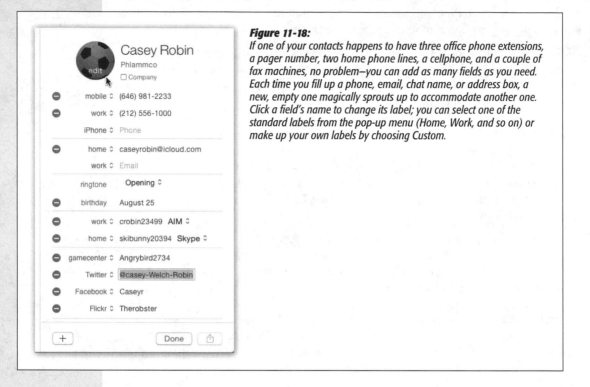

Figure 11-18:
If one of your contacts happens to have three office phone extensions, a pager number, two home phone lines, a cellphone, and a couple of fax machines, no problem—you can add as many fields as you need. Each time you fill up a phone, email, chat name, or address box, a new, empty one magically sprouts up to accommodate another one. Click a field's name to change its label; you can select one of the standard labels from the pop-up menu (Home, Work, and so on) or make up your own labels by choosing Custom.

Editing an address

When you create a new address card, you're automatically in Edit mode, which means you can add and remove fields and change the information on the card. To switch into Browse mode (where you can view and copy contact information but not change it), click the Edit button or choose Edit→Edit Card (⌘-L). You can also switch *out* of Browse Mode in the same ways.

Adding addresses from Mail

You can also make new contacts right in Mail, saving you the trouble of having to type names and email addresses manually. Select a message in Mail, and then choose Message→Add Sender to Contacts (Shift-⌘-Y). Presto: OS X adds a new card to the Contacts, with the name and email address fields already filled in. Later, you can edit the card in Contacts to add phone numbers, street addresses, and so on.

Tip: If you enter some people's birthdays in Contacts, they can show up automatically in Calendar. To make that happen, open Calendar, and then choose Calendar→Preferences→General. Turn on "Show Birthdays calendar."

Groups

A *group* is a collection of related address cards, saved under a single descriptive name (see Figure 11-19).

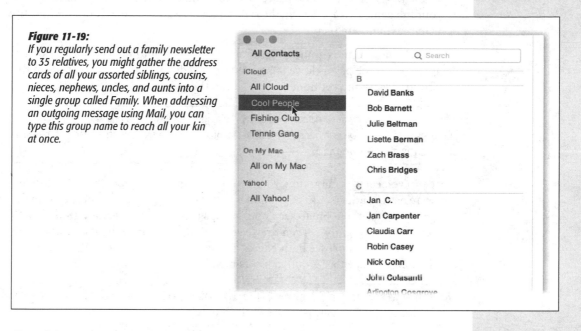

Figure 11-19:
If you regularly send out a family newsletter to 35 relatives, you might gather the address cards of all your assorted siblings, cousins, nieces, nephews, uncles, and aunts into a single group called Family. When addressing an outgoing message using Mail, you can type this group name to reach all your kin at once.

Organizing your contacts into groups can make them much easier to find and use—especially when your database of addresses climbs into the hundreds.

Tip: When you send an email message to a group en masse, how does Mail know *which* email address to use for each person?

Because you've *told* it. In Contacts, choose Edit→Edit Distribution List. A special dialog box appears, listing everyone in each group, along with each person's complete list of email addresses. (Use the tiny pop-up menu above the list to choose Phone or Address; that way, you can also indicate the preferred phone number and mailing address.) Just click the preferred email address to make it bold.

To see your groups, choose View→Groups, press ⌘-3, or click the red bookmark at the top of the page that shows individuals' names.

To create a group, click the + button at the bottom of the Group column in the Contacts window, or choose File→New Group (Shift-⌘-N.) Type a name for the newly spawned group icon in the Group column.

Now you have to fill up the group with the appropriate subset of names. There are three ways to do that:

- **To turn a set of address cards into a group very quickly** when you're in regular address-book mode (not Groups), select multiple entries from the Names column. You can do that either by Shift-clicking the names (to make contiguous selections)

or by ⌘-clicking (for noncontiguous selections)—and then choose File→New Group From Selection. You end up with a new group containing the selected names.

- **While you're on the Groups page,** click All Contacts at the top of the screen. Now your full names list appears on the right page; drag names directly onto the group names to put them there.

- **If you're not on the Groups page,** drag contacts up onto the Groups bookmark at the top of the page—leave the mouse button down as Contacts shows you the Groups page—and continue dragging onto the group's name.

Note: You're not *moving* those names; in essence, you're just creating *aliases* of them, just as you might put songs in different playlists in iTunes. The only exception is Exchange accounts; those names can exist in only one group or folder at a time.

Once you've created some groups, you can even add groups to *other* groups, as though you were nesting folders. You might find it useful to keep a Nieces group and a Nephews group, for example, but to keep both groups inside a master Family group. To do this, create the two groups. Then drag each onto the Family group. Now, whenever you select Family, you'll see both Nieces and Nephews listed among the rest of the cards; double-click either group to see its members.

Tip: If, while viewing the list of groups, you Option-click someone's name in the main list, Contacts shows you all the groups and folders that person belongs to.

Smart groups

The Finder has smart folders, Mail has smart mailboxes, and iTunes has smart playlists; inevitably, Contacts has smart *groups*.

Smart address groups, like smart folders in the Finder, automatically populate themselves with items that match criteria you specify. For example, you might create a smart group called "Apple Employees" that lists all your contacts with "apple.com" in their email addresses. Or when you visit Detroit, you could whip up a group that lists everyone you know who lives there.

To create a smart group, choose File→New Smart Group (Option-⌘-N). Then use the resulting dialog box (which looks a lot like Mail's smart mailbox dialog box) to specify how you'd like the smart group to fill itself.

Once you're done, you can use your new smart group much like you'd use a regular group. You can't add contacts to a smart group yourself, but you can still send an email to all the members of a smart group, for example, or drag one to the Finder to create a composite vCard.

Removing someone from a group

To take someone out of a group, first click the group name, and then click the person's name in the Name column and press the Delete key. If you want to remove the person from Contacts *itself,* click Delete in the resulting dialog box. Otherwise, just

click Remove from Group or press Return. Contacts keeps the card but removes it from the currently selected group.

Note: If you selected All Contacts in the Group column, rather than a specific group, you don't get a Remove from Group option. Instead, the Mac just asks you to confirm that you do, in fact, want to permanently remove the card.

Adding Pictures

You can dress up each Contacts entry with a photo. Whenever you're editing somebody's address book card, drag a digital photo—preferably 64 pixels square, or a multiple of that—onto the empty headshot square; the image shows up. Or double-click the picture well. Now you can choose from categories like Defaults (canned symbolic photos like animals and bugs); Recents (photos you've used recently); Camera (handy if this person is *with* you—take a new photo); and Linked (photos from online services like Facebook). Don't miss the swirly button next to it, which lets you apply nutty Photo Boothish effects. At that point, you can enlarge, reposition, and crop the new photo. Click Done when you're done.

You don't necessarily have to use a photo, of course. You could add any graphic that you want to represent someone, even if it's a Bart Simpson face or a skull and crossbones. You can use any standard image file format in an address card—JPEG, GIF, PNG, TIFF, or even PDF. You can drag any of these directly into one of the squares here.

From now on, if you receive an email from that person, the photo shows up right in the email message—even on your phone or iPad.

Tip: If you've got snapshots in iPhoto, it's particularly easy to add a picture to any address card. Just drag a picture directly from the main iPhoto window to the picture frame on the address card to insert it.

Replacing and removing a picture

To replace a photo on an address card, just drag a new image on top of the old one. If you want to get rid of an existing picture without replacing it, select the card, and then choose Card→Clear Custom Image (or, in Edit mode, select the picture and then press Delete).

Free headshots from Facebook

Yes, there's a little photo well on each card of your Contacts app. But here's a wild guess: Most of yours are empty. After all: Who's going to go to the trouble of hunting down headshots of 500 acquaintances, just to fully illustrate their Contacts?

Fortunately, OS X stands ready to help. With one click, it can harvest headshots from the world's largest database of names and faces: Facebook

Visit System Preferences→Internet Accounts. Click your Facebook account to see the magical button: Get Profile Photos. When you click it, OS X goes online for a massive research mission. Using your contacts' names and phone numbers as matching criteria,

it ventures off to Facebook, finds the profile photos of everyone on your Contacts, and installs them into Contacts automatically.

Crazier still, it even grabs the headshots of people in your Contacts who *aren't your Facebook friends!*

If you have already a photo for somebody, don't worry; it doesn't get replaced. Of course, you can switch to the new Facebook profile picture if you prefer. Use the Linked heading in the photo picker as described above.

Tip: You can use the Get Profile Photos button even if you don't want your Facebook friends loaded into your copy of Contacts (by turning off Contacts in System Preferences→Internet Accounts→Facebook).

Finding an Address

You can search for a Contacts entry inside the currently selected group by typing a few letters of a name (or address, or any other snippet of contact information) in the search box. To search *all* your contacts instead of just the current group, click All Contacts in the Group list.

Tip: You can press ⌘-F to jump directly to the search field and start typing. Your savings: one mouse click.

With each letter you type, Contacts filters your social circle and displays the number of matches at the bottom. The matching records themselves appear in the Name column, the first of the matching card entries appears in the far-right pane, and the matching text itself appears highlighted in the matching card.

If Contacts finds more than one matching card, use the ▼ and ▲ keys, or Return and Shift-Return, to navigate through them.

Once you've found the card you're looking for, you can perform some interesting stunts. If you click the label of a phone number (see Figure 11-20), you see the Show

Figure 11-20:
The options that become available when you click the field labels on an address card vary according to field type. Pop-up menus let you send email, open a Web page, or view a map, depending on the type of field you've clicked.

If you have an iPhone, and it's on the same WiFi network, you even see these Call Using iPhone options. They let you use your Mac as a speakerphone, as described on page 478.

The Send Message command sends an iMessage to the phone number or email address whose label you've clicked—if, in fact, it's an iMessages-registered number or address.

And the Show Map button appears when you point to an address. It opens the Maps program and shows you this address on a map.

in Large Type option: Contacts displays the number in an absurdly gigantic font, making it possible to read the number as you dial from across the room. You can also click the label of an email address to create a preaddressed email message, or click a home page to launch your Web browser and go to somebody's site.

Tip: That same pop-up menu lists FaceTime—you can begin a FaceTime video call right from Contacts.

You can also copy and paste (or drag) address card info into another program or convert it into a Sticky Note.

Tip: Once you find a street address in Contacts, you can find those coordinates on a map by pointing to the address and clicking the Show Map button. The Maps app obediently leaps open to display the address.

Changing the Contacts Display

You can't do much to customize Contacts' appearance, but Contacts→Preferences gives you at least a couple of options in the General pane that are worth checking out:

- **Show first name.** Choose to have names displayed with the first name followed by the last name, or vice versa.

- **Sort By.** Sort the entries in Contacts by either first or last name.

Printing Options

When you choose File→Print and click Show Details, the Style pop-up menu offers four ways to print whatever addresses are selected at the moment:

- **Mailing Labels.** This option prints addresses on standard sheets of sticky mailing labels—Avery, for example—that you buy at office-supply stores.

Tip: As you manipulate settings, you can see your changes in the preview pane on the left. If the preview is too small for you to see, use the Zoom slider. (It doesn't affect your printout.)

- **Envelopes.** This feature is great if you have bad handwriting; rather than hand addressing your envelopes, you can have Contacts print them out for you. Use the Layout pop-up menu to pick the size of your envelopes—it's usually listed on the outside of the envelope box.

Note: Both the Mailing Labels and Envelopes options print *only* the contacts for which you have, in fact, entered physical mailing addresses.

- **Lists.** If all you want is a paper backup of your Contacts entries, then use this setting. In the Attributes list, turn on the checkboxes of the fields you want printed—just name and phone number, for example.

- **Pocket Contacts.** This feature prints out a convenient *paper* address book from your virtual one. If you pick Indexed from the Flip Style pop-up menu, then each page's edge will even list the first letters of the last names listed on the page, mak-

ing it a cinch to find the page with the address you want. (Here again, you can pick which fields you'd like to include—phone numbers, addresses, and so on.)

As you fiddle with the options presented here, you get to see a miniature preview, right in the dialog box, that shows what you're going to get.

No matter which mode you choose, the only cards that print are the ones that were selected when you chose File→Print. If you want to print *all* your cards, therefore, click All in the Group column before you print.

Contacts Backups

Your Contacts may represent *years* of typing and compiling effort. Losing all that information to a corrupted database or a hard drive crash could be devastating. Here are three ways to protect your Contacts data:

- **Back up your entire Contacts database.** Choose File→Export→Contacts Archive. Store the resulting backup file on another drive, if you like. Later, you can use the File→Import command to find that data and slurp it back in.

- **Turn on iCloud syncing.** An iCloud account has its privileges—and one of them is automatic synchronizing with the iCloud mother ship online.

- **Back up your whole Mac with Time Machine.** Chapter 5 tells you how.

Safari

Apple's most obvious Internet friendly creation is Safari, a smartly designed window to the Web. This chapter is all about Safari—the compass icon in the Dock points the way to your Internet adventure.

Browsing Basics

You probably know the drill when it comes to Web browsers. When you click an underlined *link (hyperlink)* or a picture button, you're transported from one Web page to another. One page might be the home page of General Motors; another might contain critical information about a bill in Congress; another might have baby pictures posted by a parent in Omaha.

Tip: Text links aren't always blue and underlined. In fact, Web designers sometimes make it very difficult to tell which text is clickable and which is just text. When in doubt, move your cursor over something; if the arrow changes to a pointing finger, you've found yourself a link.

The Unified Address/Search Bar

There are all kinds of ways to begin your Web surfing session. Perform a search. Click a bookmark. On the following pages: a rundown of these starting points.

Often, of course, you'll want to type in a Web address; that's the purpose of the address/search bar identified in Figure 12-1. In OS X, a single, unified box serves as both the address bar and the search bar. (Apple just calls it the toolbar.)

If you type a Web address there, like *amazon.com,* then pressing Return takes you to that Web site; if you type anything else, like *cashmere sweaters* or just *amazon,* then pressing Return gives you the Google search results for that phrase, as described next.

In general, it's handy to have a combined address/search bar (many other browsers work this way, too). Unfortunately, it means that you can't leave off the .com when you're typing an address.

Open/close the Sidebar · Address+ Search bar · Tabs · Reload page · A text link · A graphic link

Figure 12-1:
The Safari window offers tools and features that let you navigate the Web almost effortlessly. These toolbars and buttons are described in this chapter.

Note to laptop luggers: Safari's mass of window-top strips and bars are condensed in Yosemite, leaving more vertical screen space for your actual Web-viewing pleasure.

Searching the Web

Press ⌘-L to deposit your insertion point inside the toolbar, type something you're looking for—*phony baloney,* say—and then press Return. Safari takes you directly to the results page of Google or whatever search site you've selected. As Figure 12-2 makes clear, Safari offers plenty of assistance as you type, in the form of Google suggestions, matching listings from your Bookmarks and History list, and suggestions from Maps, Wikipedia, iTunes, and other sources.

Tip: You can turn off the Google suggestions in Safari→Preferences→Search. Uncheck the box "Include search engine suggestions."

Bonus Tip: If you right-click (or two-finger click) a highlighted word or phrase on a Web page, you can choose Search with Google from the shortcut menu to search for that text. And, even cooler, this trick works in *all* Cocoa programs—not just Safari.

Figure 12-2:
As you type, Safari offers autocomplete suggestions from Google's own Suggest feature; below that, it shows the matching pages that you've either bookmarked or visited recently.

To spare yourself the tedium of typing, click the correct complete address with your mouse, or use the ▼ key to reach the desired listing and then press Return. The complete address you select pops into the toolbar.

Address/Search Bar Tips

Because typing Internet addresses and searching for things are so central to the Internet experience and such a typo-prone hassle, the address/search bar is rich with features that minimize keystrokes. For example:

- **You don't have to click there before typing;** just press ⌘-L.

- **You can highlight the entire address** (so it's ready to be typed over with a new one) by clicking anywhere inside the bar. Or press ⌘-L.

- **You don't have to type out the whole Internet address.** You can omit the *http://* and *www* portions; Safari fills in those standard address bits for you. To visit *http:// www.nytimes.com,* for example, a speed freak might press ⌘-L to highlight the address bar, type *nytimes.com,* and then press Return.

- **You don't have to use Google.** If you prefer to use Bing, Yahoo, or DuckDuckGo for searching instead of Google, then open Safari→Preferences→Search and use the "Search engine" pop-up menu. (DuckDuckGo is more limited than Google and its rivals. But it has gained a following among privacy fans, because it doesn't store any information about its visitors or the searches they conduct.)

Tip: You might wonder why the View menu even offers you the chance to hide the address/search bar. If it were hidden, how could you use the Web? Simple: Even with this bar hidden, you can briefly summon it by pressing ⌘-L. Type the address you want and then press Return to make the bar disappear again. That's good news for people with small screens—and for Mac trivia collectors.

Bookmarks, Favorites, Top Sites

Another way to begin your Web session is to click a bookmark.

In any Web browser, bookmarks are essential. They represent sites you want to visit again later. By picking one from a list, you save yourself the trouble of searching the Web or typing out an address.

Safari happens to be overrun with systems of adding and choosing bookmarks; you can't move your cursor without bumping into one. Read on.

Adding a Bookmark

When you find a Web page you might like to visit again, do yourself a favor: Bookmark it.

Here's how:

- **Press ⌘-D, or choose Bookmarks→Add Bookmark.** Proceed as shown in Figure 12-3.

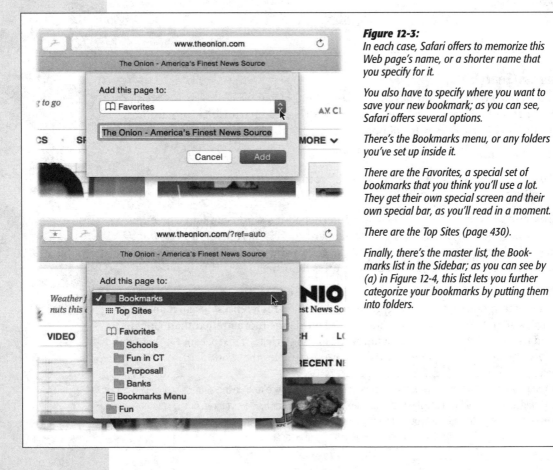

Figure 12-3:
In each case, Safari offers to memorize this Web page's name, or a shorter name that you specify for it.

You also have to specify where you want to save your new bookmark; as you can see, Safari offers several options.

There's the Bookmarks menu, or any folders you've set up inside it.

There are the Favorites, a special set of bookmarks that you think you'll use a lot. They get their own special screen and their own special bar, as you'll read in a moment.

There are the Top Sites (page 430).

Finally, there's the master list, the Bookmarks list in the Sidebar; as you can see by (a) in Figure 12-4, this list lets you further categorize your bookmarks by putting them into folders.

- **Point to the far-left edge of the address bar; hold your cursor down on the ⊕ button that appears.** This time, you get a pop-up menu of the standard locations (Reading List, Favorites, Bookmarks Menu, and so on); choose where you want this bookmark stored. This is a quick method, but it doesn't offer you the chance to rename the bookmark.

Organizing Bookmarks in the Sidebar

See the ⊞ button on the toolbar? It opens the Sidebar, the left-side pane shown at left in Figure 12-4. (You can also choose Bookmarks→Show Bookmarks, or choose View→Show Bookmarks Sidebar, or press Control-⌘-1.)

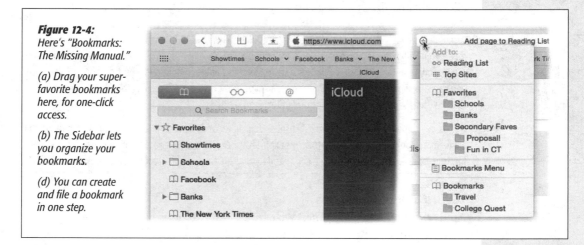

Figure 12-4:
Here's "Bookmarks: The Missing Manual."

(a) Drag your super-favorite bookmarks here, for one-click access.

(b) The Sidebar lets you organize your bookmarks.

(d) You can create and file a bookmark in one step.

At the top of this pane, three tabs await. On the first one, the ⌖ tab, you can really go to town with bookmark management. For example:

- **Rearrange bookmarks or folders** by dragging them up or down.

- **Create a folder** by choosing Bookmarks→Add Bookmark Folder. Or right-click (or two-finger click) anywhere in the list; from the shortcut menu, choose New Folder.

 Type a name for the folder, press Return, and then start filling it up by dragging existing bookmark names onto it.

- **To delete a bookmark or folder,** right-click (or two-finger click) its name. From the shortcut menu, choose Delete.

- **To edit a bookmark's name,** right-click (or two-finger click) it, or hold your cursor down in it. From the shortcut menu, choose Rename Bookmark.

- **To edit the Web address that a bookmark opens,** right-click (or two-finger click) its name. From the shortcut menu, choose Edit Address.

While you're poking around, you might notice a special folder that was here before you arrived. The Favorites folder lists the bookmarks you've installed on the Favor-

ites screen described below; it's just another way to see, choose, and organize those same items.

Organizing Bookmarks in the Editor

Before the slick new Sidebar came along, there was an earlier way to organize bookmarks: the bookmarks *editor*. You can open this special, spreadsheety window by choosing Bookmarks→Edit Bookmarks, by clicking Edit (bottom of the Sidebar), or by pressing Option-⌘-B.

In the bookmarks editor window, drag the bookmarks up and down to rearrange them. You can edit a bookmark's name or underlying address by clicking it. Delete one by clicking it and then pressing Delete. There's a New Folder button at lower left, too.

Tip: Safari is equipped to help you move out of other Web browsers. If you've been using Chrome or Firefox, for example, then the first time you use Safari, your bookmarks and browsing history get imported from the other browser automatically. (You'll see a note to that effect at the bottom of the Favorites or Top Sites view; you can click either Keep or Don't Keep. You can always import them later, using the File→Import From→ Google Chrome or File→Import From→Firefox commands.)

If you have some other weirdo browser, like Internet Explorer or OmniWeb, importing your bookmarks is only a little more complicated. Use that browser's export feature to save them to a file, and then use Safari's File→ Import From→Bookmarks HTML File command to save you the time of re-entering the bookmarks by hand.

Favorites View

Apple figures that, many times, what you'll want to do is visit one of your *favorite* sites—one of the sites you open a lot.

So whenever you open a new window, create a new tab, or click in the address bar (and don't type anything), you're shown the new Favorites page (Figure 12-5).

Yes, of course, you could choose a bookmark's name from the Bookmarks menu or the Bookmarks Sidebar, but that's a few extra clicks. Or you could get to one of your bookmarked sites by clicking the Bookmarks *bar*, if it's open—but a single horizontal bar doesn't have room for very many buttons.

The beauty of the Favorites page is that it has lots of room both horizontally and vertically. And it doesn't eat up any space—it's completely hidden—until you click in the address bar.

You can edit the icons on the Favorites page, of course:

- **Rearrange them.** You can drag any icon to a new spot.

- **Remove them.** Drag an icon out of the main Favorites view window to make it disappear in a puff of cartoon smoke.

- **View them as folders.** If you put several bookmarks into a folder, it appears on the Favorites pane as a single icon filled with even tinier icons.

- **Add an icon.** When you find a page you'd like to add to the Favorites screen, choose Bookmarks→Add Bookmark (⌘-D); on the "Where" sheet that appears, choose Favorites. Click Add.

- **Promote a frequently visited site.** At the bottom, the Favorites view lists Frequently Visited sites. You can drag one of these icons directly upward, into the Favorites area, to install it there. Now it's not just frequent; it's favorited.

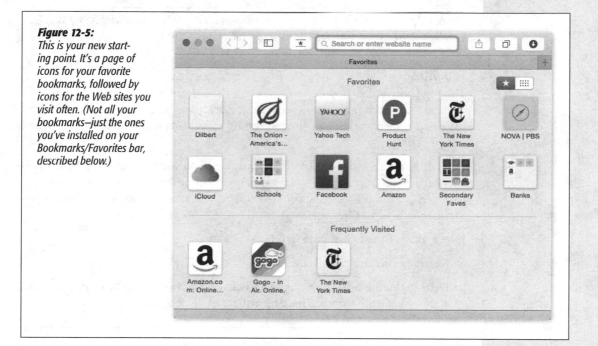

Figure 12-5:
This is your new starting point. It's a page of icons for your favorite bookmarks, followed by icons for the Web sites you visit often. (Not all your bookmarks—just the ones you've installed on your Bookmarks/Favorites bar, described below.)

Favorites Bar

The Favorites bar is a horizontal strip just beneath the address bar that lists your favorites—exactly the same ones as on your Favorites view. If you leave this bar open all the time, you have instantaneous, one-click access to a few, very special sites.

To make this bar appear or disappear, click ⊤ on the toolbar. Or choose View→Show Favorites Bar. Or press Shift-⌘-B. Then:

- **Add a favorite.** You add a bookmark to this bar exactly as described on page 426—but for the new bookmark's destination, choose Favorites.

 You can also drag your current Web page's tiny *icon* from the address/search bar directly onto the Favorites bar. You're offered the chance to type a shorter name for your new Favorite.

Tip: You can also drag a *link* from a Web page (not just the tiny Web site logo) onto your Favorites bar. In fact, you can also drag a link directly to the desktop, where it turns into an Internet location file. Thereafter, to open Safari and visit the associated Web page whenever you like, just double-click this icon.

Better yet, stash a few of these icons in your Dock or Sidebar for even easier access.

- **Remove a button** from the Favorites bar by dragging it down and away.

- **Rearrange the buttons** by dragging them horizontally.

- **Edit a button** by right-clicking (or two-finger clicking) its name. From the shortcut menu, choose Rename Bookmark or Edit Address.

Tip: Actually, you can rename a bookmark on the Favorites bar just by click-and-holding on its name. You'll see it highlighted; you can just retype. No more right-clicking necessary!

Top Sites

The Top Sites window (Figure 12-6) is exactly the same idea as the Favorites view—it's a screen full of Web site icons—except that Safari chooses them, not you. It calculates which are your favorite Web sites according to *how often* and *how recently* you've visited them.

Ordinarily, the Top Sites display changes over time, as your tastes and your activities change. But you can override Safari's attempt to curate this page in various ways. For example, you can pin a certain site so that it never leaves the Top Sites screen, or you can manually add a page.

Here's some of the fun you can have:

- **Rearrange the thumbnails** by dragging them around.

- **Delete a thumbnail** by pointing to it; click the ✖ button that appears in the corner after a couple of seconds. This page will never again appear on Top Sites.

Figure 12-6:
The Top Sites display is hiding behind the Favorites view shown in Figure 12-5. To see Top Sites, click the ⊞ icon at the top right of the Favorites view in a new window. (Or choose History→Show Top Sites.) Click a page to revisit it.

- **Pin a site**—so that it's always in Top Sites, even if you don't visit it much—point to it and click the pushpin icon that appears in the corner after a moment.

- **Add a new page to the Top Sites display.** There are a bunch of ways to go about it.

You can drag a bookmark from the Sidebar (page 35) into the Top Sites window, or even onto the Top Sites icon (▦) on the toolbar, if you've installed it there. Or, when you choose Bookmarks→Add Bookmark (⌘-D) to bookmark an open Web page, choose Top Sites as the location. You can also drag a Web address wherever it may appear—an email, Messages message, Web page, or document, for example— into the Top Sites window or onto its toolbar icon.

Full Screen and Gestures

If any app is going to remind you of an iPhone/iPad, it's Safari. Once you enter Full Screen mode by clicking the green ⊗ button at upper left (see page 160), it's almost exactly like surfing the Web on the iPad. For example:

- **Zoom in and out with pinch and spread.** That is, put two fingers on your trackpad and spread them to magnify the Web page, or pinch to zoom out. Great when the type is a little too small.

- **Magnify just a block with a two finger double-tap.** Most Web pages are subdivided into various rectangles of text and graphics. Just as on the iPhone/iPad, you can double-tap (with *two* fingers on your trackpad) to magnify only one single block of text or graphics. Repeat the process to zoom back out to regular size. (Note that this is *tapping,* not *clicking.)*

- **Use a two-finger swipe for Back and Next.** This one's really juicy. With two fingers on your trackpad, swipe left or right instead of clicking the ‹ or › buttons. The great part is that if you do this *slowly,* you pull the previous or next page onto the screen *gradually,* giving you a chance to peek at it without actually moving to it.

Tip: Each time you open Safari, it brings up whatever pages you had open last. It's part of OS X's auto-resume feature.

Scrolling

You'll rarely do more page scrolling than you do in a Web browser. Scrolling is a *constant* activity.

Fortunately, Apple gives you about 11,339 different ways to do it.

You can use the regular scroll gesture (two fingers on the trackpad). You can also press your ▲ and ▼ keys to scroll one line at a time. Page Up and Page Down scroll in full-screen increments, while Home and End whisk you to the top or bottom of the current Web page. And if your mouse has a scroll wheel, it works, too. (Hold Shift while you're rolling the wheel to scroll *horizontally.)*

But maybe the best way of all is to *tap the space bar* each time you want to see more. Press Shift-space to scroll *up*. (The space bar serves its traditional, space-making function only when the insertion point is blinking in a text box or the address bar.)

Five Ways to Magnify a Page

If it seems as though a lot of Web sites are designed with type that's too small to read, it's not just you and your aging eyes. Often, it has to do with the high resolution of today's screens, which work by packing their pixels together more tightly—and making everything look smaller.

Fortunately, Safari is well equipped to help you with this problem. In fact, it offers many solutions:

- **Enlarge the screen.** Press ⌘-plus or ⌘-minus to enlarge or reduce the entire Web page. Or use the two-finger "spread" gesture on your laptop trackpad. Or use the Zoom button, if you've added it to your toolbar. The advantage of this method is that the whole Web page's layout remains proportional.

- **Magnify a block.** Lightly double-tap (don't fully click) with *two fingers* on your trackpad to zoom into one block of text or graphics on a page, as described above.

- **Blow up just the text.** If you turn on View→Zoom Text Only, then all those shortcuts serve to magnify or shrink *only the text* on your page. Graphics remain at their original size. You're now distorting the original layout, but you're maximizing the amount of reading you can do before you have to scroll.

- **Zoom with the Control key.** Hold down the Control key and then drag two fingers up your trackpad or scroll your mouse wheel upward. That's not the same thing as the ⌘-plus or ⌘-minus tricks, which keep the window frame and menu at normal size. The Control-key zooming technique magnifies *everything*—the entire screen, menus and all. It also doesn't keep text as sharp as the ⌘-plus/⌘-minus trick.

- **Specify a minimum type size.** This may be the best option of all, because it saves you all that zooming. Open Safari→Preferences→Advanced and set the "Never use font sizes smaller than" option to, for example, 14 points. Now *every* Web page shows up with legible text. (Except a few oddballs that use weird coding to prevent text-size changing.)

Customizing the Toolbar

You can summon or dismiss individual buttons on the toolbar, customizing it to your liking (Figure 12-7).

Here's a catalog of your options:

- **Back/Forward.** Click the Back button (‹) to revisit the page you were just on, or › to return to the page you were on *before* you clicked the Back button. See the beginning of this chapter for more details.

- **iCloud Tabs** offer a way to open whatever browser windows and tabs you had open on your other Apple gadget, like an iPhone or iPad or another Mac (running OS X Mountain Lion or later). Thanks to the miracle of iCloud syncing, the last windows and tabs you had open on that other gadget (even if the gadget is turned off) show up here.

- **Share** (⬆) lets you send the current Web page to the Reading List, install it as a bookmark, or send it by email; Message, Twitter, and Facebook let you send the current Web page as a text message, a tweet, or a Facebook update with a single click. See page 239 for details.

- **Show All Tabs.** See page 451.

- **Top Sites** opens, of course, the Top Sites window (page 430).

- **Home.** Click to bring up the Web page you've designated as your home page (in the Safari→Preferences→General tab).

- **History.** Click to open the list of Web sites you've visited recently in a window—a much easier-to-navigate display than the History *menu*.

- **Sidebar** shows or hides the Sidebar, the left-side column of bookmarks, saved articles, or RSS feeds.

- **Favorites Bar.** Hides or shows the horizontal toolbar that lists your favorite bookmarks (the equivalent of choosing View→Favorites Bar).

- **AutoFill.** Click this button to make Safari fill in Web order forms with your name, address, and other information. Read on.

Figure 12-7:
To summon this toolbar-tailoring screen, choose View→Customize Toolbar. Then drag the buttons you want directly onto the address bar.

There's no way to summon text labels for these icons once they're on the toolbar. But all offer tooltip labels that you can read by pointing to the buttons without clicking.

- **Zoom.** These handy buttons make the current page's type size smaller or bigger each time you click. The keyboard shortcuts are ⌘-plus or ⌘-minus.

- **Open in Dashboard.** This icon is the key to creating Dashboard *Web clips,* as described on page 181. Click this button, and then select the part of the page you want to widgetize. It's the equivalent of the File→Open command in Dashboard.

- **Mail.** Opens a new, outgoing email message in your email program. The subject line contains the *name* of the site you were visiting; the body contains the actual Web page—not just a link, as in the olden OS X days. You can address the message, add a comment ("Re: your comment that 'no expert' recommends trampolines for children"), and send it.

- **Print.** You can add a printer icon to Safari for point-and-click paper action if you don't want to bother with ⌘-P.

Tip: Safari automatically shrinks your printouts, if necessary, by up to 10 percent, if doing so will avoid printing a second page with just one or two lines of text on it. Nice.

- **Address and Search.** Yep, it's the toolbar, where you type in the Web address you want to call up.

- **Flexible Space.** This isn't really a button. It's an invisible "tile" that you can drag between other buttons to adjust the button spacing on your toolbar.

Saved Passwords: The iCloud Keychain

Safari can remember user names, passwords, mailing addresses, and other information you type into the text boxes you encounter in your Web travels. And thanks to a glorious feature called the iCloud Keychain, Safari can even memorize your credit card details—and synchronize all of it (passwords and credit cards) with your other Apple phones, tablets, and Macs.

Memorized Contact Information

To turn on this great feature, visit the Safari→Preferences→AutoFill tab. If you turn on "Using info from my Contacts card," then whenever you're supposed to fill in your shipping address on a Web form, you can click the AutoFill button in the address bar to have Safari fill in the blanks for you automatically. (If you don't see the AutoFill button, then choose Edit→AutoFill Form to do the deed instead.)

Alternatively, just click a text box—Name, for example—and start typing. As soon as Safari recognizes a familiar scrap of your contact information, it displays a pop-up suggestion below the text box. To accept the suggestion, click it (or press the ▼ arrow key and then press Return). To decline it, press Return, or just keep typing.

Memorized Passwords

If, in Preferences, you turn on "User names and passwords," then each time you type a password into a Web page, Safari offers to memorize it for you. It's a great time-

and brain-saver. (Of course, use it with caution if you share an account on your Mac with other people.)

Turn on Other Forms if you'd like Safari to remember the terms you've typed into search engines, shopping sites, online gaming sites, and so on.

Thanks to the Passwords dialog box shown in Figure 12-8, it's easy to see all the passwords Safari has saved for you—and to delete the ones you want Safari to "forget" —for security reasons, for example.

Figure 12-8:
Choose Safari→ Preferences→ Passwords to see this list of names and passwords Safari has memorized. It's easy enough to delete one. But maybe the more useful option is "Show passwords for selected websites." After you authenticate with your account password, it shows the actual passwords for anything you click.

Auto-Filled-In Credit Cards

Safari can also store your credit card information, making it infinitely easier to buy stuff online. It's as easy as 1, 2. Figure 12-9 shows you how to store your credit cards in Safari and how to use them to buy things online.

This feature of iCloud Keychain is a lot like the popular password/credit card keeper programs 1Password and Dashlane—better, really, because it's free, and because iCloud Keychain auto-syncs your credit card information to your iPhones, iPads, and iPod Touches, too.

But in one way, it's worse: As yet another security layer, Safari doesn't memorize the security code, also known as the CVV or CV2 code, that you need to complete a credit card transaction. You have to fill that in yourself every time you buy something.

Synchronized Passwords

This is awesome: Your Mac can make up unguessable Web site passwords; fill them in automatically; and synchronize them to your other Apple gadgets, like iPhones,

iPads, iPod Touches, and other Macs. Basically, you'll never have to remember another password.

And it's not just Web site passwords, either. iCloud Keychain also memorizes your credit card information, WiFi network passwords, and online account names and passwords (Mail, Contacts, Calendar, Facebook, Twitter, LinkedIn).

Figure 12-9:
Top: Teach Safari your credit card details by choosing Preferences→ AutoFill. Click Edit to arrive at this list.

Click Add. Fill in a description for your card, the number, your name, and the expiration date. Click Done.

Bottom: Next time you're about to buy something, click inside one of the empty boxes (like Name or Credit Card Number). Safari shows this menu of your cards; click one to fill in all the boxes (except Verification Code).

Setting Up iCloud Keychain

Getting to this heavenly state, however, requires some fairly bewildering setup slogging. Apple wants to make darned sure that nobody but you is on the receiving end of this very valuable list of passwords; it would be kind of a bummer if your bank and finance passwords somehow got synced to somebody else's phone.

You probably encountered the setup steps for iCloud Keychain the first time you turned on your Mac. It's also possible that you set up your iPhone or iPad with iCloud Keychain, in which case you have only to add your Mac to the circle, as described below.

Set up the first Mac

But if this is your first iCloud Keychain setup experience, here's how it goes.

1. **Open System Preferences→iCloud. Turn on Keychain.**

 If your Mac doesn't require your password when you wake it up or log in, then OS X now recommends that you take a moment to set that up. (Otherwise, a bad guy could get in to see all your passwords.) Click either Not Now or Open Security & Privacy, and then proceed as described in Chapter 15.

 Next, the Mac asks you to supply your iCloud account password.

2. **Enter your iCloud password and click OK.**

 You're now asked to make up a new password—a security code—just for your iCloud Keychain.

POWER USERS' CLINIC

Alternatives to the Four-Digit Security Code

As you turn on the iCloud Keychain option, just when you're asked to make up a four-digit security code, there's an easy-to-overlook Advanced button. Don't overlook it.

When you click it, you're offered three other options with profound ramifications:

"Use a complex security code." The trouble with a four-digit password is, of course, that there are only 10,000 available. A really diligent thief could eventually try them all. (Well, not really; iCloud Keychain shuts you out after a certain number of wrong guesses. But just play along here.) Use this option if you'd feel more comfortable making up a longer password.

"Get a random security code" means that the Mac will make up a long, complicated password for you. Write it down and don't lose it! There's no back door; if you forget, Apple won't be able to help you. You'll have to reset your whole Keychain, losing all of your passwords in the process.

Finally, there's **"Don't create security code."**

In this scenario, there is no security code affiliated with your iCloud Keychain. Instead, you'll confirm that you're you by using another Apple product—phone, tablet, Mac.

This item is great for paranoia fans who don't want their passwords stored on Apple's iCloud servers. (Your password collection does pass *through* Apple's servers en route to your other gadgets, but they're encrypted during the transmission and then immediately deleted.) The one big downside: If you lose all your Apple gadgets, you'll have no backup of your passwords. (The security-code methods do store a backup on Apple's servers, but in an encrypted form that even Apple can't open—and it's insta-deleted if someone makes 10 unsuccessful attempts to guess the code.)

"Don't create security code" also means that you can set up additional Apple gadgets to sync with your iCloud Keychain without having to remember some code. See step 3 on page 438 for details.

Tip: If you click Advanced at this point, you're offered three alternatives to the four-digit security code. See the box on page 437.

3. **Make up a four-digit security code. Type it in; click Next. Enter it a second time, and click Next again.**

If you make up something obvious, like 0000 or 1234, you'll be scolded for your lack of creativity and offered a chance to make up something harder to guess.

Now the Mac asks you to supply a cellphone number; when you try to set up another Apple gadget to work with iCloud Keychain, Apple will send a special verification code to this phone number.

If you don't have a cellphone, you can either enter the cellphone number of somebody you trust or choose the "Don't create security code" option described in the box on page 437.

4. **Enter your cellphone number; click Done.**

You're all set. This one Mac can now auto-generate passwords for you, and your passwords are being backed up in iCloud.

But the real payoff doesn't come until you add *other* Apple gadgets to the great iCloud Keychain archipelago. That's when all your hard-won passwords are wirelessly and automatically synced to your phone, tablet, or whatever, so you don't ever have to remember them or type them. Read on.

Adding another Mac to your iCloud Keychain

To add another Mac (running OS X Mavericks or later) to your magical Keychain syncing, follow steps 1 and 2 above.

Now you're offered two ways of confirming your you-ness (Figure 12-10):

Figure 12-10:
If you opt for the Request Approval option, a message like this appears on your iPhone or iPad. You're using it to prove your authenticity instead of using the iCloud Keychain security code.

- **Request Approval.** A message appears, letting you know that a request for approval has just been sent to all your other Apple products (well, at least the ones signed in with your iCloud account). Click OK.

 And sure enough: A notification bubble now appears on your Macs and iOS 7 or 8 phones and tablets.

 If the request for approval appears on a Mac, tap View; the iCloud pane of System Preferences opens, bearing a note about another device requesting approval. Click Details; enter your iCloud password; click Allow. The deed is done.

 If the request for approval appears on an iPhone, iPad, or iPod Touch, just enter your iCloud password; click Allow. That's it.

- **Use Code.** You're asked for the four-digit security code you made up in step 3 above. Enter it, and then hit Next.

 In a moment, the phone whose number you entered in step 4 gets a text message! It bears a special message from the Apple mother ship: a six-digit verification code. Type it into the Mac, and then click OK.

You can repeat the process from additional Macs and iOS devices that you use.

Adding an iOS gadget to your iCloud Keychain

To add an iPhone, iPad, or iPod Touch (with iOS 7.0.3 or later) to the Keychain magic, open Settings→iCloud. Turn on Keychain. Turn on iCloud Keychain.

Enter your iCloud password. After a moment, you're offered an Approve with Security Code button. Tap it.

You're now asked to enter a six-digit verification code, which Apple sends to the cellphone you supplied in step 3 above.

Once you've typed that in, your new mobile gadget is part of the great syncing circle of life. Read on to find out what that means.

Auto-Generated Passwords

The problem with passwords, of course, is that they proliferate. You may visit dozens or hundreds of Web sites that require you to log in—but the security experts direly warn you not to (a) use a password that you could possibly remember, or (b) use the same password for more than one site. It's great advice, but just a little silly.

At last, though, there's a solution: Once you've turned on iCloud Keychain, Safari—both on Macs and iOS gadgets—can make up a complex, nonsensical password for you *and memorize it.* Once it's memorized, Safari can fill it in for you automatically (see Figure 12-11).

Tip: It's fine if you have more than one account per Web page—two different Gmail accounts, for example. When you log in, Safari displays a pop-up list of the different name/password combinations it knows, so you can click the one you want.

New password

Use Safari suggested password:
FK4–dzE–TN2–pTq

This password will be saved in your iCloud Keychain so it is available for AutoFill on all your devices.

Reset Password

Would you like to save this password in your iCloud Keychain for AutoFill on all your devices?

You can view and remove saved passwords in the Passwords pane of Safari preferences.

Never for This Website Not Now Save Password

Sign In

What is your e-mail address?

My e-mail address is: caseydude@icloud.com

Do you have an Amazon.com password?

○ **No, I am a new customer.**

◉ **Yes, I have a password:** ●●●●●●●●
 Forgot your password?

Sign in using our secure server ▶

Figure 12-11:
Top: Once you've turned on iCloud Keychain, clicking into any empty New Password box on a Web page makes Safari offer a suggestion like this one. Click it to make it your new password (and to make Safari memorize it).

You won't care that all your passwords are gibberish like this; the iCloud Keychain auto-syncs them to all your other gadgets, where it fills them in there, too.

Middle: Before you go on, Safari wants to know if you'd like this password passed on to all your other Apple computers and gadgets. Usually, the answer is yes, Save Password; isn't that why you went through all the rigmarole of setting up the iCloud Keychain?

Bottom: From now on, when you open a Web page that requires a name and password, Safari fills them in automatically using the telltale yellow background. If it's guessed correctly, just hit Return or "Log in" to proceed.

Tips for Better Surfing

Safari is filled with shortcuts and tricks for better speed and more pleasant surfing. For example:

The Reading List

The Reading List stores entire Web pages that you want to read later (Figure 12-12). These aren't just bookmarks (links); the Reading List downloads and stores the full contents of each page you've requested so that you can read them when you don't have an Internet connection. Better than that, actually: It stores that page *and* any other pages necessary to continue reading an article that you've flagged.

The Reading List also makes it faster to flag a Web page you like—you don't have to make up a name or a location for it, as with a bookmark. Also, the Reading List keeps track of what you've read; you can use the All/Unread buttons at the top of the list to view everything or just what you haven't yet read.

You might treat the Reading List as a list of pages you'll want to read *once* later, and use bookmarks for pages you like to revisit *frequently*.

To make matters even sweeter, iCloud synchronizes your Reading List among your Mac, iPhone, iPad, and so on (if you've turned on Safari syncing in System Preferences→iCloud). It's as though the Web always keeps your place as you move from gadget to gadget.

To add a page to the Reading List, use one of these techniques:

- **Shift-click a link.** That simple trick adds the linked page to the Reading List. You don't have to *visit* the page itself (only the link to it), or even to open the Reading List itself.

- **Click the ⊕ button.** This button appears only when you move your cursor to the left end of the address box.

- **Use the menu.** Choose Bookmarks→Add to Reading List, or press Shift-⌘-D.

- **Use the Share button.** You can also click ⬆ on the toolbar and choose Add to Reading List.

To view your saved pages, open the Sidebar (click ⬓); then click the Reading List (◯◯) tab. Or just choose View→Show Reading List Sidebar (Control-⌘-2).

To read the pages in the Reading List, you can press Option-⌘-▼ or Option-⌘-▲ to move up and down your list.

Tip: If you're reading one article in your Reading List using the Reader feature described next, and then select another article, then it, too, will appear in Reader.

Figure 12-12:
To revisit a page you've set aside in the Reading List, just click it. Screen out the pages you've already read by clicking the Unread tab at the top. Delete an entry by clicking the ⊗ button that appears at the right side when you point there, as shown here by the cursor.

The Download Manager

No browser has ever made tracking downloads simpler.

When you click a link to download something from a Web page, it *visibly* flies to the upper-right corner of the Safari window, where the Downloads button ⊕ appears. You can then monitor the progress of the download at a glance—because the Downloads button *fills up* with blue as the download completes.

As Figure 12-13 shows, you can also view and manipulate a list of everything you've downloaded recently, all without leaving the comfort of whatever page you're on.

Figure 12-13:
Click the Downloads (⊕) button to view this list of recent downloads. Double-click an icon to open the download. Drag it out of the list onto your desktop, or even onto a folder on the desktop. You can even drag it onto a Dock icon to open that file with a particular program.

Click the ⊗ button to jump to the file wherever it's sitting in the Finder. To remove an item from the list, click it and then press Delete. (The Clear button erases the whole list.)

To pause downloading, click the ⊗ button next to the download's name. Later, you can generally pick up from where you left off by clicking the Resume (⏻) button.

Tip: In Safari→Preferences→General, you can opt to have your download listings removed from the Downloads window as soon as they've been successfully downloaded, maybe for privacy reasons.

Reader

How can people read Web articles when there's Times Square blinking going on all around them? Fortunately, you'll never have to put up with that again.

The Reader button (≡) in the address/search bar is amazing. With one click (or press of Shift-⌘-R), it eliminates *everything* from the Web page you're reading except the text and photos. No ads, blinking, links, banners, promos, or anything else.

The text is also changed to a clean, clear font and size, and the background is made plain white (Figure 12-14).

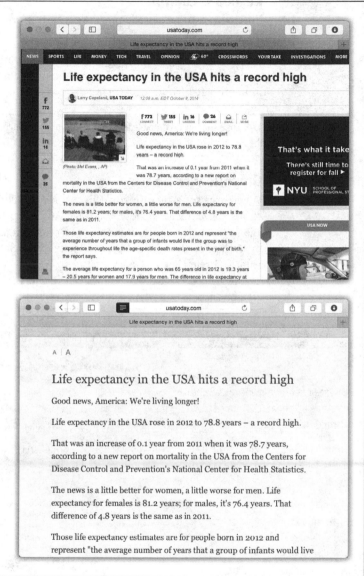

Figure 12-14:
Seriously, which way would you rather read an article? Like this (top)? Or in the calm peace of this (bottom)? Not only does Reader get rid of all the ads and clutter and blinking, it even knits multipage articles together into one seamless, scrolling page. Use the space bar or two fingers to scroll, as usual. Point near the bottom of the page to produce a palette of useful buttons: "Zoom out," "Zoom in," "Mail this page," "Print this page," and "Hide Reader."

To exit Reader, press Shift-⌘-R or press the ☰ button again. Best. Feature. Ever.

Status Bar

The status bar at the bottom of the window tells you what Safari is doing (such as "Opening page…" or "Done"). When you point to a link without clicking, the status bar also tells you which URL will open if you click it.

For those two reasons, it's a very useful strip, but it doesn't appear when you first run Safari. You have to summon it by choosing View→Show Status Bar.

Keyboard Control

Efficiency freaks generally prefer keyboard shortcuts to using the mouse, so Safari is filled with them.

Press Tab to jump from one text box or pop-up menu to the next on your Web page. Add the Option key to jump from one *link* to another (and when you highlight a link, press Return to "click" it).

Tip: For a shockingly complete list of Safari's keyboard shortcuts, open the Help menu. In the search box at the top of the menu, type *Safari shortcuts.* Wait a moment. Click "Safari shortcuts" in the list of Help topics.

Graphics Worth Saving

When you see a picture you'd like to keep, right-click (or two-finger click) it and choose Save Image to Downloads (or Add Image to iPhoto Library, or just Save Image As) from the shortcut menu. Safari stores it as a new graphics file, freed from its birthplace on the Web. (You can specify where Safari saves downloaded items on the Safari→Preferences→General tab.

Tip: You can also save a graphic to the desktop just by dragging it there, right out of the Safari window.

UP TO SPEED

Web Site Notifications

OS X can notify you when new email arrives. When a text message or phone call comes to your iPhone. When an alarm or reminder comes due.

So why shouldn't Web sites be able to notify you just as easily—when new articles are posted, for example?

They can. Often, you'll arrive on some Web site and encounter a message like the one shown here: "The website would like to send you push notifications in the Notification Center."

This is not the place to advise you on the wisdom of permitting such sites to vie for your attention during the workday. It is, however, a good idea to know how to turn these notifications on or off.

In Safari→Preferences→Notifications, you'll find a list of every site that's ever asked for such permission. And you'll see how you replied to each one: Allow or Deny.

Here you can change your mind. Or you can reset the slate by deleting some, so that you'll be asked again the next time you visit.

Above all, you can make Web sites *stop* asking for permission altogether—by turning off "Allow websites to ask for permission to send push notifications."

From now on, you won't encounter any more pushy messages asking for permission to be even pushier.

> **CNN**
>
> **The website "CNN Breaking News" would like to send you push notifications in Notification Center.**
>
> Notifications can be configured in System Preferences.
>
> [Don't Allow] [Allow]

Saving Web Pages to Disk

You don't have to be connected to the Net to read a favorite Web page; you can tuck it away for later, thanks to the newly improved Reading List feature described earlier in this chapter.

The old way of saving a page, though, is still around. You can save it to your hard drive—to archive it for good, or to send it to somebody, for example—by choosing File→Save As.

At that point, to save the *entire* page, along with all its images, movies, and so on, choose Web Archive from the Format pop-up menu. (Choose Page Source only if you intend to *edit* the raw HTML Web documents and repost them, or if you just want to study the underlying code.)

Tip: When you buy something online, don't waste paper by printing out the "This is your receipt" page. Instead, choose File→Print and, from the PDF pop-up button, choose Save PDF to Web Receipts Folder. Safari saves the page as a PDF file into a tidy folder (in your Home→Documents folder) called Web Receipts. Nice touch!

Sending a Page to a Friend

Safari provides two ways of telling a friend about the page you're looking at. You might find that useful when you come across a particularly interesting news story, op-ed piece, or burrito recipe.

- **The send-the-whole-page method.** While looking at a page, click 🖹 and choose Email This Page. You open a new Mail message with a copy of the *actual* Web page in the body. Address the message and click Send.

- **The send-a-link method.** To send just a *link* to the page you're looking at, install the Mail button (✉) onto the toolbar, as described on page 382. When you click it, Safari prepares an outgoing mail message containing only the *link* to the page you're on. Then proceed as usual, addressing the message and clicking Send.

 Links take only a split second for your recipient to download, and they're guaranteed to display properly in all email programs. All your recipients have to do is click the link to open it in their Web browsers.

Tip: Or just press Shift-⌘-I. That keystroke sends a link to an outgoing mail message.

By the way, here's a nice Yosemite touch: At the *bottom* of the 🖹 menu, you see the names of people to whom you've recently sent Web pages, and by which method. For example, you might see "Casey Robin, email" or "Kelly Switt, Messages." Those shortcuts make it incredibly easy to send more pages the same way, to the same people, again later.

Expanding Web Forms

If the customer-service comment form on that corporate Web site doesn't give you enough room to rant properly, you can resize the text box right on the page—a *very* welcome feature. Figure 12-15 tells all.

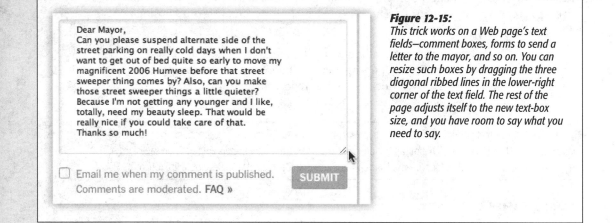

Dear Mayor,
Can you please suspend alternate side of the street parking on really cold days when I don't want to get out of bed quite so early to move my magnificent 2006 Humvee before that street sweeper thing comes by? Also, can you make those street sweeper things a little quieter? Because I'm not getting any younger and I like, totally, need my beauty sleep. That would be really nice if you could take care of that. Thanks so much!

☐ Email me when my comment is published.
Comments are moderated. FAQ »

SUBMIT

Figure 12-15:
This trick works on a Web page's text fields—comment boxes, forms to send a letter to the mayor, and so on. You can resize such boxes by dragging the three diagonal ribbed lines in the lower-right corner of the text field. The rest of the page adjusts itself to the new text-box size, and you have room to say what you need to say.

Designate Your Start Page

What's the first thing you see when you open Safari? Is it the Apple news Web site? Is it the Top Sites display (Figure 12-6)?

Actually, that's up to you.

Choose Safari→Preferences→General tab. Here the "New windows open with" pop-up menu offers choices like these:

- **Top Sites.** The Favorites view/Top Sites screen (page 430) makes a great starting point.

- **Homepage.** If you choose this option, then Safari will open up with whatever page you've specified in the "Homepage" box. Google—or its news page, *http://news. google.com*—is a good starting place. So is your favorite newspaper home page, or maybe *www.dilbert.com* for today's Dilbert cartoon.

 If you're already *on* the page you like, just click Set to Current Page.

- **Empty Page.** Some people prefer this setup, which makes Safari load very quickly when you first open it. Once this empty window opens, *then* you can tell the browser where you want to go today.

- **Same Page** opens a new window that's a duplicate of whatever window you just had open.

Note: A nearly identical pop-up menu is available for "New tabs open with." That is, you can specify one starter-page preference for new *tabs,* and another for new *windows.*

Finding Text on Web Pages

The address/search bar can help you find Web sites that match your keywords. But some pages are so long, dense, or poorly designed that finding the words *on* the page needs a whole 'nother search engine. Fortunately, Safari's search-within-the-page function shines a light on the word or phrase you're seeking.

To use it, press ⌘-F and then type your search word into the Find box (Figure 12-16). As Safari locates the word or words, it displays them within a bright-yellow box and dims the background of the rest of the page. The Find bar also tells you how many times the word or phrase occurs on the page; you can jump to each instance. Click the ⊗ to start over with new search terms, or click Done to close the Find box and return to your normal browsing activity.

Tip: When you use the Find command, are you looking for words on the page that *begin* with your search term, or that contain it *anywhere?* You can specify. Click the very tiny 🔍 in the search box and choose either Contains or Starts With from the very tiny pop-up menu.

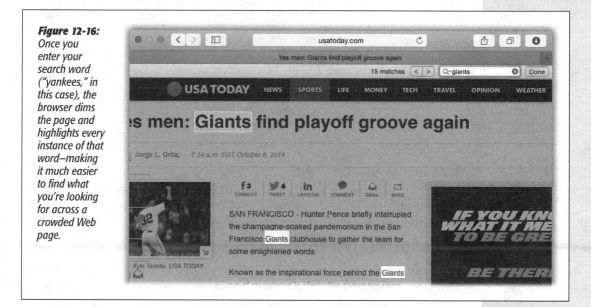

Figure 12-16:
Once you enter your search word ("yankees," in this case), the browser dims the page and highlights every instance of that word—making it much easier to find what you're looking for across a crowded Web page.

The History Menu

The History menu lists the Web sites you've visited in the past week or so, neatly organized into subfolders like Earlier Today and Yesterday. (A similar menu appears when you click *and hold* the ◄ or ► button.) These are great features if you can't recall the URL for a Web site you remember having visited recently.

Tip: See Safari's Help menu? It features a search box that lets you search all the *menu commands* in Safari—including Safari's History menu. That's just a *crazy* powerful feature. It means you can re-find a site without having to hunt through all the History submenus manually; just search for a word you remember in the title.

PDF Pages Online

PDF files are all over the Web as, among other things, forms to download, online brochures, and scanned book pages. But they aren't always especially readable in a browser window.

Unless, that is, you're using Safari. The next time you're squinting at a PDF in a window, point to the bottom edge of the document; you'll see a toolbar like the one in Figure 12-17 appear. With these four icons, you can zoom out, zoom in, open the file in Preview, or save the PDF file to your Downloads folder.

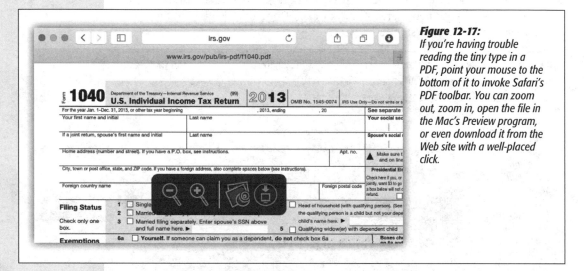

Figure 12-17:
If you're having trouble reading the tiny type in a PDF, point your mouse to the bottom of it to invoke Safari's PDF toolbar. You can zoom out, zoom in, open the file in the Mac's Preview program, or even download it from the Web site with a well-placed click.

Shared Links and RSS Feeds

You now know that when you click the ⬜ button, the Sidebar opens. As you also know now, the Sidebar offers three tabs at the top. The first displays your bookmarks; the second displays pages you've added to your Reading List.

The third, labeled @, takes some explaining (Figure 12-18).

It's a list of tweets and posts from Twitter and LinkedIn. (You can jump directly to this list by choosing View→Show Shared Links Sidebar, or pressing Control-⌘-3.) The idea is to make it easier for you to explore sites that your Twitter friends are recommending; all their Web finds are collected in one place.

These aren't just any tweets and posts. They're items that contain Web links. ("Hey guys—here's an unbelievable article about kitten gymnastics," for example.) Apple figured, instead of making you bop back and forth from your Twitter or LinkedIn program to Safari, why not extract every single tweet or message that contains a link and consolidate them in one place?

You don't have to click the link itself in these tweets; just click anywhere on the tweet. The corresponding link opens in the main part of the Safari window.

There's no indication as to which ones you've seen already. There's no way to delete one. And they don't update automatically as new tweets come along. (You have to choose View→Update Shared Links.)

There is one nifty trick, though: Right-click (or two-finger click) any item in the Shared Links list. You get some useful commands in the shortcut menu: to retweet something, to view it on Twitter.com or LinkedIn.com, and so on.

Figure 12-18:
Your RSS blurbs (middle) appear mixed in with all your Twitter links (left). That's not ideal, especially if there are hundreds of Twitter links—but at least you'll never be without a place to check for interesting stuff to read. To delete a subscription, click Subscriptions; click the ⊗ next to the subscription's name (right).

RSS subscriptions

At the bottom of the Shared Links pane, Yosemite offers a new button called Subscriptions. It's a reference to *RSS feeds*, which are something like subscriptions to Web sites. You don't have to remember to go visit your favorite blogs or news sites; notification blurbs about their newly posted articles come to you.

Here's the procedure:

1. **In Safari, open a site that offers an RSS feed.**

 News sites of all kinds offer RSS feeds (*nytimes.com, usatoday.com, engadget.com, yahootech.com,* and so on).

2. **Subscribe to it.**

 To do that, click Subscriptions, and then Add Feed.

3. **Read.**

When you want to see what's new, open the Sidebar, and then click @. Blurbs representing newly posted stories appear on the @ tab (Figure 12-18); click one to read it.

Tabbed Browsing

Beloved by hard-core surfers the world over, *tabbed browsing* is a way to keep a bunch of Web pages open simultaneously—in a single, neat window. Figure 12-19 illustrates.

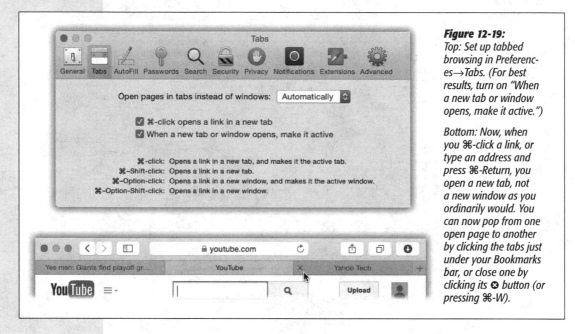

Figure 12-19:

Top: Set up tabbed browsing in Preferences→Tabs. (For best results, turn on "When a new tab or window opens, make it active.")

Bottom: Now, when you ⌘-click a link, or type an address and press ⌘-Return, you open a new tab, not a new window as you ordinarily would. You can now pop from one open page to another by clicking the tabs just under your Bookmarks bar, or close one by clicking its ⊗ button (or pressing ⌘-W).

Turning on tabbed browsing unlocks a whole raft of Safari shortcuts and tricks, which are just the sort of thing power surfers gulp down like Gatorade:

- **If there's a certain set of Web sites you like to visit daily,** put the bookmarks into one folder, using Bookmarks→Add Bookmark Folder and the Bookmarks organizer window. You can then load all of them into a single tabbed window, simply by selecting the resulting "folder" in the Bookmarks menu—or the Bookmarks bar—and choosing Open in Tabs from the submenu.

 The beauty of this arrangement is that you can start reading the first Web page while all the others load into their own tabs in the background.

- **A variation on a theme:** When you have a bunch of pages open in tabs, you can drag the tabs across the window to rearrange the order. When you have them the way you want them, right-click (or two-finger click) a tab and then choose "Add Bookmark for These [*number*] Tabs" from the shortcut menu. You can save your tabs to the Bookmarks bar and load all those pages with one click.

- **If you Option-click a tab's ⊗ button,** you close all the tabs *except* the one you clicked. The same thing happens if you hold down Option and choose File→Close Other Tabs, or if you press Option-⌘-W.

- **If you Option-⌘-click a link,** it opens in a separate window, rather than in a new tab. (When tabbed browsing is turned *off,* just ⌘-click a link to open a new window.)

- If you find yourself with a bunch of separate browser windows all over your screen, you can neatly consolidate them into one nicely tabbed Safari window by choosing Window→Merge All Windows.

- **If you ⌘-click a link,** Safari opens that page in a tab *behind* the one you're reading. That's a fantastic trick when you're reading a Web page and see a reference you want to set aside for reading next, but you don't want to interrupt whatever you're reading now.

- **If you have a lot of tabs open on your laptop**—so many that they don't all fit and some of them are getting stacked up at the right end—check out this new Yosemite trick: You can scroll through the open tabs on your trackpad. Position the cursor on the tab bar, and then swipe horizontally with two fingers.

Tab View

In the olden days, the only indication you had of your open tab collection was pieces of their names, as revealed in the tab titles across the top of your Safari window. Now, however, there's a much more visual way to survey your tab domain: Tab view.

To see these miniatures of all your open tabs, you can click the Show All Tabs button on the toolbar (⧉)—or how about this? Just pinch two fingers on your trackpad. Figure 12-20 explains all.

Tip: Once you've opened Tab view, you can perform a cool new trick: You can search all the open tabs at once (either for words in the Web page's names, or text in their addresses). You don't have to click into any search box first; just type. As you type, Safari hides all but the matching tabs.

iCloud tabs

At the bottom of Show All Tabs view (Figure 12-20), a special treat awaits: A list of whatever browser windows and tabs you had open on your *other* Apple gadgets, like iPhones or iPads. Thanks to the miracle of iCloud syncing, the last windows and tabs you had open on that other gadget (even if the gadget is turned off) show up here.

The concept is to unify your Macs and i-gadgets into one glorious, seamless Web-browsing experience. You're reading three browser windows and tabs on your phone—why not resume on the big screen when you get home and sit down in front of your Mac?

Amazingly enough, you can even *close* the tabs and windows on your other gadgets, by remote control—by clicking the ⊗ button next to each one.

You won't see these tabs unless the Macs have OS X Mountain Lion or later. And, of course, Safari has to be turned on in System Preferences→iCloud on the Mac, or Settings→iCloud on the phone or tablet.

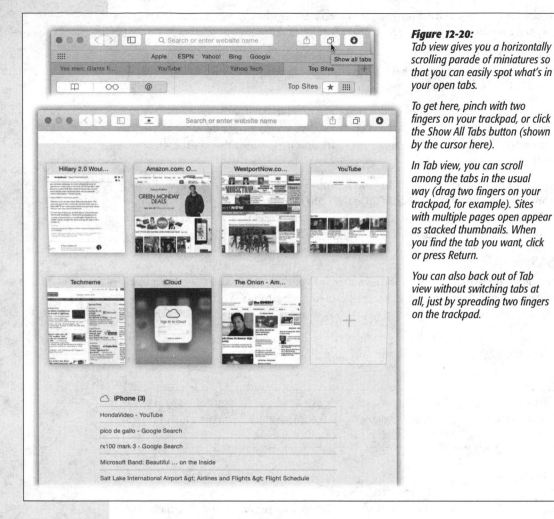

Figure 12-20:
Tab view gives you a horizontally scrolling parade of miniatures so that you can easily spot what's in your open tabs.

To get here, pinch with two fingers on your trackpad, or click the Show All Tabs button (shown by the cursor here).

In Tab view, you can scroll among the tabs in the usual way (drag two fingers on your trackpad, for example). Sites with multiple pages open appear as stacked thumbnails. When you find the tab you want, click or press Return.

You can also back out of Tab view without switching tabs at all, just by spreading two fingers on the trackpad.

Privacy and Security Features

Every year, there's another headline about some break-in where millions of credit card numbers are stolen by a hacker, sending panic into the hearts of the world's innocent Web audiences. In OS X, Apple strikes back with some very clever privacy and security features indeed.

Erasing Your History

Some people find it creepy that Safari maintains a complete list of every Web site they've seen recently, right there in plain view of any family member or coworker who wanders by.

To delete just one particularly incriminating History listing, choose History→Show History. In the resulting organizer window, highlight the offending address, and then press your Delete key. Choose History→Hide History to return to normal browsing. You've just rewritten History!

Or, to erase the entire History menu, choose History→Clear History and Website Data. In the resulting box, you can specify that you want to erase only the *last hour's* worth of history, only *today's* history, the last *two days'* worth—or your *entire* history.

Of course, the History list isn't the only set of footprints you leave as you surf. But the Clear History and Website Data command erases all other shreds of your activities: any cookies (Web-page preference files) you've accumulated, your list of past downloads, the cache files (bits of the Web pages that a browser stores on your hard drive to save time when you return to the page they came from), and so on. This is good information to know; after all, you might be nominated to the Supreme Court someday.

Private Browsing

Of course, that's a lot of work just to cover your tracks; it also erases a lot of valuable cookies, passwords, and History entries you'd probably like to keep. Is all that really necessary just so you can duck in for an occasional look at the Hot Bods of the Midwestern Tax Preparers' Association Web site?

No, it's not. A feature called *private browsing* lets you surf without adding any pages to your History list, searches to your Google search suggestions, passwords to Safari's saved password list, or autofill entries to Safari's memory. (Apple says this feature is intended for use at public Macs, where you don't want to reveal anything personal to subsequent visitors. Ha!)

The trick is to choose File→New Private Window *before* you open the naughty site. A banner across the top of your new private window explains what's happening: Within this window, Safari records nothing while you surf. When you're ready to browse "publicly" again, just close the window.

In other words, what happens in Private Browsing stays in Private Browsing.

Cookie Control—and Privacy Control

Cookies are something like Web page preference files. Certain Web sites—particularly commercial ones like Amazon.com—deposit them on your hard drive like little bookmarks so that they'll remember you the next time you visit.

Most cookies are perfectly innocuous—and, in fact, are helpful, because they help Web sites remember your tastes, your name, and so on. But fear is widespread, and the media fan the flames with tales of sinister cookies that track your movements on the Web. If you're worried about invasions of privacy, Safari is ready to protect you.

Choose Safari→Preferences→Privacy tab, where your cookie preference settings away. "Always block" means no cookies can come in, and no cookie information can go out. You'll have to re-enter your information upon every visit to every Web page.

See Figure 12-21 for some more reasonable choices.

Figure 12-21:
"Allow from websites I visit" accepts cookies from sites you want to visit but blocks cookies deposited on your hard drive by sites you're not actually visiting—cookies that an especially evil banner ad gives you, for example. "Allow from current website only," new in Yosemite, is even more restrictive.

The Details button reveals the complete list of all your cookies, and you can delete the scary ones. While you're in there, notice that there's other stuff Web sites have dumped onto your Mac. There are things like cache files and local storage files (data that Web applications leave behind on your hard drive). All of it is available for your removal with a click on the Remove All Website Data button.

Also while you're in this box: "Website use of location services" controls the behavior of Web sites that want to know your location and tailor their presentation accordingly. Do you want to be asked just once, once a day, or never?

"Ask websites not to track me" signs you up for an online "Do not track" program. The problem is that this program is voluntary—and the sleazy operators just ignore it.

Stifle Pop-Ups and Pop-Unders

The world's smarmiest advertisers inundate us with *pop-up* and *pop-under* ads—nasty little windows that appear in front of the browser window or, worse, behind it, waiting to jump out the moment you close your current window. If this kind of thing is driving you crazy, choose Safari→Preferences→Security→Block Pop-Up Windows. It's a war out there—but at least you now have some ammunition.

Tip: This feature doesn't block windows that appear when you *click a link*—only those that appear unbidden.

Messages

Somewhere between email and the telephone lies the joyous communication tool called instant messaging. Plenty of IM programs run on the Mac, but OS X comes with its very own instant messenger program called Messages. It's built right into the system and ready to connect to your friends on the iCloud, Yahoo, AIM, Jabber, Facebook, or Google Talk networks.

This chapter covers how to use Messages to communicate by video, audio, and text with your online pals.

Welcome to Messages

Messages does eight things very well:

- **Instant messaging.** Instant messaging combines the privacy of email and the immediacy of the phone. You type messages in a chat window, and your friends type back to you in real time.

- **Unified chat/text messages with phones (iMessages).** This is huge. If you and your conversation partner both have iCloud accounts, then you both can move freely from phone to tablet to Mac. Your conversation appears in real time on all your gadgets simultaneously. If you started texting someone on the train home, you can sit down at your Mac and open Messages—and pick up right from where you left off.

The messages, which Apple calls iMessages, are a lot more flexible than regular text messages. They can be much longer than 160 characters. They can include photos, movies, or other kinds of files. They give you feedback that lets you know when a message has arrived on the recipient's gadget.

And they don't count as text messages. They're routed through the Internet rather than the cellphone voice network. As far as your cellphone company is concerned, you're not texting at all, and therefore you don't have to pay for a texting plan.

- **Send text messages.** If you have an iPhone, you can also exchange text messages with *any* cellphone—from Messages, while seated at your *Mac*. That's a mind-bending violation of the usual rules that confine text messages to cellphones only.

- **Send audio clips.** Instead of just typing a line or two to somebody, you can speak it. That short recording winds up on the other person's Mac, iPhone, or iPad. It's like leaving a voicemail.

- **Free long distance.** You and a buddy can also chat *out loud,* by talking, using the Internet as a free long-distance phone. Wait, not just the two of you—the *10* of you, thanks to Messages' party-line feature.

- **Free videoconferencing.** If you and your buddies all have fast Internet connections and cameras like the ones built into most Mac models, then up to four participants can join in *video* chats, all onscreen at once, no matter where they happen to be in the world. This jaw-dropping visual stunt can bring distant collaborators face to face without plane tickets—and it costs about $99,900 less than professional videoconferencing gear.

- **File transfers.** Got an album of high-quality photos or a giant presentation file that's too big to send by email? Forget about using some online file-transfer service or networked server; you can drag that monster file directly to your buddy's Mac, through Messages, for a direct machine-to-machine transfer. (It lands in the other Mac's Downloads folder.)

- **Screen sharing.** Next time some parents or neighbors are throwing themselves upon your mercy for tech support, remember this: Messages lets you see their screen, and even control it, from across the Internet. Or you can volunteer your own screen for sharing, so you can demonstrate things to them.

More on iMessages

As hinted above, Messages is your gateway to Apple's own chat network, called iMessages. They require that both you and your chat partner have iCloud accounts (Chapter 10).

iMessages are a lot like text messages on cellphones, except:

- They're unlimited and free.

- There's almost no length limit.

- They can include photos, videos, and other huge files.

- They can go to Macs, iPhones, *and* tablets—and, in fact, they appear simultaneously on all of yours.

- Unlike in traditional chat, your pal doesn't have to be online to get your message. An iMessage will be there when he turns his gadget on again.

Setting Up Messages

When you open Messages for the first time, you're invited to enter (or sign up for) your iCloud or Apple account. Take the opportunity to set this up; you'll be glad you did.

If you click Not Now (and then click Skip in the "Are you sure?" box), then you're offered the chance to sign in to a different chat service (Figure 13-1):

Figure 13-1:
The first time you open Messages, you're supposed to enter your Apple ID (your iCloud, .mac, or .me address) and password. That way, you can join in the thrill of iMessaging.

You can also set up your account for other popular chat networks.

- **Google, Yahoo, AOL.** Click your choice, click Continue, and then enter your name and password. (If you're an America Online member, then your existing screen name and password work for AIM purposes.) Click Set Up.

- **Jabber.** Click "Other messages account." On the next screen, from the pop-up menu, choose Jabber. Enter your Jabber name and password, and then click Create.

Note: Jabber is a chat network whose key virtue is its *open-source* origins. In other words, it wasn't masterminded by some corporate media behemoth; it's an all-volunteer effort, joined by programmers all over the world. There's no one Jabber chat program (like Yahoo Messenger). There are dozens, available for OS X, Windows, Linux, Unix, iPhone, and so on. They can all chat with one another across the Internet in one glorious frenzy of typing.

- **Facebook.** Yes, you can use Messages to chat with other people on Facebook, using Facebook's own message service.

 The trick is to follow the steps above for entering a Jabber account. But in the Account Name box, type your Facebook name (with a period instead of a space),

followed by *@chat.facebook.com*. So if your name is Casey Robin, you'd type *casey. robin@chat.facebook.com.*

Enter your Facebook password. Leave everything else alone. Click Create.

If you don't have an account of those types, it's easy enough to get one. Sign up for a free account at the relevant company's Web site (at *gmail.com* or *yahoo.com*, for example).

You can also input account information later—the setup assistant isn't your only opportunity. You can do it in either of two places:

• In System Preferences, click Internet Accounts, described on page 600.

• In Messages, choose Messages→Preferences, click the Accounts button, and click the + button.

Once you've set up your accounts, you can activate or deactivate them in Messages→ Preferences→Accounts. You might want to deactivate an account when, for example, you don't want to be bugged by the rabble on that particular service.

Oh—and if you're setting up your iCloud account, in readiness for all that iMessages goodness, you have a few more options (Figure 13-2).

Figure 13-2:
You have to specify an email address to anchor your iMessages life. You can specify more than one, actually (click the + button under "You can be reached for messages at"). If you do that, you should also choose one that Messages will use as your return address (the "Caller ID" address).

Turn on "Enable this account" to make it work. Turn on "Send read receipts" if you want your correspondents to know when you've read their messages.

Note: If you're on AOL's AIM service or Yahoo's Messenger service, why would you want to use Messages instead of those companies' dedicated chat programs? Easy: Because Messages is a nice, cleanly designed program that's free of advertisements, chatbots, and clunky interface elements.

On the other hand, there are some great chat apps that Messages can't touch. One is the popular Adium, a single program that works with Messages' chat services and many others, including ICQ. And then, of course, there's Skype, the granddaddy of all chat programs, which offers audio and video chats like Messages, but also connects to Skype running on Windows, iPhones, Android phones, and so on.

The Buddy List

As noted above, most chats begin when you choose a correspondent's name from your Contacts.

But Messages also comes with a traditional chat-program Buddy List. It's like an address book whose names appear *only* in Messages—for people you don't need cluttering up your main Contacts list (Figure 13-3).

It's a *unified* Buddies list, too. It houses the chat "addresses" for all your chat partners from all the different chat services, in a single list.

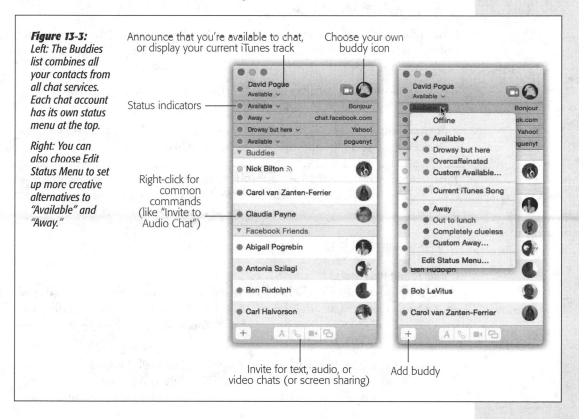

Figure 13-3:
Left: The Buddies list combines all your contacts from all chat services. Each chat account has its own status menu at the top.

Right: You can also choose Edit Status Menu to set up more creative alternatives to "Available" and "Away."

Announce that you're available to chat, or display your current iTunes track

Choose your own buddy icon

Status indicators

Right-click for common commands (like "Invite to Audio Chat")

Invite for text, audio, or video chats (or screen sharing)

Add buddy

Tip: If you'd prefer that each service (AIM, Yahoo, and so on) had its own separate buddy list window, then choose Messages→Preferences→General; turn off "Show all my accounts in one list." Now you can use the Window menu to reveal each service's buddy list separately.

A tiny icon appears next to each name in your list, indicating that person's availability to chat—and what kinds of multimedia chats are available. A phone icon means "equipped for an audio chat"; a camcorder means "equipped for a video chat." The little colored dots mean "available" (green), "away" (red), "idle" (orange), and "undetermined—probably on a cellphone" (gray). A little ᴧ icon means you're chatting with someone on a cellphone.

Filling your buddy list

If you don't see your buddy list when you open Messages (Figure 13-3), choose Window→Buddies.

Adding a buddy to this list entails knowing that person's account name/address (for example, *bunnyface23@aim.com* or *harold1968@yahoo.com*).

Once you have it, click the + in the bottom-left corner of the Buddies window; from the shortcut menu, click Add Buddy.

Down slides a sheet attached to the buddy list window, offering a window into your Contacts program (Chapter 11). Using the "Add to" pop-up menu, choose the service you want to use for chatting with this person (Yahoo, Google, AIM, whatever).

If your companion's chat address is already in Contacts, then double-click the person's name, or click it and then click Add.

If not, then enter your pal's chat address in "Account name." Enter this person's real first and last names in the appropriate boxes, if you like.

Tip: Just to make things more complicated—er, flexible—Messages lets you organize buddies into groups, like Work, Family, and Fantasy Badminton League. Use the "Add to group" pop-up menu here to specify which group you want—or just choose Buddies to leave the new person in the general sloshing bucket of humanity.

When everything looks good, click Add.

Broadcasting your status

Using the pop-up menu just below your name (Figure 13-3, right), you can display your current mental status to *other* people's chat programs. You can announce that you're Available, Away, On the Phone, Drunk, and so on. (You have to choose Edit Status Menu for that last one.)

Better yet, if you have music playing in iTunes, you can tell the world what you're listening to by choosing Current iTunes Song. (Your buddy can even click that song's name to open its screen on the iTunes Store, all for instant purchase gratification.)

For some people, by far the juiciest status option is Invisible (available for me.com and AIM accounts only). It's like a *Star Trek* cloaking device for your onscreen presence. Great for stalkers!

Tip: You can also add a Messages menulet to the top of your screen. Choose Messages→Preferences→ General, and turn on "Show status in menu bar." From now on, you can change your status even when Messages isn't running. If other people see you as anything besides Offline or Invisible, they can send you a message—and Messages will open automatically.

Sorting and sizing your friends

In View→Sort Buddies, you can rearrange your buddies as they're listed in the buddy list (by availability, name, or manually—drag the names up and down).

If you want a more space-efficient view of your buddy list, go to the View menu and turn off Show Buddy Pictures, Show Audio Status, or Show Video Status. You can turn off Buddy Groups here as well, if you'd prefer to see your buddies in one undivided list.

Bonjour buddies

See the heading in the buddy list called Bonjour? You can't add names to your Bonjour list; anyone who's on the network and running Messages appears there automatically.

Bonjour is a slick network-recognition technology. It means that you can communicate with other Macs on your own office network without signing up for any account at all—and without being online.

This is a terrific feature when you're sitting around a conference table, idly chatting with colleagues using your wireless laptop (and the boss thinks you're taking notes). It's also handy when you want to type little messages throughout the day to a family member downstairs, or to a roommate 15 feet away.

Chatting and videoconferencing work identically on all of these networks. Keep that in mind as you read the following pages.

Let the Chat Begin

If you've ever corresponded with someone in Messages before, you'll probably see that person's name in the left-side list of conversations. (Or, if you've got a *lot* of conversations listed there, you can use the search box above the list to find that person.) Click the name and then start typing into the message box. The "conversation" with that person continues, even if the last exchange was months or years ago.

To start chatting with someone you've never corresponded with before, click the Compose button (✎) next to the search box. The To: blank appears.

As you type your buddy's name into it, Messages sprouts a list of matching names from your Contacts. (If this person isn't *in* your Contacts, see "The Buddy List" on page 459.)

Some of them probably feature a blue speech bubble (●). Those are people with iCloud accounts—with whom you can exchange iMessages.

Note: An iMessage address can be either an email address or a phone number. Most people register both of those data bits as part of their iMessages setup, so that any message you send arrives on all your correspondent's Apple gadgets at once.

You can also click the ⊕ button to get a pop-up version of your Contacts, complete with a search bar at the top.

Once you've selected your lucky conversation partner(s), just type what you want to say into the message box at the bottom of the window. As the two of you correspond, the conversation appears in speech bubbles, scrolling up like a screenplay, making it easy to identify who said what—and to scroll back up to see what someone said earlier. (See Figure 13-4.)

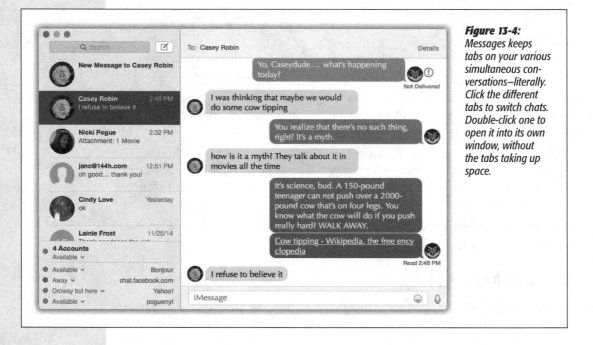

Figure 13-4:
Messages keeps tabs on your various simultaneous conversations—literally. Click the different tabs to switch chats. Double-click one to open it into its own window, without the tabs taking up space.

If This Is an iMessage Chat

If that box says iMessage in faint lettering, then you've selected a fellow iCloud member, and you'll get a few extra benefits as you chat. You can type outrageously long messages; you can use fonts and colors; you can use the smiley-face pop-up menu (at the right end of the typing box) to insert emoticons and smileys.

You can even drag photos, movies, or other files (up to 100 megabytes!) into the typing box. They'll show up on the other guy's Mac, phone, or tablet just fine.

Now, if you have multiple Apple gadgets, and you've set up your iMessages email address or phone number identically in the Settings or System Preferences of each one, then some mind-boggling stuff might start to happen. Your conversation appears simultaneously on all the gadgets.

That's extremely useful, because it means that you can (for example) start texting on your phone when you're out and about, and pick up seamlessly on your Mac when you get home, enjoying the real keyboard and big screen.

If you find that typing is losing too much emotional nuance, you can jump into a video call at any point—just click Details at the upper right of the Messages window, and then click ◻◁. The FaceTime app opens, and you can proceed as described on page 643.

As you get used to iMessages, you'll discover their advantages over regular text messages. For example, the tiny word "received" appears beneath any message you send to let you know that your recipient's gadget has received it. If the recipient has turned on "Send read receipts" (Figure 13-2), you'll even see the word "read" to let you know that the person has actually *read* the message.

If you're in a back-and-forth conversation, the text messages show up on a single screen, scrolling up in conversation balloons like a chat session. While the other guy is typing, you see "…" in his balloon, so you know he's working on a response and not just ignoring you.

Finally, Messages means that you can *keep* your text messages. They're not locked onto your phone, like regular text messages, and they don't scroll away forever, like regular text messages. You can archive them, search them, copy and paste them, print them, forward them, and so on.

GEM IN THE ROUGH

The Messages Chat Room

If everyone you want to include is a member of the same service, like Jabber, Yahoo, or me.com/AIM, there's another way to go about starting a group chat: Create a chat room. The advantage here is that you don't have to invite each member manually; you can just publicize the name of the room, and people can drop in at the appropriate time.

To create such a room, choose File→Go to Chat Room. Use the Account pop-up menu to specify which service you want, and then type a name for your room. Click Add.

Turn on Autojoin, if you like (it means "Enter this room automatically whenever I'm online with that chat service"). Click Go. You're in!

Other people can enter your secret room by choosing File→ Go to Chat Room, choosing the appropriate chat service, typing the room name, and then clicking Go.

If they don't know about the room, you can invite them yourself. Choose View→Show Chat Participants, click +, and then choose a buddy.

Messages blurs the line between text messages, chats, and email. And it gives birth to this frequently asked question: "Are you on the phone or the Mac?" Now there's no way to know.

They Invite You

If someone invites *you* to chat, a notification appears. If you point to it in time, you get a Reply button; see Figure 13-5.

Figure 13-5:
When someone messages you, a bubble like this appears in the top-right corner of your screen.

If you point to it before it vanishes, the Reply button appears, as shown here.

If you click it, you can type a quick response right there in the notification window, without having to fire up Messages at all (bottom).

If you click the notification instead, Messages opens automatically; click in the message box at the bottom and type your witty reply.

Tip: If you're getting hassled by someone on AIM or me.com, click his name in the buddy list, or in the window containing the invitation, and choose Buddies→Block Person. If the person isn't online at the time, go to Messages→Preferences→Accounts→Security and then click the button for "Block specific people." Click the Edit List button, and then type in the screen name of the person you want out of your IM life. (The other chat network types don't offer security options like this.)

Text Chats

A typed chat works like this: Each time you or your chat partner types something and then presses Return, the text appears on both of your screens.

Messages displays each typed comment next to an icon, which can be any of these three things:

- **A picture the other person added.** If the buddy added her own picture—to her own copy of Messages, a Jabber program, AOL Instant Messenger, or Yahoo Mes-

senger—then it will be transmitted to you, appearing automatically in the chat window. Cool!

- **A picture you added.** If you've added a picture of that person to the buddy list or to Contacts, you see it here instead. (After all, your vision of what somebody looks like may not match his own self-image.)

- **Generic.** If nobody's done any icon dragging of any sort, you get a generic silhouette icon.

To choose a graphic to use as your own icon, click the round picture to the right of your own name at the top of the buddy list. From the pop-up palette, you can choose, as your avatar, any of Apple's Defaults (nature shots), Recents (chat photos you've used recently), My Photo Stream (your own recently taken pictures), Faces (if you've set this feature up in iPhoto), or Camera (take a new picture right now).

In most cases, you're offered an Edit button. It opens a little adjustment window where you can fiddle with the size and centering of your headshot.

Feel free to build an array of graphics to represent yourself—and to change them in midchat, using this pop-up palette, to the delight or confusion of your conversation partner.

In-Chat Fun

Typing isn't the only thing you can do during a chat. You can also perform any of these stunts:

- **Format your text.** You can press ⌘-B or ⌘-I to make your next typed utterance bold or italic. Or change your color or font by choosing Format→Show Colors or Format→Show Fonts, which summons the standard OS X color or font palettes. (If you use some weird font that your chat partners don't have installed, then they won't see the same typeface.)

- **Insert a smiley.** When you choose a face (like Undecided, Angry, or Frown) from this quick-access menu of smiley options (at the right end of the text-reply box), Messages inserts it as a graphic into your response.

 On the other hand, if you know the correct symbols to produce smileys—typing :) produces a yellow happy face, for example, and <3 produces a red heart—you can save time by typing them instead of using the pop-up menu. Messages converts them into smiley icons on the fly, as soon as you send your reply.

- **Send a file.** Drag a file's icon from the Finder into the box where you normally type. (This trick works well with pictures and movies, because your conversation partner sees them right in his Messages window. And it can handle files as big as 100 megabytes.)

- **Adjust the type size.** Use the commands in the View menu to make all type larger or smaller—or just press ⌘-plus or ⌘-minus.

- **Get Info on someone.** If you click a name in your buddy list and then choose Buddies→Show Info, you get a little Info window about your buddy where you can edit her name, email address, and picture. (If you change the picture here, you'll see it instead of the graphic your buddy chose for herself.)

- **Send a sound clip.** A button appears whenever you're exchanging iMessages with a fellow Apple gadget owner: a 🎤 button to the right of the typing box. It lets you quickly shoot over an audio bite as easily as you'd type something.

Just click the 🎤, say what you want to say, and then click the square Stop button. Now you can play it back (▶), Cancel it, or Send it.

What you said is instantly transmitted to your buddy as an audio recording.

If the recipient has an iPhone with iOS 8 or later, he can listen just by lifting the phone to his head. And then, get this: To reply, he doesn't have to touch anything or look at the screen, either. He just holds the phone to his head again and speaks! Once he lowers the phone, his recording shoots back to you.

Sometimes, an audio recording is just better than a typed message, especially when music, children, animals, or a lot of emotion in your voice are involved.

Tip: Audio eats up a lot more disk space than text. If you do a lot of audio messaging, then, over time, those audio snippets can fill up your storage. That's why Messages comes set to delete each audio message 2 minutes after you send it—unless you click Keep within that window.

- **See all the attachments.** This one's really cool; see Figure 13-6.

Figure 13-6:
If you click the Details button at the top right of the window, you get to see a mosaic of every attachment you've ever exchanged with this correspondent—file, photo, video, whatever. Double-click one to open it. No more scrolling back through thousands of pages of typed text to find something you remember getting!

This Details pane also gets you access to buttons that begin screen sharing, phone calling, or video chatting with this lucky individual.

- **See where the other guy is.** If you're chatting with an iPhone owner, that same Details pane might reveal a map that shows his current location in the world. (The map appears only if he's turned on "Share my location" on his phone.)

- **Stop the notifications.** If this person is bombarding you with texts, you can make your Mac stop dinging and showing a notification bubble with each one. Click Details; click Do Not Disturb. Now those messages will flow into Messages, but you won't be bugged about each one.

- **Juggle conversations.** You can keep a bunch of chats going simultaneously, thanks to the individually listed chats at the left side of the window. Just don't forget which chat you're in before you say something snarky!

Tip: You can press Control-Tab to switch from chat to chat. Add the Shift key to move the other way.

Group Chats

There's nothing to stop you from inviting several people to a single chat. Just click the Compose button (✍) as usual. Enter the desired chat partners' names one at a time in the To: blank, pressing Return or the space bar after each one.

Tip: If you've created a group in Contacts, you can also just enter the group's name. Everybody in it is instantly part of the chat.

Now, you've got yourself a party line. Anything anyone types, everybody sees. Be careful what you say, will you?

The Mac's controls for group chats (defined as "three or more participants") are hiding in the pane that appears when you click Details at top right (Figure 13-7).

Figure 13-7:
If you click where it says Untitled Group Chat, you can type a new name. That should make it easier to identify this conversation later in the list of chats at the left side of the window.

You can also add or remove participants, even after the group chat is under way. To remove someone, ⌘-click his name in the Details pane; choose Remove from Conversation. To add a new member, click Add Contact.

Do Not Disturb means that new texts from this group won't trigger notifications on your Mac. And if the bickering becomes more than you can stand, you can excuse yourself and leave the chat by clicking Leave This Conversation.

Audio Chats

Messages becomes much more exciting when you exploit its AV Club capabilities. Even over slow Internet connections, you can conduct audio chats, speaking into your microphone and listening to the responses from your speaker.

If you have a broadband connection, though, you get a much more satisfying experience: Up to 10 of you can join in one massive, free conference call from across the Internet.

Starting an audio chat when you're iMessaging (chatting with a fellow iCloud member) is extremely easy. Click Details (top right); on the pane, click ✆; click FaceTime. (Or, if you have an iPhone, you can click the person's phone number and make an actual phone call, as described on page 478.)

And what if you're chatting with a non-iCloud person? In that case, click her name in the buddy list, and then click the ✆ button below the list.

Once your invitation is accepted, you can begin speaking to each other. The bars of the sound-level meter let you know that the microphone—which you've specified in the Messages→Preferences→Audio/Video tab—is working.

Tip: Although the audio is full duplex (you can hear and speak simultaneously, like a phone but unlike a walkie-talkie), there may be a delay, like you're calling overseas on a bad connection. If you can't hear anything at all, then check out Messages' Help system, which contains some suggestions.

Video Chats

The state of the art in video calling, of course, is FaceTime (page 643).

But FaceTime requires that both you and your partner be on Apple computers. Messages, on the other hand, lets you conduct free video chats with up to four people who aren't on Macs. They show up on three vertical panes, gorgeously reflected on a shiny,

The Chat Transcript

When you close a chat by clicking the ✕ in its tab, the conversation is gone forever.

Unless, that is, you've opened Messages→Preferences→General and turned on "Save history when chats are closed."

In that case, Messages autosaves the text of your conversations. Even if you close one, you can retrieve its contents by starting another chat with the same person; the history reappears.

Behind the scenes, your transcripts are saved in your Library→Messages→Archives folder. (To get to your Library folder, press Option as you choose Go→Library in the Finder.)

If you do have "Save history" turned on, and you wind up having a particularly incriminating chat, you can tell Messages *not* to save its transcript by pressing ⌘-Delete. Messages asks if you're sure. If so, that prose is hosed.

black table surface. If you've got the Mac muscle and bandwidth, your partners are as crisp, clear, bright, and smooth as television—and as big as your screen, if you like.

People can come and go; as they enter and leave the "videosphere," Messages slides their glistening screens aside, enlarging or shrinking them as necessary to fit on your screen.

Equipment Requirements

Everyone in a video chat has to be on the same service (iCloud, AIM, Yahoo, or Jabber), and everyone needs pretty high-horsepower computers and Internet connections.

Tip: For better audio quality during your video calls—both hearing and broadcasting—wear a headset. For example, you can pair a wireless Bluetooth headset with your Mac in Messages→Preferences→Audio/Video→Set Up Bluetooth Headset. This fires up the Mac's Bluetooth Setup Assistant program to guide you through the process.

After you get your Bluetooth headset married to your Mac, then go to →System Preferences→Output and select your headset in the list.

By the way, you and your buddy don't both need the gear. If only you have a camera, for example, you can choose Buddies→Invite to One-Way Video Chat (or Audio Chat). Your less-equipped buddy can see you, but has to speak (audio only) or type in response.

You need pretty decent Internet speeds, too.

Starting the Video Call

If you're in an iMessage conversation, click Details, then click ▢ to begin the video chat.

If you're chatting with a non-iCloud person, make sure there's a ▢ icon next to his name in the buddy list (meaning that he has a camera). If you see a *stacked* camcorder icon, then that person has a Mac that's capable of joining a four-way video chat.

To begin a video chat, click the ▢ icon next to a buddy's name, or highlight the name and then click ▢ at the bottom of the list. Or, if you're already in a text chat, choose Buddies→Invite to Video Chat.

A window opens, showing you. This Preview mode is intended to show what your buddy will see. (You'll probably discover that you need some kind of light in front of you to avoid being too shadowy.) As your buddies join you, they appear in their own windows.

And now, some video-chat notes:

• If your conversation partners seem unwilling to make eye contact, it's not because they're shifty. They're just looking at *you,* on the screen, rather than at the camera—and chances are you aren't looking into your camera, either.

• Don't miss the green ⊕ button in the upper-left corner of the window. It takes your video into full screen. Wild.

- If you're the one who started the call, then you can add more people by clicking the + button in the chat window or dragging a buddy's name into the window. (If that person doesn't have a camera, she can still enjoy audio or typing privileges.)

- You can have video chats with Windows computers, too, although they're often jerky, small, and slightly out of sync.

- You can capture a still "photo" of a video chat by ⌘-dragging the image to your desktop, or by choosing Video→Take Snapshot (Option-⌘-S). Or just use the Copy command (⌘-C) to copy an image of the chat to the Clipboard, ready for pasting in another program.

- Don't want to see yourself in the picture-in-picture window during your video chat? Choose Video→Hide Local Video.

- This cutting-edge technology can occasionally present cutting-edge glitches. The video quality deteriorates, the transmission aborts suddenly, the audio has an annoying echo, and so on. When problems strike, Messages Help offers a number of tips; the Video→Connection Doctor can identify your network speed. (Messages video likes lots of network speed.)

Tip: If the Messages video seems to be struggling too much to be worthwhile, consider using FaceTime instead. It's designed to deliver good video quality over less-beefy Internet connections.

Bluescreen Backdrops and Video FX

If your video chats look like a bunch of cubicle-dwellers sitting around chatting at their desks, then you can liven things up with one of Messages' most glamorous and jaw-dropping features: photo or video *backgrounds* for your talking head. Yes, now you can make your video chat partners think you're in Paris, on the moon, or even impersonating a four-panel Andy Warhol silkscreen.

Note: The Messages and Photo Booth backdrop effects require bandwidth, man, serious bandwidth—at least 128 Kbps for both upload and download speeds.

Here's how to prepare your backdrop for a video chat that's under way:

1. **Choose Video→Show Video Effects (Figure 13-8).**

 The Effects box appears, looking a lot like the one in Photo Booth (page 668); visual backdrops are the same. Click the various squares to see how each effect will transform you in real time.

 The first three pages of effects all do video magic on you and everything else in the picture. The second two pages of effects, however, don't do anything to your image. Instead, they replace the background.

 This is the really amazing part. In TV and movies, replacing the background is an extremely common special effect. All you have to do is set up a perfectly smooth, evenly lit, shadowless blue or bright-green backdrop behind the subject. Later, the

computer replaces that solid color with a new picture or video of the director's choice.

Messages, however, creates exactly the same special effect (see Figure 13-8) without requiring the bluescreen or the greenscreen. Read on.

Figure 13-8:
Top left: You have plenty of effects to choose from for your next video chat. Click an effect to add it to your chat window. Click the small arrows at the bottom of the window to advance or retreat through the various effects styles. Click the Original square in the middle of the window to erase the effect and start again from scratch.

Lower right: Let the live bluescreen action begin!

2. **Click the background effect you want.**

 Suppose, for example, that you've clicked the video loop showing the Eiffel Tower with people walking around. At this point, a message appears on the screen that says, "Please step out of the frame."

3. **Duck out of camera range (or move off to one side).**

 See, Messages intends to memorize a picture of the *real* background—without you in it. When you return to the scene, your Mac then compares each pixel of its memorized image with what it's seeing now. Any differences, it concludes, must be *you*. And *that* is how it can create a bluescreen effect without a bluescreen.

Note: To make this work, both the camera and the background must be perfectly still. If the lighting or the visuals shift or change in any way, you may get some weird, glitchy effects where your real background bleeds through.

4. **When the screen says, "Background detected," step back into the frame.**

Sacré bleu! You're now in virtual Paris. Go ahead and start the video chat with your friends, and don't forget your beret.

If you want to clear out the background, or change it, click the Original square in the middle of the Effects palette and then choose a different backdrop. (You can also change backdrops in midchat by clicking Effects again.)

If things get too weird and choppy onscreen, you can restore the normal background by choosing Video→Reset Background. (That's also handy if you suddenly have to have a video talk with your boss about your excessive use of Messages while he's away on his business trip.)

Tip: You can use one of your own photos or video clips as a Messages backdrop, too. In the Video Effects box, click the arrows on the bottom until you get to the screen with several blank User Backdrop screens. Next, drag a photo or video from the desktop directly onto one of the blank screens. Click it just like you would any of Apple's stock shots.

Sharing Your Screen

As you've seen already in this chapter, Messages lets you share your thoughts, your voice, and your image with the people on your buddy list. And now, for its next trick, it lets you share…your computer.

Messages' screen-sharing feature is a close relative of the *network* screen-sharing feature described in Chapter 16. It lets you not only *see* what's on a faraway buddy's screen, but also control it, taking command of the distant mouse and keyboard. (You can share your screen with the other guy, too.)

You can open folders, create and edit documents, and copy files on the shared Mac screen. Sharing a screen makes collaborating as easy as working side by side around the same Mac, except now you can be sitting in San Francisco while your buddy is banging it out in Boston.

And if you're the family tech-support specialist—but the family lives all over the country—screen sharing makes troubleshooting infinitely easier. You can now jump on your Mom's shared Mac and figure out why the formatting went wacky in her Word document, without her having to attempt to *explain* it to you over the phone. ("And then the little thingy disappeared and the doohickey got scrambled…")

Tip: Once you're controlling someone else's screen remotely, your keyboard shortcuts operate her Mac instead of yours. Press ⌘-Tab to bring up the application switcher, hit ⌘-Q to quit a program, use all the Mission Control and Spotlight shortcuts, and so on.

To make Messages' screen sharing work, you and your buddy must both be using an iCloud, AIM, Google Talk, Jabber, or Bonjour account; sadly, you can't share your screen using a Yahoo account.

iCloud Screen Sharing

From within an iMessages conversation (that is, a chat between two iCloud members), you can share your whole Mac screen, right there in Messages. Both people have to be using Macs running Yosemite (not, for example, an iPhone, and not an older Mac).

There are other ways to share screens, of course (page 560)—but this is by far the easiest to set up.

Once a typed chat is under way, click Details (top right), and then click ⬜. (If that icon is dimmed gray instead of blue, it's because the other person isn't using a Yosemite Mac.)

The icon sprouts two choices: "Invite to share my screen" (meaning the other guy sees *your* screen) and "Ask to share screen" (you're going to see *his* screen). Click the one you want.

He receives an invitation. If he clicks Accept, the sharing is under way. He sees your screen on his Mac, or vice versa, as though some freaky cosmic wormhole has opened up.

Once the screen sharing is going, a new ⬜ menu appears at the top of your screen. It offers tricks like these:

- **Allow [other guy] to control my screen.** He can operate your mouse and keyboard—from his Mac, thousands of miles away.

- **Mute Audio.** During a screen share, Messages automatically turns on audio chatting, so you can explain stuff to each other. Mute Audio mutes the audio.

- **Pause Screen Sharing** is like drawing a privacy curtain when you want to duck into your email program to read something. The other guy sees only a "Paused" screen until you unpause.

- **End Screen Sharing.** You guessed it.

Screen Sharing with Non-iCloud Accounts

To begin, click the sharee's name in your buddy list.

- **To share your screen,** choose Buddies→Share My Screen with [person's name].

- **To see his screen,** choose Buddies→Ask to Share [person's name]'s Screen.

Note: Similar commands are available in the Screen Sharing pop-up button—the ⬜ at the bottom of the Buddies window.

Once the invitation is accepted, the sharing begins, as shown in Figure 13-9. To help you communicate further, Messages politely opens up an audio chat with your buddy so you can have a hands-free discussion about what you're doing on the shared machine.

If you're seeing someone else's screen, you see his Mac desktop in full-screen view, right on your own machine. You also see a small window showing your own Mac; click it to switch back to your own desktop.

Tip: To copy files from Mac to Mac, drag them between the two windows. Files dragged to your Mac wind up in your Downloads folder.

To bail out, press Control-Esc on the Mac's keyboard.

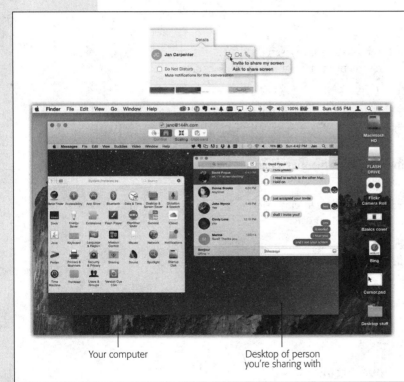

Your computer

Desktop of person
you're sharing with

Figure 13-9:
Top: You either send or receive an invitation to start sharing your screen, but make sure you know with whom you're dealing before accepting the offer and starting the sharing process.

Bottom: When you're sharing someone else's screen, you have the option to click back and forth between the two Mac screens.

You can move the cursor, click things, and even highlight text on the other guy's screen. That's great for explaining to someone, via remote control, how to perform some task.

Part Four:
Putting Down Roots

4

Mac+iPhone: Handoff, AirDrop & Continuity

pple products have always been designed to work together. Macs, phones, tablets, watches: similar software, design, wording, philosophy. That's nice for you, of course, because you have less to learn and to troubleshoot. But it's also nice for Apple, because it keeps you in velvet handcuffs; pretty soon, you've got too much invested in its own product "ecosystem" to ever consider wandering over to a rival.

In Yosemite, Apple has taken this gadget symbiosis to an astonishing extreme. If your iPhone is running iOS 8.1 or later, it can be an *accessory* to your Mac. The Mac can be a speakerphone, using the iPhone as a wireless antenna. The Mac can send and receive regular text messages. AirDrop lets you drag files back and forth, wirelessly, from phone to computer. A Mac laptop can get onto the Internet with one click, even miles from home.

Apple's name for this suite of symbiosis is "Continuity." For many people, all of this just works. For many others, there's a certain degree of setting up and troubleshooting. These are the primary rules:

- You need a Mac running OS X Yosemite and an iPhone running iOS 8.1 or later.

- The Mac and the phone have to be signed into the same iCloud account. (That's a security thing—it proves that you're the owner of both machines, and therefore unlikely to pose a risk to yourself.) On the Mac, you do that in System Preferences→iCloud. On the phone, you do that in Settings→iCloud, but also make sure that you've entered the same iCloud address in Settings→Messages and Settings→FaceTime.

- For some of these features, Bluetooth must be turned on. On the Mac, you can do that in System Preferences→Bluetooth. On the phone, it's Settings→Bluetooth. (The modern Bluetooth—called Bluetooth LE, or low energy—doesn't drain your battery the way it once did, so it's fine to leave it on. But older Macs don't have Bluetooth LE, so most Continuity features work only on 2012 and later Macs.)

All right. Setup ready? Time to experience some integration!

Mac as Speakerphone

You can now make and take phone calls on your Mac. The iPhone, sitting anywhere in your house, can be the cellular module for your Mac—even if that iPhone is asleep and locked.

When a call comes in to your iPhone's number, your *Mac* plays whatever ringtone your phone is playing. And a notice appears on your Mac screen (Figure 14-1).

Figure 14-1:
When a call comes in to your iPhone, a notification appears on your Mac (top). You can click to answer it (or decline it); your Mac's microphone and speaker become your speakerphone (bottom).

You can *place* a call the same way: Just click any phone number you find on the Mac: in Contacts, in Safari, in an email message, and so on (Figure 14-2).

After that—it just works. Even call waiting works—if a second call comes in, your Mac notifies you and offers you the chance to put the first one on hold. And on the Mac, the Contacts app now offers Ringtone and Texttone menus, so you can assign custom sounds that play when your *Mac* rings.

Crazy.

Tip: You may soon discover that there's no dialing pad on the Mac, so there's no easy way to dial a number that's not already in Contacts. The workaround: Create a temporary fake person in Contacts!

Figure 14-2:
To make Mac dialing work, the iPhone and Mac must be on the same WiFi network. They both have to be signed into the same iCloud account. And you have to open the Face-Time settings on each device and make sure they're both set to use the same iCloud account.

And if It's Not Working

"It just works" is fantastic—when it just works.

If your Mac isn't able to send and receive calls and texts through your phone, here's the checklist. One of these things, you'll discover, isn't set correctly.

- The iPhone and Mac have to be on the same network (for example, the same WiFi network).

- On the phone, open Settings→iCloud. Make sure it's signed in with the same iCloud account (Apple ID) as the Mac. (On the Mac, check the iCloud account at System Preferences→iCloud.)

- On the phone, open Settings→FaceTime. Make sure FaceTime, too, is signed into that same iCloud account. Turn on iPhone Cellular Calls.

- On the Mac, open System Preferences→General. Confirm that "Allow Handoff between this Mac and your iCloud devices" is turned on.

- On the Mac, open the FaceTime program. Choose FaceTime→Preferences. Confirm that, once again, you're signed in with the same iCloud account, that your phone number's checkbox is turned on, and that "iPhone Cellular Calls" is turned on.

- If all else fails, restart the iPhone.

Tip: If you own a bunch of Apple machines, it might drive you crazy that they all now ring at once when a call comes in. Fortunately, you can turn off the ringing on each device that you'd rather be peaceful.

To make one of your iPhones, iPads, or iPod Touches stop ringing, turn off Settings→FaceTime→iPhone Cellular Calls. To make a Mac stop ringing, open the FaceTime program; choose FaceTime→Preferences→ Settings, and turn off iPhone Cellular Calls.

Texting from the Mac

You can now send and receive text messages (and picture, audio, and video messages) on your Mac, too.

We're not talking about sending texts to other *Apple* people (with iCloud accounts). Those are called iMessages, and they're a special, Apple-only kind of message. We're talking about something much better: You can type *any* cellphone number and send a regular SMS text message to *anyone*. Or receive them when they're sent to your iPhone number.

Or you can initiate the text conversation by clicking a phone number in Contacts, Calendar, or Safari to send an SMS message. Once again, your iPhone acts as a relay station between the cellular world and your Mac.

Here's how to set it up.

First, the Mac and the phone must be on the same WiFi network and signed into the same iCloud account.

Next, on the iPhone, open Settings→Messages. Tap Text Message Forwarding. Your Mac's name appears. Turn on the switch.

Now, on the Mac, open Messages. (If all is going well, its icon is probably popping out of your Dock at this moment, trying to get your attention.) When you open Messages, a code appears. You're supposed to type into the corresponding box on your phone (Figure 14-3).

Figure 14-3.
The purpose of having to enter this setup code is to prove, really and truly, that you're the owner of both devices. You wouldn't want some bad guy reading your text messages, would you?

This same code appears right now on any iPad or iPod Touch you own. They, too, will be able to send and receive texts, with your iPhone doing the relaying.

That's it—your gadgets are paired. You can now use Messages to send standard text messages to *any* cellphone. You can also click and hold on a phone number wherever it appears—in Contacts, in a Spotlight search result, in Safari, in Mail—and choose Send Message from there. And when a text message comes in, a standard Mac notification bubble appears at top right (Figure 14-4).

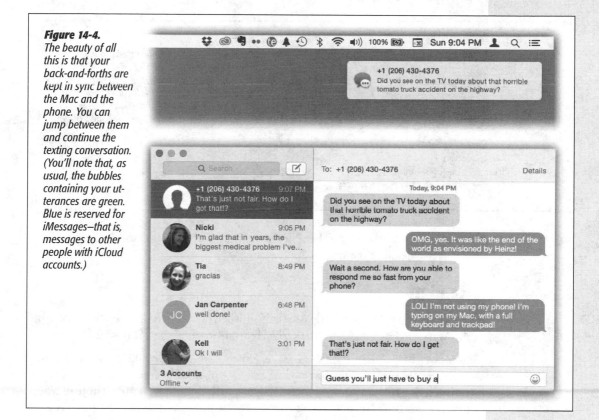

Figure 14-4.
The beauty of all this is that your back-and-forths are kept in sync between the Mac and the phone. You can jump between them and continue the texting conversation. (You'll note that, as usual, the bubbles containing your utterances are green. Blue is reserved for iMessages—that is, messages to other people with iCloud accounts.)

Instant Hotspot

Paying your cell carrier another $20 or so every month entitles you to use the iPhone's Personal Hotspot feature. That's where the phone itself acts as a portable WiFi hotspot, so that your laptop (or any other gadgets) can get online almost anywhere.

It used to be kind of a pain to get going. Each time you wanted your laptop to get online, you had to wake your iPhone, unlock it, open Settings, and turn on Personal

Hotspot. Then you had to wait about 20 seconds, until the phone's name showed up in your 🛜 menu.

Not anymore.

Now, the phone can stay in your pocket. Its name appears in your 🛜 menu, ready for choosing at any time—even if the phone is asleep and locked, and even if Personal Hotspot is turned off! Handily enough, the 🛜 menu also shows the phone's battery and signal status (Figure 14-5).

Figure 14-5.
Once your Mac is online through your iPhone's cellular connection, it tries to save you money by suspending data-intensive jobs like full backups and software updates. And it closes down the connection when you no longer need it, to save your iPhone's battery.

As usual, this works only if the iPhone and Mac both have Bluetooth turned on and are signed into the same iCloud account.

Handoff

Handoff is a new feature that passes half-finished documents between the phone and the Mac, wirelessly and automatically. Figure 14-6 shows how it works.

It doesn't have to be an email message, either. If you were reading a Web page or a Map on your phone, then that icon on the Mac opens the same Web page or map. If you were working on a Reminder; a Calendar entry; a Contacts entry; a note in Notes; or a document in Keynote, Numbers, or Pages; you can open the same in-progress item on the Mac.

Here's the setup: Once again, both gadgets must be signed into your iCloud account. Both must have Bluetooth turned on, and the Mac and phone have to be sitting within Bluetooth range of each other (about 30 feet).

On the Mac, open System Preferences→General; turn on "Allow Handoff between this Mac and your iCloud devices."

On the iPhone, the on/off switch is in Settings→General→Handoff & Suggested Apps.

Now try it out. Start an email message on your iPhone. Have a look at the Dock on your Mac: There, at the left end, pops the little icon of whatever program can finish the job.

Watch for the little lower-left icon on your screens to make it work.

Figure 14-6:
Top: Suppose you've been writing an email message on your iPhone.

Middle: When you arrive home and sit down at the Mac, a new icon appears at the left end of the Dock.

Bottom: When you click it, Mail opens, and the half-finished message is there for you to complete.

And all of it works in the other direction, too. If you're working on something on the Mac, but you're called away, an icon appears on the lower-left corner of your iPhone's Lock screen that opens the same item (Figure 14-7, left).

Tip: There's another way to find the Handoff icon that nobody ever mentions: It's in the app switcher on both devices (see Figure 14-7).

Figure 14-7.
On the phone, double-press the Home button to see the icon for a document you're handing off from the Mac (right).

On the Mac, press ⌘-Tab to open the app switcher; there, too, is the icon for the app being handed off from the phone.

AirDrop

AirDrop lets you shoot photos, videos, maps, Contacts cards, PDF files, Word documents, and all kinds of other stuff—from one Mac to another Mac. Wirelessly. Without having to set up names, passwords, or permissions. Without even having an Internet connection. That Mac-to-Mac AirDrop feature is described on page 536.

But until iOS 8 and Yosemite, you couldn't use AirDrop between a phone and a Mac. And now you can.

From iPhone to Mac

Open whatever it is you want to send: a photo, map, Web site, contact…anything with a 􀈂 button, on either the Mac or the device.

When you tap 􀈂, you see the AirDrop pane—and, after a moment, the icons of any nearby Yosemite Macs, iPhones, and iPads show up, too. Including yours (Figure 14-8, left).

If the Mac's icon *doesn't* show up, it's probably because its owner hasn't made the Mac discoverable by AirDrop.

Instruct him to open the AirDrop *window* on his Mac. (Click AirDrop in the sidebar of any Finder window.) See the small blue control at the bottom? It governs who can

"see" this Mac for AirDrop purposes: No One, Contacts Only (that is, people in the Mac's address book), or Everyone.

Once that's set up right, that Mac shows up in the iPhone's AirDrop pane ("David" in Figure 14-8). Send away. (Unlike the AirDrop of Macs gone by, in Yosemite, you don't have to start by opening the AirDrop *window.*)

Figure 14-8.
AirDrop now goes both ways: from iPhone to Mac (shown here), or Mac to iPhone. Actually, it goes many more ways than that, because the iPad and iPod Touch can do it, too.

The receiving Mac displays a note like the one shown at right in Figure 14-8. Click Accept (to download the incoming item to your Mac's Downloads folder) or Decline (to reject it).

Tip: If the phone and the Mac are both signed into the same iCloud account, then you don't encounter that Accept/Decline thing. The file goes directly into your Downloads folder without asking. You do get a notification on the Mac that lets you know how many files arrived, and it offers an Open button.

Apple figures that, since you own both the phone and the Mac, the usual permission routine isn't necessary. You're probably not trying to send yourself some evil virus of death.

Accounts, Security & Gatekeeper

I n an era when *security* is the hottest high tech buzzword, Apple was smart to make security a focal point for OS X. It was already virus-free and better protected from Internet attacks than Windows. But OS X 10.10 is the most impenetrable Mac system yet, filled with new defenses against the dark arts. This chapter covers the whole range of them.

On the premise that the biggest security threat of all comes from other people in your home or office, though, the most important security feature in OS X is the *accounts* system.

Introducing Accounts

The concept of *user accounts* is central to OS X's security approach. Like the Unix under its skin (and also like recent versions of Windows), OS X is designed from the ground up to be a *multiple-user* operating system. That is, you can set up your OS X so that everyone must log in—click his name and type his password—when the computer turns on (Figure 15-1).

Upon doing so, you discover the Macintosh universe just as you left it, including these elements:

- Your documents, files, and folders.

- Your preference settings in every program you use: Web browser bookmarks and preferred home page; desktop picture, screensaver, and language; icons on the desktop and in the Dock—and the size and position of the Dock itself; and so on.

- Email account(s), including personal information and mailboxes.

- Your personally installed programs and fonts.

- Your choice of programs that launch automatically at startup.

This system lets different people use it throughout the day, without disrupting one another's files and settings. It also protects the Mac from getting fouled up by mischievous (or bumbling) students, employees, and hackers.

If you're the only person who uses your Mac, you can safely skip most of this chapter. The Mac never pauses at startup time to demand the name and password you made up when you installed OS X, because Apple's installer automatically turns on something called *automatic login* (page 506). You *will* be using one of these accounts, though, whether you realize it or not.

Furthermore, when you're stuck in line at the Department of Motor Vehicles, you may find the concepts presented here worth skimming, as certain elements of this multiple-user system may intrude upon your solo activities—and figure in the discussions in this book—from time to time.

Tip: Even if you don't share your Mac with anyone and don't create any other accounts, you might still be tempted to learn about the accounts feature because of its ability to password-protect the entire computer. All you have to do is turn *off* the automatic login feature described on page 506. Thereafter, your Mac is protected from unauthorized fiddling when you're away from your desk or if your laptop is stolen.

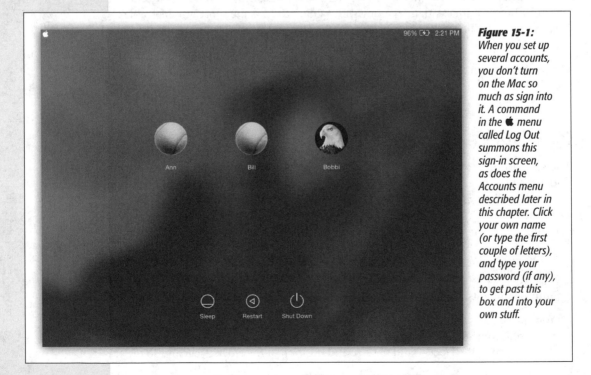

Figure 15-1:
When you set up several accounts, you don't turn on the Mac so much as sign into it. A command in the ❡ *menu called Log Out summons this sign-in screen, as does the Accounts menu described later in this chapter. Click your own name (or type the first couple of letters), and type your password (if any), to get past this box and into your own stuff.*

The First Account

When you first installed OS X, whether it was Yosemite 10.10 or an earlier version, you were asked for a name and a password. You were creating the first *user account* on your Macintosh. Since that fateful day, you may have made a number of changes to your desktop—adjusted the Dock settings, set up your folders and desktop the way you like them, added some bookmarks to your Web browser, and so on—without realizing that you were actually making those changes only to *your account.*

You've probably been saving your documents into your own Home folder, which is the cornerstone of your account. This folder, generally named after you and stashed in the Users folder on your hard drive, stores not only your own work, but also your preference settings for all the programs you use, special fonts you've installed, your own email collection, and so on.

Now then: Suppose you create an account for a second person. When she turns on the computer and signs in, she finds the desktop exactly the way it was factory-installed by Apple—stunning outer-space desktop picture, Dock along the bottom, and so on. She can make the same kinds of changes to the Mac that you've made, but nothing she does affects *your* environment the next time you log in.

In other words, the multiple-accounts feature has two components: first, a convenience element that hides everyone else's junk; and second, a security element that protects both the Mac's system software and everybody's work.

Creating an Account

Suppose somebody new joins your little Mac family—a new worker, student, or love interest, for example. And you want to make that person feel at home on your Mac.

Begin by opening System Preferences (Chapter 17). In the System Preferences window, click Users & Groups. You have just arrived at the master control center for account creation and management (Figure 15-2).

To create a new account, start by unlocking the Users & Groups pane. That is, click the 🔒 at lower left, and fill in your own account password.

Now you can click + beneath the list of accounts. The little pane shown at bottom in Figure 15-2 appears.

Phase 1: Choose an Account Type

As though this business of accounts and passwords wasn't complicated enough already, OS X offers several *types* of accounts. And you're expected to specify *which* type each person gets at the moment you create an account.

To do that, open the New Account pop-up menu (Figure 15-2, bottom). Its five account types are described on the following pages.

Administrator accounts

If this is your own personal Mac, then just beneath your name on the Users & Groups pane of System Preferences, it probably says *Admin*. This, as you could probably guess, stands for Administrator.

Figure 15-2:
Top: The screen lists everyone who has an account. From here, you can create new accounts or change passwords. If you're new at this, there's probably just one account listed here: yours. This is the account OS X created when you first installed it. You, the all-wise administrator, have to click the 🔒 to authenticate yourself before you can start making changes.

Bottom: In the account-creation process, the first step is choosing which type of account you want to create.

Because you're the person who originally installed OS X, the Mac assumes that you are its *administrator*—the technical wizard in charge of it. You're the teacher, the parent, the resident guru. You're the one who will maintain this Mac. Only an administrator is allowed to do the following:

- Install new programs into the Applications folder.

- Add fonts that everybody can use.

- Make changes to certain System Preferences panes (including Network, Date & Time, Energy Saver, and Startup Disk).

- Use some features of the Disk Utility program.

- Create, move, or delete folders outside of your Home folder.

- Decide who gets to have accounts on the Mac.

- Open, change, or delete anyone else's files.

- Bypass FileVault using a recovery key (page 510).

The administrator concept may be new to you, but it's an important pill to swallow. For one thing, you'll find certain settings all over OS X that you can change *only* if you're an administrator—including many in the Users & Groups pane itself. For another thing, administrator status plays an enormous role when you want to network your Mac to other kinds of computers, as described in the next chapter. And, finally, in the bigger picture, the fact that the Mac has an industrial-strength accounts system, just like traditional Unix and recent Windows operating systems, gives it a fighting chance in the corporations of America.

As you create accounts for other people who'll use this Mac, you're offered the opportunity to make each one an administrator just like you. Needless to say, use discretion. Bestow these powers only upon people as responsible and technically masterful as yourself.

Standard accounts

Most people, on most Macs, are ordinary *Standard* account holders. These people have everyday access to their own Home folders and to the harmless panes of System Preferences, but most other areas of the Mac are off limits. OS X won't even let them create new folders on the main hard drive, except inside their own Home folders (or in the Shared folder described starting on page 513).

A few of the System Preferences panes display a padlock icon (🔒). If you're a Standard account holder, you can't make changes to these settings without the assistance of an administrator. Fortunately, you aren't required to log out so that an administrator can log in and make changes. You can just call the administrator over, click the padlock icon, and let him type in his name and password (if, indeed, he feels comfortable with you making the changes you're about to make).

Managed accounts with Parental Controls

A *Managed* account is the same thing as a Standard account—except that you've turned on Parental Controls. (These controls are described later in this chapter.) You can turn a Managed account into a Standard account just by turning off Parental Controls, and vice versa.

That is, this account usually has even fewer freedoms—because you've limited the programs this person is allowed to use, for example. Use a Managed account for children or anyone else who needs a Mac with rubber walls.

Sharing Only account

This kind of account is extremely useful—*if* your Mac is on a network (Chapter 16).

See, ordinarily, you can log in and access the files on your Mac in either of two ways:

- In person, seated in front of it.

- From across the network.

This arrangement was designed with families and schools in mind: lots of people sharing a *single* Mac.

This setup gets a little silly, though, when the people on a home or office network each have their *own* computers. If you wanted your spouse or your sales director to be able to grab some files from you, you'd have to create full-blown accounts for them on *your* Mac, complete with utterly unnecessary Home folders they'd never use.

That's why the *Sharing Only* account is such a great idea. It's available *only* from across the network. You can't get into it by sitting down at the Mac itself—it has no Home folder!

Finally, of course, a Sharing Only account holder can't make any changes to the Mac's settings or programs. (And since they don't have Home folders, you also can't turn on FileVault for these accounts.)

In other words, a Sharing Only account exists *solely* for the purpose of file sharing on the network, and people can enter their names and passwords *only* from other Macs.

Once you've set up this kind of account, all the file-sharing and screen-sharing goodies described in Chapter 16 become available.

Group

A *group* is just a virtual container that holds the names of other account holders. You might create one for your most trusted colleagues, another for those rambunctious kids, and so on—all in the name of streamlining the *file-sharing privileges* feature described on page 512. The box on the facing page covers groups in more detail.

The Guest account

The *Guest* account is great for accommodating visitors, buddies, or anyone else who was just passing through and wanted to use your Mac for a while. When you let such people use the Guest account, your own account remains private and un-messed-with.

Note: The Guest account isn't listed among the account *types* in the New Account pop-up menu (Figure 15-2). That's because there's only *one* Guest account; you can't actually create additional ones.

But it's still an account type with specific characteristics. It's sitting right there in the list of accounts from Day One.

Best of all, any changes your guest makes while using your Mac (downloading mail, creating bookmarks, putting up a raunchy desktop picture) are automatically erased when she logs out. Files are deleted, email is nuked, setting changes are forgotten. It's like a hotel that gets demolished and rebuilt after each guest departs.

The Guest account is permanently listed in the Users & Groups pane of System Preferences. Ordinarily, though, you don't see it in the login screen list; if you're normally the only person who uses this Mac, you don't need to have it staring you in the face every day.

So to use the Guest account, bring it to life by turning on "Allow guests to log into this computer." You can even turn on the parental controls described on page 498 by clicking Open Parental Controls, or permit the guest to exchange files with your Mac from across the network (Chapter 16) by turning on "Allow guests to connect to shared folders."

Just remember to warn your vagabond friend that once he logs out (and acknowledges the warning), all traces of his visit are wiped out forever.

At least from your *Mac*.

Phase 2: Name, Password, and Status

All right. So you clicked the + button. And from the New Account pop-up menu, you chose the type of account you wanted to create.

Now, on the same starter sheet, it's time to fill in the most critical information about the new account holder:

- **Full Name.** If it's just the family, this could be "Chris" or "Robin." If it's a corporation or school, you probably want to use both first and last names.

POWER USERS' CLINIC

Creating Groups

Changing permissions settings on a networked Mac, or one with a lot of account holders, is a lot easier if you sweep all your minions into subsets called groups.

You can create a group as easily as you'd create an account. And in the same place: the Users & Groups pane of System Preferences.

Click the tiny 🔒 in the lower-left corner. When prompted, type in your administrator's name and password, and then click OK. The Mac is just making sure that somebody with a clue is at the helm.

Now click the + button as though you were about to create a new account. But from the New Account pop-up menu

(shown at bottom in Figure 15-2), choose Group. Type a name for the new group (Accounting, Kids, or whatever), and then click Create Group.

Now you see something like the list shown here: checkboxes for all this Mac's account holders. Turn on the checkboxes for the ones you consider worthy of being a part of this group.

You can create as many groups as you like. Later, when it comes time to share a folder or file, you'll save time by choosing a group name instead of setting these permissions one person at a time.

- **Account Name.** You'll quickly discover the value of this Account Name, particularly if your name is, say, Alexandra Stephanopoulos. It's meant to be an abbreviation of your actual name.

 When you sign into your Mac in person, you can use either your full name or account (short) name. But when you access this Mac by dialing into it or connecting from across the network (as described in the next chapter), the short version is more convenient.

 As soon as you tab into this field, the Mac proposes a short name for you. You can replace the suggestion with whatever you like. Technically, it doesn't even have to be shorter than the "long" name, but spaces and most punctuation marks are forbidden.

- **Use iCloud password.** You can use your *iCloud* password—the password you've already got memorized as part of your Apple ID—instead of a separate password for logging into your Mac. Why learn two passwords instead of one?

 If this appeals to you, turn on "Use iCloud password," and tell the Mac your iCloud email address (in the iCloud ID box). From now on, you'll be able to sign into the Mac using *that* password. (As a message here lets you know, you'll need an Internet connection the first time you log in this way, so the Mac can go online to confirm your iCloud account details.)

- **Use separate password.** Maybe you don't have an iCloud account. Or maybe you want a simpler password for logging into your Mac (or *no* password). In that case, choose this option.

 You're supposed to type this password twice, to make sure you didn't introduce a typo the first time. (The Mac displays only dots as you type, to guard against the possibility that somebody is watching over your shoulder.)

 The usual computer book takes this opportunity to stress the importance of a long, complex password—a phrase that isn't in the dictionary, something that's made up of mixed letters and numbers. This is excellent advice if you create sensitive documents or work in a big corporation.

 But if you share the Mac only with a spouse, or trusted colleagues in a small office, you may have nothing to hide. You may see the multiple-users feature more as a convenience (keeping your settings and files separate) than a protector of secrecy and security. In these situations, there's no particular urgency to the mission of thwarting the world's hackers with a convoluted password.

 In that case, you may want to consider setting up *no* password—leaving both password blanks empty. Later, whenever you're asked for your password, just leave the Password box blank. You'll be able to log in that much faster each day.

 (The first box says "Required," but it lies; no password is actually required. After setting up this new account and clicking Create User, the Mac asks if you're *sure* you don't want to make up a password; just click Continue and get on with your life.)

Tip: Actually, having *some* password comes in handy if you share files on the network, because Mac A can *store* your name and password from Mac B—and therefore you can access Mac B without entering your name and password *at all.* So consider making your password something very short and easy, like the apostrophe/quote mark—the ' key. It's a real password, so it's enough for Mac A to memorize. Yet when you *are* asked to enter your password—for example, when you're installing a new program—it's incredibly fast and easy to enter, because it's right next to the Return key.

- **Password Hint.** If your password is the middle name of the first person who ever kissed you, for example, your hint might be "Middle name of the first person who ever kissed me."

 Later, if you forget your password, the Mac will show you this cue to jog your memory.

When you finish setting up these essential items, click Create User.

You then return to the Users & Groups pane, where you see the new account name in the list at the left side.

Here, three final decisions await your wisdom:

- **Allow user to reset password using Apple ID.** If this person ever forgets his password, he'll be offered, on the login screen, a chance to recover it by entering his Apple ID. Nice little safety net. (Available only for accounts for which you've entered an Apple ID, of course.)

- **Allow user to administer this computer.** This checkbox lets you turn ordinary, unsuspecting Standard or Managed accounts into Administrator accounts, as described above. You know—when your kid turns 18.

- **Enable Parental Controls.** "Parental Controls" refers to the feature that limits what your offspring are allowed to do on this computer—and how much time a day they're allowed to spend glued to the mouse. Details are on page 498.

Phase 3: Choose a Picture

The usual sign-in screen (Figure 15-1) displays each account holder's name, accompanied by a little picture.

When you click the sample photo, you get a pop-up menu of Apple-supplied graphics; you can choose one to represent you. It becomes not only your icon on the sign-in screen, but also your "card" photo in the Contacts program and your icon in Messages.

If you'd rather supply your *own* graphics file—a photo of your own head, for example—just drag it directly out of its Finder window and onto the "picture well" (Figure 15-3). Use the cropping slider below the picture to frame it properly.

Or you can click the existing image to open a pop-up pane. As shown in Figure 15-3, you have three more options here:

- **Choose one of the Defaults.** Apple starts you off with a selection of account photos, intended to represent various personalities: eagles, flowers, chalkboard math, basketball, and so on.

- **My Photo Stream.** Here are the last 1,000 photos you've taken with, or imported into, your Mac (page 363). Click one, and then click Edit to adjust its size and framing within the circle.

- **Camera.** Click the 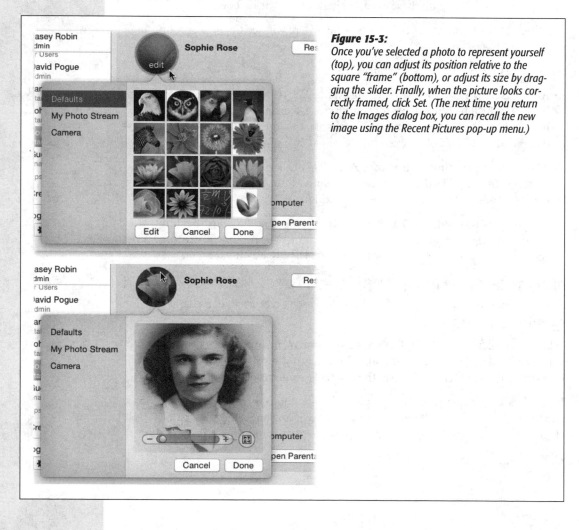 button. The Mac counts down from 3 to help you get ready, and then takes the picture. You can enlarge or shrink it; drag to move it within the circular frame; click the ⓝ button to apply a special color or distortion effect to it; or click 📷 to try again.

Figure 15-3:
Once you've selected a photo to represent yourself (top), you can adjust its position relative to the square "frame" (bottom), or adjust its size by dragging the slider. Finally, when the picture looks correctly framed, click Set. (The next time you return to the Images dialog box, you can recall the new image using the Recent Pictures pop-up menu.)

In each case, click Done to enshrine your account photo forever (or until you feel like picking a different one).

Phase 4: Login Items (Startup Items)

There's one additional setting that your account holders can set up for themselves: which programs or documents open automatically upon login. (This is one decision an administrator *can't* make for other people. It's available only to whoever is logged in at the moment.)

To choose your own crew of self-starters, open System Preferences and click Users & Groups. Click your account. Click the Login Items tab. As shown in Figure 15-4, you can now build a list of programs, documents, disks, and other goodies that automatically launch each time you log in. You can even turn on the Hide checkbox for each one so that the program is running in the background at login time, waiting to be called into service with a quick click.

Figure 15-4:
You can add any icon to the list of things you want to start up automatically. Click the + button to summon the Open dialog box, where you can find the icon, select it, and then click Choose. Better yet, if you can see the icon in a folder or disk window (or on the desktop), just drag it into this list. To remove an item, click it in the list and then click the — button.

Don't feel obligated to limit this list to programs and documents, by the way. Disks, folders, servers on the network, and other fun icons can also be startup items, so that their windows are open and waiting when you arrive at the Mac each morning.

Tip: Here's a much quicker way to add something to the Login Items list: right-click (or two-finger click) its Dock icon and choose "Open at Login" from the shortcut menu.

Parental Controls

If you're setting up a Standard/Managed account, the Parental Controls checkbox affords you the opportunity to shield your Mac—or its very young, very fearful, or very mischievous operator—from confusion and harm. This is a helpful feature to remember when you're setting up accounts for students, young children, or easily intimidated adults. (This checkbox is available for Admin accounts, too, but turning it on produces a "Silly rabbit—this is for kids!" sort of message.)

You can specify how many hours a day each person is allowed to use the Mac, and declare certain hours (like sleeping hours) off-limits. You can specify exactly who your kids are allowed to communicate with via email (if they use Mail) and instant messaging (if they use Messages), what Web sites they can visit (if they use Safari), what programs they're allowed to use, and even what words they can look up in the OS X Dictionary.

Here are all the ways you can keep your little Managed account holders shielded from the Internet—and themselves. For sanity's sake, the following discussion refers to the Managed account holder as "your child." But some of these controls—notably those in the System category—are equally useful for people of *any* age who feel overwhelmed by the Mac, are inclined to mess it up by not knowing what they're doing, or are tempted to mess it up deliberately.

Figure 15-5:
In the Parental Controls window, you can control the capabilities of any account holder on your Mac. If you turn on Limit Applications, then the lower half of the Apps tab window lets you choose applications (those from the Mac App Store and others), and even Dashboard widgets, by turning on the boxes next to their names. (Expand the flippy triangles if necessary.) Those are the only programs the account holder will be allowed to use. The search box helps you find certain programs without knowing their categories.

Note: If you apply any of these options to a Standard account, then the account type listed on the Users & Groups pane changes from "Standard" to "Managed."

To begin, click Open Parental Controls at the bottom of the Users & Groups pane. Turn on "Enable parental controls," if necessary. Now you should see the screen shown in Figure 15-5.

Apps Tab

On this tab (Figure 15-5), you can limit which programs your Managed-account flock is allowed to use. (Limiting what people can do to your Mac when you're not looking is a handy feature under any shared-computer circumstance. But if there were one word tattooed on its forehead, it would be "Classrooms!")

Use Simple Finder

If you're *really* concerned about somebody's ability to survive the Mac—or the Mac's ability to survive somebody—turn on Use Simple Finder. Then turn on the checkboxes of the programs that person is allowed to use.

Suppose you've been given a Simple Finder account. When you log in, you discover the barren world shown in Figure 15-6. There are only three menus (, Finder, and

Figure 15-6:
The Simple Finder doesn't feel like home—unless you've got one of those Spartan, space-age, Dr. Evil–style pads. But it can be just the ticket for less-skilled Mac users, with few options and a basic one-click interface. Every program in the My Applications folder is actually an alias to the real program, which is safely ensconced in the off-limits Applications folder.

File), a single onscreen window, no hard drive icon, and a bare-bones Dock. The only folders you can see are in the Dock. They include these:

- **My Applications.** This folder holds aliases of the applications that the administrator approved. They appear on a strange, fixed icon view called "pages." List and column views don't exist. As a Simple person, you can't move, rename, delete, sort, or change the display of these icons—you can merely click them. If you have too many to fit on one screen, you get numbered page buttons beneath them, which you can click to move from one set to another.

- **Documents.** Behind the scenes, this is your Home→Documents folder. Of course, as a Simple Finder kind of soul, you don't *have* a visible Home folder. All your stuff goes in here.

- **Shared.** This is the same Shared folder described on page 513. It's provided so that you and other account holders can exchange material. However, you can't open any of the folders here, only the documents.

- **Trash.** The Trash is here, but you won't use it much. Selecting or dragging any icon is against the rules, so you're left with no obvious means of putting anything into your Trash.

The only program with its own icon on the Dock is the Finder.

To keep things extra-simple, OS X permits only one window at a time to be open. It's easy to open icons, too, because *one* click opens them, not two.

The File menu is stunted, offering only a Close Window command. The Finder menu gives you only two options: About Finder and Run Full Finder. (The latter command prompts you for an administrator's user name and password, and then turns back into the regular Finder—a handy escape hatch. To return to Simple Finder, just choose Finder→Return to Simple Finder.)

The menu is *really* bare-bones: You can Log Out, Force Quit, or go to Sleep. That's it. And there's no trace of Spotlight.

Otherwise, you can essentially forget everything else you've read in this book. You can't create folders, move icons, or do much of anything beyond clicking the icons that your benevolent administrator has provided. It's as though OS X moved away and left you the empty house.

Although the Simple Finder is simple, any program (at least, any that the administrator has permitted) can run from Simple Finder. A program running inside the Simple Finder still has all its features and complexities—only the Finder has been whittled down to its essence.

In other words, Simple Finder is great for streamlining the Finder, but novices won't get far combating their techno-fear until the world presents us with Simple iMovie, Simple Mail, and Simple Microsoft Word. Still, it's better than nothing.

Limit Applications

When you turn on Limit Applications, the list shown in Figure 15-5 springs to life. It's all the programs you've bought from the Mac App Store, all other programs, all Dashboard widgets, and all the apps in your Utilities folder. Only checked items will show up in the account holder's Applications folder. (If you don't see a program listed, then use the search box, or drag its icon from the Finder into the window.)

Note: This pane gives special attention to programs you've bought from the App Store (see page 145). The Allow App Store Apps pop-up menu even lets you specify an appropriate age group for the permitted apps. If you choose "up to 9+," for example, your well-parented offspring will be allowed to use all App Store programs that have been rated for use by anyone who's 9 or older.

Web Tab

This feature is designed to limit which Web sites your kid is allowed to visit.

Frankly, trying to block the racy stuff from the Web is something of a hopeless task; if your kid doesn't manage to get around this blockade by simply using a different browser, then he'll just see the dirty pictures at another kid's house. But at least you can enjoy the illusion of taking a stand, using approaches with three degrees of severity:

- **Allow unrestricted access to Web sites.** No filtering. Anything goes.

- **Try to limit access to adult Web sites automatically.** Those words—"try to"—are Apple's way of admitting that no filter is foolproof.

 In any case, OS X analyzes what's on a Web page that you try to call up and filters out Web sites with naughty material. These sites won't appear in Safari while this account holder is logged in. By clicking Customize and then editing the "Always allow" and "Never allow" lists, you can override its decisions on a site-at-a-time basis.

- **Allow access to only these Web sites.** This is the most restrictive approach of all: It's a *whitelist*, a list of the *only* Web sites your youngster is allowed to visit. It's filled with kid-friendly sites like Disney and Discovery Kids, but of course you can edit the list by clicking the + and − buttons below the list.

People Tab

Here you can control your kid's access to three realms of people: those on email, on Messages, and on Game Center. Turn on the checkboxes as you feel it's necessary.

Then build a list of email and chat addresses, corresponding to the people you feel comfortable letting your kid exchange emails and chats with. Click the + button below the list, type the address, and then press Return. Lather, rinse, repeat.

Tip: No, you can't drag cards in from Contacts; that would be too simple. But after clicking + to create a new row in the list (in Edit mode), you can drag *just the email address* out of a Contacts card you've opened up. Or expand the resulting dialog box (click the ▾ button) and double-click someone in your address book.

For reasons explained in a moment, turn on "Send permission requests to" and plug in your own email address.

Now then: When your youngster uses Apple's Mail program to send a message to someone who's *not* on the approved list, or tries to chat with someone not on the list, she gets a message that says, "You do not have permission to send messages to this email address." If she clicks Ask Permission, then *your* email address shortly receives a permission-request message; meanwhile, the outgoing message gets placed in limbo in her Drafts folder.

If you're convinced that the would-be correspondent is not, in fact, a stalker, you can grant permission by clicking Always Allow. Your young ward gets the good news the next time she visits her Drafts folder, where the message has been awaiting word from you, the Good Parent.

Note: This feature doesn't attempt to stop email or chat using *other* programs, like Microsoft Outlook or Skype. If you're worried about your efforts being bypassed, block access to those programs using the Limit Applications feature described on page 501.

When your underling fires up Messages or Mail, she'll discover that her Buddy List is empty except for the people you've identified.

Handling the teenage hissy fit is your problem.

GEM IN THE ROUGH

Logs

On the Web tab of the Parental Controls pane, you'll find a button called Logs. That, my friends, is Big Brother Central.

It gives you a complete rundown of what your kids have been up to. Its four categories—Websites Visited, Websites Blocked, Applications, and Messages—are extremely detailed. For example, in Applications, you can see exactly which programs your kids tried to use when, and how much time they spent in each one.

It's spying, sure, but it's for the good of the child. (Right?) Use the pop-up menus at the top to change the time period being reported (Today, This Week, or whatever)

and how they're grouped in the list—by date or by application/Web site.

If you see something that you really think should be off limits—a site in the Websites Visited list, an application, a Messages session with someone—click its name and then click Restrict. You've just nipped that one in the bud.

Conversely, if the Mac blocked a Web site that you think is really OK, click its name in the list, and then click Allow. (And if you're wondering what a certain Web page *is,* click it and then click Open.)

Time Limits

Clever folks, those Apple programmers. They must have kids of their own.

They realize that some parents care about *how many* hours their kids spend in front of the Mac, and that some also care about *which* hours (Figure 15-7):

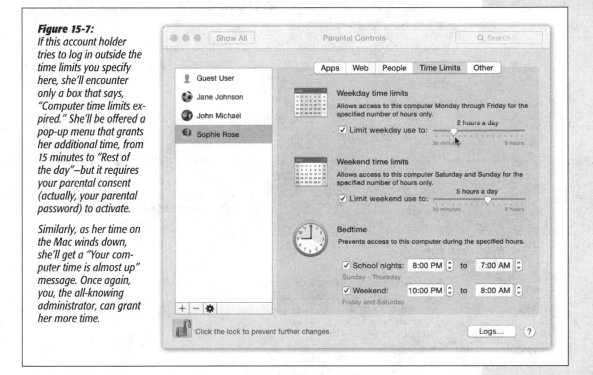

Figure 15-7:
If this account holder tries to log in outside the time limits you specify here, she'll encounter only a box that says, "Computer time limits expired." She'll be offered a pop-up menu that grants her additional time, from 15 minutes to "Rest of the day"—but it requires your parental consent (actually, your parental password) to activate.

Similarly, as her time on the Mac winds down, she'll get a "Your computer time is almost up" message. Once again, you, the all-knowing administrator, can grant her more time.

- **How much time.** In the "Weekday time limits" and "Weekend time limits" sections, turn on "Limit weekday use to" or "Limit weekend use to" and then adjust the sliders.

- **Which hours.** In the "Bedtime" section, turn on the checkbox for either "School nights" or "Weekend," and then set the hours of the day (or, rather, night) when the Mac is unavailable to your young account holder.

 In other words, this feature may have the smallest pages-to-significance ratio in this entire book. Doesn't take long to explain it, but it could bring the parents of Mac addicts a lot of peace.

Tip: When Time Limits have been applied, your little rug rats can now check to see how much time they have left to goof off on the Mac before your digital iron fist slams down. When they click the menu-bar clock (where it now says the current time), a menu appears, complete with a readout that says, for example, "Parental Controls: Time Remaining 1:29." Good parenting comes in many forms.

Other Tab

This tab offers a few miscellaneous options, including:

- **Disable built-in camera.** You've just prevented your kids from filling up your hard drive with photos of their body parts.

- **Disable Dictation.** Those kids can't turn on the Dictation feature. They can talk only to you and other humans.

- **Hide profanity in Dictionary.** OS X comes with a complete electronic copy of the *New Oxford American Dictionary.* And "complete," in this case, means "it even has swear words."

Turning on "Hide profanity in Dictionary" is like having an Insta-Censor™. It hides most of the naughty words from the dictionary whenever your young account holder is logged in (Figure 15-8).

Figure 15-8:
Something's missing from the Dictionary when the Parental Control tool is turned on: dirty words.

- **Limit printer administration.** When this checkbox is on, your underlings aren't allowed to change your Mac's printer settings. You wouldn't want them deleting or installing any printers, would you?

- **Disable changing the password.** Pretty self-explanatory. This option prevents your unruly minions from changing their passwords. That's your job, after all.

- **Limit CD and DVD burning.** When you first create Standard accounts, their holders are free to burn CDs or DVDs. But in a school lab, for example, you might want to turn off the ability to burn discs (to block software piracy). That's why this box is here.

Editing Accounts

If you're an administrator, you can change your own account in any way you like.

If you have any other kind of account, though, you can't change anything but your picture, password, Apple ID, and login items. If you want to make any other changes, you have to ask an admin to log in, make the changes you want made to your account, and then turn the computer back over to you.

Deleting Accounts

Hey, it happens: Somebody graduates, somebody gets fired, somebody dumps you. Sooner or later, you may need to delete an account from your Mac.

When that time comes, click the account name in the Users & Groups list and then click the minus-sign button beneath the list. OS X asks what to do with all the dearly departed's files and settings (Figure 15-9):

- **Save the home folder in a disk image.** This option represents the "I'll be back" approach. OS X preserves the deleted account holder's folders on the Mac, in a tidy digital envelope that won't clutter your hard drive and can be reopened in case of emergency.

Figure 15-9:
Top: This dialog box lets you know where to find the deleted account's material, should the need arise.

Bottom: The files and settings of accounts you deleted can live on in the Users→Deleted Users folder.

Are you sure you want to delete the user account "Casey Robin"?

To delete this user account, select what you want to do with the home folder for this account, and then click "Delete User".

- **Save the home folder in a disk image**
 The disk image is saved in the Deleted Users folder (in the Users folder).

- **Don't change the home folder**
 The home folder remains in the Users folder.

- **Delete the home folder**
 Erase home folder securely

Cancel Delete User

Deleted Users

Back View Arrange Action Share Edit Tags

caseyrobin.dmg

1 item, 459.05 GB available

In the Users→Deleted Users folder, you find a disk image file (.dmg). If you double-click it, a new, virtual disk icon named for the deleted account appears on your desktop. You can open folders and root through the stuff in this "disk," just as if it were a living, working Home folder.

If fate ever brings that person back into your life, you can use this disk image to reinstate the deleted person's account. Start by creating a brand-new account. Then copy the contents of the folders in the mounted disk image (Documents, Pictures, Desktop, and so on) into the corresponding folders of the new Home folder.

- **Don't change the home folder.** This time, OS X removes the *account*, in that it no longer appears in the Login list or in the Users & Groups pane of System Preferences—but it leaves the *Home folder* right where it is. Use this option if you don't intend to dispose of the dearly departed's belongings right here and now.

- **Delete the home folder.** This button offers the "Hasta la vista, baby" approach. The account and all its files and settings are vaporized forever, on the spot. (The "Erase home folder securely" option even records gibberish over the spot where that home folder was, so that its contents can't be recovered even by the NSA.)

Note: If you delete a Shared Only account, you're not offered the chance to preserve the Home folder contents—because a Shared Only account doesn't *have* a Home folder.

Setting Up the Login Process

Once you've set up more than one account, the dialog box shown in Figure 15-1 appears whenever you turn on the Mac, whenever you choose →Log Out, or whenever the Mac logs you out automatically. But a few extra controls let you, an administrator, set up either more or less security at the login screen—or, put another way, build in less or more convenience.

Open System Preferences, click Users & Groups, click the and enter an admin password to prove your worthiness, and then click the Login Options button (Figure 15-10). Here are some of the ways you can shape the login experience for greater security (or greater convenience):

- **Automatic login.** This option eliminates the need to sign in at all. It's a timesaving, hassle-free arrangement if only one person uses the Mac, or uses it most of the time.

When you choose an account holder's name from this pop-up menu, you're prompted for his password. Type it and click OK.

From now on, the dialog box shown in Figure 15-1 won't appear *at all* at startup time. After turning on the machine, you, the specified account holder, zoom straight to your desktop.

Of course, everybody else must still enter their names and passwords. (And how can they, since the Mac rushes right into the Automatic person's account at startup time? Answer: The Automatic thing happens only at startup time. The usual

login screen appears whenever the current account holder logs out—by choosing ⌘→Log Out, for example.)

- **Display login window as.** Under normal circumstances, the login screen presents a list of account holders when you power up the Mac, as shown in Figure 15-1. That's the "List of users" option in action.

If you're especially worried about security, however, you might not even want that list to appear. If you turn on "Name and password" (Figure 15-10), then each person who signs in must type both his name (into a blank that appears) *and* his password—a very inconvenient, but more secure, arrangement.

Figure 15-10:
These options make it easier or harder for people to sign in, offering various degrees of security. By the way: Turning on "Name and password" also lets you sign in as >console, an advanced geeky troubleshooting technique. It's also one way to sign in with the root account, if you're Unixy enough to know what that is.

- **Show the Sleep, Restart, and Shut Down buttons.** Truth is, the OS X security system is easy to circumvent. Truly devoted evildoers can bypass the standard login screen in a number of different ways: restart in FireWire disk mode, restart at the Unix Terminal, and so on. Suddenly, these no-goodniks have full access to every document on the machine, blowing right past all the safeguards you've so carefully established.

One way to thwart them is to use FileVault (page 519). Another is to turn off this checkbox. Now there's no Restart or Shut Down button to tempt mischief-makers. That's plenty of protection in most homes, schools, and workplaces; after all, Mac people tend to be *nice* people.

But if you worry that somebody with a pronounced mean streak might restart simply by pulling the plug, then either use FileVault or set the *firmware password*, as described in the box below.

- **Show Input menu in login window.** If the Input menu is available at login time, it means that people who use non-U.S. keyboard layouts and alphabets can use the login features without having to pretend to be American. (You can't use fancy non-Roman alphabets like Japanese or Russian for your password. But at least this option will let you enter your full name in the language of your choice. Greetings, Mr. Bond-san.)

- **Show password hints.** OS X is kind enough to display your password hint ("middle name of the first person who ever kissed me") after you've typed it wrong three times when trying to log in. This option lets you turn off that feature for an extra layer of security. The hint will never appear.

The Firmware Password Utility

After all this discussion of security and passwords, it may come as a bit of a shock to learn that enterprising villains can bypass all of OS X's security features in 10 seconds. If you haven't turned on FileVault, their nefarious options include using the Unix console described in Appendix B, single-user mode, FireWire disk mode, and so on.

But there is one way to secure your Mac completely: by turning on the very secret, little-known firmware password.

To find it, restart your Mac while pressing ⌘-R. That starts up OS X's Recovery console (page 732).

Once you've chosen your language, choose Utilities→Firmware Password Utility.

When you run this utility, enter an administrator's password. Now turn on "Require password to change firmware settings," as shown here. Then make up a password—your firmware password—that will be required to start up from anything but the internal drive.

Next, you're asked for an administrator's password. Finally, a message tells you, "The settings were successfully saved." Restart the Mac.

From now on, whenever you attempt to start up in anything but the usual way, you're asked to type the firmware password. Holding down the C key to start up from a CD, holding down N to start up from a NetBoot server, pressing T to start up in Target Disk Mode, pressing D to start up from the installation DVD in diagnostic mode, pressing ⌘-V to start up in Verbose mode, ⌘-S to start up in Single-user mode, ⌘-Option-P-R to reset the parameter RAM, pressing Option to start up from a different system disk, pressing Shift to enter Safe Boot mode—none of it works without the master firmware password.

> **Firmware Password Utility**
>
> The firmware password is used to prevent others from starting your computer with a different disk. This makes your computer even more secure.
>
> ☑ Require password to change firmware settings
>
> Password: [_____]
> Type a password or phrase
>
> Verify: [_____]
> Retype the password or phrase
>
> (Cancel) (OK)

- **Show fast user switching menu as:** The fast user switching feature lets you switch to another account without having to log out of the first one, as described on page 514.

 If you do turn on fast user switching, a new menu appears at the upper-right corner of your screen, listing all the account holders on the machine. Thanks to this pop-up menu, you can now specify what that menu looks like. It can display the current account holder's full name (Name), the short name (Short Name), or only a generic torso-silhouette icon (Icon) to save space on the menu bar.

- **Use VoiceOver in the login window.** The VoiceOver feature (page 714) is all well and good if you're blind. But how are you supposed to log in? Turn on this checkbox, and VoiceOver speaks the features on the Login pane, too.

Tip: Actually, there's one more, rather secret login option—and if you're a laptop lugger, you might really like it. You can create a message that appears on the login screen whenever you—or, rather, *not* you—turns on the computer. For example, it could be an "If found, contact…" message. Or a "$500 reward" message.

To set it up, open System Preferences→Security & Privacy→General. Click the 🔒, authenticate yourself, and then turn on "Show a message when the screen is locked." Click Set Lock Message, and then type your message. (Press Option-Return to create a new paragraph.) And hope whoever finds your laptop has a conscience.

Signing In, Logging Out

Once somebody has set up your account, here's what it's like getting into, and out of, an OS X machine. (For the purposes of this discussion, "you" are no longer the administrator—you're one of the students, employees, or family members for whom an account has been set up.)

Identifying Yourself

When you first turn on the Mac—or when the person who last used this computer chooses →Log Out—the login screen shown in Figure 15-1 appears. At this point, you can proceed in any of several ways:

- **Restart.** Click if you need to restart the Mac for some reason. (The Restart and Shut Down buttons don't appear here if the administrator has chosen to hide them as a security precaution.)

- **Shut Down.** Click if you're done for the day, or if sudden panic about the complexity of user accounts makes you want to run away. The computer turns off.

- **Log In.** To sign in, click your account name in the list. If you're a keyboard speed freak, you can also type the first letter or two—or press the up or down arrow keys—until your name is highlighted. Then press Return.

 Either way, the password box appears now (if a password is required). If you accidentally click the wrong person's name on the first screen, you can click Back. Otherwise, type your password, and then press Return (or click Log In).

You can try as many times as you want to type the password. With each incorrect guess, the entire password box shudders violently from side to side, as though shaking its head no. (If you see a strange ⇧ icon in the password box, guess what? You've got your Caps Lock key on, and the Mac thinks you're typing an all-capitals password.)

If you try unsuccessfully three times, your hint appears—if you've set one up. And if even that safety net fails, you can use your Apple ID as the key to resetting your password. See the box below.

Once you're in, the world of the Mac looks just the way you left it (or the way an administrator set it up for you). Everything in your Home folder, all your email and bookmarks, your desktop picture and Dock settings—all of it unique to you.

Unless you're an administrator, you're not allowed to install any new programs (or, indeed, to put anything at all) into the Applications folder. That folder, after all, is

FREQUENTLY ASKED QUESTION

The Forgotten-Password Survival Guide

Help—I forgot my password! And I never told it to anybody, so even the administrator can't help me!

No problem. Your administrator can simply open up System Preferences, click Users & Groups, click your account name, and then click Reset Password to re-establish the password.

But you don't understand. I am the administrator! And I'm the only account!

Lucky for you, Apple has provided you with not one, not two, but three safety nets. None of them work, however, unless your friendly neighborhood administrator turned them on in advance.

First: On your third attempt to type your password correctly, the Mac shows you your password hint (if you have one, and if the administrator left the Hint option turned on).

Second: If the administrator has turned on the "Allow user to reset password using Apple ID" in System Preferences→ Users & Groups, then you can click the ? button right there in the Password box when you're logging in. A tiny message appears, letting you know that, "If you forgot your password, you can reset it using your Apple ID."

To proceed, click the ⊕ button to bring up the Reset Password dialog box. Enter your Apple ID and password, and

then click Reset Password. A message appears to let you know that changing your account password will also create a new Keychain (page 526). (The old one is still around, ready to be unlocked if you remember the old password at some point.) Click OK. Now enter a new password (twice) and password hint, and then click Reset Password.

You've just reset your account password. Click Continue Log In to finish logging in with your new, improved, not-forgotten password.

Third: If the administrator has turned on FileVault, described later in this chapter, then you can use its recovery key to log in, in a pinch. It's the master password: a last-ditch, emergency, backup password.

If you have your recovery key, read on. (If not, and you opted to store it with Apple, call Apple tech support; they'll give it to you. If not, and you didn't store it with Apple, you're completely out of luck. Your hard drive is encrypted, and you can't do anything but erase it and kiss your files goodbye.)

Anyway, restart the Mac. On the login screen, click your name; then click the ? button. If the hint appears and it helps you out, great. If not, click "Reset it using your Recovery Key," type in your recovery key, and then praise the Apple gods that this final safety net actually worked.

a central software repository for *everybody* who uses the Mac, and the Mac forbids everyday account holders from moving or changing all such universally shared folders.

Logging Out

When you're finished using the Mac, choose →Log Out (or press Shift-⌘-Q). A confirmation message appears; if you click Cancel or press Esc, you return to whatever you were doing. If you click Log Out or press Return, you return to the screen shown in Figure 15-1, and the entire sign-in cycle begins again.

Tip: If you press Option as you choose →Log Out (or as you press Shift-⌘-Q), the confirmation box doesn't appear.

Logout Options

When you choose →Log Out and confirm your intention to log out, the login screen appears, ready for the next victim.

But sometimes people forget. You might wander off to the bathroom for a minute, but run into a colleague there who breathlessly begins describing last night's date and proposes finishing the conversation over pizza. The next thing you know, you've left your Mac unattended but logged in, with all your life's secrets accessible to anyone who walks by your desk.

You can tighten up that security hole, and many others, using the options in the Security & Privacy→General pane of System Preferences:

- **Require password [immediately] after sleep or screen saver begins.** This option gives you a password-protected screensaver that locks your Mac when you wander away. Now, whenever somebody tries to wake up your Mac after the screensaver has appeared (or when the Mac has simply gone to sleep according to your settings in the Energy Saver pane of System Preferences), the "Enter your password" dialog box appears. No password? No access.

 The pop-up menu here (which starts out saying "immediately") is a handy feature. Without it, the person most inconvenienced by the password requirement would be *you,* not the evil snitch from Accounting; even if you just stepped away to the bathroom or the coffee machine, you'd have to unlock the screensaver with your password. It would get old fast.

 Instead, the password requirement can kick in only after you've been away for a more serious amount of time—5 minutes, 15 minutes, an hour, whatever. You can still put the Mac to sleep, or you can still set up your screensaver to kick in sooner than that. But until that time period has passed, you'll be able to wake the machine without having to log in.

 (Super-geeky bonus fact: You can use a Unix command in Terminal, described in the free downloadable appendix called "Terminal Crash Course.pdf" on this book's "Missing CD" page at *www.missingmanuals.com*, to specify *any* time interval—not just the canned choices in the pop-up menu. The magic command is *defaults -cur-*

rentHost write com.apple.screensaver askForPasswordDelay -int 1800, where the final
number specifies how many seconds should elapse before a password is required.)

- **Show a message when the screen is locked.** Whatever you type into this box will
 appear on the login screen (where you click your name in the list) or the screen-
 saver. It could be, "Getting coffee..." or your name and cellphone number or
 anything you like.

- **Disable automatic login.** This is just a duplicate of the Automatic Login on/off
 switch described on page 506. Apple figured that this feature really deserved *some*
 presence on a control panel called Security & Privacy.

If you click the Advanced button (at the bottom of the Security & Privacy pane of
System Preferences), you get these three bonus tweaks:

- **Log out after [60] minutes of inactivity.** You can make the Mac sign out of your
 account completely if it figures out that you've wandered off (and it's been, say,
 15 minutes since the last time you touched the mouse or keyboard). Anyone who
 shows up at your Mac will find only the standard login screen.

- **Require an administrator password to access system-wide preferences.** Ordinarily,
 certain System Preferences changes require an administrator's approval—namely,
 the ones that affect the entire computer and everyone who uses it, like Date & Time,
 Users & Groups, Network, Time Machine, and Security & Privacy. If you're *not* an
 administrator, you can't make changes to these panes until an administrator has
 typed in her name and password to approve your change.

 However, once Mr. Teacher or Ms. Parent has unlocked *one* of those secure prefer-
 ence settings, they're *all* unlocked. Once the administrator leaves your desk, you
 can go right on making changes to the *other* important panes (Network *and* Time
 Machine *and* Security & Privacy) without the administrator's knowledge.

 Unless this "Require an administrator password" box is turned on, that is. In that
 case, an Administrative account holder has to enter her name and password to
 approve *each* of those System Preferences panes individually.

Sharing Across Accounts

It's all fine to say that every account is segregated from all *other* accounts. It's nice to
know your stuff is safe from the prying eyes of your coworkers or family.

But what about collaboration? What if you *want* to give some files or folders to an-
other account holder?

You can't just open up someone else's Home folder and drop it in there. Yes, every
account holder has a Home folder (all in the Users folder on your hard drive). But if
you try to open anybody else's Home folder, you'll see a tiny red ⊖ icon superimposed
on almost every folder inside, telling you, "Look, but don't touch."

Fortunately, there are a couple of wormholes between accounts (Figure 15-11):

- **The Shared folder.** Sitting in the Users folder is one folder that doesn't correspond to any particular person: Shared. Everybody can freely access this folder, inserting and extracting files without restriction. It's the common ground among all the account holders on a single Mac. It's Central Park, the farmers' market, and the grocery-store bulletin board.

- **The Public folder.** In your Home folder, there's a folder called Public. Anything you copy into it becomes available for inspection or copying (but not changing

Figure 15-11:

Top: In other people's Home folders, the Public folder is available for your inspection. It contains stuff that other people have "published" for the benefit of their coworkers.

Middle: In the Public folder is the Drop Box, which serves the opposite purpose. It lets anyone else who uses this Mac hand in files to you; they, however, can't see what's in the box.

Bottom: Inside the Users folder (to get there from a Home folder, press ⌘-▲) is the Shared folder, a wormhole connecting all accounts. Everybody has full access to everything inside.

or deleting) by any other account holder, whether they log into your Mac or sign in from across the network.

- **The Drop Box.** And *inside* your Public folder is another cool little folder: the Drop Box (not to be confused with the free online Dropbox service). It exists to let *other* people give files to *you*, discreetly and invisibly to anyone else. That is, people can drop files and folders into your Drop Box, but they can't actually *open* it. This folder, too, is available both locally (in person) and from across the network.

Fast User Switching

The account system described so far in this chapter has its charms. It keeps everyone's stuff separate, it keeps your files safe, and it lets you have the desktop picture of your choice.

Unfortunately, it can go from handy to hassle in one split second. That's when you're logged in, and somebody else wants to duck in just for a second—to check email or a calendar, for example. What are you supposed to do—log out completely, closing all your documents and quitting all your programs, just so the interloper can look something up? Then afterward, you'd have to log back in and fire up all your stuff again, praying that your inspirational muse hasn't fled in the meantime.

Fortunately, that's all over now. Fast user switching lets Person B log in and use the Mac for a little while. All *your* stuff, Person A, simply slides into the background, still open the way you had it; see Figure 15-12.

When Person B is finished working, you can bring your whole work environment back to the screen without having to reopen anything. All your windows and programs are still open, just as you left them.

FREQUENTLY ASKED QUESTION

Shared Data Files

My wife and my 8-year-old kid share my Mac. Over the years, we've amassed a fabulous collection of MP3 files, but at the moment, I'm the only one who sees them in iTunes. This business of separate environments for every account holder is all well and good, but what about when we want to access the same files—like our iTunes Library?

The problem is that the iTunes Library is stored in the Music folder of just one person. Fortunately, the solution is easy enough.

Whoever is the administrator—probably your 8-year-old—should move the iTunes Music folder (currently inside

somebody's Music→iTunes folder) to the Users→Shared folder. Now it's available to everybody.

At this point, each account holder can log in, fire up iTunes, choose iTunes→Preferences→Advanced, and click the Change button to choose the relocated iTunes Music folder in the Shared folder. To update the list of songs, you should also drag the folder into each account holder's iTunes window.

From now on, each person will be able to see and access the entire library of iTunes tunes. Your underlings won't be able to rename songs, convert them to other formats, and so on, but they'll still enjoy the flexibility to build individual playlists.

Do you see your own account name, or a human silhouette, in the upper-right corner of the screen (Figure 15-12)? It lists all account holders.

(If you don't see this Fast User Switching menu, open the Users & Groups pane of System Preferences; click the 🔒, if necessary, to unlock the pane. Click Login Options, and turn on the "Show fast user switching menu as" checkbox. And while you're at it: You can change what this menu looks like by using the "Show fast user switching menu as" pop-up menu.)

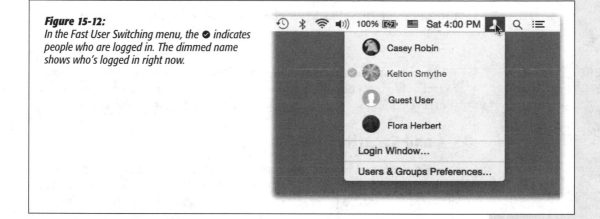

Figure 15-12:
In the Fast User Switching menu, the ⊘ *indicates people who are logged in. The dimmed name shows who's logged in right now.*

Next time you need a fellow account holder to relinquish control so you can duck in to do a little work, just choose your name from the Accounts menu. Type your password, if one is required, and feel guiltless about the interruption.

And now, the finer points of fast user switching:

- Depending on how many programs are open and how much memory the Mac has, switching accounts may entail a delay and some hard drive activity. That's OS X's virtual memory scheme "setting down" what was in memory in *your* account to make room for the incoming account's stuff.

- To exit an open account, choose →Log Out as usual. Or just choose Login Window from the Accounts menu. It ensures that you can get to your own account no matter whose is running at the moment.

- Weirdly enough, a bunch of account holders can be using the same program simultaneously in their own parallel universes.

- You can't make changes to accounts (in System Preferences) that are still logged in. You can't turn off fast user switching or turn on FileVault while other people are logged in, either.

- If you try to shut the Mac down or restart it while other people are logged in, a dialog box tells you, "There are currently logged in users who may lose unsaved changes if you shut down this computer." And you're asked to type in an administrator's name and password to establish that you know what you're doing.

Here's a moral dilemma for the modern age: If you proceed by typing the password and clicking Shut Down, you shut down all accounts that were open in the background *and* any open documents. If you click Cancel, you can't shut down the Mac until you hunt down the account holders whose stuff is still open in the background so they can log out.

Tip: You can avoid this awkward situation in either of two ways: (1) Trust one another completely, or (2) Save all your documents before you let anyone else cut in and send your account to the background.

* Remember the Shared folder (in the Users folder on the hard drive)? It's still the wormhole connecting all accounts. If you want to share a file with another account holder, put it there.

* Your account isn't anesthetized completely when it's switched into the background. In fact, it keeps on doing whatever you set it to doing. If you were downloading some big file, for example, it keeps right on downloading when the next guy logs in.

OS X and Security

OS X has a spectacular reputation for stability and security. At this writing, there still hasn't been a single widespread OS X virus. There's also no Windows-esque plague of spyware (downloaded programs that do something sneaky behind your back).

The usual rap is, "Well, that's because Windows is a much bigger target. What virus writer is going to waste his time on a computer with 8 percent market share?"

That may be part of the reason OS X is virus-free. But OS X was also built more intelligently from the ground up. Listed below are a few of the many drafty corners of a typical operating system that Apple has solidly plugged:

* OS X has always come from the factory with all of its *ports* shut and locked.

POWER USERS' CLINIC

Virtual Memory, Security, and You

Virtual memory is a trick that computers use to keep a lot of programs open at once—more, in fact, than they technically have enough memory (RAM) for. How do they manage to keep so many software balls in the air? Easy: They set some of them down on the hard drive.

When you bring Photoshop to the front, OS X frees up the necessary memory for it by storing some of the *background* programs' code on the hard drive. When you switch back to, say, Safari, OS X swaps Photoshop for the Safari code it needs from the hard drive, so that the frontmost program always has full command of your actual memory.

Sophisticated software snoopers could, in theory, sneak up to the Mac while you're logged in but away from your desk. Using a built-in Unix command called *strings,* the no-goodniks could actually *read* what's stored on the hard drive in that virtual-memory swap file—in particular, your passwords.

Lucky for you, your *virtual memory swap files* are encrypted, automatically and invisibly, so nobody can read them.

Ports are channels that remote computers use to connect to services on your computer: one for instant messaging, one for Windows' remote-control feature, and so on. It's fine to have them open if you're expecting visitors. But if you've got an open port that exposes the soft underbelly of your computer without your knowledge, you're in for a world of hurt. Open ports are precisely what permitted viruses like Blaster in 2003 to infiltrate millions of PCs.

- In OS X, no program (like a virus) can install itself without your awareness. You're notified at every juncture when anything is trying to install itself on your Mac. In fact, every time you try to download something, either in Safari or Mail, that contains *executable code* (a program, in other words), a dialog box warns you that it could conceivably harbor a virus—even if your download is compressed as a .zip file.

- Unlike certain other operating systems, OS X doesn't even let an administrator touch the files that drive the operating system itself without pestering you to provide your password and grant it permission to do so. An OS X virus could theoretically wipe out all your files, but it wouldn't be able to access anyone else's stuff—and it couldn't touch the operating system itself.

- You probably already know about the Finder's Secure Empty Trash option (page 113). But an option on the Erase tab of the Disk Utility program can do the same super-erasing of *all free space* on your hard drive. We're talking not just erasing, but recording gibberish over the spots where your files once were—once, seven times, or *35* times—utterly shattering any hope a hard-disk recovery firm (or spy) might have had of recovering passwords or files from your hard drive.

- Safari's Private Browsing mode means you can freely visit Web sites without leaving any digital tracks—no history, no nothing.

Those are only a few tiny examples. Here are a few of OS X's big-ticket defenses.

Gatekeeper

This security feature is going to send every Eastern European teenage hacker into therapy.

Nasty programs aren't very common on the Mac to begin with. But now, unless you turn Gatekeeper off, downloading a program that's secretly designed to damage your Mac is virtually impossible.

Gatekeeper won't even let you install programs that haven't been proved to be safe (Figure 15-13).

There's no Gatekeeper app or even a Gatekeeper System Preferences icon. Instead, to find Gatekeeper, you open System Preferences→Security & Privacy→General. At the bottom of this screen (Figure 15-13, top), you see three options. These three humble buttons are Gatekeeper.

Click the 🔒 and enter your password to unlock this pane. Now your choices, under "Allow applications downloaded from," are as follows:

- **Mac App Store.** This is the safest option. *Every* program that Apple allows into its Mac App store is safe. Each has been tested by Apple to make sure that, among other things, it's both *sandboxed* (blocked from accessing parts of the Mac that it doesn't need) and *digitally signed* (set up to notify that Mac if it's been altered in any way since it left the software company).

 So what happens if you try to download a program that didn't come from the App Store? The Mac won't let you install it, period.

Figure 15-13:
Top: The "Allow apps downloaded from" options are, in fact, the face of Gatekeeper.

Bottom: If you try to open a downloaded program that Apple can't vouch for, you get this admonishing dialog box.

- **Mac App Store and identified developers.** This option, the factory setting, lets you download and install both App Store programs and those from "identified developers." That means software companies that have registered with Apple and received, in turn, an encrypted code (a "certificate") that's embedded in their programs.

 This certificate lets Apple track who created the app, and also digitally signs it, as described above. Now, Apple may not know this software company, and Apple

doesn't inspect its software. But if anybody reports that some program is actually a virus in disguise, Apple can instantly add that program to its blacklist—and prevent millions of other people from installing it. (OS X updates its blacklist once a day.)

- **Anywhere.** This button turns Gatekeeper off (after presenting an "Are you sure?" message). You're free to download and install any programs you want, with no checking for their hygiene.

Tip: Don't turn on Anywhere just because there's one particular non-kosher app you want to run. In that case, it's smarter to leave Gatekeeper turned on—and override Gatekeeper just for that one app. To do so, right-click (or two-finger click) the program's icon; from the shortcut menu, choose Open.

Gatekeeper is a pretty powerful disincentive for the world's bad eggs; if millions of people leave Gatekeeper turned on, the bad guys might as well not even bother. Their apps will never be downloaded and can therefore never spread.

There are, however, some important limitations to note:

- Gatekeeper doesn't uninstall programs you've already installed. (Once you've run any program once, Gatekeeper never checks it again.)
- Gatekeeper is intended to stop bad software that you get by *downloading*. It doesn't do anything about programs you've installed from, for example, a DVD or USB drive.
- It doesn't stop Flash and Java programs.

Overall, Gatekeeper is a pretty convincing barrier to a Windows-like nightmare scenario, where some virus breaks out into the wild and takes down hundreds of thousands of computers. If most people leave the factory setting selected—and they will—that outcome is virtually impossible.

FileVault

FileVault is one of OS X's most powerful security features. Understanding what it does, however, may take a little slogging.

As you know, the accounts system is designed to keep people out of one another's stuff. Ordinarily, for example, Chris isn't allowed to go rooting through Robin's email and files.

Until FileVault came along, though, there were all kinds of ways to circumvent this protection system. A sneak or a show-off could start up the Mac in FireWire disk mode, for example, or even remove the hard drive and hook it up to a Linux machine or another Mac.

In each case, they'd then be able to run rampant through everybody's files, changing or trashing them with abandon. For people with sensitive or private files, the result was a security hole bigger than Kim Kardashian's bank account.

FileVault is an extra line of defense. When you turn on this feature, your Mac automatically *encrypts* (scrambles) *everything* on your startup hard drive—not just what's in your Home folder. Every time you create or save a new file, it, too, is insta-encrypted.

Note: FileVault uses something called XTS-AES 128 encryption. How secure is that? It would take a password-guessing computer *149 trillion years* before hitting pay dirt. Or, in more human terms, slightly longer than two back-to-back *Transformers* movies.

This means that unless someone knows (or can figure out) your password, FileVault renders your files unreadable for anyone but you and your computer's administrator—no matter what sneaky tricks they try to pull. (You can, if you like, authorize other account holders to get in, too.)

You won't notice much difference when FileVault is turned on. You log in as usual, clicking your name and typing your password. Only a slight pause as you log out indicates that OS X is doing some housekeeping on the encrypted files: freeing up some space and/or backing up your home directory with Time Machine.

Tip: This feature is especially useful for laptop owners. If someone swipes or "borrows" your laptop, they can't get into your stuff without the password.

Here are some things you should know about FileVault's protection:

- **It's useful only if you've logged out.** Once you're logged in, the entire drive is unlocked and accessible. If you want the protection, log out before you wander away from the Mac.

- **An administrator can access your files, too.** According to OS X's caste system, anyone with an Administrator account can theoretically have unhindered access to his peasants' files—even with FileVault on—if that administrator has the master password (the recovery key) described below.

- **FileVault relies on the Recovery HD partition.** You can read about this secret chunk of your hard drive on page 519. For now, the point is that if you've deliberately reformatted your hard drive in some nonstandard way, you may not be able to use FileVault.

- **FileVault can encrypt external drives, too—even flash drives.** The controls to do this, though, are in a different place—not in System Preferences at all. Instead, open Disk Utility (in your Utilities folder). Erase the external drive using Mac OS Extended (Journaled, Encrypted) format. (And, yes, you have to *erase* the drive before you can encrypt it.)

Note: Pre-OS X Lion machines won't be able to access a drive you've encrypted in this way.

- **You can turn FileVault off at any time.** Just revisit the FileVault pane in System Preferences. (It takes time to decrypt your drive, but you can keep right on working.)

To turn FileVault on, proceed like this:

1. **In System Preferences, click Security & Privacy, and then click FileVault. Click the 🔒, authenticate yourself, and then click Turn On FileVault.**

 Now, remember, FileVault encrypts all your files. If you forget your Mac account password—well, that would be bad.

 Yeah, yeah, the peons with Standard accounts forget *their* account passwords all the time. But with FileVault, a forgotten password would mean *the entire hard drive is locked forever.* So Apple gives you, the technically savvy administrator, a back door, for use in that situation.

 It offers to let you use your iCloud password (your Apple ID password) as the back door. That's a much more reasonable option than the alternative, the *recovery key.*

 The recovery key is a long, complicated override password like UK84-LVT5-YFX9-XN3K-LT53-PL9N. It gives you another way to unlock the encrypted drive, even without knowing the account holder's password.

Figure 15-14:
Top: You have to explicitly give permission to each person you want to allow to log into your FileVault-protected Mac.

Bottom: Here's your recovery key: a skeleton key that can get you into your encrypted Mac even if the idiot administrator forgets his password. (You have no idea how often this happens.)

2. **Choose the backdoor method you prefer: "my iCloud account" or "recovery key." Click Continue.**

 If you chose the recovery key, the Mac now shows it to you: a long, complicated string of numbers and letters and hyphens. Write it down in a place you'll never lose it! Then click Continue.

 Either way, a list of account holders now appears (Figure 15-14, top). The button next to each one, Enable User, might sound like you're about to lead someone into drug addiction, but it's actually your chance to specify who else can unlock the disk by logging in.

3. **For each person you want to be able to log into this Mac with her own password, click Enable User. Type in that person's password and click OK. When you're finished, click Continue.**

 (Anyone in this list to whom you *don't* give access can still use the Mac—but only after persuading an administrator to come over and type in his name and password.)

4. **Click Restart.**

 When you log in again, the Mac begins the process of encrypting your entire hard drive. This process takes a long time (the FileVault pane in System Preferences shows you the estimated remaining time), but you can keep using your Mac in the meantime. In theory, you won't feel much of a slowdown at all while the encrypting is going on. You can even restart or shut down the computer.

 You shouldn't notice any speed hit as you *work* with an encrypted disk, either. You'll notice only a few small security-related changes. For example, you'll be asked for your password every time you wake the computer or exit the screensaver.

UP TO SPEED

Password Hell

In OS X, you have quite a few different passwords to keep straight. Each one, however, has a specific purpose:

Account password. You type this password in at the normal login screen. You can't get into anyone else's account with it—only yours. Entering this password unlocks FileVault, too.

Administrator password. You're asked to enter this password whenever you try to install new software or modify certain system settings. If you're the only one who uses your computer (or you're the one who controls it), your administrator password *is* your account password. Otherwise, you're supposed to go find an administrator (the parent, teacher,

or guru who set up your account to begin with) and ask that person to type in his name and password once he's assessed what you're trying to do.

Recovery key. Think of this password as a master key. If anyone with FileVault forgets her account password, the administrator who knows the master password can unlock the account. This master password also lets an administrator change an account's password right at the login screen, whether FileVault is turned on or not.

Root password. This password is rarely useful for anything other than Unix hackery; you know who you are.

Note: Actually, there's one more change. When FileVault is turned on, you won't see the icon for the Recovery HD appear when you hold down the Option key at startup. It's still there, though, and you can still start up with the Recovery HD by pressing ⌘-R as your Mac starts up.

The Firewall

If you have a broadband, always-on connection, you're open to the Internet 24 hours a day. It's theoretically possible for some cretin to use automated hacking software to flood you with data packets or take control of your machine. OS X's *firewall* feature puts up a barrier to such mischief. To turn it on, click the 🔒 on the Firewall pane, authenticate yourself, and then click Start.

Note: You don't need to turn on this firewall if your Mac connects to the Internet through a wired or wireless router (including the AirPort base station). Virtually every router already has a built-in firewall that protects your entire network. (Similarly, if you're using the Internet Sharing feature described on page 359, turn on the firewall only for the *first* Mac, the one connected right to the Internet.)

In short: Use the firewall only if your Mac is connected *directly* to a cable modem, DSL box, or dial-up modem.

Fortunately, it's not a *complete* barrier. One of the great joys of having a computer is the ability to connect to other computers. Living in a cement crypt is one way to avoid getting infected, but it's not much fun.

Therefore, you can turn the firewall on by opening System Preferences→Security & Privacy→Firewall tab, authenticating, and clicking Turn On Firewall. But you can also fine-tune the blockade.

To do that, click Firewall Options; you see something like Figure 15-15. As you can sort of tell, OS X lets you allow or block Internet connections individually for *each program* on your Mac. Here's what you'll find there:

- **Block all incoming connections.** This option might be better known as Paranoid Mode. You're allowed to do email and basic Web surfing and a few other deep-seated services that OS X needs to get by. But all other kinds of network connections are blocked, including screen sharing, iTunes music sharing, and so on. This is a hardcore, meat-fisted firewall that, for most people, is more trouble than it's worth.

Tip: As you can tell from the wording of this item, OS X's firewall blocks only *incoming* connections, which covers most of the dangerous stuff. But if you'd also like your Mac to block *outgoing* Internet connections, you can install a shareware firewall program like Little Snitch. It's available on this book's "Missing CD" page at *www.missingmanuals.com*.

- **[List of individual programs].** If the firewall is on but you haven't turned on "Block all," then the Mac uses this list of individual programs and features to determine

what's allowed to accept network connections (Figure 15-15, bottom). They get added to this list automatically when you turn them on in System Preferences: File Sharing, Printer Sharing, and so on.

Figure 15-15:
Top: The OS X firewall starts with a simple button click. The fun stuff doesn't begin until you click Firewall Options.

Bottom: This pane lists the programs that have been given permission to receive communications from the Internet. At any point, you can change a program's Block/Allow setting, as shown here. You can also click the + button to navigate to your Applications folder and manually choose programs for inclusion.

Non-Apple programs can gain passage through your firewall, too. You can add one to the list manually by clicking the + below the list and choosing it by hand; or you can simply respond to the request box that pops up whenever a new program wants to accept incoming Internet connections.

Click Allow for each such request (unless, of course, you see a request for an app called SneakyPoisonVirus or something). As you do so, their names get added to the list of programs in this dialog box.

For each program, you can use the pop-up menu beside its name to specify either "Allow incoming connections" or "Block incoming connections," depending on your level of paranoia.

Note: From time to time, some program will ask for permission to accept incoming messages from its mother ship online. If it's a program you trust, click Allow.

- **Automatically allow signed software to receive incoming connections.** *Signed* software means programs that Apple recognizes as coming from legitimate companies. Anything from Adobe or Microsoft, for example, has got to be OK, right? (Insert your own wisecrack here.)

Note: OK, technically, a signed program is one whose authenticity is confirmed by a third party—a "certificate authority" company like Verisign or GoDaddy. A system of invisible *keys* (security numbers) confirms that the software did indeed come from the creators it claims it came from, no matter how many detours it took to reach you.

One more point: When you explicitly grant permission to a program, as described below, *you're* signing that program.

If this checkbox is *not* turned on, then each time you run a new program for the first time, you'll be interrupted so that the Mac can ask if it's OK to permit Internet connections. The "signed software" box cuts down on the interruptions, since well-known apps are assumed not to be viruses or spyware.

- **Enable stealth mode.** This is designed to slam shut the Mac's back door to the Internet. See, hackers often use automated hacker tools that send out "Are you there?" messages. They're hoping to find computers that are turned on and connected full time to the Internet. If your machine responds, and they can figure out how to get into it, they'll use it, without your knowledge, as a relay station for pumping out spam or masking their hacking footsteps.

"Enable stealth mode," then, makes your Mac even more invisible on the network; it means your Mac won't respond to the electronic signal called a *ping*. (On the other hand, *you* won't be able to ping your machine, either, when you're on the road and want to know if it's turned on and online.)

Note: You might have noticed that there doesn't seem to be any option to turn on *firewall logging,* which creates a little text file where OS X records every attempt that anyone from the outside makes to infiltrate your Mac. Logging is available, though—in fact, it's turned on all the time. To view the log, open the Applications→Utilities→Console program. In the left-side list, expand the */private/var/log* heading, and click *appfirewall.log.*

The Password Assistant

Plenty of software features require you to make up a password: Web sites, accounts, networked disks, and so on. No wonder most people wind up trying to use the same password in as many situations as possible. Worse, they use something easily guessable like their names, kids' names, spouse's names, and so on. Even regular English words aren't very secure, because hackers routinely use *dictionary attacks*—software that tries to guess your password by running through every word in the dictionary—to break in.

To prevent evildoers from guessing your passwords, OS X comes with a good-password suggestion feature called the Password Assistant (Figure 15-16). It cheerfully generates one suggestion after another for impossible-to-guess passwords (*recharges8@exchangeability*, anyone?).

Figure 15-16:
Anyplace you're supposed to make up a password, including in the Users & Groups pane of System Preferences, a key icon appears. When you click it, the Password Assistant opens. Use the pop-up menu and the Length slider to specify how long and unguessable the password should be. The Quality graph shows you just how tough it is to crack this password.

(In the Type pop-up menu, you might wonder about FIPS-181. It stands for the Federal Information Processing Standards Publication 181, which sets forth the U.S. government's standard for password-generating algorithms.)

Fortunately, *you* won't have to remember most of them, thanks to the Keychain password-memorizing feature described next. The only password you have to memorize is your account password.

The Keychain

The information explosion of the computer age may translate into bargains, power, and efficiency, but as noted above, it carries with it a colossal annoyance: the proliferation of *passwords* we have to memorize. Shared folders on the network, Web sites, FTP sites—each requires another password.

Apple has done the world a mighty favor with its *Keychain* feature. (It's an earlier, not-Internet-based version of the iCloud Keychain described on page 434.) Whenever you log into OS X and type in your password, you've typed the master code that tells the computer, "It's really me. I'm at my computer now." From that moment on, the Mac *automatically* fills in every password blank you encounter, whether it's a Web site in Safari, a shared disk on your network, a wireless network, an encrypted disk image, or an FTP (File Transfer Protocol) program like Transmit or Cyberduck. With only a few exceptions, you can safely forget *all* your passwords except your login password.

All kinds of programs and services know about the Keychain and offer to store your passwords there. For example:

• In Safari, whenever you type your name and password for a certain Web page and then click OK, a dialog box asks: "Would you like to save this password?" (See Figure 15-17, top.)

Note: This offer is valid only if, in Safari→Preferences→AutoFill tab, "User names and passwords" is turned on. If not, the "Would you like to save this password?" message never appears.

Note, too, that some Web sites use a nonstandard login system that doesn't produce the "Would you?" message. Unless the Web site provides its own "Remember me" or "Store my password" option, you're out of luck; you'll have to type in this information with every visit.

Figure 15-17:
Top: Safari is one of several Internet-based programs that offer to store your passwords in the Keychain; just click Yes. The next time you visit this Web page, you'll find your name and password already typed in.

At any time, you can see a complete list of the memorized Web passwords by choosing Safari→Preferences→Passwords.

Bottom: When you connect to a server (a shared disk or folder on the network), just turn on "Remember this password in my keychain."

- When you connect to a shared folder or disk on the network, the opportunity to save the password in your Keychain is equally obvious (Figure 15-17, bottom).

- You also see a "Remember password (add to Keychain)" option when you create an encrypted disk image using Disk Utility.

- Mac email programs, like Mail and Outlook, store your email account passwords in your Keychain. So do FTP programs; check their Preferences dialog boxes.

- Your iCloud account information is stored in the Keychain, too (as you entered it on the iCloud pane of System Preferences).

- A "Remember password" option appears when you type in the password for a wireless network or an AirPort base station.

- The iTunes program memorizes your iTunes Store password, too.

Locking and unlocking the Keychain

If you work alone, the Keychain is automatic, invisible, and generally wonderful. Login is the only time you have to type a password. After that, the Mac figures, "Hey, I know it's you; you proved it by entering your account password. That ID is good enough for me. I'll fill in all your other passwords automatically." In Apple parlance, you've *unlocked* your Keychain just by logging in.

But there may be times when you want the Keychain to *stop* filling in all your passwords, perhaps only temporarily. Maybe you work in an office where someone else might sit down at your Mac while you're getting a candy bar.

Of course, you can have OS X lock your Mac—Keychain and all—after a specified period of inactivity (page 512).

But if you want to lock the Keychain *manually*, so that no passwords are autofilled in until you unlock it again, you can use any of these methods. Each requires the Keychain Access program (in your Applications→Utilities folder):

- **Lock the Keychain manually.** In the Keychain Access program, choose File→Lock Keychain "login" (⌘-L), or just click the big 🔒 button in the toolbar (Figure 15-18).

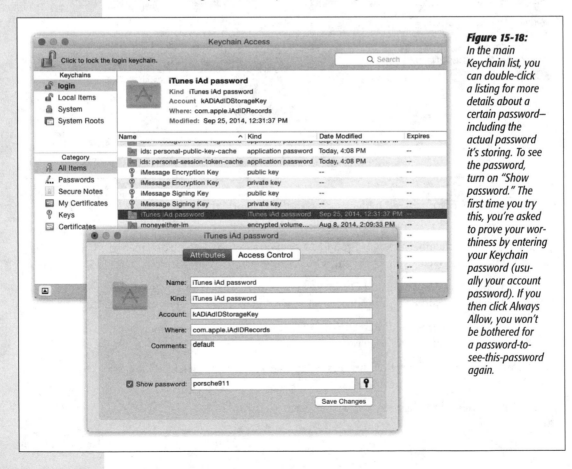

Figure 15-18:
In the main Keychain list, you can double-click a listing for more details about a certain password– including the actual password it's storing. To see the password, turn on "Show password." The first time you try this, you're asked to prove your worthiness by entering your Keychain password (usually your account password). If you then click Always Allow, you won't be bothered for a password-to-see-this-password again.

- **Choose Lock Keychain "login" from the Keychain menulet.** To put the Keychain menulet on your menu bar, open Keychain Access, choose Keychain Access→Preferences→General. Turn on "Show keychain status in menu bar."
- **Lock the Keychain automatically.** In the Keychain Access program, choose Edit→ Change Settings for Keychain [your name]. The resulting dialog box lets you set up the Keychain to lock itself, say, 5 minutes after the last time you used your Mac, or whenever the Mac goes to sleep. When you return, you're asked to re-enter your account password in order to unlock the Keychain.

Whenever the Keychain is locked, OS X no longer fills in your passwords.

Note: As noted above, you unlock your Keychain using the same password you use to log into OS X, but that's just a convenience. If you're really worried about security, you can choose Edit→Change Password for Keychain [your name], thereby establishing a *different* password for your Keychain, so that it no longer matches your login password.

Managing Keychain

To take a look at your Keychain, open the Keychain Access program. By clicking one of the password rows, you get to see its attributes—name, kind, account, and so on (Figure 15-18).

Tip: The primary purpose of the Keychain is, of course, to type in passwords for you automatically. However, it's also an excellent place to record all kinds of private information just for your own reference: credit card numbers, ATM numbers, and so on. Simply choose File→New Password Item (if it's a name and password) or File→New Secure Note Item (if you just want to type a blob of very, very private text).

No, the Mac won't type them in for you automatically anywhere, but it will maintain them in one central location that is, itself, password-protected.

Multiple Keychains

By choosing File→New Keychain, you can create more than one Keychain, each with its own master password. On one hand, this might defeat the simplicity goal of the Keychain. On the other hand, it's conceivable that you might want to encrypt all your business documents with one master password and all your personal stuff with another, for example.

If you do have more than one Keychain, you can view all of them by clicking the little Show Keychains button at the lower-left corner of the Keychain Access window; now you see a list of all your Keychains (including some maintained by OS X itself). Click their names to switch among them.

Keychain files

Keychains are represented by separate files in your Home→Library→Keychains folder. Knowing that can be handy when you want to delete a Keychain or copy it to another Mac—your laptop, for example. (Then again, the File→Export command may be even more convenient.)

Privacy Shields

In Apple's mind, there's a difference between *security* (protecting your Mac) and *privacy* (protecting your information from distribution). The Privacy tab in the Security & Privacy pane of System Preferences harbors five fairly random privacy-related options:

Location Services

Location Services means "knowing where I am." It's the feature that lets your laptop figure out its own time zone automatically, for example, or that lets a weather Web site show your *local* weather the first time you visit.

Every time a program wants to use your current location for its own features, you'll be asked about it. (The Mac figures out your location based on its proximity to known WiFi networks.) Each time you say OK, the program that did the asking installs its own name into the list here.

You can turn off the checkboxes of the programs you'd rather didn't know where you are, or you can turn off location tracking altogether by turning off the "Enable location services" box.

Contacts, Calendars, Reminders

Some programs work better if you allow them to access your address book, calendar, or to-do list. For example, Skype wants access so that it can incorporate *your* address book into *its* address book. This list shows all the programs that access your Contacts, Calendar, or Reminders apps—and offers checkboxes to turn off that access.

Twitter, Facebook

Here, you'll see programs that want to access your Twitter and Facebook accounts. Once again, you can turn off their access, if you like.

Accessibility

Many programs that have nothing to do with assisting the disabled nonetheless rely on the Mac's built-in accessibility features to work, including Parallels Desktop, Skype, TextExpander, and even Apple programs like Safari and System Preferences.

Diagnostic and Usage Data

If you turn on this box, your Mac will automatically and quietly send data to Apple about what's going on with your Mac (anonymously, of course—Apple won't know it's you). The transmissions include details about crashes and freezes, what programs and hardware you use, what software versions and peripherals you have, and so on.

None of this is transmitted unless you turn this box on.

Networking, File Sharing & AirDrop

etworks are awesome. Once you've got a home or office network, you can copy files from one machine to another—even between Windows PCs and Macs—just as you'd drag files between folders on your own Mac. You can send little messages to other people's screens. Everyone on the network can consult the same database or calendar, or listen to the same iTunes music collection. You can play games over the network. You can share a single printer or cable modem among all the Macs in the office. You can connect to the network from wherever you are in the world, using the Internet as the world's longest extension cord back to your office.

In OS X, you can even do *screen sharing,* which means that you, the wise computer whiz, can see what's on the screen of your pathetic, floundering relative or buddy elsewhere on the network. You can seize control of the other Mac's mouse and keyboard. You can troubleshoot, fiddle with settings, and so on. It's the next best thing to being there—often, a lot *better* than being there.

Note: This chapter concerns itself with *local* networking—setting up a network in your home or small office. But don't miss its sibling, Chapter 10, which is about hooking up to the somewhat larger network called the Internet.

Wiring the Network

Most people connect their computers using one of two connection systems: Ethernet or WiFi.

Note: Until recently, Apple had its own name for WiFi: AirPort. That's what it said in System Preferences→Network, for example, and that's what the 📶 menulet was called.

AirPort was a lot cleverer, wordplay-wise, than the meaningless "WiFi." Unfortunately, not many people realized that AirPort was the same thing as what the rest of the world called WiFi. So at least in the onscreen references, these days, Apple gives AirPort a new name: WiFi.

Ethernet Networks

Every Mac (except the MacBook Air) has an Ethernet jack (Figure 16-1). If you connect all the Macs and Ethernet printers in your small office to a central Ethernet hub, switch, or *router*—a compact, inexpensive box with jacks for five, 10, or even more computers and printers—you've got yourself a very fast, very reliable network. (Most people wind up hiding the hub in a closet and running the wiring either along the edges of the room or inside the walls.) You can buy Ethernet cables, plus the hub, at any computer store or, less expensively, from an Internet-based mail-order house; none of this stuff is Mac-specific.

Tip: If you want to connect only two Macs—say, your laptop and your desktop machine—you don't need an Ethernet hub. Instead, you just need a standard Ethernet cable. Run it directly between the Ethernet jacks of the two computers. Then connect the Macs as described in the box on page 534.

Or don't use Ethernet at all; just use a person-to-person WiFi network.

Figure 16-1:
Every Mac except the Air has a built-in Ethernet jack (left). It looks like an overweight telephone jack. It connects to an Ethernet router or hub (right) via an Ethernet cable (also known as Cat 5 or Cat 6), which ends in what looks like an overweight telephone-wire plug (also known as an RJ-45 connector).

Ethernet jack Ethernet hub

Ethernet is the best networking system for many offices. It's fast, easy, and cheap.

WiFi Networks

WiFi, known to the geeks as 802.11 and to Apple fans as AirPort, means wireless networking. It's the technology that lets laptops get online at high speed in any WiFi "hotspot." Hotspots are everywhere these days: in homes, offices, coffee shops, hotels, airports, and thousands of other places.

When you're in a WiFi hotspot, your Mac has a very fast connection to the Internet, as though it's connected to a cable modem or DSL.

Every Mac has WiFi circuitry. It lets you connect to your network and the Internet wirelessly, as long as you're within about 150 feet of a *base station* or (as Windows people call it) *access point*. That box, in turn, must in turn be physically connected to a network and Internet connection.

The base station can take any of these forms:

- **AirPort base station.** Apple's sleek, white, squarish base stations ($100 to $180) permit as many as 50 computers to connect simultaneously.

 The less expensive one, the AirPort Express, is so small it looks like a small white power adapter. It also has a USB jack so you can share a USB printer on the network. It can serve up to 10 computers at once.

- **A Time Capsule.** This Apple gizmo is exactly the same as the AirPort base station, except that it also contains a huge hard drive so that it can back up your Macs automatically over the wired or wireless network.

UP TO SPEED

AirPort a, b, g, and n: Regular or Supersized?

In the short history of wireless networking, WiFi gear has come in several variants, bearing the absurdly user-hostile names 802.11b, 802.11g, 802.11a, 802.11n, and so on.

The difference involves the technical specs of the wireless signal. Original AirPort uses the 802.11b standard; AirPort Extreme uses 802.11g; the current AirPort cards and base stations use 802.11n.

So what's the difference? Equipment bearing the "b" label transfers data through the air at up to 11 megabits per second; the "g" system is almost five times as fast (54 megabits a second); and "n" is supposed to be four times as fast as that.

(Traditionally, geeks measure network speeds in megabits, not megabytes. If you're more familiar with megabytes, though, here's a translation: The older AirPort gear has a top speed of 1.4 megabytes per second, versus more than 6 megabytes per second for the AirPort Extreme stuff.)

(Oh, and while we're using parentheses here: The only place you'll get the quoted speeds out of this gear is on the moon. Here on earth, signal strength is affected by pesky things like air, furniture, walls, floors, wiring, phone interference, and antenna angles. Speed and signal strength diminish proportionally as you move away from the base station.)

Now, each successive version of the WiFi base station/laptop circuitry standard is backward-compatible. For example, you can buy a new, 802.11n base station, and still connect to it from your ancient 802.11g PowerBook. You won't get any greater speed, of course—that would require a laptop with an 802.11n transmitter—but you'll enjoy the greater range in your house.

It's important to understand, though, that even the most expensive, top-tier cable modem or DSL service delivers Internet information at only about half a megabyte per second. The bottleneck is the Internet connection, not your network. Don't buy newer AirPort gear thinking that you're going to speed up your email and Web activity.

Instead, the speed boost you get with AirPort Extreme is useful only for transferring files between computers and gadgets on your own network (like the bandwidth-hungry Apple TV)—and playing networkable games.

And one more note: All WiFi gear works together, no matter what kind of computer you have. There's no such thing as a "Windows" wireless network or a "Macintosh" wireless network. Macs can use non-Apple base stations, Windows PCs can use AirPort base stations, and so on.

- **A wireless broadband router.** Linksys, Belkin, and lots of other companies make less expensive WiFi base stations. You can plug the base station into an Ethernet router or hub, thus permitting 10 or 20 wireless-equipped computers, including Macs, to join an existing Ethernet network without wiring. (With all due non-fanboyism, however, Apple's base stations and software are more polished and satisfying to use.)

Tip: It's perfectly possible to plug a WiFi base station into a regular router, too, to accommodate both wired and wireless computers.

- **Another Mac.** Your Mac can also *impersonate* an AirPort base station. In effect, the Mac becomes a software-based base station, and you save yourself the cost of a separate physical base station.

- **A modem.** A few, proud people still get online by dialing via modem, which is built into some old AirPort base station models. The base station is plugged into a phone jack. Wireless Macs in the house can get online by triggering the base station to dial by remote control.

Tip: If you connect through a modern router or AirPort base station, you already have a great firewall protecting you. You don't have to turn on OS X's firewall.

You use the AirPort Utility (in your Applications→Utilities folder) to set up your base station; if you have a typical cable modem or DSL, the setup practically takes care of itself.

Whether you've set up your own wireless network or want to hop onto somebody else's, Chapter 10 has the full scoop on *joining* WiFi networks.

GEM IN THE ROUGH

Networking Without the Network

In a pinch, you can connect two Macs without any real network at all. You can create an Ethernet connection without a hub or a router—or an AirPort connection without a WiFi base station.

To set up the wired connection, just run a standard Ethernet cable between the Ethernet jacks of the two Macs. (You don't need to use an Ethernet crossover cable, as you did in days of old.)

To set up a wireless connection, from your 🛜 menulet, choose Create Network. Make up a name and password for your little private network, and then click OK. On the second Mac, choose 🛜→Join Network, enter the same private network name, and then click Join.

At this point, your two Macs belong to the same ad hoc micro-network. If you've shared some folders on the first Mac, its name (like "Casey's iMac") now appears in the Sidebar of the second Mac. Click it to see what's on it. From here, proceed exactly as described on page 546.

Cell Networks

If you have an iPhone or a similar cellphone, you may be able to get your Mac online even when you're hundreds of miles from the nearest Ethernet jack or WiFi hotspot. Thanks to *tethering,* your phone can act as an Internet antenna for your laptop, relying on the slow, expensive, but almost ubiquitous *cellular* network for its connection. Details are on page 356.

FireWire Networks

Apple is busily phasing out the convenient, fast *FireWire* jacks on its Macs. But if you have two FireWire-equipped Macs, you can create a blazing-fast connection between them with nothing more than a FireWire cable. Details are in the free downloadable appendix to this chapter called "FireWire Networking." It's available on this book's "Missing CD" page at *www.missingmanuals.com.*

File Sharing: Three Ways

When you're done wiring (or not wiring, as the case may be), your network is ready. Your Mac should "see" any Ethernet or shared USB printers, in readiness to print (Chapter 9). You can now play network games or use a network calendar. And you can now turn on *File Sharing,* one of the most useful features of all.

In File Sharing, you can drag files back and forth between different Macs (or even Windows PCs) on the network, exactly as though the other computer's folder or disk is a hard drive connected to your own machine. You can see the idea in Figure 16-2.

The thing is, it's not easy being Apple. You have to write *one* operating system that's supposed to please *everyone,* from the self-employed first-time newbie to the network administrator for NASA. You have to design a networking system simple enough for the laptop owner who just wants to copy things to a desktop Mac when returning from a trip, yet secure and flexible enough for the network designer at a large corporation.

Clearly, different people have different attitudes toward the need for security and flexibility.

That's why OS X offers *three ways* to share files, striking three different positions along the Simplicity-to-Flexibility Spectrum:

- **The easiest way: AirDrop.** This feature is dreamy—if there are other people in your house or office who have wireless Macs running Lion or later. Imagine this: You open the AirDrop folder, where you see everybody else's icons. To give someone a file, you drop its icon on that person's face. Done.

- **Slightly harder way: the Public folder.** Every account holder has a Public folder. It's free for anyone else on the network to access. Like a grocery store bulletin board, there's no password required. Super-convenient, super-easy.

 There's only one downside, and you may not care about it: You have to move or copy files *into* the Public folder before anyone else can see them. Depending on

how many files you want to share, this can get tedious, disrupt your standard organizational structure, and eat up disk space.

- **The flexible way: any folder.** You can also make *any* file, folder, or disk available for inspection by other people on the network. This method means that you don't have to move files into the Public folder, for starters. It also gives you elaborate control over who is allowed to do what to your files. You might want to permit your company's executives to see *and* edit your documents, but allow the peons in Accounting just to see them. And Andy, that unreliable goofball in Sales? You don't want him even *seeing* what's in your shared folder.

Of course, setting up all those levels of control means more work and more complexity.

The following pages tackle these three methods one at a time.

AirDrop

AirDrop is one of OS X's star attractions. It's a breakthrough in speed, simplicity, and efficiency. There's no setup, no passwords involved. It lets you copy files to someone else's Mac, iPhone, iPad, or iPod Touch up to 30 feet away, instantly and wirelessly; you don't need an Internet connection or even a WiFi network. It works on a flight, a beach, or a sailboat in the middle of the Atlantic. It also works if you are on a WiFi network, doing other things online.

You can exchange files with any Mac running OS X Lion or later, and any i-gadget running iOS 7 or later.

Sending by AirDrop

Usually, you'll begin the sending process in one of two ways:

- **From the Finder.** Right-click (or two-finger-click) the file's icon. From the shortcut menu, choose Share→AirDrop. The box shown in Figure 16-2 appears.

Figure 16-2:
The icons of nearby AirDrop-friendly Apple gadgets and Macs show up in this fun-sized window. You've already said what you want to send; now you just have to specify who gets it. Click the destination device's icon and then click Send.

Note: Here's a second way to send something in the Finder: Open the AirDrop *window*. (It's listed in the sidebar at the left side of every Finder window. Or choose Go→AirDrop, or press Shift-⌘-R.) Drag the icon(s) you want to send onto the icon of the receiving device (Figure 16-3).

Figure 16-3:
If there are other recent Lion or later Macs within about 30 feet, you see their logged-in owners' icons here. Usually, the icons display the Mac owners' account pictures; but if they have facial photos in your Contacts, then you see those instead.

- **From an app.** When you're looking at whatever you want to send, click the ⬆ button. From the shortcut menu, choose AirDrop.

 And where is that ⬆ button? Everywhere. It's at the top of every Finder window, and at the top of every Quick Look window. It's in Open and Save boxes on the Mac. It's available on every page in Safari, map in Maps, photo in Photos, contact in Contacts, and note in Notes. Lots of non-Apple apps offer that ⬆ button, too. (See page 239 for more on the Share button.)

In each case, you should now proceed as shown in Figure 16-2.

A message appears on the other gadget's screen, asking if the owner wants to accept your file. If she chooses Accept, then the transaction is complete. Quick, effortless, wireless, delightful.

Note: Until Yosemite came along, you and your recipient's Mac both had to have their AirDrop windows open. That's no longer true; AirDrop works whether that window is open or not.

Eight Reasons AirDrop Might Seem Not to Work

Miraculous though AirDrop may seem when it's working, certain stars do have to be in alignment. If AirDrop isn't working as advertised, here are some things to check:

- Both sender and receiver must have Bluetooth and WiFi turned on. They have to be within about 30 feet of each other.

- AirDrop works only with fairly recent Apple models. For example, it works with the MacBook Pro (made since late 2008), MacBook Air (since late 2010), MacBook (late 2008), iMac (early 2009), Mac mini (mid-2010), and Mac Pro (mid-2010).

 And among i-devices, it requires an iPhone 5 or later, iPad mini (any generation), iPad (4th generation or later), or iPod Touch (5th generation or later).

- If your Mac can't seem to "see" other nearby, older Macs (pre-2012 models)—either when sending or receiving an AirDrop file—the process may require an extra step. If you've right-clicked (or two-finger clicked) an icon or used the ⬆ button in a program, click "Don't see who you're looking for?" at top right (shown in Figure 16-2), and then click Search for an Older Mac.

 The "Don't see who you're looking for?" link also appears in the AirDrop *window* in the Finder (you can see it in Figure 16-3). Here again, only by clicking "Search for an Older Mac" will you see the icons for pre-2012 Mac models show up.

 And, by the way: When your Mac is seeing those *older* Macs, it can't see *newer* ones—and vice versa.

- On the Mac, AirDrop requires OS X Lion or later. On an iPhone, iPad, or iPod Touch, it requires iOS 7 or later.

- If you don't see the AirDrop icon in your Finder's sidebar, it's because somebody turned off its checkbox in Finder→Preferences→Sidebar. (You can still use Air-Drop, though.)

- If your lucky recipient's icon still isn't showing up on your Mac, he may have AirDrop turned off or restricted.

 Ask him to swipe up from the bottom of his screen and tap AirDrop (iOS device) or open the AirDrop window (Mac). Here you can control who can see you: Off (nobody), Contacts Only (people in your address book), or Everyone. It's supposed to be a security precaution, but you may as well leave it set to Everyone; after all, you have to approve every file individually, so it's not as though some passing hacker can shove evil files down your throat without your knowing.

 And if one of you has turned on Contacts Only, you still won't be able to participate in AirDrop transactions unless you're also logged into your iCloud account.

- AirDrop doesn't work if you've turned on "Block all connections" in your firewall (page 523).

- AirDrop requires both sending and receiving gadgets to be on (awake).

Receiving a File by AirDrop

If someone's sending *you* a file by AirDrop, the steps depend on whether you're using a Mac or an i-device:

- **Receiving on the Mac.** You get a notification (see Figure 16-4).

Tip: Actually, if you're sending something to *yourself*—from your own phone to your own Mac, for example—this confirmation doesn't appear. Apple notices that both devices are signed into the same iCloud account and figures that you don't need protection from *yourself*. So it just dumps the incoming file directly into your Downloads folder without making you accept it first. (You still get a notification that the transaction has happened.) It's very nice.

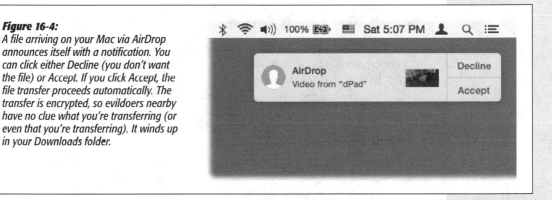

Figure 16-4:
A file arriving on your Mac via AirDrop announces itself with a notification. You can click either Decline (you don't want the file) or Accept. If you click Accept, the file transfer proceeds automatically. The transfer is encrypted, so evildoers nearby have no clue what you're transferring (or even that you're transferring). It winds up in your Downloads folder.

The file lands in your Downloads folder. This folder generally sits on the Dock, so it's easy to find. But you can also choose Go→Downloads, or press Option-⌘-L, to jump there.

- **Receiving on an iPhone/iPad/iPod Touch.** A message says, "[Other guy's name] would like to share [the file's name]." Tap Decline or Accept.

If your iOS device knows what to do with the file, it opens automatically in the appropriate app (a photo in Photos, a Web page in Safari, and so on).

If it's not sure what to do with the file, it offers a list of apps that can open your newly acquired item. For example, suppose someone's just sent you a Word document. You're offered a choice of apps that can handle Word files (either to open or to store them), like Evernote and Dropbox. Tap the one you want.

If you don't have any app that can open the file, iOS sometimes offers you the chance to download an app that *can*. And if even that trick comes up empty-handed, your i-device rejects the incoming file altogether.

There's a lot of great stuff in AirDrop:

- If you see someone's *name* beneath her icon in the AirDrop window, that means that she's in your Contacts *and* has signed in with her Apple ID. That's an extra bit of confidence that she is who her icon says she is.

- AirDrop works by creating a temporary two-computer wireless network. That's why it works even if you're not in a WiFi hotspot.

- If *you're* the one receiving a file, you can cancel a half-finished transfer by clicking the ⊗ button on the progress bar that wraps around the sender's icon in the AirDrop window. (Another way: If your Downloads folder is set to Stack view, you can click the ⊗ button in the corner of the file's icon.)

Sharing Your Public Folder

All right. So if AirDrop is so great, why doesn't it wipe out all other forms of file transfer and save this book a bunch of pages? Because (a) it works only on *Macs running Lion or later,* (b) it works only *wirelessly,* and (c) it's a one-way street. Other people can't *take* files from your Mac—you have to shove the files to them.

The next simplest file-sharing method eliminates all those limitations. It's the Public-folder method.

Figure 16-5:
Here's the master switch that makes your Public folder (and any other folders you designate) available to other people on the network. You can edit the Computer Name, if you like. Your Mac will appear on the network with this name. Make it nice and descriptive, such as Front Desk iMac.

Inside your Home folder, there's a folder called Public. (Inside *everybody's* Home folder is a folder called Public.)

Anything you put into this folder is automatically available to everyone else on the network. They don't need a password, they don't need an account on your Mac—they just have to be on the same network, wireless or wired. They can put files here *or* copy things out.

To make your Public folder available to your networkmates, you have to turn on the File Sharing master switch. Choose →System Preferences, click Sharing, and then turn on File Sharing (as shown in Figure 16-5).

Now round up the files and folders you want to share with all comers on the network and drag them into your Home→Public folder. That's all there is to it.

Note: You may notice that there's already something in your Public folder: a folder called Drop Box. It's there so that other people can give *you* files from across the network, as described later in this chapter.

So now that you've set up Public-folder sharing, how are other people supposed to access your Public folder? See page 546.

Sharing Any Folder

If the Public-folder method seems too simple and restrictive, then you can graduate to the "share any folder" method. In this scheme, you can make *any* file, folder, or disk available to other people on the network.

The advantage here is that you don't have to move your files into the Public folder; they can sit right where you have them. And this time, you can set up elaborate *sharing privileges* (also known as *permissions*) that grant individuals different amounts of access to your files.

This method is more complicated to set up than that Public-folder business. In fact, just to underline its complexity, Apple has created two different setup procedures. You can share one icon at a time by opening its Get Info window; or you can work in a master list of shared items in System Preferences.

The following pages cover both methods.

The Get Info Method

Here's how to share a Mac file, disk, or folder disk using its Get Info window.

The following steps assume that you've turned on →System Preferences→Sharing→File Sharing, as shown in Figure 16-5.

1. **Highlight the folder or disk you want to share. Choose File→Get Info.**

 The Get Info dialog box appears (Figure 16-6). Expand the General pane, if it's not already visible.

Note: Sharing an entire disk means that every folder and file on it is available to anyone you give access to. On the other hand, by sharing only a folder or two, you can keep *most* of the stuff on your hard drive private, out of view of curious network comrades. Sharing only a folder or two does *them* a favor, too, by making it easier for them to find the files they're supposed to have. This way, they don't have to root through your entire drive looking for the folder they actually need.

Figure 16-6:
The file-sharing permissions controls are here, in the Get Info box for any file, folder, or disk.

2. **Turn on "Shared folder."**

 Enter your administrative password, if necessary.

Tip: To help you remember what you've made available to other people on the network, a banner labeled "Shared Folder" appears across the top of any Finder window you've shared. It even appears at the top of the Open and Save dialog boxes.

OK, this disk or folder is now shared. But with whom?

3. **Expand the Sharing & Permissions pane, if it's not already visible. Click the 🔒 icon and enter your administrator's password.**

 The controls in the Sharing & Permissions area spring to life and become editable. At the bottom of the Info pane is a little table. The first column can display the names of individual account holders, like Casey or Chris, or *groups* of account holders, like Everyone or Accounting Dept.

The second column lists the *privileges* each person or group has for this folder.

Now, the average person has no clue what "privileges" means, and this is why things get a little hairy when you're setting up folder-by-folder permissions. But read on; it's not as bad as it seems.

4. **Edit the table by adding people's names. Then set their access permissions.**

At the moment, your name appears in the Name column, and it probably says Read & Write in the Privilege column. In other words, you're currently the master of this folder. You can put things in, and you can take things out.

If you just want to share files with *yourself*, so you can transfer them from one computer to another, you can stop here.

If you want to share files with *other* people—well, at the moment, the privileges for Everyone are probably set to "Read only." Other people can see this folder, but they can't do anything with it.

Your job is to work through this list of people, specifying *how much* control each person has over the file or folder you're sharing.

To add the name of a person or group, click the + button below the list. The list shown in Figure 16-7 appears.

Now click a name in the list. Then, from the Privilege pop-up menu, choose a permissions setting.

Figure 16-7:
This list includes every account holder on your Mac, plus groups you've set up, plus the contents of your address book. One by one, you can add them to the list of lucky sharers of your files or folders—and then change the degree of access they have to the stuff you're sharing.

- **Read & Write** has the most access of all. This person, like you, can add, change, or delete any file in the shared folder, or make any changes she likes to a document. Give Read & Write permission to people you trust not to mess things up.

- **Read only** means "Look, but don't touch." This person can see what's in the folder (or file) and can copy it, but he can't delete or change the original. It's a good setting for distributing company documents or making source files available to your minions.

- **Write only (Drop Box)** means that other people can't even open the folder. They can drop things *into* it, but it's like a mail slot: The letter disappears into the slot, and then it's too late for them to change their minds. As the folder's owner, you can do what you like with the deposited goodies. This drop-box effect is great when you want students, coworkers, or family members to be able to *turn things in* to you—homework, reports, scandalous diaries—without running the risk that someone else might see those documents. (This option doesn't appear for documents—only disks and folders.)

- **No access** is an option only for Everyone. It means that other people can see this file or folder's icon but can't do a thing with it.

Tip: Usually, you'll want the privileges for the folder to also apply to everything *inside* it; it would be a real drag to have to change the sharing privileges of the contents one icon as a time. That's why the ✿ menu at the bottom of the Get Info box has a command called "Apply to enclosed items."

5. **Close the Get Info window.**

 Now the folder is ready for invasion from across the network.

The System Preferences Method

It's very convenient to turn on sharing one folder at a time, using the Get Info window. But there's another way in, too, one that displays *all* your shared stuff in one handy master list.

To see it, choose →System Preferences. Click Sharing. Click File Sharing (and make sure it's turned on).

Now you're looking at a slightly different kind of permissions table, shown in Figure 16-8. It has *three* columns:

- **Shared folders.** The first column lists the files, folders, and disks you've shared. You'll probably see that every account's *Public* folder is already listed here, since they're all shared automatically. (You can turn *off* sharing for a Public folder, too, just by clicking it and then clicking the − button.)

 But you can add more icons to this list. Either drag them into the list directly from the desktop or a Finder window, or click the + sign, navigate to the item you want to share, select it, and then click Add. Either way, that item now appears in the Shared Folders list.

- **Users.** When you click a shared item, the second column sprouts a list of *who* gets to work with it from across the network. You're listed here, of course, since it's your stuff. There's also a listing here for Everyone, which really means "everyone *else*"—that is, everyone who's not specifically listed here.

 You can add to this list, too. Click + to open the person-selection box shown in Figure 16-7. It lists the other account holders on your Mac, and some predefined groups, as well as the contents of your Contacts.

Note: Most of the Contacts people don't actually have accounts on this Mac, of course. If you choose somebody from this list, you're asked to make up an account password. When you click Create Account, you've actually created a *Sharing Only* account on your Mac for that person, as described on page 491. When you return to the Users & Groups pane of System Preferences, you'll see that new person listed.

Figure 16-8:
Hiding in System Preferences is a list of every disk and folder you've shared. To stop sharing something, click it and click the — button. To share a new disk or folder, drag its icon off the desktop, or out of its window, directly into the Shared Folders list.

Double-click a person's name to add her to the list of people who can access this item from over the network, and then set up the appropriate privileges (described next).

To *remove* someone from this list, just click the name and then click the — button.

- **Users.** This *third* column lets you specify how much access each person in the *second* column has to this folder. Your choices, once again, are **Read & Write** (full access to change or delete this item's contents); **Read Only** (open or copy, but can't edit or delete); and **Write Only (Drop Box)**, which lets the person put things *into* this disk or folder, but not open it or see what else is in it.

For the Everyone group, you also get an option called **No Access,** which means that this item is completely off limits to everyone else on the network.

And now, having slogged through all these options and permutations, your Mac is ready for invasion from across the network.

Accessing Shared Files

The previous pages have described *setting up* a Mac so people at other computers can access its files. There's an easy, limited way (use the Public folder) and a more elaborate way (turn on sharing settings for each folder individually).

Now comes the payoff to both methods: sitting at another computer and *connecting* to the one you set up. There are two ways to go about it: You can use the Sidebar, or you can use the more flexible Connect to Server command. The following pages cover both methods.

Connection Method A: Use the Sidebar

Suppose, then, that you're seated in front of your Mac, and you want to see the files on another Mac on the network. Proceed like this:

1. **Open any Finder window.**

 In the Shared category of the Sidebar at the left side of the window, icons for all the computers on the network appear. See Figure 16-9.

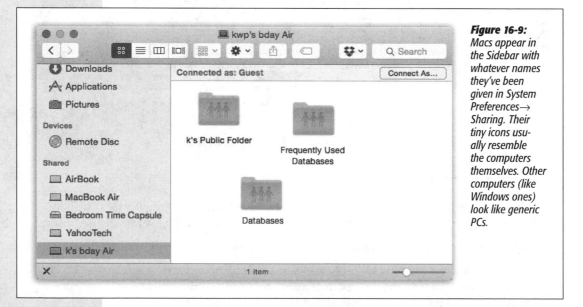

Figure 16-9:
Macs appear in the Sidebar with whatever names they've been given in System Preferences→Sharing. Their tiny icons usually resemble the computers themselves. Other computers (like Windows ones) look like generic PCs.

Tip: The same Sidebar items show up in the Save and Open dialog boxes of your programs, too, making the entire network available to you for opening and saving files.

If you don't see a certain Mac's icon here, it might be turned off, it might not be on the network, or it might have File Sharing turned off.

Note: Or it might not have the right file-sharing *type* turned on. To check, open System Preferences→Sharing; click Sharing, and then Options. You'll see checkboxes for AFP and SMB; your computers can't see each other if they don't have one of these options in common.

If you don't see any computers at all in the Sidebar, then *your* computer might not be on the network. Or maybe you've turned off the checkboxes for Connected Servers and Bonjour Computers in Finder→Preferences→Sidebar.

Tip: If the other Mac is just asleep, it still shows up in the Sidebar, and you can wake it up to get at it. How is that possible? Through the miracle of the Wake for Network Access feature described on page 594.

If there are a lot of computer icons in the Sidebar, or if you're on a corporate-style network that has the sub-chunks known as *workgroups*, you may also see an icon called All. Click it to see the full list of network entities that your Mac can see: not just individual Mac, Windows, and Unix machines, but also any "network neighborhoods" (limbs of your network tree). For example, you may see the names of network zones (clusters of machines, as found in big companies and universities).

Or, if you're trying to tap into a Windows machine, open the icon representing the *workgroup* (computer cluster) that contains the machine you want. In small office networks, it's usually called MSHOME or WORKGROUP. In big corpora-

POWER USERS' CLINIC

What You Can See

Precisely which other folders you can see on the remote Mac depend on what kind of account you have there: Guest, Standard, or Administrator. (See the previous chapter.)

If you're using the Guest account, you can see only the Public folders. The rest of the Mac is invisible and off limits to you. (You may see additional folders if somebody turned on sharing for them.)

If you have a Standard account, you can see other people's Public and Drop Box folders, plus your own Home folder. (Again, somebody may have made other folders available.)

If you're an administrator, you get to see icons for the account holders' Public folders and the hard drive itself to

which you're connecting. In fact, you even get to see the names of any other disks connected to that Mac.

If you, O lucky administrator, open the hard drive, you'll discover that you also have the freedom to see and manipulate the contents of the Applications, Desktop, Library, and Users→Shared folders.

You can even see what folders are in other users' Home folders, although you can't open them or put anything into them.

Finally, there's something called the root user. This account has complete freedom to move or delete any file or folder anywhere, including critical system files that could disable your Mac. It also requires a degree in Unix.

tions, these workgroups can be called almost anything—as long as it's no more than 15 letters long with no punctuation. (Thanks, Microsoft.)

If you *do* see icons for workgroups or other network "zones," double-click until you're seeing the icons for individual computers.

> **Note:** If you're a network nerd, you may be interested to note that OS X can "see" servers that use the SMB/CIFS, NFS, FTP, and WebDAV protocols running on OS X Server, Unix, Linux, Novell NetWare, and Windows servers (NT, 2000, XP, Vista, and Windows 7 or 8). But the Sidebar reveals *only* the shared computers on your *subnet* (your local, internal office network). (It also shows Back to My Mac if it's set up; see page 567.)

2. Click the computer whose files you want to open.

In the main window, you now see the Public Folder icons for each account holder on that computer: Mom, Dad, Sissy, whatever, as shown in Figure 16-9. (They *may* have shared other folders with you, too.) If you have an account on the other computer, you'll see a folder representing *your* stuff, too. At this point, you're considered a guest.

> **Note:** This amount of access depends on a setting in System Preferences→Users & Groups. Click the Guest account to see it: "Allow guests to connect to shared folders." That checkbox is usually turned on—but it's something to check if you can't seem to connect.

From here, the remaining instructions diverge, depending on whether you want to access *other* people's stuff or *your* stuff. That's why there are two alternative versions of step 3 here:

3a. If you want to access the stuff that somebody else has left for you, double-click that person's Public folder.

Instantly, that folder's contents appear in the Finder window.

In this situation, you're only a guest. You don't have to bother with a password. On the other hand, the only thing you can generally see inside the other person's account folder is his Public folder.

> **Tip:** Actually, you *might* see other folders here—if the account holder has specifically shared them *and* decided that you're important enough to have access to them.

One thing you'll find inside the Public folder is the Drop Box folder. This folder exists so that you can *give* files and folders to the other person. You can drop any of your own icons onto the Drop Box folder—but you can't open the Drop Box folder to see what *other* people have put there. It's one-way, like a mail slot in somebody's front door.

If you see anything else at all in the Public folder you've opened, then it's stuff the account holder has copied there for the enjoyment of you and your networkmates. You're not allowed to delete anything from the other person's Public folder or make changes to anything in it.

You can, however, open those icons, read them, or even copy them to *your* Mac—and then edit *your* copies.

Tip: Every now and then, you'll click the name of a Mac in the Finder Sidebar, hoping to see its contents—and instead of seeing a list of the shared Public folders, you get a Not Connected or Connection Failed message at the top of your window.

In that case, go to the shared Mac and do this: Open System Preferences→Sharing. Click File Sharing, then Options. Turn off "Share files and folders using SMB." Close System Preferences. Often, that's all it takes to make your Mac visible and connectable from other Macs on the network. (If not, then try restarting the shared Mac to make the SMB change stick.)

3b. To access your own Home folder on the other Mac, click the Connect As button (Figure 16-10). Sign in as usual.

When the "Connect to the file server" box appears, you're supposed to specify your account name and password (from the Mac you're tapping into). This is the same name and password you'd use to log in if you were actually sitting at that machine.

Type your account name (long or short version) and password. And if you didn't set up a password for your account, leave the password box empty.

Figure 16-10:
You can sign into your account on another Mac on the network (even while somebody else is using that Mac in person). Click Connect As and then enter your name and password. Turn on "Remember this password in my keychain" to speed up the process for next time. The Change Password button lets you change your account password on the other machine. No matter which method you use to connect to a shared folder or disk, its icon shows up in the Sidebar.

Tip: The dialog box shown in Figure 16-10 includes the delightful and timesaving "Remember this password in my keychain" option, which makes the Mac memorize your password for a certain disk so you don't have to type it—or even see this dialog box—every darned time you connect. (If you have no password, though, the "Remember password" doesn't work. You'll have to confront—and press Return to dismiss—the "Connect to the file server" box every time.)

When you click Connect (or press Return), the other Mac's icon shows up in your Sidebar, and its contents appear in the main window. (The other Mac's icon may also show up on the desktop, if you've turned on the "Connected Servers" option in Finder→Preferences→Sidebar.)

Tip: Once you've connected to a Mac using your account, the other Mac has a lock on your identity. You'll be able to connect to the other Mac over and over again during this same computing session, without ever having to retype your password.

In the meantime, you can double-click icons to open them, make copies of them, and otherwise manipulate them exactly as though they were icons on your own hard drive. Depending on what permissions you've been given, you can even edit or trash those files.

Tip: There's one significant difference between working with "local" icons and working with those that sit elsewhere on the network. When you delete a file from another Mac on the network, either by pressing the Delete key or by dragging it to the Trash, a message appears to let you know that you're about to delete that item instantly and permanently. It won't simply land in the Trash "folder," awaiting the Empty Trash command.

You can even use Spotlight to find files on that networked disk. If the Mac across the network is running Leopard or a later OS X version, in fact, you can search for words *inside* its files, just as though you were sitting in front of it. If not, you can still search for text in files' names.

GEM IN THE ROUGH

Faster Ways to Connect Next Time

If you expect that you might want to access a shared disk or folder again later, take a moment to make an alias of it. The easiest way is to press Option-⌘ as you drag it out of the window where it first appears.

Next time, you can bring it back to your screen just by double-clicking the alias. And if you turned on "Remember this password in my keychain," you won't even be asked for your name and password again.

Similarly, if you put an alias like this onto the Dock, you can bring it back to your screen later just by clicking its icon.

You can even drag the alias into the Login Items window described on page 497. Now the disk appears on your desktop automatically each time you log in—the most effortless arrangement of all.

Connection Method B: Connect to Server

The Sidebar method of connecting to networked folders and disks is practically effortless. It involves nothing more than clicking your way through folders—a skill that, in theory, you already know.

But the Sidebar method has its drawbacks. For example, the Sidebar doesn't let you type in a disk's network address. As a result, you can't access any shared disk *on the Internet* (an FTP site, for example), or indeed anywhere beyond your local subnet (your own small network).

Fortunately, there's another way. When you choose Go→Connect to Server, you get the dialog box shown in Figure 16-11. You're supposed to type in the address of the shared disk you want.

Figure 16-11:
The Sidebar method of connecting to shared disks and folders is quick and easy, but it doesn't let you connect to certain kinds of disks. The Connect to Server method entails plodding through several dialog boxes, but it can find just about every kind of networked disk.

For example, from here you can connect to the following:

- **Everyday Macs on your network.** If you know the IP address of the Mac you're trying to access (you geek!), you can type nothing but its IP address into the box and then hit Connect. Or you can just type its Bonjour name, something like this: *afp://upstairs-PowerMac.local/.*

Tip: To find out your Mac's IP address, open the Network pane of System Preferences. There, near the top, you'll see a message like this: "WiFi is connected to Tim's Hotspot and has the IP address 192.168.1.113." That's your IP address.

To see your Bonjour address, open the Sharing pane of System Preferences. Click File Sharing. Near the top, you'll see the computer name with ".local" tacked onto its name—and hyphens instead of spaces—like this: Little-MacBook.local.

After you enter your account password and choose the shared disk or folder you want, you're connected exactly as though you had clicked Connect As (Figure 16-10).

The next time you open the Connect to Server dialog box, OS X remembers that address, as a courtesy to you, and shows it pre-entered in the Address field.

• **Macs across the Internet.** If your Mac has a permanent (static) IP address, the computer itself can be a server, to which you can connect from anywhere in the world via the Internet.

• **Windows machines.** Find out the PC's IP address or computer name, and then use this format for the address: *smb://192.168.1.34* or *smb://Cheapo-Dell*.

After a moment, you're asked to enter your Windows account name and password, and then to choose the name of the shared folder you want. When you click OK, the shared folder's contents appear in the window, ready to use, and the computer's icon appears in your Sidebar. (More on sharing with Windows PCs later in this chapter.)

Tip: If you know the name of the shared folder, you can add that after a slash, like this: *smb://192.168.4.23/ sharedstuff.* You save yourself one dialog box.

• **NFS servers.** If you're on a network with Unix machines, you can tap into one of their shared directories using this address format: *nfs://Machine-Name/pathname,* where *Machine-Name* is the computer's name or IP address, and *pathname* is the folder path to the shared item you want.

• **FTP servers.** OS X makes it simple to bring *FTP servers* onto your screen, too. (These are the drives, out there on the Internet, that store the files used by Web sites.)

In the Connect to Server dialog box, type the FTP address of the server you want, like this: *ftp://www.apple.com*. If the site's administrators have permitted *anonymous* access—the equivalent of a Guest account—that's all there is to it. A Finder window pops open, revealing the FTP site's contents.

GEM IN THE ROUGH

Hello, Bonjour

Throughout this chapter, and throughout this book, you'll encounter rituals in which you're supposed to connect to another Mac, server, or printer by typing in its IP address (its unique network address).

But first of all, IP addresses are insanely difficult to memorize (192.179.248.3, anyone?). Second, networks shouldn't require you to deal with them anyway. If a piece of equipment is on the network, it should announce its presence, rather than making you specifically call for it by name.

Now you can appreciate the beauty of Bonjour, an underlying OS X networking technology that lets networked gadgets de-

tect one another on the network automatically and recognize one another's capabilities.

It's Bonjour at work, for example, that makes other Macs' names show up in your iTunes program so you can listen to their music from across the network. Bonjour is also responsible for filling up your Bonjour buddy list in Messages automatically, listing everyone who's on the same office network; for making shared Macs' names show up in the Sidebar's Shared list; and for making the names of modern laser printers from HP, Epson, or Lexmark appear like magic in the list of printers in the Print dialog box.

If you need a password for the FTP site, however, you're now asked for your name and password.

Tip: You can eliminate that password-dialog-box step by using this address format: *ftp://
yourname:yourpassword@www.apple.com.*

Once you type it and press Return, the FTP server's icon appears in the Sidebar. Its contents appear, too, ready to open or copy.

- **WebDAV server.** This special Web-based shared disk requires a special address format, something like this: *http://Computer-Name/pathname.*

In each case, once you click OK, you may be asked for your name and password.

And now, some timesaving features in the Connect to Server box:

- Once you've typed a disk's address, you can click + to add it to the list of server favorites. The next time you want to connect, you can just double-click its name.

- The clock-icon pop-up menu lists Recent Servers—computers you've accessed recently over the network. If you choose one of them from this pop-up menu, you can skip having to type in an address.

Tip: Like the Sidebar network-browsing method, the Connect to Server command displays each connected computer as an icon in your Sidebar, even within the Open or Save dialog boxes of your programs. You don't have to burrow through the Sidebar's Network icon to open files from them, or save files onto them.

Figure 16-12:
To disconnect from a shared network disk or folder, click the other computer's icon in the Sidebar. Then click Disconnect at the top-right corner of the window.

Disconnecting Yourself

When you're finished using a shared disk or folder, you can disconnect from it as shown in Figure 16-12.

Disconnecting Others

In OS X, you really have to work if you want to know whether other people on the network are accessing *your* Mac. You have to choose System Preferences→Sharing→File Sharing→Options. There you'll see something like, "Number of users connected: 1."

Maybe that's because there's nothing to worry about. You certainly have nothing to fear from a security standpoint, since you control what they can see on your Mac. Nor will you experience much computer slowdown as you work, thanks to OS X's prodigious multitasking features.

There may be users connected to this computer.
Enter the number of minutes before file sharing is turned off.

5 Minutes

Cancel OK

Figure 16-13:
This dialog box asks you how much notice you want to give your coworkers that they're about to be disconnected.

Still, if you're feeling particularly antisocial, you can slam shut the door to your Mac. Just open System Preferences→Sharing and turn off File Sharing.

If anybody is, in fact, connected to your Mac at the time (*from* a Mac), you, the door-slammer, get to see the dialog box in Figure 16-13, which sends a little warning message to whomever's connected to your Mac.

If nobody is connected right now, your Mac instantly becomes an island once again.

Networking with Windows

Macs and Windows PCs can see each other on the network, with no special software (or talent) required. In fact, you can go in either direction. Your Mac can see shared folders on a Windows PC, and a Windows PC can see shared folders on your Mac.

It goes like this.

Seated at the Mac, Seeing the PC

Suppose you have a Windows PC and a Mac on the same wired or wireless network. Here's how you get the Mac and PC chatting:

1. **On your Windows PC, share some files.**

 This isn't really a book about Windows networking (thank heaven), but here are the basics.

 On a recent Windows 8 (or 8.1) PC, there may be nothing to it. All your personal files probably come pre-shared. You can skip to step 2.

 If step 2 doesn't seem to work, then maybe your PC files aren't already shared, and you have some reading ahead of you:

 Just as on the Mac, there are two ways to share files in Windows. One of them is super-simple: You just copy the files you want to share into a central, fully accessible folder. As long as nobody has turned off the Guest access feature, no passwords, accounts, or other steps are required.

 In **Windows Vista,** that's the Public folder, which appears in the Navigation pane of every Explorer window. (In Vista, there's one Public folder for the whole *computer,* not one per account holder.)

 In **Windows 7,** there's a Public folder in each library. That is, there's a Public Documents, Public Pictures, Public Music, and so on.

Note: There is no system of Public folders in Windows 8 and 8.1—but if you upgraded your PC from an earlier Windows version, the Public folders are still there and work the same way.

The second, more complicated method is the "share any folder" method, just as in OS X. In Vista, you right-click the folder you want to share, choose Properties from the shortcut menu, click the Sharing tab, and turn on "Share this folder on the network" (Figure 16-14, top).

In Windows 7, use the Share With menu at the top of any folder's window; in Windows 8 or 8.1, use the Share tab on the ribbon at the top of any Explorer window at the desktop.

Repeat for any other folders you want to make available to your Mac.

2. **On the Mac, open any Finder window.**

 The shared PCs appear as individual computer names in the Sidebar (Figure 16-14).

 (If you work in a big company, you may have to click the All icon to see the icons of their *workgroups*—network clusters. Unless you or a network administrator changed it, the workgroup name is probably MSHOME or WORKGROUP. Double-click the workgroup name you want.)

Tip: You can also access the shared PC via the Connect to Server command, as described on page 551. You could type into it *smb://192.168.1.103* (or whatever the PC's IP address is) or *smb://SuperDell* (or whatever its name is) and hit Return—and then skip to step 5. In fact, using the Connect to Server method often works when the Sidebar method doesn't.

3. Click the name of the computer you want.

If you're using one of the simple file-sharing methods on the PC, as described above, that's all there is to it. The contents of the Shared Documents or Public folder now appear on your Mac screen. You can work with them just as you would your own files.

If you're using one of the "shared folder" methods, read on.

4. Click Connect As.

This button appears in the top-right corner of the Finder window. Now you're asked for your name and password (Figure 16-14, top).

Note: In Windows 8 and 8.1, there are two ways to log into a computer—two kinds of user accounts. You can sign in with a *Microsoft ID* (which is just like an Apple ID) or with a regular *local* account. (Microsoft pushes you very hard to use a Microsoft ID; many features of Windows 8 won't work without it.)

If you're trying to connect to a Windows 8/8.1 account with a Microsoft ID, be sure to use *that* as the account name in this step (it looks like an email address), along with the corresponding password. If you enter the account's human name, you won't be able to connect.

Figure 16-14:
Bottom: Click the PC's name in the Sidebar. (If it's part of a workgroup, click All and then your workgroup name first.)

Next, enter the account name and password that you'd enter if you were seated at the PC—your regular login password (top).

When you click Connect, you get to see all your PC files in the Finder window.

5. **Enter the name and password for your account on the PC, and then click OK.**

The contents of the shared folder on the Windows machine appear in your Finder window, just as though you'd tapped into another Mac (Figure 16-14, bottom). The icon of the shared folder appears on your desktop, too, and an Eject button (⏏) appears next to the PC's name in your Sidebar.

From here, it's a simple matter to drag files between the machines, open Word documents on the PC using Word for the Mac, and so on—exactly like you're hooked into another Mac.

Tip: Finally, for heaven's sake, make an alias of the Windows folder you've finally opened. That way, you can just double-click to open it the next time!

TROUBLESHOOTING MOMENT

When the Mac Doesn't See the PC

Are you having trouble getting your PC's icon to show up in your Finder's Sidebar?

Now, you can probably connect to the PC using the Mac's Go→Connect to Server command, but the Sidebar would be a lot more convenient.

And the problem is probably that the Mac doesn't know anything about Windows *workgroups*.

Even a lowly home PC is part of a workgroup (a corporate cluster), whether it knows it or not. And until your Mac is part of that very tiny club, it won't be able to see your PCs, and they won't be able to see it.

So if you're having no luck with this whole Mac-PC thing, try this. First, find out what your PC thinks its workgroup is. (It's usually either WORKGROUP or MSHOME.) Windows 8/8.1: At the desktop, right-click the Start-menu icon (⊞); from the shortcut menu, choose System. Scroll down to see the workgroup's name.

Older Windows versions: Click Start, and then right-click Computer. From the shortcut menu, choose Properties. In the resulting info screen, you'll see the workgroup's name.

To find out the Mac's idea of its workgroup, open System Preferences→Network. Click the connection you're using (like WiFi or Ethernet)→Advanced→WINS.

Now you see the peculiar controls shown here. Make sure that the Workgroup box shows the same name as the one on the PC. Click OK, and then click Apply.

Now your Windows PCs should show up in the Sidebar, like magic.

If they're *still* not showing up, then your PC's firewall software is probably turned on. Make sure it's turned off—and turn off your Mac's firewall, too (page 523). You can't do much connecting if there's a virtual wall between the computers.

Seated at the PC, Seeing the Mac

Cross-platformers, rejoice: OS X lets you share files in *both directions*. Not only can your Mac see other PCs on the network, but they can see the Mac, too.

On the Mac, open ■→System Preferences→Sharing. Click File Sharing (make sure File Sharing is turned on), and then click Options to open the dialog box shown in Figure 16-15.

Figure 16-15:
Prepare your Mac for visitation by the Windows PC. It won't hurt a bit. The system-wide On switch for invasion from Windows is the second checkbox shown here, in the System Preferences→Sharing→File Sharing→Options box.

Next, turn on the individual accounts of people you want to allow to connect from the PC. You'll be asked to enter their account passwords, too. Click Done when you're done.

Turn on "Share files and folders using SMB." Below that checkbox, you see a list of all the accounts on your Mac. Turn on the checkboxes to specify *which* Mac user accounts you want to be able to access. You must type in each person's password, too. Click Done.

Now you're ready to open your Mac files on the PC.

If your PC has **Windows Vista,** choose Start→Network; if it's **Windows 7 or 8/8.1,** expand the Network heading in the sidebar of any desktop (Explorer) window. If you've sacrificed the proper animals to the networking gods, your Mac's icon should appear in the network window, as shown in Figure 16-16, top.

Double-click the Mac's icon. Public-folder stuff is available immediately. Otherwise, you have to sign in with your Mac account name and password; Figure 16-16, middle, has the details.

In the final window, you see your actual Home folder—on a Windows PC! You're ready to open its files, copy them back and forth, or whatever (Figure 16-16, bottom).

Figure 16-16:

Top: Double-click the Mac you want to visit from your PC (Windows 8.1 is shown here).

Middle: Type your Mac's name and password.

(If you're using Vista or earlier, it's more complicated. Enter your Mac's NetBIOS name in all capitals, or its IP address, and then a backslash, and then your Mac account short name. You can find out your Mac's NetBIOS name—what Windows calls it—on the Network pane of System Preferences. Click Advanced, then WINS.)

Turn on "Remember my password" if you plan to do this again someday. Click OK.

Bottom: Here's your Mac Home folder—in Windows! Open it up to find all your stuff.

More Mac-Windows Connections

The direct Mac-to-Windows file-sharing feature of OS X is by far the easiest way to access each other's files. But it's not the only way. Chapter 6 offers a long list of other options, from flash drives to the third-party service Dropbox.

Screen Sharing

OS X has answered the prayers of baffled beginners and exasperated experts every-where. Now, when a novice needs help from a guru, the guru doesn't have to run all the way downstairs or down the hall to assist. Thanks to OS X's screen-sharing feature, you can see exactly what's on the screen of another Mac, from across the network—and even seize control of the other Mac's mouse and keyboard (with the newbie's permission, of course).

(Anyone who's ever tried to help someone troubleshoot over the phone knows *exactly* how helpful this is. If you haven't, this small example may suffice: "OK, open the Apple menu and choose 'About This Mac.'" Pause. "What's the Apple menu?")

Nor is playing Bail-Out-the-Newbie the only situation when screen sharing is useful. It's also great for collaborating on a document, showing something to someone for approval, or just freaking each other out. It can also be handy when *you* are the owner of both Macs (a laptop and a desktop, for example), and you want to run a program that you don't have on the Mac that's in front of you. For example, you might want to adjust the playlist selection on the upstairs Mac that's connected to your sound system.

Or maybe you just want to keep an eye on what your kids are doing on the Macs upstairs in their rooms.

The controlling person can do *everything* on the controlled Mac, including running programs, messing around with the folders and files, and even shutting it down. You

GEM IN THE ROUGH

Logging In with an Apple ID

In the bad old days, you couldn't share your screen or your files with other people unless you first created full-blown accounts for them on your Mac. You know: a Home folder, Music and Movies folders, and so on. That was an awful lot of disk space sacrificed, just so other people could visit your Mac over the network.

Nowadays, you can create a Sharing Only account for them. They can now share your screen or your files without actually having a presence on your hard drive.

In fact, there's even a third option: They can exploit your shared screen or shared folders just by logging in with their Apple IDs. This way, you don't even have to set up a name and password for them on your Mac, and they don't have to learn another name and password. They don't have an account on your Mac at all—just a Contacts card.

To set this up, open Contacts. Make sure there's a card in

there for the person who will be visiting your Mac over the network. Make sure, furthermore, that the card includes the email address that person uses as an Apple ID.

Now visit System Preferences→Sharing. Click Screen Sharing. As shown in Figure 16-17, click the + sign. In the pane that appears, click Contacts, and double-click the name of the prospective visitor. You're asked to enter a screen-sharing password for this person (twice) and then click Create Account.

The visitor should make sure he's registered his Apple ID in his own account details for System Preferences→Users & Groups.

If so, then the setup is ready. When he attempts to connect to your Mac, he'll be able to use the "Using an Apple ID" option as his credentials. No account on your Mac is necessary!

can even press keystrokes on *your* Mac—⌘-Tab, ⌘-space, ⌘-Option-Escape, and so on—to trigger the corresponding functions on the *other* Mac.

OS X is crawling with ways to use screen sharing. You can do it over a network, over the Internet, and even during a Messages chat.

Truth is, the Messages method, described in Chapter 13, is much simpler and better than the small-network method described here. It doesn't require names or passwords, it doesn't require the same OS X version on both Macs, it's easy to flip back between seeing the other guy's screen and your own, and you can transfer files by dragging them from your screen to the other guy's (or vice versa).

Then again, the small-network method described here is built right into the Finder and doesn't require logging into Messages.

In the modern OS X screen sharing, you can log into a distant Mac and control it as though you were logged into your own account—*while somebody else is using it* and seeing a totally different screen! Read on.

Other Mac: Give Permission in Advance

Trying to understand meta concepts like seeing one Mac's screen on the monitor of another can get confusing fast. So in this example, suppose that you're seated at Your Mac, and you want to control Other Mac.

Now, it would be a chaotic world if any Mac could randomly take control of any other Mac (although it sure would be fun). Fortunately, though, nobody can share your screen or take control of your Mac without your explicit permission.

To give such permission, sit down at Other Mac. Choose →System Preferences→ Sharing, and then turn on Screen Sharing.

At this point, there are three levels of security to protect your Mac against unauthorized remote-control mischief:

- **Secure.** If you select All Users, then *anyone with an account on your Mac* will be able to tap in and take control anytime they like, even when you're not around. They'll just have to enter the same name and password they'd use if they were sitting in front of your machine.

 If "anyone" means "you and your spouse" or "you and the other two fourth-grade teachers," then that's probably perfectly fine.

- **Securer.** For greater security, though, you can limit who's allowed to stop in. Click "Only these users" and then click the + sign. A small pane appears, listing everyone with an account on your Mac. Choose the ones you trust not to mess things up while you're away from your Mac (Figure 16-17).

Tip: You can permit people to see your Mac's screen remotely by entering their Apple ID and passwords. That's a lot simpler and less disk space than before, when each person had to have a full-blown *account* on your Mac, complete with Pictures folder, Movies folder, and so on. To set this up, see the box on page 560.

• **Securest.** If you click "Only these users" and then don't add *anyone* to the list, then only people who have Administrator accounts on your Mac (page 490) can tap into your screen.

Figure 16-17:
Your Mac is now ready to be observed and even controlled by other machines across the network. The people listed here are allowed to tap in anytime they like, even when you're not at your machine.

Alternatively, if you're only a *little* bit of a Scrooge, you can set things up so that they can request permission to share your screen—as long as you're sitting in front of your Mac at the time and feeling generous.

To set this up, click Computer Settings and then turn on "Anyone may request permission to share screen." Now your fans will have to request permission to enter, and you'll have to grant it (by clicking OK on the screen), in real time, while you're there to watch what they're doing.

Your Mac: Take Control

All right, Other Mac has been prepared for invasion. Now suppose you're the person on the other end. You're the guru, or the parent, or whoever wants to take control.

Sit at Your Mac elsewhere on your home or office network, and proceed like this:

1. **Open a Finder window. Expand the Shared list in the Sidebar, if necessary, so that you see the icon of Other Mac. Click it.**

 The strip at the top of the main window displays a button that wasn't there before: Share Screen (Figure 16-18, top).

2. **Click Share Screen.**

Now you see the box shown at middle in Figure 16-18. It offers as many as three different ways for you to prove that you're not some East German teenage hacker.

Figure 16-18:
Top: Start by clicking Share Screen in the strip at the top of your Mac's window.

If you've been pre-added to the VIP list of authorized screen sharers, you can sign in with either your account name and password or your Apple ID. If not, you can request permission to share Other Mac's screen (provided the Mac owner has turned on that option in System Preferences→ Sharing→Screen Sharing→Computer Settings). You'll be granted permission only if Other Mac's owner is present and OKs you.

Bottom: If you request permission, the other person (sitting at Other Mac) sees your request like this.

"By asking for permission" sends the other Mac's current operator a message asking if it's OK for you to take over. If that person grants permission, that's it; the Other Mac's screen image appears on *your* screen, and you can skip the rest of these steps.

But what if nobody's seated at the other Mac to grant permission? If you sometimes use the Other Mac yourself, and you have an account on it, then you can choose "As a registered user."

And what if nobody's at the other Mac to grant you permission *and* you don't have a user account on that machine? In that case, you can use the "Using an Apple ID" option. If Other Mac's owner wants you to have access and has set you up that

way (following the steps in the box on page 560), then you can connect just by entering your Apple ID and password.

Tip: In theory, you can also connect from across the Internet, assuming you left your Mac at home turned on and connected to a broadband modem, and assuming you've worked through the port-forwarding issue mentioned on page 568.

In this case, though, you'd begin by choosing Go→Connect to Server in the Finder; in the Connect to Server box, type in *vnc://123.456.78.90* (or whatever your home Mac's public IP address is). The rest of the steps are the same.

3. **If you have a user account on Other Mac, click "As a registered user" and log in. If not, but your Apple ID has been pre-approved, click "Using an Apple ID" and supply your sharing password.**

Your Mac, of course, *knows* your Apple ID already (because you've entered it in your account screen in System Preferences→User Accounts). It shows up here in the dialog box; all you have to do is enter your password.

4. **Click Connect.**

If you've signed in with the same account that's already logged into the Other Mac (for example, if they're both your Macs), then that's all there is to it. The other Mac's screen image fills yours.

But if you've just connected using a *different* account, you see the dialog box shown in Figure 16-19. If you choose "Connect to a virtual display," then you can use your account on the Other Mac even while somebody else is using her account. Simultaneously. Crazy stuff.

(The only evidence she'll have that you're rooting around behind the scenes is a tiny menu-bar icon that looks like this: ▣.)

Figure 16-19:
The Mac wants to know if you want to view or control the screen that's in use right now by whomever's using Other Mac—or if you want to use the "virtual display" option, where you take control of your account on the other Mac without disturbing the totally different activity of whomever is seated there.

Note: If *nobody* is using Other Mac at the moment, then it doesn't matter which option you click.

5. Click either "Ask to share the display" (to see the same thing as the Other Mac person) or "Connect to a virtual display" (to log into a different account and work independently).

And now a weird and wonderful sight appears. As shown in Figure 16-20, your screen now fills with a *second* screen—from the other Mac. You have full keyboard and mouse control to work with that other machine exactly as though you were sitting in front of it.

Figure 16-20:
Don't be alarmed. You're looking at the Other Mac's desktop in a window on your Mac desktop. You have keyboard and mouse control, and so does the other guy (if he's there); when you're really bored, you can play King of the Cursor. (Note the Screen Sharing toolbar, which has been made visible by choosing View→Show Toolbar.)

Well, maybe not *exactly.* There are a few caveats and options.

- **Full Screen mode.** There it is, in its customary upper-left spot: the green ⊙ button. If you click it, then your view of Other Mac expands to fill your screen, edge to edge; now there's *no sign at all* that you're actually using a different computer.

- **The speed-vs.-blurriness issue.** Remember, you're asking the other Mac to pump its video display across the network—and that takes time. Entire milliseconds, in fact.

So ordinarily, the Mac uses something called *adaptive quality,* which just means that the screen gets blurry when you scroll, quit a program, or do anything else that creates a sudden change in the picture. You can turn off this feature by choosing View→Full Quality. Now you get full sharpness all the time—but things take longer to scroll, appear, and disappear.

- **Mismatched screen sizes.** If the other screen is *smaller* than yours, no big deal. It floats at actual size on your monitor, with room to spare. But if it's the same size as yours or larger, then the other Mac's screen gets shrunk down to fit in a window.

 If you'd prefer to see it at actual size, choose View→Turn Scaling Off. Of course, now you have to *scroll* in the Screen Sharing window to see the whole image.

Tip: Another way to turn scaling on and off is to click the "Fit screen in window" button on the Screen Sharing *toolbar* (identified in Figure 16-20).

- **Observe Mode.** In Observe Mode, your cursor turns white, and you give up all your typing and clicking powers. In other words, you're playing "look, but don't touch." (To enter this mode, choose View→Switch to Observe Mode, or click the corresponding toolbar icon.)

 This is a handy option when the person at Other Mac just wants to give you a slideshow or a presentation, or when you just want to watch what he's doing when you're on a troubleshooting hunt, or when he's freaked out by having you move the mouse or type stuff by remote control.

- **Manage the Clipboard.** You can actually *copy and paste* material from the remote-controlled Mac to your own—or the other way—thanks to a freaky little worm-hole in the time-space continuum. In the Edit menu, choose Send Clipboard to put what's on *your* Clipboard onto *Other* Mac's Clipboard, or Get Clipboard to copy Other Mac's Clipboard contents onto *your* Clipboard. Breathe slowly and drink plenty of fluids, and your brain won't explode. (There are toolbar-button equivalents, too.)

- **Dragging files between computers.** You can now transfer files from one Mac to the other, just by dragging their icons. Drag the icon from the distant Mac clear out of its window, and pause over your own desktop until your cursor sprouts a green ✪ icon. When you let go, the files get copied to your own Mac.

- **Quitting.** When you hit the ⌘-Q keystroke, you *don't* quit Screen Sharing; you quit whatever program is running on the other Mac! So when you're finished having your way with the other computer, choose Screen Sharing→Quit Screen Sharing to return to your own desktop (and your own sanity).

The Toolbar

If you don't see the screen-sharing toolbar, you can summon it by choosing View→Show Toolbar. It starts out with buttons for Control (click to enter Observe Only mode), Fit to Window, Screen Capture (takes a picture of the screen), Get Clipboard, and Send Clipboard.

But if you right-click (or two-finger click) the toolbar, you're offered a shortcut menu containing the usual controls over how the toolbar buttons appear (Icon and Text, Icon

Only, Use Small Size, and so on), plus a Customize Toolbar command that produces the box shown in Figure 16-21.

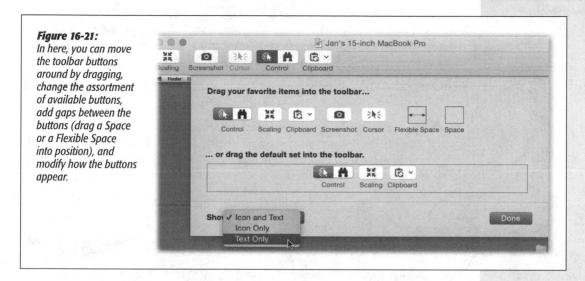

Figure 16-21:
In here, you can move the toolbar buttons around by dragging, change the assortment of available buttons, add gaps between the buttons (drag a Space or a Flexible Space into position), and modify how the buttons appear.

Variations on Screen Sharing

The steps above guide you through screen sharing between two Macs running Mac OS 10.5 or later. But screen sharing is based on a standard technology called VNC, and OS X is bristling with different permutations.

Screen sharing through Messages

Two people who both have Mac OS 10.5 or later can perform exactly the same screen-sharing stunt *over the Internet*. No accounts, passwords, or setup are required—only the granting of permission by the other guy. Just initiate a Messages chat, and then proceed as described on page 472. It's really awesome.

Screen sharing the manual way

Screen Sharing is an actual, double-clickable program, with its own icon on your Mac. (It's in the System→Library→CoreServices folder.) When you double-click it, you can type in the public IP address or domain name of the computer you want to connect to, and presto: You're connected!

Screen sharing with Back to My Mac

Back to My Mac is intended to simplify the nightmare of remote networking. It works only if you have two Macs (OS X 10.7.2 or later), and you've signed into the same iCloud account on both. Also, open System Preferences→iCloud on each machine and turn on "Back to My Mac." Finally, set up the "Allow access for" settings in System Preferences→Screen Sharing.

Once that's all in place, your Macs behave exactly as though they're on the same home network, even though they can be thousands of miles apart across the network.

Now, suppose you're on your laptop in New Zealand. Choose Finder→Preferences→ Sidebar; turn on Back to My Mac.

Now an entry for Back to My Mac is supposed to appear in the Sharing section of your Sidebar. Click to see the icon of your Mac back at home. At this point, you can connect to it for file sharing by clicking Connect As or take control of it by clicking Share Screen.

In theory, Back to My Mac spares you an awfully long visit to networking hell, because Apple has done all the configuration work for you.

In practice, not everyone can get Back to My Mac to work. Apple says the problems are related to firewalls, port-forwarding issues, and router incompatibilities. Apple also says you'll have the best luck on networks that involve only an AirPort base station—and not a hardware router.

All the technical details are available online. Visit *http://support.apple.com/kb/HT1109* to read more about the Back to My Mac issues.

GEM IN THE ROUGH

Screen Sharing with Windows and Other Machines

The beauty of Apple's screen-sharing technology is that it isn't Apple's screen-sharing technology. It's a popular open standard called VNC (Virtual Network Computing).

Once you've turned on Screen Sharing on your Mac, any computer on earth with a free VNC client program—sort of a viewer program—can pop onto your machine for a screen share. VNC clients are available for Windows, Linux, pre-Leopard Macs, and even some cellphones. (Not all VNC programs work with the Yosemite version of screen sharing, alas; some require updates.)

To prepare your Mac for invasion, open the Sharing pane of System Preferences. Click Screen Sharing, and then click Computer Settings. Turn on "VNC viewers may control screen with password," and make up a password. (VNC doesn't know anything about OS X account passwords, so you're making up one password for sharing your whole Mac.)

Give that password to the lucky few who have your trust. Let them plug your Mac's public IP address into their VNC clients—or let them connect over your office network, using the address displayed on the Screen Sharing pane (*vnc:// MacBook-Pro,* for example)—and let the sharing begin.

System Preferences

The hub of Mac customization is System Preferences, the equivalent of the Control Panel (Windows) or the Settings app (iPhone, iPad, Android). Some of its panes are extremely important, because their settings determine whether or not you can connect to a network or go online to exchange email. Others handle the more cosmetic aspects of customizing OS X.

This chapter guides you through the entire System Preferences program, pane by pane.

Tip: Only an administrator (page 490) can change settings that affect everyone who shares a certain machine: most of its Network settings, Energy Saver settings, and so on. If you see a bunch of controls that are dimmed and unavailable, now you know why. If you, a nonadministrator, would like to edit a settings, then call an administrator over to your Mac and ask him to click the 🔒, input his password, and supervise your tweaks.

The System Preferences Window

You can open System Preferences in dozens of ways:

- Choose its name from the menu.

- Jump directly to a System Preferences pane by pressing Option as you tap keys on the top row of your keyboard: Option-⊞ for Mission Control preferences, Option-volume key (◀, ◀), or ◀))) for Sound prefs, Option-brightness keys (☀ or ☀) or Option-keyboard-brightness key (⋅⋅ or ⋅⋅) for the Displays prefs. At that point, you can click Show All (⠿) or press ⌘-L to see the full spread.

- If you know the name of the System Preferences pane you want, it's often quicker to use Spotlight. To open the General System Preferences pane, for example, hit

⌘-space, type *gen,* and then press Return. See Chapter 3 for more on operating Spotlight from the keyboard.

- If you put the System Preferences icon in your *Dock* (Chapter 2), you can open it *and* jump to a particular pane in one smooth move: Click-and-hold the System Preferences icon. You get a pop-up menu of every System Preferences pane.

Suppose, then, that by hook or by crook, you've figured out how to open System Preferences. At first, the rows of icons are grouped according to function, as shown in Figure 17-1, bottom. But you can also view them in tidy alphabetical order, as shown at top in Figure 17-1. That can spare you the ritual of hunting through various rows just to find a certain pane icon whose name you already know. (Quick, without looking: Which row is Date & Time in?) This chapter describes the various panes following this alphabetical arrangement.

Either way, when you click one of the icons, the corresponding controls appear. To access a different preference pane, you have a number of options:

- **Fast:** When System Preferences first opens, the insertion point is blinking in the System Preferences search box. (If the insertion point is *not* blinking there, then press ⌘-F.) Type a few letters of *volume, resolution, wallpaper, wireless,* or whatever

Figure 17-1:
You can view System Preferences icons alphabetically (top), rather than in rows by function (bottom); just choose View→Organize Alphabetically. Non-Apple preference panes appear in a final row.

Super-top-secret trick: If you choose Customize (from the View menu or, believe it or not, the Show All button), the icons here sprout checkboxes. You can turn off—and hide—the icons you never use. (You can still choose their names from the View menu.)

feature you want to adjust. In a literal illustration of Spotlight's name, the System Preferences window darkens *except* for the icons where you'll find relevant controls (Figure 17-2). Click the name or icon of the one that looks the most promising.

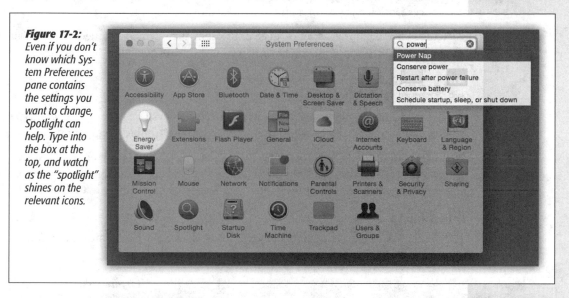

Figure 17-2:
Even if you don't know which System Preferences pane contains the settings you want to change, Spotlight can help. Type into the box at the top, and watch as the "spotlight" shines on the relevant icons.

System Preferences: Under the Hood

The entire System Preferences program is nothing more than a series of graphical front ends for underlying Unix settings.

The individual preferences panes are represented by package icons in your various Library folders. For example, icons that Apple supplies with Yosemite are in System→Library→PreferencePanes. OS X also looks for preferences modules in the Network→Library→PreferencePanes folder, if there is one.

Now suppose you've downloaded some new preferences module and you want to install it. Just double-clicking a downloaded System Preferences pane does the trick.

If you prefer manual control, you can put a downloaded module into your Home→Library→PreferencePanes folder. (To get to your Library folder, which is usually invisible, press the Option key; choose Go→Library in the Finder.) The beauty of this arrangement, of course, is that everyone who shares the Mac now can see a different assortment of customized preference panes.

If you're an administrator, you can use the PreferencePanes folder in the Mac's main Library folder; it lets everyone with an account on the Mac (Chapter 15) access your newly added panes.

When you install some new System Preferences pane like Growl, Perian, or TiVo Desktop, it takes the form of a new icon in one of those four PreferencePanes folders. That's good to know when the day comes when you want to remove one of these add-on panes. Usually, you remove these non-Apple preference panes by right-clicking (or two-finger clicking) them and choosing Remove Preference Pane from the shortcut menu; but in a pinch, you could also delete one by removing it from one of these special folders.

Within the System Preferences program, any new panes you add in this way appear in a new row of icons labeled Other (when you're viewing System Preferences in Category view).

- **Faster:** Click the Show All icon in the upper-left corner of the window (or press ⌘-L, a shortcut worth learning). Then click the icon of the new pane you want.

- **Fastest:** Choose any pane's name from the View menu—or from the System Preferences Dock icon pop-up menu described above.

Here, then, is your grand tour of all 28 of the built-in System Preferences panes. (You may have a couple more if you've installed any non-Apple panes.)

Accessibility

The Accessibility pane (formerly Universal Access) is designed for people who type with one hand, find it difficult to use a mouse, or have trouble seeing or hearing.

Accessibility is a huge focus for Apple. In fact, there's a whole Apple Web site dedicated to explaining all these features: *www.apple.com/accessibility*. Here, though, is an over-view of the noteworthiest features, broken down according to the tabs at the left side.

Display

If you have trouble seeing the screen, then, boy, does OS X have features for you.

Figure 17-3:
When you turn on "Reduce transparency," those semi-transparent menu bars, window edges, and panes (top) become opaque (bottom). The translucence is a trademark feature of Yosemite, but it doesn't actually help you use the Mac; plenty of people find opaque menus and windows less visually confusing.

- **Invert colors** swaps the colors of the screen, so that text appears white on black—an effect that some people find easier to read. (This option also freaks out many Mac fans who turn it on by *mistake*.)

- **Use grayscale** banishes all color from your screen. This is another feature designed to improve text clarity, but it's also a dandy way to see how a color document will look when printed on a monochrome laser printer.

- **Differentiate without color** is intended for color-blind people, but it's fairly pointless. The only thing it affects is the "unavailable" status indicators (like "Away" and "Out to lunch") in Messages. They're denoted by red *squares* instead of circles.

- **Increase contrast** (Figure 17-3) affects two aspects of the Mac's design. First, it darkens the lines that form buttons, sliders, and checkboxes on the screen, making them easier to distinguish. Second, it turns on the next checkbox, **Reduce transparency**.

- **Reduce transparency** eliminates all of Yosemite's translucency; see Figure 17-3.

- **Display contrast.** As you drag this slider toward Maximum, OS X's gray shades gradually bleach out, becoming closer and closer to pure black and white, which may be easier to see if you have limited vision.

- The **Cursor size** slider is a godsend not only to people with failing vision, but also to anyone using one of Apple's large, super-high-resolution screens; as the pixel density increases, the arrow cursor gets smaller and smaller. This slider lets you make the arrow cursor larger—much larger, if you like—making it much easier to see.

Zoom

This feature, shown in Figure 17-4, lets you enlarge the area surrounding your cursor in any increment. It's incredibly useful incredibly often, especially if you have over-40 eyes.

Figure 17-4:
You'll be amazed at how much you can zoom using this Accessibility pane. In fact, there's nothing to stop you from zooming in so far that a single pixel nearly fills the entire monitor. (That may not be especially useful for people with limited vision, but it can be handy for graphic designers learning how to reproduce a certain icon, dot by dot.)

You can start enlarging things in either of two ways:

- **From the keyboard.** To set this up, turn on "Use keyboard shortcuts to zoom."

- **With the trackpad or mouse wheel.** To prepare, turn on "Use scroll gesture with modifier keys to zoom."

In either case, nothing visible has happened yet.

Now look at the Zoom Style control. If it's set to Fullscreen, then zooming magnifies the entire screen. (And that, as many Apple Genius Bar employees can tell you, freaks out a lot of people who don't know what's happened.) If it's set to Picture-in-picture, then zooming will produce a movable rectangular magnifying lens (Figure 17-5).

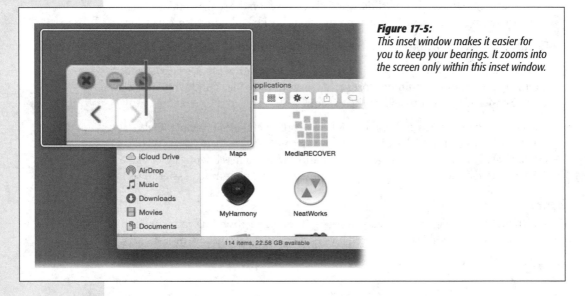

Figure 17-5:
This inset window makes it easier for you to keep your bearings. It zooms into the screen only within this inset window.

All right; you're ready to zoom. Next time you need to magnify things, do this:

- **From the keyboard.** Press Option-⌘-8. You've either opened up the magnifying lens or magnified the entire screen. The magnification is 200 percent of original size. You can increase or decrease the amount of zooming by pressing Option-⌘-plus (the = key) or Option-⌘-minus (the - key). With each press, the screen image gets larger or smaller, creating a virtual monitor that follows your cursor around.

- **Using the trackpad or mouse wheel.** While pressing the Control key, drag two fingers up your trackpad, or turn your mouse wheel upward. The amount of dragging or turning controls the degree of magnification.

Once you're zoomed in, you can pan around inside the lens (or pan the entire virtual giant screen) by dragging with two fingers on your trackpad. The lens moves to follow your cursor; in Picture-in-picture mode, the whole screen scrolls when your cursor hits the edge of the magnified area.

Or, if you turn on "Zoom follows the keyboard focus," then the area of magnification jumps when you press the Tab key to highlight different areas of whatever program you're using.

You have a huge array of customization options. For example, you can substitute the Option or ⌘ key, if Control isn't working out for you. And you can turn on a pixel-smoothing feature that adds a certain blurriness to the zoomed-in image ("Smooth images").

If you click More Options, you find yet another raft of choices. What you see here depends on whether you've chosen Fullscreen or Picture-in-picture zoom mode. In Fullscreen, you get choices like these:

- **Maximum Zoom, Minimum Zoom.** Turns out that pressing Option-⌘-8 isn't the only way to turn on zooming. These sliders establish starting points for two other magnification keystrokes: a large zoom that you'll get when you press Option-⌘-plus, and a smaller degree of zoom when you press Option-⌘-minus. (At either point, you can adjust the zoom in either direction by pressing Option-⌘-plus or Option-⌘-minus *again*.)

- **Show preview rectangle when zoomed out.** If you turn this option on, a black rectangle appears on the screen at all times when you *haven't* magnified the screen. It shows you what part of the screen image will fill your monitor when you press the "zoom-in" keystroke, Option-⌘-8. (This rectangle appears only if you've changed the Maximum Zoom slider to something larger than 1x.)

- **When zoomed in…** specifies how you want to scroll around within your zoomed-in screen image. The first setting, "Continuously with pointer," is actually pretty frustrating; the whole screen shifts around whenever you move the cursor. ("So the pointer is at or near the center of the screen" is very similar.) "Only when the pointer reaches an edge" is a lot less annoying and lets you *use* the cursor (to click buttons, for example) without sending the entire screen image darting away from you.

When Picture-in-picture is turned on, the More Options are different. They offer these choices:

- **Magnification.** Use this slider to specify the initial amount of zoom. (You can always zoom in more or less by pressing Option-⌘-plus or Option-⌘-minus.)

- **Window position.** If you choose Stationary, then the lens remains parked on the screen. You can't move or resize it—at least not once you've left the Options dialog box.

Tip: You *can* change its size and position for good, though, by clicking Adjust Size and Location in the corner of the Options dialog box. You'll be offered the chance to drag the little inset window (Figure 17-5) to move it, or drag its edges to change its shape. When you like the result, click OK.

"Follow mouse cursor" makes the inset window follow your cursor around, as though you're moving a high-tech magnifying glass over a map. And if you choose "Tiled along edge," then the lens becomes much bigger—in fact, it becomes an

enormous rectangular swath at the left side of your screen. The image scrolls as you move your cursor around.

- **Cursor style.** Within the magnification lens, your cursor can look like it always does, or it can take on the look of a big crosshairs ($+$) for more precision.

- **Invert colors** turns your screen into a color negative: black is white, blue is yellow, and so on—within the magnification "lens," for greater clarity.

- **Enable temporary zoom.** This one's great. It means that at any time, in any program, you can summon the magnified lens at your cursor location by holding down your Control and Option keys together. (It works only if Zoom is turned *on*.) It's a great way to dip into a magnified view of something on your screen, briefly.

- **Speak items under mouse after delay.** Just what it says. Use the slider to adjust the pause before the Mac speaks aloud whatever text your mouse rests on.

VoiceOver

VoiceOver makes the Mac *read out loud* every bit of text that's on the screen. See page 714

Descriptions

This new option, "Play video descriptions when available," is for Internet movies that come, or may someday come, with a narration track that describes the action for the blind.

Captions

This option controls the look of subtitles in movies, TV shows, videos, and podcasts you've bought, rented, or streamed from Apple. (Subtitles are an option in iTunes, QuickTime, and DVD Player.)

Tip: In the iTunes Store, videos equipped with subtitles bear a small CC icon.

When you first click Captions, you can see that Apple has supplied you with three different caption styles—Default, Classic, and Large Text; each has its own font, color, and background color. If you click the $+$ button, though, you can whip up a new subtitle style to your own taste; you get an insane number of font, size, opacity, and color options.

A few videos have been subtitled specifically for deaf people. Those subtitles, called closed captioning or SDH (Subtitles for the Deaf and Hard of Hearing), are the same thing as regular subtitles, except that they also identify nonspoken sounds ("Glass breaking") and who's speaking ("Captain Picard: Engage!"). If you'd prefer to see these SDH captions instead of the regular ones, turn on "Prefer Closed Captions and SDH."

Audio

If you have trouble hearing the Mac's sounds, the obvious solution is to increase the volume, which is why this pane offers a link to the Sound Preferences pane.

Audio is especially important when the Mac tries to get your attention by beeping. For those situations, turn on "Flash the screen when an alert sound occurs" (an effect you can try out by clicking the Test Flash Screen button). Now you'll see a white flash across the entire monitor whenever the Mac would otherwise beep—not a bad idea on laptops, actually, so that you don't miss beeps when you've got the speakers muted.

The "Play stereo audio as mono" option is intended for people with hearing loss in one ear. This way, you won't miss any of the musical mix just because you're listening through only one headphone.

Keyboard

This pane offers two clever features designed to help people who have trouble using the keyboard.

- **Sticky Keys** lets you press multiple-key shortcuts (involving keys like Shift, Option, Control, and ⌘) one at a time instead of all together.

 To make Sticky Keys work, first turn on Enable Sticky Keys. Then go to work on the Mac, triggering keyboard commands as shown in Figure 17-6.

Figure 17-6:
To press a multiple-key keystroke like Shift-⌘-D, press them one at a time. You see ghost images of these keys on your screen, as though to show you which keystrokes you've added to your temporary collection. To "unpress" a key you've already pressed, press it again twice.

If you press a modifier key *twice*, meanwhile, you lock it down. (Its onscreen symbol gets brighter to let you know.) When a key is locked, you can use it for several commands in a row. For example, if a folder icon is highlighted, you could double-press ⌘ to lock it down—and then type O (to open the folder), look around, and then press W (to close the window). Press the ⌘ key a third time to "un-press" it.

Tip: The checkbox called "Press the Shift key five times to turn Sticky Keys on or off" (click Options to see it) gives you the flexibility of turning Sticky Keys on and off at will, without even taking a trip to System Preferences. Whenever you want to turn on Sticky Keys, press the Shift key five times in succession. You'll hear a special clacking sound effect alerting you that you just turned on Sticky Keys. (Repeat the five presses to turn Sticky Keys off again.)

• **Slow Keys,** on the other hand, doesn't register a key press at all until you've held down the key for more than a second or so—a feature designed to screen out accidental key presses.

If you click Options and then turn on "Use click key sounds," you'll hear a little typing sound each time you press a key—but none of these key presses registers unless you hold the key down for a moment. (Use the Acceptance Delay slider to govern this threshold.)

You hear a different sound when the Mac actually accepts the key press—and, of course, you see the letter you typed appear onscreen.

Mouse & Trackpad

Mouse Keys is designed to help people who can't use the mouse—or who want more precision when they can. It lets you click, drag, and otherwise manipulate the cursor by pressing the keys on your numeric keypad. (It's not very useful on keyboards that don't *have* separate numeric keypads, like laptops.)

When Mouse Keys is turned on, the 5 key acts as the clicker—hold it down for a moment to "click the mouse," do that twice to double-click, and so on. Hold down the 0 key to lock down the mouse button, and the period key to unlock it. (The amount of time you have to hold them down depends on how you've set the Initial Delay slider.)

Move the cursor around the screen by pressing the eight keys that surround the 5 key. (For example, hold down the 9 key to move the cursor diagonally up and to the right.) If you hold one of these keys down continuously, the cursor, after a pause, begins to move smoothly in that direction—according to the way you've adjusted the sliders called Initial Delay and Maximum Speed.

Tip: The checkbox, in Options, called "Press the Option key five times to turn Mouse Keys on or off" saves you the trouble of opening System Preferences.

If you do have a trackpad, you can find some happy surprises hiding behind the Trackpad Options button. Here you can adjust your Mac's response when you scroll by dragging across the trackpad—do things keep scrolling a little after you lift your finger ("inertia")?

You can also enable *trackpad dragging,* which means moving things across the screen without having to keep the trackpad button down. To drag, tap *twice* (don't fully click); leave your finger touching the trackpad on the second tap. At this point, your "mouse button" is down. Swipe across the trackpad to move the object. (If "with Drag Lock" is turned on, then the "mouse button" remains down until you repeat the double-tap business. In "without Drag Lock" mode, *one* tap ends the dragging.)

Switch Control

Apple has also made the Mac available to people whose physical skills are limited to very simple gestures, like puffing on an air pipe, pressing a foot switch, blinking an

eye, or turning the head, for example. A hardware accessory called a *switch* lets you operate certain gadgets this way.

When you turn on Enable Switch Control, you're asked to authenticate; a row of icons then appears on a floating bar. More importantly, the Mac sequentially highlights one object on the screen after another; you're supposed to puff, tap, or blink at the right moment to say, "Yes, *this* one."

If you don't have a physical switch apparatus, you can use the one that came with your keyboard: the space bar (the factory setting). Each time the Mac is highlighting the button, control, or key you want, tap the space bar.

You can specify how fast the sequential highlighting proceeds, whether or not it pauses on the screen's first item, how many times the highlighting cycles through each screenful, and so on.

For details on adding your own switch and customizing how it works, read *http://support.apple.com/kb/PH18393*.

Dictation

Confusingly enough, OS X offers two different features called Dictation. One of them is text-to-speech—where the Mac types what you're saying. That feature is described on page 218.

This Dictation feature, new in Yosemite, lets you control the Mac by speaking *commands*. Yosemite understands dozens of commands for selecting and formatting text, navigating and editing documents, and operating the Mac itself (quitting apps, searching with Spotlight, opening documents, and so on). You can create your own commands, too.

To make all this work, you have to turn on Enhanced Dictation. That feature is primarily designed to let you speak-to-type without an Internet connection (page 219); but as a handy side effect, it also makes possible the new speak-commands feature. If Enhanced Dictation isn't already turned on, the Mac lets you know ("Enhanced Dictation must be enabled") and offers you a button that lets you go turn it on ("Open Dictation & Speech Preferences").

Once that's done, you're ready to speak some commands. To make the Mac start listening, tap the fn key twice. (You can change that keystroke if you like; see page 199.)

The "listening" button appears, as shown at left in Figure 17-7. Say, "Show commands" to open a list of commands you can say (Figure 17-7, right).

If you've turned on "Enable advanced commands" (there's no reason not to), you open up another batch of possibilities. Now you can control programs and documents, too, with commands like these: "Switch to Safari." "Quit Calendar." "Click File menu." "Save document." "Close window."

You may discover that you're triggering some commands accidentally. In that case, you can turn off a command in the list (in System Preferences→Accessibility→Dictation). Click the command, and then click the − button below it.

The + button is there so that you can *add* to the list of commands the Mac recognizes.

When you click +, you're offered three boxes to fill in:

- **When I say.** Type what you're going to say to trigger this command. It has to include at least two words; otherwise, the Mac might think you're speaking text you want typed out. Don't use proper names and words that the Mac might confuse with similar-sounding ones.

- **While using.** Specify which program you want this command to work in (or leave it set to Any Application).

- **Perform.** From this pop-up menu, specify what you want the Mac to do. It can open a file, open an app, run an Automator workflow, paste a certain blob of text, or "press" a certain keystroke.

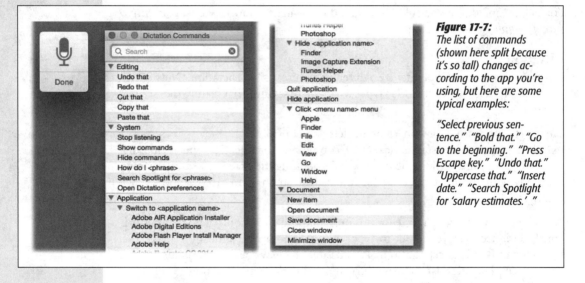

Figure 17-7:
The list of commands (shown here split because it's so tall) changes according to the app you're using, but here are some typical examples:

"Select previous sentence." "Bold that." "Go to the beginning." "Press Escape key." "Undo that." "Uppercase that." "Insert date." "Search Spotlight for 'salary estimates.'"

For example, suppose you want to create a command that types out your mailing address when you're composing email. In the "When I say" box, type "Paste my address." In the "While using," choose Mail. From the Perform pop-up menu, choose Paste Text; then type your mailing address into the text box.

When you click Done, your new command is ready to use, and it appears at the top of the command list at left.

Speaking to control your Mac doesn't quite have the flexibility or accuracy of, say, the computer in *Star Trek*. Then again, the Mac's spoken-command feature can save you time, is easy to set up and use, and has the distinct advantage of not being fictional.

App Store

This System Preferences pane governs when and how your Mac auto-downloads new versions of software you've acquired from the App Store (Chapter 4).

Whenever Apple improves or fixes some piece of OS X or some Apple-branded program, the Mac can notify you, download the update, and install it into your system automatically. These updates may include new versions of programs like iPhoto and iMovie; drivers for newly released printers, scanners, cameras, and such; bug fixes and security patches; and so on. These checkboxes that govern the process:

- **Automatically check for updates.** You grant permission to your Mac to ping the mother ship periodically to see if there are updates available. Turn it off, and you're stuck with today's software versions forever.

- **Download newly available updates in the background.** If you leave this option turned on, you'll still be notified before anything gets installed, but you won't have to wait for the downloading—the deed will already be done.

- **Install app updates.** If you turn this off, you won't get updates to your apps automatically installed.

 It's hard to think of a reason why you wouldn't want the latest, most refined versions of your apps. But maybe you want to read online about some update online before installing it.

- **Install OS X updates.** If you turn this off, you won't automatically get OS X updates as they come along.

- **Install system data files and security updates.** These files are part of OS X's automatic, ongoing virus protection. If you turn off this option, your Mac won't know how to recognize and fight the latest viruses. Also, you're nuts.

- **Automatically download apps purchased on other Macs.** Fascinating, Captain. This checkbox ensures that if you buy an app from the App Store on one of your other Macs, this Mac will download it automatically, so that you have it everywhere (assuming that both Macs are signed in with the same Apple ID).

At the bottom of this dialog box, a message lets you know the last time updates were automatically installed. And you can click Check Now to open the App Store to its Updates page.

Tip: In case this automatic-update thing feels a little too automatic, you can always see a list of what updates have been installed while you weren't looking. Open the App Store app and click the Updates tab to see everything that's been installed in the past 30 days.

Bluetooth

Bluetooth is a short-range, low-power, wireless *cable-elimination* technology. It's designed to connect gadgets in pairings that make sense, like cellphone+earpiece,

Mac+wireless keyboard, phone+portable speaker, or Mac+cellphone. In Yosemite, Bluetooth is the key to the Continuity features described in Chapter 14; it's the wireless link between your Mac and your iPhone.

Pairing

Now, you wouldn't want the guy in the next cubicle to be able to operate *your* Mac using *his* Bluetooth keyboard. So the first step in any Bluetooth relationship is *pairing*, or formally introducing the two gadgets that will be communicating. Figure 17-8 shows how that goes.

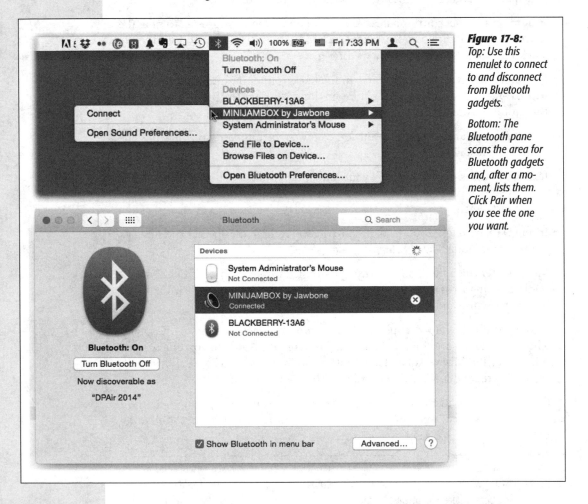

Figure 17-8:
Top: Use this menulet to connect to and disconnect from Bluetooth gadgets.

Bottom: The Bluetooth pane scans the area for Bluetooth gadgets and, after a moment, lists them. Click Pair when you see the one you want.

To do that, open System Preferences→Bluetooth. Make sure that Bluetooth is On. (The only reason to turn it off is to save laptop battery power.)

You don't have to turn on a Discoverable switch to make the Mac "visible" to other Bluetooth gadgets in range; whenever the Bluetooth pane of System Preferences is open, it's discoverable.

In fact, you don't have to click some Add New Device button, either. When the Bluetooth pane is open, the Mac automatically starts searching for nearby Bluetooth gadgets within range (see Figure 17-8, bottom)—nearby headsets, laptops, cellphones, and so on. Usually, it finds the one you're trying to pair. Just click the one you want, and then click Pair.

When it's all over, the new gadget is listed in the pane, in the list of Bluetooth stuff that you've previously introduced to this Mac. (You can click it and then click ⊗ to get rid of the pairing, when that day comes.)

A few footnotes:

- If you're pairing a mobile phone or something else that has a keypad or a keyboard, the Mac may display a large, multiple-digit *passcode*. It's like a password, except that you'll have to input it only this once, to confirm that *you* are the true owner of both the Mac and the gadget. (If it weren't for this passcode business, some guy next to you at the airport could enjoy free laptop Internet access through the cellphone in *your* pocket.)

 At this point, the phone, computer, or palmtop displays a message to the effect that you have 30 seconds to type that passcode. Do it. When the gadget asks if you want to pair with the Mac and connect to it, say yes. (If you're pairing one Mac with another, just click Continue on both machines; you *see* the same passcode on both but don't have to type it.)

- If you intend to send a file to another Mac, set up that other machine by visiting System Preferences→Sharing; turn on Bluetooth Sharing.

Advanced Options

If you click Advanced, you arrive at a few more tweaky Bluetoothisms:

- **Open Bluetooth Setup Assistant at startup if no keyboard is detected.** Here's where you can tell the Bluetooth Setup Assistant to open up automatically when the Mac thinks no keyboard is attached (because it assumes that you have a wireless Bluetooth keyboard that has yet to be set up).

- **Open Bluetooth Setup Assistant at startup if no mouse or trackpad is detected.** Same deal, this time suggesting that the Assistant will open if the Mac can't find a trackpad or mouse. Once again, the Mac is assuming that you'll be wanting to connect a *wireless* one.

- **Allow Bluetooth devices to wake this computer.** Turn this on if you want to be able to wake up a sleeping Mac when you press a key, just like a wired keyboard does.

Tip: If you Option-click the Bluetooth menulet (✳), you get a couple of lines of secret Bluetooth details. The menu reveals the name of your Mac, as it will appear to other Bluetooth wireless gadgets; and the version of Bluetooth you're running.

The Bluetooth Menulet

The Bluetooth menulet (Figure 17-8, top) gives you an easy way to turn Bluetooth on and off, to connect to Bluetooth gadgets, to disconnect from them, and to send files to them (page 237). If you don't see this menulet, then turn on "Show Bluetooth in menu bar" (Figure 17-8, bottom).

CDs & DVDs

This pane appears only if your Mac does, in fact, have a DVD drive. It lets you tell the Mac what it should do when it detects that you've inserted a CD or DVD. For example, when you insert a music CD, you probably want iTunes to open automatically so you can listen to the songs or convert them to MP3 or AAC files on your hard drive. Similarly, when you insert a picture CD (such as a Kodak Photo CD), you probably want iPhoto to open in readiness to import the pictures into your photo collection. And when you insert a movie on DVD, you probably want the Mac's DVD Player program to open.

For each kind of disc (blank CD, blank DVD, music CD, picture CD, or video DVD), the pop-up menu lets you choose options like these:

- **Ask what to do.** A box asks what you want to do with a newly inserted blank disc.

- **Open (iDVD, iTunes, iPhoto, DVD Player…).** The Mac can open a certain program automatically when you insert the disc. When the day comes that somebody writes a better music player than iTunes, or a better digital shoebox than iPhoto, then you can use the "Open other application" option.

- **Run script.** If you've become handy writing or downloading AppleScript programs, you can schedule one of your own scripts to take over from here. For example, you can set things up so that inserting a blank CD automatically copies your Home folder onto it for backup purposes.

- **Ignore.** The Mac won't do anything when you insert a disc except display its icon on the desktop. (If it's a blank disc, the Mac does nothing at all.)

Date & Time

Your Mac's conception of what time it is can be very important. Every file you create, save, or even open is stamped with this time, and every email you send or receive is marked with it. As you might expect, setting your Mac's clock is what the Date & Time pane is all about.

Date & Time Tab

Click the Date & Time tab. If "Set date & time automatically" is turned on, your Mac sets its own clock by consulting a highly accurate online scientific clock. (No need to worry about daylight saving time, either; the time servers take that into account.)

If you're not online and have no prospect of getting there, you can also set the date and time manually. To change the month, day, or year, click the digit that needs changing and then either (a) type a new number, (b) press the ▲ or ▼ keys on the keyboard, or (c) click the little arrow buttons. Press the Tab key to highlight the next number. (You can also specify the day of the month by clicking a date on the minicalendar.)

To set the time of day, use the same technique—or, for more geeky fun, you can set the time by dragging the hour, minute, or second hands on the analog clock.

Finally, click Save. (If you get carried away with dragging the clock hands around and lose track of the *real* time, click the Revert button to restore the pane settings.)

Tip: If you prefer seeing 24-hour "military time" notation on your menu bar (that is, *17:30* instead of *5:30 p.m.*)–click the Clock tab and turn on "Use a 24-hour clock."

Note, however, that this affects only the menu bar clock. If you'd like to reformat the menu bar clock *and* all other dates (like the ones that show when your files were modified in list views), click the Open Language & Region button at the bottom of the Date & Time pane. Once there, you'll see an Advanced button; its Times tab leads you to a whole new world of time-format customization. You can drag elements of the current time (Hour, Minute, Second, Millisecond, and so on) into any order, and separate them with any desired punctuation. This way, you can set up your date displays in (for example) the European format, expressing April 13 as 13/4 instead of 4/13).

Time Zone Tab

You'd be surprised how important it is to set the time zone for your Mac. If you don't do so, the email and documents you send out—and the Mac's conception of what documents are older and newer—could be hopelessly skewed.

OS X can set its own time zone *automatically.* That's an especially useful feature if you're a laptop warrior who travels a lot.

If you turn on "Set time zone automatically using current location" (Figure 17-9), the Mac will think for a moment. Then, if the WiFi gods are smiling, it will, before your eyes, drop a pin onto the world map to represent your location—and set the time zone automatically. (The world map dims to show that you can no longer set your location manually.)

Often, though, you'll be told that the Mac is "Unable to determine current location at this time." In that case, specify your location manually, as shown in Figure 17-9.

Clock Tab

In the Clock pane, you can turn the menu-bar clock on or off. You can choose between two different clock styles: digital (3:53 p.m.) or analog (a round clock face). You also get several other options for the digital clock display: whether to show seconds, designations for a.m. and p.m., the day of the week, a blinking colon, and a 24-hour clock.

Tip: At the bottom of the dialog box, you'll find a feature called "Announce the time." At the intervals you specify, the Mac can speak, out loud, the current time: "It's 10 o'clock." If you tend to get so immersed in "working" that you lose track of time, OS X just removed your last excuse. The menu-bar clock can show not just the time and day of the week, but also today's *date.* Turn on the "Show the day of the week" and "Show date" checkboxes if you want to see, for example, "Wed May 9 7:32 PM" on your menu bar.

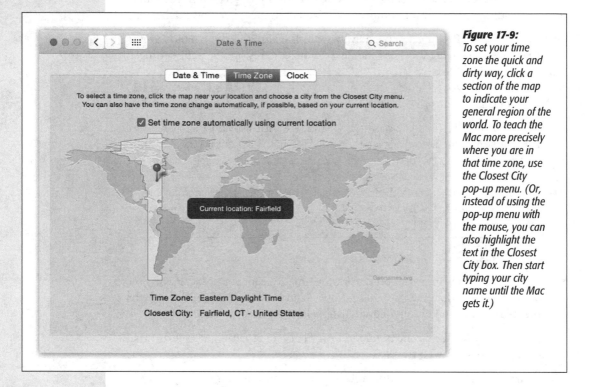

Figure 17-9:
To set your time zone the quick and dirty way, click a section of the map to indicate your general region of the world. To teach the Mac more precisely where you are in that time zone, use the Closest City pop-up menu. (Or, instead of using the pop-up menu with the mouse, you can also highlight the text in the Closest City box. Then start typing your city name until the Mac gets it.)

If you decide you don't need all that information—if your menu bar is crowded enough as it is—you can always look up today's day and date just by *clicking* the time on your menu bar. A menu drops down revealing the complete date. The menu also lets you switch between digital and analog clock types and provides a shortcut to the Date & Time Preferences pane.

Tip: This one's for Unix geeks only. Use *sudo*, type date *mmddhhmmyyyy.ss*, and press Return. (Of course, replace that code with the actual date and time you want, such as *040517552015*.00 for April 5, 2015, 5:55 p.m.) You might find this method faster than the System Preferences route.

Desktop & Screen Saver

This pane offers two ways to show off OS X's glamorous graphics features: *desktop pictures* and *screensavers.*

Desktop Pictures

OS X comes with mountain of desktop pictures, ranging from *National Geographic*–style nature photos to plain solid colors. To install a new background picture, first choose one of the image categories in the list at the left side of the window, as shown in Figure 17-10.

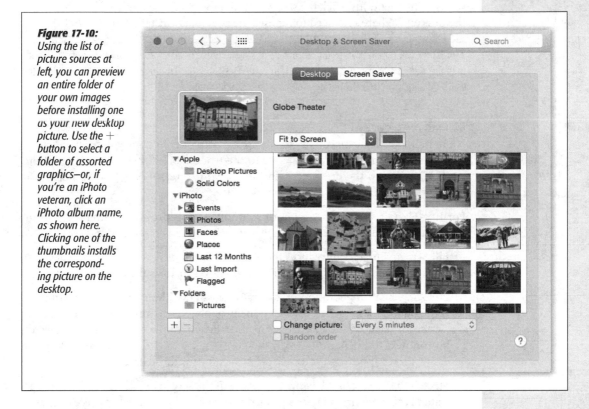

Figure 17-10:
Using the list of picture sources at left, you can preview an entire folder of your own images before installing one as your new desktop picture. Use the +button to select a folder of assorted graphics—or, if you're an iPhoto veteran, click an iPhoto album name, as shown here. Clicking one of the thumbnails installs the corresponding picture on the desktop.

Your choices include Desktop Pictures (muted, soft-focus swishes and swirls and a few nature shots—like the new Yosemite cliff shot); Nature (bugs, water, outer space); Plants (flowers, soft-focus leaves); Art (a collection of famous paintings by Monet, Degas, Seurat, and other canvas superheroes); Black & White (breathtaking monochrome shots); Abstract (swishes and swirls with wild colors); Patterns (a pair of fabric closeups); and Solid Colors (simple grays, blues, and greens).

Tip: You can choose *any* solid color—not just one of the preselected shades Apple gives you. Click Custom Color and go nuts.

Using your own pictures

Of course, you may feel that decorating your Mac desktop is much more fun if you use one of your *own* pictures. You can use almost any graphics file: JPEG, GIF, TIFF,

Photoshop, and even PDF. (Guess you could use the PDF option to help teach yourself your camera's user guide by staring at your desktop every morning.)

That's why icons for your own Pictures folder and iPhoto and Aperture albums also appear here, along with a + button that lets you choose *any* folder of pictures. When you click one of these icons, you see thumbnail versions of its contents in the main screen to its right. Just click the thumbnail of any picture to apply it immediately to the desktop. (There's no need to remove the previously installed picture first.)

Tip: If there's a certain picture you like, but it's not in any of the listed sources, you can drag its image file onto the *well* (the miniature desktop displayed in the Desktop pane). A thumbnail instantly appears in the well, and a moment later the picture is plastered across your monitor.

Making the picture fit

No matter which source you use to choose a photo of your own, you have one more issue to deal with. Unless you've gone to the trouble of editing your chosen photo so that it matches the precise dimensions of your screen (1920 × 1080 pixels, for example), it probably isn't exactly the right size.

Fortunately, OS X offers a number of solutions to this problem. Using the pop-up menu just to the right of the desktop preview well, you can choose any of these options:

- **Fill Screen.** Enlarges or reduces the image so that it fills every inch of the desktop. Parts may get chopped off, but this option never distorts the picture.

- **Fit to Screen.** Your photo appears as large as possible without distortion *or* cropping. If the photo doesn't precisely match the proportions of your screen, then you get "letterbox bars" on the sides or at top and bottom. Apple provides a color-swatch button next to the pop-up menu shown in Figure 17-10. When you click it, the Color Picker appears so you can specify a color for those letterbox bars.

- **Stretch to Fill Screen.** Makes your picture fit the screen exactly, come hell or high water. Larger pictures may be squished vertically or horizontally as necessary, and small pictures are drastically blown up *and* squished, usually with grisly results.

- **Center.** Centers the photo neatly on the screen. The edges of the picture may be chopped off. If the picture is smaller than the screen, it sits smack in the center of the monitor at actual size, leaving a swath of empty border all the way around. (Use the swatch button just to the right of the pop-up menu to specify a color for that border.)

- **Tile.** This option makes your picture repeat over and over until the multiple images fill the entire monitor. (If your picture is larger than the screen, no such tiling takes place. You see only the top center chunk of the image.)

Auto picture changing

The novelty of any desktop picture, no matter how interesting, is likely to fade after several months of all-day viewing. That's why the randomizing function is so delightful.

Turn on "Change picture" at the bottom of the dialog box (Figure 17-10, bottom). From the pop-up menu, specify when you want your background picture to change: "every day," "every 15 minutes," or, if you're *really* having trouble staying awake at your Mac, "every 5 seconds." (The option called "when waking from sleep" refers to the *Mac* waking from sleep, not you.)

Finally, turn on "Random order," if you like. If you leave it off, your desktop pictures change in alphabetical order by file name.

Now, at the interval you specified, your desktop picture changes automatically, smoothly cross-fading between the pictures like a slideshow. You may never want to open another window, because you'll hate to block your view of the show.

Screen Saver

On the Screen Saver pane, you can create your own screensaver slideshows—an absolute must if you have an Apple Thunderbolt Display and a cool Manhattan loft apartment.

Tip: Of course, a screensaver doesn't really save your screen. Flat-panel screens, the only kind Apple sells, are incapable of "burning in" a stationary image of the sort that originally inspired the creation of screensavers years ago.

No, these screensavers serve two unrelated functions. First, they mask what's on your screen from passersby whenever you leave your desk. Second, they're kind of fun.

When you click a module's name in the Screen Saver list, you see a mini version of it playing back in the preview screen. Click the preview to give the module a dry run on your full screen. When you've had enough of the preview, just move the mouse or press any key.

The Screen Saver module offers two categories of screensavers.

Slideshows

At the top of the scrolling list of icons at left, Apple has installed 14 "slideshows"—attractive animations that gracefully fling photos around in different show-offy ways—that began life in programs like iPhoto.

At right, use the Source pop-up menu to specify which photos you want included in the slideshow. You can use any of the photo sets that Apple provides (National Geographic, Aerial, Cosmos, Nature Patterns); you can choose Choose Folder to specify some photos of your own from a folder on your Mac; or you can choose Photo Library to see a list of your iPhoto or Aperture albums. Each creates an amazingly dramatic, almost cinematic experience, worthy of setting up to "play" during dinner parties like the lava lamps of the '70s.

"Shuffle slide order," of course, scrambles the photo sequence so that it's different every time. Wouldn't want you to get bored staring at your screen, now.

Tip: Once a slideshow screensaver kicks in, you can control it as you would a real slideshow. Press the ◄ and ► keys to visit previous or subsequent photos. That's great for those times when someone passing your Mac says, "Hey, what was that?"

Nonphotographic displays

Beneath the list of slideshows, you'll find the icons for seven more traditional, non-photographic slideshow displays. Each has options worth exploring. For example:

- **Flurry.** Flaming, colorful, undulating arms of fire, which resemble a cross between an octopus and somebody arc welding in the dark. If you click Screen Saver Options, you can control how many streams of fire appear at once, the thickness of the arms, the speed of movement, and the colors.

- **Arabesque.** Patterns of small circles that come and go, shrink and grow; drugged-out randomness.

- **Shell.** Five swirling fireworksy spinners, centered around a bigger one.

- **Message.** The Apple logo and the computer's name, faintly displayed on the monitor. (These elements shift position every few minutes.) Lets corporate supervisors glance over at the screens of unattended Macs to find out which employees aren't at their desks.

Tip: If you click Options, you can type in replacement text. Instead of your Mac's name bouncing around, your supervisor can see, for example, "This Mac temporarily unassigned."

- **iTunes Artwork.** This module builds a gigantic mosaic of album art from your music collection. The tiles periodically flip around, just to keep the image changing. (The Options button lets you specify how many rows of album-art squares appear, and how often the tiles flip.)

Tip: If you point to an album cover while this screensaver is playing, a big ► button appears. If you click it, the Mac starts playing the corresponding album. (Of course, that means clicking no longer exits the screensaver. Press a key to wake up the Mac instead.)

- **Word of the Day.** A parade of interesting words drawn from the Dictionary program. You're invited to tap the D key to open the dictionary to that entry to read more. Build your word power!

Tip: Click Options to specify *which* dictionary you want: the standard New Oxford American or the Japanese one.

- **Random.** The Mac chooses a different screensaver each time. Surrender to the power of chance!

No matter which screensaver mode you choose, you can also turn on "Show with clock." This option superimposes the current time on whatever screensaver you've

selected. You'd be surprised at how handy it can be to use your Mac as a giant digital clock when you're getting coffee across the room.

Activating the screensaver

You can control when your screensaver takes over your monitor in a couple of ways:

- **After a period of inactivity.** Using the "Start after" pop-up menu, you can set the amount of time that has to pass without keyboard or mouse activity before the screensaver starts. The duration can be as short as 1 minute or as long as 1 hour, or you can choose Never to prevent the screensaver from ever turning on by itself.

- **When you park your cursor in the corner of the screen.** If you click the Hot Corners button, you can turn each corner of your monitor into a *hot corner* (Figure 17-11).

Figure 17-11:
This "sheet" lets you set certain corners of your screen as instant-activation spots, or never-come-on spots. Sliding the mouse to the Start Screen Saver corner, for example, turns on your screensaver.

If you work in a business, or in a nosy family, it might be worth noting here that you can set things up so that your password is required to exit the screensaver. Visit System Preferences→Security & Privacy, and turn on "Require password immediately after sleep or screensaver begins."

Dictation & Speech

Your Mac's ability to speak—and to be spoken to—is described in juicy detail within other chapters. To learn about OS X's speak-to-type feature, see page 218; for spoken commands, see page 579; for details on its ability to speak to you, see page 714.

Displays

This panel controls your screen settings. It's described on page 340.

Dock

See Chapter 2 for details on the Dock and its System Preferences pane.

Energy Saver

The Energy Saver program helps you and your Mac in a number of ways. By blacking out the screen after a period of inactivity, it prolongs the life of your monitor. By putting the Mac to sleep after you've stopped using it, Energy Saver cuts down on electricity costs and pollution. On a laptop, Energy Saver extends the length of the battery charge by controlling the activity of the hard drive and screen.

Best of all, this pane offers the option to have your computer turn off each night automatically—and turn on again at a specified time in anticipation of your arrival at the desk (Figure 17-12).

Figure 17-12:
Top: Here's what Energy Saver looks like on a laptop. In the "Display sleep" option, you can specify an independent sleep time for the screen.

Bottom: Here are the Schedule controls—the key to the Mac's self-scheduling abilities.

Sleep Sliders

The Energy Saver controls are different on a laptop Mac and a desktop Mac. In fact, they differ depending on which laptop or desktop model you have.

- **Computer sleep.** This slider exists only on pre-2013 Macs. (The processors in newer models sleep automatically.) It controls when the Mac will automatically go to sleep—anywhere from 1 minute after your last activity to Never. (Activity can be mouse movement, keyboard action, or Internet data transfer; Energy Saver won't put your Mac to sleep in the middle of a download.)

At that time, the screen goes dark, the hard drive stops spinning, and your processor chip slows to a crawl. Your Mac is now in *sleep* mode, using only a fraction of its usual electricity consumption. To wake it up when you return to your desk, press any key. Everything you were working on, including open programs and documents, is still onscreen, exactly as it was. (To turn off this automatic sleep feature entirely, drag the slider to Never.)

- **Turn off display after** (or **Display sleep**): This slider controls when the *screen* goes black to save power.

Checkbox Options

Below the sliders, you see a selection of additional power-related options. On a laptop, the two tabs at the top of the dialog box let you create different settings for the two states of life for a laptop: when it's plugged in (Power Adapter) and when it's running on battery power (Battery). That's important, because on a laptop, every drop of battery power counts. Here's what you may see:

- **Put the hard disks to sleep when possible.** This saves even more juice—and noise—by letting your drives stop spinning when not in use. This option appears on both the Battery and Power Adapter tabs, so you can control it independently for each power source.

- **Slightly dim the display while on battery power.** You see this checkbox only on the Battery tab for a laptop. It means "Don't use full brightness, so I can save power."

Tip: And when your laptop is plugged in, the sudden dimming of the screen becomes a handy signal that you've lost power. Maybe your power cord needs replugging, the power strip went out, or there's a massive blackout in your half of the country.

- **Wake for Wi-Fi network access.** This option (on the Power Adapter tab) lets you access a sleeping Mac from across the network. How is that possible? See the box on the next page.

Note: The wording of this option reflects how your Mac can connect to a network. If it can connect either over an Ethernet cable or a wireless hotspot, it says, "Wake for network access." If it's not a wireless Mac, you'll see, "Wake for Ethernet network access." If it's a MacBook without an Ethernet adapter, it says, "Wake for Wi-Fi network access." On a laptop, the "wake" feature is available only when the machine's lid is left open and you're plugged into a power outlet.

- **Enable Power Nap.** Power Nap is an ingenious and extremely useful feature for laptops—specifically, flash-storage laptop models that were introduced in 2012 or later, like the Retina Display laptops or recent MacBook Airs. (On older laptops, it doesn't appear at all.)

 Anyway, when you turn on Enable Power Nap, the Mac keeps updating Internet data even while it's closed and asleep. About once every hour, it wakes itself—without activating any fans or lights—long enough to check for mail, calendar updates, Photo Stream updates, software updates, and so on. When you wake up

the laptop later, you'll be delighted to find that it's completely up to date, with new email waiting and all of your iCloud programs (Notes, Messages, Reminders, and so on) up to date. And the lid was closed the whole time!

Power Nap comes set to work only when your laptop is plugged into a power outlet, but you can make it work on battery power, too (Apple says that the battery hit is very slight). You'll find separate on/off switches on each of the Energy Saver tabs. On the Battery tab, it says "Enable Power Nap while on battery power"; on the Power Adapter tab, it says "Enable Power Nap while plugged into a power adapter."

Most of those network functions take place even when the laptop's on battery power. But when it's plugged in, Power Nap also performs two more time-consuming functions: Time Machine backups and App Store software updates.

Of course, Power Nap means that your laptop isn't quite as somnolent as it used to be while the lid was closed—it's using a little more battery power.

- **Restart automatically if the computer freezes.** This checkbox appears only on desktop Macs. It's handy if you leave your Mac unattended and access it remotely, or if you use it as a network file server or Web server. It ensures that, if your lonely Mac seizes up or crashes, it will start itself right back up again.

GEM IN THE ROUGH

Auto-Wake for Network Access

You should put your Mac to sleep as much as possible; you'll save power, money, and pollution. Unfortunately, a sleeping Mac is useless on your network. For example, you can't access files on it from another machine.

But Wake on Demand gives you the best of both worlds. It keeps a sleeping Mac available on the network, so you can wake it up remotely when you need it.

How can you do that? Is the Mac sleeping, or isn't it?

Yes, it's sleeping. But before it dozes off, it hands off its list of available network services—file sharing, screen sharing, printer sharing, and so on—to your Apple wireless base station. The base station becomes your sleeping Mac's agent, continuing to broadcast the available features of the sleeping Mac (via Apple's Bonjour networking technology) to the rest of the network.

To make this work, you need an AirPort wireless base station or a Time Capsule, running the latest Apple firmware. If

you're using a WPA or WPA2 password on your base station or Time Capsule, it can't be in "bridge mode" (you'd know if you'd turned that on). Only Macs made since late 2008 can be awakened over a wireless network (all Macs can be awakened over an Ethernet wired network). To find out if yours is eligible, open System Information (page 623); under the Network heading, click Wi-Fi and look to see if Wake on Wireless is listed as Supported.

(Longtime Mac nuts may observe that "Wake for network access" has been available in Energy Saver for years. That older method, however, worked only on wired networks, not wireless.)

Once you've turned on Wake on Demand, by the way, you might hear brief sounds from the DVD drive, hard drive, or fans, even when the Mac is asleep. That's normal; it means the Mac is checking in with the Bonjour sleep switchboard.

That's right: Even your Mac sometimes stirs in its sleep.

Tip: If you've also turned off (or left off) "Ask to keep changes when closing documents" and "Close windows when quitting an application" in System Preferences→General, then your Mac will both restart *and* restore everything you were doing. You may, in fact, never even realize that a crash or freeze occurred while you were away! (The telltale sign: Any Web pages you had logged into, like a banking Web site, will have logged you out.)

- **Show battery status in the menu bar.** This on/off switch (laptops only) controls the battery menulet described in the box below.

Scheduled Startup and Shutdown

By clicking Schedule, you can set up the Mac to shut itself down and turn itself back on automatically (Figure 17-12, bottom).

If you work from 9 to 5, for example, you can set the office Mac to turn itself on at 8:45 a.m. and shut itself down at 5:30 p.m.—an arrangement that conserves electricity, saves money, and reduces pollution, but doesn't inconvenience you in the least. In fact, you may come to forget that you've set up the Mac this way, since you'll never actually see it turn itself off.

Note: The Mac doesn't shut down automatically if you've left unsaved documents open onscreen. It will go to sleep, though.

Mysteries of the Battery Menulet

If you've got a laptop, don't miss the checkbox in Energy Saver called "Show battery status in the menu bar." It puts a handy status indicator (⎘) in the menu bar.

Without clicking the menulet, all you see is an icon that represents the battery charge. If you turn on Show Percentage from the menulet's actual menu, then the menulet can also show how much charge remains, in percentage form.

Here's what the menulet icon may show:

Lightning bolt in the battery. The laptop is plugged in and the battery is charging or charged.

Superimposed X. The laptop is plugged in, but the battery isn't in right, is missing, or isn't getting a charge for some other reason.

Emptying black battery. The laptop is on battery and has at least 25 percent power left. (The width of the bar reveals how much charge is left.)

Emptying red battery. The laptop is running off of battery

power but has less than 25 percent charge remaining.

A nearly invisible red bar means you have less than 9 minutes left. Save those documents, buddy.

If you click the menulet, you see an estimate of actual time remaining on your battery charge, in hours:minutes form. (If the battery is charging, then you see how much time *remains* until the battery is fully recharged, like this: "0:24 Until Full.") Either way, the readout is counting down (or up) to that joyous moment.

The menu also offers a terrific list: Apps Using Significant Energy. When your battery is running low, it's a great way to see which apps are guzzling down your juice.

Finally, if you Option-click the menulet, you get a health report for your battery. It might say, for example, "Condition: Normal." When the condition needs your attention—when it says "Service Battery," "Replace Soon," "Replace Now," or "Check Battery," you don't have to press Option. You'll see that message every time you open the menulet.)

Extensions

One of Yosemite's unsung new features is the ability to install *extensions*. These are add-on features—plug-ins—that expand what your Mac can do. Each is associated with a full-blown program you've installed on your Mac; they can come from Apple or anybody else. This System Preferences pane lists the ones you've got installed so far, and lets you turn off the ones you don't use.

Extensions (Figure 17-13) can modify four parts of the Mac:

Figure 17-13:
Once you click the category name, you can operate on the individual extensions listed within. You can hide or show them by turning their checkboxes off or on, and you can change the order in which they appear in your menus by dragging them up or down.

- **Actions.** You probably have only one item here, called Markup. That's Apple's own extension, and it lets you mark up attachments in Mail, TextEdit, and some other programs. In theory, these extensions do *something* to whatever text or graphics you've selected.

- **Finder.** These features operate on files at the desktop. The most common example is Dropbox; its extension adds Dropbox commands (like Share Dropbox Link) to the shortcut menu when you right-click or two-finger click an icon in your Dropbox folder, and adds a green checkmark icon to each file that's been synced with Dropbox online.

- **Share Menu.** You know the Share button that appears all across OS X (page 239)? It produces a list of different ways (Mail, Messages, or Facebook) that you can share whatever you've got selected (a map, a Web page, a photo). Well, that list is now extensible. Your programs can insert their own sharing options into this list.

- **Today.** The Today pane of the Notification Center is described on page 616—but what's fascinating is that you can now install new information chunks (widgets, as Apple calls them) to that display. Everybody can choose from the starter widgets like Calculator, Calendar, and Weather—but other programs can install additional info-bits here.

Each of these extension categories works in the same way, as shown in Figure 17-13.

General

This pane is mostly about how things look on the screen: windows, menus, buttons, scroll bars, and fonts.

Changing Colors

Two pop-up menus let you crank up or tone down OS X's overall colorfulness:

- **Appearance.** Choose between Blue and Graphite. Blue refers to OS X's factory setting—bright, candy-colored progress bars,  menu, and pulsing OK buttons—and those red, yellow, and green buttons in the corner of every window. If you, like some graphics professionals, find this circus-poster coloring a bit distracting, then choose Graphite, which renders all those interface elements in various shades of gray.

- **Use dark menu bar and Dock.** When you turn this checkbox on, the backgrounds of your menu bar and Dock turn dark gray. Here again, Apple probably had visual artists in mind—but it looks cool and calming no matter who you are.

- **Highlight color.** When you drag your cursor across text, its background changes color to indicate that you've selected it. *Which* color the background becomes is up to you; choose a shade from the pop-up menu. The Highlight color also affects such subtleties as the lines on the inside of a window as you drag an icon into it.

If you choose Other, the Color Picker palette (see the box on the next page) appears, from which you can choose any color your Mac is capable of displaying.

Sidebar Icon Size

This pop-up menu controls the size of the icons in the Sidebar (page 35), as you'd expect. But you might not guess that it also controls the *type size* of those icons. And you'd *definitely* not guess that it simultaneously adjusts the size and type of the mailbox icons in the Mail program.

Tweaking the Scroll Bars

These options control the scroll bars of all your windows—including the controversial *removal* of scroll bars.

- **Show scroll bars.** If you choose "Automatically based on mouse or trackpad," then whether the scroll bars appear or not depends on what you have plugged in.

 If you have a trackpad or a Magic Mouse, for example, Apple assumes that you'll scroll by dragging your fingers—so you won't be needing the scroll bars at the

edges of the windows. Therefore, the scroll bars appear only when you're actually scrolling (and then only to show you where you are in the window). But if you have no way of using touch gestures—for example, if you have a regular mouse or Apple's Mighty Mouse—then scroll bars are always visible, so you don't freak out.

"When scrolling" means that the scroll bars pop into view during the actual scroll, when your mouse or fingers-on-trackpad are actually in motion. And "Always," of course, means that the scroll bars never disappear.

The Color Picker

Here and there—in System Preferences, iMovie, TextEdit, Microsoft Office, and many other programs—OS X offers you the opportunity to choose a *color* for some element: for your desktop background, a window, and so on.

The dialog box that appears offers a miniature color lab that lets you dial in any color in the Mac's rainbow—several color labs, actually, arrayed across the top, each designed to make color choosing easier in certain circumstances:

Color wheel. Drag the scroll bar vertically to adjust the brightness, and then drag your cursor around the ball to pick the shade.

Color sliders. From the pop-up menu, choose the color-mixing method you prefer. CMYK stands for cyan, magenta, yellow, and black. People in the printing industry will feel immediately at home, because these four colors are the component inks for color printing. (These people may also be able to explain why K stands for black.)

RGB is how a TV or computer monitor thinks of colors: as proportions of red, green, and blue light. Grayscale means shades of gray, like a black-and-white TV. And HSB stands for hue, saturation, and brightness—a favorite color-specifying scheme in scientific circles.

In each case, just drag the sliders to mix up the color you want, or type in the percentages of each component.

Color palettes. This option presents canned sets of color swatches. They're primarily for programmers who want quick access to the standard colors in OS X. The Web Safe

Colors list is useful for Web designers, too; they can use it to ensure that the colors they choose will display properly on other computers.

Image palettes. Here's the visible rainbow arrayed yet another way: in cloudy, color-arranged streaks. (Cool tip: If you drag a graphics file directly into the dialog box, it appears in the spectrum's place. That's a handy trick if you're trying to identify the color of a certain spot of an image, for example. And don't miss the pop-up button at the bottom of the dialog box, which offers a few other stunts.)

Crayons. Now this is a good user interface. You can click each crayon to see its color name: Mocha, Fern, Cayenne, and so on. (Some interior decorator in Cupertino had a field day naming these crayons.)

In any of these color pickers, you can also "sample" a color that's outside the dialog box—a color you found on a Web page, for example. Just click the magnifying-glass icon and then move your cursor around the screen. You'll see the sliders and numbers change inside the dialog box automatically when you click.

Finally, note that you can store frequently used (or frequently admired) colors in the tiny palette squares at the bottom. To do that, drag the big rectangular color swatch (next to the magnifying glass) directly down into one of the little squares, where it will stay fresh for weeks.

If you don't have space for all the colors you want at the bottom of the window, you can drag the small circular dot down to make room for more.

• **Click in the scroll bar to.** For details on "Jump to the next page" and "Jump to the spot that's clicked," see the box on page 39.

Default Web Browser

When you click a link in, for example, an email message—or on Twitter or Facebook—which Web browser should open? Safari? Chrome? Firefox? Here's where you decide.

Ask to Keep Changes When Closing Documents

If you turn this item on, then you'll be *asked* whether you want to preserve the changes you've made since your last manual Save. (Auto Save will still be there in case your program crashes, as described on page 206.)

Close Windows When Quitting an App

Here's the master on/off switch for the OS X feature responsible for reopening your last-used documents and windows each time you open a window. Usually, the auto-reopening feature saves you time and helps you resume your mental flow. But if you find it disturbing (or if you're worried about someone else discovering what you're up to), turn on this checkbox.

Number of Recent Items

Just how many of your recently opened documents, networked servers, and programs do you want the Mac to show using the Recent Items command in the menu? Pick a number from the pop-up menus.

Allow Handoff Between This Mac and Your iCloud Devices

You know that fantastic synergy that you gain if you own both an iPhone and a Mac—the features described in Chapter 14? This is the master on/off switch.

Use LCD Font Smoothing When Available

The Mac's built-in text-smoothing (*antialiasing*) feature is supposed to produce smoother, more commercial-looking text anywhere it appears on your Mac: in word processing documents, email messages, Web pages, and so on (Figure 17-14).

Figure 17-14:
Experiment with Font Smoothing to see how you like the effect; it's fairly subtle. Furthermore, it has no effect until the next time you open the program in question. In the Finder, for example, you won't see a difference until you log out and back in again.

(These settings don't affect your printouts, only the onscreen display.)

Smoothing is turned off.

Smoothing is turned on.

iCloud

This pane is, of course, the master setup page for Apple's free iCloud synchronization service. For complete details on setting up iCloud and using it, see Chapter 10.

Internet Accounts

This is a single, handy, central place to tell OS X your user names and passwords for all kinds of Internet services: Gmail, Yahoo, Exchange, Twitter, Vimeo, Flickr, LinkedIn, and so on.

To get started entering your account names and passwords, click one of the big-name logos (Gmail, Yahoo, whatever)—or click the + button below the list. The Mac is smart enough to feed the account information here into the right programs (Mail, Calendar, Contacts, and the Share buttons described on page 239).

Keyboard

The changes you make on this pane are tiny but can have a cumulatively big impact on your daily typing routine.

Keyboard Tab

On this pane, you have these choices:

- **Key Repeat Rate, Delay Until Repeat.** In OS X, holding down letter and number keys don't make them repeat, much to the disappointment of people who like to type, for example, "AAAAAARRRRRRGGGGHHH!" Instead, holding down a key produces a palette of alternative accented versions of that letter, like é, è, ê, ë, and so on.

 Only the punctuation keys still repeat, so at least you can still type ****** or ????? or !!!!!!!.

 There are sneaky ways to make your regular keys repeat, as they did in days gone by; see page 217. In the meantime, these two sliders govern the repeating behavior of the punctuation keys. On the right: a slider that determines how long you must hold down a key before it starts repeating (to prevent triggering repetitions accidentally). On the left: a slider that governs how fast each key spits out characters once the spitting has begun.

- **Use all F1, F2, etc. keys as standard function keys.** This option appears *only* on laptops and aluminum-keyboard Macs. It's complicated, so read page 187 slowly.

- **Adjust keyboard brightness in low light.** This setting appears only if your Mac's keyboard does, in fact, light up when you're working in the dark—a showy feature of most Mac laptops. You can specify that you want the internal lighting to shut off after a period of inactivity (to save power when you've wandered away, for example), or you can turn the lighting off altogether. (You can always adjust the keyboard brightness manually, of course, by tapping the ∴ and ∴ keys.)

- **Show Keyboard & Character Viewers in menu bar.** You can read all about these special symbol-generating windows on page 227. Here's the on/off switch for the menulet that makes them appear.

- **Set Up Bluetooth Keyboard.** Yes, you're absolutely right: This button lets you set up a Bluetooth (wireless) keyboard.

- **Modifier Keys.** This button lets you turn off, or remap, the functions of the Option, Caps Lock, Control, and ⌘ keys. It's for Unix programmers whose pinkies can't adjust to the Mac's modifier-key layout; for anyone using a PC keyboard on which the Option (Alt) and ⊞ (Windows) keys are in the "wrong" positions relative to each other; and for anyone who keeps hitting Caps Lock by accident during everyday typing.

Text Tab

Here's where you set up the Mac's automatic abbreviation-expansion feature, described on page 215.

Shortcuts Tab

This pane lets you make up new keystrokes for just about any function on the Mac, like capturing a screenshot, operating the Dock, triggering one of the Services, or operating a menu in *any program* from the keyboard. You can come up with keyboard combinations that, for example, are easier to remember, harder to trigger by accident, or easier to hit with one hand.

Step-by-step instructions for using this pane appear on page 197.

Input Sources

These are the keyboard layouts for various languages. See page 226.

Language & Region

The primary job of this pane is to set up your Mac to work in other languages. If you bought your Mac already set up in your own language—you're already using the only language, number format, and keyboard layout you'll ever need—then you can ignore most of this pane. But when it comes to showing off OS X to your friends and loved ones, the "wow" factor on the Mac's polyglot features is huge.

Details appear on page 225.

Mission Control

Mission Control, the joint venture of the Exposé, Spaces, and Dashboard window-management features, is described in detail in Chapter 4—and so is this joint-venture control pane.

Mouse

This pane looks different depending on what kind of mouse (if any) is attached to your Mac.

Tracking Speed, Double-Click Speed

It may surprise you that the cursor on the screen doesn't move five inches when you move the mouse five inches on the desk. Instead, the cursor moves farther when you move the mouse faster.

How *much* farther depends on how you set the first slider here. The Fast setting is nice if you have an enormous monitor, since you don't need an equally large mouse pad to get from one corner to another. The Slow setting, on the other hand, forces you to pick up and put down the mouse frequently as you scoot across the screen. It offers very little acceleration, but it can be great for highly detailed work like pixel-by-pixel editing in Photoshop.

The Double-Click Speed setting specifies how much time you have to complete a double-click. If you click too slowly—beyond the time you've allotted yourself with this slider—the Mac "hears" two *single* clicks instead.

Note: On a laptop without any mouse attached, the Mouse pane still appears in System Preferences—but its sole function is to help you "pair" your Mac with a wireless Bluetooth mouse. At that point, the Mouse pane looks just as it does on a desktop Mac.

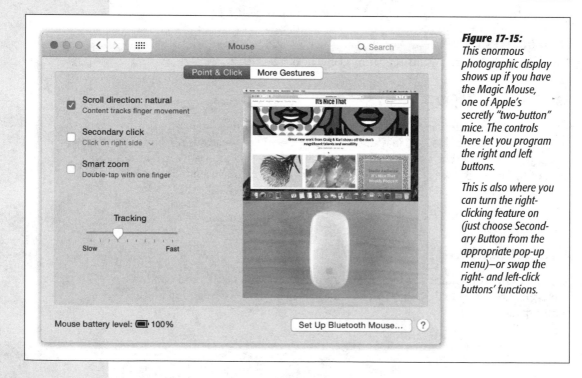

Figure 17-15:
This enormous photographic display shows up if you have the Magic Mouse, one of Apple's secretly "two-button" mice. The controls here let you program the right and left buttons.

This is also where you can turn the right-clicking feature on (just choose Secondary Button from the appropriate pop-up menu)—or swap the right- and left-click buttons' functions.

The Mighty Mouse and Magic Mouse

Just by looking, you'd never know that these Apple mice have both a right button and a left button. Once you turn on the two-button feature in System Preferences (Figure 17-15), though, each side clicks independently.

The unusually flat, broad top surface of the Magic Mouse is also a trackpad. You can drag your finger across its surface to trigger many of OS X's trackpad gestures.

The Mighty Mouse is the white mouse that has come with desktop Macs since 2005.

Network

See Chapter 16 for the settings you need to plug in for networking.

Notifications

Here's where you customize the Notification Center, which gets its own big writeup in Chapter 18.

Parental Controls

These controls are described at length in Chapter 15.

Printers & Scanners

Chapter 9 describes printing, scanning, and faxing. This pane offers a centralized list of the printers, scanners, and fax modems you've introduced to the Mac.

Security & Privacy

See Chapter 15 for details on locking up your Mac.

Sharing

OS X is an outstanding, upstanding network citizen, flexible enough to share its contents with other Macs, Windows PCs, people dialing in from the road, and so on. On this pane, you'll find on/off switches for each of these sharing channels.

In this book, many of these features are covered in other chapters. For example, Screen Sharing and File Sharing are in Chapter 16, Printer Sharing is in Chapter 9, and Internet Sharing is in Chapter 10.

Here's a quick rundown on the other items:

- **DVD or CD Sharing.** This feature was added to accommodate Mac models that don't have CD/DVD drives—which, these days, is all of them. When you sit at a Mac that *does* have a drive and turn on this option, those driveless computers on

the network can "see," and borrow, your Mac's DVD drive for the purposes of installing new software or running Mac disk-repair software. (Your drive shows up under the Remote Disc heading in the driveless Mac's Finder Sidebar.)

- **Remote Management.** Lets someone else control your Mac using Apple Remote Desktop, a popular add-on program for teachers and system administrators.

- **Remote Apple Events.** Lets AppleScript gurus send commands to Macs across the network.

- **Bluetooth Sharing.** This pane lets you set up Bluetooth file sharing, a way for other people near you to shoot files over to (or receive files from) your laptop—without hassle, or passwords. Page 581 has the details.

Sound

Using the panes of the Sound pane, you can configure the sound system of your Mac in any of several ways.

Tip: Here's a quick way to jump directly to the Sound pane of System Preferences—from the keyboard, without ever having to open System Preferences or click Sound. Just press Option as you tap the ◀, ◀), or ◀)) key on the top row of your Apple keyboard.

Sound Effects Tab

"Sound effects" means *error beeps*—the sound you hear when the Mac wants your attention, or when you click someplace you shouldn't.

Just click the sound of your choice to make it your default system beep. Most of the canned choices here are funny and clever, yet subdued enough to be practical as alert sounds (Figure 17-16).

The other controls on the Sound Effects pane include these:

- **Play sound effects through:** Intriguingly enough, in Yosemite, you can now specify one sound source (a speaker or headset) for most sound playback—and a different one just for your error beeps. That's the one you specify with this pop-up menu.

- **Alert volume.** The *main* volume slider for your Mac is the "Output volume" slider at the bottom of the Sound pane. The "Alert volume" slider is *just* for error beeps; Apple was kind enough to let you adjust the volume of these error beeps independently.

- **Play user interface sound effects.** This option produces a few subtle sound effects during certain Finder operations: when you drag something off the Dock, into the Trash, or into a folder, or when the Finder finishes a file-copying job.

- **Play feedback when volume is changed.** Each time you press one of the volume keys (◂, ◂», ◂»)), the Mac beeps (or, rather, pops) to help you gauge the current volume. (The popping sound has been toned down and de-obnoxified in Yosemite.)

That's all fine when you're working at home. But more than one person has been humiliated in an important meeting when the Mac made a sudden, inappropriately loud sonic outburst—and then amplified that embarrassment by furiously and repeatedly pressing the volume-down key, beeping all the way.

If you turn off this checkbox, the Mac won't make any sound at all as you adjust its volume. Instead, you'll see only a visual representation of the steadily decreasing (or increasing) volume level.

Tip: The Shift key reverses the logic. So if you have "Play feedback" turned *on,* holding down Shift as you tap the volume keys makes them silent. If it's turned *off,* you can force the volume-gauging beeps to play by pressing Shift as you tap the volume keys.

Figure 17-16:
You can adjust your overall speaker volume independently from the alert-beep volume, thank goodness.

Output Tab

"Output" means speakers or headphones. For most people, this pane lists only Internal Speakers (and a Balance slider for left-to-right stereo balancing). This pane is more useful when you've connected external speakers, a Bluetooth or USB phone headset, or an AirPlay receiver like an Apple TV—and then clicked its name. All Mac

audio now flows to that device. OS X will even remember your volume setting for each gadget independently.

Tip: Here's a much quicker way to change your audio input or output: Press Option as you click the ◀)) menulet. You get a secret pop-up menu that lists your various microphones, speakers, and headphones, so you can switch things without a visit to System Preferences.

Input Tab

This pane lets you specify which sound source you want the Mac to "listen to," if you have more than one connected: external microphone, internal microphone, line input, USB headset, or whatever. It also lets you adjust the sensitivity of that microphone—its *input volume*—by dragging the slider and watching the real-time Input level meter above it change as you speak. Put another way, it's a quick way to see if your microphone is working.

The "Use ambient noise reduction" is great if you make podcasts or use dictation software. It turns any mike into what amounts to a noise-canceling microphone, deadening the background noise while you're recording.

If you'd prefer even more control over your Mac's sound inputs and outputs, don't miss the Audio MIDI Setup program in your Applications→Utilities folder.

Spotlight

Here's how you tell the Mac (a) which categories of files and information you want the Spotlight search feature to search, (b) which folders you *don't* want searched, for privacy reasons, and (c) which key combination you want to use for summoning the Spotlight menu or dialog box. Details are in Chapter 3.

Startup Disk

Use this pane to pick the System folder your Mac will use the next time it starts up—when you're swapping between OS X and Windows (running with Boot Camp), for example. Check out the details in Chapter 9.

Time Machine

Here's the master on/off switch and options pane for Time Machine, which is described in Chapter 5.

Trackpad

You may love your Mac laptop now, but these special features make your laptop *crazy* better. Turns out you can point, click, scroll, right-click, rotate things, enlarge things, hide windows, and switch programs, all on the trackpad itself, without ever having

to lift your fingers. (You can do most of this on a desktop Mac, too, if it has an Apple Magic Mouse, or an external trackpad like Apple's Magic Trackpad.)

The options here depend on your Mac model, but usually you see something like Figure 17-17: three tabs. Each governs how you do pointing, clicking, scrolling, and other mouselike maneuvers. Each time you click one, the right half of the dialog box plays a looping movie that shows you that technique clearly and visibly.

Here's what's on the three main tabs.

Point & Click

- **Tap to Click.** Usually, you touch your laptop's trackpad only to move the cursor. For clicking and dragging, you're supposed to push down on the clicker (the lower half of the actual trackpad surface).

 Many people find, however, that it's more direct to tap and drag directly on the trackpad, using the same finger that's been moving the cursor. That's the purpose of this checkbox. When it's on, you can tap the trackpad surface to register a mouse click at the location of the cursor. Double-tap to double-click.

- **Secondary click.** This means "right-click." As you know, right-clicking is a huge deal on the Mac; it unleashes useful features just about everywhere.

 This pop-up menu offers you three options. You can click with two fingers; click once in the lower-right corner of the trackpad; or click once in the lower-left corner. You can also trigger a right-click by clicking with your thumb while resting your index and middle fingers on the trackpad. Weird, but wonderful.

- **Look up.** This gesture lets you tap the trackpad (*don't* click—just touch the surface without clicking) to bring up a handy dictionary definition for the word you're double-tapping. It doesn't work in all programs.

- **Three-finger drag.** This option lets you move a window around the screen, or change its size and shape, without actually clicking. Instead, you rest three fingers on the trackpad and drag. For example, move a window by pointing to the title bar and then dragging three fingers. Make it wider by pointing to its right or left edge and then dragging three fingers. Change its shape by pointing to the lower-right corner and then dragging three fingers.

- **Tracking speed.** This is a duplicate of the Tracking Speed slider described under "Mouse" earlier in this chapter—but it lets you establish an independent tracking speed for the *trackpad.*

Scroll & Zoom

- **Scroll direction: natural.** Here's the heart of OS X's most controversial recent feature: scrolling *up* when you drag your fingers (or the scroll wheel, or the scroll bar) *up.* That's exactly the opposite of what we've been doing for years.

If you can't stand this arrangement, designed to make the Mac work more like the iPhone and iPad, then turn it off here (Figure 17-17).

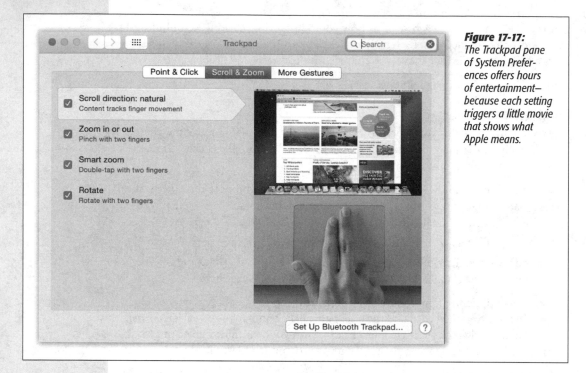

Figure 17-17:
The Trackpad pane of System Preferences offers hours of entertainment—because each setting triggers a little movie that shows what Apple means.

- **Zoom in or out.** If you've used an iPhone or iPad, this one will seem familiar. What it means is, "Put two fingers on the trackpad and spread them apart to *enlarge* what's on the screen. Slide two fingers *together* to shrink it down again." It doesn't work in every program—it affects pictures and PDFs in Preview, photos in iPhoto, text in Safari, text in a TextEdit window—but it's great when it does.

- **Smart zoom.** On the iPhone/iPad, you can double-tap a block of text or a graphic on a Web page to enlarge just that block to full-screen size. The "smart" element of this is the way the software senses that block's borders and zooms in exactly right.

 Now you can do that on your Mac, too. Double-tap your trackpad (touch, don't click) with *two* fingers to do it.

- **Rotate.** Place two fingers on the trackpad, and then twist them around an invisible center point, to rotate a photo or a PDF document. This doesn't work in all programs or in all circumstances, but it's great for turning images upright in Preview, iPhoto, Image Capture, and so on.

More Gestures

- **Swipe between pages**. Drag two fingers horizontally across the trackpad to skip to the next or previous page or image in a batch. Great for flipping through images or PDF pages in Preview or iPhoto, or to go back or forward a page in Safari.

 The tiny pop-up menu here lets you *change* the swiping gesture. You can swipe with two fingers, three fingers, or—if you're a fan of variety—two *or* three fingers.

- **Swipe between full-screen apps.** If you've embraced OS X's Full Screen feature, or its Mission Control feature, you'll want to learn this one. You can flip between full-screen apps either with three or four fingers on the trackpad.

- **Notification Center.** You can summon the Notification Center by swiping leftward with two fingers onto the trackpad from beyond its right edge (page 614).

- **Mission Control.** This gesture lets you enter and exit Mission Control (Chapter 4) by swiping up or down with three fingers. (You can change it to *four* fingers.)

- **App Exposé.** If this checkbox is on, you can trigger App Exposé (page 184) by swiping three fingers downward. (You can change the setting to *four* fingers.)

Note: If you study those last two paragraphs carefully, you'll realize that the four-finger swipe has different *levels*. Starting from whatever you're doing, a four-finger swipe *up* takes you into Mission Control. From there, *two* swipes down takes you into App Exposé.

Similarly, from within App Exposé, *two* swipes upward enters Mission Control.

- **Launchpad.** Launchpad (page 152) wouldn't be very useful if it took several steps to open. Fortunately, this option lets you fire up Launchpad by pinching on the trackpad with three fingers and your thumb. (You can also exit Launchpad by *spreading* those four fingers.)

- **Show Desktop.** You can spread three fingers and your thumb to trigger Desktop Exposé (page 186). Once there, *pinch* those fingers to return to what you were doing.

Note: Here again, Apple has created *levels* of four-finger pinching. Pinching once opens Launchpad; spread *twice* from there to show the desktop. Likewise, pinching *twice* from Show Desktop takes you straight into Launchpad.

At the bottom of the Trackpad pane, a Set Up Bluetooth Trackpad button appears. Use it to pair your Mac with a wireless external trackpad—like Apple's own Magic Trackpad.

Users & Groups

This is the master list of people who are allowed to log into your Mac. (In previous Mac OS X versions it was called Accounts.) It's where you can adjust their passwords, startup pictures, self-opening startup items, permissions to use various features of the Mac, and other security tools. All of this is described in Chapter 15.

Notifications

A notification is an important status message or warning. On a smartphone, you get one every time a text message comes in, an alarm goes off, a calendar appointment is imminent, or your battery is running low.

Phone *apps* use this mechanism, too. You get a message when your friends post updates on Facebook or Twitter. When your flight is two hours from takeoff. When a new Groupon discount becomes available. When your online Scrabble or chess opponent makes another move.

It's no different on your Mac. Mail and Messages might want to let you know that a new message has arrived. Game Center might want you to realize that it's your move. The Calendar app might want to remind you that an important meeting is about to start.

In OS X, you know when some app is trying to get your attention: A message bubble slides into view at the top right of your screen (Figure 18-1, top). Some of these alerts slide away again after 5 seconds; others require you to click a button, like Close, Snooze, or Show (which opens the program that's waving its little hand in your face).

Note: Only apps you got from the Mac App Store can tap into the Notification Center. Other programs will use whatever alert mechanisms they always have—pop-up dialog boxes, for example.

You're also notified this way when one of your App Store apps has been automatically updated, or when that update requires you to quit the app or restart the Mac (and you're offered a Later button).

All kinds of warnings—dying battery, failed Time Machine backups, disks ejected improperly—now appear in these subtle notification bubbles.

Insta-Respond to Bubbles

Some of those notification bubbles aren't just the Mac's way of speaking to you; they're interactive. That's particularly handy when the bubble represents an incoming iMessage, FaceTime call, or email—because you can reply to them. See Figure 18-1.

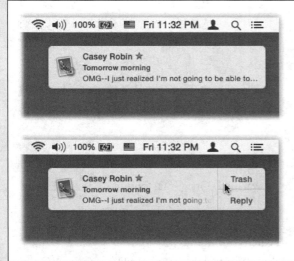

Figure 18-1:
Top: Whenever possible, OS X tries to get your attention using these subtle, upper-right-corner notifications.

Bottom: If you point to these bubbles before they disappear, they sometimes offer buttons that let you take action. For example, if it's an incoming instant message, you can hit Reply and then type your response right in the bubble. If it's a FaceTime call, you can answer it or decline it.

And if it's an email message, you can click either Trash or Reply. If you hit Reply, an outgoing, floating email message window opens, already addressed, already set up as a response. Just type your reply and hit Send.

Shutting Up the Bubbles

Of course, little bubbles sliding into the top-right corner of your screen may not always be what you want, especially if you're trying to beat a deadline.

Dismiss One Bubble

If you're in a hurry, you can get rid of one of these bubbles with a right swipe on it (two fingers on a trackpad, one on a Magic Mouse, or just drag it off to the right).

Do Not Disturb (Manual)

But to truly shut up all notifications, turn on Do Not Disturb (Figure 18-2, top).

Tip: If you're an efficiency nut, you may prefer to simply Option-click the ☰ button at the right end of your menu bar. It turns gray, indicating that you've just stifled all bubbles until midnight (or until you Option-click it again).

When Do Not Disturb is on, your messages quietly pile up in the Notification Center (described in a moment); they don't pop up on your screen individually as they happen, and they certainly don't make any noises.

Do Not Disturb (Automatic)

The Mac can also shut up the bubbles automatically, either according to a daily schedule (like when you're asleep) or when you're giving a presentation.

To see it, open System Preferences→Notifications (Figure 18-2). You'll find that this version of Do Not Disturb offers all kinds of useful options:

- **On a schedule.** Here you can specify starting and ending hours for Do Not Disturb to kick in automatically. It's handy if you'd like the Mac to go dark during the same hours you do every night. (There's no separate setting for weekends; Do Not Disturb will turn on and off for the same hours every day of the week.)

Figure 18-2:
Top: In the Notification Center, on the Today tab, scroll to the very top to see this Do Not Disturb on/off switch.

Meanwhile, the little ⊗ icon at the bottom of the Notifications pane takes you directly to the Do Not Disturb pane of System Preferences, shown here at bottom.

Bottom: You can set up Do Not Disturb on a schedule, allowing exceptions in case of emergency.

- **When the display is sleeping.** When the screen is dark, it means you're not at your Mac. You probably don't need passersby to see your incoming love notes; besides, you're not there to witness them arriving anyway.

- **When mirroring to TVs and projectors.** If you're showing an audience something from your Mac, chances are pretty good that you don't want little notice bubbles to interrupt the show. There's nothing worse than an audience of 500 witnessing the embarrassing subject lines of your incoming email.

- **Allow calls from everyone.** If you use your Mac as a speakerphone (Chapter 14), you might still want it to ring for incoming calls. In that case, turn on this option. All other notifications are still silenced when Do Not Disturb is engaged—just not phone calls and FaceTime calls.

- **Allow repeated calls.** If you turn this on, and somebody tries to call you more than once within three minutes, it will ring through. The idea here is that nobody *would* call you multiple times unless it was urgent. You certainly wouldn't want Do Not Disturb to block somebody trying to tell you that there's been an accident, that you've overslept, or that you've just won the lottery.

The Notification Center

All right, now you know how to dismiss, stifle, or respond to notification bubbles. But what if you miss one? Or you decide to act on it later?

Thought you'd never ask.

All of those "Hey you!" messages collect on a single screen called the Notification Center (Figure 18-3).

To make it appear on a laptop, swipe two fingers *onto* the trackpad from the right. (Start the swipe off to the right of the trackpad.)

You can also open the Notification Center by clicking the ☰ in the upper-right corner of your screen. That's a handy trick if your Mac doesn't have a trackpad—if it's an iMac, for example. (You can also set up a keystroke or a "hot corner" to open the Notification Center, if you like. See pages 197 and 164.)

Either way, the Notification Center slides onto the screen like a classy black window shade, printed in white with every recent item of interest; whatever *was* on your screen gets shoved temporarily off to the left side.

Tip: To close the Notification Center, swipe the opposite way (left to right) with two fingers. Or just click any other part of the screen. Or click the ☰ again. Or press the Esc key. Or just blink really hard.

The Notification Center has two tabs at the top (Figure 18-3):

- **Today.** On the Today tab, you see today's weather, all your upcoming appointments and reminders, and an assortment of widgets (calculator, stock report, news headlines) that you've installed there. More on this in a moment.

- **Notifications.** This tab lists all your apps' notifications, as well as all your Mac's messages, reminders, upcoming appointments, and so on.

Each produces a scrolling pane; read on.

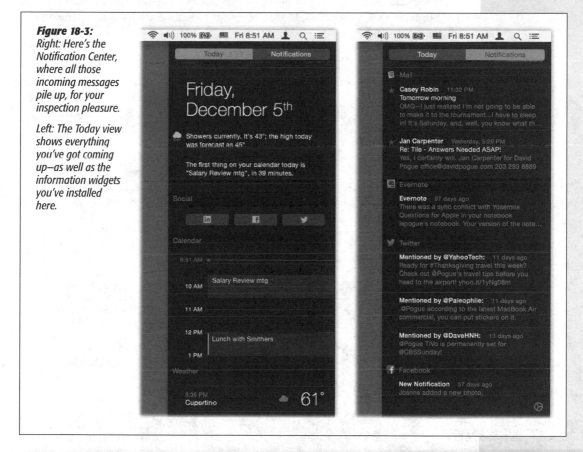

Figure 18-3:
Right: Here's the Notification Center, where all those incoming messages pile up, for your inspection pleasure.

Left: The Today view shows everything you've got coming up—as well as the information widgets you've installed here.

Notifications Tab

On the Notifications tab (Figure 18-3, right), you can have two kinds of fun:

- Click an item to open the relevant app for more details. For example, click an appointment listed there to open its information pane in Calendar. Click the name of a software update to open the Mac App Store program to read about it and download it. Click a message's name to open Mail, where you can read the entire message.

- Click the little ✕ to dismiss one app's entire list of notifications once you've seen them. (The app is free to fill up your Notification Center again once it has something to say.)

And if you have no interest in a certain app's notifications showing up here, you can make them stop appearing for good, as described below.

Today Tab

The Today pane presents an executive summary of everything you need to know today, in plain English: your upcoming appointments (" 'Personnel meeting' is next up on your calendar, at 2 PM"); reminders coming due; weather and stock information; and a preview of your schedule for tomorrow. It's identical to the Today pane on the iPhone or iPad, if you're scoring at home.

Intriguingly, Apple also allows apps to add their *own* sections to the Today list.

For example, Dropbox can show a list of files that have been added to your Dropbox folder; Evernote can add buttons for creating new notes or reminders; The New York Times, Yahoo Digest, and Huffington Post apps can add headlines; the Kindle app offers links to the books you're reading right now; and so on.

To manage all of this, click Edit at the bottom of the pane; proceed as described in Figure 18-4.

Tip: If you're feeling widget-deprived, click App Store. It opens a special section of the Mac App Store dedicated to apps that install widgets on your Today pane.

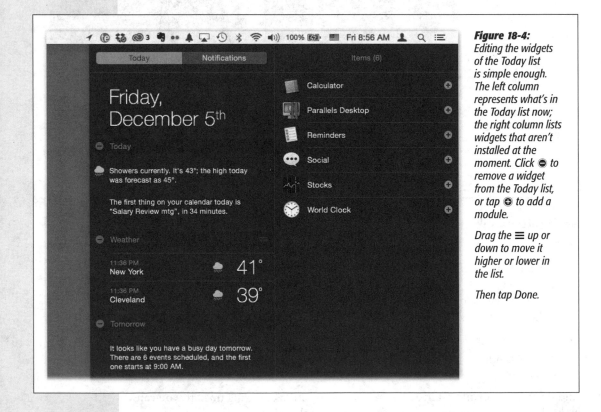

Figure 18-4:
Editing the widgets of the Today list is simple enough. The left column represents what's in the Today list now; the right column lists widgets that aren't installed at the moment. Click ⊖ to remove a widget from the Today list, or tap ⊕ to add a module.

Drag the ☰ up or down to move it higher or lower in the list.

Then tap Done.

Messaging, Tweeting, or Facebooking

If you've told OS X the details of your iCloud, Twitter, Facebook, or LinkedIn accounts, then a strange little surprise awaits you at the top of the Notification Center's Today list: buttons that let you send a Messages or LinkedIn message, post a tweet, or post a Facebook item—right from there, without having to open an app or go to a Web page.

Note: You can hide these buttons, if you like. You can uninstall this row just as you'd remove any Today widget, as shown in Figure 18-4.

When you click one of these buttons, you get the little pop-up card illustrated in Figure 18-5.

Figure 18-5:
To send a tweet or a message (Facebook, LinkedIn, Messages), click the corresponding icon in the Today pane. Type your message; click Post or Send. (If you haven't yet told OS X your name and password for that account, you have the chance to do that now.)

If you're sending a Facebook message, you can use the pop-up menus to specify which audience sees this note (Friends, everyone, and so on), and whether or not you'd like your current geographical location to be included.

And what do these buttons have to do with notifications? Absolutely nothing. They're here in the Notification Center because Apple wanted them to be available anytime, anywhere, no matter what program you're using—and the Notification Center is a perfect always-available dashboard.

Customizing the Notification Center

You can (and should) specify *which* apps are allowed to junk up your Notification
Center. Open System Preferences→Notifications to see the list of apps that might
want to get your attention in the master Notifications list (Figure 18-6).

Tip: A faster way to get to the proper System Preferences pane is built right into the Notification Center itself.
Click the tiny ❂ icon at the very bottom of the pane.

Figure 18-6:
Here in System Prefer-
ences, you can specify
which apps are per-
mitted to intrude on
the precious billboard
that is your Notifica-
tion Center—and how
they're permitted to
intrude.

Some individual
apps, including Mail
and Calendar, offer
additional controls
in their Preferences
boxes. For example,
in Calendar, you can
turn off notifications
from shared calendars
and from meeting
invitations.

This is also the place where you can specify the *order* of the various apps' notifications
in the center. Use the Sort Notification Center pop-up menu at the bottom of the
window. If you choose By Time, then the apps with the newest alerts appear at the
top. But if you tap Manually, you can simply drag the app names up or down in the
list to specify their top-to-bottom order on the Notification Center list.

Out of the box, the following OS X programs are listed in the Notification Center:

- **Calendar** lets you know about imminent appointments.

- **FaceTime** tells you when you've missed an incoming call.

- **Game Center** flags you when somebody has invited you to a game or wants to
become your friend.

- **Mail** lets you know when you've received a new message. You can also specify
whether or not the notification displays the beginning of the message itself when

you're not seated at your Mac, which you may consider to be either useful or a scary privacy violation. (Mercifully, Mail's Preferences→General tab lets you limit these alerts, so you won't be buried in a barrage of meaningless heads-up bubbles. You can tell Mail to alert you only when somebody in your Contacts list has written to you, only when a message lands in a smart mailbox folder, only when you get email from someone you've designated as a VIP—or whenever any message lands in any mailbox.)

- **Messages** lets you know when somebody has sent you an instant message.

- **Reminders**—well, you can guess.

- **Safari.** Certain Web sites, if they're open in Safari, can send you notifications (known as HTML Web notifications).

- **Twitter** pops up whenever somebody has mentioned you on Twitter or tried to reach you with a direct message.

- **Facebook** governs the appearance of updates from your Facebook friends.

- **iCloud Photos** lets you know when somebody has subscribed to a stream of pictures you've shared (or has commented on one, or added one).

Other companies' apps may appear in this list, too: BusyCal, Evernote, Skype, and so on.

Now it's time to change the settings for one app at a time. Click an app's name to see its individual Notifications settings (Figure 18-6—the Calendar app, in this example).

For example, as hinted above, different apps can get your attention in different ways:

- **None.** If certain apps seem to bug you with news you really don't care about, you can make them shut up forever. They won't bother you with pop-up messages, although they can still insert items into the Notification Center pane.

- **Banners.** This option (Figure 18-6) makes incoming notifications slide quietly and briefly onto the top right of your screen. Each message holds still long enough for you to read it, but it goes away automatically after a few seconds. Banners are a good option for things like Facebook and Twitter updates and incoming email messages.

- **Alerts.** These notifications don't go away until you click a button to dismiss them. Good for important messages, like alarms and flight updates.

At the bottom of the Notifications window, you get more settings for each app:

- **Show notifications on lock screen.** Do you want summaries of all your missed notifications to appear on your Login screen ("5 email notifications") when you wake up the Mac after having been away? It's a great feature, as long as you don't mind passing busybodies knowing how popular you are.

- **Show in Notification Center: __ Recent Items.** This pop-up menu specifies how *many* rows of information you want to reserve for this app in the Notification Center: one from your Scrabble app, for example, but all 20 of your recent Reminders.

Tip: If you turn off this checkbox, the app disappears from the Notification Center completely. You can still get its alert messages, but you won't see them listed in the Notification Center pane. Another way to achieve the same effect: Drag the app's name down to the bottom of the list, below the "Not in Notification Center" heading.

- **Badge app icon.** If you turn this option on, then each app's actual icon (in your Launchpad and on your Dock) sprouts a red, circled number. This number lets you know how many times it's tried to flag you about something.

- **Play sound when receiving notifications.** Some apps play a sound when a new notification arrives. For example, Calendar dings to remind you of an upcoming event. It's a little extra insurance that you won't miss a nudge; here's where you can turn these sounds off.

Tip: If this Notification Center thing gets you fired up, then you should probably know about Growl, too. It's a free program that creates an effect very similar to Notification Center—but with far more customization. You can make the alerts appear in a different corner of your screen, for example, or change how they look. Growl is available on this book's "Missing CD" page at *www.missingmanuals.com*.

The Free Programs

Right out of the box, OS X comes with a healthy assortment of about 50 freebies: programs for sending email, writing documents, doing math, even playing games. Some have been around for years. Others, like Maps and iBooks, are newer. They're designed not only to show off some of OS X's most dramatic technologies, but also to let you get real work done without having to invest in additional software.

Your Free OS X Programs

A broad assortment of programs sits in the Applications folder in the main hard drive window, and another couple dozen less frequently used apps await in the Applications→Utilities folder.

This chapter guides you through every item in your new software library, one program at a time. (Of course, your Applications list may vary. Apple might have blessed your particular Mac model with some bonus programs, or you may have downloaded or installed some on your own.)

Tip: A reminder: You can jump straight to the Applications folder in the Finder by pressing Shift-⌘-A (the shortcut for Go→Applications), or by clicking the Applications folder icon in the Sidebar. You might consider adding the Application folder's icon to the Dock, too, so you can access it no matter what program you're in. Shift-⌘-U (or Go→Utilities) takes you, of course, to the Utilities folder.

App Store

See the beginning of Chapter 4 for full details on the Mac App Store.

Automator, AppleScript

The software-robot program and language are described in a free downloadable PDF appendix to this chapter, "Automator & AppleScript.pdf." You can download it from this book's "Missing CD" page at *missingmanuals.com*.

Calculator

The Calculator is much more than a simple four-function memory calculator. It can also act as a scientific calculator for students and scientists, a conversion calculator for metric and U.S. measures, and even a currency calculator for world travelers.

The little Calculator widget in the Today pane of the Notification Center is quicker to open, but the standalone Calculator program is far more powerful. For example:

- Calculator has three modes: Basic, Advanced, and Programmer (Figure 19-1). Switch among them by choosing from the View menu (or pressing ⌘-1 for Basic, ⌘-2 for Advanced, or ⌘-3 for Programmer).

Figure 19-1:
The Calculator program offers a four-function Basic mode, a full-blown scientific calculator mode, and a programmer's calculator (shown here, and capable of hex, octal, decimal, and binary notation). The first two modes offer a "paper tape" feature (Windows→Paper Tape) that lets you correct errors made way back in a calculation. To edit one of the numbers on the paper tape, drag through it, retype, and then click Recalculate Totals. You can also save the tape as a text file by choosing File→Save Tape As, or print it by selecting File→Print Tape.

- You can operate Calculator by clicking the onscreen buttons, but it's much easier to press the corresponding number and symbol keys on your keyboard.

- Press the C key to clear the calculator display.

- As you go, you can make Calculator speak each key you press. The Mac's voice ensures that you don't mistype as you keep your eyes on the receipts in front of you, typing by touch.

Just choose Speech→Speak Button Pressed to turn this feature on or off. (You choose *which* voice does the talking in the Speech pane of System Preferences.)

- Once you've calculated a result, you can copy it (using Edit→Copy, or ⌘-C) and paste it directly into another program.

- Calculator even offers Reverse Polish Notation (RPN), a system of entering numbers that's popular with some mathematicians, programmers, and engineers, because it lets them omit parentheses. Choose View ›RPN to turn it on and off.

Tip: How cool is this? In most programs, you don't need Calculator or even a Today widget. Remember that the Spotlight menu is a calculator, too. Type or paste an equation into the Spotlight search box; instantly, the answer appears in the results menu.

Conversions

Calculator is more than a calculator; it's also a conversion program. No matter what units you're trying to convert—meters, grams, cubic inches, miles per hour, euros—Calculator is ready.

Now, the truth is, the Units Converter widget in Spotlight is simpler and quicker to open than this older Calculator feature. But if you've already got Calculator open, here's the drill:

1. **Clear the calculator (type C on your keyboard). Type in the starting measurement.**

 To convert 48 degrees Celsius to Fahrenheit, for example, type *48*.

2. **From the Convert menu, choose the kind of conversion you want.**

 In this case, choose Temperature. When you're done choosing, a dialog box appears.

3. **Use the pop-up menus to specify which units you want to convert to and from.**

 To convert Celsius to Fahrenheit, choose Celsius from the first pop-up menu, and Fahrenheit from the second.

4. **Click OK.**

 That's it. The Calculator displays the result—in degrees Fahrenheit, in this example.

The next time you want to make this kind of calculation, you can skip steps 2, 3, and 4. Instead, just choose your desired conversion from the Convert→Recent Conversions submenu.

Calculator is especially amazing when it comes to *currency* conversions—from pesos to American dollars, for example—because it actually does its homework. It goes online to download up-to-the-minute currency rates to ensure that the conversion is accurate. (Choose Convert→Update Currency Exchange Rates.)

Tip: If you're working with big numbers, don't forget to turn on View→Show Thousands Separators. Calculator will add commas (like 1,242,939) to help you read your big numbers more easily.

Calendar

The calendar program that was called iCal for many years is now called Calendar, so that it matches the iPhone and iPad.

Calendar is not so different from those "Hunks of the Midwest Police Stations" paper calendars that people leave hanging on the walls for months past their natural life span.

Tip: Calendar's Dock icon displays today's date—even when Calendar isn't running.

But Calendar offers several advantages over paper calendars:

- It can automate the process of entering repeating events, such as weekly staff meetings or gym workouts.

- Calendar can give you a gentle nudge (with a sound, a dialog box, or even an email) when an important appointment is approaching.

- Calendar can share information with Contacts, with Mail, with your iPod/iPad/iPhone, with other Macs, or with "published" calendars on the Internet. Some of these features require one of those iCloud accounts described in Chapter 10. But Calendar also works fine on a single Mac, even without an Internet connection.

- Calendar can subscribe to other people's calendars. For example, you can subscribe to your spouse's calendar, thereby finding out when you've been committed to after-dinner drinks on the night of the big game on TV. You can also tell Calendar to display your online calendars from Google and Yahoo, or even your company's Exchange calendar.

Working with Views

When you open Calendar, you see something like Figure 19-2. By clicking one of the View buttons above the calendar, or by pressing ⌘-1, ⌘-2, ⌘-3, or ⌘-4, you can switch among these views:

- **Day** looks exactly like a day-at-a-time desk calendar. On the left side, you see today's schedule on an hour-by-hour chart. On the right, you see the details of whichever appointment is selected.)

 If you choose Calendar→Preferences, you can specify what hours constitute a workday. This is ideal both for those annoying power-life people who get up at 5 a.m. for two hours of calisthenics and for the more reasonable people who sleep until 11 a.m.

Tip: Calendar provides three quick ways to get to the current day's date. Click Today (upper-left corner, between the ◀ and ▶), choose View→Go to Today, or press ⌘-T.

- **Week** fills the main display area with seven columns, reflecting the current week. (You can establish a five-day workweek instead in Calendar→Preferences.)

Tip: If you double-click the date above the calendar, you open the Day view for that day.

- **Month** shows the entire current month. The time of each appointment is listed in gray off to the right of each square. Double-click a date number to open the Day view for that date.

Figure 19-2:
In Calendar, the ‹ and › buttons at top right take you to the previous or next day, week, month, or year (depending on your current view). In the Day view, shown here, you can click the tiny numbers on the mini-calendars to change days.

If a Month-view square is too small to show everything you've got scheduled that day, you'll see a notation at the bottom of the square like, "3 more…" Sometimes, making the window bigger (or full screen) helps make more room, or you can just double-click the date's number to switch to Day view and see everything at once.

Tip: Month view scrolls endlessly vertically—and not necessarily a month at a time, either. You can park any week of the month at the top of the screen—not just the first week. That's a refreshing change from paper calendars.

- **Year** view displays the date numbers for the entire year (Figure 19-3).

In Week or Month view, *double-click* an appointment to see more about it, or even make changes to it.

Tip: In Week or Day view, Calendar sprouts a handy horizontal line that shows where you are in time right now. (Look in the hours-of-the-day "ruler" down the left side of the window to see this line's little red bulb.) A nice touch, and a handy visual aid that can tell you at a glance when you're already late for something.

Also in any view, you can switch into Full Screen view by clicking the green ⊙ button (top left). See page 160 for more on Full Screen mode.

Figure 19-3:
Year view shows the entire year. In Calendar→Preferences→Advanced, you can turn on "Show events in year view," which actually means "Show me a 'heat map' to indicate how hectic my schedule is."

You can single-click a date number to see a pop-out list of the appointments scheduled for that date.

Making an Appointment

The basic Calendar is easy to figure out. After all, with the exception of one unfortunate Gregorian incident, we've been using calendars successfully for centuries.

Even so, there are two ways to record a new appointment: using the mouse, or using the Quick Event box.

The mousy way

You can quickly record an appointment using any of several techniques, listed here in order of decreasing efficiency:

- **In Month view,** double-click a blank spot on the date you want. Type the name of the event and a time slot—for example, *Sales meeting 9am-4:30*. (See "The Quick Event way," below, for details on how Calendar interprets these time notations.)

- **In Day or Week view,** double-click the starting time to create a one-hour appointment. Or drag vertically through the time slots that represent the appointment's duration. Either way, type the event's name inside the newly created colored box.

- **In Day, Week, or Month view,** right-click (or two-finger click) a date and choose New Event from the shortcut menu. Type the event's name.

Unless you use the drag-over-hours method, a new event believes itself to be one hour long. But in Day or Week view, you can adjust its duration by dragging the bottom edge vertically. Drag the dark top bar up or down to adjust the start time.

In many cases, that's all there is to it. You've just specified the day, time, and title of the appointment. Now you can get on with your life.

Tip: If the Edit balloon is blocking a part of the calendar you need to see, no biggie: Just drag the balloon out of the way, using any blank spot as a handle. It "tears off" and becomes independent.

The Quick Event way

In the *Quick Event* method, the program spares you the trouble of manually selecting dates, start times, and end times. Instead, the program understands notations like "7 pm Friday," and puts your new appointment into the right time slot automatically.

To use this feature, press ⌘-N. Or click + (top left of the window) or choose File→New Event. The Quick Event box appears. Proceed as shown in Figure 19-4.

Note: Calendar proposes adding the new appointment to your *default calendar*—that is, the category you use most often (read on for details on these calendar categories). Supposedly, you've already told it which category is your preferred one by using the Calendar→Preferences→General→Default Calendar pop-up menu.

But as you add a new appointment this way, you can override that setting by *holding down* the + button. You get a pop-up menu of your calendar categories; only after you click one do you see the Quick Event box shown in Figure 19-4.

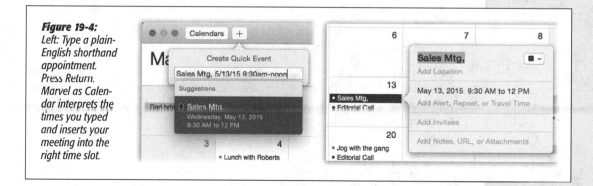

Figure 19-4:
Left: Type a plain-English shorthand appointment. Press Return. Marvel as Calendar interprets the times you typed and inserts your meeting into the right time slot.

Into the Quick Event box, type the name of your appointment and its date and time. For example, you could type *Report deadline Aug 12,* or *"Titanic 2: The Return" Sat 7 pm,* or *Cara date 11-11:15am.*

When you press Return, Calendar interprets what you typed, using these rules:

- If you didn't specify an ending time, Calendar sets the appointment to 1 hour long.

- If you didn't enter *any* time information, Calendar figures you meant an all-day event like a birthday, holiday, or deadline.

- If you typed *breakfast* or *morning*, Calendar sets the appointment to start at 9 a.m.; *lunch* or *noon*, it starts at 12 p.m.; *dinner* or *night*, it starts at 8 p.m.

- If you enter a weekday (for example, *Chicago Monday*), Calendar assumes you mean the very next occurrence of that day. (If that's not what you want, enter the date, like *Chicago Jul 3.*)

- If you enter a time but not a date or day (for example, *Fishing 3:30 pm*), Calendar assumes you mean today.

As you type, Calendar displays a menu of similar appointments you've entered in the past (Figure 19-4, left). If you click one, Calendar fills in all the details of the new appointment in one fell swoop, copying them from the earlier event.

As soon as Calendar interprets your shorthand and turns it into a real appointment, its details balloon opens automatically (Figure 19-4, right), so that you can clean up any errors and add more details.

Location, alarms, travel time, and other details

No matter which method you use to create the basic event (the mouse way or the Quick Event way), you're now presented with the information balloon shown at right in Figure 19-4. Here's where you go to town filling in the details. (This same balloon will appear when you double-click any existing appointment later.)

Tip: You can also open the Info balloon by clicking an appointment and then pressing ⌘-E (which is short for Edit→Edit Event).

For each appointment, you can Tab your way to the following information areas:

- **subject.** That's the large, bold type at the top—the name of your appointment. For example, you might type *Fly to Phoenix.*

- **calendar.** A *calendar,* in Calendar's terminology, is a subset—a category—into which you can place appointments. You can create one for you, one for family-only events, one for book-club appointments, and so on. You can hide and show these categories at will. Details begin on page 635; for now, note that the tiny colored square in the top-right corner of the Info bubble is a pop-up menu of your calendars.

Tip: Use this same pop-up menu to *change* an appointment's category. If you filed something in "Company Memos" that should have been in "Sweet Nothings for Honey-Poo," then open the event's information balloon and reassign it. Quick.

- **location.** This field makes a lot of sense; if you think about it, almost everyone needs to record *where* a meeting is to take place. You might type a reminder for yourself like *My place,* a specific address like *212 East 23,* or some other helpful information, like a contact phone number or flight number.

As you type, Calendar busily consults Apple's worldwide database of street addresses—and proposes a few matches, as shown in Figure 19-5 (top left). You're under no obligation to choose one of these; you can ignore the suggestions and type "Casey's treehouse," for all Apple cares. But if you *do* choose from Apple's list of proposals, some cool things happen.

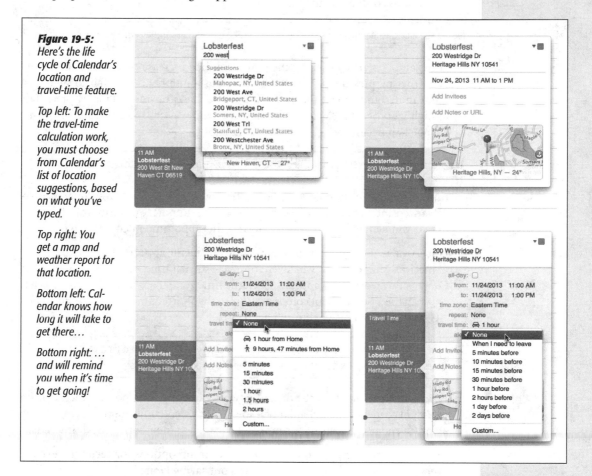

Figure 19-5:
Here's the life cycle of Calendar's location and travel-time feature.

Top left: To make the travel-time calculation work, you must choose from Calendar's list of location suggestions, based on what you've typed.

Top right: You get a map and weather report for that location.

Bottom left: Calendar knows how long it will take to get there…

Bottom right: … and will remind you when it's time to get going!

For example, you get a little map (which you can click to open the Maps app for a bigger view), as shown in Figure 19-5 (top right). You get to see the current weather, so you know how much to bundle up. And you get to use the travel-time feature described below.

Note: The next few controls appear only when you expand the Info bubble to see the time and date information. To do that, click whatever time is listed now—or, if you've just tabbed your way to the times, press Return.

- **all-day.** An "all-day" event, of course, refers to something that has no specific time of day associated with it: a holiday, a birthday, a book deadline. When you turn on

this box, you see the name of the appointment jump to the top of the Calendar screen, in the area reserved for this kind of thing.

- **starts, ends.** You can adjust the times shown here by typing, clicking buttons, or both. Press Tab to jump from one setting to another, and from there to the hours and minutes of the starting time.

Note: The little calendar that pops up when you click the date is handier than typing a date manually.

For example, start by clicking the hour, and then increase or decrease this number either by pressing ▲ and ▼ or by typing a number. Press Tab to highlight the minutes and repeat the arrow-buttons-or-keys business. Finally, press Tab to highlight the AM/PM indicator, and type either *A* or *P*—or press ▲ or ▼—to change it, if necessary.

Tip: If you specify a different ending date, a *banner* appears across the top of the calendar.

- **time zone.** This option appears only after you choose Calendar→Preferences→ Advanced and then turn on "Turn on time zone support." And you would do *that* only if you plan to be traveling on the day this appointment comes to pass.

 Once you've done that, a time zone pop-up menu appears. It starts out with "America/New York" (or whatever your Mac's usual time zone is); if you choose Other, a tiny world map appears. Click the time zone that represents where you'll be when this appointment comes due. From the shortcut menu, choose the major city that's in the same zone you'll be in.

Tip: The time zone pop-up menu remembers each new city you select. The next time you travel to a city you've visited before, you won't have to do that clicking-the-world-map business.

Now, when you arrive in the distant city, use the time zone pop-up menu at the top-right corner of the Calendar window to tell Calendar where you are. You'll see all of Calendar's appointments jump, like magic, to their correct new time slots.

- **repeat.** The pop-up menu here contains common options for recurring events: every day, every week, and so on. It starts out saying None.

 Once you've made a selection, you get an *end* pop-up menu that lets you specify when this event should *stop* repeating. If you choose "Never," you're stuck seeing this event repeating on your calendar until the end of time (a good choice for recording, say, your anniversary, especially if your spouse might be consulting the same calendar). You can also turn on "After (a certain number of times)," which is a useful option for car and mortgage payments. And if you choose "On date," you can specify the date when the repetitions come to an end; use this option to indicate the last day of school, for example.

 "Custom" lets you specify repeat schedules like "First Monday of the month" or "Every two weeks."

Tip: If you don't see the following items in the editing bubble, click the gray lettering that says "Add Alert, Repeat, or Travel Time" to make them appear.

- **travel time.** This item represents a breakthrough in common sense: It automatically builds travel time into Calendar's understanding of any appointment. After all, it's not very useful to get a reminder like "Lunch with Jenkins at 1 p.m." 10 minutes beforehand if it takes half an hour to get there.

 Now, then: If Calendar is to calculate travel time, it has to know where you're starting out and where you're going.

 To figure out your starting point, the Mac consults your "me" card in the Contacts app (page 411), and uses either your home address or your work address, depending on the time of day. (How does Calendar know when you're at work? It cleverly uses the "Day starts at" and "Day ends at" settings in Calendar→Preferences→General.)

 If you haven't specified home and work addresses on your "me" card, then Calendar uses the current location of your Mac as the starting point. (And *that* works only if you've allowed the Mac to track your location.)

 For the arrival location, the Travel Time feature requires that you've accepted one of the Mac's address suggestions, as described above (Figure 19-5, top left).

 Once all that's done, the "travel time" pop-up menu shows you both the driving and walking times to your appointment. You can override these suggestions if you like; you can choose any time interval from 5 minutes to 2 hours, or choose Custom to plug in something not listed here.

 The real payoff, of course, comes when you set a reminder for yourself; read on.

- **alert.** This pop-up menu tells Calendar to notify you when a certain appointment is about to begin. Choose how much notice you want: "At time of event," "5 minutes before," all the way up to "2 days before." If it's a TV show, a reminder 5 minutes before airtime is fine. If it's a birthday, you might set up a two-day warning, so there's time to buy a present.

 Actually, you can get a lot more particular than that. If you choose Custom, you can specify any advance-warning interval at all: "16 minutes before," or "15 days after," or whatever. (Yes, you can even set up an alarm to ring after the event—great if you want to follow up with something or check the oven.)

 Here, in Custom land, you can also set any of four *kinds* of flags to get your attention. It can display a message (with a sound, if you like), send you an email, or open a file on your hard drive. (You could use this unusual option to ensure that you don't forget a work deadline by having Calendar fling the relevant document open in front of your face at the eleventh hour.)

And if you've used the travel-time feature described above, Calendar even offers a choice called "When I need to leave" (Figure 19-5, lower right), which factors travel time into the reminder. (Alas, the Mac does *not* factor in traffic conditions.)

Tip: You can set up more than one alarm for the same appointment, each with its own advance-warning interval. Just click the + button to add a new one.

- **show as (busy/free/tentative/out of office).** This little item shows up only if you've subscribed to a calendar server, like an Internet-based calendar (in geek-speak, a CalDAV server) or your company's Exchange calendar. It communicates to your colleagues when you might be available for meetings.

Note: If your calendar comes from a CalDAV server, then your only options are "busy" and "free." The factory setting for most appointments is "busy," but for all-day events it's "free." Which is logical; just because it's International Gecko Appreciation Day doesn't mean you're not available for meetings (rats!).

You might think: "Well, *duh*—if I've got something on the calendar, then I'm obviously busy!" But not necessarily. Some Calendar entries might just be placeholders, reminders to self, TV shows you wanted to watch, appointments you'd be willing to change—not things that would necessarily render you unavailable if a better invitation should come along.

- **invitees.** If the appointment is a meeting or some other gathering, you can type the participants' names here. If a name is already in your Contacts program, Calendar proposes autocompleting the name for you.

If you separate several names with commas, Calendar automatically turns each into a shaded oval button. You can click it for a pop-up menu of commands like Remove Attendee and Send Email. (That last option appears only if the person in

UP TO SPEED

Inviting Guests

When you click Send at the bottom of the info balloon, your guests receive your invitation. If they use Calendar, the invitation appears in their Notifications panes. (To open the Notifications pane, click the tiny Inbox icon in the top-left corner of the window.) They can click Accept, Decline, or Maybe.

In your Notifications window, you then see the status of each invitee's name: a green checkmark for Accepted, red X for Declined, orange question mark for Maybe, and gray question mark for Not Yet Responded. (Your guests, meanwhile, will be delighted to find that the appointment automatically appears on their calendars once they commit.)

Now, suppose you send an invitation to your sister, who doesn't have a Mac. She just gets an email message that says, "Chris Smith has invited you to the event: Company Hoedown, scheduled for February 02, 2015 at 3:00 PM. To accept or decline this invitation, click the link below." Unfortunately, there generally *is* no link. She just has to know to open the .ics attachment.

If she uses a calendar program that understands this attachment, the appointment appears on her calendar, and her RSVP shows up in your Calendar Notification pane.

Contacts has an email address, or if you typed a name *with* an email address in brackets, like this: *Chris Smith <chris@yahoo.com>.*)

Tip: If you and your invitees are on the same CalDAV or Exchange calendar service—usually, coworkers at the same company—Calendar can show a "time map" of the invitees' days, all in a handy scrolling window, so you can find a time when everybody's free. To see this map, click the Available Meeting Times link beneath the addresses of the invitees you've specified, or choose Window→Availability Panel (see Figure 19-6).

Figure 19-6:
Drag the vertical block (your proposed meeting) to a different time slot, or click Next Available Time to find when everybody's free. Good luck.

Once you've specified some attendees, a Send button appears in the Info box. If you click it, Calendar fires up Mail and prepares ready-to-send messages, each with an *iCal .ics* attachment: a calendar-program invitation file. See the box on the facing page.

- **url.** A *URL* is a Uniform Resource Locator—a Web address, like *www.apple.com.* If there's a URL relevant to this appointment, by all means type it here. Type more than one, if it'll help you; just be sure to separate them all with commas.

- **note.** You can type, paste, or drag any text you like in the note area—driving directions, contact phone numbers, a call history, or whatever.

Your newly scheduled event now shows up on the calendar, complete with the color coding that corresponds to the calendar category you've assigned.

What to Do with an Appointment

Once you've entrusted your agenda to Calendar, you can start putting it to work. Calendar is only too pleased to remind you (via pop-up messages) of your events, reschedule them, print them out, and so on. Here are a few of the possibilities.

Editing events

To edit a calendar event's details, click to open its Info balloon (Figure 19-4).

And if you want to change only an appointment's "calendar" category, right-click (or two-finger click) anywhere on the appointment and choose from the resulting Calendar shortcut menu. That way, you bypass the need to open the Info balloon.

Rescheduling events

If an event in your life gets rescheduled, you can drag an appointment block vertically in a Day- or Week-view column to make it later or earlier the same day, or horizontally

to another date in any view. (If you reschedule a recurring event, Calendar asks if you want to change only *this* occurrence, or this *and* all future ones.)

If something is postponed for, say, a month or two, you're in trouble, since you can't drag an appointment beyond its month window. You have no choice but to open the Info balloon and edit the starting and ending dates or times—or just cut and paste the event to a different date.

Lengthening or shortening events

If a scheduled meeting becomes shorter or your lunch hour becomes a lunch hour-and-a-half (in your dreams), changing the length of the representative calendar event is as easy as dragging the bottom border of its block in any column view (see Figure 19-7).

Tip: In Week view, if you've grabbed the *bottom* edge of an appointment's block so that the cursor changes, you can drag *horizontally* to make an appointment cross the midnight line and extend into a second day.

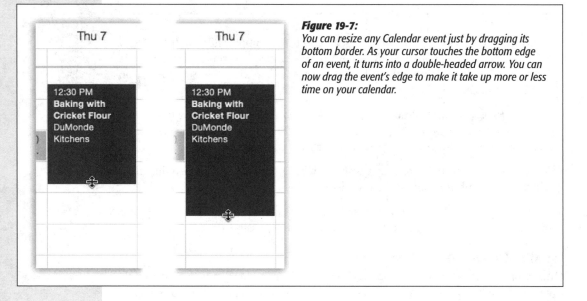

Figure 19-7:
You can resize any Calendar event just by dragging its bottom border. As your cursor touches the bottom edge of an event, it turns into a double-headed arrow. You can now drag the event's edge to make it take up more or less time on your calendar.

Printing events

To commit your calendar to paper, choose File→Print, or press ⌘-P. The resulting Print dialog box lets you include only a certain range of dates, only events on certain calendars, with or without To Do lists or mini-month calendars, and so on.

Searching for events

When you type into the search box at the top right of the Calendar screen, you're offered some "search tokens" that indicate where you want to search for that phrase (in the name of an event, in its notes, location, and so on). The right-hand column offers a clickable list of search results. Figure 19-8 has the details.

Deleting events

To delete an appointment, click it and then press the Delete key. If you delete a recurring event (like a weekly meeting), Calendar asks whether you want to delete only that particular instance of the event, or the whole series from that point forward.

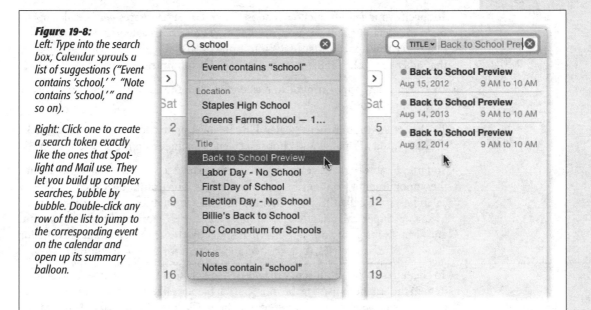

Figure 19-8:
Left: Type into the search box, Calendar sprouts a list of suggestions ("Event contains 'school,'" "Note contains 'school,'" and so on).

Right: Click one to create a search token exactly like the ones that Spotlight and Mail use. They let you build up complex searches, bubble by bubble. Double-click any row of the list to jump to the corresponding event on the calendar and open up its summary balloon.

The "Calendar" Category Concept

Calendar has *calendars* that let you organize appointments into subsets. They can be anything you like. One person might have calendars called Home, Work, and TV Reminders. Another might have Me, Spouse 'n' Me, and Whole Family. A small business could have categories called Deductible Travel, R&D, and R&R.

And now, the Calendars Tip-O-Rama:

- **To create a calendar**, choose File→New Calendar. You now have to specify *where* you want this category to live: On My Mac (meaning on your Mac), or on one of your online accounts, like iCloud, Google, Yahoo, or Exchange. Type a name that defines the category in your mind.

Note: When you set up an iCloud account either in System Preferences or when you first run Yosemite, Calendar automatically transfers your "On My Mac" categories to iCloud. You can no longer create categories that live only on your Mac. (There's one exception: If you created your iCloud account in Calendar Preferences, then you *can* have an "On My Mac" category.)

- **To see your list of categories**, click the Calendars button (upper left of the window). A sidebar list appears, if it wasn't already open.

- **Hide or show an entire category of appointments at once** by turning on or off the appropriate checkbox in the Calendars sidebar.

- **To change the color of a category,** right-click (or two-finger click) its name in the sidebar list. In the pop-up bubble, you choose a new color.

- **To specify your** *default* **calendar,** choose Calendar→Preferences→General. Choose from the Default Calendar pop-up menu. (The Default calendar is the category that every new appointment falls into unless you change it. It's also the category that *other* apps, like Mail, propose putting new appointments into.)

- **To assign a new appointment to a calendar,** click the color swatch in the corner of its Info balloon.

- **To change an appointment's calendar category,** right-click (or two-finger click) the appointment's name and choose a calendar name from the shortcut menu.

- **You may be able to make calendar** *groups,* **too.** That's a container that consolidates the appointments from several *other* calendars. For example, you could have a calendar group called Kids, containing the individual calendars for each of your offspring. Super-calendars like this make it easier to manage, hide, show, print, and search subsets of your appointments. (Sadly, this feature is available only for "On My Mac" categories, as described above—not for online accounts.)

 To create a calendar group, choose File→New Calendar Group. Name the resulting item in the Calendar list; for the most part, it behaves like any other calendar. Drag other calendar names onto it to include them. Click the flippy triangle to hide or show the component calendars.

"Publishing" Calendars to the Web

One of Calendar's best features is its ability to post your calendar on the Web, so that other people can subscribe to it, which adds *your* appointments to *their* calendars. Anyone with a Web browser—or only people you designate—can also *view* your calendar, right online.

For example, you might use this feature to post the meeting schedule for a club that you manage, or to share the agenda for a series of upcoming financial meetings that all your coworkers will need to consult.

Publishing

The steps for sharing a calendar depend on whether or not you have an iCloud account. Observe:

If you have iCloud account: Proceed as shown in Figure 19-9. Note that you can specify whether each person can just *see* the appointments, or be able to edit them, too. That's a delightful, two-way collaboration—a terrific way for a couple or a family to coordinate everyone's calendars, for example.

Behind the scenes, Calendar sends an invitation to the recipient. If she has a Mac, iPhone, or iPad, she'll see a notification right in Calendar (■); otherwise, she'll get

the invitation by email. Once she clicks the invitation and clicks Accept, your shared calendar shows up on her machine.

Later, you can modify the settings (Figure 19-9, bottom). Or you can stop sharing with someone by clicking the next to a calendar name; clicking a person's name; and then pressing the Delete key.

Tip: You can also share an iCloud calendar at *icloud.com*. Just click the ⋙ icon beside a calendar's name.

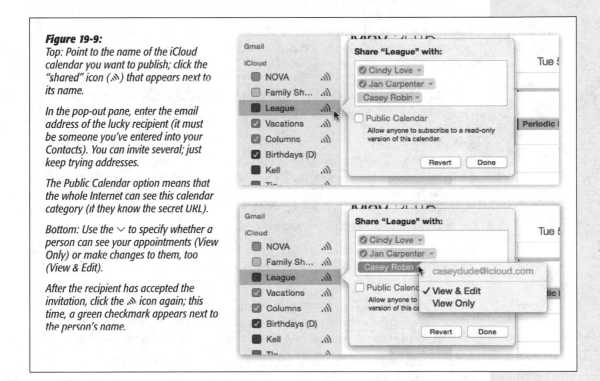

Figure 19-9:
Top: Point to the name of the iCloud calendar you want to publish; click the "shared" icon (⋙) that appears next to its name.

In the pop-out pane, enter the email address of the lucky recipient (it must be someone you've entered into your Contacts). You can invite several; just keep trying addresses.

The Public Calendar option means that the whole Internet can see this calendar category (if they know the secret URL).

Bottom: Use the ⌄ to specify whether a person can see your appointments (View Only) or make changes to them, too (View & Edit).

After the recipient has accepted the invitation, click the ⋙ icon again; this time, a green checkmark appears next to the person's name.

If you don't have iCloud: If you don't have an iCloud account, then you'll need a Web site of your own, where your online calendar can be hung. And it has to be a WebDAV-compatible server (ask your Web-hosting company). You know what? It might just be easier to sign up for a free iCloud account and do it that way.

In any case, begin by making sure that the Calendars list is open. Click the calendar you want to share. Choose Edit→Publish Calendar. (This command doesn't appear if you have an iCloud account, since the sharing mechanism is so much simpler with iCloud.)

Tip: You have to perform this step individually for each calendar category. If you want to publish more than one calendar simultaneously, then create a calendar *group*, and publish *that*.

A dialog box appears. This is where you specify your Web address, its password (if necessary), and how your saved calendar is going to look and work. If you turn on "Publish changes automatically," then whenever you edit the calendar, Calendar connects to the Internet and updates the copy there. (Otherwise, you can right-click the calendar's name and choose Refresh whenever you want to update the Web copy.)

When you click Publish, your Mac connects to the Web and then shows you the Web address (the URL) of the finished page, complete with a Send Mail button that lets you fire the URL off to your colleagues.

Tip: Whenever you want to send someone the subscription information, click the calendar category you've published and choose Edit→Send Publication Email. Calendar will prepare an outgoing email message containing details on subscribing to your calendar.

To stop publishing that calendar, click its name in the Calendars pop-up list and then choose Edit→Stop Publishing.

Subscribing

Often, Web sites publish calendars that you can bring into Calendar. Maybe you use Tripit.com to manage your flights and hotel reservations. Maybe you've found a calendar you like at *www.icalshare.com*—a schedule of rocket launches, trade shows, National Hockey League games, NASCAR races, soccer matches, the *Iron Chef* and *Survivor* TV shows, holidays, or whatever.

Each of these Web calendars has its own address. To subscribe, choose File→New Calendar Subscription. In the Subscribe to Calendar dialog box, paste the address of the published calendar.

You can also provide your own name for this category, specify how often you want your own copy to be updated (assuming you have a full-time Internet connection), and indicate whether or not you want to be bothered with the publisher's alarms and notes.

When it's all over, you see a new "calendar" category in your left-side list, representing the published appointments.

Google, Yahoo, and Facebook Calendars

If you maintain a calendar online—at Google, Yahoo, or Facebook, for example—you may take particular pleasure in discovering how easy it is to bring those appointments into Calendar. It's one handy way to keep, for example, a husband's and wife's appointments visible on each other's calendars.

Setting this up is ridiculously easy. Choose Calendar→Preferences→Accounts. Click + below the list. Enter your Google, Yahoo, or Facebook address (for example, *psmithers@gmail.com*) and password. Click Create.

In a minute or so, you'll see all your Google, Yahoo, or Facebook events show up in Calendar. (Each Web calendar has its own heading in the left-side list.) Better yet: It's a two-way sync; changes you make to these events in Calendar show up on the Web, too.

Syncing Calendar with Your iPhone, iPad, and Other Computers

Here's the real magic of Calendar, iCloud, and the rest of Apple's software archipelago: Your calendar can be autosynced among all your machines, like your iPhone, iPad, and Macs. Add an appointment on your phone, change an appointment on your iPad, whatever—all your other gadgets are wirelessly and automatically synced to match. See Chapter 10 for details on this amazing setup.

Note: Wondering where the To Do list feature went? It was in iCal—it's gone in Calendar. Well, that's because OS X has its own full-blown Reminders app now, described later in this chapter.

Chess

OS X comes with only one game, but it's a beauty (Figure 19-10). It's a traditional chess game played on a gorgeously rendered board with a set of realistic 3-D pieces.

Note: The program is actually a sophisticated Unix-based chess program, Sjeng, that Apple packaged up in a new wrapper.

Figure 19-10:
You don't have to be terribly exact about grabbing the chess pieces when it's time to make your move. Just click anywhere within a piece's current square to drag it into a new position on the board (shown here in its Marble incarnation). And why is this chessboard rotated like this? Because you can grab a corner of the board and rotate it in 3-D space. Cool!

Playing a Game of Chess

When you launch Chess, you're presented with a fresh, new game that's set up in Human vs. Computer mode—meaning that you, the Human (light-colored pieces) get to play against the Computer (your Mac, on the dark side). Drag the chess piece of your choice into position on the board, and the game is afoot.

If you choose Game→New Game, however, you're offered a pop-up menu with choices like Human vs. Computer, Human vs. Human, and so on. If you switch the pop-up menu to Computer vs. Human, then you and your Mac trade places; the Mac takes the white side of the board and opens the game with the first move, and you play the black side.

Tip: The same New Game dialog box also offers a pop-up menu called Variant, which offers three other chess-like games: Crazyhouse, Suicide, and Losers.

On some night when the video store is closed and you're desperate for entertainment, you might also want to try the Computer vs. Computer option, which pits your Mac against itself. Pour yourself a beer, open a bag of chips, and settle in to watch until someone—either the Mac or the Mac—gains victory.

Chess Prefs

Choose Chess→Preferences to find some useful controls like these:

- **Style.** Apple has gone nuts with the computer-generated materials options in this program. (Is it a coincidence that Steve Jobs was also the CEO of Pixar, the computer-animation company?)

 In any case, you can choose all kinds of wacky materials for the look of your game board (Wood, Metal, Marble, or *Grass*) and for your playing pieces (Wood, Metal, Marble, or *Fur*).

- **Computer Plays.** Use this slider to determine how frustrated you want to get when trying to win at Chess. The farther you drag the slider toward the Stronger side, the more calculations the computer runs before making its next move—and, thus, the harder it gets for you to outthink it. At the Faster setting, Chess won't think more than one move ahead. Drag the slider all the way to the right, however, and the program may analyze each move for as long as 4 or 5 minutes. This hardest setting, of course, makes it all but impossible to win a game.

 Choosing the Faster setting makes it only mildly impossible.

- **Speech.** The two checkboxes here let you play Chess using the Mac's built-in voice-recognition features, *telling* your chess pieces where to go instead of dragging them, and listening to the Mac tell you which moves it's making.

Tip: If your Chess-playing skills are less than optimal, the Moves menu will become your fast friend. The three commands there undo your last move (great for recovering from a blunder), suggest a move when you're stuck, and display a previous move (in case you failed to notice what the computer just did).

Studying Your Games

You can choose Game→Save to save any game in progress, so you can resume it later.

To analyze the moves making up a game, use the Moves→Game Log command, which displays the history of your game, move by move. A typical move would be recorded

as "Nb8 – c6," meaning the knight on the b8 square moved to the c6 square. Equipped with a Chess list document, you could recreate an entire game, move by move.

Tip: If you open this window before you begin a new game, you can see the game log fill in the moves *as they happen.*

Contacts

See the end of Chapter 11 for details.

Dashboard

Dashboard, is a true-blue, double-clickable application that's described in Chapter 4.

Dictionary

For word nerds everywhere, the Dictionary (and thesaurus) is a blessing—a handy way to look up word definitions, pronunciations, and synonyms (Figure 19-11). To be precise, OS X comes with electronic versions of multiple reference works in one:

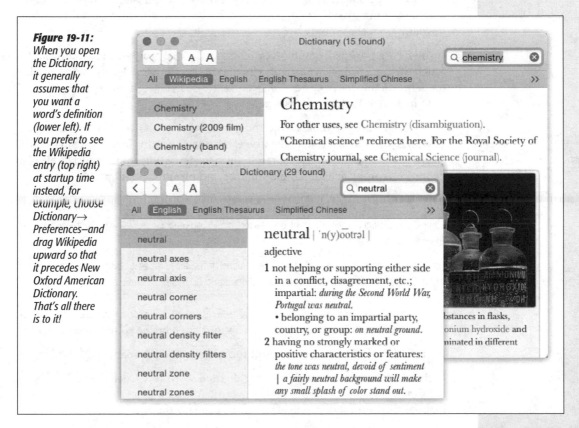

Figure 19-11:
When you open the Dictionary, it generally assumes that you want a word's definition (lower left). If you prefer to see the Wikipedia entry (top right) at startup time instead, for example, choose Dictionary→ Preferences—and drag Wikipedia upward so that it precedes New Oxford American Dictionary. That's all there is to it!

- **The entire New Oxford American Dictionary.** The *third* edition, actually. You'll note that its entries give you more examples and background.

- **The complete Oxford American Writer's Thesaurus.**

- **Two venerable guides to British English:** the Oxford Dictionary of English and Oxford Thesaurus of English.

- **A dictionary of Apple terms,** from "A/UX" to "Xsan." (Apparently there aren't any Apple terms that begin with Y or Z.)

- **Wikipedia.** This famous citizen-created encyclopedia isn't actually on your Mac. Dictionary just gives you an easy way to search the *online* version, and display the results right in the comfy Dictionary window.

- **Foreign language dictionaries:** Japanese, French, Spanish, German, Dutch, Korean, Italian, and Chinese.

Tip: You don't ordinarily see these reference books. You have to turn them on in Dictionary→Preferences.

OS X also comes with about a million ways to look up a word:

- **Search it in Spotlight.** Press ⌘-space, type the word you want into the Spotlight search box, and marvel as the dictionary entry appears in the results list. To read the definition, click it once.

- **If you have a trackpad, point to a word in a basic Mac program, and then double-touch the trackpad (don't actually click) with three fingers.** That's the gesture for the same dictionary pane described above. (It doesn't work unless you've turned it on in System Preferences→Trackpad.)

- **Double-click the Dictionary icon.** You get the window shown at bottom in Figure 19-11. As you type into the Spotlight-y search box, you home in on matching words; click a word, or highlight it and press Return, to view a full, typographically elegant definition, complete with sample sentence and pronunciation guide.

Tip: And if you don't recognize a word in the definition, click *that word* to look up *its* definition. (Each word turns blue and underlined when you point to it, as a reminder.) You can then click again in *that* definition—and on, and on, and on.

(You can then use the ⊖ and ⊕ buttons on the toolbar, or the ⌘-[and ⌘-] keystrokes to go back and forward in your chain of lookups. Hold down the ⊖ for a pop-up menu of recent lookups.)

It's worth exploring the Dictionary→Preferences dialog box, by the way. There you can choose U.S. or British pronunciations and choose your reference books.

- **Press ⊙.** Yes, the Dictionary is one of the widgets in Dashboard (page 170).

- **Right-click (or two-finger click) a highlighted word in a Cocoa program.** From the shortcut menu, choose Look Up [word]. You get a pane that pops out of the highlighted word, showing the Dictionary page for that word.

- **Use the *dict://* prefix in Safari.** This might sound a little odd, but it's actually ultra-convenient, because it puts the dictionary right where you're most likely to need it: on the Web.

 Turns out that you can look up a word (for example, *preposterous)* by typing *dict://preposterous* into the address bar. When you hit Return, Dictionary opens automatically and presents the search results from all of its resources (dictionary, thesaurus, Apple terms, and Wikipedia).

- **Point to a word in a basic Mac program, and then press Control-⌘-D.** That keystroke makes the definition pane sprout right from the word you were pointing to. (The advantage here, of course, is that you don't have to highlight the word first.) "Basic Mac program," in this case, means one of the Apple standards: Mail, Stickies, Safari, TextEdit, Messages, and so on.

The *front matter* of the Oxford American Dictionary (the reference section at the beginning) is here, too. It includes some delicious writers' tools, including guides to spelling, grammar, capitalization, punctuation, chemical elements, and clichés, along with the full text of the Declaration of Independence and the U.S. Constitution. Just choose Go→Front/Back Matter—and marvel that your Mac comes with a built-in college English course.

Tip: Got a big screen or poor eyesight? Then bump up the type size. Dictionary's toolbar has bigger/smaller buttons.

DVD Player

DVD Player, your Mac's built-in movie projector, is described in Chapter 9.

FaceTime

If you have a Mac laptop or iMac, then it's got a built-in microphone and camera. And that means it's equipped to make free, very high-quality audio and video calls to other Apple computers, phones, and tablets (Figure 19-12).

There's very little delay, and it works the first time and every time. Now Grandma can see the baby, or you can help someone shop from afar, or you can supervise brain surgery from thousands of miles away (some medical training recommended).

From your Mac, you'll probably make FaceTime calls over a WiFi network. But your callees, using iPhones or cellular iPads, can even conduct video chats over the cellular airwaves, when they're out and about.

Placing a Call

Ironically, the FaceTime experience often begins with a more old-fashioned communication—a phone call or a text message, for example. ("Want to FaceTime now?")

In any case, FaceTime couldn't be easier to fire up—in many different ways:

- **From Contacts.** If you're in the Contacts app, and you've recorded the iPhone number or Apple ID of someone in your Mac's Contacts program, you'll see the the ☐◁ button next to that person's name. Click it to place a video call. Or, to place an audio call, click ✆, and then click FaceTime Audio.

- **From the FaceTime app.** This app presents a list of your recent FaceTime calls (Figure 19-12, top left). Click the ☐◁ button next to a name on the Video tab to place a video call. For an audio call, click the Audio tab, and then click ✆, next to the person's name.

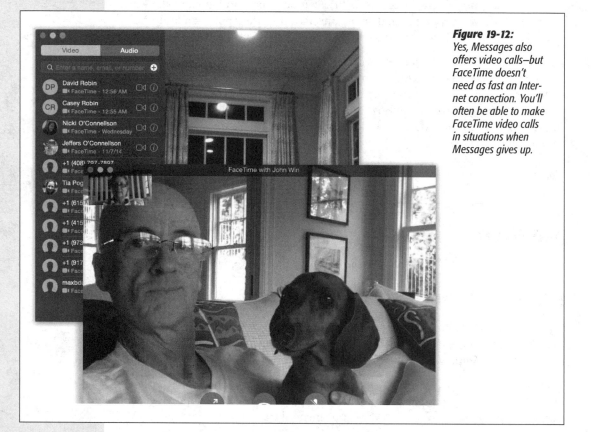

Figure 19-12:
Yes, Messages also offers video calls—but FaceTime doesn't need as fast an Internet connection. You'll often be able to make FaceTime video calls in situations when Messages gives up.

- **From Messages.** If you're chatting away with somebody by text and you realize that typing is no longer appropriate for the conversation, then click Details at the top of the screen. Then click ☐◁ (for a video call) or ✆ and then FaceTime (for a video call).

Tip: If you right-click (or two-finger click) FaceTime's Dock icon, you get a handy pop-up menu of Recent Calls. In other words, if you keep FaceTime in your Dock, you can place a new call to somebody on the spur of the moment, whatever you're doing, without having to open FaceTime first.

At this point, the other guy receives an audio and video message inviting him to a chat. If he taps Accept, then you're on. You're on each other's screens, seeing and hearing each other in real time. (You appear on your own screen, too, in a little inset window. It's spinach-in-your-teeth protection.)

Once the chat has begun, here's some of the fun you can have:

- **Resize the window.** Drag any window edge, or choose Window→Zoom.

- **Go full-screen.** Click the ⤢ button (or the green Ⓢ button) to make the window fill your entire screen. (Click it again to restore the window.)

- **Move the inset.** The little picture-in-picture rectangle shows *you*. You can drag it to a different corner of the video window, if you like.

- **Rotate the screen.** FaceTime works in either portrait (upright) or landscape (widescreen) view. Turn View→Use Landscape on or off to choose, or click the curved arrow in the inset that shows your face. (If you're calling someone using an iPhone or iPad, your Mac picture rotates automatically when your partner's gadget rotates. You don't have to turn the monitor 90 degrees.)

- **Mute the mike.** Either choose Video→Mute, or click the 🎤 button at the bottom of the video window. The video continues. This is handy when you have to make throat-clearing sounds or yell at your kid in the background.

- **Pause the call.** You can also mute (black out) the *video*, for use when you have to perform small acts of personal grooming. To do that, choose FaceTime→Hide FaceTime, or right-click (two-finger click) the FaceTime icon in the Dock and choose Hide from the shortcut menu.

Tip: The call is also paused whenever you minimize FaceTime.

When you and your buddy have had quite enough, tap the End button to terminate the call. (Although it's easy to jump from phone call to videochat, there's no way to go the other direction.)

And marvel that you were alive to see the day.

UP TO SPEED

The Apple (iCloud) ID

Once you become a member of the Apple cult, the key that unlocks all Apple doors is your Apple ID. The same email address and password gets you into iCloud, the iTunes Store, the Apple Store, the App Store, Messages, FaceTime, and almost any other Apple service that requires you to log in. In the unlikely event that you don't yet have an Apple ID, you can get one by opening System Preferences→iCloud and clicking "Create new Apple ID."

FaceTime Audio Calls

You might imagine that, on the great timeline of Apple technologies, audio calling would have arrived before video calling. But no; free Internet audio calls didn't come to the iPhone until iOS 7.

And it's a big deal. Video calling is neat and all, but be honest: Don't you find yourself making phone calls more often? Video calling forces us to be "on," neatly dressed and well behaved, because we're on camera. Most of the time, we're perfectly happy (in fact, happier) with audio only.

To place an audio call, you start out exactly as you would when making a video call, as described earlier: in the FaceTime app, Contacts, or Messages. Click ☎, and then click FaceTime Audio (as opposed to whatever phone numbers are listed there).

When you place an audio FaceTime call, the other person's phone, tablet, or Mac rings. If he accepts your call, it's better than being on a phone call in two ways. First, you don't have the usual lag time that throws off your comic timing. And, second, the audio quality is amazing—more like FM radio than cellular. It sounds like the other person is right next to your head; you hear every breath, sniff, and sweater rustle.

Receiving Calls

Life is even simpler when somebody calls *you*. A notification bubble appears on your screen, and you hear an incoming-call sound. (Which ringtone? That's up to you; in the FaceTime app, choose FaceTime→Preferences→Settings. Use the Ringtone pop-up menu.) If iTunes is playing music, it pauses automatically. Sweet.

If the Mac is asleep, it wakes; you can even answer the call on the Login screen, without having to enter your password.

Click Accept to start the call, or Decline if now is not the time. (In that case, the caller will be told that you're not available.)

FaceTime doesn't have to be running for you to receive a call. That's generally a cool feature—but if you really don't want to be interrupted, you can hang up a digital "Do Not Disturb" sign in any of these ways:

• In FaceTime, choose FaceTime→Turn FaceTime Off.

• Use the Do Not Disturb feature (page 612).

• Sign out of FaceTime. (Choose FaceTime→Preferences→Settings, and then click Sign Out.)

Font Book

For details on this font-management program, see Chapter 9.

Game Center

The Mac has had its share of games over the years, but it's never been much of a haven for gamers. But the Game Center app does make the Mac a little bit more of a hospitable place for the games people play.

Game Center began life on iPhones and iPads in 2010 as a way to compare scores with friends and challenge buddies to games. Several updates and 130 million people later, Game Center on iPhones/iPads is a certified hit.

Little wonder then, that Apple would want to create a Mac version of Game Center to promote gaming on the Mac. It performs the same functions as the iPhone version of Game Center—but opens up the possibility of playing games on your Mac against people with phones and tablets. (That miracle, of course, is possible only in cases when the same game is available on those different gadgets.) Someday soon, Apple hopes, there will be one glorious, universal game ecosystem of Apple machines.

Getting Started

When you open the Game Center app, start by signing in. If you've used Game Center on your phone or tablet, your Apple ID appears automatically; just type your password. From there, Game Center imports everything—your nickname, your list of existing Game Center friends, and even the photo you use to identify yourself.

If this is your first time with Game Center, fill in your Apple ID (page 645) and password. You're asked to create a nickname—"AngriestBird" or "BobSmith2000," for example. This nickname is public and can appear on the leaderboards for games (scoreboards that show the highest point winners); you can also use this nickname when you play games against other people. Within your Game Center account, you can also turn two settings on and off: One lets friends invite you to play games; the other makes your public profile visible to other Game Center members.

That public profile includes space for a short description and photo of yourself. You can grab a picture from a list of recent photos (any images you've used as your Messages icon, for example), Apple's standard OS X icons, or a photo you take with your Mac's built-in camera. The Mac's Game Center gives you a few more photo editing options than you get in the iOS version: In addition to zooming and placing the image, you can also apply a filter, giving your photo a tinted, distorted, or pixelated look.

Tip: Any change you make to your Game Center profile on a Mac will also show up on Game Center on your iPhone or iPad—and vice versa.

Once all that's in place, the Me tab in Game Center displays your nickname, that clever little phrase you wrote, and your picture. Beneath that, multicolored banners display the number of Game Center–compatible games you own (either iOS or Mac games), the number of Game Center friends you have, and—perhaps most significantly—the number of points you've accrued from your gaming activities.

Points and Achievements

Points play a leading role in Game Center. You earn them by racking up achievements in Game Center–compatible apps. Smash enough blocks in one of the many versions of Angry Birds, or expand your territory in Civilization, and you unlock achievements in those games; those achievements translate to points, which show up in your Game Center profile.

Those points also provide a way to measure your personal worth against your friends'. On Game Center's Friends tab, your friends appear in a pane on the left side of the Friends window (Figure 19-13).

Figure 19-13:
You can sort the Friends list alphabetically, by how recently your friends have played a game, or by the total points they've accumulated in Game Center apps.

If you click a friend's name in that left pane, you get a choice of three views: the games your friends play, the names of their friends, and the number of points they've tallied. The points view features a side-by-side comparison showing your respective accomplishments in commonly played games, so you can settle once and for all who's tops at Cubemen. (Game Center also shows the points your friends have racked up in games you don't own, which is Apple's way of suggesting that maybe you should download more games.)

Making Friends

Of course, before you can compare your scores with your friends', it helps to *have* some friends. (Insert your own joke about hard-core gamers here.)

You can invite your real-life pals to join you in Game Center by clicking the Add Friends banner near the top of the left-hand pane on the Friends window. You get a pop-up message window, where you can type in a person's Game Center nickname or email address to send a friend invitation. (Email is probably the better choice, as you may not know your friend's Game Center nickname; he might not even be signed up to the service.) You can also issue invitations from the Requests tab, which

is where you typically accept invitations that come in from other Game Center users who want to befriend you.

But what if you don't have any existing friends, or at least none who you know are on Game Center? Above the Add Friends banner, a Friend Recommendations button brings up a list of potential buddies. These are strangers, of course, but they're based on friends and games you have in common. Clicking on one of those names takes you to a page that shows common friends, if any, and a Send Friend Request banner.

You can also find gaming companions through your other Game Center friends. Just click one of your friends' names, and then select the Friends view on her page to see who she hangs out with in Game Center (when she's not matching scores with you, of course). The list of her Game Center friends appears under a list of shared friends and notes how many games you have in common with this would-be buddy.

Finding Games

Game Center can also help you find games to play—well, at least games that are designed to tie in with Game Center. The top of the Games tab features a Recommendations section that takes you to a list of suggested games. Game Center bases these recommendations on what you already own, what your friends play, and popular App Store downloads.

While you decide what games you want to learn, you can always fool around with the Chess game that comes with Yosemite; it's Game Center–ready.

Managing Game Center

You get to most of the Game Center management features from the Me tab. That's where you can change your photo and status message, manage your privacy settings, and even sign out of Game Center. But there's another aspect of Game Center that you manage in a completely different place.

Game Center notifies you whenever anyone asks to friend you or accepts your Game Center invitation. These notifications usually appear as banners, flashing in your upper-right corner briefly before they disappear. You can, of course, shut them up; open System Preferences→Notifications, click Game Center, and customize the settings as described on page 612.

GarageBand

GarageBand, Apple's do-it-yourself music construction kit, isn't actually part of OS X. If you have a copy, that's because it's part of the iLife suite that comes on every new Mac (along with iMovie and iPhoto).

iBooks

iBooks is Apple's ebook reading program. For years, it's turned the iPhone or iPad into a sort of pocket-sized Kindle. It lets you carry around dozens or hundreds of

books in your pocket, which, in the pre-ebook days, would have drawn some funny looks in public.

Inevitably, it finally came to the Mac.

The beauty of all this is iCloud syncing. If you're reading a book on your iPhone in line for the Department of Motor Vehicles, you'll find that your iPad opens up to exactly the same page when you're on the train home. And when you open your MacBook at home, it'll be on the same page as where you left the iPad. Your books, documents, notes, highlighting, and other details are synced among your Apple gadgets, too. (You can turn that syncing feature off in iBooks→Preferences→General if it spooks you.)

Most people think of iBooks as a reader for books that Apple sells on its iTunes bookstore—bestsellers and current fiction, for example—and it does that very well. But you can also load it up with your own PDF documents, as well as thousands of free, older, out-of-copyright books.

Tip: iBooks is very cool and all. But in the interest of fairness, it's worth noting that Amazon's free Kindle app, and Barnes & Noble's free B&N eReader app, are much the same thing—but offer much bigger book libraries at lower prices than Apple's.

Downloading Books

To shop the iBooks bookstore, open the iBooks app. Click iBooks Store in the upper-left corner; the iBooks app becomes the literary equivalent of the App Store, complete with the icons across the bottom. The links here offer everything you'd need in your bibliographic quest: "NY Times" (bestseller lists), "Top Authors," "Best of the Month," "Books Made into Movies," "Free Books," and so on. You can also search by name or click Purchased to see what you've bought.

Tip: Once you've bought a book from Apple, you can download it again on other Macs, iPhones, iPod Touches, and iPads. Buy once, read many times. That's the purpose of the Not In My Library tab, which appears when you click Purchased.

But unless you have some kind of privacy concern, you may as well tell iBooks to download your books *automatically* as you buy them on your other Apple gadgets. Open iBooks→Preferences→Store and turn on "Download new purchases automatically." That way you'll never forget what you bought on your iPad as you sit down at your Mac.

Once you find a book that looks good, you can click Get Sample to download a free chapter, read ratings and reviews, or click the price itself to buy the book and download it straight to the phone.

If you see a book cover bearing the ⌀ icon, that's a book you own—it's available in your online locker—but you haven't downloaded it to this Mac yet. Click to download.

ePub Files

Apple's bookstore isn't the only way to get books. You can also load up your ebook reader from your computer, feeding it with ePub files.

Actually, ePub is the normal iBooks format. It's a very popular standard for ebook readers, Apple's and otherwise. The only difference between ePub documents you create and the ones Apple sells is that Apple's are copy protected.

To add your own ePub documents to your iBooks library, just drag their icons off the desktop and into the iBooks window. Or choose File→Add to Library.

And where are you supposed to get all these files? Free (and not free) ebooks in ePub format are everywhere. There are 33,000 free downloadable books at *gutenberg.org*, for example, and over a million at *books.google.com*—oldies, but classic oldies, with lots of Mark Twain, Agatha Christie, Herman Melville, H.G. Wells, and so on. (Lots of these are available in the Free pages of Apple's own iBook store, too.)

PDF Files

iBooks can display and catalog PDF documents, too. PDFs are everywhere—people send them as attachments, and you can turn any document into a PDF file. (For example, on the Mac, in any program, choose File→Print; in the resulting dialog box, click PDF→Save as PDF.) You bring them into iBooks by dragging them into its window, or with File→Add to Library.

When you double-click one, though, it doesn't open in iBooks; it opens into *Preview*. Which is, after all, a program expressly designed for reading PDF documents.

You've been warned.

Your Library

When you open iBooks, you see your own personal library represented as little book covers (Figure 19-14). Mostly what you'll do here is click a book to open it. But there are all kinds of other activities waiting for you:

- **You can reorganize your bookshelf.** Use the Sort By pop-up menu to choose Most Recent or Title—or Sort Manually, which means that you can drag books around into any order you like.

- **You can view your library as a compact list.** Click List at the top to switch the book-cover view to a much more boring (but more compact) list view. The column headings let you sort the list by author, title, category, and so on. And there's a search box, too, which lets you search your books' titles—helpful if you have an enormous library.

- **To delete a book**, click it and then press the Delete key; confirm in the warning box. Of course, deleting a book from the Mac doesn't delete your safety copy on your other gadgets or online.

- **Organize your books into folders.** In iBooks, the "folders" are called collections, but it's the same idea. You might have one for school, one for work, and a third for somebody who shares your Mac, for example.

To see your collections, click Collections; the Collections list opens at the left side. Make a new collection by clicking the + button (or choose Use File→New Collection; type to name it.

Now, to file your books away, select them (you can press ⌘ as you click to select multiple books); then choose File→Add to Collection and choose the name of the collection you want them in.

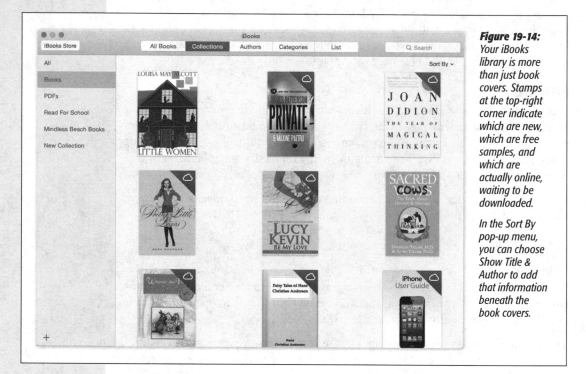

Figure 19-14:
Your iBooks library is more than just book covers. Stamps at the top-right corner indicate which are new, which are free samples, and which are actually online, waiting to be downloaded.

In the Sort By pop-up menu, you can choose Show Title & Author to add that information beneath the book covers.

Reading

But come on—you're a reader, not a librarian. Here's how you read an ebook.

Open the book by double-clicking the book cover. Now the book opens, ready for you to read. Looks great, doesn't it (Figure 19-15)? If you're returning to a book you've been reading, iBooks remembers your place.

Tip: You can open several books at once, you multitasking maniac.

In general, reading is simple: Just read. Turn pages like this:

- Press the space bar. (Add Shift to turn back a page.)

- Tap the ▶ key. (Press ◀ to turn back.)

- Point to the right margin; click the > button that appears. (Left margin to go back.)

- Swipe two fingers across the trackpad—to the right (to go forward) or left (to go back a page).

You should also take a moment to adjust your reading environment. For example:

- **Enter Full Screen mode** for the biggest, least distracting view of your book (see page 160).

- **Specify either a one-page or a two-page spread** (use the Single Page or Two Pages commands in the View menu). In Full Screen mode, Single Page isn't available.

- **Adjust the type size** using the ₐA button. That's a huge feature for people with tired or over-40 eyes. And it's something paper books definitely can't do.

 The same pop-out pane offers a Fonts button, where you can choose from five different typefaces for your book.

- **Adjust the background color.** The ₐA button also offers a Themes button, which lets you specify whether the page itself is white, black (with white text, for nighttime reading), or Sepia (off-white).

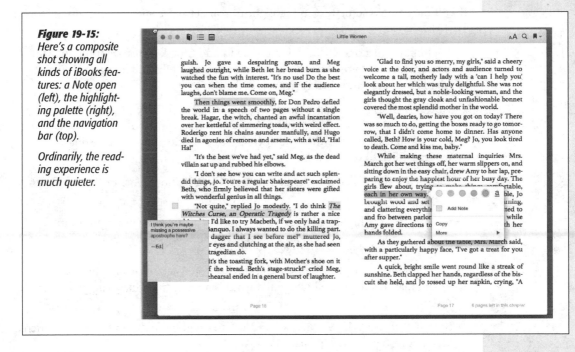

Figure 19-15:
Here's a composite shot showing all kinds of iBooks features: a Note open (left), the highlighting palette (right), and the navigation bar (top).

Ordinarily, the reading experience is much quieter.

While you're reading, iBooks makes all the onscreen controls fade away so you can read in peace. But if you move your mouse to the top of the window, a row of additional controls appears (Figure 19-15):

- 📖 takes you back to the bookshelf (Library view).

- ☰ opens the Table of Contents pane. The chapter or page names are "live"— you can click one to jump there.

- ▤ opens the Notes pane, described below.

- 🔍 opens the search box. It lets you search for text within the book you're reading, which can be extremely useful.

- 🔖 adds a bookmark to the current page. This isn't like a physical bookmark, where there's only one in the whole book; you can use it to flag as many pages, for as many reasons, as you like.

 Once you've accumulated a bookmark or two, use the ⌄ next to the 🔖 menu to see a list of them—and to jump back to one.

Tip: An iBook can include pictures and even videos. Double-click a picture in a book to zoom in on it.

Notes, Bookmarks, Highlighting, Dictionary

Here are some more stunts that you'd have trouble pulling off in a printed book. If you *double-click* a word, you get a graceful, elegant page from iBooks' built-in dictionary. You know—in the unlikely event that you encounter a word you don't know.

If you drag across some text to highlight it, you get some surprise options (Figure 19-15):

- **Highlight.** Click one of the colored dots to add tinted, transparent highlighting, or underlining, to the word you clicked. (To remove highlighting, click inside a highlighted area and click Remove Highlighting.)

- **Note.** When you click Add Note, iBooks creates highlighting on the selected passage *and* opens an empty, colored sticky note so you can type in your own annotations. When you click outside the note, it collapses down to a tiny Post-it square in the margin. Click to reopen it.

 To delete a note, click the highlighted text. Click Remove Note or Remove Highlight & Note.

- **Copy** copies the highlighted text, ready for pasting in some other program.

In the More menu, a few additional options lurk:

- **Search Book** opens the same search box that you'd get by clicking the 🔍 icon—except that this time, the highlighted word is already filled in, saving you a bit of typing.

- **Search Web, Search Wikipedia** hand off the highlighted text to Safari, which searches Google or Wikipedia.

- **Facebook, Messages, Twitter, Email** opens the share sheet (page 241) so you can send the highlighted material to somebody else by message or email, or post a favorite quote on Twitter or Facebook.

- **Start speaking** reads the highlighted passage aloud.

Tip: The Mac's speaking feature isn't limited to a blob of text that you've highlighted. You can use the Edit→Speech→Start Speaking command to have the *entire book* read to you—in a voice that's only a *little* robotic. Yes, this is exactly the feature that debuted in the Amazon Kindle and was then removed when publishers screamed bloody murder—but somehow, so far, Apple has gotten away with it.

Once you've added bookmarks, notes, and highlighting to your book, they're magically and wirelessly synced to any other copies of that book—on other gadgets, like the iPad or iPod Touch, other iPhones, or other Mavericks or Yosemite Macs. Very handy indeed.

Furthermore, if you click the ▤ button, you'll see the Notes pane. It presents a tidy list of all your bookmarked pages, notes, and highlighted passages. You can click one of the listings to jump to the relevant page.

iBooks Settings

If you've embraced the simple joy of reading electronic books, then you deserve to know where to make settings changes: in iBooks→Preferences. Here are the options waiting there.

General tab

- **Let lines break naturally.** Ordinarily, iBooks presents text with ragged-right margins. Select "Justify text" if you like the text to stretch from edge to edge of the screen.

- **Auto-hyphenate words.** Sometimes, typesetting looks better if hyphens allow partial words to appear at the right edge of each line. Especially if you've also turned on "Justify text."

- **Sync.** Turn this on if you'd like your bookmarks, highlighting, and book collections to be synced with your other Apple gadgets.

Store tab

Read about shopping for iBooks on page 650.

Parental tab

If you're a parent, you might wish to shield your impressionable offspring from dirty reading material—or to shield your credit card from wild teenage book-spending sprees (we should all have that problem!).

Click the 🔒 and enter your administrator's password; now you can turn on "Disable the iBooks Store" to prevent purchases, or "Restrict books with explicit content" to block the downloading of raunchy material.

Image Capture

This unsung little program was originally designed to download pictures from a camera and then process them automatically (turning them into a Web page, scaling

them to emailable size, and so on). Of course, after Image Capture's birth, iPhoto came along, generally blowing its predecessor out of the water.

Even so, Apple includes Image Capture with OS X for these reasons:

• Image Capture is a smaller, faster app for downloading all or only some pictures from your camera (Figure 19-16). iPhoto can do that nowadays, but sometimes that's like using a bulldozer to get out a splinter.

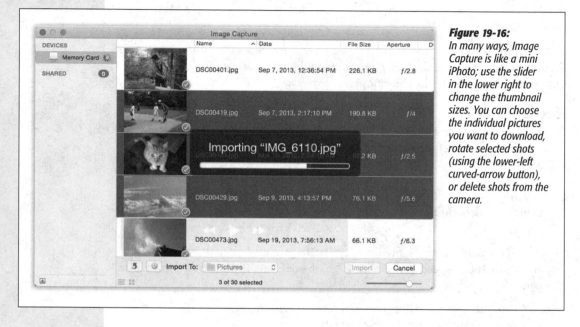

Figure 19-16:
In many ways, Image Capture is like a mini iPhoto; use the slider in the lower right to change the thumbnail sizes. You can choose the individual pictures you want to download, rotate selected shots (using the lower-left curved-arrow button), or delete shots from the camera.

• Image Capture can grab images from scanners, too, not just cameras.

• Image Capture can download your *sounds* (like voice notes) from a digital still camera; iPhoto can't.

You can open Image Capture in either of two ways: You can simply double-click its icon in your Applications folder, or you can set it up to open automatically whenever you connect a digital camera and turn it on. To set up that arrangement, open Image Capture manually. Using the "Connecting this camera opens:" pop-up menu at the bottom of the pane, choose Image Capture.

Tip: Image Capture remembers your setting here separately for each camera. For example, you can set it up so that when you connect your fancy SLR camera, Aperture opens; when you connect your spouse's pocket camera, iPhoto opens; and when you connect your iPhone, Image Capture opens, so you can quickly grab the best shots and email them directly.

Once Image Capture is open, it looks like Figure 19-16. When you connect your camera, cellphone, or scanner, its name appears in the left-side list. To begin, click it.

After a moment, Image Capture displays all the photos on the camera's card, in either list view or icon view (your choice).

Import To:

Use this pop-up menu to specify what happens to the imported pictures. Image Capture proposes putting photos, sounds, and movies from the camera into your Home folder's Pictures folder. But you can specify any folder (choose Other from the pop-up menu).

Furthermore, there are some other very cool options here:

- **iPhoto.** Neat that you can direct photos from your camera *to* iPhoto *via* Image Capture. Might come in handy when you didn't *expect* to want to load photos into your permanent collection, but you change your mind when you actually look them over in Image Capture.

- **Preview** opens the fresh pictures in Preview so you can get a better (and bigger) look at them.

- **Mail** sends the pix directly into the Mac's email program, which can be handy when the whole point of getting the photos off the camera is to send them off to friends.

- **Build web page** creates an actual Web page of your downloaded shots. Against a dark-gray background, you get thumbnail images of the pictures in a Web page document called *index.html.* Just click one of the small images to view it at full size, exactly as your Web site visitors will be able to do once this page is actually on the Web. (Getting it online is up to you.)

Note: Image Capture puts the Web page files in a Home folder→Pictures→Webpage on [today's date and time] folder. It contains the graphics files incorporated into this HTML document; you can post the whole thing on your Web site, if you like.

Image Capture automatically opens up this page in your Web browser, proud of its work.

- **MakePDF.** When you choose this option, you wind up with what looks like a Preview window, showing thumbnails of your photos. If you choose Save right now, you'll get a beautiful, full-color PDF of the selected photos, ready to print out and then, presumably, cut apart with scissors or a paper cutter. But if you use the Layout menu, you can choose different layouts for your photos: 3 × 5, 4 × 6, 8 × 10, and so on.

And what if a photo doesn't precisely fit the proportions you've selected? The Crop commands in the Layout menu (for example, "Crop to 4 × 6") center each photo within the specified shape and then trim the outer borders if necessary. The Fit commands, on the other hand, *shrink* the photo as necessary to fit into the specified dimensions, sometimes leaving blank white margins.

Note: The "crop" commands never touch the actual downloaded photos. The downloaded image files themselves retain their full sizes and resolutions.

- **Other.** The beauty of the Image Capture system is that people can, in theory, write additional processing scripts. Once you've written or downloaded them, drop them into your System→Library→Image Capture→Automatic Tasks folder. Then enjoy their presence in the newly enhanced Import To pop-up menu.

Tip: You can set up Image Capture to download everything on the camera *automatically* when you connect it. No muss, no options, no fuss.

To do that, connect the camera. Click its name in the Devices list. Then, from the "Connecting this camera opens" pop-up menu, choose AutoImporter. From now on, Image Capture downloads all pictures on the camera each time it's connected. When the downloading process is complete, a little green checkmark appears on the thumbnail of each imported photo.

Import Some, Import All

Clicking Import All, of course, begins the process of downloading the photos to the folder you've selected. A progress dialog box appears, showing you thumbnail images of each picture that flies down the wire.

If you prefer to import only *some* photos, select them first. (In list view, you click and Shift-click to select a bunch of *consecutive* photos, and ⌘-click to add *individual* photos to the selection. In icon view, you can both ⌘-click and *Shift*-click to select individual photos.) Then click Import.

Scanning

Image Capture's scanning function is described starting on page 342.

iMovie

Apple's video-editing program is big enough and complex enough that it gets a book all its own: *iMovie: The Missing Manual*, of course.

iPhoto/Photos

Well, *this* is awkward. For years, iPhoto was the photo organizing/editing program that came free with every Mac. But in the fall of 2014, Apple announced that iPhoto would be going away. It would be replaced by a new program called Photos—but not until sometime in 2015!

So if you have OS X Yosemite, you might have iPhoto, and you might have Photos, depending on when you're reading this. What a nightmare for people who write computer books!

In any case, you can read about the new Photos app once it becomes available. At that point, you'll be able to download a free PDF appendix to this chapter called "Photos. pdf" from this book's "Missing CD" page at *www.missingmanuals.com*.

iTunes

iTunes is Apple's beloved digital music–library program. Chapter 9 tells all.

Launchpad

See Chapter 4 for the full story about the program-opening Home screen.

Mail

See Chapter 11 for the missing Mail manual.

Maps

When Apple brought its own Maps app to the iPhone in 2012, the underlying databases had a lot of problems. They didn't include nearly as many points of interest (buildings, stores, landmarks) as Google. Addresses were sometimes wrong. Satellite view showed bridges and roads melting into the sea. In a remarkable apology letter, CEO Tim Cook recommended using one of Maps' rivals.

But some of Maps' features are pretty great—and now that Maps is a Mac app, too (Figure 19-17), there's some handy synergy with the iPhone or iPad. You can look up an address on the Mac and then wirelessly shoot it over to the phone for navigation

Figure 19-17:
Maps lets you type in any address or point of interest and see it on a map, with turn-by-turn directions, just like a $300 windshield GPS unit. It also gives you a live national Yellow Pages business directory and real-time traffic-jam alerts. You have a choice of a street-map diagram or actual aerial photos, taken by satellite.

in the car, for example. Or simply walk over to your Mac; thanks to Handoff (page 482), whatever map was on your phone is now on your Mac. And Maps' smarts are wired into other OS X programs, like Calendar, Contacts, and Safari.

Meet Maps

When you open Maps, you see a blue dot that represents your current location. You can manipulate the map in all the usual ways:

- **Zoom in or out** using the keyboard (press ⌘-plus or ⌘-minus), the mouse (double-click to zoom in, add the Option key to zoom out—or just click the + or − buttons), or the trackpad (pinch two fingers to zoom out, spread them to zoom in).

- **Scroll around the map** using the keyboard (press the arrow keys), the mouse (drag), or the trackpad (swipe two fingers in any direction).

- **Rotate the map** using the mouse (drag the small compass at lower right) or the trackpad (rotate two fingers). You can return the map to "North is up" by pressing ⌘-▲, by clicking the compass, or by double-tapping two fingers on the trackpad.

- **You can tilt into a 3-D view**, which makes it look more like you're surveying the map at an angle instead of straight down. You can do that with the mouse (click the 3D button), keyboard (press ⌘-0), or the trackpad (press Option and drag with two fingers).

At any time, you can click any of the buttons above the map for your choice of amazing map views: Standard (street-map illustration) and Satellite (aerial photos superimposed with street names).

There's no guarantee that the Satellite view provides a very *recent* photo—different parts of the Maps database use photography taken at different times—but it's still very cool.

Finding Yourself

All right—now that you know how the Mac gets its location information, here's how you can use it. Its first trick is to show you where you are.

Click the ➤ button at the top left of Maps. When the button is blue, the Mac is showing you your location. (Click it to turn it black, which makes it stop showing your dot.)

Searching the Maps

You're not always interested in finding out where you are; often, you know that much perfectly well. Instead, you want to see where something *else* is.

Click in the search box and type what you're seeking. (If there's already something in the box, click ⊗ to clear it out.) Here's what Maps can find for you:

- **An address.** You can skip the periods (and usually the commas, too). And you can use abbreviations. Typing *710 w end ave ny ny* will find 710 West End Avenue, New York, New York. (In this and any of the other examples, you can type a Zip code instead of a city and a state.)

- **An intersection.** Type *57th and lexington, ny ny.* Maps will find the spot where East 57th Street crosses Lexington Avenue in New York City.

- **A city.** Type *chicago il* to see that city. You can zoom in from there.

- **A Zip code or a neighborhood.** Type *10024* or *greenwich village.*

- **A point of interest.** Type *washington monument* or *niagara falls.*

- **A business type.** Type *drugstores in albany ny* or *hospitals in roanoke va.* (Figure 19-17 shows this idea.)

When Maps finds a specific address, an animated, red-topped pushpin comes flying down onto its precise spot on the map. A bubble identifies the location by name.

Click outside the bubble to hide it. Click the map pin to bring the bubble back. Click Directions for instant driving directions.

Tip: Or walking directions. Click the Walk button at the top of the directions pane.

Click ⓘ to open the Location page; read on.

The Details Screen

Once you've found something on the map—your current position, say, or something you've searched for—you can drop a pin there for future reference. Choose Edit→→ Drop Pin. A purple pushpin appears. (You can drag the pin to move it, if your aim wasn't exact.)

Red pushpins represent addresses you've looked up. And the tiny icons represent restaurants, stores, and other establishments in Apple's (actually Yelp's) database.

All of these pushpins and nano-icons are clickable. You get little labels that identify them. And if you click the ⓘ on a label, you open a details screen (Figure 19-18).

Bookmarks, Recents, Contacts

Maps is also plugged into your Contacts list, which makes it especially easy to find a friend's house (or just to see how ritzy his neighborhood is).

When you click into the empty search bar, the Bookmarks/Recents/Contacts menu appears; it can save you a lot of typing.

The list as it first appears displays Recents (locations you've looked up recently—on your Mac or your iOS gadgets). If you click Favorites, you get to see a list of Favorites (locations you've bookmarked) and Contacts. Yes, your master address book (page 411) is accessible here; you can search All Contacts or any one of your accounts.

When you click an entry in any of these lists, Maps drops a red, animated pushpin onto the map to identify that address.

Finding Friends and Businesses

That pushpin business also comes into play when you use Maps as a glorified national Yellow Pages. If you type, for example, *pharmacy 60609*, then those red pushpins show you all the drugstores in that Chicago Zip code. It's a great way to find a gas station, a cash machine, or a hospital in a pinch. Click a pushpin to see the name of the corresponding business.

As usual, you can click the ⓘ in the map pin's bubble to open a details screen. If you've searched for a friend, then you see the corresponding Contacts card. If you've searched for a business, then you get a screen containing its phone number, address, Web site, and so on; often, you get a beautiful page of Yelp information (photos, reviews, ratings).

Remember that you can click a Web address to open it or send the phone number to your phone to dial it. ("Hello, what time do you close today?")

Figure 19-18:
On the Details screen that sprouts when you click a red pushpin, buttons let you bookmark the spot, get directions, or add the information to Contacts.

If the location is a restaurant or a business, you might strike gold: The details screen might offer several screens full of useful information, courtesy of Yelp.com. You'll see customer reviews, photos, hours of operation, delivery and reservation information, and so on.

Best of all, the ⬆ button lets you share this location with other people—via AirDrop, email, text message, Facebook, or Twitter—or with yourself; your iPhones, iPads, and iPod Touches show up here, if they're signed into the same iCloud account.

An identical ⬆ button appears at the top of the Maps main window, so you can send whatever route or location you've summoned.

Directions

The Directions pane opens when you click the Directions button (top left of Maps), or when you click the Directions To Here (or From Here) button on any location's information pane.

The Directions pane actually offers *two* search bars: Start and End. Plug in two addresses—the Start address may already say "Current Location"—and let Maps guide you from the first to the second.

Tip: The ʊ button swaps the Start and End points. That's a great way to find your way back after a trip.

When everything looks good, Maps displays an overview of the route you're about to follow. In fact, it may propose several different routes, labeled with tags that show how long they'll take: "1 hr 9 min," "1 hr 15 min," and "1 hr 28 min," for example.

If you click one of these tags, the top of the Directions pane lets you know the distance and estimated time for that option and identifies the main roads you'll be on.

Now, nobody expects you to use your Mac as a portable GPS device. You're not going to park it on your dashboard and have it tell you when to turn.

What you can do, though, is send your selected directions to an iPhone or an iPad and use *that* as your GPS. See Figure 19-18.

Or, if you're just planning your trip, click any of the steps in the Directions pane; the map zooms in to that particular turn. Your route looks like it's been drawn in with a blue highlighter.

Traffic

How's this for a cool feature? Free, real-time traffic reporting. From the Show pop-up menu (bottom of the screen), choose Show Traffic. Now traffic jams appear on the relevant roads, for your stressing pleasure; orange dotted lines for slow traffic, and red ones for true stop-and-go nightmares.

If you don't see any dotted lines, it's either because traffic is moving fine or because Apple doesn't have any information for those roads. Usually, you get traffic info only for highways, and only in metropolitan areas.

Tiny icons also appear, representing accidents, construction sites, closed roads, and general alerts. Click the icon to make a quick description tag appear (like "Accident, Park Ave at State St"); click that tag to read a full-screen account of what's going on.

Flyover

You don't need to be headed somewhere to use Flyover, the Maps app's most dazzling feature; it has nothing to do with navigation, really. You can operate it even while you're lying on your couch like a slug; see Figure 19-19.

To engage Flyover, switch into either Hybrid or Satellite view. Choose View→Show 3D Map (or click the 3D logo in the lower-right corner).

Now you can go nuts, conducting your own virtual chopper tour of the city using the zooming and rotating tricks described earlier. Only a couple of things are different:

 • To move around the map, drag it—or use two fingers on the trackpad.

- To change your camera angle relative to the ground, press Option as you use two fingers on the trackpad—or drag up or down on the compass at lower right.

- To zoom in, spread two fingers on the trackpad—or click the + and − buttons.

It's immersing, completely amazing, and very unlikely to make you airsick.

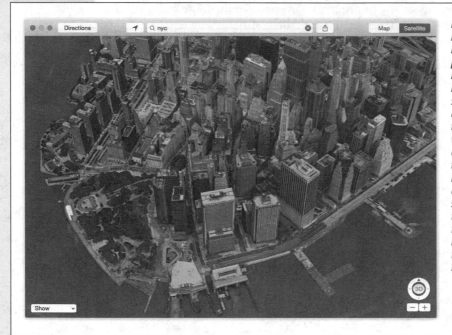

Figure 19-19:
Flyover is a dynamic, interactive, photographic 3-D model of certain major cities. It looks something like an aerial video, except that you control the virtual camera. You can pan around these scenes, looking over and around buildings to see what's behind them. To create this feature, Apple says, it spent two years filming cities from helicopters.

Flyover Tours

In Yosemite, Apple wasn't satisfied with letting you pan around virtual 3-D city models using your finger. Now it's prepared to give you city *tours* in 3-D.

Use the search box to enter the name of a big city or major landmark. (Some examples: San Francisco, New York, Tokyo, London, Paris, Rome, Madrid, Vancouver, San Jose, Cape Town, Stockholm. Or places like Yosemite National Park, Sydney Opera House, Stonehenge, St. Peter's Basilica, or the Brooklyn Bridge.)

When you hit Search, a new control appears just beneath the Start box; "3D Flyover Tour." When you tap Start, you're in for a crazy treat: a fully automated video tour of that city or place. The San Francisco tour shows you the baseball park, the famous Transamerica Pyramid, the Alcatraz prison island, and so on. It's slow, soothing, cool, and definitely something that paper maps never did.

Messages

See Chapter 13 for details on Messages, the Mac's instant-messaging/audiochat/videochat/text-messaging program.

Mission Control

Chapter 4 covers OS X's window-management tool.

Notes

The Notes app, a clone of the one on the iPhone/iPad, lets you jot down lists, recipes, driving directions, and brainstorms—and they all sync effortlessly among your Apple phones, tablets, and other computers. It's lost its yellow-lined-paper look but, at heart, it's the same old Notes.

To create a new page of notes, choose File→New Note (⌘-N), or click the ☑ button at top left. Once the new page appears, type away (Figure 19-20).

Tip: Notes works with Handoff (page 482). So if you're editing a note on your Mac, iPhone, or iPad, you'll be offered the chance to jump to the same note on any *other* Mac, iPhone, or iPad you own (if it's on the same WiFi network).

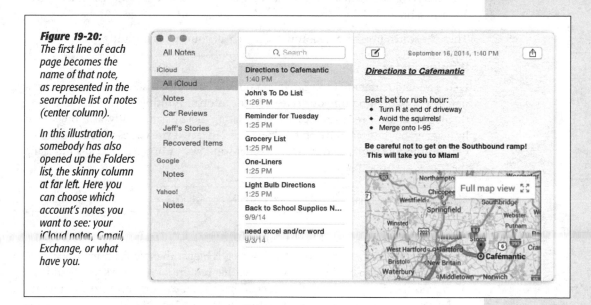

Figure 19-20:
The first line of each page becomes the name of that note, as represented in the searchable list of notes (center column).

In this illustration, somebody has also opened up the Folders list, the skinny column at far left. Here you can choose which account's notes you want to see: your iCloud notes, Gmail, Exchange, or what have you.

Interior Design

You can dress up your Mac's Notes pages far more elaborately than you can on the iPhone. For example:

- You have control over fonts, type sizes, colors, paragraph alignment, and indentation, using the commands in the Format menu. Notes can even create automatic bulleted, dashed, or numbered lists; check out the Format→Lists submenus.

- You can paste or drag photos and other graphics into your notes, too—or even documents, like PDF files, Word documents, or Excel spreadsheets. Drag such a

document into a note from the desktop; there it becomes an icon that you can double-click to open later.

- You can drag or paste a link into a note. Later, when you click it, it opens into the corresponding Web site.

Note: Not all interior decoration gets synced to your phone or tablet. Pictures, for example, don't survive the transition, and not all of your Mac fonts are available on your phone. But for the first time, Notes' typographical skills extend beyond Marker Felt and Helvetica.

A handy icon appears at the top right of each Notes page. You can click ⬆ to send the note to someone, either by email (Chapter 11) or in Messages (Chapter 13).

Tip: You can also print a note; choose File→Print. Just pointing that out.

As you create more pages, the Notes list (the center column in Figure 19-20) becomes more useful. It's your table of contents for the Notes pad. It displays the first lines of your notes (most recent at the top), along with the time or date you last edited them. To open a note, click its name.

There's a search box here, too. You can search all your notes instantly.

Pinning Notes

Here's an undocumented special: If you double-click a note's name, it opens into a new window, floating on your screen. You can open multiple notes this way, drag them around the screen, and leave them floating there permanently, as though held by magnets on the great refrigerator door of life. In fact, if you choose Window→Float On Top, the note remains in front of all other windows. (You can drag it around using the title as a handle.)

Tip: Notes is a card-carrying Full Screen app, as described on page 160.

Notes Folders

Chances are fairly good that your Mac's screen is bigger than your phone's. So Apple gave the Mac version of Notes a few features that require some extra space—and one of them is the side pane of Notes folders. That is, you can organize your notes into various categories, for ease of wading through them. (Any folders you create on the Mac also show up on your iPhone/iPad.)

The key to understanding this feature is the slide-out Folders list, which you can see in Figure 19-20. You can make it appear by choosing View→Show Folders List. Then you can adjust the Folder list's width by dragging the vertical line at its right edge.

To make a new folder, choose File→New Folder; name the folder and then press Return. You can then drag existing notes into its name in the Folders list. (The usual rules apply: You can select a swath of notes in a list by clicking the first and then

Shift-clicking the last. Or you can click individual, nonconsecutive notes by clicking with the ⌘ key pressed.)

Tip: If you press Option as you drag a note, you make a copy of it in the new folder instead of moving the original.

Click a folder's name to see the notes inside it. (Click "All [account name]" to see all the notes in that account.)

To create a new note within a folder, click the folder's name first. If you don't click any folder's name before you create the note, it goes into the general Notes category.

You can also rename a folder (right-click or two-finger click its name; choose Rename Folder), delete one (right-click or two-finger click its name; choose Delete Folder), put one inside another (drag its name), and move a folder to a different account—for example, from your iCloud account to your Google one—by dragging it.

Syncing Notes

The real beauty of this app is that it can synchronize your collection of Notes with all kinds of other Apple gear—iPhones, iPads, and other Macs (Mountain Lion or later)—so the same notes are waiting for you everywhere you look.

Just make sure Notes is turned on in System Preferences→iCloud (on your Mac), and in Settings→Mail, Contacts, Calendars→iCloud (on your phone or tablet). The rest is automatic.

Tip: If you're using the Folders feature, here's how to see them on your phone or tablet: Click the Accounts button in the upper-left corner of the Notes window. The list of accounts and folders appears, much as it does on your Mac.

Notes Accounts

Notes can also show you the contents of the Notes modules on Google, Yahoo, AOL, or another IMAP email account. You'll see each account's worth of notes in the Folder list, as you can see in Figure 19-20—and from there, you can drag notes hither and yon, among accounts, with abandon.

To set this up, open System Preferences→Internet Accounts. Click the account you want (Exchange, Gmail, Yahoo, AOL, or whatever); finally, turn the Notes switch On.

That should do it. Now each account's notes appear under its own heading in the Folders list. And your notes are synced, both ways.

All of this makes life a little more complex, of course. For example, when you create a note, you have to worry about which account it's about to go into. To do that, be sure to specify an account name (and a folder within it, if necessary) *before* you create the new note.

Numbers, Pages

Numbers and Pages are Apple's spreadsheet and word processing programs, something like Apple-flavored versions of Microsoft Excel and Word. They're part of Apple's iWork suite, which comes preinstalled on every new Mac. And they're big enough and complicated enough that there's a whole book about them: *iWork: The Missing Manual*.

Photo Booth

It may be goofy, it may be pointless, but the Photo Booth program is a bigger time drain than Solitaire, the Web, and *Dancing with the Stars* put together.

It's a match made in heaven for any Mac with a camera above the screen. (Photo Booth doesn't even open if your Mac doesn't have *some* kind of camera.)

Open this program and then peer into the camera. Photo Booth acts like a digital mirror, showing whatever the camera sees—that is, you.

GEM IN THE ROUGH

Still and Video Backdrops

Photo Booth and Messages are cousins, and they're closer than ever. One particular feature, in fact, is identical in each: custom backdrops. You can replace the actual, mundane background of your office or den with something far more exciting: a rushing waterfall, for example, or a rider's-eye view of a roller coaster. In fact, you can use any photo or video you want as the background.

It's just like the bluescreen or greenscreen technology that Hollywood uses to put actors someplace they're not—but without the bluescreen or greenscreen.

To replace your background in Photo Booth, click Effects. The fourth page of effects offers eight *canned* backgrounds, prepared by Apple: various spectacular stills (cloudscape, color dots, the moon) and videos (Eiffel Tower plaza, aquarium, roller coaster, tropical beach, Yosemite waterfall).

The final page offers eight empty preview squares. You're supposed to drag a still or a video from your desktop (or iPhoto) into these empty squares, making them not so empty.

In any case, prepare the backdrop by clicking one of the preview squares. Photo Booth says, "Please step out of the frame." Do it. Photo Booth is going to memorize what its field of view looks like without you in it, so that when you reappear, it can tell *you* apart from your boring office background.

Now, when you record the movie or take the photo, you'll be amazed to discover that Photo Booth has just transplanted you to the far more exotic locale you selected. (Alas, blotches may result if the background includes movement or highly contrasting elements.)

But then click the Effects button. You enter a world of special visual effects—and we're talking *very* special. Some make you look like a pinhead, or bulbous, or like a Siamese twin; others simulate Andy Warhol paintings, fisheye lenses, and charcoal sketches (Figure 19-21). In fact, there are five whole pages of effects, nine previews on a page. (The last two pages hold *backdrop* effects, described below.)

Figure 19-21:
The Photo Booth effects must have been dreamed up one night in the midst of a serious beer party at Apple. They're disturbingly creative. If you decide that you really look best without any help from Apple's warped imagery, click the Normal icon in the center.

Click an effect

4-Up | Movie
Still

Finished shots

Effects pages

To page through them, click the left or right arrow buttons, or press ◀ or ▶, or swipe with two fingers on your trackpad (one finger on the Magic Mouse).

The first page contains eight effects, some of which use sophisticated face-recognition smarts to track your face as it moves around the frame. That's how Dizzy and Lovestruck are able to keep the animated birds or hearts circling your head, and how Chipmunk, Nose Twirl, and Bug Out are able to distort your cheeks, nose, and eyeballs even as you move around.

Some of the effects have sliders that govern their intensity; you'll see them appear when you click the preview.

Still Photos

When you find an effect that looks appealing (or unappealing, depending on your goals here), click the camera button, or press ⌘-Return. You see and hear a 3-second countdown, and then *snap!*—your screen flashes white to add illumination, and the resulting photo appears on your screen. Its thumbnail joins the collection at the bottom.

Tip: If that countdown is getting on your nerves, *Option*-click the camera button. You can get rid of the screen flash, too, by *Shift*-clicking. Needless to say, if you press Option *and* Shift, you get neither the countdown nor the flash.

4-Up Photos

If you click the 4-Up button identified in Figure 19-21, then when you click the Camera icon (or press ⌘-Return), the 3-2-1 countdown begins, and then Photo Booth snaps *four* consecutive photos in 2 seconds. You can exploit the timing just the way you would in a real photo booth—make four different expressions, horse around, whatever.

The result is a single graphic with four panes, kind of like what you get at a shopping-mall photo booth. (In Photo Booth, they appear rakishly assembled at an angle; but when you export the image, they appear straight, like panes of a window.) Its icon plops into the row of thumbnails at the bottom of the window, just like the single still photos.

Movies

Photo Booth can also record *videos,* complete with those wacky distortion effects. Click the third icon below the screen, the Movie icon (Figure 19-21), and then click the camera button (or press ⌘-Return). You get the 3-2-1 countdown—but this time, Photo Booth records a video, with sound, until you click the Stop button. (The little digital counter at left reminds you that you're still filming.) When it's over, the movie's icon appears in the row of thumbnails, ready to play or export.

Tip: If you click a movie's thumbnail after recording it and then hit ⌘-T, yellow trim handles appear at both ends of the scroll bar (the same ones you'd see when trimming a video on the iPhone or iPad, or in iPhoto). Drag them inward to trim off any dead air at the beginning or end of your video clip. Hit the space bar to check your work. If the trim is OK, click the Trim button to confirm.

GEM IN THE ROUGH

De-Mirrorizing Your Photos

Technically, Photo Booth acts like a mirror, not a camera. That is, every picture you take is actually flipped, left-to-right. If there's ever text in the picture—something written on your T-shirt, for example—or if you ever examine the way your hair is parted, you'll realize that every image is backward.

That's why you can click a thumbnail at the bottom of the window and then choose Edit→Flip Photo (⌘-F). You've just made the photo match what a camera would have seen.

Or choose Edit→Auto Flip New Items if you want Photo Booth to do the flipping for you from now on.

Exporting Shots and Movies

To look at a photo or movie you've captured, click its thumbnail in the scrolling row at the bottom of the screen. (To return to camera mode, click the ⊙ or ◼◂.)

Fortunately, these masterpieces of goofiness and distortion aren't locked in Photo Booth forever. You can share them with your adoring public in any of these ways:

- **Click the ⬆ button.** The pop-up menu offers the usual offerings of the Share menu (page 239): Mail, Messages, AirDrop, Twitter, Facebook, Vimeo, Flickr, and more, plus Add to iPhone and Add to Aperture, if you use those programs.

 There's also a "Change profile picture" command (to make this photo represent you on the Login screen), and a More button that opens the System Preferences→ Extensions screen described on page 596.

 And speaking of interesting headshots: If you export a 4-up image and choose it as your Buddy Picture, you'll get an *animated* buddy icon. That is, your tiny icon cycles among the four images, creating a crude sort of animation. It's sort of annoying, actually, but all the kids are doing it.

- Click the photo or movie, and then choose File→Export. (Or just right-click or two-finger-click the photo or movie itself; choose Export from the shortcut menu.) You're asked to name and save the exported image or video.

Tip: If you choose File→Export Original instead, the exported photo or video lacks any of the effects that you've applied. You get the original, undistorted, underlying photo.

- Drag a thumbnail out of the window to your desktop.

Note: These files are stored in a single icon, a package file, that sits in your Home→Pictures folder. It's called Photo Booth Library. You'll find one JPEG apiece for single shots, four JPEG files for a 4-up, and a MOV file for videos.

As you set off on your Photo Booth adventures, a note of caution: Keep it away from children. They won't move from Photo Booth for the next 12 years.

Tip: Photo Booth is one of the certified Full Screen apps. Click the green ⊗ button at upper left to make the app fill your screen, for added graphic juiciness.

Preview

Preview is OS X's scanning software, graphics viewer, fax viewer, and PDF reader. It's always been teeming with features that most Mac owners never even knew were there—but now it's a flagship OS X program, offering all of Apple's pet cutting-edge features like Autosave, Versions, Full Screen mode, saving to iCloud (page 211), and a Share icon (⬆) that lets you send a document to somebody else by email, AirDrop, or Messages, or via Facebook, Twitter, or Flickr (page 239).

Tip: Preview can even open Microsoft Office documents (Word, PowerPoint, Excel) and iWork documents (Pages, Numbers, Keynote). You can't edit them in Preview, but you can read them, search them, and print them. No longer must you pay homage to Microsoft's bottom line just to have a look at the documents people send you.

Importing Camera Photos

Preview can import pictures directly from a digital camera (or iPhone), meaning that there are now *three* OS X apps that can perform that duty. (iPhoto and Image Capture are the other two.) It's sometimes handy to use Preview for this purpose, though, because it has some great tools for photos: color-correction controls, size/resolution options, format conversion, and so on.

The actual importing process, though, is *exactly* like using Image Capture. Connect your camera, choose File→Import from [your camera's name], and carry on as described on page 655.

Operating Your Scanner

Preview's scanning features are described starting on page 342.

Multiple Pages, Multiple Views

One hallmark of Preview is its effortless handling of *multiples:* multiple fax pages, multiple PDF files, batches of photos, and so on. The key to understanding the possibilities is mastering the Sidebar, shown in Figure 19-22. The idea is that these thumbnails let you navigate pages or graphics without having to open a rat's nest of individual windows.

Figure 19-22:
The Sidebar can display thumbnails, a table of contents, or annotations, or it can appear as a full-screen array of thumbnail images. Drag the central scroll bar to make the Sidebar bigger; drag the lower-right corner of the Sidebar to make the whole Preview window bigger.

Tip: You can drag these thumbnails from one Preview window's Sidebar into another. That's a great way to mix and match pages from different PDF documents into a single new one, for example.

To hide or show the Sidebar, chose one of these three commands from the View menu:

- **Thumbnails.** This standard view (Figure 19-22, left) offers a scrolling vertical list of miniature pages or photos. Click one to see it at full size in the main window. Make the thumbnails larger or smaller by dragging the window/Sidebar dividing line.

- **Highlights & Notes.** Preview is a better PDF editor than ever. If you add comments and highlighting to a PDF document, as described later in this section, you can view all of them in this tidy list—and click one to jump to it.

- **Table of Contents.** If you're looking over photos, this option turns the Sidebar into a scrolling list of their names. If you've opened a group of PDFs all at once, you see a list of them. Or, if you have a PDF that contains chapter headings, you see them listed in the Sidebar as, yes, a table of contents.

- **Contact Sheet.** When you choose this view, the *main* window scrolls away, leaving you with a full screen of thumbnail miniatures. It's like a light table where you can look over all the photos or PDF pages at once. Make them bigger or smaller using the slider in the lower left.

Tip: You can also change among these views by pressing the keyboard shortcuts Option-⌘-1, -2, -3, and -4.

Preview as Graphics Viewer

Preview is surprisingly versatile. It can display and manipulate pictures saved in a wide variety of formats, including common graphics formats like JPEG, TIFF, PICT, and GIF; less commonly used formats like BMP, PNG, SGI, and TGA; and even Photoshop, EPS, and PDF graphics.

Tip: Don't miss the Tools→Show Magnifier command. It gives you a loupe: a magnifying circle (or, in a PDF document, a magnifying rectangle) that lets you inspect part of your graphic or PDF file more closely.

Bunches o' graphics

If you highlight a group of image files in the Finder and open them all at once (for example, by pressing ⌘-O), Preview opens the first one but lists the thumbnails of the whole group in the Sidebar. You can walk through them with the ▲ and ▼ keys, or you can choose View→Slideshow (Shift-⌘-F) to open a full-screen slideshow.

Tip: You can change the order of the photos just by dragging them around in the Sidebar, in any of its views.

Cropping graphics

To crop graphics in Preview, drag across the part of the graphic that you want to keep. To redraw, drag the round handles on the dotted rectangle; or, to proceed with the crop, choose Tools→Crop. (The keyboard shortcut is ⌘-K.)

Since Preview is an Autosave program, you can always return to the original if you change your mind someday.

Tip: You can also rotate an image in 90-degree increments and then flip it vertically or horizontally, using the commands in the Tools menu. In fact, if you select several thumbnails in the Sidebar first, you can rotate or flip them all simultaneously.

Fixing up photos

Preview is no Photoshop, but it's getting closer every year. Let us count the ways:

- **Choose Tools→Show Inspector.** A floating pane appears. Click the first tab to see the photo's name, when it was taken, its pixel dimensions, and so on. Click the second one for even more geeky details, including camera settings like the lens type, ISO setting, focus mode, whether the flash was on, and so on. The third tab lets you add keywords, so you'll be able to search for this image later using Spotlight. (The fourth is for PDF documents only, not photos; it lets you add annotations. A fifth tab appears only in PDF documents—for rotating, cropping, and resizing the file.)

- **Choose Tools→Adjust Color.** A translucent, floating color-adjustment palette appears, teeming with sliders for brightness, contrast, exposure, saturation (color intensity), temperature and tint (color cast), sharpness, and more. See Figure 19-23.

Figure 19-23:
Humble little Preview has grown up into a big, strong mini-Photoshop. You can really fix up a photo if you know what you're doing, using these sliders. Or you can just click the Auto Levels button. It sets all those sliders for you, which generally does an amazing job of making almost any photo look better.

- **Choose Tools→Adjust Size.** This command lets you adjust a photo's resolution, which comes in handy a lot. For example, you can scale an unwieldy 10-megapixel, gazillion-by-gazillion-pixel shot down to a nice 640 × 480 JPEG that's small enough to send by email. Or you can shrink a photo down so it fits within a desktop window, for use as a window background.

There's not much to it. Type in the new print dimensions you want for the photo, in inches or whatever units you choose from the pop-up menu. If you like, you can also change the resolution (the number of pixels per inch) by editing the Resolution box.

Cutting backgrounds out

Here's a Photoshoppy feature you would never, ever expect to find in a simple viewer like Preview: You can extract a person (or anything, really) from its background. That's handy when you want to clip yourself out of a group shot to use as your Messages portrait, when you want to paste somebody into a new background, or when you break up with someone and want them out of your photos.

If the background is simple—mostly a solid color or two—you can do this job quickly. Start by making sure the Markup toolbar is visible (Shift-⌘-A). Choose the Instant Alpha button, which looks like a wand doing some magic.

This feature is extremely weird, but here goes: Drag over the first background color you want to eliminate. Preview automatically dims out *all* the adjacent pixels that

POWER USERS' CLINIC

Scaling and Resampling

When you're fooling around with a picture's size and resolution in the Adjust Size dialog box, you might find that a couple of the options take a little explaining.

If "Scale proportionally" is turned on, Preview changes the Height number when you change the Width number, and vice versa. In other words, it won't let you change the *shape* of the photo; that's why a little padlock icon appears to bracket the Height and Width boxes.

If "Resample image" is turned off, then Preview adjusts the image's size by making the exist-

Image Dimensions	
Fit into:	Custom ⬍ pixels
Width:	0
Height:	6.67
Resolution:	72
	inches ⬍
	pixels/inch ⬍

☑ Scale proportionally
☑ Resample image

Resulting Size

52.8 percent

93 KB (was 253 KB)

Cancel OK

ing dots bigger or smaller—but never changes the *number* of dots. (That's why a padlock bracket links all three boxes together. For example, you can make the image larger—but you'll lower the number of dots per inch.)

If "Resample image" is turned *on,* then you're giving Preview permission to add or subtract pixels as necessary to scale the photo up or down. Of course, it can't create detail that wasn't there in the original, but if you're scaling the picture *up,* it does a decent job of generating new pixels by averaging the colors of the neighboring ones.

match the color you clicked. Hit Delete. Continue selecting and deleting until you have successfully isolated the subject from the background.

You've just created a graphic with an *alpha channel,* which, in computer-graphics terms, is a special mask that can be used for transparency or blending. The background you deleted—the empty gray part—appears transparent when you export it (File→Export) and then import it into certain graphically sophisticated programs. For example:

- **iMovie.** You can drag your exported graphic directly onto a filmstrip in an iMovie project. The white areas of the exported Preview image become transparent, so whatever video is already in the filmstrip plays through it. Great for opening credits or special effects.

- **Preview.** Yes, Preview itself recognizes incoming alpha channels. So after you cut the background out of Photo A, you can select what's left (press ⌘-A), copy it to the Clipboard (⌘-C), open Photo B, and then paste (⌘-V). The visible part of Photo A gets pasted into the background of Photo B.

- **Photoshop, Photoshop Elements.** Of course, these advanced graphics programs recognize alpha channels, too. Paste in your Preview graphic; it appears as a layer, with the existing layers shining through the empty areas.

Tip: Here's a great way to create a banner or headline for your Web page: Create a big, bold-font text block in TextEdit. Choose File→Print; from the PDF pop-up button, choose Open PDF in Preview.

In Preview, crop the document down and save it as a PNG-format graphic (because PNG recognizes alpha channels). Then use the Instant Alpha feature to dab out the background and the gaps inside the letters. When you import this image to your Web page, you'll find a professional-looking text banner that lets your page's background shine through the empty areas of the lettering.

Converting file formats

Preview doesn't just open all these file formats—it can also convert among most of them. You can pop open some old Mac PICT files and turn them into BMP files for a Windows user, pry open a TIFF file from a scanner and turn it into a JPEG for use on your Web site, and so on.

Tip: What's even cooler is you can open raw PostScript files right into Preview, which converts them into PDF files on the spot. You no longer need a PostScript laser printer to print out high-end diagrams and page layouts that come to you as PostScript files. Thanks to Preview, even an inkjet printer can handle them.

All you have to do is open the file you want to convert and choose File→Export. In the dialog box that appears, choose the new format for the image using the Format pop-up menu (JPEG, TIFF, PNG, or Photoshop, for example); if you press the Option key, you're offered even more file types. Finally, click Save to export the file.

Preview as PDF Reader

Preview is a nearly full-blown equivalent of Adobe Reader, the free program used by millions to read PDF documents. It lets you search PDF documents, copy text out of

them, add comments, fill in forms, click live hyperlinks, add highlighting, circle certain passages, type in notes—features that used to be available only in Adobe's Acrobat Reader. You can even fill out *PDF forms*, typing into boxes on the electronic document.

Tip: Don't forget that Preview is one of OS X's certified Full Screen apps, as described on page 160. You can also flip through the pages of a PDF using the "next page" gesture: a two-finger swipe on the trackpad.

Here are the basics:

- Zoom in and out using ⌘-plus and ⌘-minus.

Tip: Another way to get a closer look: Press the ` key (upper left of your keyboard), or choose Tools→Show Magnifier. Now a big magnifying glass follows your cursor; you can even press + or − to zoom in or out within it. Dismiss the magnifier by pressing ` again.

- Use the View menu commands to control how the PDF document appears: as two-page spreads; as single scrolling sheets of "paper towel"; with borders that indicate ends of pages; and so on.

- Press the space bar to page through a document (add Shift to page *upward*. The Page Up and Page Down keys do the same thing.)

Tip: Some PDF documents include a table of contents, which you'll see in Preview's Sidebar, complete with flippy triangles that denote chapter headings. Use the ▲ and ▼ keys to walk through these chapter headings, and then expand one that looks good by pressing the ▶ key. Collapse it again with the ◀ key. In other words, you expand and collapse flippy triangles in Preview just as you do in a Finder list view. (The View→Sidebar submenu also includes Expand All and Collapse All commands.)

- Bookmark your place by choosing Tools→Add Bookmark (⌘-D). You'll be able to return to that spot by choosing its name from the Bookmarks menu.

 These remain living, editable entities even after the document is saved and re-opened. These are full-blown Acrobat annotations; they'll show up when your PDF document is opened by Acrobat Reader or even on Windows PCs.

- Turn smoothing on or off to improve readability. To find the on/off switch, choose Preview→Preferences, and click the PDF tab. Turn on "Smooth text and line art." (Though antialiased text generally looks great, it's sometimes easier to read very small type with antialiasing turned off. It's a little jagged, but clearer nonetheless.)

- If you want to copy material out of a PDF document—for pasting into a word processor, for example, where you can edit it—click the Text tool (the letters Aa on the Markup toolbar) or choose Tools→Text Selection. Now you can drag through some text (and even graphics) and then choose Edit→Copy, just as though the PDF document were a Web page. You can even drag across page boundaries.

Tip: Ordinarily, dragging across text selects the text from one edge of the page to the other, even if the PDF document is laid out in columns. But Preview is a bit smarter. It can tell if you're trying to get the text in only one column and highlights just that part automatically.

- To find a word or phrase somewhere in a PDF document, press ⌘-F (or choose Edit→Find) to open the Find box—or just type into the �querybox. Proceed as shown in Figure 19-24.

Figure 19-24:
Type into the search box. Matches appear in the Sidebar, with page numbers; click one to go there. You can sort the found list either by rank (how likely Preview thinks it is to be what you're looking for) or in page order; click the appropriate button to sort.

The search results show a snippet of the actual text surrounding each "find," along with the number of matches per page, and even a thumbnail of the page itself. It's all about context, baby.

- You can save a single page from a PDF as a TIFF file to use it in other graphics, word processing, or page layout programs that might not directly recognize PDF.

To extract a page, use the usual File→Export command, making sure to choose the new file format from the pop-up menu. (If you choose a format like Photoshop or JPEG, Preview converts only the currently selected page of your PDF document. That's because there's no such thing as a multipage Photoshop or JPEG graphic. But you already knew that.)

Tip: You can also scan a new page directly into an open PDF document. Just choose File→Import from Scanner.

- Add keywords to a graphic or PDF (choose Tools→Show Inspector, click the ⌒ tab, click the + button). Later, you'll be able to call up these documents with a quick Spotlight search for those details.

Annotations and Drawing Tools

Preview in Yosemite has become the Godzilla of PDF editing programs. It is, in fact, a full-blown drawing program now, with a choice of shapes, colors, lines, arrows, and text boxes to dress up a PDF document. These are identical to the new drawing tools in Mail, so they're worth getting to know.

You can type notes (in a box or a bubble), add clickable links (to Web addresses or other spots in the document), or use circles, arrows, rectangles, strikethroughs, underlining, or colored highlighting to draw your PDF readers' attention to certain sections. (You can dress up photos this way, too.) In fact, in Yosemite, you can even use your laptop's trackpad to draw on a document—or to sign one.

To highlight text in a PDF document, click the ✎ button on the toolbar, and then drag across the text. Use the pop-up menu next to ✎ to choose a different highlighter color, or to choose underlining or strikethrough styles.

For the more ambitious annotation styles, like signing a document or drawing on it, open the Markup toolbar, shown in Figure 19-25. To do that, click ⊜ on the toolbar.

At this point, the icons on the toolbar offer these features:

- **AaI, ⊡ Text Selection, Rectangular Selection.** These tools let you highlight text in a document (so that you can copy it, for example) or select a chunk of a graphic.

- **✐ Sketch.** This remarkable new tool lets you draw freehand in your document—and marvel as Preview cleans up your lines. For example, if you draw what's more or less a diagonal line, Preview straightens it and makes it a perfect 45 degrees. If you draw what seems to be a box or a circle, Preview zaps it into perfection. Use the ≡˅, ▢˅, and ▨˅ buttons to specify the line thickness, add a colored border, or fill the interior with a background color. Figure 19-25 shows the process.

- **Shapes.** Use this pop-up menu to choose what kind of perfect shape you want to draw: line, arrow, circle, square, and so on. It will use whatever thickness and color you've chosen from the ≡˅ and ▢˅ pop-up menus.

Once you've selected a tool, drag diagonally on your document to place the shape.

The two icons at the bottom of this palette are unusual for a drawing program, but handy when you want to draw attention to some part of a document or photo.

At lower left in the Shapes pop-up menu, the Mask dims out the entire document except the rectangular portion you enclose. The one at lower right, the loupe, magnifies a circular area to draw the viewer's eye to it (Figure 19-25). Whatever attention-flagging markings you enclose using these tools become part of the finished, exported PDF or graphic.

- **T Text.** Click to place a text box on the image. You can drag it or reshape it—and, of course, you can replace the word "Text" inside it with much superior words of your own. Use the A˅ pop-up menu to choose a font, color, size, and style; use the ▢˅ and ▨˅ buttons to add a colored border or fill the interior with a background color.

- ⌒ **Signature.** See the next section for details.

- ▤ **Note.** Click to place a Post-it note onto the document. As you type or paste into it, the note expands; you can't otherwise control its size or shape. But when you click outside the note, it collapses down into a little square button. At this point, you can change the note's background color (right-click or two-finger click; choose a color from the shortcut menu); drag the little square to move the note; or open the note back up by double-clicking.

Tip: You can view a tidy list of all your notes and highlighted passages by choosing View→Highlighting and Notes. Preview ordinarily displays each text note with your name and the date. If you'd rather not have that info, then choose Preview→Preferences, click PDF, and then turn off "Add name to annotations."

Figure 19-25:
Top: As you draw a freehand shape, OS X helpfully straightens your straight lines and makes your curved ones perfect (middle).

If you actually prefer your imperfect original, then you can click the original (or any other variation) from the little floating palette (shown at left in the middle illustration).

Bottom: The Shapes pop-up menu (⬡⌄) offers a range of fascinating drawing options. They include the classic Speech Bubble (left) and the loupe, which produces a magnified view of one circular area (center).

While you're editing a loupe, you see a tiny green dot. Drag it to adjust the magnification inside the circle; drag the blue one to change the circle's size.

- ☰⌄ **Shape Style.** This palette governs the line thickness and line style of whatever line or shape you're drawing (or that you've selected). There are some very cool options here, including dashed lines, shadowed ones, or chalky-looking ones—and ones with arrowheads.

- ▣⌄, ⊘⌄ **Border Color, Fill Color.** These palettes affect the border color (line color) and interior background color of whatever shape you're drawing (or have selected).

- *A*⌄ **Text Style.** Here are your font, size, and style commands for whatever text you're about to type (or have selected).

Once you've made an annotation, you can drag it around, drag its blue control dots to change its shape, edit the text inside it, and so on.

Signing PDF Documents with Your Real Signature

Of OS X's 47,000 features, few are quite as slick or useful as the PDF signature option. It lets your Mac memorize your signature, either by taking a picture of it—or by letting you sign with your finger on your laptop's trackpad (a new feature in Yosemite).

Once Preview has stored your signature, you can slap it into the PDF documents that will come through your life.

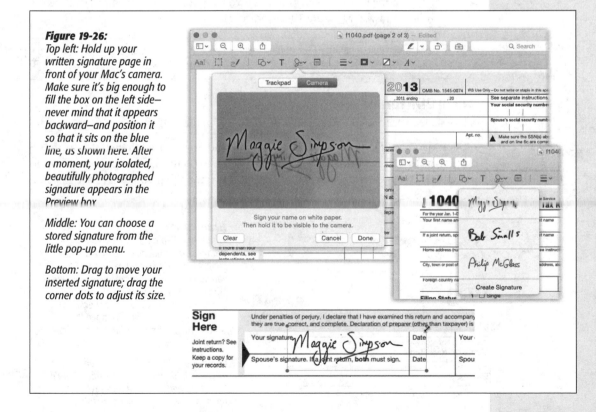

Figure 19-26:
Top left: Hold up your written signature page in front of your Mac's camera. Make sure it's big enough to fill the box on the left side—never mind that it appears backward—and position it so that it sits on the blue line, as shown here. After a moment, your isolated, beautifully photographed signature appears in the Preview box.

Middle: You can choose a stored signature from the little pop-up menu.

Bottom: Drag to move your inserted signature; drag the corner dots to adjust its size.

The first step is to teach Preview what your signature looks like. On the Markup toolbar, click the Signature pop-up menu, ⚲∨. In the resulting window, you're offered two tabs:

- **Trackpad.** If your Mac has a trackpad, this option lets you write out your signature with your finger! Click where it says "Click Here to Begin," and then draw away.

 Plan ahead; the width of the trackpad is all the space you've got. When you're done, press any key, and then click Done. The result may not look exactly like your pen-and-paper signature, but it'll do for most purposes.

- **Camera.** Sign your name on a piece of white paper; hold it up to your Mac's camera, as shown in Figure 19-26. When the positioning looks good, click Done. You've just stored your signature. (You have to do this only once—per signature, anyway.)

Tip: As a handy bonus, whatever signatures you've saved this way also appear in Preview on all your *other* Macs. (At least those that are signed into your same iCloud account and are running Yosemite—and have iCloud Keychain turned on in Settings→iCloud.)

Now then. When the time comes to sign a document, make the Markup toolbar visible. From the ⚲∨ pop-up menu, choose the signature's name (Figure 19-26, middle.)

The signature appears in its own graphics box. Drag it to a new position, or drag the blue handles to resize it (Figure 19-26, bottom).

Tip: To delete a signature, open the ⚲∨ pop-up menu, point to the signature, and click the ⊗ next to it in the menu.

Fill in PDF Forms

Here's a feature that could save a lot of trees: fill-inable PDF forms.

Lots and lots of PDF documents are forms that you're supposed to fill out—from IRS tax forms to school permission slips. Preview is smart enough to recognize boxes to fill in, lines to type on, and checkboxes to click, meaning that you don't have to print,

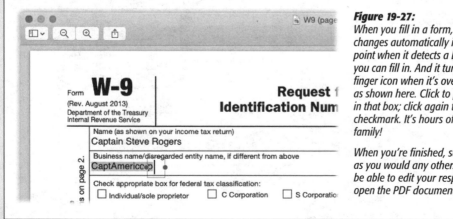

Figure 19-27:
When you fill in a form, the cursor changes automatically into an insertion point when it detects a box or a line that you can fill in. And it turns into a pointing-finger icon when it's over a checkbox, as shown here. Click to put a checkmark in that box; click again to remove the checkmark. It's hours of fun for the whole family!

When you're finished, save the document as you would any other. Amazingly, you'll be able to edit your responses when you open the PDF document again later.

fill out, and then scan these things anymore. And it manages to find those lines, text boxes, and checkboxes on *any* PDF document, not just those that were originally designed to be filled in by PDF form-filling software. See Figure 19-27.

The Toolbar

There's a lot you can do with Preview's toolbar. You can customize it (by choosing View→Customize Toolbar), rearrange its icons (by ⌘-dragging them sideways), and remove icons (by ⌘-dragging them downward).

QuickTime Player

This little app opens when you double-click any kind of movie file. Press Play to play and stop the show. The control toolbar at the bottom of the window fades away after a few seconds and reappears anytime your mouse moves back into the movie frame. Click the Full Screen button (⊘)to make the video fill your entire monitor, just as though you'd chosen View→Enter Full Screen.

But wait, there's more! QuickTime Player is also QuickTime Editor. You can:

- **Edit movies** using the Trim, Split, Cut, Copy, and Paste commands in the Edit menu.

- **Record movies** (using your Mac's camera) using File→New Movie Recording.

- **Record screen activity** by choosing File→New Screen Recording and then clicking the red Record button. Click the ■ button to stop recording.

- **Export your video** directly to YouTube, Vimeo, Flickr, or Facebook by choosing from the ⬆ menu. Sign into your online account, enter keywords and so on, and then click Share. (The same ⬆ menu lets you send the movie as an email attachment, an iMessage, or a transmission to a nearby Mac by AirDrop.) Or use File→Export to save the movie to your hard drive.

Reminders

Reminders is a To Do-list program. It not only records your life's little tasks, but also reminds you about them when the time comes. On a laptop, Reminders can even remind you about something based on *where you are,* just as it does on the iPhone. For example, when you arrive home each day, it can remind you to feed your cats—or when you leave your vacation house, it can ask you if you've turned off the gas burners.

If you have an iCloud account, your reminders sync across all your gadgets. Create or check off a task on your iPhone, and you'll also find it created or checked off on your Mac, iPhone, iPad, iPod Touch, or PC. (Yes, PC. See *www.apple.com/icloud/setup/pc.html*).

The syncing business also explains why the location feature is useful even if you have a desktop Mac that doesn't move around a lot. You can program a reminder on your Mac—and your *phone or tablet* will alert you when you move into or away from a specified place.

Tip: If you have an iPhone—oh, wow. Siri and Reminders are a match made in heaven. "Remind me to file the Jenkins report when I get to work." "Remind me to set the TiVo for tonight at 8." "Remind me about Timmy's soccer game a week from Saturday." "Add waffles to my Groceries list." Speech recognition rocks when it comes to leaving notes for yourself. And iCloud will take care of copying those reminders to your Mac.

Once you've opened Reminders (Figure 19-28), you record a new task by clicking the + button in the upper right, or choose File→New Reminder (⌘-N). A new blank line appears in your list. Type your reminder.

Later, as you go through life completing tasks, click the checkbox next to each one. Doing that makes the item seem to disappear—but in fact, it whips into a separate list called Completed (the top of the list, shown in Figure 19-28).

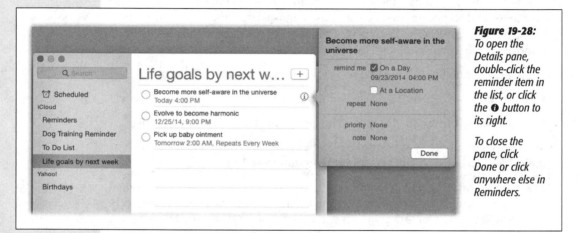

Figure 19-28:
To open the Details pane, double-click the reminder item in the list, or click the ❶ button to its right.

To close the pane, click Done or click anywhere else in Reminders.

The Details Bubble

If you click an item's ⓘ button, you open the Details bubble. See Figure 19-28.

Here are the options you'll find:

- **On a Day.** Reminders can remind you at a certain time on a certain date. In the Details bubble, next to "remind me," turn on On a Day. The proposed time is the next "o'clock"—if it's 12:15 now, the app suggests 1:00. But you can click the date to open a clickable mini-calendar (to change the date), or click the digits of the time to edit them.

- **At a location.** If you turn on this checkbox, your Mac or phone will use its location circuits to remind you of this item when you arrive at a certain place or leave a certain place. (Your laptop will remind you, if it's turned on and within a WiFi hotspot. But more often, this option will be useful if you have an iPhone or iPad that's on the same iCloud account. Record the reminder on your Mac—receive the reminder on your phone.)

The little pop-up menu here proposes Current Location—wherever you are at the moment. That's handy if, for example, you're dropping off your dry cleaning and want to remember to pick it up the next time you're driving by.

But you can click that line to specify Home (your home address, as you've set it up in Contacts). You can also start typing any city name, or the name of any person in your Contacts whose address you've specified. You'll even see "Porky Pig Home" and "Porky Pig Work," if Porky has a couple of addresses on file.

The final step here is to click either Leaving or Arriving. Later, your gadgets will remind you at the appointed time, or as you approach (or leave) the appointed address. It's fairly mind-blowing the first few times it happens.

- **Repeat.** Reminders can remind you about things that recur in your life, like quarterly tax payments, haircuts, and anniversaries. Click Repeat if you want this reminder to appear every day, week, two weeks, month, or year. (This option appears only if you've turned on the On a Day option.)

- **Priority.** Click this pop-up menu to specify whether this item has High, Medium, or Low priority—or None. You'll see one, two, or three exclamation marks (!!!) next to each item in your Reminders list, indicating its urgency. In some of the calendar programs that sync with Reminders, you can sort your task list by priority.

- **Notes.** Here's a handy place where you can record freehand notes about this item: an address, a phone number, details of any kind.

Click Done to close the Details bubble and record your changes.

The Calendar of Deadline Hell

As you now know, Reminders can give you warnings of upcoming deadlines and to-do items. You don't have to wait until it gives you a reminder, though. Click Scheduled at the top of the list to review a list of all upcoming reminders.

Lists

Handily enough, you can create *more than one* to-do list, each with its own name: a Groceries list, Kids' Chores, a running tally of expenses, and so on. Here's a great way to log what you eat if you're on a diet, or to keep a list of movies people recommend.

If you share an iCloud account with another family member, you might create a different Reminder list for each person. (Of course, now you run the risk that your spouse might sneakily add items to *your* to-do list!)

If you have an Exchange account, one of your lists can be synced to your corporate Tasks list. It doesn't offer all the features of the other lists in Reminders, but at least it's kept tidy and separate. (Just set up your Exchange account in System Preferences→Internet Accounts.)

The list of lists is at the left side of Reminders; it's visible in Figure 19-28.

At the outset, the list of lists lists only one list: Reminders. But you can create others. Click the + button at the bottom-left corner, or choose File→New List. (If you have

more than one online account set up, like an iCloud account and a Yahoo account, you'll then have to specify which account gets this list).

In any case, you've just made a new list called New List. Type to rename it to "Groceries list," "Movies list," whatever you like. (You can also get rid of a list by clicking it and then pressing the Delete key.)

Tip: You can view the contents of more than one list simultaneously. Just Shift-click the names of the lists you want in the left column; the right-side pane displays a unified, combined list of all their contents.

You can also open a list into a window of its own, just by double-clicking its name in the left column.

Once you've created some lists, you have two ways to switch among them:

- **Swipe two fingers across the trackpad.** The lists slide into view as though they're successive photos in a slideshow.

- **Click a different list in the list of lists.** Or press the ▲ and ▼ keys to "walk" through the list.

You can assign a task to a different list by dragging it. Click any blank part of its line (not the text itself), and drag carefully onto the name of a different list in the List list at left.

Syncing Reminders

Once you've set up a few reminders in Reminders, you'll marvel as it gracefully integrates with the Notification Center when it wants your attention.

But the real power of Reminders becomes apparent when you see it auto-synchronize your to-do lists across other gadgets, like iPhones, iPads, iPod Touches, other Macs, and even Windows PCs.

To give it permission for that kind of sharing, open System Preferences→iCloud and turn on the Reminders checkbox.

Note, however, that Reminders can also coordinate with the to-do list features of Exchange and so-called CalDAV services (Yahoo is one). To set them up, open System Preferences→Internet Accounts. Click the account you want (like Exchange or Yahoo); finally, turn the Reminders switch On.

That should do it. Now your to-do lists are synced, both ways.

Tip: You can also export your lists as .ics files, which you can then import into Google Calendar or another program. Just click the list and then choose File→Export. You can also *import* an existing .ics file (from another computer, for example) into a Reminders list you've selected: It's File→Import, of course.

Safari

The secrets of Apple's Web browser are revealed in Chapter 12.

Stickies

Even in the age of the far more modern Notes program, the old Stickies app is still creaking along. It creates virtual Post-it notes that you can stick anywhere on your screen.

You can use Stickies for quick notes and to-do items, Web addresses or phone numbers you need to remember, or any other little scraps and snippets of text you come across. They all show up whenever the Stickies program is running (Figure 19-29).

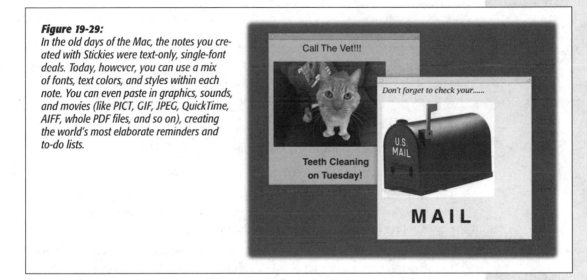

Figure 19-29:
In the old days of the Mac, the notes you created with Stickies were text-only, single-font deals. Today, however, you can use a mix of fonts, text colors, and styles within each note. You can even paste in graphics, sounds, and movies (like PICT, GIF, JPEG, QuickTime, AIFF, whole PDF files, and so on), creating the world's most elaborate reminders and to-do lists.

Creating Sticky Notes

The first time you launch Stickies, a couple of sample notes appear automatically, describing some of the program's features. You can quickly dispose of each sample by clicking the close button in the upper-left corner of each note or by choosing File→Close (⌘-W). Each time you close a note, a dialog box asks if you want to save it. If you click Don't Save (or press ⌘-D), the note disappears permanently.

To create a new note, choose File→New Note (⌘-N). Then start typing or:

- **Drag text in from any other program.** Or drag text clippings from the desktop directly into your note. You can also drag a graphics file into a note to add a picture. You can even drag a sound or movie in.

- **Drag the icon of a PDF file into a note.** (Stickies can even accommodate multipage PDF files. At first, you see only the first page, but the scroll bar reveals the rest.)

- **Choose File→Import Text** and select any plain text file or RTF (Rich Text Format) document to bring it into a note.

- **Drag URLs** into a note directly from a Web browser's address bar.

Tip: If one particular note contains your most important information—your to-do list, say—you can force it to remain in front of all other windows, even if Stickies itself gets shunted to the background. Just click the note, and then choose Note→Floating Window.

- **In many Apple programs, you can select a chunk of text** and then choose Make New Sticky Note from the program's Services menu, or press Shift-⌘-Y. This command launches Stickies, creates a new note, and fills it with your selected text—all in one step.

Note: All your notes are stored in a file called *StickiesDatabase*, located in your Home→Library folder. You're free to copy it, pass it along, and so on, just as you would any file.

Have a favorite style for your sticky notes? First create a new note, choosing the color and text style you like and setting it to the size you prefer. Then choose Note→Use as Default. All new notes you create now appear in the size, font, and color you've chosen.

Growing and Shrinking Notes

Stickies includes a few built-in tricks for managing a deskful of notes:

- **Drag any point of the perimeter of the sticky note to resize it.**

- **Use the small triangle in the upper-right corner** of each note to zoom and shrink note windows with a single click. The first click expands a note nearly to full-screen size. Another click pops the note back down to normal size.

- **The best option: Double-click anywhere** along the dark strip at the top of each note to collapse it into a compact one-line mini-note. You also can collapse a selected note by choosing Window→Collapse (⌘-M).

Tip: The most efficient way to use Stickies is to keep the notes in their collapsed state. When a note is collapsed, the first line of text shows up in tiny type in the collapsed title bar of the note, so you don't have to expand the note to remember what's in it. Plenty of notes can be summed up in a couple of words ("Pick up dry cleaning," "Call Mom"), so you may even be able to leave your notes this way.

Formatting Notes

Stickies has word processor–like commands for creating designer sticky notes, with any combination of fonts, colors, and styles (explore the Font menu). You can also choose from six background colors from the Color menu.

Saving Sticky Notes

The notes you create in Stickies last only as long as you keep them open. If you close a note to get it out of the way (and click Don't Save in the confirmation box), it vanishes permanently.

If you want to preserve the information you've stuffed into your notes in a more permanent form, use File→Export Text to save each note as a standalone TextEdit document. When you use the Export Text command, you have the following options:

- **Plain Text.** This option saves your note as a plain text file, with neither formatting nor pictures.

- **RTF.** RTF stands for Rich Text Format, a special exchange format that preserves most formatting, including font, style, and color choices. You can open the resulting RTF file in just about any word processor with all your formatting still intact.

- **RTFD.** RTFD, a strange and powerful variant of RTF, is a Rich Text Format document *with attachments.* How do you "attach" items to an RTFD file? Drag the icon of an actual application (Preview, Calculator, or whatever) or a multipage PDF file, into a sticky note. The icon for the program or document appears in the note, but double-clicking the icon doesn't do anything. When you export the note as an RTFD file, the result is a TextEdit document that has embedded within it the *entire* program or document you dragged in. The program icon appears just as it did in the sticky note, but if you double-click the icon, the program actually opens.

You can also paste a graphic into your sticky note. When you export the note as an RTFD document, the resulting *package* file includes a graphics file of the format you pasted.

System Preferences

This program opens the door to the nerve center of OS X's various user preferences, settings, and options. Chapter 17 covers every option in detail.

TextEdit

TextEdit is a basic word processor—but it's not nearly as basic as people think it is. You can create real documents with real formatting, using style sheets, colors, automatic numbering and bullets, tables, and customized line spacing. You can even open, edit, and create Microsoft Word documents. If you had to, you could write a children's book in TextEdit, and it would look pretty decent.

Better yet, TextEdit (Figure 19-30) is now a showcase for OS X's iPaddish features, like Full Screen mode, Auto Save, and Versions (see Chapter 4). It can also save your files into your iCloud Drive, as described on page 211.

And TextEdit works with OS X's long list of built-in text-editing features: smart links, smart quotes, smart dashes, smart copy/paste, abbreviation expansion, auto–typo correction, data detectors, and so on. They're all described in Chapter 5.

Tip: You can magnify the type size of a TextEdit document just the way you do on an iPhone or an iPad: by pinching or spreading. That is, spread two fingers on your trackpad to enlarge the type, or pinch on the trackpad to shrink it. Best. Tip. Ever.

TextEdit's Two Personalities

The one confusing aspect of TextEdit is that it's both a *plain text editor* (no formatting; globally compatible) and a true *word processor* (fonts, sizes, styles; compatible with other word processors). Here's the scheme:

- You can change a plain text document to a formatted one by choosing Format→ Make Rich Text. The ruler appears automatically to remind you that a new world of formatting has just become available.

- Conversely, you can change a formatted document (a Word file you've opened, for example) to a plain text document by choosing Format→Make Plain Text. An alert message appears to point out that you're about to lose all formatting.

- If you know what kind of document you *always* want to open, go to the TextEdit→ Preferences dialog box; on the New Document tab, select Rich Text or Plain Text. That's what you'll get each time you choose File→New.

Tip: Here's also where you can turn on smart links, smart quotes, smart dashes, and the other smart text-processing features described in Chapter 5.

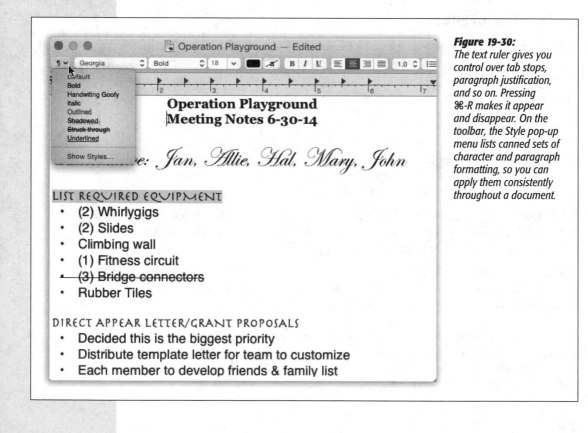

Figure 19-30:
The text ruler gives you control over tab stops, paragraph justification, and so on. Pressing ⌘-R makes it appear and disappear. On the toolbar, the Style pop-up menu lists canned sets of character and paragraph formatting, so you can apply them consistently throughout a document.

Working in TextEdit

As you begin typing, all the usual word processing rules apply, with a few twists:

- Choose bold, italic, and font sizes using the new formatting toolbar. (You can still use the commands in the Format menu.) You can even create subscripts or superscripts, change the color of the text (Format→Font→Show Colors), and so on.

- Common paragraph-alignment options—Align Left, Align Right, Center, Justify—are all available as toolbar buttons and also reside in the Format→Text submenu. Adjust the line spacing (single, double, or any fraction or multiple) using the Spacing pop-up menu in the toolbar.

- The toolbar also offers automatic bulleting and numbering of paragraphs. Just choose the numbering style you prefer from the pop-up menu at the right end of the toolbar.

- You can select several nonadjacent bits of text *simultaneously*. To pull this off, highlight your first piece of text by dragging, and then press ⌘ as you use the mouse to select more text. Bingo: You've highlighted two separate chunks of text.

When you're done selecting bits of text here and there, you can operate on them en masse. For example, you can make them all bold or italic in one fell swoop. You can even use the Cut, Copy, and Paste commands, as described in the next section. When you cut or copy, the command acts upon all your selections at once.

UP TO SPEED

The Deal with Microsoft Word

Yes, it's true: Humble TextEdit can open and create Microsoft Word documents! Your savings: the $400 price of Microsoft Office!

Well, sort of.

When you open a Microsoft Word document in TextEdit, most of the formatting comes through alive: bold, italic, font choices, colors, line spacing, alignment, and so on. Even very basic tables make it into TextEdit, although with different column widths.

A lot of Word-specific formatting does not survive crossing the chasm, however: borders, style sheets, footnotes, and the like. Bullets and numbered lists don't make it, either, even though TextEdit can create its own versions of these. And TextEdit doesn't recognize the comments and tracked changes your collaborators might use to mark up your manuscript.

Saving a new TextEdit document as a Word document is a better bet, because Word understands the many kinds of formatting that TextEdit can produce—including bullets, numbering, and tables. (You can create a Word file the first time you save it from TextEdit, or you can convert a document into Word format later by choosing File→Duplicate and then File→Save.)

The one disappointment is that Word doesn't recognize any style sheets you've set up in TextEdit. The formatting applied by those style names survives—just not the style names themselves.

Even so, a built-in Word-document editor is a huge, huge step for the Mac operating system. It means that in many cases, you can be a first-class citizen on the playing field of American business. Nobody ever needs to know that you're (a) using a Mac, and (b) not using the real Microsoft Word.

You can also drag any *one* of the highlighted portions to a new area, confident that the other chunks will come along for the ride. All the selected areas wind up consolidated in their new location.

Tip: If you *Option*-drag one of the highlighted bits, you *copy* all selected chunks, leaving the originals in place.

- Similarly, you can use the Find command. To do that, choose Edit→Find→Find (or just press ⌘-F). Fill in the search box; the sought-for term appears highlighted everywhere in your document at once. (You can also search and *replace,* using the other commands in the Edit→Find submenu.)

- If you Option-drag vertically, you can freely select an arbitrary column of text (not necessarily the entire page width). This technique is very useful when you want to select only one column in a multicolumn layout, or when you want to select the numbers in a list and format them all at once.

Style Sheets

A *style* is a prepackaged collection of formatting attributes that you can apply and reapply with a click of the mouse (bold, 24-point Optima, double-spaced, centered, for instance). You can create as many styles as you need: chapter headings, sidebar styles, and so on. You end up with a collection of custom-tailored styles for each of the repeating elements of your document.

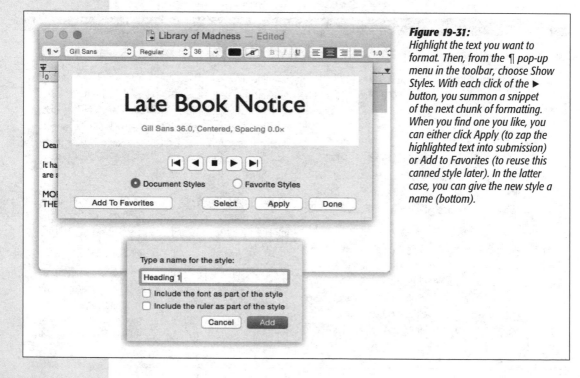

Figure 19-31:
Highlight the text you want to format. Then, from the ¶ pop-up menu in the toolbar, choose Show Styles. With each click of the ▶ button, you summon a snippet of the next chunk of formatting. When you find one you like, you can either click Apply (to zap the highlighted text into submission) or Add to Favorites (to reuse this canned style later). In the latter case, you can give the new style a name (bottom).

Once you've created your styles, you can apply them as you need them, safe in the knowledge that they'll be consistent throughout the document. During the editing process, if you notice that you accidentally styled a *headline* using the *Subhead* style, you can fix the problem by simply reapplying the correct style.

Note: Unlike a real word processor, TextEdit doesn't let you *change* a style's formatting and thereby update every occurrence of it. Fortunately, you *can* search for all occurrences of a style and change them all simultaneously (see page 693).

- **Creating a named style.** To create a style, format some text so it looks the way you like it, complete with font, color, line spacing, tab settings, and so on.

POWER USERS' CLINIC

Advanced Typography in TextEdit

If you just sprayed your coffee upon reading the heading of this sidebar, you're forgiven. Advanced typography in TextEdit? Isn't that a little bit like saying, "advanced page layout in Notepad"?

Not at all. TextEdit is a gleaming showcase for OS X's typographical smarts.

Most of the commands in the Format→Font submenu should be familiar to you: Bold, Italic, Underline, and so on. But a few were once found only in expensive page-layout programs like InDesign and QuarkXPress. For example:

Kern. Use these commands, such as Tighten and Loosen, to nudge the letters of the selected text closer together or farther apart—an especially useful feature when you're fiddling with headlines and headings.

There are no controls to set how much you want to kern the text, but you can apply these commands repeatedly to the same text selection to intensify them. If you want your text to be very tight, for example, just keep choosing the Tighten command. The characters creep closer and closer together until they crash into one another.

Ligature. Ligatures are letter pairs, such as fl and ff, that, in fancy typesetting, are often conjoined into special combi-

nation characters, as shown here. If you choose Format→ Font→Ligature→Use Default (or Use All), then TextEdit displays these letter pairs with the appropriate ligatures. (This works only if the font you're using has those ligatures built into it. New York, Charcoal, Apple Chancery, and all Adobe Expert fonts do, for example, but many other fonts don't.)

Baseline. The baseline is the imaginary "floor" for text characters in a line of type. You can push text above this line or sink it below the baseline using the Raise and Lower commands in the Baseline submenu. The Superscript and Subscript commands, meanwhile, shift characters far above or below the baseline, so you can write stuff like "H_2O."

Character Shape. In a few fonts, such as Adobe Expert fonts, this submenu offers a choice between Traditional Form and specialized type treatments like Small Caps.

Copy Style/Paste Style. If mastering styles is just too much effort, then these commands offer another way to copy and paste just the font formatting to other text—the font, color, style, and size, but none of the actual text or paragraph attributes, such as alignment.

Then, from the ¶ pop-up menu at the left end of the toolbar, choose Show Styles (Figure 19-31). Click Add to Favorites, type a name for the style, turn on both checkboxes, and then click Add.

Figure 19-32:
Note to Web designers: TextEdit may not be Dreamweaver, but it's great for spinning out quick Web pages, thanks to the table features. Here you can see that a big table forms the underlying structure for this Web page, along with a couple of nested ones and color selections.

- **Applying a style.** Later, when you want to reuse the formatting you set up, highlight some text and then choose the appropriate name from the ¶ pop-up menu. TextEdit applies the formatting immediately.

Tip: *If you simply click inside a paragraph, applying a style affects only paragraph attributes, like line spacing, tab stops, and alignment. If you highlight a random chunk of text instead, applying a style affects only character attributes, like the font and type size. If you highlight an entire paragraph, however, both text and paragraph formatting appear.*

- **Deleting a style.** To delete a superfluous style, choose Show Styles from the ¶ pop-up menu on the toolbar. Click the Favorite Styles button, choose the unwanted style's name from the pop-up menu, and then click Remove From Favorites. (Deleting a style doesn't affect any formatting that's already in your document; it just removes the name from the Styles menu.)

- **Replacing all occurrences.** You can highlight every occurrence of a certain style at once—and then change, copy, or delete them all at once.

To make this work, choose Show Styles from the ¶ pop-up menu. Choose the style you want to work on. (If "Document styles" is selected, click the ▶ button to page through the styles; if "Favorite styles" is selected, choose from the pop-up menu.) Then click Select.

In the little details sheet that appears, click the options you want, and then click Select. TextEdit highlights every occurrence of that style in the entire document (or selection). At this point, you can use any of the usual text-formatting controls to modify them all simultaneously.

- **Formatting by example.** In TextEdit, you can also use Option-⌘-C and Option-⌘-V (Format→Font→Copy Style and Format→Font→Paste Style) to grab formatting from one place in your document and reuse it elsewhere. (Of course, you can't apply styles in text-only documents.)

Tables

Tables can make life a lot easier when you want to create a resumé, agenda, program booklet, list, multiple-choice test, Web page, or another document where numbers, words, and phrases must be aligned across the page. In the bad old days, people did it by pressing the Tab key to line up columns—a technique that turned into a nightmare as soon as you tried to add or delete text. But using a word processor's *table* feature is light-years easier and more flexible, because each row of a table expands to contain whatever you put into it. Everything else in its row remains aligned.

Tip: Tables are sometimes used for designing Web pages. Even though you can't see the table outlines, many a Web page is filled with columns of text that are aligned invisibly by tables. And now that TextEdit can save your work as an HTML document, it's suddenly a viable candidate for designing basic Web pages.

- **Create a table** by choosing Format→Table. The floating Table palette appears (Figure 19-32). Use it to specify how many rows and columns you want. The placeholder table in your document adjusts itself in real time.

- **Format the table** using the other controls in the Table palette. The Alignment controls let you specify how the text in the table cells hugs its border. Cell Border controls the thickness of the line around the selected cells' borders (or, if you enter *0*, makes the table walls invisible). The color swatch next to Cell Border specifies the color of the solid lines. The Cell Background controls let you color in the table cells with colors of your choice. (Choose Color Fill from the pop-up menu, and then click the color swatch.) This is an especially valuable option for Web designers.

- **Adjust the rows and columns** by dragging the cell borders.

- **Merge two selected cells** by clicking Merge Cells in the Table palette. Once you've done that, you can use the Split Cell button to split them apart again. (Split Cell doesn't work except in cells you've previously merged.)

- **Nest one table inside a cell of another** by clicking in the cell and then clicking Nest Table. Change the numbers in the Rows and Columns boxes to set up its dimensions (Figure 19-32).

TextEdit as Web Designer

The Table palette isn't the only clue that Apple intends TextEdit to be a quick-and-dirty Web page design program. Consider these other tools:

- You can easily add graphics to the page by dragging or pasting them into a document. The program understands TIFF, PICT, JPEG, and GIF formats.

- You can add Web-style hyperlinks by highlighting "Click here" (or whatever the link says), choosing Edit→Add Link, and then entering the Web address in the resulting dialog box. Or just drag a link in from Safari, Mail, or another program. (To edit the link later, right-click it (or two-finger click it), and then choose Edit Link.)

Tip: Of course, you can also have TextEdit convert typed links into clickable ones *automatically* as you type them. That's the purpose of the Smart Links option in TextEdit→Preferences.

- To save a brand-new document as an HTML (Web page) file, choose File→Save; from the File Format pop-up menu, choose Web Page. (To save an existing TextEdit document as an HTML file, choose File→Duplicate and then File→Save; choose Web Page from the pop-up menu.)

- Don't miss the HTML options in TextEdit→Preferences. On the Open and Save tab, you can specify what kind of HTML document you want to produce, what cascading style sheets (CSS) setting you want, and whether or not you want TextEdit to include code to preserve blank areas (white space) in your layout.

Tip: When you open a Web page document—that is, an HTML document—TextEdit is faced with a quandary. Should it open up the page as though it's a Web page, interpreting the HTML code as though it's a browser? Or should it reveal the underlying HTML code itself?

Actually, that's up to you. When you choose File→Open, turn on "Ignore rich text commands" to make the document open up as HTML code. (To make this change permanent, turn on the "Display HTML files as HTML code instead of formatted text" checkbox on the Open and Save pane of the TextEdit→Preferences dialog box.)

Time Machine

This marquee feature of OS X is described in Chapter 5.

Utilities: Your OS X Toolbox

The Utilities folder (inside your Applications folder) is home to another batch of freebies: a couple of dozen tools for monitoring, tuning, tweaking, and troubleshooting your Mac.

The truth is, you're likely to use only about six of these utilities. The rest are very specialized gizmos primarily of interest to network administrators or Unix geeks who are obsessed with knowing what kind of computer-code gibberish is going on behind the scenes.

Tip: Even so, Apple obviously noticed that as the sophistication of OS X fans grows, more people open the Utilities folder more often. That's why there's a menu command and a keystroke that can take you there. In the Finder, choose Go→Utilities (Shift-⌘-U).

Activity Monitor

Activity Monitor is designed to let the technologically savvy Mac fan see how much of the Mac's available power is being tapped at any given moment.

The Processes table

Even when you're only running a program or two on your Mac, dozens of computational tasks (*processes*) are going on in the background. The top half of the dialog box, which looks like a table, shows you all the different processes—visible and invisible—that your Mac is handling at the moment.

Check out how many items appear in the Process list, even when you're just staring at the desktop. It's awesome to see just how busy your Mac is! Some are easily recognizable programs (such as Finder), while others are background system-level operations you don't normally see. For each item, you can see the percentage of the CPU being used, who's using it (either your account name, someone else's, or *root*, meaning the Mac itself), whether or not it's been written as a 64-bit app, and how much memory it's using.

Or use the View menu above the list to see views like these:

- **All Processes.** This is the complete list of running processes; you'll notice that the vast majority are little Unix applications you never even knew you had.

- **All Processes, Hierarchically.** In Unix, one process launches another, creating a tree-like hierarchy. The big daddy of them all is the process called *launchd*. Here and there, you'll see some other interesting relationships. For example, the Dock launches DashboardClient.

- **My Processes.** This list shows only the programs that pertain to *your* world, your login. There are still plenty of unfamiliar items, but they're all running to serve *your* account.

- **System Processes.** These are the processes run by *root*—that is, opened by OS X itself.

- **Other User Processes.** Here's a list of all *other* processes—"owned" by neither root nor you. Here you might see the processes being run by another account holder, for example (using fast user switching), or people who have connected to this Mac from across a network or the Internet.

- **Active Processes, Inactive Processes.** Active processes are the ones that are actually doing something right now; inactive are the ones that are sitting there, waiting for a signal (like a keypress or a mouse click).

- **Windowed Processes.** Now *this* is probably what you were expecting: a list of actual programs with actual English names, like Activity Monitor, Finder, Safari, and Mail. These are the only ones running in actual windows, the only ones that are *visible*.

The System monitor tabs

At the top of Activity Monitor, you're offered five tabs that reveal intimate details about your Mac and its behind-the-scenes efforts (Figure 19-33):

Figure 19-33:
The many faces of Activity Monitor.

Top: It can be a graph of your processor (CPU) activity, your RAM usage at the moment, your disk capacity, and so on. For most people, only the processes listed here with tiny icons beside their names are actual windowed programs—those with icons in the Finder, the ones you actually interact with.

The top-left Quit Process button (⊗) is a convenient way to jettison a locked-up program when all else fails.

Bottom: If you double-click a process's name, you get a dialog box that offers stunningly complete reams of data (mostly of interest only to programmers) about what that program is up to. (The Open Files and Ports tab, for example, shows you how many files that program has opened, often invisibly.)

- **CPU.** As you go about your usual Mac business, opening a few programs, playing QuickTime movies, playing a game, and so on, you can see the CPU graphs rise and fall, depending on how busy you're keeping the CPU. You see a different graph color for each of your Mac's cores (independent sub-chips on your processor), so you can see how efficiently OS X is distributing the work among them.

Tip: You may also want to watch this graph right in your Dock (choose View→Dock Icon→Show CPU Usage) or in a small floating window that you can move around your screen (choose Window→CPU Usage, or click ⌘-2).

Finally, there's the Window→CPU History command. It makes a resizable, real-time monitor window float on top of all your other programs, so you can't miss it.

- **Memory.** Here's a glorious revelation of the state of your Mac's RAM at the moment.

 The graph shows "memory pressure"—how much your programs are straining the Mac's memory. If, when your Mac is running a typical complement of programs, this graph is nearly filled up, it's time to consider buying more memory. You're suffocating your Mac.

- **Energy.** How much battery power is each of your programs responsible for sucking away? This fascinating tab tells all—including which programs are currently enjoying an App Nap (page 21).

- **Disk.** Even when you're not opening or saving a file, your Mac's hard drive or flash storage is frequently hard at work, shuffling chunks of program code into and out of memory, for example. Here's where the savvy technician can see exactly how frantic the disk is at the moment.

- **Network.** Keep an eye on how much data is shooting across your office network with this handy tsunami of real-time data.

AirPort Utility

You use the AirPort Utility to set up and manage AirPort base stations (Apple's wireless WiFi networking routers).

If you click Continue, it presents a series of screens, posing one question at a time: what you want to name the network, what password you want for it, and so on. Once you've followed the steps and answered the questions, your AirPort hardware will be properly configured and ready to use.

Audio MIDI Setup

This program has a split personality; its name is a description of its two halves:

- **Audio.** When you first open Audio MIDI Setup, you see a complete summary of the audio inputs and outputs available on your Mac right now. It's a lot like the Sound pane of System Preferences, but with a lot more geeky detail. Here, for example, you can specify the recording level for your Mac's microphone, or even change the audio quality it records.

 For most people, this is all meaningless, because most Macs have only one input (the microphone) and one output (the speakers). But if you're sitting in your darkened music studio, which is humming with high-tech audio gear whose software has been designed to work with this little program, you'll smile when you see this tab.

There's even a Configure Speakers button, for those audiophilic Mac fans who've attached stereo or even surround-sound speaker systems to their Macs.

Tip: Using the ✿ menu at the bottom of the window, you can turn your various audio inputs (that is, microphones, line inputs, and so on) on or off. You can even direct your Mac's system beeps to pour forth from one set of speakers (like the one built into your Mac), and all other sound, like music, through a different set.

- **MIDI.** MIDI stands for Musical Instrument Digital Interface, a standard "language" for inter-synthesizer communication. It's available to music software companies who have written their wares to capitalize on these tools.

 When you choose Window→Show MIDI Studio, you get a window that represents your recording-studio configuration. By clicking Add Device, you create a new icon that represents one of your pieces of gear. Double-click the icon to specify its make and model. Finally, by dragging lines from the "in" and "out" arrows, you teach your Mac and its MIDI software how the various components are wired together.

Bluetooth File Exchange

One of the luxuries of using a Mac that has Bluetooth is the ability to shoot files (to colleagues who own similarly clever gadgets) through the air, up to 30 feet away. Bluetooth File Exchange makes it possible, as described on page 238.

Boot Camp Assistant

This program helps you create (or destroy) a partition of your hard drive to hold a copy of Microsoft Windows. Details in Chapter 8.

ColorSync Utility

If you use ColorSync, then you probably know already that this utility is for people in the high-end color printing business. Its tabs include these two:

- **Profile First Aid.** This tab performs a fairly esoteric task: repairing ColorSync profiles that may be "broken" because they don't strictly conform to the *ICC profile* specifications. (ICC [International Color Consortium] profiles are part of Apple's ColorSync color management system.) If a profile for your specific monitor or printer doesn't appear in the Profiles tab of this program when it should, Profile First Aid is the tool you need to fix it.

- **Profiles.** This tab lets you review all the ColorSync profiles installed on your system. The area on the right side of the window displays information about each ColorSync profile you select from the list on the left.

Console

Console is a viewer for all of OS X's logs—the behind-the-scenes, internal Unix record of your Mac's activities.

Opening the Console log is a bit like stepping into an operating room during a complex surgery: You're exposed to stuff the average person just isn't supposed to see. (Typical Console entries: "kCGErrorCannotComplete" or "doGetDisplayTransferBy-Table.") You can adjust the font and word wrapping using Console's Font menu, but the truth is that the phrase "CGXGetWindowType: Invalid window -1" looks ugly in just about *any* font!

Console isn't useless, however. These messages can be of significant value to programmers who are debugging software or troubleshooting a messy problem, or, occasionally, to someone you've called for tech support.

For example, your *crash logs* are detailed technical descriptions of what went wrong when various programs crashed, and what was stored in memory at the time.

Unfortunately, there's not much plain English here to help you understand the crash, or how to avoid it in the future. Most of it runs along the lines of "Exception: EXC_BAD_ACCESS (0x0001); Codes: KERN_INVALID_ADDRESS (0x0001) at 0x2f6b657d." In other words, it's primarily for the benefit of programmers. Still, tech-support staff may occasionally ask to see the information in one of these logs.

DigitalColor Meter

DigitalColor Meter can grab the exact color value of any pixel on your screen, which can be helpful when matching colors in Web page construction or other design work. After launching the DigitalColor Meter, just point anywhere on your screen. A magnified view appears in the meter window, and the RGB (red-green-blue) color value of the pixels appears in the meter window.

Here are some tips for using the DigitalColor Meter to capture color information from your screen:

- To home in on the exact pixel (and color) you want to measure, drag the Aperture Size slider to the smallest size—one pixel.

- Press ⌘-X (View→Lock X) to freeze your cursor at its current horizontal position; you can now move it only horizontally. Or press ⌘-Y (View→Lock Y) to freeze your cursor at its current vertical position. You can also lock the cursor in both directions. (Press the keystroke again to unlock.) The idea is to make it easier for you to snap exactly the pixel you want.

- When the Aperture Size slider is set to view more than one pixel, DigitalColor Meter measures the *average* value of the pixels being examined.

Disk Utility

This important program serves two key functions:

- It serves as OS X's own disk-repair program: a powerful administration tool that lets you repair, erase, format, and partition disks. You'll probably use Disk Utility most often for its *Repair Permissions* feature, which solves an uncanny number of weird little Mac glitches. But it's also worth keeping in mind in case you ever find yourself facing a serious disk problem.

• Disk Utility also creates and manages *disk images,* electronic versions of disks or folders that you can exchange electronically with other people.

The following discussion tackles the program's two personalities one at a time.

Disk Utility, the hard drive repair program

Here are some of the tasks you can perform with this half of Disk Utility:

• Repair folders, files, and programs that don't work because you supposedly don't have sufficient "access privileges." This is by far the most common use of Disk Utility, not to mention the most reliable and satisfying. Using the Repair Disk Permissions button fixes an *astonishing* range of bizarre OS X problems, from programs that won't open to menulets that freeze up the works.

• Get size and type information about any disks attached to your Mac.

• Fix disks that won't appear on your desktop or behave properly.

• Completely erase disks—including rewritable CDs and DVDs (such as CD-RW and DVD-RW discs).

• Partition a disk into multiple *volumes* (that is, subdivide a drive so that its segments appear on the desktop with separate disk icons).

Tip: Disk Utility can even create or enlarge disk partitions without requiring you to erase the entire hard drive. Details below.

• Set up a *RAID array* (a cluster of separate disks that acts as a single volume).

Note: Disk Utility can perform *some* of its magic on the startup disk—the disk that's running OS X at the moment. For example, it can check the disk for damage, fix the permissions of the disk, or even adjust its partitions.

But any other operation, like reformatting, erasing, or actually repairing the disk, still requires the Mac to start up from a different disk (an external hard drive, for example, or Yosemite's secret recovery partition). Otherwise, it'd be like a surgeon performing an appendectomy on himself—not a great idea.

The left Disk Utility pane lists your hard drive and any other disks in or attached to your Mac at the moment. When you click the name of your hard drive's mechanism, like "500 GB Hitachi iC25N0…" (not the "Macintosh HD" volume label below it), you see a pane with five tabs, one for each of the main Disk Utility functions:

• **First Aid.** This is the disk-repair part of Disk Utility, and it does a terrific job at fixing many disk problems. When you're troubleshooting, Disk Utility should always be your first resort.

To use it, click the icon of a disk and then click either Verify Disk (to get a report on the disk's health) or Repair Disk (which fixes whatever problems the program finds). In other words, First Aid attempts to perform the same healing effects on a sick hard drive as, say, a program like Norton Utilities.

If Disk First Aid reports that it's unable to fix the problem, *then* it's time to invest in a program like DiskWarrior (*www.alsoft.com*).

You may wind up using the Verify and Repair Disk *Permissions* buttons even more often. Their function is to straighten out problems with the invisible Unix file permissions that keep you from moving, changing, or deleting files or folders. (The occasional software installer can create problems like this.) You'd be surprised how often running one of these permission checks solves little OS X glitches.

Chapter 15 has a more detailed discussion of permissions.

- **Erase.** Select a disk, choose a format—*always* Mac OS Extended (Journaled), unless you're formatting a disk for use on a Windows PC—give it a name, and then click Erase to wipe a disk clean.

Tip: The Erase tab is the key to using FileVault on flash drives and other external drives, as described on page 520. In other words, you can encrypt external disks so that nobody can access them without a password. The trick is to erase the drive using "Mac OS Extended (Journaled, Encrypted)" format.

- **Partition.** With the Partition tools, you can erase a hard drive in such a way that you subdivide its surface. Each chunk is represented on your screen by another hard drive icon (Figure 19-34).

Figure 19-34:
Partitioning your drive with Disk Utility no longer involves erasing it completely. Select the drive you want to partition from the list on the left, and then click the Partition tab. Click the + for each new partition you want.

Now drag the horizontal dividers in the Volume Scheme map to specify the relative sizes of the partitions you want to create. Assign a name and a format for each partition in the Volume Information area, and then click Apply.

There are some very good reasons *not* to partition a drive these days: A partitioned hard drive is more difficult to resurrect after a serious crash, requires more navigation when you want to open a particular file, and offers no speed or safety benefits.

On the other hand, there's one very good reason *to* do it: Partitioning is the only way to use Boot Camp, described in Chapter 8. When you're using Boot Camp, your Mac is a Mac when running off of one partition, and a Windows PC when starting up from another one. (But you don't use Disk Utility in that case; use Boot Camp Assistant.)

- **RAID.** RAID stands for Redundant Array of Independent Disks and refers to a special formatting scheme in which a group of separate disks are configured to work together as one very large, very fast drive. In a RAID array, multiple disks share the job of storing data—a setup that can improve speed and reliability.

 Most Mac owners don't use or set up RAID arrays, probably because most Mac owners have only one hard drive (and Disk Utility can't make your startup disk part of a RAID array).

 But if you're using multiple hard disks—in a Mac Pro, for example—you can use Apple RAID to merge them into one giant disk. Just drag the icons of the relevant disks (or disk partitions) from the left-side list of disks into the main list (where it says, "Drag disks or volumes here to add to set"). Use the RAID Type pop-up menu to specify the RAID format you want to use. (Stripe is a popular choice for maximizing disk speed; Mirror RAID is extra safe, because it creates a perfect

POWER USERS' CLINIC

Partition Adjustments on the Fly

You can expand, shrink, or create partitions without having to erase the whole hard drive. If you're into partitioning at all, this is a *huge* convenience.

Expanding a partition. Suppose, for example, that your main hard drive has two partitions: a main one (200 gigs) and a secondary one (50 gigs) that used to hold all your photos and movies. But you've outgrown the second partition and have moved all those photos and movies to their own external hard drive. Wouldn't it be nice to add the newly unoccupied 50 gigs to your main partition?

You can do that without having to erase the whole hard drive. (This process, however, nukes everything on the *second* partition, so make sure you're prepared to lose it all.)

Open Disk Utility. Click the name of the hard drive (for example, "Hitachi HTS541616J9SA00"–*not* "Macintosh HD"). Click Partition. You see a display like the one in Figure 19-35.

Click the second partition (or third, or whatever partition is *just after* the one you want to expand) and then click the — button below the list. Poof! It's gone.

Now you can drag the main partition's bottom edge downward (or type a new size into the Size box), expanding it into the free area. Take a deep breath, and then click Apply.

Shrinking a partition. In Figure 19-35, you can see that a portion of the first partition is lightly shaded. (It's blue in real life.) The blue represents data; you can't shrink a partition so much that it crowds out your files. You can, however, shrink the partition to eliminate empty space. Just drag the lower edge of its map chunk upward.

Creating new partitions. Anytime there's leftover space on the drive, you can create *new* partitions from it. To do that, click the + button and proceed as described in Figure 19-35.

backup clone of your main drive.) Name your new mega-disk, and then click Create. The result is a single "disk" icon on your desktop that actually represents the combined capacity of all the RAID disks.

- **Restore.** This tab lets you make a perfect copy of a disk or a disk image, much like the popular shareware programs Carbon Copy Cloner and SuperDuper. You might find this useful when, for example, you want to make an exact copy of your old Mac's drive on your new one. You can't do that just by copying your old files and folders manually. If you try, you won't get the thousands of *invisible* files that make up OS X. If you use the Restore function, though, they'll come along for the ride.

 Start by dragging the disk or disk image you want to copy *from* into the Source box. Then drag the icon of the disk you want to copy *to* into the Destination box.

Tip: If you want to copy an online disk image onto one of your disks, you don't have to download it first. Just type its Web address into the Source field.

If you turn on Erase Destination, then Disk Utility obliterates all the data on your target disk before copying the data. If you leave this checkbox off, however, Disk Utility simply copies everything onto your destination, preserving all your old data in the process (although it replaces files that have the same names and locations as the ones you're copying).

Finally, click the Restore button. (You might need to type in an administrator password.) Restoring can take a long time for big disks, so go ahead and make yourself a cup of coffee while you're waiting.

Disk Utility, the disk-image program

Disk images are very cool. Each one is a single icon that behaves precisely like an actual disk—a flash drive or hard drive, for example—but can be distributed electronically. For example, a lot of OS X apps arrive from your Web download in disk-image form.

Disk images are popular for software distribution for a simple reason: Each image file precisely duplicates the original master disk, complete with all the necessary files in all the right places. When a software company sends you a disk image, it ensures that you'll install the software from a disk that *exactly* matches the master disk.

As a handy bonus, you can password-protect a disk image, which is the closest OS X comes to offering the ability to password-protect an individual folder.

By the way: There's a difference between a *disk-image file* and the *mounted disk* (the one that appears when you double-click the disk image). You can drag the disk to the Trash after using it; the disk-image file (.dmg) will still be there to summon it.

Tip: After you double-click a disk image, click Skip in the verification box that appears. If something truly got scrambled during the download, you'll know about it right away—your file won't decompress correctly, or it'll display the wrong icon, for example.

In fact, you can make Disk Utility always skip that verification business, which is a relic from the days of floppy disks. To do so, choose Disk Utility→Preferences, and turn off "Check images on locked media."

You can create disk images, too. Doing so can be very handy in situations like these:

- **You want to create a backup of an important CD.** By turning it into a disk-image file on your hard drive, you'll always have a safety copy, ready to burn back onto a *new* CD. (This is an essential practice for educational CDs that kids will be handling soon after eating peanut butter and jelly.)

- **You want to replicate your entire hard drive**—complete with all its files, programs, folder setups, and so on—onto a new, bigger hard drive (or a new, better Mac), using the Restore feature described earlier.

- **You want to back up your entire hard drive,** or maybe just a certain chunk of it, onto an iPod or another disk. (Again, you can later use the Restore function.)

- **You want to send somebody else a copy of a disk via the Internet.** You simply create a disk image, and then send *that*—preferably in compressed form.

Here's how to make a disk image.

- **To image-ize a disk or partition.** Click the name of the disk in the list, where you see your currently available disks. (The topmost item is the name of your *drive*, like "484.0 MB MATSHITA DVD-R" for a DVD drive or "74.5 GB Hitachi" for a hard drive. Beneath that entry, you generally see the name of the actual partition, like "Macintosh HD," or the CD's name as it appears on the screen.)

 Then choose File→New→Disk Image from [the disk or partition's name].

- **To image-ize a folder.** Choose File→New→Disk Image from Folder. In the Open dialog box, click the folder you want, and then click Image. Either way, the next dialog box (Figure 19-35) offers some fascinating options.

Figure 19-35:
These two pop-up menus let you specify (a) what kind of disk image you want, and (b) whether you want it password-protected. The latter option is great when you want to password-protect one folder, without bothering with your entire Home folder.

- **Image Format.** If you choose "read/write," your disk image file, when double-clicked, turns into a superb imitation of a hard drive. You can drag files and folders onto it, drag them off of it, change icons' names on it, and so on.

 If you choose "read-only," however, the result behaves more like a CD. You can copy things off of it but not make any changes to it.

 The "compressed" option is best if you intend to send the resulting file by email, post it for Web download, or preserve the disk image on some backup disk for a rainy day. It takes a little longer to create a simulated disk when you double-click the disk image file, but it takes up a lot less disk space than an uncompressed version.

 Finally, choose "DVD/CD master" if you're copying a CD or a DVD. The resulting file is a perfect mirror of the original disc, ready for copying onto a blank CD or DVD when the time comes.

- **Encryption.** Here's an easy way to lock private files away into a vault that nobody else can open. If you choose one of these two AES encryption options (choose AES-128, if you value your time), you'll be asked to assign a password to your new image file. Nobody can open it without the password—not even you. On the other hand, if you save it into your Keychain (page 434), it's not such a disaster if you forget the password.

- **Save As.** Choose a name and location for your new image file. The name you choose here doesn't need to match the original disk or folder name.

When you click Save (or press Return), if you opted to create an encrypted image, you're asked to make up a password at this point.

Otherwise, Disk Utility now creates the image and then *mounts* it—that is, turns the image file into a simulated, yet fully functional, disk icon on your desktop.

When you're finished working with the disk, eject it as you would any disk (right-click or two-finger click it and choose Eject, for example). Hang onto the .dmg disk image file itself, however. This is the file you'll need to double-click if you ever want to recreate your "simulated disk."

Turning an image into a CD

One of the other most common disk-image tasks is turning a disk image *back* into a CD or DVD—provided that you have an external CD or DVD burner, of course.

All you have to do is drag the .dmg file into the Disk Utility window, select it, and click the Burn icon on the toolbar (or, alternatively, right-click or two-finger click the .dmg icon and choose Burn from the shortcut menu). Insert a blank CD or DVD, and then click Burn.

Grab

Grab takes pictures of your Mac's screen, for use when you're writing up instructions, illustrating a computer book, or collecting proof of some secret screen you found buried in a game. You can take pictures of the entire screen (press ⌘-Z, which for

once in its life does *not* mean Undo) or capture only the contents of a rectangular selection (press Shift-⌘-A). When you're finished, Grab displays your snapshot in a new window, which you can print, close without saving, or save as a TIFF file, ready for emailing or inserting into a manuscript.

Now, the Mac operating system has long had its *own* built-in shortcuts for capturing screenshots: Press Shift-⌘-3 to take a picture of the whole screen, and Shift-⌘-4 to capture a rectangular selection. (See page 281 for all the details.)

Tip: Don't forget that you can choose different, easier-to-remember keyboard shortcuts for these functions, if you like. Just open System Preferences→Keyboard→Shortcuts, click Screen Shots, click where it now says Shift-⌘-3 (or whatever), and then press the new key combo.

So why use Grab instead? In many cases, you shouldn't. The Shift-⌘-3 and Shift-⌘-4 shortcuts work like a dream. But there are some cases when it might make more sense to opt for Grab. Here are two:

- Grab can make a *timed* screen capture (choose Capture→Timed Screen, or press Shift-⌘-Z), which lets you enjoy a 10-second delay before the screenshot is actually taken. After you click the Start Timer button, you have an opportunity to activate windows, pull down menus, drag items around, and otherwise set up the shot before Grab shoots the picture.

- With Grab, you have the option of including the *cursor* in the picture, which is extremely useful when you're showing a menu being pulled down or a button being clicked. (OS X's screenshot keystrokes, by contrast, always eliminate the pointer.) Use the technique described in Figure 19-36 to add the pointer style of your choice to a Grab screenshot.

Tip: If you're really going to write a book or manual about OS X, the program you need is Snapz Pro X; a trial version is available from this book's "Missing CD" at *www.missingmanuals.com*. It offers far more flexibility.

Figure 19-36:
Unlike the Shift-⌘-3 or Shift-⌘-4 keystrokes, Grab lets you include the pointer/cursor in the picture—or hide it. Choose Grab→Preferences and pick one of the eight pointer styles, or choose to keep the pointer hidden by activating the blank button in the upper-left corner.

Grapher

This little unsung app is an amazing piece of work. It lets you create 2-D or 3-D graphs of staggering beauty and complexity.

When you first open Grapher, you're asked to choose what kind of virtual "graph paper" you want: two-dimensional (standard, polar, logarithmic) or three-dimensional (cubic, spherical, cylindrical). Click a name to see a preview; when you're happy with the selection, click Open.

Now the main Grapher window appears (Figure 19-37). Do yourself a favor. Spend a few wow-inducing minutes choosing canned equations from the Examples menu, and watching how Grapher whips up gorgeous, colorful, sometimes animated graphs on the fly.

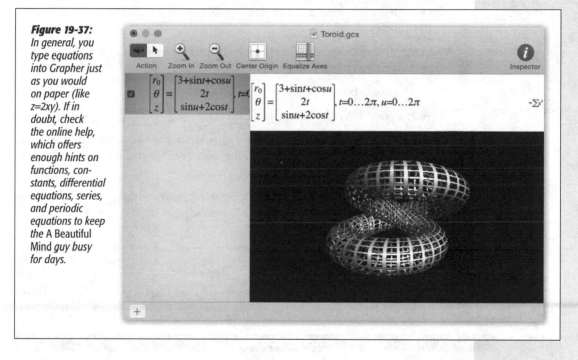

Figure 19-37:
In general, you type equations into Grapher just as you would on paper (like z=2xy). If in doubt, check the online help, which offers enough hints on functions, constants, differential equations, series, and periodic equations to keep the A Beautiful Mind guy busy for days.

When you're ready to plug in an equation of your own, type it into the text box at the top of the window. If you're not such a math hotshot, or you're not sure of the equation format, work from the canned equations and mathematical building blocks that appear when you choose Equation→New Equation from Template or Window→Show Equation Palette (a floating window containing a huge selection of math symbols and constants).

Tip: If you don't know the keystroke that produces a mathematical symbol like π or θ, you can just type *pi* or *theta*. Grapher replaces it with the correct symbol automatically.

Once the graph is up on the screen, you can tailor it like this:

- **To move a 2-D graph** in the window, choose View→Move Tool and then drag; to move a 3-D graph, ⌘-drag it.

- **To rotate a 3-D graph,** drag in any direction. If you add the Option key, you flip the graph around on one axis.

- **To change the colors, line thicknesses, 3-D "walls," and other graphic elements,** click the ❶ button (or choose Window→Show Inspector) to open the formatting palette. The controls you find here vary by graph type, but rest assured that Grapher can accommodate your every visual whim.

- **To change the fonts and sizes,** choose Grapher→Preferences. On the Equations pane, the four sliders let you specify the relative sizes of the text elements. If you click the sample equation, the Fonts pane appears, so you can go to town fiddling with the type.

- Add your own captions, arrows, ovals, or rectangles to 2-D graphs using the Object menu.

When it's all over, you can preserve your masterpiece using any of these techniques:

- **Export a graphic** by choosing File→Export.

- **Copy an equation to the Clipboard** by right-clicking or two-finger clicking it and choosing Copy As→TIFF (or EPS, or whatever) from the shortcut menu. Now you can paste it into another program.

- **Export an animated graph** by choosing Equation→Create Animation. The resulting dialog box lets you specify how long you want the movie to last (and a lot of other parameters).

Tip: If you Shift-drag the starting or ending images at the bottom, you can change their size.

Finally, click Create Animation. After a moment, the finished movie appears. If you like it, choose File→Save As to preserve it on your hard drive for future generations.

POWER USERS' CLINIC

For Mathematicians (and Physicists, Scientists, and Students) Only

If you're into math, science, or studying math or science, Grapher is a tremendous addition to OS X. There's a whole lot to it—but if you're just getting started, here are a few features not to miss.

You can calculate values, intercepts, derivatives, and integrals (even indefinite integrals) by using the Equation→Evaluation and Equation→Integration commands.

Some useful ready-made equation components await in the pop-up button at the right side of the equation text box. Using the Sum and Product symbols, for example, you can quickly calculate summations and products.

That same pop-up menu can help you generate piecewise, parametric, and other specialized kinds of graphs (this means you, math students).

Keychain Access

Keychain Access memorizes and stores all your secret passwords. For instructions on using it, see page 526.

Migration Assistant

This little cutie automates the transfer of all your stuff from a Windows PC or another Mac to your current Mac: your Home folder, network settings, programs, and more. This comes in extremely handy when you buy a Mac—or when you need Time Machine to recover an entire dead Mac's worth of data. The instructions on the screen guide you through the process (see Appendix A).

Network Utility

Network Utility isn't actually in Yosemite's Utilities folder. It now lives in a deeply nested folder where you'd never think to look (System→Library→CoreServices→Applications). But you can quickly find and open it with a Spotlight search, or from within System Information, described below (choose Window→Network Utility).

In any case, it gathers information about Web sites and network citizens. It offers a suite of standard Internet tools like netstat, ping, traceroute, DNS lookup, and whois—advanced tools, to be sure, but ones that even Mac novices may be asked to fire up when calling a technician for Internet help.

Otherwise, you probably won't need to use Network Utility to get your work done. However, Network Utility can be useful when you're doing Internet detective work.

- **Whois** ("who is") can gather an amazing amount of information about the owners of any particular domain (such as apple.com)—including name and address info, telephone numbers, and administrative contacts. It uses the technique shown in Figure 19-38.

Figure 19-38:
The whois tool is a powerful part of Network Utility. First enter a domain that you want information about, and then choose a whois server (you might try whois. networksolutions.com). When you click the whois button, you get a surprisingly revealing report about the owner of the domain, including phone numbers and contact names.

• Use **Ping** to enter an address (either a Web address like *www.google.com* or an IP address like 192.168.1.110), and then "ping" (send out a "sonar" signal to) the server to see how long it takes for it to respond to your request. Network Utility reports the response time in milliseconds—a useful test when you're trying to see if a remote server (a Web site, for example) is up and running. (The time it takes for the ping to report back to you also tells you how good your connection to it is.)

• **Traceroute** lets you track how many "hops" are required for your Mac to communicate with a certain server (an IP address or Web address). You'll see that your request actually jumps from one *trunk* of the Internet to another, from router to router, as it makes its way to its destination. You'll learn that a message sometimes crisscrosses the entire country before it arrives at its destination. You can also see how long each leg of the journey took, in milliseconds.

Script Editor

This little program is where you can type up your own *AppleScripts*. You can read about these programmery software robots in the free online appendix to this chapter, "Automator & AppleScript.pdf," available at *www.missingmanuals.com*.

System Information

System Information is a great tool for learning exactly what's installed on your Mac and what's not—in terms of both hardware and software. The people who answer the phones on Apple's tech-support line are particularly fond of System Profiler, since the detailed information it reports can be very useful for troubleshooting nasty problems.

There are actually two versions of System Information: a quick, easy snapshot and a ridiculously detailed version:

• **Snapshot.** Choose →About This Mac. You get a concise, attractive summary info screen that reveals your OS X version, your Mac's memory amount, its serial number, what processor it has inside, and so on (Figure 19-39, top).

The tabs across the top reveal similarly precise details about your Displays and Storage. The Support tab offers links to various sources of online help, and the Service tab reveals your options for getting the Mac fixed.

• **Ridiculously detailed.** Open Applications→Utilities; double-click System Information. (You can also open the System Information program from inside the About This Mac dialog box shown in Figure 19-39; just click System Report.)

When System Information opens, it reports information about your Mac in a list down the left side (Figure 19-40). The details fall into these categories:

• **Hardware.** Click this word to see precisely which model Mac you have, what kind of chip is inside (and how many), how much memory it has, and its serial number.

If you expand the flippy triangle, you get to see details about which memory slots are filled and the size of the memory module in each slot; what kind of disc burning your Mac can do; what PCI cards are installed in your expansion slots; what

graphics/displays circuitry you have (graphics card and monitor); what's attached to your SATA bus (internal drives, like your hard drive); what's connected to your Thunderbolt, USB, and FireWire chains, if anything; and much more.

- **Network** reveals details what WiFi components you have, what Internet connection Locations you've established, and so on.

- **Software** shows which version of OS X you have and what your computer's name is, as far as the network is concerned ("Chris's Computer," for example). The Applications list documents every program on your system, with version information. It's useful for spotting duplicate copies of programs.

Figure 19-39:
This dialog box gives you a plain-English display of the Mac details you probably care the most about: memory, screen, storage, serial number, OS X version, and so on. (Click the tabs across the top for more details.) To proceed from here to the full System Information program, click System Report.

Similar information shows up in the Extensions pane. Extensions are the drivers for the Mac's various components, which sit in the System→Library→Extensions folder. Whatever is in that folder is what you see listed in this pane. Other categories include self-explanatory lists like Fonts, Preference Panes, and Startup Items.

Finally, the Logs pane reveals your Mac's secret diary: a record of the traumatic events that it experiences from day to day. (Many of these are the same as those revealed by the Console utility; see page 700.)

Tip: If any of these screens is showing you more technical information than you'd like, use the File→Show Less Information command to pare down the overload to just the human-recognizable items.

Figure 19-40:
Does your MacBook's chip run at 2 GHz or 2.6? What percentage of your external hard drive is filled up? What are the version numbers of every program installed on your Mac? Can your DVD burner burn dual-layer discs? Does your laptop have any open slots for extra RAM?

Terminal

Underneath its skin, OS X is actually Unix, one of the oldest and most respected operating systems in use today. But you'd never know it by looking; Unix is a world without icons, menus, or dialog boxes. You operate it by typing out memorized commands at a special prompt, called the command line. The mouse is almost useless here.

Terminal is your keyhole into OS X's Unix innards. There's a whole chapter on it waiting for you on this book's "Missing CD" page at *www.missingmanuals.com*.

VoiceOver Utility

The Mac has always been able to read stuff on the screen out loud. But Apple has turned this feature into a full-blown *screen reader* for the benefit of people who can't see. VoiceOver doesn't just read every scrap of text it finds on the screen—it also lets you control everything (menus, buttons, and so on) without ever needing the mouse.

On a Mac with a multitouch trackpad, you can interact with what's visible on the screen by using the trackpad itself as a map of the current window or screen area; VoiceOver speaks whatever's under your finger. OS X can also read entire Web pages, navigate Web tables, hop from link to link, and so on. You can navigate by pressing arrow keys, using the mouse, or using the trackpad.

Obviously, learning VoiceOver is a *huge* task—but if it's your ticket to being able to use a computer at all, you'll probably be happy to have such a monster of a program. You'll find a detailed Apple user guide at *http://www.apple.com/voiceover/info/guide*.

5

Part Five:
Appendixes

Installing OS X Yosemite

I f your computer came with Yosemite already installed on it, you can skip this appendix—for now. But if you're running an earlier version of the Mac OS and want to savor the Yosemite experience, this appendix describes how to install the new operating system on your Mac.

If you're new in these parts, you may be in for quite a shock: You can't buy Yosemite in a box, or on a DVD. You're supposed to download it from the Mac App Store.

There are some very attractive elements to the download-only system. For example, there's no copy protection and no serial numbers to type in. There's no cost to Apple for manufacturing or shipping, which may explain why Yosemite isn't even $20 or $30, like its predecessors—it's free.

Now there's no disc to hunt down later, when you want to install OS X again (onto a new Mac, for example). And when you do need a copy again, you'll download the

POWER USERS' CLINIC

The Partitioning Question

Before you install Yosemite, you might want to confront the issue of *partitioning* your Mac's hard drive–dividing its space so that it shows up on your desktop with two different icons and two different names. You can keep Yosemite on one and Mavericks on the other, for example.

Now you can live like a king, enjoying all the advantages of having two separate hard drives. As a bonus, the Mac even comes with a partitioning program: Disk Utility. And it no longer requires first erasing the drive completely; you can repartition on the fly, without disturbing whatever is already on the drive.

latest version—10.10.3 or whatever it is—instead of having to install whatever updates have come out since you got your DVD.

(And what if you don't have a fast Internet connection for downloading Yosemite? The world won't come to an end; read on.)

Hardware Requirements

For starters, you need to make sure you and your Mac have what it takes to handle Yosemite—specifically:

- **A Mac that's not a geezer.** Yosemite can run on any Mac that Mavericks or Mountain Lion could. That list includes the iMac (mid-2007 or newer), aluminum MacBook (late 2008 or newer), plastic MacBook (early 2009 or newer), MacBook Pro (mid-2007 or newer), MacBook Air (late 2008 or newer), Mac mini (early 2009 or newer), or Mac Pro (early 2008 or newer).

Note: Some features, like AirDrop, Power Nap, AirPlay mirroring, and Handoff, work only on more recent models.

- **Snow Leopard or later.** Your Mac has to be running OS X 10.6.8 or later (Snow Leopard, Lion, Mountain Lion, or Mavericks). Even if you have one of those, run Software Update to make sure you have the *latest* version of that edition.

- **Free storage space.** You need at least 8 GB free on your hard drive or flash storage to install Mac OS X 10.10. More is much better.

- **A lot of memory.** Apple recommends at least 2 GB of memory, but OS X absolutely *loves* memory. For the greatest speed, install 4 gigabytes—more if you can afford it. (And these days, you probably can.)

- **The latest firmware.** *Firmware* describes the low-level, underlying software instructions that control the actual circuitry of your Mac. Every now and then, Apple

POWER USERS' CLINIC

Reinstalling: Tricks of the Trade

You can install Yosemite on as many Macs as you own. To install it on a second Mac, for example, open the App Store, find Yosemite, and download it again.

That's what most people will do, anyway. Unfortunately, downloading the 5.3-gigabyte installer again and again takes a lot of time and eats up a lot of your monthly Internet data allotment.

There is, fortunately, a trick that saves you the trouble of

re-downloading Yosemite over and over again: Copy the Install OS X Yosemite installer program from the *first* Mac to all your other Macs (over the network or on a flash drive, for example). There's also a tricky part to this trick: Ordinarily, installing Yosemite on the first Mac *deletes* that installer program once it's finished, to save you the disk space.

The trick to this trick, then, is to copy the installer to another Mac or drive (or at least to take it out of your Applications folder) *before* you install Yosemite on the first Mac.

updates it for certain Mac models, and it's very important that your Mac have the absolute latest. If yours doesn't, a message will appear to let you know during the installation. Quit the installer and grab the latest update from *http://support. apple.com/kb/HT1237*.

- **A full backup.** It's a really, *really* good idea to back up your entire Mac before you begin this, or any, upgrade. Even if things go wrong for only, say, 0.01 percent of Mac owners, that's still thousands of people. If you don't have a second hard drive, this is your excuse to buy one; they're dirt cheap these days. You can use Time Machine in your current version of OS X to make a complete, automatic backup of your Mac as it is now.

Psychological Requirements

Upgrading an operating system is always a traumatic experience for a computer—and, too often, for its owner. If you can rein in your excitement long enough to perform just a few extra steps, you'll be glad you did.

- **Check your hard drive.** Open Disk Utility (page 701), click your main hard drive's name and then click Verify Disk. If the program reports that you have problems, you'll have to start up from a different disk (like your recovery disk—page 735), run Disk Utility again, and use the Repair Disk button this time.

- **Turn off FileVault, if you're using it.** (You'd remember turning on this Home folder–encryption feature.)

- **Make sure your software will run.** Most modern programs run very smoothly on Yosemite. But some older ones won't run—in particular, programs like AppleWorks and Microsoft Office 2004 that relied on the old Rosetta translation technology. Find out for sure by visiting *http://roaringapps.com/apps:table* and looking up the programs you own.

Tip: You can also look up your own programs using the System Profiler program in your Applications→ Utilities folder. In the left-side column, click Applications. Click the Kind column heading to sort your programs. The programs listed as *PowerPC* or *Classic* won't run in Yosemite.

The Standard Installation

To do the actual installation, open the App Store program on your Mac. If you don't see "OS X Yosemite" advertised right there on the home page, you can find it by searching for *Yosemite*. Click the Free Upgrade button, and then click again when it changes to say "Install App" (Figure A-1).

When the download begins, behind the scenes, the App Store puts a 5.3-gigabyte program called *Install OS X Yosemite* into your Applications folder and on your Launchpad, if you have it.

Tip: If you don't have a fast Internet connection, or if your Internet provider imposes monthly data limits, you might not be thrilled about the prospect of waiting for a 5-gigabyte download.

Your best bet is to take your Mac to an Apple Store and use *its* free, fast WiFi to download Yosemite (or a friend's house, a library, a coffee shop…).

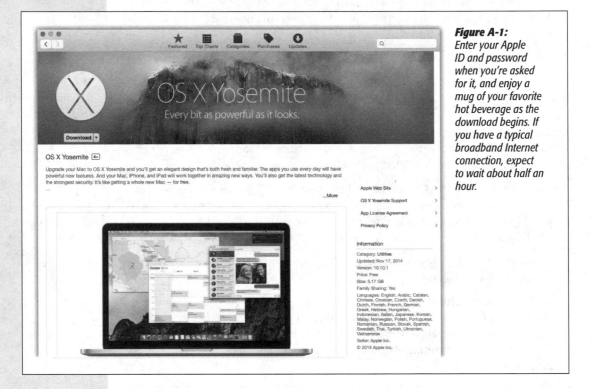

Figure A-1:
Enter your Apple ID and password when you're asked for it, and enjoy a mug of your favorite hot beverage as the download begins. If you have a typical broadband Internet connection, expect to wait about half an hour.

You'll know when the downloading is over, because the actual installer opens up automatically and presents you with the logo shown in Figure A-2.

The procedure from here:

1. **Click Continue.**

 The installer follows a pattern: Read the instructions, make a couple of choices, and then click Continue to advance to the next screen. As you go, the list on the left side of the screen reveals where you are in the overall procedure.

2. **Click Agree to pass the Software License Agreement screen, and then Agree again.**

 The software license agreement requires you to agree with whatever Apple's lawyers say.

3. **Choose the disk or partition where you want to install OS X.**

 The installer proposes the obvious hard drive: the main one inside your Mac.

If you have other drives, you can click Show All Disks to see their icons and choose one. Yellow exclamation-mark icons mean "You can't install here," for one technical reason or another. You can install Yosemite only onto a blank hard drive, formatted as a Mac drive (technically, "Mac OS Extended [Journaled]" format), or onto a drive that has Snow Leopard, Lion, Mountain Lion, or Mavericks on it.

4. **Click Install. Enter an administrator's account name and password when you're asked for it.**

 Now you're in for a 20- to 30-minute wait as the installer copies software onto your hard drive. (That's why, if you're using a laptop and it's not plugged in, you'll be encouraged to plug it in.) At one point, it restarts the Mac and carries right on.

OS X 10.10 is now installed on your Mac. That, if you hadn't noticed, was a far less harrowing experience than it was in previous OS X installations. You were never asked what kind of installation you wanted, which language translations or printer drivers you wanted installed, which optional components you wanted, and so on.

Still, you're not quite ready to use Yosemite yet. Read on.

Figure A-2:
Your installation adventure is about to begin. You've never experienced such a simple operating-system installation. You don't even have to restart the computer before you start. You have far fewer options and decisions to make.

The Setup Assistant

What you see depends on whether you installed Yosemite onto an older OS X drive or an empty drive. Either way, it's called the Setup Assistant (Figure A-3), and it's meant to interview you about which features you'd like turned on.

After Installing over Snow Leopard, Lion, Mountain Lion, or Mavericks

If you installed onto a drive that already had OS X stuff on it—accounts, files, settings, and so on—then after the Mac restarts, all you have to do is log in as usual.

You're asked for your Apple (iCloud) name and password, or you can sign up for one now. You're asked if you want to turn on Find My Mac (page 368) and if you'd like to use the iCloud Keychain feature (page 434).

Note: It's possible, at this point, that Yosemite will tell you that it found some incompatible software during the installation. This outdated software has been summarily tossed into a folder called Incompatible Software.

You may also be asked if it's OK for certain programs to access your calendar, reminders, or contacts—non-Apple programs you already own. Other programs may require that the Assistive Devices feature of OS X be turned on; you're directed to the appropriate pane of System Preferences, where you're supposed to turn on the appropriate checkboxes. All of these are security steps, new in Yosemite.

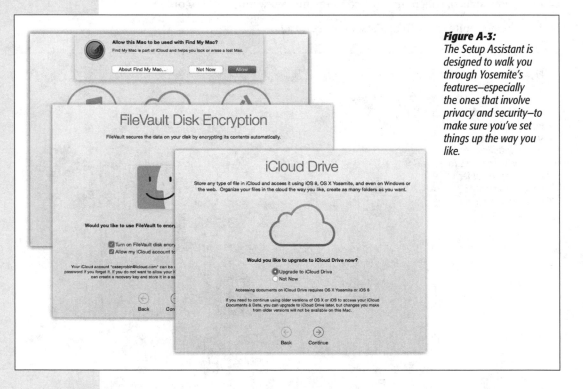

Figure A-3:
The Setup Assistant is designed to walk you through Yosemite's features—especially the ones that involve privacy and security—to make sure you've set things up the way you like.

Finally, a little notification bubble appears on the desktop, offering to show you a "What's New in OS X Yosemite" Web page.

After Installing onto a Blank Drive

If you installed Yosemite onto an empty drive, then the Setup Assistant is a little more involved.

Once again, you're in for a click-through-the-screens experience, this time with the aim of setting up your Mac's various options. After answering the questions on each screen, click Continue. The number of information screens you encounter may vary, but here are some of the possibilities:

- **Welcome.** Click the name of the country you're in.

- **Select Your Keyboard.** Different countries require different keyboard layouts. For example, if you choose the Canadian layout, pressing the] key on a U.S. keyboard produces the ç symbol. Click Continue.

- **Select a Network Connection.** This is your chance to introduce the Mac to any networks in the vicinity. Click the name of the WiFi hotspot you want to join, for example. If there's no wireless hotspot at all—hey, it could happen—click Different Network Setup to specify, say, a wired or cellular network hookup.

POWER USERS' CLINIC

The Clean Install

For years, there were two ways to install OS X: the *automatic* way and the *clean install*.

The automatic way preserved everything on your Mac. Every program, setting, and file stayed exactly as you had it. In essence, this kind of installation just worked through your System folder, updating each component and disturbing nothing else.

The *clean install* was preferred by power users, especially in times of troubleshooting, because it erased the entire hard drive and *then* installed OS X. Any minor corruptions or ancient software crumbs were swept away, leaving you with a clean, perfect system.

The clean-install option is gone now; Apple says its automatic installation method is perfect enough that the erase-and-install business is no longer useful.

Sometimes, though, a clean install *is* still useful. For one thing, some people just like the idea of starting fresh. For another, this process lets you install Yosemite onto a Mac that's running *Leopard* (Mac OS X 10.5), without having to upgrade it to Snow Leopard first. (This method saves you time, but not money—you'll still need a Mac running Snow

Leopard or later to *get* the Yosemite installer, since you need Snow Leopard to use the App Store to get Yosemite in the first place.)

Anyway, start by making a *complete backup* of the Mac you want to Yosemitize. In case you missed it, the clean-install process *erases everything on it.*

Now make a homemade Yosemite startup drive, as described on page 725. Use it to start up the Mac you just backed up.

The first thing you'll see is a Utilities screen; you can read more about this Recovery Mode in Appendix B. Click Disk Utility, and then click Continue. In Disk Utility, click the Mac's hard drive name at the left side; click Erase; choose "Mac OS Extended (Journaled)" from the Format pop-up menu; click Erase.

When the erasing is over, quit Disk Utility. You return to the Utilities screen.

Now click Reinstall OS X. Click Continue to trigger the Yosemite installation described on these pages. At the end of it, you'll be offered the chance to copy everything from your backup back onto the empty hard drive.

- **Transfer Information to This Mac.** The Setup Assistant can suck all your old programs, files, folders, and settings from the old Mac to the new one—or even from an old *Windows PC* to your new Mac. Meet the Migration Assistant.

 Your choices here are **From another Mac** (connect your old Mac to this one over a network, even a wireless one); **From a Windows PC** (ditto); **From Time Machine or other disk** (connect your new Mac to your backup drive); and **Don't Transfer now.**

Tip: You can always perform this sluggish task later. Just open the Migration Assistant program, in your Applications→Utilities folder, when it's a better time. See Chapter 6 for more on migrating from Windows.

If you choose one of the first options and then click Transfer, the data-copying process begins. It can take a *wicked* long time.

- **Enter Your Apple ID.** Here you're offered the chance to type in an Apple ID (an email address and password for all your Apple dealings), which is more essential in Yosemite than ever before. If you don't have one, just click Continue; you can get one and fill it in later.

- **Registration Information.** This is your chance to become a grain of sand on the great beach of the Apple database (and to set up your own "card" in OS X's Contacts program).

TROUBLESHOOTING MOMENT

Journaling

If you decide to erase your hard drive before installing Yosemite, you're offered a choice of several formats for it. But you should stick with the factory setting, "Mac OS Extended (Journaled)." It turns on a special background feature of OS X known as *file journaling*.

When file journaling is turned on, your Mac keeps a personal diary of everything you do on your hard drive—opening, saving, deleting files, and so on. Journaling offers two benefits: a shorter startup time and safety in the event of a crash.

Here's how it works: When you press the power button, OS X checks to see whether your computer was shut down properly (by choosing →Shut Down, for example, instead of just pulling out the plug).

If you didn't shut down properly, OS X examines your hard drive the next time you start up to see if it needs repair. It has to scan the whole drive–which can take quite a while. Thanks to file journaling, however, OS X can tell what was happening when your computer shut down–and therefore spend a lot less time checking your hard drive.

There are some downsides to the journaled format, however. First, this procedure doesn't actually recover what you were working on when your Mac shut down; it can only try to keep files you already saved from getting corrupted. Second, file journaling can make it take slightly longer for your programs to save files.

OS X doesn't prevent you from having different hard drives with different formats. You can use the journaled format on your main hard drive but not on your external FireWire drive–or vice versa. (If you ever want to change the format of one of your disks, use Disk Utility, although you'll have to erase all the information on the disk first.)

If you leave your Mac on all the time (if you run it as a Web server, for example), it's a good idea to use the journaled hard drive format. Keep in mind, too, that blackouts affect your hard drive just as much as pulling the plug. So if you live in Iraq, a solar-powered house, or anywhere else where power is inconsistent, journaling can be a lifesaver.

Note: If you're not interested in providing your personal information to Apple, or if you've already done so during a previous installation, press ⌘-Q. A message offers you Skip, Shut Down, and Cancel buttons. If you click Skip, you jump straight ahead to Create Your Computer Account, below.

- **Create Your Computer Account.** Most of the steps up to this point have been pretty inconsequential, but this is a big moment. You're about to create your *account*—your Administrator account, in fact, as described in Chapter 15.

 All you have to do is make up a name, usually a short variation of your name, and a password. Choose your account name carefully; you can't easily change it later.

 What you come up with here is extremely important, especially if several people use this Mac at different times, or if other people connect to it on a network.

 If you're the only one who uses your Mac, it's perfectly OK to leave the password blank empty.

- **Select a Picture For This Account.** If your Mac has a built-in camera (laptops and iMacs do), you can take a photo of yourself to use as your account icon. Just click "Take a video snapshot." You get a 3-second countdown, and then the Mac snaps your photo. (You can always reshoot it.) Adjust the cropping by dragging inside the photo, and adjust the size by dragging the slider beneath it.

 If you're camera-shy, of course, you can choose "Choose from the picture library" and find an Apple-provided icon instead.

- **Thank You.** When you click Start Using Yosemite, you wind up at the OS X desktop, just as described in Chapter 2.

The Homemade Installer Disk

Yosemite's download-only shtick is revolutionary and, in most cases, incredibly convenient. But sometimes, you'll miss having a physical disk with the installer on it. You might wish you had one if, for example, you want to install Yosemite on a huge array of Macs, like the ones at a school or in a business; downloading that 5-gig installer over and over again would drive you crazy.

You might also wish you had an installation disk when your Mac starts acting up and the tricks described in Appendix B don't seem to work.

As it turns out, you can make a Yosemite installation disk fairly easily. All you need is a hard drive, a flash drive, or even a blank DVD. (Hard drives and flash drives are much faster at performing the actual installation.)

Phase 1: Format the Drive

If you're planning to use a flash drive or a hard drive, the first step is to format it so that the Mac will be able to start up from it. To do that, connect or insert the drive. (It needs at least 5 gigabytes of free space. These steps assume that there's nothing else on it.)

Now open Disk Utility (it's in your Applications→Utilities folder). In Disk Utility, click the drive's name in the left-side list (not the partition name beneath it). Then click the Partition tab in the main window.

Under Partition Layout, choose 1 Partition. Then click the actual partition—the big rectangle "map" in the middle of the window—and then click Options beneath it. In the resulting dialog box, click GUID Partition Table; click OK.

Tip: Actually, it's fine to create multiple partitions, so you don't wind up wasting a lot of disk space. Just give the installation partition at least 5 gigabytes so it will have room for the installer.

Now, back at the Partition window, you can type a name for your drive. From the Format menu, choose "Mac OS Extended (Journaled)." Click Apply. Click Partition in the confirmation window. The process may take a minute or two.

Phase 2: Build Your Installer

Now you'll turn your formatted drive into a Yosemite installer.

Start by grabbing the *Install OS X Yosemite.app* program that winds up in your Applications folder when you first get Yosemite. (You have to think of this *before* you actually run it, as described in the box on page 718. That box also tells you how you can re-download the Yosemite installer app if it's too late for that.)

Right-click (or two-finger click) the installer's icon. From the shortcut menu, choose Show Package Contents.

In the resulting folder, open Contents, and then open Shared Support. Inside is a disk-image file called *InstallESD.dmg*. Double-click it to make the OS X Install ESD "disk" appear on your desktop. (It stands for Electronic Software Delivery, in case you were wondering.)

Your next step requires you to work with some of the Mac's usually invisible files. The easiest way to do that is using TinkerTool, the free utility program that's on this book's "Missing CD" page at *www.missingmanuals.com.* Open it, turn on "Show hidden and system files," and click Relaunch Finder. Your Finder is now filled with light-gray icons, representing files that are usually hidden. One of them, on that ESD "disk," is called BaseSystem.dmg.

Back in Disk Utility, drag the *BaseSystem.dmg* file from the Finder (in the ESD "disk" window) into the Source box in Disk Utility; you can see it in Figure A-4.

Insert the flash drive, or connect the hard drive, that you formatted in Phase 1. See the name of the partition you made earlier? Drag it out of the left-side list into the Destination box (Figure A-4). Click Restore and then Erase; enter your administrator name and password when you're asked.

When the "restoring" process is complete, you wind up with an actual Yosemite flash drive or disk that you baked all by yourself.

Phase 3: Replace the "Packages" Alias

In the Finder, in the flash drive's window, open the System folder. Delete the alias icon called Packages; you have to replace it with the actual Packages folder that's sitting on that OS X Install ESD "disk" from the previous step. Drag it into the window where the Packages alias was a minute ago.

Figure A-4:
This is what the setup should look like in Disk Utility just before you actually create the installation disk.

To finish up, open TinkerTool, turn off "Show hidden and system files," and click Relaunch Finder, so that all those invisible files are once again invisible.

How to Use Your Emergency Disk

When disaster strikes, and you need to repair or reinstall your Yosemite installation, go find your emergency installer drive.

Turn off the Mac. Connect the emergency drive. When you turn on the Mac, hold down the Option key so that a choice of startup disks appears. Click your homemade installer to start up from it.

Now you can install Yosemite as usual, or use any of the recovery features described in Appendix B.

Troubleshooting

W hether it's a car engine or an operating system, anything with several thousand parts can develop the occasional technical hiccup. OS X is far more resilient than its predecessors, but it's still a complex system with the potential for occasional glitches.

Most freaky little glitches go away if you just try these two steps, one at a time:

- Quit and restart the wayward program.
- Log out and log back in again.

It's the *other* problems that'll drive you batty.

Minor Eccentric Behavior

All kinds of glitches may befall you, occasionally, in OS X. A menu doesn't open when you click it. A program doesn't open—it just bounces in the Dock a couple of times and then stops. A program freezes.

When a single program is acting up like this, but quitting and restarting it does no good, try the following steps, in the following sequence.

First Resort: Repair Permissions

An amazing number of mysterious glitches arise because the *permissions* of either that item or something in your System folder—that is, the complex mesh of interconnected Unix permissions described in Chapter 15—have become muddled.

When something doesn't seem to be working right, therefore, open your Applications→Utilities folder and open Disk Utility. Proceed as shown in Figure B-1.

This is a really, *really* great trick to know.

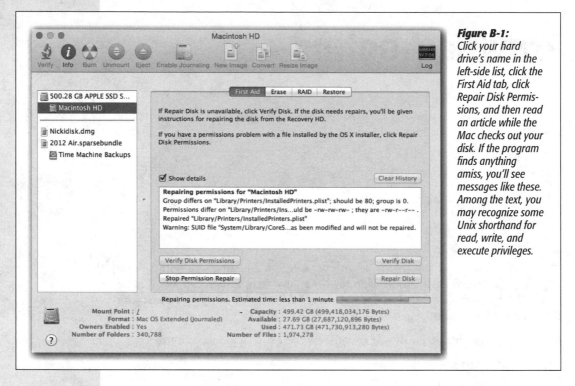

Figure B-1:
Click your hard drive's name in the left-side list, click the First Aid tab, click Repair Disk Permissions, and then read an article while the Mac checks out your disk. If the program finds anything amiss, you'll see messages like these. Among the text, you may recognize some Unix shorthand for read, write, and execute privileges.

Second Resort: Look for an Update

If a program starts acting up immediately after you've installed OS X 10.10, chances are good that it has some minor incompatibility. Chances are also good that you'll find an updated version on the company's Web site.

Third Resort: Toss the Prefs File

A corrupted preference file can bewilder the program that depends on it.

Before you go on a dumpfest, however, take this simple test: Log in using a *different account* (perhaps a dummy account that you create just for testing purposes). Run the problem program. Is the problem gone? If so, then the glitch exists only when *you* are logged in—which means it's a problem with *your* copy of the program's preferences.

Return to your own account. Open your Home→Library→Preferences folder, where you'll find neatly labeled preference files for all the programs you use. (To open the hidden Library folder, press the Option key as you open the Go menu; choose Library.)

Each preference file ends with the file name suffix .plist. For example, *com.apple. finder.plist* is the Finder's preference file, *com.apple.dock.plist* is the Dock's, and so on.

Put the suspect preference file into the Trash, but don't empty it. The next time you run the recalcitrant program, it will build itself a brand-new preference file that, if you're lucky, lacks whatever corruption was causing your problems.

If not, quit the program. You can reinstate its original .plist file from the Trash, if you find that helpful as you pursue your troubleshooting agenda.

Remember, however, that you actually have *two* Preferences folders. In addition to your own Home folder's stash, there's a second one in the Library folder in the main hard drive window (which administrators are allowed to trash; this one contains system-wide preferences, like your network configuration).

In any case, the next time you open the sick program or log in, the Mac creates fresh, virginal preference files.

Fourth Resort: Restart

Sometimes you can give OS X or its programs a swift kick by restarting the Mac. It's an inconvenient step, but not nearly as time-consuming as what comes next. And it can fix problems that cropped up when you started up the computer.

Last Resort: Trash and Reinstall the Program

Sometimes reinstalling the problem program clears up whatever the glitch was.

First, however, throw away all traces of it. Open the Applications folder and drag the program's icon (or its folder) to the Trash. In most cases, the only remaining pieces to discard are its .plist file (or files) in your Home→Library→Preferences folder, and any scraps bearing the program's name in your Library→Application Support folder. (You can do a quick Spotlight search to round up any other pieces.)

Then reinstall the program from its original disc or installer—after first checking the company's Web site to see if there's an updated version, of course.

Frozen Programs (Force Quitting)

The occasional unresponsive application has become such a part of OS X life that, among the Mac cognoscenti online, the dreaded, endless "please wait" cursor has been given its own acronym: SBOD (Spinning Beachball of Death). When the SBOD strikes, no amount of mouse clicking and keyboard pounding will get you out of the recalcitrant program.

Here are the different ways you can go about *force quitting* a stuck program (the equivalent of pressing Ctrl+Alt+Delete in Windows), in increasing order of desperation:

- **Force quit the usual way.** Choose →Force Quit to terminate the stuck program, or use one of the other force-quit methods described on page 158.

- **Force quit the sneaky way.** Some programs, including the Dock, don't show up at all in the usual Force Quit dialog box. Your next attempt, therefore, should be to open the Activity Monitor program (in Applications→Utilities), which shows *everything* that's running. Double-click a program and then, in the resulting dialog box, click Quit to force quit it. (Unix hounds: You can also use the *kill* command in Terminal.)

- **Force quit remotely.** If the Finder itself has locked up, you can't very well get to Activity Monitor (unless it occurred to you *beforehand* to stash its icon in your Dock—not a bad idea). At this point, you may have to abort the locked program from another computer across the network, if you're on one, by using the *SSH* (secure shell) command.

Tip: If all of this seems like a lot to remember, you can always force restart the Mac. On most Macs, you do that by holding down the power button for 5 seconds. If that doesn't work, press Control-⌘-power button.

Recovery Mode: Three Emergency Disks

OS X, as you've probably heard, no longer comes on a DVD. When your Mac won't even start up, there's no DVD to insert as a backup startup disk, as there used to be. That's a scary place to be; if your hard drive is sick, then everything on it may be inaccessible to you. What you need is an emergency drive that can repair the hard drive and get you back in operation.

Apple is way ahead of you on this one. It offers *three* simulated repair disks: three ways to supply disk-repair and system software–repair tools in times of crisis.

The Recovery HD

Here's the sneaky surprise: When you install Yosemite, it automatically creates an invisible hidden "hard drive" (a partition of your main drive that has its own icon) called Recovery HD. It's a 650-megabyte "drive" that's generally invisible to you. It's even invisible to Disk Utility, so even if you erase your hard drive, the Recovery HD is still there to help you.

But if you can't seem to start up your Mac properly, or if your hard drive is acting a little flaky, you'll be glad you had this "separate" startup disk. On it, Apple has provided some emergency tools for fixing drive or software glitches, restoring files, browsing the Web, and even reinstalling OS X.

Note: The OS X installer creates the Recovery HD partition only if your startup drive is an internal drive. In certain other situations, it won't create the partition—for example, if you're installing OS X onto a RAID volume or one with a non-standard Boot Camp partition setup.

You can power up your Mac from the Recovery HD in either of two ways:

- **Hold down ⌘-R as the Mac is starting up.** You can let go when you see the Apple logo appear.

- **Hold down the Option key as the Mac is starting up.** When you see the Startup Manager (Figure B-2, top), let go. Click the up-arrow button below the Recovery HD icon.

Either way, you wind up at the Utilities screen shown in Figure B-2, bottom.

Figure B-2:
Top: This simple display of disk icons is known as the Startup Manager. It's an easy way to specify which disk you want to start up from.

Bottom: Here's the point of the Recovery HD partition: a screen full of emergency utilities that can fix your Mac's regularly scheduled hard drive. If there's a pop-up menu at the bottom, it's for choosing a WiFi hotspot so that you can access the rest of your network. That might be useful when, for example, you want to access your Time Machine backups.

Here, Apple has supplied you with four important tools:

- **Restore From Time Machine Backup.** If your Mac is really hosed, this is the option you want. It restores your *entire* software world—programs, data, settings, OS X itself—from the Time Machine backup you carefully set up as you read Chapter 5.

This option *completely erases* your existing hard drive, so—you know. Be sure.

Once you choose this option, click Continue. You're now asked to choose the Time Machine drive, then the time-stamped backup you want to restore from, and, finally, the drive or partition you want to wipe out. You get one more warning that you're about to wipe out the destination drive. When you click Continue, the restoration begins. When it's all over—usually a couple of hours later—the Mac restarts as though nothing ever happened.

- **Reinstall OS X.** You can use this option to install a copy of OS X onto any hard drive—for example, you could reinstall it on your main internal drive.

Note: This option will download the actual copy of Yosemite from the Internet—all 5.3 gigabytes of it. In other words, it requires an Internet connection and a *lot* of patience.

- **Get Help Online.** This option opens your Safari Web browser, which presents you with some helpful information about using the Recovery Mode that you've fired up. You're actually online at this point, so you can also visit any other Web site you might find helpful.

 Quit Safari when you're finished browsing; you return to the main OS X Utilities window.

- **Disk Utility.** Use this option to open Disk Utility, the Mac's hard drive diagnostics-and-repair program. You can use it to check, fix, erase, or partition any of your hard drives.

 For example, you can repair the main startup disk, which is often the most useful option.

Those four options are the big-ticket items, but don't miss the menu bar. The commands here let you open the Firmware Password Utility (page 508), Network Utility (page 711), and Terminal (page 714).

Yosemite Internet Recovery

OK, the Recovery HD concept is clever. And most of the time, it's all you need.

But what if your hard drive is *completely* hosed? What then, smart guy? You can't very well boot up from the Recovery HD if it's sitting on the same dead hard drive.

Or what if you've just installed a brand-new, bigger, or faster hard drive? It doesn't have OS X on it. It doesn't have Recovery HD on it. How are you supposed to install Yosemite?

In those situations, recent Mac models—those released in 2011 and later—offer an even cleverer option: Internet Recovery. This mode offers the same exact options that the Utilities screen of Recovery HD would have—but you're connecting to that software *online,* over a high-speed Internet connection. You're literally starting up from *Apple's* hard drives, thousands of miles away.

So even if your hard drive is dead as a doornail, you can still repair it, reinstall OS X, and so on.

To fire up Internet Recovery, make sure your computer is in a WiFi hotspot or connected to an Ethernet network. Then hold down ⌘-R as the computer is starting up. You can let go when you see the screen that asks you to choose a WiFi network. Do that, and then enter the password for the network, if necessary.

Now your Mac downloads a disk image containing just enough software to get you to the Utilities screen described in the previous section.

Note: Once you're up and running, you can re-download the copies of iPhoto (or Photos), iMovie, and GarageBand that came with your Mac. Just open the App Store program, log in with your Apple ID, click Purchases, and click Accept to download those iLife programs. You won't be charged for them.

Physical Recovery Disks

But what if the hard drive is so sick that you can't start up from the Recovery HD—*and* your Mac isn't new enough to offer the Internet Recovery feature? (Or what if it *does* offer that feature, but you'd rather repair your Mac a quicker way?)

One solution is to build yourself a bootable OS X flash drive, DVD, or hard drive, as described on page 732. Not only is it capable of starting up or reinstalling OS X, but it also has a complete set of recovery tools on board.

But creating a bootable drive takes a lot of steps, and it requires sacrificing an 8-gigabyte (or bigger) flash drive. If you have any flash drive, even a 2-gigabyte one that somebody handed you at a trade show, you can load it up with just the recovery tools, to use in times of trouble. Creating this kind of emergency flash drive is somewhat easier than creating the kind of full-blown reinstallation flash drive described in Appendix A.

Note: To create an emergency "disk," your Mac must have OS X on it already, including the invisible Recovery HD partition. That's because it *relies* on the data and software on that partition.

It's OK if the flash drive is partitioned; just leave at least 2 gigs for the recovery partition.

To get started, download Apple's free OS X Recovery Disk Assistant. (It's available from this book's "Missing CD" page at *www.missingmanuals.com*. It may seem to be intended for Mountain Lion, but it still works fine in Yosemite.)

Insert your flash drive into the Mac. Open the OS X Recovery Disk Assistant; click Agree to get through the legalese screen.

Click the name of the flash drive, and then click Continue. You're warned that this process will *erase* the flash drive (or its partition), and you're asked to authenticate yourself with an administrator name and password.

When you click OK, your Mac begins creating the recovery disk. After a minute or so, a message congratulates you, and the newly created drive's icon appears in the Recovery Disk Assistant program, bearing the name Recovery HD.

To use this emergency disk, hold down the Option key as the Mac starts up. You wind up at the Startup Manager screen shown in Figure B-2, top. From the pop-up menu, choose your WiFi hotspot.

Now click the up-arrow button below the Recovery HD icon. (You may even see *two* Recovery HD icons—one of them is the USB flash drive, and the other is the invisible partition on your hard drive.) Your Mac is starting up from the flash drive! After a moment, you wind up at the Utilities screen described earlier in this appendix.

Note: The recovery flash drive you made will work only on the Mac model you used to make it.

Application Won't Open

If a program won't open (if its icon bounces merrily in the Dock for a few seconds, for instance, but then nothing happens), begin by trashing its preference file, as described earlier. If that doesn't solve it, reinstalling the program, or installing the Yosemite-compatible update for it, usually does.

Startup Problems

Not every problem you encounter is related to running applications. Sometimes trouble strikes before you even get that far. The following are examples.

Kernel Panic

When you see the cheerful, multilingual dialog box shown in Figure B-3 you've got yourself a *kernel panic*—a Unix nervous breakdown.

(In such situations, *user panic* might be the more applicable term, but that's programmers for you.)

If you experience a kernel panic, it's almost always the result of a *hardware* glitch—most often a bad memory (RAM) board, but possibly an accelerator card, graphics card, or USB hub that OS X doesn't like. A poorly seated AirPort card can bring on a kernel panic, too, and so can a bad USB or FireWire cable.

If simply restarting the machine doesn't help, detach every shred of gear that didn't come from Apple. Restore these components to the Mac one at a time until you find out which one was causing OS X's bad hair day. If you're able to pinpoint the culprit, seek its manufacturer (or its Web site) on a quest for updated drivers, or at least try to find out for sure whether the add-on is compatible with OS X.

Tip: This advice goes for your Macintosh itself. Apple periodically updates the Mac's *own* "drivers" in the form of a *firmware update.* You download these updates from the Support area of Apple's Web site (if indeed OS X's own Software Update mechanism doesn't alert you to their existence).

Figure B-3:
A kernel panic is almost always related to some piece of add-on hardware. And look at the bright side: At least you get this handsome dialog box. That's a lot better than the Mac OS X 10.0 and 10.1 effect: random text gibberish superimposing itself on your screen.

You need to restart your computer. Hold down the Power button for several seconds or press the Restart button.

Veuillez redémarrer votre ordinateur. Maintenez la touche de démarrage enfoncée pendant plusieurs secondes ou bien appuyez sur le bouton de réinitialisation.

Sie müssen Ihren Computer neu starten. Halten Sie dazu die Einschalttaste einige Sekunden gedrückt oder drücken Sie die Neustart-Taste.

コンピュータを再起動する必要があります。パワーボタンを数秒間押し続けるか、リセットボタンを押してください。

There's one other cause for kernel panics, by the way, and that's moving, renaming, or changing the access permissions for OS X's essential system files and folders—the Applications or System folder, for example. (See Chapter 15 for more on permissions.) This cause isn't even worth mentioning, of course, because nobody would be that foolish.

Safe Mode (Safe Boot)

In times of troubleshooting, Windows fans press an F-key to start up in Safe Mode. That's how you turn off all nonessential system-software nubbins in an effort to get a sick machine at least powered up.

Although not one person in a hundred knows it, OS X offers the same kind of emergency keystroke. It can come in handy when you've just installed some new piece of software and find that you can't even start up the machine, or when one of your fonts is corrupted, or when something you've designated as a login item turns out to be gumming up the works. With this trick, you can at least turn on the computer so that you can uninstall the cranky program.

The trick is to *press the Shift key* as the machine is starting up. Hold it down from the startup chime until you see the words "Safe Boot," in red lettering, on the login screen.

Welcome to Safe Mode.

What have you accomplished?

- **Checked your hard drive.** The Shift-key business makes the startup process seem to take a very long time; as the progress bar suggests, OS X is actually scanning your entire hard drive for problems.

- **Brought up the login screen.** When you do a safe boot, you must click your name and enter your password, even if you normally have Automatic Login turned on.

- **Turned off noncritical kernel extensions (drivers).** All kinds of software nuggets load during the startup process. Some of them you choose yourself, like icons you add to the Login Items list in the System Preferences→Users & Groups pane. Others are normally hidden, including a large mass of *kernel extensions,* which are chunks of software that add various features to the basic operating system. (Kernel extensions live in your System→Library→Extensions folder.)

 If you're experiencing startup crashes, some non-Apple installer may have given you a kernel extension that doesn't care for OS X 10.10—so in Safe Mode, they're all turned off.

- **Turned off your fonts.** Corrupted fonts are a chronic source of trouble—and because you can't tell by looking, they're darned difficult to diagnose. So just to make sure you can at least get into your computer, Safe Mode turns them all off (except the authorized, Apple-sanctioned ones that it actually needs to run, which are in your System→Library→Fonts folder).

- **Trashed your font cache.** The font cache is a speed trick. OS X stores the visual information for each of your fonts on the hard drive so the system won't have to read every single typeface off your hard drive when you open your Font menus or the Fonts pane.

 When these files get scrambled, startup crashes can result. That's why a Safe Boot moves all these files into the Trash. (You'll even see them sitting there in the Trash after the startup process is complete, although there's not much you can do with them except walk around holding your nose and pointing.)

- **Turned off your login items.** Safe Mode also prevents any Finder windows from opening *and* prevents your own handpicked startup items from opening—that is, whatever you've asked your Mac to auto-open by adding them to the System Preferences→Users & Groups→Login Items list.

 This, too, is a troubleshooting tactic. If some login item crashes your Mac every time it opens, you can squelch it just long enough to remove it from your Login Items list.

Tip: If you don't hold down the Shift key until you click the Log In button (after entering your name and password at the login screen), you squelch *only* your login items but *not* the fonts and extensions.

Once you reach the desktop, you'll find a long list of standard features inoperable. You can't use DVD Player, capture video in iMovie, use a wireless network, or use certain microphones and speakers. (The next time you restart, all this goodness will be restored, assuming you're no longer clutching the Shift key in a sweaty panic.)

In any case, the beauty of Safe Mode is that it lets you get your Mac going. You have access to your files, so at least the emergency of crashing-on-startup is over. And you can start picking through your fonts and login items to see if you can spot the problem.

Gray Screen During Startup

Confirm that your Mac has the latest firmware, as described earlier. Detach and test all your non-Apple add-ons. Finally, perform a disk check (see below).

Blue Screen During Startup

Most of the troubleshooting steps for this problem (which is usually accompanied by the Spinning Beachball of Death cursor) are the same as those described under "Kernel Panic" on page 736.

Forgotten Password

If you or one of the other people who use your Mac have forgotten the corresponding account password, no worries: Just read the box on 510.

Fixing the Disk

The beauty of OS X's design is that the operating system itself is frozen in its perfect, pristine state, impervious to conflicting system extensions, clueless Mac users, and other sources of disaster.

That's the theory, anyway. But what happens if something goes wrong with the complex software that operates the hard drive itself?

Fortunately, OS X comes with its own disk-repair program. In the familiar Mac universe of icons and menus, it takes the form of a program in Applications→Utilities called Disk Utility. In the barren world of Terminal and the command-line interface, there's a utility that works just as well but bears a different name: *fsck* (for file system check).

In any case, running Disk Utility or its alter ego *fsck* is a powerful and useful troubleshooting tool that can cure all kinds of strange ills, including these problems, among others:

- Your Mac freezes during startup, either before or after the login screen.
- The startup process interrupts itself with the appearance of the text-only command line.
- You get the "applications showing up as folders" problem.

Method 1: Disk Utility

The easiest way to check your disk is to use the Disk Utility program. Use this method if your Mac can, indeed, start up. (See Method 2 if you can't even get that far.)

Disk Utility can't fix the disk it's *on* (except for permissions repairs, described at the beginning of this appendix). That's why you have to restart the Mac into Recovery Mode and run Disk Utility from there. The process goes like this:

1. **Start up the Mac from the Recovery HD, or a recovery flash drive.**

They're both described earlier in this appendix. You wind up, after some time, at the Utilities screen.

2. **Click "Disk Utility: Repair or erase a disk using Disk Utility."**

 After a moment, the Disk Utility screen appears.

3. **Click the disk or disk partition you want to fix, click the First Aid tab, and then click Repair Disk.**

 The Mac whirls into action, checking a list of very technical disk-formatting parameters.

If you see the message, "The volume 'Macintosh HD' appears to be OK," that's meant to be *good* news. Believe it or not, that cautious statement is as definitive an affirmation as Disk Utility is capable of making about the health of your disk.

Disk Utility may also tell you that the disk is damaged but that it can't help you. In that case, you need a more heavy-duty disk-repair program like DiskWarrior (*www. alsoft.com*).

Method 2: fsck at the Console

Techier folk can also boot into the Mac's raw Unix underlayer to perform some diagnostic (and healing) commands.

Specifically, you can run the Unix program *fsck,* for which Disk Utility is little more than a pretty faceplate.

Note: Even so, Apple recommends that you use Disk Utility if at all possible. Use *fsck* only if all else fails.

Like any Unix program, *fsck* runs at the command line. You launch it from the all-text, black Unix screen by typing *fsck* and pressing Return. (You can also use *fsck -f.*)

You can't, however, just run *fsck* in Terminal. You have to run it when the usual arsenal of graphic-interface programs—like the Finder and its invisible suite of accessory programs—isn't running.

Single-user mode (⌘-S at startup)

The Terminal program is the best-known form of OS X's command line, but it's not the only one. In fact, there are several other ways to get there.

In general, you don't hear them mentioned except in the context of troubleshooting, because the Terminal program offers many more convenient features for doing the same thing. And because it's contained in a OS X–style window, Terminal is not as disorienting as the three methods you're about to read.

All these techniques take you into *console mode,* shown in Figure B-4. In console mode, Unix takes over your screen completely, showing white type against black, no windows or icons in sight. Abandon the mouse, all ye who enter here; in console mode, you can't do anything but type commands.

To get there in times of startup troubleshooting, press ⌘-S while the Mac is starting up. (If you're stuck at the frozen remnants of a previous startup attempt, you may first have to force restart your Mac; hold down the ⏻ button for 5 seconds.)

Instead of arriving at the usual desktop, you see technical-looking text scrolling up a black screen as the Mac runs its various startup routines. When it finally stops at the *localhost#* prompt, you're ready to type commands. You're now in what's called *single-user mode,* meaning that the Unix multiple-accounts software has yet to load. You won't be asked to log in.

Figure B-4:
In console mode, your entire screen is a command line interface. Unix jockeys can go to town here. Everyone else can timidly type fsck -y *after the local-host:/root # prompt—see this prompt on the very last line?—and hope for the best.*

```
Found old device 0x0cdea00
IOFireWireDevice,    ROM unchanged 0x0cdea00
IOFireWireDevice 0x0cdea00,   ROM generation  zero
Got boot device =
IOService:/Core99PE/pc@f20000000/AppleMacRiscPCI/mac-
io@17/KeyLargo/ata-4@1f000/KeyLargoATA/ATADeviceNub@0/IOA
TABlockStorageDriver/IOATABlockStorageDevice/IOBlockStorageDr
iver/QUANTUM  FIREBALL  CX13.6A
Media/IOApplePartitionScheme/Untitled
@9
BSD root: disk0s9, major 14, minor 9
Rereading  ROM up to 25 quads
devfs on /dev
USB:     4.947: AppleUSBKeyboard[0xD0E80014::start    USB  Generic
Keyboard @ 3 (0x18110000)
Mon Nov 19 23:18:53 EST 2001
Singleuser boot -- fsck not done
Root device is mounted read-only
If you want to make modifications  to files,
run '/sbin/fsck -y' first and then '/sbin/mount -uw/'
localhost#
```

At the *root#* prompt, type *fsck -y* (note the space before the hyphen) and press Return. (The *y* means "yes," as in "yes, I want you to fix any problems automatically.")

Now the file-system check program takes over, running through five sets of tests. When it's complete, you'll see one of two messages:

- **The volume Macintosh HD appears to be OK.** All is well. Type *exit* and press Return to proceed to the usual login screen and desktop.

- **File system was modified.** A good sign, but just a beginning. You need to run the program again. One *fsck* pass often repairs only one layer of problems, leaving another to be patched in the next pass. Type *fsck -y* a second time, a third time, and so on, until you finally arrive at a "disk appears to be OK" message.

Type *exit* at the prompt and press Return to get back to the familiar world of icons and windows.

Where to Get Troubleshooting Help

If the basic steps described in this appendix haven't helped, the universe is crawling with additional help sources. The Apple's Support Web site is a great resource. But the truth is, you'll find more answers faster using Google than you ever will using individual help sites. That's because Google *includes* all those help sites in its search!

Suppose, for example, that you've just installed the 10.10.2 software update, and it's mysteriously turned all your accounts into Standard ones. You could go to one Web site after another, hunting for a fix, repeating your search—or you could just type *Yosemite 10.10.2 standard accounts* into Google. You'll get your answers after just a few more seconds of clicking and exploring the results.

Help Online

These Web sites contain nothing but troubleshooting discussions, tools, and help:

- **Apple Discussion Groups** (*http://discussions.apple.com*). The volume and quality of question-and-answer activity here dwarfs any other free source. If you're polite and concise, you can post questions to the multitudes here and get more replies from them than you'll know what to do with.

- **Apple's help site** (*www.apple.com/support*). Apple's help site includes downloadable manuals, software updates, frequently asked questions, and many other resources.

 Its search box is your ticket to the Knowledge Base, a collection of 100,000 technical articles that the Apple technicians themselves consult when answering calls for help.

Help by Telephone

Finally, consider contacting whoever sold you the component that's making your life miserable: the printer company, scanner company, software company, or whatever.

If it's an OS X problem, you can call Apple at 800-275-2273 (that's 800-APL-CARE). For the first 90 days after your purchase of OS X, the technicians will answer your questions for free.

After that, unless you've paid for AppleCare for your Mac (a three-year extended warranty program), Apple will charge you to answer your questions. Fortunately, if the problem turns out to be Apple's fault, they won't charge you.

The "Where'd It Go?" Dictionary

Maybe you were convinced by the old Apple "Switch" ad campaign. Maybe you like the looks of today's Macs. Or maybe you've just endured one virus, spyware download, or service pack too many. In any case, if you're switching to OS X from Windows, this appendix is for you. It's an alphabetical listing of every common Windows function and where to find it in OS X. After all, an operating system is an operating system. The actual functions are pretty much the same—they're just in different places.

Tip: If this listing only whets your appetite for information about making the switch, read *Switching to the Mac: The Missing Manual,* Yosemite Edition. In addition to an expanded version of this appendix, it also contains useful information on moving your files from the PC to the Mac, copying over your email, transferring your contacts to Contacts, and so on.

About [this program]

To find out the version number of the program you're using, don't look in the Help menu. Instead, look in the *application* menu next to the menu—the one that bears the name of the program you're in. That's where you find the About command for Macintosh programs.

Active Desktop

The Mac never displays Web pages directly on the desktop—and knowing Apple, that's probably a point of pride. But Dashboard (Chapter 4) keeps Internet data only a keystroke away.

All Programs

There's no Programs menu built into OS X, like the one on the Windows Start menu. If you'd like one, drag your Applications folder into the end of the Dock. Now its icon is a tidy pop-up menu of every program on your machine.

Alt key

On the Mac, it's the Option key, although the key usually says "Alt" on it, too. (In some countries, it says *only* Alt.) You can substitute Option for Alt in any keystroke in most popular programs. The Option key has a number of secondary features on the Mac, too: It hides the windows of one program when you click into another, and so on.

Automatic Update

The App Store's automatic updates feature does exactly the same thing (page 581).

Backspace key

It's in the same place on the Macintosh keyboard, but it's called the Delete key.

Battery level

The battery-level graph () for your Mac laptop appears in the menu bar, rather than in the system tray. (If you don't see it, open System Preferences→Energy Saver and turn it on.)

BIOS

You'll never have to update or even think about the ROM of your Macintosh (the approximate equivalent of the BIOS on the PC). It's permanent and unchanging. The very similar *firmware* of your Macintosh does occasionally have to be updated in order to work with a new version of the Mac operating system or some dramatic new feature—once every four years, perhaps. You'll be notified on the screen when the time comes.

Briefcase

The Briefcase is a Windows invention designed to help you keep your files in sync between a laptop and a desktop computer. You can use iCloud Drive (page 211) to achieve exactly the same result with your Mac.

Calculator

The Calculator program in OS X is almost identical to the one in Windows. It sits in your Applications folder and is described on page 622. (There's a simpler Calculator in Dashboard, too; see page 174. And don't forget that you can type quick math equations into the ⚲ Spotlight menu.)

Camera and Scanner Installation Wizard

When you connect a digital camera or scanner to your Mac, iPhoto or Image Capture opens automatically and prepares to download the pictures. Details are on page 655.

CDs and DVDs

Modern Macs don't come with CD/DVD drives, but if you have an external drive, to spit out the disc that's in it, right-click (or two-finger click) its desktop icon and then choose Eject from the shortcut menu. There are various other ways to eject a disc, but the point is that you never do so by pushing the Eject button on the disc drive itself.

Character Map

This Windows program helps you find out what keys you need to press to trigger trademark symbols, copyright symbols, and other special characters. The equivalent on the Mac is called the Character Viewer (page 227).

Clean install

The OS X installer can give you a fresh copy of the operating system, just as the Windows installer can. Instructions are in Appendix A.

Clipboard

The Mac's Clipboard works much like the one in Windows. In the Finder, you can choose Edit→Show Clipboard to see whatever you most recently copied or cut.

Command prompt

In OS X, the command prompt is alive and well—but it speaks Unix, not DOS. You get to it by opening Terminal; see 714.

Control Panel

The Control Panel in OS X is called System Preferences, and you open it from your menu. As in Windows, you can view these icons either by category or in a simple alphabetical list: Just choose either Organize by Categories or Organize Alphabetically from the View menu.

Copy, Cut, Paste

When you're editing in a word processor or graphics program, the OS X Cut, Copy, and Paste commands work exactly as they do in Windows.

At the desktop, however, there are a few differences. You can indeed copy icons and paste them into a new window using the Copy and Paste commands—but *cutting* them out of a window, as you can in Windows, works slightly differently: After you've copied the icons from the first window, open the destination window. Then press the Option key, open the Edit menu, and choose Move Items Here.

Ctrl key

On the Macintosh, you generally substitute the ⌘ key in keystrokes that would involve the Ctrl key in Windows. In other words, the Save command is now ⌘-S instead of Ctrl+S, Open is ⌘-O instead of Ctrl+O, and so on.

Date and Time

To set your Mac's calendar and clock, open Date & Time in System Preferences.

Delete Key (Forward Delete)

Most desktop Mac keyboards have a forward-delete key (labeled ⌦ or *Del*) exactly like the ones on PCs. On Mac laptops, and on Apple's aluminum keyboards, you trigger the forward-delete function by pressing the Delete key while simultaneously pressing the fn key.

Desktop

The Macintosh desktop is pretty much the same idea as the Windows desktop, with a few key differences:

- Disk icons show up on the Mac desktop as soon as they are inserted or connected. You don't have to open a window to see their icons.

- You change the desktop picture using the Desktop & Screen Saver pane of System Preferences. (Or just right-click or two-finger click the desktop.)

- The Trash is an icon in the Dock, not on the desktop.

Device Stage

The Mac requires no program for installing the driver for a new external gadget. If you plug something into the Mac and find that it doesn't work immediately, just install the driver from the manufacturer's Web site.

Directories

Most people call them *folders* on the Mac.

Disk Defragmenter

There's no such utility included with OS X; the system auto-defragments in the background. (A *defragmenting* program moves around the pieces of files on your hard drive in an effort to optimize their placement and speed of opening.)

Disks

Working with disks is very different on the Mac. Every disk inside, or attached to, a Macintosh can be represented on the screen by an icon. OS X does have something like the Computer or My Computer window (choose Go→Computer), but the icons there reflect only the disks currently inserted in your Mac. You'll never see an icon for an empty drive, as you do on Windows, and there's no such thing as drive letters (because the Mac refers to *disks,* not to *drives*—and calls them by name).

Yosemite doesn't display icons for disks on the desktop, as earlier OS X versions did—but you can bring them back by choosing Finder→Preferences→General and turning on the checkboxes for different kinds of disks.

Display control panel

The functions of the Windows Display control panel lurk in the OS X System Preferences program—just not all in one place. You set up your desktop picture and screensaver using the Desktop & Screen Saver pane and adjust your monitor settings using

the Displays pane. (OS X offers no equivalent to the Appearance tab in Windows, for changing the system-wide look of your computer.)

DLL files

The Macintosh equivalent of DLL files—shared libraries of programming code—are invisible and off limits. As a result, no Macintosh user ever experiences DLL conflicts or out-of-date DLL files.

DOS prompt

There's a command line in OS X, but it's Unix, not DOS. See page 714.

Drivers

See "Add or Remove Programs."

Ease of Access Center

The special features that let you operate the computer even with impaired vision, hearing, or motor control are called Accessibility in Yosemite. They're in System Preferences (see Chapter 17).

End Task dialog box

If some Macintosh program is hung or frozen, you escape it pretty much the same way you would in Windows: by forcing it to quit. To bring up the Force Quit dialog box, you press Option-⌘-Esc or choose →Force Quit.

Exiting programs

You can quit a program either by choosing Quit from the menu bearing its name (next to the menu), or by right-clicking (or two-finger clicking) its Dock icon and then choosing Quit from the pop-up menu.

Explorer

The Mac has its own "tree" view of the files and folders on your hard drive: list view. By expanding the "flippy triangles" of your folders, you build a hierarchy that shows you as much or as little detail as you like.

If you prefer the Explorer effect of clicking a folder in *one* pane to see its contents in the next, try column view instead. Both views are described in Chapter 2.

Favorites

In OS X, there isn't one single Favorites menu that lists both favorite Web sites and favorite icons. The Bookmarks menu of Safari, the Web browser, lists only Web sites, and the Sidebar at the desktop (page 35) lists only favorite files, folders, disks, and other icons.

Faxing

Faxing is no longer built into OS X, but you can always buy a non-Apple fax modem and use the software that comes with it.

File Sharing

See Chapter 16 for an in-depth look at the Macintosh networking and file-sharing system.

Folder Options

The Folder Options control panel in Windows is a collection of unrelated settings that boil down to this:

- **General tab.** Exactly as in Windows, it's up to you whether or not double-clicking a folder opens up a second window—or just changes what's in the first one. On the Mac, you make these changes using the Finder→Preferences command. There you'll find the option called "Open folders in tabs instead of new windows."

- **View tab.** Most of the options here don't exist on the Mac. For example, system files are *always* hidden on the Mac; you can't opt to make them visible (at least not with the built-in controls). You can, however, choose whether you want to see the file name extensions in your desktop windows (like .doc and .html). Choose Finder→Preferences→Advanced, and turn "Show all file extensions" on or off.

- **Search tab.** These tweaky Windows options let you control what and how to search. You can find similar customizations for the Mac's Spotlight search feature in System Preferences→Spotlight.

Fonts

The Mac and Windows PCs both use TrueType, PostScript, and OpenType fonts. (In fact, your Mac can even use the exact font files you had in Windows.) On the Mac, however, there are actually three different folders that can contain them. A complete discussion is in Chapter 9.

Help and Support

At the desktop, choose Help→Mac Help. In other programs, the Help command is generally at the right end of your menus, exactly as in Windows.

Hibernation

The Mac can't hibernate at all, as modern PCs do, cutting all power but remembering what programs and documents you had open for a faster restart later. Sleep mode is the closest it gets; see "Standby mode."

Installing and uninstalling software

Installing a program onto the Mac is described in Chapter 4. Removing a program simply involves dragging its icon to the Trash. (For a clean sweep, inspect your Home→Library→Preferences and Home→Library→Application Support folders to see if any preference files got left behind. Note that your Home→Library folder is normally hidden. The quickest way to see it is to press Option as you choose Go→ Library in the Finder.)

Internet Explorer

Microsoft has abandoned the Mac version of Internet Explorer. Apple would prefer, of course, that you try Safari, its own Web browser, but many a power user prefers Firefox or Chrome, which are nearly identical to the Windows version.

Internet Options

On the Mac, you find the options for your Web browser by choosing Safari→Preferences.

IRQs

They don't exist on the Mac.

Java

This interpreter of tiny Web page programs is alive and well in OS X. Java programs run fine in all Mac Web browsers.

Keyboard control panel

You can make exactly the same kinds of settings—and more—on the Keyboard pane of System Preferences.

Logging in

The multiple-accounts feature of OS X is extremely similar to that of Windows 2000, XP, Vista, 7, and 8/8.1. In each case, you can, if you wish, create a requirement to log in with a name and password before using the computer. This arrangement keeps separate the documents, email, and settings of each person who uses the computer. Chapter 15 tells all.

Mail control panel

OS X comes with its own email program (described in Chapter 11); all of its settings are contained within the program.

Maximize button

On the Mac, clicking the Zoom button (the green button in the upper-left corner of a window) does something like the Maximize button in Windows: It makes your window larger. On the Mac, however, clicking the zoom button never makes the window expand to fill the entire screen. Instead, the window grows—or *shrinks*—precisely enough to enclose its contents.

Of course, if you see the ⊗ button in the upper-right corner of your window, you can do even better: You can take that program into *Full Screen mode,* where every last pixel of screen space is put to work displaying your document.

Menus

On the Macintosh, there's only one menu bar, always at the very top of the screen. The menus change depending on the program and the window you're using, but the point is that the menu bar is no longer inside each window you open.

Tip: Just because you don't see the little underlines in the menus doesn't mean you can't operate all the menus from the keyboard, as in Windows. See page 195 for details.

Minimize button

You can minimize an OS X window to the Dock, just the way you would minimize a Windows window to the taskbar. You do so by double-clicking its title bar, pressing ⌘-M, choosing Window→Minimize, or clicking the yellow Minimize button at the top left of a window. (Restore the window by clicking its icon in the Dock.)

Mouse control panel

The equivalent settings can be found in the Mouse pane of System Preferences.

(My) Computer

The Mac's Computer window is very similar (choose Go→Computer), in that it shows the icons of all disks (hard drive, CD, and so on). On the other hand, it shows *only* the disks that are actually inserted or connected. (See "Disks.")

(My) Documents, (My) Pictures, (My) Music

The equivalent buckets for your everyday documents, music files, and pictures are the Documents, Music, and Pictures folders in your Home folder.

(My) Network Places

On the Mac, the network is almost always on the screen: It's the Sidebar, the panel at the left side of every Finder window. All the Macs and PCs on your network are always listed here, in the Shared category (unless you turned this feature off in Finder→Preferences, of course).

Network

See the previous entry.

Notepad

Page 665 documents the Notes app, which is far more powerful than the Notepad of old.

Phone and Modem control panel

To find the modem settings for your Mac, see the free appendix to this book, "Setting Up a Dial-Up Connection," available on the "Missing CD" page at *www.missingmanuals.com*.

Power Options

To control when your Mac goes to sleep and (if it's a laptop) how much power it uses, use the Energy Saver pane of System Preferences (Chapter 17).

Printer Sharing

To share a USB inkjet printer with other Macs on the network, open the Sharing pane of System Preferences on the Mac with the printer. Turn on Printer Sharing.

To use the shared printer from across the network, open the document you want to print, choose File→Print, and choose the name of the shared printer from the first pop-up menu.

Printers and Faxes

For a list of your printers, open the Printers & Scanners pane of System Preferences. Faxing is no longer built into OS X.

PrntScrn key

You capture pictures of your Mac screen by pressing Shift-⌘-3 (for a full-screen grab) or Shift-⌘-4 (to grab a selected portion of the screen). There are many options available; see the end of Chapter 19.

Program Files folder

The Applications folder (Go→Applications) is like the Program Files folder in Windows—except that you're not discouraged from opening it and double-clicking things. On the Macintosh, every program bears its true name; Microsoft Word, for example, is called Microsoft Word, not WINWORD.EXE.

Properties dialog box

You can call up something very similar for any *icon* (file, folder, program, disk, printer) by highlighting its icon and then choosing File→Get Info. But objects in Macintosh *programs* generally don't contain Properties dialog boxes.

Recycle Bin

OS X has a Trash icon at the end of the Dock. In general, it works exactly like the Windows Recycle Bin—and why not, since the Macintosh Trash was Microsoft's inspiration?—but there are a couple of differences. The Macintosh never automatically empties it, for example. That job is up to you: The simplest way is to right-click it, or two-finger click it, and then choose Empty Trash from the shortcut menu.

The Mac never bothers you with an "Are you sure?" message when you throw something into the Trash, either. The Mac interrupts you for permission only when you choose Finder→Empty Trash. And you can even turn that confirmation off, if you like (in Finder→Preferences→Advanced).

To put icons into the Trash, drag them there, or highlight them and then press ⌘-Delete.

Regional and Language control panel

The equivalent is the Language & Region pane of System Preferences.

Registry

There is no registry. Let the celebration begin!

Run command

The Mac's command line is Terminal (page 714).

Safe Mode

You can press the Shift key during startup to suppress the loading of certain software libraries, but OS X's "safe mode" isn't quite as massively stripped down as Windows' Safe Mode.

ScanDisk

Just like Windows, the Mac automatically scans and, if necessary, repairs its hard drive every time your machine starts up. To run such a check on command, open Disk Utility (located in the Applications→Utilities folder), click the name of your hard drive, and then click the First Aid tab.

Scheduled Tasks

To schedule a task to take place unattended, use the *launchd* Unix command in Terminal (page 714).

Scrap files

On the Mac, they're called *clipping files,* and they're even more widely compatible. You create them the same way: Drag some highlighted text, or a graphic, out of a program's window and onto the desktop. There it becomes an independent clipping file that you can drag back in—to the same window or a different one.

Screen saver

The Mac's screensavers are impressive. Open System Preferences and click the Desktop & Screen Saver icon.

Search

In OS X, you have the ultimate file-searching tool: Spotlight (Chapter 3). Get psyched!

To find Web sites, use the Google search box at the top of the Safari browser.

Shortcut menus

They work exactly the same as they do in Windows. You produce a shortcut menu by right-clicking (or two-finger clicking, or Control-clicking) things like icons, list items, and so on.

Shortcuts

On the Mac, they're known as *aliases*. See page 105.

Sounds and Audio Devices

Open System Preferences; click the Sound icon. You may also want to explore the Audio MIDI Setup program in Applications→Utilities.

Speech control panel

The Mac's center for speech recognition and text-to-speech is the Dictation & Speech pane of System Preferences. As Chapter 5 makes clear, the Mac can read aloud any text in any program, and it also lets you speak to type.

Standby mode

On the Mac, it's called Sleep, but it's the same idea. You make a Mac laptop sleep by closing the lid. You make a Mac desktop sleep by choosing →Sleep, or just walking away; the Mac goes to sleep on its own, according to the settings in the Energy Saver pane of System Preferences.

Start menu

There's no Start menu in OS X. Instead, you stash the icons of the programs, documents, and folders you use frequently onto the Dock at the edge of the screen, or into the Places section of the Sidebar at the left edge of every Finder window.

Exactly as with the Start menu, you can rearrange these icons (drag them horizontally) or remove the ones you don't use often (drag them away from the Dock and then release). To add new icons of your own, just drag them into place (applications go to the left of the Dock's divider line, documents and folders to the right).

StartUp folder

To make programs launch automatically at startup, include them in the list of Login Items in the System Preferences→Users & Groups pane.

Sync Center

Sync Center is feature of Windows designed to help you keep your files in sync between your computer and files stored on network servers or Sync Center–compatible devices, such as smartphones. You can use iCloud Drive (page 211) to achieve the same result with your Mac.

System Properties control panel

The Mac has no central equivalent of the System window on a Windows PC. But its functions have analogs here:

- **Computer Name tab.** Open System Preferences, click Sharing, and edit your computer's network name here.

- **Hardware tab.** The closest thing the Mac has to the Device Manager is System Profiler (in your Applications→Utilities folder).

- **Advanced tab.** In OS X, you can't easily adjust your virtual memory, processor scheduling, or user profile information.

• **Remote tab.** OS X offers remote control in the form of Screen Sharing, described on 560.

System Tray

The OS X equivalent of the system tray (also called the notification area) is the row of *menulets* at the upper-right corner of your screen.

Taskbar

OS X doesn't have a taskbar, but it does have something very close: the Dock (Chapter 2). Open programs are indicated by a small, shiny dot beneath their icons in the Dock. If you hold down your cursor on one of these icons (or right-click it, or two-finger click it), you get a pop-up list of the open windows in that program, exactly as in Windows.

On the other hand, some conventions never die. Much as in Windows, you cycle through the various open Mac programs by holding down the ⌘ key and pressing Tab repeatedly.

Taskbar and Start Menu control panel

To configure your Dock (the equivalent of the taskbar and the Start menu), choose the Dock icon in System Preferences.

"Three-fingered salute"

Instead of pressing Ctrl-Alt-Delete to jettison a stuck program on the Mac, you press Option-⌘-Esc. A Force Quit dialog box appears. Click the program you want to toss, click Force Quit, confirm your choice, and then relaunch the program to get on with your day.

ToolTips

Small, yellow identifying balloons pop up on the Mac almost as often as they do in Windows. Just point to a toolbar icon or truncated file name without clicking. (There's no way to turn these labels off.)

Tweak UI

The closest equivalent for this free, downloadable, but unsupported Microsoft utility for tweaking the look of your PC is TinkerTool for OS X.

User Accounts control panel

Like Windows 2000, XP, Vista, and 7, OS X was designed from Square One to be a multiuser operating system, keeping each person's files, mail, and settings separate. You set up and manage these accounts in System Preferences→Users & Groups (page 610).

Windows (or WINNT) folder

OS X's operating system resides in a folder simply called System, which sits in your main hard drive window. Exactly as in recent Windows versions, you're forbidden to

add, remove, or change anything inside. Also as in Windows, most of it is invisible anyway.

Windows logo key

The Mac has no equivalent for the ⊞ key on most PC keyboards.

Windows Media Player

The Mac comes with individual programs for playing multimedia files:

- **QuickTime Player** (page 683) to play back movies and sounds.

- **iTunes** (page 323) to play CDs, Internet radio, MP3 files, and other audio files.

- **DVD Player** (page 320) for playing DVDs. This program is in the Applications folder.

Windows Messenger

OS X's instant-messaging, audioconferencing and videoconferencing software is called Messages, and it's described in Chapter 13.

WordPad

The TextEdit program (in the Applications folder) is a word processor along the lines of WordPad. It can even open and save Word files, as WordPad can.

Zip files

Zip files exist on the Mac, too, and you create them almost the same way: Right-click (or two-finger click) a file or folder and choose Compress from the shortcut menu.

The Master Secret Keystroke List

Here it is, by popular, frustrated demand: the master list of every secret (or not-so-secret) keystroke in OS X, including all the keys you can press during startup. Clip and post to your monitor (unless, of course, you got this book from the library).

Note: For the most part, the following list doesn't include the keystrokes already listed in your menus, like ⌘-P for Print, ⌘-S for Save, and so on.

Startup Keystrokes

Keys to Hold Down	Effect
C	Starts up from a bootable CD, DVD, or USB thumb drive
N	Starts up from a network server
R	Resets the laptop screen
⌘-R	Starts Recovery Mode
T	Puts the Mac into FireWire or Thunderbolt Target Disk mode
Option	Shows icons of all startup disks and partitions, so you can choose one for starting up
Option-⌘-P-R	Zaps the parameter RAM (PRAM) (hold down until you hear the second chime)
⌘-V	Shows Unix console messages during startup, logout, and shutdown

⌘-S Starts up in single-user (Unix command-line)
 mode

Mouse down or F12 Ejects a stuck CD or DVD

Shift Just after logging in: Prevents Finder windows
 and startup items from opening (they'll return
 the next time you start up)

In the Finder

⌘-space Opens Spotlight box

Option-⌘-space Opens Spotlight window

▶, ◀ Expands or collapses a selected folder in list
 view

Option-▶ Expands a folder in a list view *and* all folders
 inside it

Option-◀ Collapses a folder *and* all folders inside it

⌘-▲ Opens parent folder

⌘-▼ (or ⌘-O) Opens the selected icon

Option-click the flippy triangle Expands or collapses all folders within that
 window

Tab Selects next icon alphabetically

Shift-Tab Selects previous icon alphabetically

space bar Opens Quick Look preview of highlighted
 icon(s)

space bar During a spring-loaded folder drag, opens the
 disk or folder under the mouse immediately

Option-click Zoom button Enlarges the window (but not into Full Screen
 mode)

Option-click Close button Closes all Finder windows

Option-click Minimize button Minimizes all windows (works in most apps)

⌘-drag an icon Moves it into, or out of, the System folder
 (administrator password required)

Option Changes Quick Look button to Slideshow button

⌘-drag Rearranges or removes menulets or toolbar
 icons

⌘-click window title Opens a pop-up menu showing the folder
 path

Menu

Option	Changes "About This Mac" to "System Information"
Shift-⌘-Q	Logs out
Shift-Option-⌘-Q	Logs out without confirmation box

Finder Menu

Option	Eliminates the confirmation box from Empty Trash and Secure Empty Trash
Shift-⌘-Delete	Empties the Trash
Shift-⌘-Delete	Puts back a highlighted icon now in the Trash
Shift-Option-⌘-Delete	Empties the Trash without confirmation box
Option-Empty Trash	Empties the Trash without confirmation box
⌘-comma	Opens Preferences
⌘-H	Hide this program
Option-⌘-H	Hide other programs

File Menu

⌘-N	New Finder window
⌘-T	New Finder tab
Shift-⌘-N	New folder
Option-⌘-N	New smart folder
⌘-O or ⌘-▼	Open
Control-⌘-O	Open in new window and close previously open window
Option-click File menu	Changes "Open With" to "Always Open With"
⌘-W	Close window
Option-⌘-W	Close All
⌘-I	Get Info
Option-⌘-I	Show Inspector
Control-⌘-I	Summary Info (of selected icons)
⌘-D	Duplicate
⌘-L	Make Alias
⌘-Y	Quick Look
Option-⌘-Y	Slideshow (of selected icons)
⌘-R	Show Original (of alias)
Control-⌘-T	Add to Sidebar
Shift-Control-⌘-T	Add to Dock

⌘-Delete	Move to Trash
⌘-E	Eject
⌘-F	Find
Shift-⌘-F	Search All My Files

Edit Menu

⌘-Z	Undo
⌘-C, ⌘-X, ⌘-V	Copy, Cut, Paste
Option-⌘-V	Move copied icons to this window
⌘-A	Select All
Option-⌘-A	Deselect All

View Menu

⌘-1, -2, -3, -4	Icon, list, column, Cover Flow views
Control-⌘-1, -2, -3, -4, -5, -6, -7, -0	Arrange by Name, Kind, Date Last Opened, Date Added, Date Modified, Size, Tags, None
Option	Changes "Clean Up Selection" to "Clean Up"
Option	Changes "Arrange By" to "Sort By"
Shift-⌘-T	Show/hide Tabs bar
Shift-⌘-P	Show/hide preview pane
Option-⌘-P	Show/hide Path bar
Option-⌘-T	Show/hide Toolbar
Option-⌘-S	Show/hide Sidebar
⌘-/	Show/hide status bar
⌘-J	Show/hide View Options palette
Control-⌘-F	Full Screen mode

Go Menu

⌘-[, ⌘-]	Back, Forward
⌘-▲	Enclosing folder
Control-⌘-▲	Enclosing folder in new window
Shift-⌘-F	All My Files window
Shift-⌘-O	Documents window
Shift-⌘-D	Desktop window
Option-⌘-L	Downloads window
Shift-⌘-H	Home window
Option	Makes Library command appear
Shift-⌘-C	Computer window

Shift-⌘-R	AirDrop window
Shift-⌘-K	Network window
Shift-⌘-I	iCloud Drive menu
Shift-⌘-A	Applications window
Shift-⌘-G	Go to Folder
⌘-K	Connect to Server

Window Menu

⌘-M	Minimize
Option-⌘-M	Minimize All

Help Menu

Shift-⌘-?	Opens help search box

Power Keys

Control-⏏	Brings up dialog box for Shut Down, Sleep, or Restart
Option-⌘-⏏	Sleep
Control-Option-⌘-⏏	Shut Down
Control-⌘-⏏	Restart

The Dock

Option-click a Dock icon	Switches to new program and hides previous one
Option-⌘-D	Hides/shows the Dock
⌘-click a Dock or Stacks icon	Reveals its actual Finder icon
Option-⌘-click a Dock icon	Switches to this program and hides all others
Control-click a Dock icon	Opens a shortcut menu
Hold mouse down on Dock app icon	Triggers Exposé (shows all windows of that app in miniature)
⌘-drag an icon onto a Dock icon	Prevents Dock icons from moving, so you can drop your icon onto one of them
⌘-drag a Dock icon	Drags the actual item
Option-⌘-drag an icon onto the Dock	Forces a Dock program to open the icon you're dropping on it

Managing Programs

Option-click a Dock icon	Switches to new program and hides the previous one
Option-click in a window	Switches to new program and hides the previous one

⌘-H	Hide this program's windows (works in most apps)
Option-⌘-H	Hide all *other* programs' windows (most apps)
Control-◄, ►	Previous/next Spaces screen
F9	Exposé: Shrinks and tiles all windows in all programs
Shift-F9	Exposé: Shrinks and tiles all windows in slow motion
F10	Exposé: Shrinks and tiles all windows in front-most program
F11	Exposé: Flings all windows in all programs to edges of screen, revealing desktop
F12	Dashboard widgets
⌘-Tab	Press and release: Switches back and forth between current and previous open programs
⌘-Tab	Hold down ⌘: Displays floating icons of open programs. Press Tab repeatedly to cycle through them. (Add Shift to cycle *backward* through open programs.)
⌘-~	Switches to next open window in this program. (Add Shift to cycle in the opposite direction.)
Option-⌘-Esc	Opens the Force Quit dialog box (to close a stuck program)
Shift-⌘-3	Captures the screen image as a PNG file on your desktop
Shift-⌘-4	Produces a crosshairs; drag to capture a selected portion of the screen as a PNG graphics file. (Press space to get the "camera" cursor that snips out just a menu, icon, or window.)

Dialog Boxes

⌘-comma	Opens Preferences dialog box (any Apple program)
Esc	"Clicks" the Cancel button in a dialog box
Return	"Clicks" the OK button (or other blue, highlighted button) in a dialog box
Option-⌘-F	Moves the insertion point to the search box in most Apple programs
⌘-D, ⌘-R	"Clicks" the Don't Save or Replace button

Trackpad Gestures

You can change many of these gestures, or turn them on and off, in the Trackpad pane of System Preferences. But here are the factory settings:

Two-finger click	Right-click
Two-finger drag up/down	Scroll up/down
Two-finger swipe left-/right	Move among open Web or document pages
Two-finger swipe from right edge	Open Notification Center
Two-finger pinch or spread	Zoom in or out of a picture, PDF, or Web page
Two-finger rotate	Rotate photo or PDF
Two-finger double-tap (not click)	"Smart zoom" into Safari or Preview page
Three-finger swipe up	Mission Control
Three-finger swipe down	Show all windows in this app (Exposé)
Three-finger swipe left/right	Previous/next Spaces screen or full-screen app
Three-finger drag	Move window
Three-finger tap (not click)	Look up this word in Dictionary
Four-finger pinch	Open Launchpad
Four-finger spread	Reveal desktop (Exposé)

Magic Mouse Gestures

A few important gestures also work on the top surface of the Magic Mouse:

One-finger double-tap (not click)	"Smart zoom" into Safari or Preview page
Two-finger double-tap (not click)	Mission Control
One-finger swipe left-/right	Move between open Web or document
Two-finger swipe left/right	Previous/next Spaces screen or full-screen app

SWITCHING TO THE MAC: THE MISSING MANUAL

Index

Index

L

M

Colophon

This book was written on a 13-inch 2012 MacBook Air that remained attached to David Pogue like an appendage. It was updated from the Mavericks edition of the same book directly in Adobe InDesign, with substantial assistance from the typing-shortcut program TextExpander *(www.smileonmymac.com)*.

The book's screen illustrations were captured with Ambrosia Software's Snapz Pro X *(www.ambrosiasw.com)*, edited in Adobe Photoshop CS5.5 *(www.adobe.com)*, and overlaid with labels, lines, and circles in Adobe Illustrator.

The book was designed and laid out in Adobe InDesign CS5.5 on a Mac Pro. The fonts include Formata (as the sans-serif family) and Minion (as the serif body face). To provide the symbols (, ⌘, ⏏, and so on), Phil Simpson designed four custom fonts using FontLab Fontographer.

The book was then exported as Adobe Acrobat PDF files for final transmission to the printing plant.